The European Union 2004–2024

Indrė Isokaitė-Valužė · Haroldas Šinkūnas
Volume Editors

The European Union 2004–2024

Twenty Years of Legal Experience, Challenges and Growth after Unprecedented EU Enlargement

ASSER PRESS

Springer

Volume Editors
Indrė Isokaitė-Valužė
Faculty of Law
Vilnius University
Vilnius, Lithuania

Haroldas Šinkūnas
Faculty of Law
Vilnius University
Vilnius, Lithuania

ISBN 978-94-6265-719-9 ISBN 978-94-6265-718-2 (eBook)
https://doi.org/10.1007/978-94-6265-718-2

Published by T.M.C. ASSER PRESS, The Hague, The Netherlands www.asserpress.nl
Produced and distributed for T.M.C. ASSER PRESS by Springer-Verlag Berlin Heidelberg

This T.M.C. ASSER PRESS imprint is published by the registered company Springer-Verlag GmbH, DE, part of Springer Nature.
The registered company address is: Heidelberger Platz 3, 14197 Berlin, Germany

Foreword

All opinions expressed herein are personal to the author.

Becoming a Member of the European Union: A Constitutional Moment

1 May 2004 represented the fulfilment of a struggle for freedom, justice and democracy that was six decades in the making, becoming unstoppable in 1989 with the Solidarity movement, the Baltic Chain, the fall of the Berlin Wall, and the Velvet Revolution. What united that generation of Europeans was their unbreakable resolve to tear down the Iron Curtain, which had immersed them in the darkness of authoritarian rule since the end of World War II.

Above all, the 2004 accession, the largest single enlargement ever, put to rest the idea of a divided Europe. The European family was again reunited in a project that revolves around building together a "common legal order" based on the values of freedom, democracy and justice.[1] For the Czech Republic, Estonia, Cyprus, Latvia, Lithuania, Hungary, Malta, Poland, Slovenia and Slovakia, becoming a member of the EU was a constitutional moment.

I used the expression "constitutional moment" because, *looking back*, those ten Member States had to undergo institutional reforms and adopt new laws that sought to demolish the remains of an authoritarian past and replace it with a democratic system of governance, while implementing the EU *acquis*. It was a constitutional moment because, *looking forward*, those ten Member States had, as an act of national sovereignty, decided to take part in European integration. This meant being loyal to the EU, by respecting the values on which it is founded and the principles on the basis of which it operates.

---

[1] Judgments of 16 February 2022, Hungary v Parliament and Council, C-156/21, EU:C:2022:97, para 127, and of 16 February 2022, Poland v Parliament and Council, C-157/21, EU:C:2022:98, para 145.

To some extent, this idea of "looking back" and "looking forward" underpins my speech. In constitutional terms, that idea has been translated into two founding constitutional principles that are attached to EU membership: the principle of constitutional alignment and the principle of no regression in value protection. I will examine these two principles in the light of the case law of the Court of Justice of the European Union (the "Court of Justice").

Before accession, the constitution—and even the national identity—of the candidate State for EU membership must align itself with the values on which the EU is founded. The *raison d'être* of that principle is to prevent any conflicts between the national identity of that State and the EU identity, whilst creating synergies between them. Based on common values, both types of identity enter into a mutually reinforcing dynamic, which allows room for mutual trust. *After* accession, compliance with the principle of no regression in value protection precludes a Member State from passing reforms that lead to democratic backsliding. In the EU legal order, there is no room for authoritarian drifts. More freedom, more democracy and more justice are the only way forward.

I shall now explore the meaning, content and impact of those two constitutional principles.[2]

I. The Principle of Constitutional Alignment

A candidate State for EU membership must align its own constitution and national identity with the values on which the EU is founded as a *condidío sine qua non* for accession. It must commit itself to respecting "the values of respect for human dignity, freedom, democracy, equality, the rule of law and respect for human rights", which are contained in Article 2 TEU.

As the Court of Justice held in the ***Conditionality Judgments***, "[the] values contained in Article 2 TEU have been identified and are shared by the Member States. They define *the very identity of the European Union as a common legal order*. Thus, the European Union must be able to defend those values, within the limits of its powers as laid down by the Treaties".[3] This means, in essence, that those values draw inspiration from the constitutional traditions common to the Member States. Those values are not the result of a "top-down" approach but follow a "bottom-up" dynamic. They encapsulate the struggle of previous generations of Europeans who

---

[2] See, generally, Lenaerts K (2023) On Checks and Balances: the Rule of Law Within the EU 29(2) *Columbia Journal of European Law*, p. 25, and On Values and Structures: The Rule of Law and the Court of Justice of the European Union. In: Södersten A and Hercock E (eds) (2023) *The Rule of Law in the EU: Crisis and Solutions* (Stockholm, Swedish Institute for European Policy Studies), p. 12.

[3] Judgments of 16 February 2022, Hungary v Parliament and Council, C–156/21, EU:C:2022:97, para 127, and of 16 February 2022, Poland v Parliament and Council, C–157/21, EU:C:2022:98, para 145 (emphasis added).

strived for freedom, democracy and justice. They form part of our common heritage as Europeans.

For example, the values contained in Article 2 TEU can be found in the Lithuanian Constitution. Its preamble contains references to "the innate rights of the human being" and to "an open, just, and harmonious civil society under the rule of law".

The "Copenhagen Criteria" require, *inter alia,* strict adherence to that alignment. The decision to align its own constitutional arrangements with EU values is a sovereign choice of a candidate State for EU membership.[4] And, if a candidate State fails to do so, Article 49 TEU bars it from becoming a member of the EU.[5]

Whilst EU law protects the national identity of the Member States within the meaning of Article 4(2) TEU, a Member State may not invoke its national identity in order to disregard the values contained in Article 2 TEU and the Treaty provisions that give concrete expression to those values.[6] This normative conflict is precisely what the principle of constitutional alignment seeks to avoid.

For example, national identity may not be invoked as a means of calling into question the principles of effective judicial protection and judicial independence, as provided for by Article 19(1) TEU, which gives concrete expression to the value of respect for the rule of law. This was made crystal clear by the Court of Justice in ***Commission v Poland (Independence and private life of judges)***. There, the Court held—and I quote—that "there is no ground for maintaining that the requirements arising, as conditions for both accession to and participation in the European Union, from respect for values and principles such as the rule of law, effective judicial protection and judicial independence ... are capable of affecting the national identity of a Member State, within the meaning of Article 4(2) TEU".[7]

What the Court is really saying is that, by acquiring membership status, the national identity of a Member State, as protected under EU law, is deemed to be in keeping with the values contained in Article 2 TEU. This is because, otherwise, the Member State in question would not have been able to join the EU in the first place. Logically, this means that a Member State is precluded from relying on its own identity in order to breach those values.

Therefore, Article 4(2) TEU must be read taking into account the provisions, of the same rank, enshrined in Article 2 and Article 19(1) TEU, and cannot exempt

---

[4] The same applies where a Member State decides to withdraw from the EU. See judgment of 10 December 2018, Wightman and Others, C-621/18, EU:C:2018:999, para 50.

[5] That provision states that "[a]ny European State *which respects the values referred to in Article 2* and is committed to promoting them may apply to become a member of the Union." (emphasis added). Judgment of 20 April 2021, Repubblika, C-896/19, EU:C:2021:311, para 61.

[6] Judgment of 5 June 2023, Commission v Poland (Independence and private life of judges), C-204/21, EU:C:2023:442, para 72. The same holds true for the provisions of the Charter giving concrete expression to the values on which the EU is founded. See, in this regard, judgment of 5 June 2018, Coman and Others, C-673/16, EU:C:2018:385, paras 42 to 51, and judgment of 14 December 2021, Stolichna obshtina, rayon 'Pancharevo', C-490/20, EU:C:2021:1008, paras 53 to 65.

[7] Judgment of 5 June 2023, Commission v Poland (Independence and private life of judges), C-204/21, EU:C:2023:442, para 72.

Member States from the obligation to comply with the requirements arising from those provisions.

It follows that acquiring membership status is a "constitutional moment" for the Member State concerned since, at that very moment, the legal order of that new Member State is deemed by the "Masters of the Treaties" to uphold the values on which the EU is founded. As a result, mutual trust between the new Member State and the others and, in particular, between their courts and tribunals may take place, since "[it] is based on the fundamental premiss that [all] the Member States [, the old and the new ones,] share those common values".[8]

As a matter of fact, mutual trust is one of the key features that distinguish the relationship between the 27 Member States from that between a Member State and a third country. That explains in particular why the Court, in ***Achmea***, rejected the idea that "mistrust" concerning access to effective judicial protection could become the premise between two or more Member States, even in the specific context of disputes between an investor and a public authority.[9] The principle of mutual trust thus serves to draw the dividing line between the Member States and third countries. Unlike its findings in *Achmea*, the Court suggested in **Opinion 1/17** that a third country does not necessarily share the same degree of commitment towards those values and in respect of which "trust" therefore cannot be presumed.[10] Such a third country may, however, gain that trust by building a special relationship with the EU and by being equally committed to the values on which the EU is founded.[11]

Moreover, the principle of constitutional alignment does not rule out diversity altogether. This is because the values contained in Article 2 TEU do not impose a "particular constitutional model".[12] They only impose a framework of reference within which a Member State may make its own constitutional choices in keeping with its culture, history and tradition. The concept of a "framework of reference" is also referred to by academics as "not crossing red lines".[13] Allow me to illustrate this point by looking at an example taken from the case law of the Court.

---

[8] Judgment of 5 June 2023, Commission v Poland (Independence and private life of judges), C-204/21, EU:C:2023:442, para 66.

[9] Judgment of 6 March 2018, Achmea, C–284/16, EU:C:2018:158.

[10] Opinion 1/17 (EU-Canada CET Agreement), of 30 April 2019, EU:C:2019:341, para 129 (holding that "the principle of mutual trust, with respect to, inter alia, compliance with the right to an effective remedy before an independent tribunal, is not applicable in relations between the [EU] and a non-Member State").

[11] Judgment of 2 April 2020, Ruska Federacija, C–897/19 PPU, EU:C:2020:262, paras 44 and 77.

[12] Judgments of 21 December 2021, Euro Box Promotion and Others, C–357/19, C–379/19, C–547/19, C–811/19 and C–840/19, EU:C:2021:1034, para 229 and the case-law cited, and of 22 February 2022, RS (Effect of the decisions of a constitutional court), C–430/21, EU:C:2022:99, para 43.

[13] Von Bogdandy A (2021) Towards a Tyranny of Values? In: Von Bogdandy A and Others (eds) *Defending Checks and Balances in EU Member States,* Berlin, Springer, p. 91 (observing that the values contained in Article 2 TEU "do not constitute "laws of construction", but rather "red lines"").

In ***Runevič-Vardyn and Wardyn***,[14] which involved a reference made by the First District Court of the City of Vilnius, the Court of Justice was asked to examine the compatibility of national rules requiring names and surnames on civil status certificates to follow the spelling rules of the host Member State's official language with the right of EU citizens to move freely within the EU. The Court held that it was legitimate for Lithuania to protect and promote its official language. Referring to Article 3(3) TEU and Article 22 of the Charter, it observed that the EU is committed to respecting its rich cultural and linguistic diversity. Most importantly, it stated that the protection of a State's official language is part and parcel of its national identity which, in accordance with Article 4(2) TEU, the EU must protect. Subject to compliance with the principle of proportionality, a Member State may therefore adopt such spelling rules. Needless to say, the fact that other Member States may consider it unnecessary to adopt those spelling rules in order to protect their official language has no bearing on the application of the principle of proportionality. That principle does not require national courts to embark on a comparative study of the national laws on the protection of the official language in order to identify the one that is the most practical for free movers. Instead, it focuses on striking the right balance between individual interest (a person's name is a constituent element of his or her identity and of his or her private life, the protection of which is enshrined in Article 7 of the Charter) and a collective interest (the protection and promotion of the host Member State's official language).

In the EU legal order, the importance of national identity is not limited to protecting the official languages of the Member States, given that, as Article 4(2) TEU states, it also guarantees their fundamental structures and essential functions. The EU is not a State,[15] nor does it seek to become one. On the contrary, it serves to protect the Member States' statehood by creating a "pool of sovereignty" amongst them. Member States become stronger together, since they can achieve goals that would be unachievable acting alone. The protection of national identity is of paramount importance for States that have lived under Soviet occupation or that were within the Soviet Union's sphere of influence. Unfortunately, the war in Ukraine has resurrected old demons, showing that the threat of military aggression against the EU exists. That is why the EU and its Member States must be able to defend themselves effectively.

For example, disinformation is a serious threat to our democracies and to the European way of life. That is why EU law, as interpreted by the Court of Justice, serves to protect our democratic societies against that threat. For example, in ***Baltic Media Alliance***,[16] the Regional Administrative Court of Vilnius asked the Court of Justice to interpret the Audiovisual Media Services Directive.[17] In that case, the Court of Justice interpreted the directive in a way that enabled the Lithuanian authorities to

---

[14] Judgment of 12 May 2011, Runevič-Vardyn and Wardyn, C–391/09, EU:C:2011:291.

[15] Opinion 2/13 (Accession of the European Union to the ECHR) of 18 December 2014, EU:C:2014:2454, para 156 ("the EU is, under international law, precluded by its very nature from being considered a State").

[16] Judgment of 4 July 2019, Baltic Media Alliance, C–622/17, EU:C:2019:566.

[17] Directive 2010/13/EU of the European Parliament and of the Council of 10 March 2010 on the coordination of certain provisions laid down by law, regulation or administrative action in

combat Russian propaganda targeting the Russian-speaking minority in Lithuania, whilst upholding the application of the country of origin principle. This meant, in concrete terms, that those authorities could oblige Lithuanian media providers to distribute a channel broadcast by a UK-based company only in pay-to-view packages, on the ground that its programmes incited hatred based on nationality.

Another example in this regard is ***RT France v Council***.[18] In that case, the General Court dismissed an action for annulment, brought by a media outlet that was wholly funded by the Russian State, against a Council Regulation that temporarily prohibited that media outlet from broadcasting content, on the grounds that it had engaged in a propaganda campaign, targeting civil society in the EU, justifying and supporting Russia's military aggression against Ukraine. The General Court reasoned *inter alia* that the Council had limited RT France's freedom of expression in a way that was in keeping with the Charter, since the challenged Regulation pursued two legitimate aims—namely, the protection of the Union's public order and security and the application of pressure on the Russian authorities in order to bring an end to the war—whilst also complying with the principle of proportionality.

In my view, the *Baltic Media Alliance* and *RT France* judgments show that in interpreting EU law, the Court of Justice and the General Court strive to protect civil society from disinformation that can cause civil unrest and threaten the democratic process, whilst guaranteeing that any restrictions on the freedom of expression are limited to what is strictly necessary. When war is at the EU's doorstep, that protection serves to maintain law and order and safeguard national security, which are components of the Member States' essential functions and thus, of their national identities.

II. The Principle of No Regression in Value Protection

After accession, the Member State in question commits itself to respecting the values contained in Article 2 TEU for as long as it remains a member of the EU. That ongoing commitment means that there is "no turning back the clock" when it comes to respecting those values. Accession is the starting point in value protection, not the finish line. A Member State can always improve its level of value protection.

The principle of no regression in value protection precludes a Member State from drifting towards an authoritarian regime or from falling into democratic backsliding. "Compliance with those values", the Court of Justice has held, "cannot be reduced to an obligation which a candidate State must meet in order to accede to the [EU]

Member States concerning the provision of audiovisual media services (Audiovisual Media Services Directive), [2010] OJ L 95/ 1.

[18] Judgment of 27 July 2022, RT France v Council, T-125/22, EU:T:2022:483.

and which it may disregard after its accession".[19] The Member States must respect those values "at all times".[20]

The prohibition of value regression is highlighted by contrasting the judgments of the Court of Justice in *A. K. and Others (Independence of the Disciplinary Chamber of the Supreme Court)* and *A.B. and Others (Appointment of judges to the Supreme Court – Actions)*, with that in *Repubblika*. In those cases, the Court of Justice held that the principle of judicial independence does not prevent the executive from appointing judges, provided that "once appointed, they are free from influence or pressure when carrying out their role".[21] That proviso means, in essence, that the substantive conditions and procedural rules governing the adoption of those appointment decisions must not give rise to reasonable doubts as to the internal and external independence of those judges.[22] Those doubts arise where the reforms at issue bring about a regression of the rule of law. This may occur where the constitutional body in charge of evaluating the suitability of candidates for judicial office is no longer independent.

In ***A. K. and Others (Independence of the Disciplinary Chamber of the Supreme Court)*** and ***A.B. and Others (Appointment of judges to the Supreme Court – Actions)***, that appeared to be the case since the reforms at issue sought—subject to confirmation by the referring courts – to undermine the independence of the Polish National Judicial Council (the "KRS"), which, as the constitutional body entrusted with protecting judicial independence, submits proposals for appointment to judicial positions to the Polish President. Following the judgment of the Court of Justice in *A. K. and Others (Independence of the Disciplinary Chamber of the Supreme Court)*, the referring court found that the KRS was not an independent body.[23] Similarly, in the context of an infringement action brought by the Commission that challenged the new disciplinary regime for Polish judges, the Court made the same findings in respect to the KRS.[24] It noted, drawing on its previous case law, that the law reforming the KRS had shortened the mandate of incumbent members, and that 23 of the 25 members of the KRS were appointed by the Polish executive or legislature (or were

[19] Judgments of 16 February 2022, Hungary v Parliament and Council, C-156/21, EU:C:2022:97, para 126, and of 16 February 2022, Poland v Parliament and Council, C-157/21, EU:C:2022:98, para 144.

[20] Judgments of 16 February 2022, Hungary v Parliament and Council, C-156/21, EU:C:2022:97, para 234, and of 16 February 2022, Poland v Parliament and Council, C-157/21, EU:C:2022:98, para 266.

[21] Judgments of 19 November 2019, *A. K. and Others (Independence of the Disciplinary Chamber of the Supreme Court)*, C585/18, C624/18 and C625/18, EU:C:2019:982, para 133; of 2 March 2021, *A.B. and Others (Appointment of judges to the Supreme Court—Actions)*, C824/18, EU:C:2021:153, para 122, and of 20 April 2021, Repubblika, C896/19, EU:C:2021:311, para 56.

[22] Judgments of 19 November 2019, *A. K. and Others (Independence of the Disciplinary Chamber of the Supreme Court)*, C585/18, C624/18 and C625/18, EU:C:2019:982, paras 134 and 135; of 2 March 2021, *A.B. and Others (Appointment of judges to the Supreme Court—Actions)*, C824/18, EU:C:2021:153, para 123, and of 20 April 2021, Repubblika, C896/19, EU:C:2021:311, para 57.

[23] Polish Supreme Court, judgment of 5 December 2019. For a summary of that judgment, see order of 8 April 2020, Commission v Poland, C791/19 R, EU:C:2020:277, para 19.

[24] Judgment of 15 July 2021, *Commission v Poland (Disciplinary regime for judges)*, C791/19, EU:C:2021:596.

members thereof), whereas previously 15 out of 25 were elected by the Polish judges themselves.[25] Moreover, it observed that some of the new members of the KRS had, according to the referring court, been appointed in spite of significant irregularities. When compared with the appointment process in force at the time Poland acceded to the EU in 2004, the reforms at issue – which were passed in 2017 and 2018 – were a step backward.

Similarly, the finding of regression in protecting judicial independence was crucial in the seminal judgment of the Court in ***Krajowa Rada Sądownictwa (Continued holding of a judicial office)***, in which it ruled, for the first time, that a chamber of a court, namely the Chamber of Extraordinary Control and Public Affairs of the Polish Supreme Court, was not independent and, as a result, could not be considered to be a "court or tribunal of a Member State" within the meaning of Article 267 TFEU. It therefore could not make a reference for a preliminary ruling to the Court of Justice.[26]

By contrast, in ***Repubblika***, the reforms in question had actually strengthened the guarantee of judicial independence in Malta.[27] They established a body, the Judicial Appointments Committee, that gave advice to the Prime Minister of Malta about the eligibility and merit of the candidates for appointment to judicial positions. Since the independence of that body was not questioned by the referring court, it contributed to objectivising the appointment process to judicial positions. When compared with the appointment process in force at the time Malta acceded to the EU in 2004, the reforms at issue – which were passed in 2016 – were a step forward.

I would like to make three additional remarks regarding the principle of no regression in value protection. First, regarding its scope *ratione personae*, I do not believe that it only applies to Member States that have acceded to the EU. In the light of the principle of equality of Member States before the Treaties, which is enshrined in Article 4(2) TEU, the principle of no regression in value protection applies to all Member States, including the original six. As a matter of fact, the judgment in ***Asociaţia 'Forumul Judecătorilor din România' and Others*** and subsequent case law contain no reference to accession.[28] In the relevant passage of that judgment, the Court held – and I quote – that "[a] Member State cannot … amend its legislation in such a way as to bring about a reduction in the protection of the value of the rule of law… The Member States are thus required to ensure that, in the light of that value, any regression of their laws on the organisation of justice is prevented, by refraining

[25] *Ibid*, para 104.

[26] Judgment of 21 December 2023, Krajowa Rada Sądownictwa (Continued holding of a judicial office), C–718/21, EU:C:2023:1015.

[27] Judgment of 20 April 2021, Repubblika, C–896/19, EU:C:2021:311, para 69.

[28] Judgments of 18 May 2021, Asociaţia 'Forumul Judecătorilor din România' and Others, C–83/19, C–127/19, C–195/19, C291/19, C–355/19 and C–397/19, EU:C:2021:393, para 162; of 15 July 2021*Commission v Poland (Disciplinary regime for judges)*, C–791/19, EU:C:2021:596, para 51, and of 21 December 2021, Euro Box Promotion and Others, C–357/19, C–379/19, C–547/19, C–811/19 and C–840/19, EU:C:2021:1034, para 162.

from adopting rules which would undermine the independence of judges".[29] Accession is therefore a relevant benchmark for examining the existence or absence of regression, but it is not the only one.

Second, regarding the scope *ratione materiae*, the principle of no regression in value protection is not limited to the value of respect for the rule of law, but may include the other values contained in Article 2 TEU, such as respect for democracy. That principle therefore precludes democratic backsliding that, for example, undermines the freedom of the press.

Third and last, in the ***Conditionality Judgments***, the Court of Justice held that "Article 2 TEU is not merely a statement of policy guidelines or intentions, but contains values which... are an integral part of the very identity of the European Union as a common legal order, values which are given concrete expression in principles containing legally binding obligations for the Member States".[30] Logically, this raises the question of whether a value contained in Article 2 TEU, such as human dignity or democracy, requires a Treaty provision that gives it concrete expression in order for that value to be operational or whether Article 2 TEU may operate as a stand-alone provision. In a pending case, ***Commission v Hungary***,[31] it appears that the Court of Justice will be confronted with that complex question.

III. Concluding Remarks

The 2004 accession is a success story, for both the ten Member States concerned and the EU as a whole. Membership has brought freedom, prosperity and progress to all. In particular, the Baltic States have become one of the most prosperous regions in Europe, leading the way in digital transformation. At the same time, the EU has been reinvigorated in its fight for freedom, democracy and justice, given that the recent history of those Member States reminds us that those values cannot be taken for granted.

EU membership is, in my view, a "two-way street". On the one hand, the Member States must strive to keep the Union strong, by showing to their citizens the added value of working together and the importance of building and maintaining an area without internal borders where citizens may move freely and securely. On the other hand, the EU protects the Member States against "value backsliding", by preventing them from deviating from the constitutional traditions common to the Member States. This means, in essence, that the values on which the EU is founded are here to stay.

---

[29] Judgments of 18 May 2021, Asociaţia 'Forumul Judecătorilor din România' and Others, C–83/19, C–127/19, C–195/19, C–291/19, C–355/19 and C–397/19, EU:C:2021:393, para 162.

[30] Judgments of 16 February 2022, Hungary v Parliament and Council, C–156/21, EU:C:2022:97, para 232, and of 16 February 2022, Poland v Parliament and Council, C–157/21, EU:C:2022:98, para 264.

[31] Case C-769/22 *Commission v Hungary* (pending).

They must operate as a moral compass that allows both the EU and its Member States to navigate through the uncharted waters of an ever-changing world.

Civil society, and in particular academics must be active in shaping future generations so that one day, they become active citizens who know “the real value of European values”, share and cherish them and are willing to defend them. It is not only in the courtroom where values become a living truth, but also in the classroom. There is no bigger danger to freedom, democracy and justice than to have citizens who take everything for granted and who cannot be bothered to stand up for what is right. Paraphrasing the famous words of Benjamin Franklin, the EU is a Union of liberal values, if we, Europeans, “can keep it”.

May 2024

Koen Lenaerts
President of the Court of Justice
of the European Union
Luxembourg/Leuven, Belgium

Professor of European Union Law
Leuven University
Luxembourg, Belgium

Contents

Editors and Contributors

About the Editors

Indrė Isokaitė-Valužė Associate Professor, Advisor to the Dean for international development at the Law Faculty of Vilnius University, Vilnius, Lithuania

Haroldas Šinkūnas Professor and the Dean of the Law Faculty of Vilnius University, Vilnius, Lithuania

Contributors

Magdalena Bainczyk The Institute for Western Affairs, Poznań, Poland; Andrzej Frycz Modrzewski University, Kraków, Poland

Lina Beliūnienė Institute of Law at the Lithuanian Centre for Social Sciences, Constitutional Court of the Republic of Lithuania, Vilnius, Lithuania

Edmunds Broks Faculty of Law, University of Latvia, Riga, Latvia

Danguolė Bublienė Faculty of Law, Vilnius University, Vilnius, Lithuania

Arnis Buka Faculty of Law, University of Latvia, Riga, Latvia

Lolita Buka Faculty of Law, University of Latvia, Riga, Latvia

Ewelina Cała-Wacinkiewicz Faculty of Law and Administration, University of Szczecin, Szczecin, Poland

Tomas Davulis Faculty of Law, Vilnius University, Vilnius, Lithuania

Kalvis Engīzers University of Latvia, Riga, Latvia

Kinga Flaga-Gieruszyńska University of Szczecin, Szczecin, Poland

Ligita Gasparėnienė Faculty of Law, Vilnius University, Vilnius, Lithuania

Gintaras Goda Faculty of Law, Vilnius University, Vilnius, Lithuania

Vitalii Gutnyk Faculty of Law, Vilnius University, Vilnius, Lithuania; Ivan Franko National University of Lviv, Lviv, Ukraine

Irmantas Jarukaitis Faculty of Law, Vilnius University, Vilnius, Lithuania

Stefan Kadelbach Goethe University Frankfurt am Main, Frankfurt am Main, Germany

Saulius Lukas Kalėda Faculty of Law, Vilnius University, Vilnius, Lithuania

Aleksandra Klich Faculty of Law, Vilnius University, Vilnius, Lithuania

Egidijus Kūris Faculty of Law, Vilnius University, Vilnius, Lithuania

Ārija Meikališa University of Latvia, Riga, Latvia

Ewa Michałkiewicz-Kądziela Faculty of Law and Administration, University of Szczecin, Szczecin, Poland

Volodymyr Motyl Faculty of International Relations, Ivan Franko National University of Lviv, Lviv, Ukraine

Mykhailo Mykiyevych Faculty of Law, Vilnius University, Vilnius, Lithuania; Faculty of International Relations, Ivan Franko National University of Lviv, Lviv, Ukraine

Rimvydas Norkus Court of Justice of the European Union, Luxembourg, Luxembourg

Jānis Pleps University of Latvia, Riga, Latvia

Rita Remeikienė Faculty of Law, Vilnius University, Vilnius, Lithuania

Jānis Rozenbergs University of Latvia, Riga, Latvia

Christoph Schewe University of Applied Sciences Kiel-Altenholz/Reinfeld, Altenholz, Germany

Viktorija Soņeca Riga Graduate School of Law, Riga, Latvia

Kristīne Strada-Rozenberga University of Latvia, Riga, Latvia

Wojciech Sz. Staszewski Faculty of Law and Administration, University of Szczecin, Szczecin, Poland

Volodymyr Venher Faculty of Law, National University "Kyiv-Mohyla Academy", Kyiv, Ukraine

Part I
Introduction

Chapter 1
The European Union as a Peace-Orientated Integration Through (the Rule of) Law and EU Membership in a Shifting International Landscape: An Introduction

Indrė Isokaitė-Valužė and Haroldas Šinkūnas

Contents

Abstract This chapter as an introduction to the book refers to the European Union ("EU" or "Union") as a law-based European project created to contribute to peace, security and stability in Europe, with a focus on EU membership. First, the EU is characterised as an integration through law, emphasizing the principle of the rule of law, and a value-based Union's identity is addressed as reflected in EU membership. Some insights on the largest EU enlargement of 2004 are provided demonstrating the interrelation between the Union's evolving identity and the accession of new Member States. Thereafter the Union's role in strengthening peace and security and regional stability is revealed, taking complicated and fragile international landscape into account. After more than 70 years since the establishment of the then European Coal and Steal Community peace seams to remain the underlying aim of the Union permeating all other goals—economic prosperity, social cohesion, sustainable development, scientific and technological progress, among others. The EU's role contributing to (regional and international) peace and security is revealed in the framework of its relations with other main organisations in the field, namely,

I. Isokaitė-Valužė (✉) · H. Šinkūnas
Faculty of Law, Vilnius University, Vilnius, Lithuania
e-mail: indre.isokaite@tf.vu.lt

H. Šinkūnas
e-mail: haroldas.sinkunas@tf.vu.lt

I. Isokaitė-Valužė and H. Šinkūnas (eds.), *The European Union 2004-2024*,
https://doi.org/10.1007/978-94-6265-718-2_1

the United Nations ("UN") and NATO, and with an emphasis of the significance of international landscape for further EU enlargement.

Keywords European Union · EU membership · EU enlargement · EU law · EU values · EU identity · European integration · Rule of law · International peace and security

1.1 Introduction

The EU is an historic achievement, and the membership of each State is a unique story contributing to the journey of European integration built on the ideas, values and principles without which it could have never started. Throughout already more than seven decades the EU has developed from a peace-orientated but mostly economic community to a value-based entity dealing with a huge range of regional and even global issues in its labyrinths of EU—Member States competence division and firmly standing in a fragile and fragmented international landscape. There has been much of everything on that journey: failures and victories, mistakes and lessons learned, inspiration and disappointment. Today, being open for accession of new States, the Union seems to be still an attractive European project and EU membership—a constitutional value.[1]

The only component without which the EU could not exist is its Member States (and their people) which define not only a geopolitical map of the EU, but also form the Union's identity, uphold or sometimes test its values trying to balance national aspirations and a common gain. New Member States not only expand the area open for free movement of people, widening opportunities for investment and trade and providing conditions for big achievements, but also bring new issues to be solved by the Union, the solutions of which could either foster development of some advanced measures and better regulation or hinder progress and impair the Union's effective

[1] The Constitutional Court of the Republic of Lithuania in its ruling of 24 January 2014 on the Compliance of the Republic of Lithuania's Law Amending Article 125 of the Constitution and Article 170 (Wording of 15 March 2012) of the Statute of the Seimas of the Republic of Lithuania with the Constitution of the Republic of Lithuania emphasized that "the fundamental constitutional values consolidated in Article 1 of the Constitution – the independence of the state, democracy, the republic – are closely interrelated with the geopolitical orientation of the State of Lithuania, which is consolidated in the Constitution and implies European and transatlantic integration pursued by the Republic of Lithuania. <…> the geopolitical orientation of the State of Lithuania means the membership of the Republic of Lithuania in the EU and NATO as well as the necessity to fulfil the corresponding international commitments related with the said membership. It should also be noted that such geopolitical orientation of the State of Lithuania is based upon the recognised and protected universal constitutional values which are common with the values of other European and North American states" (para 6.2). Thus EU membership was "deemed to be a constitutional value and imperative based on the structural compatibility of the fundamental values of both the Constitution and EU primary law". Jarukaitis and Švedas 2019, p. 1010.

functioning. However, in general, the EU expansion is an occasion to celebrate this as an achievement and a sign of growth.

Such was the EU enlargement in 2004, when ten countries became EU Member States: the accession of Cyprus, the Czech Republic, Estonia, Hungary, Latvia, Lithuania, Malta, Poland, Slovakia and Slovenia remains the largest EU enlargement in EU history. It was an unprecedented event by its scale and long-lasting effects on stability and prosperity in Europe. To celebrate this significant occasion, the Law Faculty of Vilnius University on 24 May 2024 held an international conference entitled "The Republic of Lithuania in the European Union: Twenty Years of Experience, Challenges and Growth" in Vilnius.[2] The event, honoured by the participation of distinguished guests, including the President of the EU Court of Justice and Doctor Honoris Causa of Vilnius University Dr. Koen Lenaerts[3] and other prominent EU law scholars, was the inspiration for this book.

This chapter serves as an introduction aimed to address some fundamental issues uniting the whole edited volume and permeating the value-based Union's legal identity and its role, the meaning of EU membership and key legal developments throughout two decades since the unprecedented EU enlargement. In particular, it seeks to emphasize the Union as a value-based entity integrated through law with a focus on the rule of law and basic EU membership-related implications in a two-decade period. Thereafter the Union's role for peace and security and regional stability is revealed, given the complicated and fragile current international landscape. After a brief reference to the Union's relations with other international organisations, namely the UN and NATO, some insights on further EU enlargement are made.

The editors would like to express their gratitude to all the authors of this book, for their contribution to this edited volume, and to the speakers of the 24 May 2024 conference in Vilnius. We appreciate working together in preparation of and contributing to this edited volume and believe it to be a significant opportunity of uniting the insights and expertise of prominent scholars and a meaningful contribution in a time of important decisions for Europe turning its new page of history.

This book is a comprehensive and extensive research of basic legal developments of the EU and the Member States of the 2004 enlargement during a two-decade period reflected in the preface and four structural parts, including Part I (first chapter) as an introduction. Part II, "European Union Membership and Values", reveals EU

[2] A film "Lithuania – 20 years of European Union membership" was produced especially for this event, the film and the event recording were published on the Youtube channel of the Law Faculty of Vilnius University (the film: https://www.youtube.com/watch?v=Ws3q9y-GOHc&t=1s, the conference: https://www.youtube.com/watch?v=swwSdW-Tyr8). Law Faculty of Vilnius University (2024) Twenty years of Lithuania in the European Union: the development of the law, the progress of the state and the challenges ahead. https://www.tf.vu.lt/science_events_archives/2024-3/twenty-years-of-lithuania-in-the-european-union-the-development-of-the-law-the-progress-of-the-state-and-the-challenges-ahead/. Accessed 2 April 2025.

[3] Being awarded the title in 2022, K. Lenaerts gave this comparison: "The Vilnius University mission statement mirrors what the European Union stands for: openness to diversity and respect for national and regional identities while focusing on what unites the peoples of Europe. United in Diversity as the European motto states". Lenaerts 2022, p. 1.

identity as a value-based legal entity and EU membership as a constitutional value among other aspects such as an accession treaty and the experience of particular States (Latvia, Lithuania, Poland) with some historical discourse. Thereafter, Part III, "European Integration: A Closer Look into Several Areas", explores different aspects of European integration, such as principles of effectiveness and proportionality, issues of external relations, common foreign and security policy and the rule of law, jurisdiction of the EU Court of Justice and EU law-affected developments in national criminal law, civil law and procedure, *etc*. Finally, Part IV, "The Future of the European Union: Thinking Ahead", addresses crucial issues pending for the Union in the nearest future, mainly the further enlargement of the Union with a focus on Ukraine's accession (and the related issue of seeking justice) as well as the topics of the relation between EU law and national law and EU future reform.

1.2 Several Insights on the Union's Identity, EU Membership and the 2004 Enlargement

The issue of how much the EU should expand has been evolving in parallel with the discussion of the desirable, needed or optimal scale and depth of European integration. These developments were reflected in the Union's founding treaties, which introduced legal and institutional amendments and are closely related to EU membership.

The destination towards an "ever closer union" indicated in the preamble of the Treaty of Rome[4] (1957) almost five decades thereafter intended to reach even a greater scale of unity within a constitutional framework foreseen by the draft Treaty establishing a Constitution for Europe (2004), which acknowledged that "the peoples of Europe are determined to transcend their former divisions and, united ever more closely, to forge a common destiny".[5] The European Parliament in its resolution of 18 December 2003 recalled "the general acknowledgement of the need for a deepening of European integration in the process of the enlargement of the Union" and expressed the view that "failure to resolve the issue of the enlarged Union's capability to act could result in a 'variable-speed Europe'" referring to the risk of "the fragmentation of the Union".[6] The Treaty of Lisbon (2009) did not include the provision of the draft Treaty establishing a Constitution for Europe, retaining the reference to the continuation of "the process of creating an ever closer union among the peoples of Europe" and "further steps to be taken in order to advance European integration".[7]

---

[4] Treaty establishing the European Economic Community (entered into force on 1 January 1958). OJ C 224, 31.8.1992, pp. 6–79.

[5] The Treaty has not entered into force. OJ C 310, 16.12.2004, pp. 1–474.

[6] European Parliament resolution on the outcome of the Intergovernmental Conference, P5_TA (2003)0593, Meeting of heads of state and/or government on the IGC. https://www.europarl.europa.eu/doceo/document/TA-5-2003-0593_EN.pdf?redirect. Accessed 2 April 2025.

[7] Preamble. Treaty on European Union (consolidated version). OJ 2016 C 202, pp. 15–45.

However, it listed the EU values explicitly, although leaving some ambiguity as to the final list.[8] In addition to discussion on (or fear of) the EU's federalisation, attempts were made to enhance democracy. The Treaty of Lisbon introduced a European citizens' initiative and strengthened the role of national parliaments, also the EU Charter of Fundamental Rights became part of EU law.[9] Since then, the Union, being built on two founding treaties—the Treaty on EU[10] and the Treaty on the Functioning of the EU[11]—has become a single entity holding international legal personality and is a community based on values that remains integrated through law. Recently A. von Bogdandy referred to "European republicanism",[12] explaining that his contribution "does not categorize the EU as a republic, nor does it define its 'legal nature'",[13] and that "argument for a European renaissance of republicanism is not apologetic of European integration".[14] A. von Bogdandy explored republicanism in its relation with democratic constitutionalism, through civic focus and understanding of the common good.

The Union's history witnessed by the founding treaties, seen in legal and institutional developments, reflected in political discourse and scholarly research shows that the European integration-related issues remain open for discussion and this process of evolution is an unfinished story.

Accession to the EU is always a beginning of something advanced and promising but the journey may be more challenging than expected. The depiction of joining the EU as a "European family" is usually positive in general as EU membership is related to progress and growth. However, each new EU membership or membership anniversary is not only celebratory: they contain many legal and institutional, theoretical and practical implications, which may be explored in a wide range of fields, from data protection to environment, from foreign and security policy to a common market. EU membership means not only a promise of a common gain, but also a responsibility of navigating together through stormy waters. Responding to crises and strengthening resilience to new threats is how the EU develops. As noticed by P. M. Maduro, "in response to crises, new challenges and enduring changes in the

[8] Article 2 of the Treaty on European Union (consolidated version): "The Union is founded on the values of respect for human dignity, freedom, democracy, equality, the rule of law and respect for human rights, including the rights of persons belonging to minorities. These values are common to the Member States in a society in which pluralism, non-discrimination, tolerance, justice, solidarity and equality between women and men prevail." The paragraph is structured of two sentences, the first of which lists the values, however, the second provides certain related implications. The topic on EU values is explored by the editors (authors) in Chapter 4 of this edited volume.

[9] Factsheets on the European Union: The Treaty of Lisbon (2025) https://www.europarl.europa.eu/factsheets/en/sheet/5/the-treaty-of-lisbon. Accessed 2 April 2025.

[10] Treaty on European Union (consolidated version).

[11] Treaty on the Functioning of the European Union (consolidated version). OJ C 326, 26.10.2012, pp. 47–390.

[12] Von Bogdandy 2024.

[13] *Ibid.*, p. 34.

[14] *Ibid.*, p. 32.

economic environment, the EU has embarked on a process of transformation to an extent unforeseen by its architects".[15]

As to the 2004 enlargement, the accession of ten Member States not only demanded enormous work, including the implementation of countless EU legal acts into domestic legal systems, but also contained a strong implication of the choice for European values, including democracy and freedom, the rule of law and the protection of human rights. The two-decade period reflects a fundamental transformation of the then new EU Member States into equal partners, thereafter at times even leading EU countries. EU membership meant the need for structural reforms and a fundamental transition in law, economy, political culture and the minds of people. For example, aligning governance with the rule of law requirements after a decade-long Soviet rule was hardly achievable at once, as well as making land and forests available for acquisition by EU subjects just after the restoration of private property was not easy to perceive as common or natural. Each accession contains peculiarities, and each membership contributes a unique experience; however, in general, the enlargement by ten new Member States made not only them grow, but also asked for adjustments from the EU and its older Member States and brought new challenges to all. This was also the period when the EU had to respond to crises: the migration crisis, the economic crisis, the security crisis (terrorist attacks in EU Member States (Islamic State's terrorist attacks in Belgium, Germany, Spain, *etc.*) and the war in Ukraine), the public health crisis, democracy backsliding and "Brexit", which demonstrated that EU membership is not only a one-way street. These Member States already participated in negotiations which led to the adoption of the Treaty of Lisbon and the enlargement took place in the same year as the draft Treaty establishing a Constitution for Europe was adopted (Lithuania was the first to ratify it).[16]

A common area for joint and shared action, expected benefit and possible losses means Member States are committed to finding unity in diversity and to seeking compromise in clashes of different, even opposing views. But above all, EU membership means the determination for integration through law. Many acknowledge law as an instrument to reach goals and safeguard values. The President of the European Parliament R. Metsola emphasised the Union as being based on values and law: "EU law was indeed created in order to bring lasting peace and prosperity, based on the principles of freedom, democracy, rule of law and respect for human rights and human dignity in Europe".[17]

The Union is not merely institutional structures and provisions in treaties, it is how it is applied by domestic institutions, interpreted by national courts and supervised by the EU Court of Justice, but also how it is perceived by the European community. In a certain sense, the implementation of EU law is a culture, in particular, speaking about EU values, especially the rule of law, among others—respect for human dignity and human rights, freedom, democracy and equality.[18] As was put by A. Sajó, "like

[15] Maduro *et al.* 2021, p. 1.

[16] Jarukaitis 2006, p. 59.

[17] Metsola 2024, p. 9.

[18] Article 2 of the Treaty on European Union (consolidated version).

constitutionalism in general, the existence and observance of the [rule of law] is to a great extent a matter of mentality, tradition, and culture. There is a spirit of the [rule of law] that must be shared by the actors of the law, and to some extent society, for the [rule of law] to be meaningful and efficient".[19]

The rule of law is one of the fundamental values of the EU, inseparable from democracy and the protection of human rights, which all together also form the three pillars of the Council of Europe as the foundations of the European legal order. "The rule of law is established as a European value, political ideal and a legal concept" and "there is no need to invent formal definitions of the rule of law to fully implement it as something that works effectively".[20] The rule of law encompasses the principles of good democratic governance, equal protection under law, transparent, accountable, democratic and pluralistic law-making process, effective judicial protection, among others. All these elements are interrelated and closely linked with EU values.

K. Lenaerts emphasized the role of courts and judicial independence as an essential element of the rule of law and its importance for European integration:[21] in this "defining moment in the history of integration" Europeans "must stand up for the values – such as democracy, the rule of law and fundamental rights – that we share in order to emphasize the point that what brings us together remains stronger than what pulls us apart".[22] K. Lenaerts concluded that "if the next generation of Europeans is to explore new horizons for an ever-closer Union where citizens may continue to enjoy a sphere of individual liberty free from public interferences, integration through the rule of law is the only way forward".[23]

Being multifaceted and comprehensive, the rule of law is relevant in different fields, from the application of EU law to the area of freedom, security and justice, from social cohesion to an investment-friendly business environment. Although crises usually pose a risk to EU values and may negatively affect trust in the Union, its law and institutions, recent surveys show a high level of belief that the EU plays an important role in upholding the rule of law (74%) and that it is important for all EU Member States to respect the EU's core values (89%).[24] Adherence to the rule of law is a condition for the accession and membership in both the EU and the Council of Europe as it is "the basic feature of the European constitutional order".[25]

It is important to emphasize that the rule of law is applicable not only on a domestic or regional (European) level, but also on an international universal level—the UN, where it is primarily linked with the key aim of international legal order—international peace and security.

---

[19] Sajó 2023, p. 7.

[20] Holovaty 2021, p. 23.

[21] Lenaerts 2020.

[22] *Ibid.*, p. 34.

[23] *Ibid.*

[24] European Commission. 2024 Rule of Law Report. https://commission.europa.eu/document/download/27db4143-58b4-4b61-a021-a215940e19d0_en?filename=1_1_58120_communication_rol_en.pdf. Accessed 2 April 2025, p. 1.

[25] Polakiewicz and Kirchmayr 2021, p. 363.

1.3 The EU as a Peace Project: The Role of the Union (and Its Enlargement) in the International Landscape

From a 70 years' perspective, "it is symbolic that both—the quest for peace, necessary in the face of Russia's aggression against Ukraine, and the principle of the rule of law—still are the most significant part of the European project".[26] This war was a clear reminder of the significance of the peace-orientated foundations underlying the idea of European integration as well as the role of the Union built after years of casualties and division.

Devastating disasters and wars (in particular Russia's war in Ukraine and the Israeli - Palestine ("Hamas") military conflict-related situation in the Gaza Strip) demonstrate, and reports confirm, a decrease in peace and stability on a global scale: "many of the conditions that precede major conflicts are higher than they have been since the end of the Second World War"[27] and "there has been a significant rise in both conflicts and battle deaths in the past two decades".[28]

In the framework of increased competition, polarisation and decreased international peace, security and trust, regional organisations may play a significant role. The Secretary General of the UN emphasized "the need of strong partnerships between the UN and regional organizations" and that the latter "are urgent in regions where long-standing security architectures are collapsing or where they have never been built".[29]

The Union's contribution to regional stability and even international peace and security should be admitted. Economic dimension and social cohesion contribute to human rights protection, democracy and the rule of law helps strengthen stability, and EU competence in the field of foreign and security policy places the Union among the actors entrusted with ensuring international peace and security. One should acknowledge that "the scale of atrocities and damage caused by Russia in and to Ukraine are immense and have already united many states to take unprecedented measures needed to respond to grave violations of international law and to seek the aggressor state's accountability".[30] Unprecedented sanctions applied in respect of Russia (its subjects) and joint efforts to collect evidence of international crimes as well as fully-fledged participation in the Register of Damage for Ukraine show unity in seeking for the aggressor state's liability and justice for Ukraine; political, humanitarian, military and financial support for Ukraine demonstrate that the EU has

[26] Calleja and Rusche 2024, p. 16.

[27] Institute for Economics & Peace. Global Peace Index 2024: Measuring Peace in a Complex World, Sydney, June 2024. http://visionofhumanity.org/resources. Accessed 2 April 2025, p. 2.

[28] *Ibid.*, p. 3.

[29] United Nations (2023) A New Agenda for Peace. Our Common Agenda Policy Brief 9. https://www.un.org/sites/un2.un.org/files/our-common-agenda-policy-brief-new-agenda-for-peace-en.pdf. Accessed 2 April 2025, p. 12.

[30] Isokaitė-Valužė and Grigaitė-Daugirdė 2024, p. 41.

put solidarity in action.[31] This does not, however, eliminate the difficulties in finding unity on specific issues or maintaining that unity in the long run.

The EU is ready to support peace-orientated multilateral solutions based on the UN Charter which demand international cooperation. The recommitment to the rule-based international legal order and support for international peace and security naturally prevails (in addition to advancement of sustainable development; addressing the triple planetary crisis (climate change, pollution and biodiversity loss) and fostering trust through a more effective multilateral system).[32]

The rule of law on the UN level calls for adherence to international law and is also the foundation for peace. In the New Vision for the Rule of Law,[33] the rule of law (together with the 2030 Agenda for Sustainable Development) should be seen as placed in the centre of the international community's efforts to increase trust and solidarity, is needed for people's engagement, equal access to justice for all, free and independent media, *etc.*

The Union is also an essential partner for NATO (majority of Member States coincide, Russia's aggression against Ukraine persuaded Finland to join NATO in 2023 and Sweden in 2024):[34] both organisations share common values,[35] strategic interests and some similar threats (e.g. hybrid, cyber, nuclear, terrorism, Russia's aggression, among others). The main fields of cooperation are crisis management, capability development in addressing hybrid threats and challenges posed by growing strategic competition, as well as in building the capacities of their common partners in the east and south.[36] NATO membership means coverage by its deterrence (including nuclear), a forum for consultations on any security issue, a mechanism to act in cooperation with the UN and to implement UN resolutions, having at your disposal capabilities to be used in situations demanding humanitarian efforts and also as a forum for interaction with other international organisations and stakeholders.[37] In the face of threats posed by an aggressor state, the need to increase resilience and strengthen military capabilities of European States has increased during recent years, in particular fostering integration and increasing the importance of unity in its

---

[31] European Union. EU Support for Ukraine (2025) https://european-union.europa.eu/priorities-and-actions/eu-support-ukraine_en. Accessed 2 April 2025.

[32] EU Priorities at the United Nations (2023) https://www.eeas.europa.eu/eeas/eu-priorities-united-nations_en. Accessed 2 April 2025.

[33] United Nations (2023) New Vision of the Secretary-General for the Rule of Law. https://www.un.org/ruleoflaw/wp-content/uploads/2023/10/Rule-of-Law-New-Vision-English.pdf. Accessed 2 April 2025.

[34] 23 out of 27 EU Member States are also NATO members. EU-NATO Cooperation (2025) https://www.consilium.europa.eu/en/policies/eu-nato-cooperation/#:~:text=EU%20countries%20that%20are%20NATO%20members&text=NATO%20and%20the%20EU%20have,%2C%20Slovenia%2C%20Spain%20and%20Sweden. Accessed 2 April 2025.

[35] The Preamble of the North Atlantic Treaty (UNTS 34, p. 243) declares the determination "to safeguard the freedom, common heritage and civilisation of their peoples, founded on the principles of democracy, individual liberty and the rule of law."

[36] NATO (2025) Relations with the European Union. https://www.nato.int/cps/en/natohq/topics_49217.htm. Accessed 2 April 2025.

[37] Isokaitė-Valužė 2024, p. 42.

turn. Researchers suggest that "[d]efence, therefore, becomes the driver of deeper European unification, in which the EU is the essential partner for Ukraine".[38]

Opening the door for new Member States, the Union needs to rethink itself; not only acceding countries, but also the EU should be prepared, as well as its current Member States. The EU enlargement is not only a legal process but also a geopolitical tool. It consolidates dimensions of security, democracy and prosperity (economic-social implications). This was witnessed by the applications of three East European countries—Ukraine, Moldova, and Georgia—to accede to the EU, submitted shortly after Russia's aggression against Ukraine started.[39]

On the day of opening accession negotiations with Ukraine and Moldova in June 2024, President of the European Commission U. von der Leyen emphasized that "we celebrate the values and principles that bind us together. The EU has always been more than a political and economic union. It is a testament to our collective aspiration for peace, for security, for democracy and for prosperity".[40]

Although it can be easier to look from a distance and experience-based learning seems attractive, we can hardly align the anticipated accessions with the 2004 enlargement. Today EU membership bears the same meaning of the choice for EU values, no less important as it was for the countries which joined the Union in 2004. On the one hand, part of the issues, including, e.g., legislative, judicial, economic and social reforms, remain among the accession clusters, on the other hand, current candidate countries need to address more and novel issues related to, e.g. green energy, digital transformation and climate change, among many others. However, the world has changed and it is difficult to predict the course of history. For example, Georgia in December 2023 was granted EU candidate status,[41] but the State suspended its accession negotiations and the decision was followed by mass protests.[42]

---

[38] Duff 2024, p. 7.

[39] Without any intention here to explore the foreseen accession of all current candidate countries (Albania, Bosnia and Herzegovina, Georgia, Moldova, Montenegro, North Macedonia, Serbia, Turkey, Ukraine (and Kosovo as potential candidate country)) the emphasis is made on Ukraine, encompassing Moldova as well as Georgia, as countries affected by Russia's aggressive policy.

[40] Directorate-General for Neighbourhood and Enlargement Negotiations, 25 June 2024. https://enlargement.ec.europa.eu/news/statement-president-von-der-leyen-opening-accession-negotiations-ukraine-and-moldova-video-message-2024-06-25_en. Accessed 2 April 2025.

[41] "[o]n the understanding that the relevant steps set out in the Commission recommendation of 8 November 2023 are taken". European Commission. Georgia. Membership status: candidate country (2025) https://enlargement.ec.europa.eu/european-neighbourhood-policy/countries-region/georgia_en. Accessed 2 April 2025. Twelve priorities were outlined for the State and, according to one of assessments, "[i]n the first group of politically fundamental priorities, the most challenging are political polarisation, judicial reforms and de-oligarchisation. Most of the problems here link to the unresolved and central issue of de-oligarchisation, which holds the key to resolving the other fundamental political shortcomings". Akhvlediani 2023, p. 29.

[42] Mackintosh T, Davies M, Demytrie R (2024) Police use water cannon as Georgia EU protests erupt for second night, 30 November 2024, BBC News. https://www.bbc.com/news/articles/c62jp68p315o. Accessed 2 April 2025.

The international geopolitical landscape plays a role when deciding on the enlargement of the EU, of course, in addition to the progress of fulfilment of the EU accession criteria.

Moldova has been facing significant challenges related to Russia's aggression against Ukraine: large numbers of refugees, economic problems, threats to energy supplies, hybrid threats, *etc.* In order to address this impact, EU launched a Support Package for the Republic of Moldova aimed at facilitating economic development and connectivity, strengthening administrative capacity and energy and overall security, as well as countering foreign interference.[43]

The case of Ukraine is unique: a state being torn apart by war, living under martial law, seeking justice before international courts and fighting hard on the battlefield as well as dealing with numerous social, economic and other problems, needs to implement a long list of reforms and meet numerous requirements. Despite the progress made,[44] the way towards the EU is neither fast nor easy, even if "fast-tracked" and with a promise of European leaders to "continue to support Ukraine and its people for as long as it takes".[45]

The EU enlargement today is to be discussed and decided in a shifting international peace and security environment, witnessing historic attempts to establish a special tribunal for the crime of aggression, unprecedented support for (intervention in) Ukraine's proceedings instituted against Russia before international courts[46] and discussion on the importance of strengthening military capabilities and resilience of European States (among other challenges, such as energy transition, environmental, technological and digital issues, *etc.*). Although, as history witnesses, alliances were limited in time, moreover, the reason for their disintegration often was new military conflicts, the meaningfulness of EU membership has even increased. Retaining the Union and possibly expanding EU borders means maintaining stability and enhancing security, even if fragile, as it is today; responding to crises together and overcoming challenges means the development of experience enabling the EU to be more resilient to threats and better prepared to ensure a sustainable and lasting peace.

---

[43] European Commission. Moldova. Membership status: candidate country (2025) https://enlargement.ec.europa.eu/european-neighbourhood-policy/countries-region/moldova_en. Accessed 2 April 2025.

[44] See, e.g. Report on Ukraine of 30 October 2024. Directorate-General for Neighbourhood and Enlargement. https://enlargement.ec.europa.eu/ukraine-report-2024_en. Accessed 2 April 2025.

[45] European Policy Centre (2025) How to fast-track Ukraine's membership of the European Union. https://www.epc.eu/publication/-Ukraines-membership-EU-6230b8/. Accessed 2 April 2025.

[46] For example, the case before the International Court of Justice concerning Allegations of Genocide under the Convention on the Prevention and Punishment of the Crime of Genocide (Ukraine v. Russian Federation) with 32 States intervening. www.icj-cij.org/case/182/intervention. Accessed 2 April 2025. The situation in Ukraine investigated before the International Criminal Court was referred to by 43 countries. Situation in Ukraine, ICC-01/22. https://www.icc-cpi.int/situations/ukraine. Accessed 2 April 2025.

1.4 Concluding Remarks

The evolution of the Union's identity, witnessed by the founding treaties and legal and institutional developments, reflected in political discourse and scholarly research, show that European integration is a continuous journey. Accession of new Member States not only changes the geopolitical map of the Union, but also has an impact on EU identity, the scale and depth of European integration and the Union's role on a global level. Accession to the EU is not only celebrative: EU membership demands profound changes in law, it means commitment and responsibility which may not only be rewarding and inspiring but challenging as well.

The accession of ten new Member States in 2004 was unprecedented in its scale and long-lasting effects on stability and prosperity in Europe. For the States which had recovered from Soviet rule, the accession was also a choice for European values, a geopolitical orientation. During the two-decade period the Union was called to respond to economic, migration, public health, democracy and security crises and "Brexit" showed that EU membership can be a two-way street. However, the EU provides for a comprehensive framework to flexibly react to challenges. New tasks tested the unity of the EU and its values, each challenge was reflected in separate countries, each Member State created an individual contribution shifting the change.

EU law has a profound impact on domestic legal orders and serves as a means to reach goals and make the principles and values respected. The EU is a value-based entity and EU membership means integration through law with a particular focus on the rule of law. The rule of law, democracy and human rights form the foundations of the European legal order. The rule of law is multifaceted and being applicable in many different fields it is relevant not only for European integration, but plays a significant role on the domestic and global levels as well. On the latter, it calls for peace and respect for the international legal order.

In a fragile and less stable international environment of increased polarisation, fragmentation, decreased security and trust, regional organisations can make a change. With both the UN and NATO the EU has space to cooperate, contribute or adapt. In response to Russia's aggression against Ukraine the EU has demonstrated its unity and ability to act so far, but this is not the end of the story. EU Member States should be determined to address the challenges and seek opportunities, being flexible to react to and develop in the face of an ever-changing landscape. EU enlargement is to be discussed in the light of evolving international relations and many political, diplomatic, social, economic, security and other issues pending. EU enlargement remains also a political decision related with questions "how" and "when". Taking into account the price Ukraine has already been paying for years in order to protect freedom and democracy not only in Ukraine, but also in Europe, its membership should not be confined to merely formal accession criteria, but be perceived encompassing everything what is left beyond. For all countries, becoming an EU Member State still carries the same meaning regarding the choice for EU values. Most important is that currently, facing increased threats to the international legal order and European values, the EU remains not only a Union of Law, but also a Union of Peace.

References

Akhvlediani T (2023) Georgia. In: Emerson M, Akhvlediani T, Cenusa D, Movchan V, Remizov A (authors) The EU Accession Prospects of Ukraine, Moldova and Georgia. First responses to the conditions set by the European Commission. March, 2023–06. https://cdn.ceps.eu/wp-content/uploads/2023/03/CEPS-In-depth-analysis-2023-06_EU-Accession-Prospects-of-Ukraine-Moldova-and-Georgia.pdf. Accessed 2 April 2025, pp 29–40

Calleja D, Rusche T M (2024) Įvadas. In: ES teisei – 70 metų. Savo piliečių labui veikianti Sąjunga. Europos Sąjungos leidinių biuras, Liuksemburgas [Introduction. In: 70 Years of EU Law. Union acting for the benefit of its Citizens. Publications Office of the European Union, Luxemburg], pp 15–32

Duff A (2024) NATO and the European Union: Bridging the Gap. Discussion Paper. European Politics and Institutions Programme. European Policy Centre

Holovaty S (2021) Measuring the Seemingly Immeasurable. In: Koziubra M (ed) Rule of Law Checklist at National Level. Case of Ukraine. Kyiv

Isokaitė-Valužė I (2024) Beyond the procedures: several aspects of a true meaning of NATO membership. In: Balatska O, Balashov E, Khudoliy A (eds) EU-NATO and the Ukrainian Status-QUO: panel discussion, Publishing House of the National University of Ostroh Academy, Ostroh, pp 41–45. https://doi.org/10.25264/5.03.2024

Isokaitė-Valužė I, Grigaitė-Daugirdė G (2024) Invocation of International (Treaty) Law Principles against an Aggressor State: Suspension, Restriction of Membership Rights, Expulsion? Kyiv-Mohyla Law & Politics Journal 10:19–50

Jarukaitis I (2006) Ratification of the treaty establishing a constitution for Europe in Lithuania and its impact on the national constitutional system. Teisė, 61:57–70

Jarukaitis I, Švedas G (2019) The Constitutional Experience of Lithuania in the Context of European and Global Governance Challenges. In: Albi A, Bardutzky S (eds) National Constitutions in European and Global Governance: Democracy, Rights, the Rule of Law: National Reports. T.M.C. Asser Press, The Hague, pp 997–1046

Lenaerts K (2020) New Horizons for the Rule of Law Within the EU. German Law Journal 21(1):29–34. https://doi.org/10.1017/glj.2019.91

Lenaerts K (2022) Speech delivered on the occasion of the acceptance of a doctorate Honoris Causa, 25 October 2022. Law Faculty of Vilnius University 2022. https://www.tf.vu.lt/wp-content/uploads/2022/10/Speech-of-prof.-Koen-Lenaerts.pdf. Accessed 2 April 2025

Maduro P M, Martin P, Piris J, Pisani-Ferry J, Reichlin L, Steinbach A, Weder di Mauro B (2021) Policy Insight 114: Revisiting the EU framework: Economic necessities and legal options. CEPR Policy Insight No 114, CEPR Press, Paris/London

Mackintosh T, Davies M, Demytrie R (2024) Police use water cannon as Georgia EU protests erupt for second night, 30 November 2024, BBC News. https://www.bbc.com/news/articles/c62jp68p315o. Accessed 2 April 2025

Metsola R (2024) Žodis svečiui. In: ES teisei – 70 metų. Savo piliečių labui veikianti Sąjunga. Europos Sąjungos leidinių biuras, Liuksemburgas [A Foreword. In: 70 Years of EU Law. Union acting for the benefit of its Citizens. Publications Office of the European Union, Luxemburg], pp 8–10

Polakiewicz J, Kirchmayr J K (2021) Sounding the Alarm: The Council of Europe As the Guardian of the Rule of Law in Contemporary Europe. In: von Bogdandy A, Bogdanowicz P, Canor I, Grabenwarter C, Taborowski M, Schmidt M (eds) Defending Checks and Balances in EU

Member States. Beiträge zum ausländischen öffentlichen Recht und Völkerrecht, Vol 298. Springer, Berlin/Heidelberg. https://doi.org/10.1007/978-3-662-62317-6_14
Sajó A (2023) On the Difficulties of Rule of Law Restoration. Working Papers. Central European University Democracy Institute
Von Bogdandy A (2024) The European Renaissance of Republicanism: On the Future of EU Law in Light of Article 2 TEU. Max Planck Institute for Comparative Public Law & International Law (MPIL) Research Paper No. 2024-02

Indrė Isokaitė-Valužė is a doctor of law, an associate professor, and Advisor to the Dean for international development at the Law Faculty of Vilnius University.

Haroldas Šinkūnas is a doctor of law, a professor and the Dean of the Law Faculty of Vilnius University.

Part II
European Union Membership and Values

Chapter 2
From the Union of Lublin to the European Union—The Common Path of Poland and Lithuania in the Process of Integration Through Law

Ewelina Cała-Wacinkiewicz and Wojciech Sz. Staszewski

Contents

Abstract The 20 years of both Lithuania's and Poland's membership in the European Union provides a special occasion to do some summing up of this period and to take into account not only factual aspects of the European integration process and integration through law, but also its special dimension, which is legal integration. The history of Poland and Lithuania may be used symbolically to serve as an example of widely understood integration processes occurring in Europe. Both these

E. Cała-Wacinkiewicz (✉) · W. Sz. Staszewski
Faculty of Law and Administration, University of Szczecin, Szczecin, Poland
e-mail: ewelina.cala-wacinkiewicz@usz.edu.pl

W. Sz. Staszewski
e-mail: wojciech.staszewski@usz.edu.pl

I. Isokaitė-Valužė and H. Šinkūnas (eds.), *The European Union 2004-2024*,
https://doi.org/10.1007/978-94-6265-718-2_2

countries have experienced multiculturalism, multiple religions, tolerance, and the building and modelling of national identity. Three historical events had a significant importance in their history and integration process: The Act of the Union of Lublin, declared on 1 July 1569, and in recent history the Treaty between the Republic of Poland and the Republic of Lithuania on friendly relations and good-neighbourly cooperation, signed in Vilnius on 26 April 1994, and the Treaty of Accession of Poland and Lithuania to the European Union, signed in Athens on 16 April 2003. These events and an analysis of documents signed then will allow us to shed light on the on-going processes in Central and Eastern Europe and the common efforts to become EU members. It will also allow an assessment of the essential aspect of integration, namely integration that is taking place in the legal realm. The commitments made and historic moments marked by treaties (such as the three legal acts referred to above) makes this assessment comprehensive and very much desired from the perspective of the activity of both these countries within EU structures; an activity which is celebrating its 20th anniversary this year.

Keywords Member States · Candidate country · Accession · European integration process · Integration through law · Lithuania's and Poland's membership in the European Union

2.1 Introduction

Context-sensitive analyses of the particular value, which is an integrated (united) Europe, must not ignore findings on integration, understood as a state, a process and a certain phenomenon alike. Europe is not only "an object of history, but its product, and what we call Europe is, in fact, a historically created reality with ever-changing forms and dynamics".[1] And although this dynamic is clearly connected with the integration process, the historically conditioned past determining reality, is evident in the 20th anniversary of Lithuania's and Poland's membership in the European Union in 2024. This timeline provides an opportunity to do some summing up, taking into account factual aspects of the European integration process, while at the same time contributing to the presentation of its specific dimension, which is integration by law (also understood as integration through law). Giving the law the status of a tool through which one of the planes of integration materializes is part of the main research objective of this study; it has also been given the attribute of scholarly intuition suggesting that the history of Poland and Lithuania should be symbolically presented as an example of broadly understood integration processes taking place in Europe.

These countries have experienced multiculturalism, multiple religions, tolerance, and building and modelling national identity. The following three historical events had a significant importance in their history, also in the integration process: The Act

[1] Delanty 1999, p. 9.

of the Union of Lublin, proclaimed on 1 July 1569,[2] and in recent history: the Treaty between the Republic of Poland and the Republic of Lithuania on friendly relations and good-neighbourly cooperation, signed in Vilnius on 26 April 1994,[3] and the Treaty on the Accession of Poland and Lithuania to the European Union, signed in Athens on 16 April 2003[4] (hereinafter also referred to as the Accession Treaty). These events and the analysis of the documents concluded at that time will allow us to present the ongoing processes in Central and Eastern Europe and the common aspirations for membership in the European Union. Their analysis is not an end in itself, however. It serves to allow an assessment of the essential aspect of integration, namely integration that is taking place in the legal realm, pursuant to the objective set out above. The commitments made and historic moments marked by treaties (such as the three legal acts referred to above) make this assessment comprehensive and very much desired from the perspective of today's activity of both these countries in the EU structure, which is celebrating its 20th anniversary this year.

The jubilee character of the study is worth comparing with seemingly incompatible events associated with the "From the Union of Lublin to the European Union" relation, which is reflected in the proposed title. These words, as emphasized in the literature, were uttered in Rome on 19 June 2003 by Pope John Paul II, just before the accession referendum in Poland, which decided on its accession to the European Union. This statement is an apt metaphor spanning 400 years of history of a large part of Central and Eastern Europe.[5]

A kind of communalization of the history of Poland and Lithuania, for which the membership of both countries in the European Union may be the culmination, materialized through the adopted treaties. This shows Europe as a community of law, governed by law and developed by law. There is no doubt that the international agreements—by virtue of their provisions—marked the common path of Poland and Lithuania, integrating through law.

---

[2] Act of the Union of Lublin of 1 July 1569, for the text, see: Szarek-Zwijacz 2019, pp. 180–187.

[3] The Treaty between the Republic of Poland and the Republic of Lithuania on friendly relations and good-neighbourly cooperation, signed in Vilnius on 26 April 1994, Dz. U. (Journal of Laws) of 1995 no. 15, item 71.

[4] This has been done on the basis of the Treaty between the Kingdom of Belgium, the Kingdom of Denmark, the Federal Republic of Germany, the Hellenic Republic, the Kingdom of Spain, the French Republic, Ireland, the Italian Republic, the Grand Duchy of Luxembourg, the Kingdom of the Netherlands, the Republic of Austria, the Portuguese Republic, the Republic of Finland, the Kingdom of Sweden, the United Kingdom of Great Britain and Northern Ireland (Member States of the European Union) and the Czech Republic, the Republic of Estonia, the Republic of Cyprus, the Republic of Latvia, the Republic of Lithuania, the Republic of Hungary, the Republic of Malta, the Republic of Poland, the Republic of Slovenia, the Slovak Republic concerning the accession of the Czech Republic, the Republic of Estonia, the Republic of Cyprus, the Republic of Latvia, the Republic of Lithuania, the Republic of Hungary, the Republic of Malta, the Republic of Poland, the Republic of Slovenia and the Slovak Republic into the European Union, signed at Athens on 16 April 2003. Pursuant to Article 2(2) of the Treaty, it entered into force on 1 May 2004. Text: Dz. U. (Journal of Laws) of 2004 no. 90, item 864.

[5] Przeździecki 2015, p. 7.

2.2 Integration by Law (Integration Through Law) and Its Importance in the Process of Integration *in Genere*

Against the background of the factually presented process of European integration, determined by historically conditioned events, such as those indicated in the title of this study (including the very important accession of Poland and Lithuania to the structures of the European Union), particular importance should be attributed to the category that is not very obvious, but that maps the rudimentary—from the perspective of the integration process—meaning of integration by law or, more precisely, integration through law.[6] The specific nature of law, as it is aptly noted in the literature, as a certain ontological category, requires that the legal plane of social phenomena be treated as a separate object of analysis and evaluation.[7] Therefore, if—understood as a state, a process, and above all as a phenomenon—the category of integration were to be placed into the framework of contemporary social phenomena, proving the existence of its legal plane appears not only as a prerequisite for in-depth analyses of the integration process *per se*, but it also shifts their vector toward presenting law as a particular tool through which one of the planes of integration, namely integration by law (also understood as integration through law), materializes. Giving the analyses devoted to it the status of a separate subject of research gives an impetus to a better understanding of the essence of the treaties that define common moments in the history of Poland and Lithuania. Such an optics fits into the assumptions of this chapter.

The law as an ontological category is a focus of many studies which do not only investigate countless semantic intuitions attributed to law, but, above all, offer deeper insights that situate law in the wider context of phenomena of the cultural world.[8] Indeed, law, being a product of culture (and at the same time a cultural factor)[9]—together with culture—creates the "central aspect of Europe's identity".[10] Europe, which—as K. Łastawski sees it—based on the achievements of civilization, using ancient Greek ideas, Roman law, Christian universalism and abundant achievements of nation states, through integration has led to the fact that European nations—of different identities—have strengthened cooperation. Europe has remained a "nation of many nations", but at the same time forms a modern community, relying on common goals and principles of conduct and on common legal norms and institutions that cover more and more states and regulate more and more planes.[11] This, in turn,

---

[6] The "integration through law" category is not a new one. See more on this in Cappelletti *et al.* 1986, Vol. 1; Azoulai 2016, pp. 449–463; Augenstein 2012.

[7] Sowiński 2003, p. 22.

[8] The term adopted after Rot 1995, p. 18. Law and culture jointly are also considered by Zumbansen 1999, pp. 114–126. See more in Cała-Wacinkiewicz 2006, pp. 113–128.

[9] Cf. Tokarczyk 2000a, p. 61 and Rot 1995, p. 18.

[10] Tokarczyk 2000b, p. 18.

[11] Łastawski 2003, p. 385.

on juridical grounds, makes it possible to treat Europe both as a community and as a specific value.[12]

The process of European integration, initiated in the 1950s and taking place on various levels (i.e. political, economic and cultural), has been the subject of multi-faceted analyses. Results of these scholarly investigations have appeared in the literature, varying in quantity and subject matter and even a cursory analysis of[13] it might suggest that almost everything has been said about it. Therefore, when analysing the integration process, it is worth focusing on the formative role and significance of law, highlighted by a particularly important category, i.e. integration through law. This is justified by at least a few reasons.

First, law has undoubtedly accompanied integration processes since their inception, materializing political assumptions and concepts, expressing the unanimous will of states for a common European project. In this angle, "“integration through law" is what may be called a "conjunctural concept": one that takes on a new meaning depending on the historical time in which it is formulated".[14] The implementation of the integration process will therefore be reflected in the adopted law. It stimulates integration[15] while being its particular effect.[16] Integration needs the law as a tool, as a vehicle of intentions and political plans. As emphasised in the literature, "we might conclude rather quickly that law is both the object of integration—the focus being on the legal process of bringing distinct national legal systems together such as to create a new legal order—and the agent or instrument of integration – the focus being on the process of framing through legal instruments (institutions, concepts, doctrines) the economic, social, and political spheres such as to achieve the basic goals of integration".[17]

Secondly, in the context of integration through law, attention should be focused on law as a tool for bringing states together into a community of goals, values or intentions. In fact, legal norms are not only the formal basis for their cooperation, implemented through the adoption of specific normative provisions on the basis of which the Member States of the European Union act in the various fields of integration, but above all through law, which constitutes a certain "coherence" of the integration processes for which it is at the same time a basis and a reference point.

The legal level of European integration is one of the most expressive planes. The integration of states in this area aims to unify legal systems within the European Union, which through the legal acts issued has an integrative effect on these legal systems. However, this is not just about harmonizing national law. Integration through

---

[12] The understanding of Europe as a community and a value and as an axiological category can be found in the message of John Paul II, who sees Europe as a Europe of homelands, safeguarding culture as an expression of man. See more in: Bortkiewicz 2000, pp. 101–111.

[13] For example, see: Sandholtz and Stone Sweet 1998, pp. 27–58; Heukels *et al.* 1998; Wallace 2000, pp. 3–37; de Búrca 2003, pp. 55–81.

[14] Azoulai 2016, p. 450.

[15] Biernat 2002, pp. 14, 53–61.

[16] Sowiński 2003, p. 24. Apart from the law of integration and integration by law, the author also distinguishes legal integration and integration in law. Cf. also: Möllers 2000, pp. 679–713.

[17] Azoulai 2016, p. 451.

law is something more than harmonization of rules. In this view, in the context of the economic, political and cultural spheres, law plays an important role in establishing a normative system of organizing the processes of integration.[18]

2.3 The Act of the Union of Lublin of 1 July 1569

2.3.1 The Circumstances Prior to the Conclusion of the Act

The relations between Poland and Lithuania have a long history, and the agreement concluded in Krewo on 14 August 1385 (called the "Union of Krewo") is considered to be the formal tightening of relations. It provided for the adoption of Jagiełło as a son by Elizabeth of Bosnia, Queen of Hungary (widow of Louis the Hungarian of the House of Anjou) and the marriage of her daughter Queen Jadwiga of Poland, to him. In addition, Jagiełło committed to: (a) conversion to Roman Catholicism for himself and for all his unbaptized brothers-princes and for all the residents; (b) pay William, Duke of Austria, compensation for breaking his engagement with Queen Jadwiga; (c) use the treasury to rebuild the destruction in Poland and Lithuania; (d) recover and rebuild by its own effort and at his own expense the territorial losses and destruction suffered by Poland; (e) permanently attach the lands of Lithuania and Ruthenia to the Crown of the Kingdom of Poland; (f) free all Christian prisoners taken by Lithuania on Polish lands and imprisoned there in the possessions of princes, lords and warriors.[19] In January 1386, the Polish delegation went to Lithuania and met with Jagiełło in Wołkowysk. Documents confirming the election of Jagiełło as king of Poland were issued there and an invitation to the meeting of the Polish nobility, which was planned in Lublin, was given. Jagiełło arrived at the meeting, where he was already welcomed as the king of Poland. He then went to Cracow and on 15 February 1386 was baptized and given the name Władysław. Three days later (18 February) his marriage to Jadwiga took place, and the solemn coronation of Władysław Jagiełło as king of Poland took place on 4 March 1386. The union of both countries, after many efforts, became a fact.[20] It is noted that the most important feature of the union of Poland and Lithuania was solidarity, which in the realities of that time could be understood as striving to create a secure future together which allowed them to win the Battle of Grunewald.[21] The documents signed in Krewo and Wołkowysk gave rise to special relations between the two countries, and also launched the process of interpenetration and influence, which undoubtedly contributed to the integration of this part of the continent. These Polish-Lithuanian relations, which worked differently (sometimes better, sometimes worse), were developed and deepened by the successive European

[18] The term adopted after Armstrong 1998, p. 89.

[19] Bardach 1999, p. 12; Uruszczak 2017, pp. 26–27.

[20] Myśliński 2004, p. 17.

[21] Meilūnas 2010, p. 17.

treaties, which regulated relations between the two countries, including the Vilnius-Radom Union of 1401 or the Union of Horodło of 1413. They were an expression of the changing balance of power in Central and Eastern Europe.[22] In the middle of the 16th century, the Polish reform movements undertook intensified actions aimed at tightening the union, and in turn in Lithuania they were preceded by legal changes that made the Duchy's system similar to the one in force in the Kingdom of Poland. King Sigismund II Augustus was aware that the extinction of the male line in the dynasty would be a serious threat to both countries. Wishing to permanently unite Lithuania with Poland, in 1564 he handed over to the Crown the hereditary rights of the Jagiellonian dynasty to the Grand Duchy. It is noted that this move was important because it meant detaching the notion of power in the state from a person.[23]

King Sigismund Augustus decided to convene a common Sejm in Lublin and arrived there in December 1568. The session began on 10 January 1569—two separate Sejm sessions were held: of the Crown and of the Grand Duchy, which contacted each other and only occasionally held joint hearings. Unfortunately, differing visions of the future union, as well as the lack of willingness to convene a joint session of the common Sejm, caused the majority of Lithuanians to leave Lublin on 28 February and 1 March 1569. The king decided to use his prerogatives and began intensive efforts to support arguments in favour of the union. Then he issued four incorporate acts, attaching Podlasie (5 March 1569), Volhynia and Bracław Land (27 May 1569) and Kiev Voivodeship (6 June 1569) to the Crown. These actions, combined with the threat from Moscow, prompted the delegates of the Grand Duchy to return to negotiations and on 7 June 1569 the Sejm resumed its sessions. The terms of the union were adopted on 27 June 1569 and the following day a meeting between the two parties and a joint final agreement were held, with a view to finally agreeing on the text of the act on 29 June 1569.[24] Technical matters related to the preparation of parchment paper, the writing of documents and their sealing took a few days.[25]

2.3.2 *Characterization of the Act*

The Act of Union was issued separately by the Sejms of the Crown and of the Grand Duchy on 1 July 1569 and then approved by King Sigismund Augustus on 4 July 1569. When discussing this act, it is worth noting that the Sejm of Lublin adopted a number of legal regulations defining the shape of relations between the Polish Crown and the Grand Duchy of Lithuania. One should agree with the expressed view that the Act of Union itself was a document of key importance, but it was preceded by acts changing the territorial structure of the common state, and after 1 July the joint

---

[22] Bardach 1999, p. 15.

[23] Krochmal 2020, pp. 13–14.

[24] Szarek-Zwijacz 2019, pp. 177–178.

[25] Krochmal 2020, p. 18.

Polish-Lithuanian Sejm adopted several subsequent constitutional resolutions which clarified and set the details of the Act of Union itself.[26]

One of the key provisions of the Act was Section 3, which stated that "the Kingdom of Poland and the Grand Duchy of Lithuania are one indivisible and not differing body, and also a not differing but one and common Republic, which was made and united out of two states and nations into one people". On the basis of the Act of the Union of Lublin, the Republic was created—a federal state, formed from two equal members and based on the real union. This equivalence of the joining countries was expressed, among others, by the common coat of arms, in which the Polish Eagle and the Lithuanian Vytis were alternately placed on the four-pole shield. Such a coat of arms was already present on the seal which was affixed to the document approving the Union by the King on 4 July 1569.[27]

The Polish-Lithuanian Commonwealth had a common ruler, chosen during a free election by the Polish and Lithuanian nobility, and who then was crowned at Wawel. The Sejm and Senate, defence and foreign policy, as well as the monetary system were also shared, although it should be noted that Poland and Lithuania kept their own armies and minted coins with their own seals. Distinctiveness was preserved in offices, titles and dignitary matters.[28] In addition, courts, laws and treasuries remained separate.[29]

As mentioned earlier, the Act of the Union of Lublin was complemented by a number of legal acts adopted later. One of the most important was the act of the Confederation of Warsaw adopted by the Sejm on 28 January 1573, which is described as an act of religious tolerance in force in the Republic of Poland and thanks to which the Republic was considered a "state without stakes".[30]

2.3.3 The Consequences of the Act and Integration by Law

The Union of Lublin, which was an act ending the long process of developing and deepening integration between Poland and Lithuania, and which was expressed by a number of agreements, starting from the Union of Krewo in 1385, permanently connected the two neighbouring countries. This process of strengthening relations was closely intertwined with the social, cultural and economic changes taking place in both states. It is also worth noting that the legal changes following the conclusion of the Union of Lublin required the introduction of legal regulations in the Grand Duchy of Lithuania. They were introduced in 1588 and written down in the Third Statute of Lithuania. The legal measures adopted and applied in the Duchy, also proved useful to the Crown, in which they were used when there were insufficient

[26] Gmiterek 2020, p. 104.

[27] Krochmal 2020, p. 20.

[28] *Ibid.*, p. 21.

[29] Szarek-Zwijacz 2019, p. 175.

[30] Krochmal 2020, p. 22.

provisions in Polish law. For this reason, the Third Statute of Lithuania was translated into Polish in 1614.[31] This proves the mutual penetration of law and its impact on the consolidation of the integration process of the two countries. One can therefore also speak of inculturation and thus mutual enrichment of the political and legal cultures of both the Crown and the Grand Duchy.[32]

The joining of the two countries on a voluntary basis and on equal footing undoubtedly contributed to the fact that the established Polish-Lithuanian commonwealth turned out to be a permanent, multi-ethnic, multicultural and multi-religious federal state. In addition, unlike many European countries engaged in religious wars, it was an extremely tolerant country. One may repeat after prof. J. Bardach that "the Union of Lublin was an outstanding work, because it defined for several centuries the further development of Central and Eastern Europe".[33]

The union of the two states was later strengthened by the Four-Year Sejm, which on 20 October 1791 adopted the Act of the Reciprocal Guarantee of Two Nations, which formed part of the Constitution of 3 May.[34] As a result of possessive aspirations of its neighbours, i.e. Austria, Prussia and Russia, the Polish-Lithuanian Commonwealth ceased to exist in 1795.[35]

2.4 The Treaty Between the Republic of Poland and the Republic of Lithuania on Friendly Relations and Good-Neighbourly Cooperation, Signed in Vilnius on 26 April 1994

2.4.1 The Circumstances Prior to the Conclusion of the Treaty

Transformations in the Central and Eastern European countries, motivated by *perestroika* in the USSR and the success of the opposition in the 1989 elections to the Parliament in Poland (4 June), initiated by events known as the "Autumn of Nations",[36] led to political changes in many states and the international environment in this part of Europe, including the disintegration of the Union of Soviet

[31] Bardach 1999, pp. 31–32; Krochmal 2020, p. 23.

[32] Bardach 1999, p. 32.

[33] Bardach 1969, p. 616.

[34] Meilūnas 2010, p. 19.

[35] Krochmal 2020, pp. 26–27; Meilūnas 2010, p. 20.

[36] Kukułka 2007, p. 389 ff. See also Trembicka 2005, p. 41 ff.

Socialist Republics.[37] Already on 18 May 1989, the Supreme Council of the Lithuanian SSR adopted the Declaration on State Sovereignty of Lithuania[38] and on 11 March 1990 the Supreme Council of the Republic of Lithuania adopted the Act of the Re-Establishment of the State of Lithuania.[39] There were conditions for the resumption of inter-state relations between Poland and Lithuania at that time. On 13 March 1990, the Government of the Republic of Poland issued a statement on the "Declaration on the Restoration of the State of Lithuania" adopted by the Supreme Council of Lithuania[40] and interparliamentary contacts were established. On 22 March 1990, the Sejm of the Republic of Poland adopted a resolution concerning Lithuania, which stated, among others: "[…] We welcome the return of the Lithuanian people to the family of free nations with all the greater joy because we are aware both of the centuries-old bonds that unite our nations liberated from totalitarianism, and of the fact that only free nations will be able to establish their relations on the basis of authentic fraternity, good neighbourly relations and partnerships […]".[41] Unfortunately, for more than a year Poland could not fully resume diplomatic ties with Lithuania, which resulted from existing international determinants and the need for Poland to pursue a policy of two-track[42] relations, consisting in maintaining links with the USSR as a whole and systematically expanding relations with the republics, especially Poland's neighbours.[43] The situation changed after the defeat of the coup in Moscow in August 1991 and on 26 August 1991 the Prime Minister of the Republic of Poland, J.K. Bielecki, informed the Prime Minister of Lithuania G. Vagnorius by a letter about his readiness to establish inter-state relations with the Republic of

[37] See Zieliński 1993a (in this study, in particular: Zieliński 1993, p. 7 ff; Górowska 1993, p. 115 ff). See also Antonowicz 1992, p. 20 ff.

[38] Declaration on state sovereignty of Lithuania, adopted by the Supreme Council of the Lithuanian Soviet Socialist Republic on 18 May 1989, for the text, see: Zieliński 1993a, p. 273.

[39] Act on the restoration of the independence of the State of Lithuania, adopted by the Supreme Council of the Republic of Lithuania on 11 March 1990, for the text, see: Zieliński 1993a, p. 278.

[40] It stated that "the Government of the Republic of Poland supports self-determination of nations, including self-determination leading to the acquisition of a separate statehood. Poles care about good relations with the Lithuanian nation, as well as with all other neighbours. The Government of the Republic of Poland believes that the interest of the peoples of Central and Eastern Europe requires that any changes, taking into account legitimate national aspirations, should be carried out peacefully with respect for the stability of our part of the continent". It was also highlighted, that "The Polish Government expresses its hope and conviction that Lithuania and the USSR will solve each other's problems while respecting the above principles" (Council of Ministers of the Republic of Poland 1991, pp. 47–48).

[41] Resolution of the Sejm of Republic of Poland of 22 March 1990, Dz. U. (Journal of Laws) of 1990 no. 11, item 79.

[42] This concept, authored by the Polish Ministry of Foreign Affairs, has been applied by numerous so-called Western countries. Skubiszewski 1993, p. 21.

[43] The USSR still existed and such actions could have been perceived as interference in the internal affairs of this country. It is also worth noting that the actions taken by Lithuania and other Baltic republics met with strong political and military repression. The Polish Government and Polish parliamentarians (The Sejm and the Senate of the Republic of Poland 1992, pp. 13–14) gave their support to Lithuania and the changes that followed in that country. Modzelewski 2012, p. 288; Nowakowski 1993, pp. 78–80.

Lithuania.[44] After that, an agreement was concluded through the exchange of notes of foreign ministers on the resumption of diplomatic relations between Poland and Lithuania.[45] On 13 January 1992, during the official visit of the Minister of Foreign Affairs of the Republic of Poland K. Skubiszewski in Vilnius, the Declaration on friendly relations and good-neighbourly cooperation was adopted, which laid down the principles of mutual relations and indicated the areas of cooperation, without, however, creating a legal international basis for them.

The events that took place in 1994 had a breakthrough significance in Polish-Lithuanian relations. At that time, the difficult and long-lasting negotiations[46] of the Treaty on friendly relations and good-neighbourly cooperation were completed. It was initialled by the Ministers of Foreign Affairs of Poland and Lithuania on 18 March 1994 and signed by the President of Poland, L. Wałęsa, and the President of Lithuania, A. Brazauskas, on 26 April 1994.

2.4.2 Characterization of the Treaty

Pursuant to the provisions of Article 27 of the Treaty, the instruments of ratification were exchanged in Marijampolė on 26 November 1994 and the Treaty entered into force on that date.[47] In the preamble, the signatories referred to the complex history of both nations and the possibility of "a different understanding of common history by both [of them]", while "stressing that the awareness of good and bad cards from the history of our countries is to serve to consolidate mutual understanding between the Polish and Lithuanian peoples in a uniting democratic Europe". The two countries also expressed their desire to contribute to the ongoing process of European integration "conscious of their common interests and their shared responsibility for peace, security, understanding and cooperation in a democratic, free and human rights-respecting Europe". They also reaffirmed their desire to pursue the comprehensive development of mutual relations and friendly cooperation based on the principle of good-neighbourly relations and declared their will to cooperate within international organizations and institutions, as well as to develop collaboration in the Baltic region.

The Parties committed to develop their relations in a spirit of mutual respect, trust, equality and good-neighbourly relations, based on the primacy of international law, in

---

[44] Widacki 1997, p. 151.

[45] Agreement through the exchange of notes of foreign ministers on the resumption of diplomatic relations between the Republic of Poland and the Republic of Lithuania, Warsaw, 28 August 1991, Vilnius, 2 September 1991; Staszewski and Szarek-Zwijacz 2015, p. 341.

[46] Major problems during the negotiations concerned divergent assessments of the historical Polish-Lithuanian relations and the issue of the rights of the Polish minority in Lithuania. Brodowski 1995, pp. 115–116; Chajewski 2018, p. 151 ff.

[47] The Government statement of 29 November 1994 on the exchange of documents of ratification of the Treaty between the Republic of Poland and the Republic of Lithuania on friendly relations and good-neighbourly cooperation, signed in Vilnius on 26 April 1994, Dz. U. (Journal of Laws) of 1995 no. 15, item 72.

particular on the principles of respect for sovereignty, inviolability of borders, prohibition of armed aggression, territorial integrity, non-interference in internal affairs and respect for human rights and fundamental freedoms (Article 1). The agreement confirmed the existing border between the Parties and stated that the Parties had no territorial claims against each other and will not have such claims in the future (Article 2). The Parties to the Treaty undertook to resolve their disputes solely by peaceful means and confirmed that they would refrain from using force or threatening to use it in their mutual relations (Article 3(1)). In addition, they agreed that neither of them will allow a third country or countries to commit an act of aggression from its territory against the other Party (Article 3(2)). The Treaty also provided for the possibility of immediate consultations in the event of a dispute or situation which, in the opinion of Parties, is likely to threaten or threaten the maintenance of peace or security in the world or violate international peace or security, in particular where such a dispute or situation affects both Parties. Such consultations shall be held with a view to seeking possible means of settling the dispute or the situation arising, in accordance with the provisions of the Charter of the United Nations. It was also agreed that in the event that a third state or third states attack one of the Parties-Signatories in armed conflict, the other Party shall refrain from providing any assistance or support to that third state or states throughout the duration of the armed conflict and shall take steps to resolve that conflict (Article 6). The Treaty also laid down the basis for cooperation in all relevant areas in which both Parties hold interest, including: security and defence; economy; scientific, cultural, technical and educational cooperation; youth and their exchange; environmental protection and the rational use of natural resources; safety and environmental cooperation; transport links and their modernization and telecommunications; health and sanitation; labour relations, insurance and welfare; legal transactions in civil, family, criminal and administrative matters; in the fight against organized crime, terrorism, economic crime, illicit drug and arms trafficking and illicit trafficking in works of art; breaches of civil air and maritime security; production and circulation of counterfeit means of payment, and illegal migration.

The Treaty also contains regulations concerning national minorities and the protection of their rights. Article 13(2) of the agreement defines the Polish minority in the Republic of Lithuania and the Lithuanian minority in the Republic of Poland. The Polish minority is understood as persons having Lithuanian citizenship, who are of Polish origin or admit to the Polish nationality, culture or tradition and recognize Polish as their mother tongue. The agreement defines the Lithuanian minority residing in the territory of Poland similarly.[48] They were granted the right, individually or jointly with other members of their group, to freely express, preserve or develop their national, cultural, linguistic and religious identity, without discrimination of any kind and with full equality before the law. The Parties undertook to respect international principles and standards for the protection of the rights of national minorities.[49]

---

[48] Wójcik 2010, p. 222.

[49] *Ibid.*, p. 225 ff.

The Parties to the Treaty undertook to provide special care for places and objects of culture in their territories bearing witness to historical events and cultural and scientific achievements and traditions of the other Party-Signatory. The basis for cooperation in the protection of graves and cemeteries located or in the future discovered on the territory of one Party and constituting the object of veneration and commemoration of the other Party was also established.

The agreement also regulated cooperation between municipalities, cities and other administrative-territorial units and regions, while committing to take action to integrate this cooperation into the activities of the relevant European institutions and declaring that they will be guided by the relevant Council of Europe conventions, which directly refers to the processes of integration through law in Europe and which both countries have joined. The Parties have also established the basis for cooperation between state bodies (including inter-parliamentary cooperation, heads of state and government, foreign ministers, as well as bilateral commissions).

While characterizing the provisions of the Treaty, it is also worth mentioning that it was concluded for a period of 15 years and adopted a renewal clause, which automatically extends it for five-year periods if neither party terminates it by notification at least one year before the expiry of the period of validity. The Treaty was drafted in Polish and Lithuanian. Unfortunately, it was not decided to draw it up in a third language of international importance, which could possibly facilitate its interpretation and application[50] in the future.

2.4.3 The Consequences of the Treaty and Integration Through Law

The Treaty on friendly relations and good-neighbourly cooperation, which was an expression of the compromise, proved that Poland and Lithuania are able to communicate with their neighbours and resolve previous misunderstandings. It played an important role in bilateral relations and in this part of Europe in general. It allowed for the exchange of experience and joint implementation of many projects and activities on many levels, which contributed to close cooperation and integration processes between the parties, such as in cross-border collaboration. The Treaty provided the basis for the two countries to build their strategic partnership and support Poland and Lithuania's aspirations to participate in international organizations and to become members of the European Communities/European Union. It was also the basis for the conclusion of a number of bilateral agreements, in which the areas of cooperation indicated in the Treaty were regulated in detail. These are for example the Agreement between the Government of the Republic of Poland and the Government of the Republic of Lithuania on cross-border cooperation of 16 September 1995; Agreement between the Government of the Republic of Poland and the Government of the Republic of Lithuania on youth exchange and cooperation of 14 February 1997;

[50] Walkowiak 2014, p. 88 ff.

Agreement between the Government of the Republic of Poland and the Government of the Republic of Lithuania on the establishment of a joint military unit for the maintenance and restoration of international peace and security of 25 June 1997. It is also worth mentioning that in 1997 the Consultative Committee of the Presidents of Poland and Lithuania was established, at whose meetings the current problems of bilateral cooperation and issues of integration of Poland and Lithuania with the European Union and with the structures of the North Atlantic Treaty Organization[51] were discussed.

2.5 Treaty of Accession of Poland and Lithuania to the European Union, Signed in Athens on 16 April 2003

2.5.1 Legal Status of the Accession Treaties

Accession treaties in a multi-centric legal system are undoubtedly a kind of international agreement of underestimated scientific interest.[52] Their particularly important normative status is manifested not only in the fact that the provisions contained in the treaty make accession, understood as the accession of the state to an international organization, but above all, that this treaty is the legal emanation of a community of law, which at the moment of accession becomes the participation of the state or states, as was the case with the analysed Treaty on the accession of Poland and Lithuania to the European Union. This highlights the importance of such agreements, also in the context of the aforementioned integration by law.

The accession treaties, being international agreements, fall under the regime of the Vienna Convention on the Law of Treaties of 23 May 1969.[53] Their international relevance is therefore beyond doubt, although the particular importance of such treaties is evident in the context of the relationship between the state(s) acceding to an international organization and the existing Member States, as well as in national law, through the requirement of ratification, in accordance with the constitutional provisions of the individual Member States.

This is no different in the case of the Treaty discussed here. As the literature emphasizes—where an international agreement is an element of a specific legal regime, e.g. a system established within a specific group of states, it is also important to determine the place of the agreement within it.[54] The Treaty on the accession of

[51] Staszewski 2002, p. 6 ff.

[52] On the uniqueness of accession protocols in the context of the WTO see: Liu 2014, pp. 751–771, who points out that "accession protocols are unique legal instruments in the World Trade Organization (WTO) legal system".

[53] Dz. U. (Journal of Laws) of 1990 no. 74, item 439, annex.

[54] Wyrozumska 2003, p. 13.

Poland and Lithuania to the European Union is undoubtedly a source of international law, as stated above, but also a source of primary law of the European Union. To the extent that it introduces changes to existing legal provisions, it also acts as an amending (modifying) treaty, which from a legislative perspective significantly shapes the legal system. Indeed, the provisions of a single treaty do not only bring about the accession of the state(s) to the structure of an international organization, but also "adapt" the existing legislation to this fact. This type of action is based on the provisions of Article 49 of the Treaty on European Union as established by the Treaty of Lisbon of 13 December 2007,[55] pursuant to which the conditions of admission and the adjustments to the Treaties on which the Union is founded are the subject of an agreement between the Member States and the applicant state.

2.5.2 *The Normative Essence of the Treaty of Accession of Poland and Lithuania to the European Union and Integration Through Law*

The signing of the accession treaty and the accession of Poland and Lithuania to the structures of the European Union were preceded not only by a multi-thread negotiation process, but above all by the signing of association agreements, which are a formal manifestation of the will to establish full cooperation and acquire membership in this organization.[56] Poland signed the Association Agreement on 16 December 1991, and in the case of Lithuania this took place on 12 June 1995.[57] The formal completion of the application process for Poland and Lithuania to join the EU structures took place when the Accession Treaty was signed in Athens on 16 April 2003. The structure of this Treaty was not uniform though.

---

[55] Consolidated version, OJ C 202/13, 7.06.2016.

[56] The Europe Agreement establishing an association between the Republic of Poland, of the one part, and the European Communities and their Member States, of the other part, done at Brussels on 16 December 1991. Pursuant to Article 121 of the Agreement, it entered into force on 1 February 1994 (Text: Dz. U. (Journal of Laws) of 1994 no. 11, item 38). The Agreement was supplemented with effect from 1 July 2002 by an Additional Protocol setting out a trade agreement on certain fish and fishery products relating to the Europe Agreement establishing an association between the Republic of Poland, of the one part, and the European Communities and their Member States, of the other part, done at Brussels on 14 June 2002. Pursuant to Article 6 of the Protocol, it entered into force on 1 July 2002 (Text: Dz. U. (Journal of Laws) of 2003 no. 78, item 704).

[57] Europe Agreement establishing an Association between the European Communities and their Member States, of the one part, and the Republic of Lithuania, of the other part—Protocol 1 Referred to in Article 16 (2) laying down other arrangements applicable to textile products—Protocol 2 On trade between the Community and Lithuania in processed agricultural products—Protocol 3 Concerning the definition of originating products and methods of administrative cooperation—Protocol 4 On specific provisions relating to trade between Lithuania and Spain and Portugal—Protocol 5 On mutual assistance between administrative authorities in customs matters—Final Act—Joint Declarations—Unilateral Declarations, OJ L 51, 20.02.1998, pp. 3–242.

It included the Accession Treaty, the Act concerning the conditions of accession and the Final Act. The first of them—key, although quite general in its content—constituted the accession to the European Union of 10 countries applying for membership (i.e. the Czech Republic, the Republic of Estonia, the Republic of Cyprus, the Republic of Latvia, the Republic of Lithuania, the Republic of Hungary, the Republic of Malta, the Republic of Poland, the Republic of Slovenia and the Slovak Republic), which by virtue of the provisions of Article 1 thereof became members of the European Union and parties to the Treaties on which the Union is founded, as amended and supplemented. The Accession Treaty, containing, inter alia, the ratification clause and the entry into force clause, at the same time in Article 1(2) regarding the conditions of acceptance and the resulting adjustments to the Treaties on which the Union is founded, referred to the provisions of the Act concerning the conditions of accession.

This act—much more normatively complex—set out a number of specific issues related to accession (i.e. being bound by the founding treaties—Article 2, being bound by and applying the provisions of the Schengen acquis—Article 3), etc. It also specified the scope of changes (adjustments) in the founding treaties of the European Union, the adaptation of secondary legislation (including the free movement of goods, persons and services, but also company law, competition policy, agriculture, fisheries, transport policy, taxation, social and employment policies, energy, small and medium-sized enterprises, education and training, environment, consumers and health, justice and home affairs cooperation, customs union, external relations or common foreign and security policy). The Act also includes temporary provisions, provisions on the implementation of the Act, as well as annexes—specifying detailed technical issues, or lists of adjustments from permanent and temporary provisions in the field of specific sectoral regulations. It is worth noting that the provisions of the Act form an integral part of the Treaty (Article 1(2) of the Accession Treaty).

This is not the case with the Final Act, which, while not part of the Treaty, contains declarations, statements and positions of the parties to the Treaty concerning the interpretation and application of its provisions.

From the perspective of the integration process, a particular role should be given to the Act concerning the conditions of Accession. It obliged the new Member States to be bound by the provisions of the founding treaties and secondary legislation, as it were, ipso jure introducing them into the adoption and application of the EU acquis. Thus, the Act harmonized the legal orders of the individual Member States, allowing the substance of the Accession Treaty to be deemed as executing integration through law most fully. On the one hand, its provisions forced the obligation to harmonize the national law of the new Member States. As emphasized in the introduction, Europe is a certain product of history; therefore, the fact of caring for a certain community of law connecting the Member States should be considered significant. However, the integration through law named in the title is something more, it is a tool of integration (approximation) not only of legislation, but above all of countries, and Poland and Lithuania exemplify its special dimension.

2.6 Conclusion

A united Europe is undoubtedly a special value worth pointing out at such moments as the 20th anniversary of Poland and Lithuania's membership in the European Union celebrated in 2024. Without a doubt, as the above analyses have shown, interlocking with crucial moments reflected in the discussed treaties, the history of Poland and Lithuania can be symbolically taken as an example of broadly understood integration processes taking place in Europe. Processes that are so difficult that they confront both countries with multiculturalism, multiple religions, the need for far-reaching tolerance and building and shaping national identity, closing in on the "united in diversity" characteristic of the European Union.

Within the framework of these broadly defined integration processes, equipping a category of law with the status of a tool through which one of the planes of integration materializes not only meets the research objective of this study, but also allows us to look from a slightly different perspective both at Europe and at integration itself, which is a state of the art, a process but also a kind of *signum temporis* of post-war Europe. This Europe has become not only a community of law, a community governed and developed by law, but also a value enabling states to integrate through law.

The considerable function of law as a tool for materializing political assumptions and concepts shows—as seen in the example of Poland and Lithuania—that even in the case of countries with difficult pages of common history, it is possible to jointly participate in the European project of building Europe as a common value. If it is a truism to assume that integration needs law, then the conclusion that integration without law would not have been realized or becomes only an illusory project, gives importance and meaning to law as a certain ontological category.

Law, as a tool that unites states into a certain community of goals, values and intentions, is thus a certain "coherence" of integration processes, being the foundation and a point of reference for them. It is a specific normative system ordering the process of integration, without which a United Europe would not have been achieved. Taking care of it does not only mean paying off a certain historical debt incurred by those who made history. It is also a special commitment and responsibility to future generations, and Russian aggression against Ukraine shows this with increased force.

References

Antonowicz L (1992) Rozpad ZSRR ze stanowiska prawa międzynarodowego [Dissolution of the USSR from the point of view of international law]. Państwo i Prawo 9:20–29

Armstrong K (1998) New Institutionalism and European Union Legal Studies. In: Craig P, Harlow C (eds) Lawmaking in the European Union. Wolters Kluwer (Kluwer Law International), London/The Hague/Boston

Augenstein D (ed) (2012) "Integration through Law" Revisited. The Making of the European Polity. Routledge, London/New York

Azoulai L (2016) "Integration through law" and us. International Journal of Constitutional Law 14(2):449–463

Bardach J (1969) Krewo i Lublin. Z problemów unii polsko-litewskiej [Krewo and Lublin. On the problems of the Polish-Lithuanian union]. Kwartalnik Historyczny, LXXVI (3):583–619

Bardach J (1999) Od aktu w Krewie do Zaręczenia Wzajemnego Obojga Narodów (1385–1791) [From the act of Krewo to the Reciprocal Guarantee of Two Nations (1385–1791)]. In: Kłoczowski J, Kras P, Łaszkiewicz H (eds) Unia Lubelska i tradycje integracyjne w Europie Środkowo-Wschodniej [The Union of Lublin and integration traditions in the Central-Eastern Europe]. Instytut Europy Środkowo-Wschodniej, Lublin, pp 12–44

Biernat T (2002) Wspólnota prawa. O osobliwościach systemu europejskiego [Community of law. On the peculiarities of the European system]. Wydawnictwo Adam Marszałek, Toruń

Bortkiewicz P (2000) W stronę etosu zjednoczonej Europy [Towards the ethos of united Europe]. In: Mikołajczak AW, Mrozewicz L (eds) Poszukiwanie Europy. Zjazd gnieźnieński a idea zjednoczonej Europy [Searching for Europe. The Meeting in Gniezno and the idea of a united Europe]. Wydawnictwo Naukowe Uniwersytetu im. Adama Mickiewicza (Poznań), Poznan, pp 101–111

Brodowski L (1995) Stosunki z Litwą [Relations with Lithuania]. In: Wizimirska B (ed) Rocznik Polskiej Polityki Zagranicznej – 1995 [Polish Foreign Policy Annals - 1995]. Polski Instytut Spraw Międzynarodowych, Warsaw, pp 115–118

Cała-Wacinkiewicz E (2006) Kulturowa i prawna płaszczyzna integracji europejskiej (rozważania w kontekście wielopłaszczyznowego charakteru Unii Europejskiej) [Cultural and legal plane of European integration (reflections in the context of the multifaceted nature of the European Union)]. In: Smoliński T (ed) Modele integracji międzynarodowej – uniwersalny, kontynentalny, sektorowy a państwo, prawo, idee. Zbiór studiów [Models of international integration – universal, continental, sectoral vis-a-vis state, law and ideas. Collection of studies]. Wydawnictwo Uniwersytetu Szczecińskiego, Szczecin, pp 113–128

Cappelletti M, Seccombe M, Weiler J (eds) (1986) Integration Through Law: Europe and the American Federal Experience. Vol. 1: Methods, Tools and Institution. Walter De Gruyter And Co., New York

Chajewski A (2018) Kwestia zaszłości historycznych w rokowaniach nad traktatem między Rzecząpospolitą Polską a Republiką Litewską o przyjaznych stosunkach i dobrosąsiedzkiej współpracy [The question of past events in negotiations over the Treaty between the Republic of Poland and the Republic of Lithuania on friendly relations and good-neighbourly cooperation]. In: Lis W (ed) Polacy na Litwie. Przeszłość i teraźniejszość [Poles in Lithuania. Then and now]. Wydawnictwo Adam Marszałek, Toruń, pp 151–183

Council of Ministers of the Republic of Poland (1991) Oświadczenie Rady Ministrów Rzeczypospolitej Polskiej w związku z rozwojem sytuacji na Litwie z dnia 14 stycznia 1991 r. [Declaration of the Council of Ministers of the Republic of Poland on the development of the situation in Lithuania of 14 January 1991], Zbiór Dokumentów 1:15–16

de Búrca G (2003) The Institutional Development of the EU. A Constitutional Analysis. In: Craig P, de Búrca G (eds) The Evolution of EU Law. Cambridge University Press, Oxford, pp 55–81

Delanty G (1999) Odkrywanie Europy. Idea, tożsamość, rzeczywistość [Discovering Europe. Idea, identity, reality]. Wydawnictwo Naukowe PWN, Warsaw/Krakow

Gmiterek H (2020) Dokumenty unii polsko-litewskiej z 1569 r. – analiza treści i znaczenie dla Rzeczypospolitej Obojga Narodów [Documents of the 1569 Polish-Lithuanian union – analysis of the content and the importance for the Polish-Lithuanian Commonwealth] In: Szczygieł R (ed) Unia Lubelska i jej tradycje [The Union of Lublin and its traditions]. Wojewódzka Biblioteka Publiczna im. Hieronima Łopacińskiego w Lublinie, Lublin, pp 101–115

Górowska B (1993) Tworzenie struktur władzy państwowej republik [Creating structures of state authorities in republics] In: Zieliński E (ed) Przeobrażenia ustrojowe w republikach dawnego ZSRR [Political transformations in the republics of the former USSR]. Dom Wydawniczy i Handlowy "ELIPSA", Warsaw, pp 115–133

Heukels T, Blokker N, Brus M (eds) (1998) The European Union after Amsterdam. A Legal Analysis. Wolters Kluwer (Kluwer Law International), The Hague/London/Boston

Krochmal J (2020) Unia Lubelska aktem założycielskim Rzeczypospolitej [The Union of Lublin as a founding act for the Republic]. In: Krochmal J (ed) Unia Lubelska 1569 roku i unie w Europie Środkowo-Wschodniej [The Union of Lublin of 1569 and other unions in Central and Eastern Europe]. Archiwum Główne Akt Dawnych, Warsaw, pp 13–64

Kukułka J (2007) Historia współczesnych stosunków międzynarodowych 1945–2000 z kalendarium 2001–2006 [History of modern international relations 1945–2000: from the 2001–2006 annals]. Wydawnictwo Naukowe Scholar, Warsaw

Łastawski K (2003) Od idei do integracji europejskiej [From the idea to European integration]. Wydawnictwo Wyższej Szkoły Pedagogicznej TWP, Warsaw

Liu J (2014) Accession Protocols: Legal Status in the WTO Legal System. Journal of World Trade 48(4):751–771

Meilūnas E (2010) Litwa – Polska: od Unii do Unii [Lithuania – Poland: from a Union to a Union]. In: Gil A (ed) Unia Lubelska – dziedzictwo wielu narodów [The Union of Lublin – heritage of many nations]. Towarzystwo Instytutu Europy Środkowo-Wschodniej, Instytut Europy Środkowo-Wschodniej, Lublin, pp 15–34

Modzelewski WT (2012) Dwie dekady stosunków Polski z Litwą – wymiar polityczny [Two decades of Poland's relations with Lithuania – political dimension]. Środkowoeuropejskie Studia Polityczne 3:287- 312

Möllers T (2000) The Role of Law in European Integration. American Journal of Comparative Law 48: 679–713

Myśliński K (2004) Losy związku polsko-litewskiego od Unii Krewskiej do Unii Lubelskiej [The course of the Polish-Lithuanian relations from the Union of Krewo to the Union of Lublin]. In: Witusik A (ed) Unia Lubelska 1569 roku w dziejach Polski i Europy [The 1569 Union of Lublin in the history of Poland and Europe]. Wydawnictwo Multico, Lublin, pp 13–38

Nowakowski J M (1993) Polska polityka wschodnia w 1991 roku [Poland's eastern policy in 1991], In: Wizimiska B (ed) Rocznik Polskiej Polityki Zagranicznej – 1991 [Polish Foreign Policy Annals – 1991]. Polski Instytut Spraw Międzynarodowych, Warsaw, pp 77–88

Przeździecki M (2015) Od Unii Lubelskiej do Unii Europejskiej [From the Union of Lublin to the European Union]. Państwowa Wyższa Szkoła Informatyki i Przedsiębiorczości, Łomża

Rot H (1995) Główne kultury prawne współczesnego świata [Main legal cultures of today's world]. Wydawnictwo Naukawe PWN, Warsaw

Sandholtz W, Stone Sweet A (eds) (1998) The Path to European Integration: A Historical – Institutionalist Analysis. In: European Integration and Supranational Governance. Wydawca: Państwowe Wydawnictwo Naukowe, New York

Skubiszewski K (1993) Polska polityka zagraniczna w 1991 roku [Poland's foreign policy in1991]. In: Wizimirska B (ed) Rocznik Polskiej Polityki Zagranicznej – 1991 [Polish Foreign Policy Annals – 1991]. Polski Instytut Spraw Międzynarodowych, Warsaw, pp 15–25

Sowiński R (2003) Integracja prawna jako składnik europejskiej tożsamości [Legal integration as an element of European identity]. In: Drozdowicz Z (ed) Współczesna Europa w poszukiwaniu swojej tożsamości [Today's Europe in search for its identity]. Poznań

Staszewski W Sz (2002) Komitet Konsultacyjny Prezydentów Polski i Litwy [Consultation Committee of the President of Poland and the President of Lithuania]. Studia i Materiały Centrum Badań Wschodnich Uniwersytetu Warszawskiego 93, Warsaw

Staszewski W Sz, Szarek-Zwijacz A (2015) Instytucja uznania państwa i jej stosowanie w praktyce polskiej oraz Wspólnot Europejskich (Unii Europejskiej) w stosunku do państw powstałych po rozpadzie ZSRR [The institution of the recognition of a state and its application in the Polish practice and the Practice of European Communities (European Union) towards states that were established after the dissolution of the USSR]. In: Brodowski L, Kuźniar-Kwiatek D (eds) Unia Europejska a prawo międzynarodowe. Księga Jubileuszowa dedykowana Prof. Elżbiecie Dyni [European Union and international law. Commemorative book for prof. Elżbieta Dynia]. Oficyna Wydawnicza "Zimowit" Sp. z o.o., Rzeszów, pp 333–343

Szarek-Zwijacz A (ed) (2019) Akt Unii Lubelskiej, proklamowany dnia 1 lipca 1569 r. [Act of the Union of Lublin, promulgated on 1 July 1569], In: Stasiak K, Staszewski W Sz, Szarek-Zwijacz

A (eds) Prawo międzynarodowe publiczne. Studia i materiały [Public international law. Studies and materials], vol. II, Towarzystwo Naukowe KUL, Lublin, pp 175–187
The Sejm and the Senate of the Republic of Poland (1992) Wspólne Oświadczenie Sejmu i Senatu Rzeczypospolitej Polskiej dotyczące sytuacji na Litwie z dnia 11 stycznia 1991 r. [Joint Statement of the Sejm and the Senate of the Republic of Poland on the situation in Lithuania of 11 January 1991], Zbiór Dokumentów 1:13–14
Tokarczyk R (2000a) Współczesne kultury prawne [Modern legal cultures], Zakamycze, Kraków
Tokarczyk R (2000b) Kultura prawa europejskiego [European law culture]. In: Mik C (ed) Europeizacja prawa krajowego. Wpływ integracji europejskiej na klasyczne dziedziny prawa krajowego [Europeanization of domestic law. The impact of European integration on classical fields of domestic law]. TNOiK, Toruń
Trembicka K (2005) Zmiana systemu władzy w Europie Środkowo-Wschodniej (1989–1990): uwarunkowania i prawidłowości [Change in the system of power in Central and Eastern Europe (1989–1990): determinants and regularities]. Annales Universitatis Mariae Curie-Skłodowska. Sectio K, Politologia 12:41–61
Uruszczak W (2017) Unio regnorum sub una Corona non causat eorum unitatem: Unia Polski i Litwy w Krewie w 1385 r.: studium historyczno-prawne [Unio regnorum sub una Corona non causat eorum unitatem: the Union of Poland and Lithuania in Krewo of 1358: a historical and legal study]. Jagiellonian University in Krakow. Chair of the History of Polish Law. https://khpp.wpia.uj.edu.pl/documents/106750129/0/unia_polski_i_litwy_v3/a46ba21f-340d-411f-8c67-962e0e9c90a1. Accessed 30 March 2025
Walkowiak J (2014) One word, two languages, two interpretations: the Polish-Lithuanian treaty of 1994 and how it was (mis)understood. Comparative Legilinguistics 18:88–101
Wallace H (2000) The Institutional Setting. In: Wallace H, Wallace W (eds) Policy-Making in the European Union. Oxford University Press, Oxford, pp 3–37
Widacki J (1997) Stosunki z Litwą [Relations with Lithuania]. In: Wizimirska B (ed) Rocznik Polskiej Polityki Zagranicznej – 1997 [Polish Foreign Policy Annals – 1997]. Polski Instytut Spraw Międzynarodowych, Warsaw, pp 147–158
Wójcik K (2010) Ochrona mniejszości narodowych w świetle dwustronnych traktatów zawartych przez Polskę [Protection of national minorities in the light of bilateral treaties signed by Poland]. Studia Iuridica Lublinensia 14: 217–235
Wyrozumska A (2003) Charakter prawny traktatu o przystąpieniu do Unii Europejskiej z 2003 r. [Legal nature of the 2003 Accession Treaty]. In: Biernat S, Dudzik S, Niedźwiedź M (eds) Przystąpienie Polski do Unii Europejskiej. Traktat akcesyjny i jego skutki [Poland's accession to the European Union. Accession Treaty and its effects]. Zakamycze, Krakow/Zakamycze
Zieliński E (ed) (1993a) Przeobrażenia ustrojowe w republikach dawnego ZSRR [Political transformations in the republics of the former USSR]. Dom Wydawniczy i Handlowy "ELIPSA", Warsaw
Zieliński E (1993b) Proces odrodzenia narodowego i państwowego republik [The process of national and state revival of republics]. In: Zieliński E (ed) Przeobrażenia ustrojowe w republikach dawnego ZSRR [Political transformations in the former USSR]. Dom Wydawniczy i Handlowy "ELIPSA", Warsaw, pp 7–52
Zumbansen P (1999) Semantics of European Law. European Law Journal 5(2): 114–126

Ewelina Cała-Wacinkiewicz is dr. hab., professor at the Faculty of Law and Administration of the University of Szczecin. Author of Sects. 2.1, 2.2, 2.5 and 2.6.

Wojciech Sz. Staszewski is dr. hab., professor at the Faculty of Law and Administration of the University of Szczecin. Author of Sects. 2.3 and 2.4.

Chapter 3
Membership in the European Union as a Constitutional Value and Obligation

Tomas Davulis

Contents

Abstract This chapter explores the constitutional dimensions of Lithuania's membership in the European Union (EU), emphasizing that attention to EU law is not merely ceremonial, but reflects deep theoretical and practical legal engagement. Membership takes on new significance in the broader context of the EU's efficiency, integration prospects, and responses to contemporary challenges—such as security, climate, and technology. The relationship between EU law and national law, particularly in Lithuania, has evolved beyond interest to a complex and nuanced field of daily legal practice. Debates in legal scholarship and at academic forums, including interpretations of the openness of the Constitution of the Republic of Lithuania to EU and international law, reveal a dynamic discourse. Notably, scholars such as T. Birmontienė question whether openness to EU law constitutes a principle of constitutional interpretation, while others emphasize the idea of EU law priority rather than supremacy, pointing to shared or transferred competencies. This chapter identifies and discusses four key constitutional aspects that, in the author's view, reveal how Lithuania's EU membership functions as both a constitutional value and a legal obligation, as interpreted by the Constitutional Court.

Keywords EU Membership · Lithuania's EU membership · Constitutional value · EU law · Relationship between EU law and national law · Constitutional Court of the Republic of Lithuania · Geopolitical orientation

T. Davulis (✉)
Faculty of Law, Vilnius University, Vilnius, Lithuania
e-mail: tomas.davulis@tf.vu.lt

I. Isokaitė-Valužė and H. Šinkūnas (eds.), *The European Union 2004-2024*,
https://doi.org/10.1007/978-94-6265-718-2_3

3.1 Introduction

European Union law and the case law of the Court of Justice of the European Union have for some time now become the sources of law used by European constitutional courts. The Lithuanian Constitutional Court has noted not once that European Union law and the jurisprudence of the CJEU are inevitable sources for the interpretation and application of Lithuanian law.[1] In the decision of 20 December 2017 it was also concluded by the Constitutional Court that European Union law is a source of the interpretation of the law of the Republic of Lithuania, *inter alia*, the Constitution in the areas where (under Article 1 of the Constitutional Act of the Republic of Lithuania on Membership of the Republic of Lithuania in the European Union), the Republic of Lithuania shares with or confers on the European Union the competences of its state institutions.[2] The decision of 20 December 2017 is of particular importance because, for the first time, the Court has expressed the need to consider EU law when interpreting the Constitution and formulating official constitutional doctrine. The Constitutional Court's decision of 20 December 2017 and its ruling of 11 January 2019 has prompted scholarly debate regarding the extent to which European Union law should serve as a source for interpreting the Constitution. It has been argued that the newly articulated constitutional doctrine broadens the application of EU law and necessitates further development of the boundaries governing the interaction between national and EU legal systems.

Numerous views have been voiced in legal scholarship and academic conferences concerning how the Constitution of the Republic of Lithuania is receptive to international and EU law. For instance, T. Birmontienė has questioned whether openness to EU law should be recognized as a constitutional principle of interpretation.[3] In contrast, E. Kūris has sharply criticized specific rulings, characterizing them as a "deliberate capitulation of the Constitutional Court to the CJEU".[4]

The present contribution focuses on the constitutional assessment of the State's membership in the European Union to show that the Euro-integration processes gain more potential thanks to their value-laden constitutional importance. The chapter aims to highlight the legal foundations of membership in the European Union and the development of the perception of membership as a constitutional value in the case law of the Constitutional Court. The chapter defends the hypothesis that Lithuania's membership in the EU shall be understood in the framework of all constitutional values, and solutions must be found to ensure that none of such values will be denied or unreasonably restricted.

[1] Rulings of, *inter alia*, 27 March 2009, 21 June 2011 and 22 December 2011, Constitutional Court of the Republic of Lithuania.

[2] It was repeated in the Rulings of 6 January 2020 and 7 June 2023, Constitutional Court of the Republic of Lithuania.

[3] Birmontienė 2020, pp. 92–95; Birmontienė 2023, pp. 36–37.

[4] Kūris 2024, pp. 23–25.

3.2 International Cooperation and Lithuania's Geopolitical Orientation as Constitutional Imperatives

The constitutional framework of Lithuania's international cooperation, including its membership in the EU, is grounded in the general principles articulated in Chapter XIII of the Lithuanian Constitution, titled "*Foreign Policy and National Defence*". These provisions collectively reflect Lithuania's commitment to international law, democratic values, and the rule of law as core constitutional principles.

Article 135 of the Constitution states that "[i]n the implementation of its foreign policy, the Republic of Lithuania shall follow the universally recognized principles and norms of international law, shall seek to ensure the security and independence of the country, the welfare of its citizens, and their fundamental rights and freedoms, and shall contribute to the creation of an international order based on law and justice". This provision encapsulates Lithuania's voluntary commitment to its international obligations, the adherence to *pacta sunt servanda* and the integration of international legal norms into its domestic legal order, collectively representing the legal tradition of the restored independent Lithuanian state.

Complementing this, Article 136 establishes that "[t]he Republic of Lithuania shall participate in international organizations, provided this does not contradict the interests of the State and its independence". Furthermore, Article 138(3) of the Constitution explicitly affirms that international treaties ratified by the *Seimas* constitute an integral part of the Lithuanian legal system. These provisions together affirm the constitutional openness of the Republic of Lithuania to international cooperation and legal integration, provided it aligns with the national interest and sovereignty.

Notably, the constitutional principle of the rule of law encompasses respect for international law. This principle is closely linked to the aspiration for an open, fair, and harmonious civil society. This ambition presupposes openness to universal democratic values and integration into the international community founded upon those values. This interpretation has been affirmed by the Constitutional Court,[5] which emphasized the intrinsic connection between the rule of law and the observance of international legal commitments.

Lithuania's geopolitical orientation, as reflected in its constitutional identity, includes EU membership as a fundamental element of its international engagement. This orientation is not merely political but is grounded in the Constitution's recognition of shared universal democratic values such as human dignity, freedom, democracy, equality, the rule of law, and human rights—values constituting the foundation of the EU legal and political order.

Accordingly, the constitutional interpretation supports the conclusion that Lithuania's EU membership is consistent with the geopolitical direction democratically chosen by the Lithuanian people and that fulfilling obligations arising from this membership is a constitutional expression of the state's international cooperation principles.

---

[5] Ruling of 16 May 2016, Constitutional Court of the Republic of Lithuania.

3.3 Membership in the European Union as a Constitutional Value

The citizens of the Republic of Lithuania in the referendum held on 10 and 11 May 2003 voted in favour of the membership of the Republic of Lithuania in the European Union. The *Seimas* of the Republic of Lithuania, fulfilling the will of the citizens, adopted the Constitutional Act "On the Membership of the Republic of Lithuania in the European Union". The Act entered into force on 14 August 2004 and, according to the Constitutional Court,[6] became an integral part of the Constitution. The constitutional amendments related to EU membership, including adopting the Constitutional Act, were essential for ensuring the compatibility of Lithuanian law with EU obligations. Still, the late date of adoption and entry into force of this Act may raise legitimate questions about Lithuania's ability to apply EU law in full from the first day of EU membership. Several constitutional scholars have expressed concerns regarding the timing of the adoption and entry into force of Lithuania's Constitutional Act on EU Membership, particularly concerning the country's capacity to fully implement EU law from the first day of membership. These critiques focus on the potential legal and practical challenges of the delayed constitutional adjustments necessary for EU accession.

Without going into this debate, it is essential to emphasize the particular legal and symbolic significance of the Act's provisions: namely, that it constitutionally affirmed the Republic of Lithuania's membership in the European Union.[7] The Constitutional Court emphasizes that Lithuania's full membership in the European Union holds particular constitutional significance as it constitutes an integral element of the national system of constitutional values. The constitutional imperative of Lithuania's participation in the EU presupposes that it must be full, rather than partial, engagement—both in the Union's institutional activities and in the broader processes of European integration.[8]

Articles 1 and 2 of the Constitutional Act "On Membership of the Republic of Lithuania in the European Union" establish the constitutional foundations of Lithuania's membership in the European Union. If they were not based on the Constitution, Lithuania would not be able to be a full member of the European Union.

Article 1 of this Constitutional Act enshrines the principle that the Republic of Lithuania, being a member state of the European Union, shares or entrusts the European Union with the competence of state institutions in the (founding) treaties in the areas provided for and to the extent that, together with other European Union member states, they jointly fulfil the obligations of membership in these areas, as well as use the rights of membership.

---

[6] Ruling of 24 January 2014, Constitutional Court of the Republic of Lithuania.

[7] Ruling of 13 December 2004, Constitutional Court of the Republic of Lithuania.

[8] Ruling of 24 January 2014, Constitutional Court of the Republic of Lithuania.

Article 2 of the Constitutional Act provides that the legal norms of the European Union form an integral part of the legal system of the Republic of Lithuania. This provision also establishes a conflict-of-laws rule, affirming the precedence of EU legal acts over national legislation. However, the applicability of this rule is expressly limited to those EU law provisions that derive from the founding treaties of the European Union. This qualification leaves interpretative space for the Constitutional Court, particularly in determining the scope and limits of such precedence.

In its jurisprudence, the Constitutional Court has provided clear interpretative guidance on applying the conflict-of-laws rule outlined in the Constitutional Act. It has affirmed the priority of European Union legal acts where EU law norms conflict with national legal provisions, irrespective of their hierarchical position within the domestic legal system. However, an explicit exception is maintained concerning the Constitution, which retains a distinct and superior normative status.[9] I. Jarukaitis aptly observes that the provisions of the Constitutional Act acknowledge the *sui generis* character of the European Union and its legal order. However, he also contends that these provisions do not permit the unconditional acceptance of the supremacy of European Union law over the Constitution of the Republic of Lithuania. Consequently, the relationship between the EU legal system and the Lithuanian constitutional order may be more accurately characterized as horizontal rather than hierarchical.[10] Moreover, as E. Jarašiūnas has pointed out, the recognition of the full membership of the Republic of Lithuania in the EU as a constitutional value that shall be counterbalanced with other values protected by the Constitution means that solutions must be found to ensure that none of such values will be denied or unreasonably restricted.[11]

Following the adoption of the Constitutional Act, the foundations of Lithuania's membership in the European Union were constitutionally enshrined. The Republic of Lithuania's participation in the EU has since acquired the status of a constitutional imperative grounded in the Nation's sovereign will as expressed through democratic procedures. This elevates Lithuania's EU membership to the level of constitutional value and provides a robust basis for an EU-friendly interpretative approach by the Constitutional Court.

3.4 European Union Law in the Jurisprudence of the Constitutional Court

The constitutional imperative of the Republic of Lithuania's full participation in the European Union entails a corresponding constitutional obligation to ensure the proper implementation of European Union law. Moreover, this imperative necessitates that EU law serves as a source for interpreting the legal norms of the Republic

[9] Ruling of 14 March 2006, Constitutional Court of the Republic of Lithuania.

[10] Jarukaitis 2006, p. 30.

[11] Jarašiūnas 2018, p. 35.

of Lithuania—including, where appropriate, the Constitution itself—in those areas where, under Article 1 of the Constitutional Act "On the Membership of the Republic of Lithuania in the European Union", the Republic of Lithuania has transferred or shared competences with the European Union.[12] Furthermore, the jurisprudence of the Court of Justice of the European Union (CJEU) is beginning to play a significant role as a source of legal interpretation in the interpretation and application of Lithuanian law.[13] In other words, the Constitution begins to impose an obligation on the Constitutional Court to consider EU law in cases of constitutional adjudication. The case law of the Constitutional Court of Lithuania demonstrates an increasingly active reliance on the provisions of EU law and their application, as well as on the jurisprudence of the Court of Justice of the European Union in interpreting those provisions.

The Constitutional Court's engagement with European Union law is notably exemplified by its referrals to the Court of Justice of the European Union (CJEU) for preliminary rulings. To date, there have been two such referrals concerning the interpretation of EU legal acts in the context of constitutional justice. In submitting these questions, the Constitutional Court sought authoritative clarification on the meaning of relevant EU law provisions central to the constitutional review proceedings. The EU Treaties established this referral mechanism and further regulated it by the Law of the Constitutional Court of the Republic of Lithuania. Only upon receiving the CJEU's interpretation did the Constitutional Court proceed to determine the constitutionality of the contested legal norms in the respective cases.

The first reference to the CJEU was made by the decision of the Constitutional Court of 8 May 2007, adopted in the constitutional justice case in which the question decided concerned the connection to electricity networks. In this case, the Constitutional Court was requested to assess the constitutionality of Article 20 of the law implementing Directive 2003/54/EC of the EU concerning standard rules for the internal market in electricity and repealing Directive 96/92/EC. At that time, the Constitutional Court decided that the impugned provision of the Law on Electricity must be interpreted in the context of the legal regulation of the directive; therefore, it referred to the CJEU to clarify both the meaning of the provisions of the directive and the limits of the application of the principle of subsidiarity, which allows the relevant issues to be resolved by the state itself. And only after receiving the ruling of the Court of Justice of the European Union the Constitutional Court decided that the impugned legal regulation was not in conflict with the Constitution.[14]

The second reference to the CJEU was made in 2017 in the constitutional justice case regulating the trade in raw milk.[15] The Constitutional Court referred to the CJEU, requesting an interpretation of the content of Article 148 of Regulation No 1308/2013, which regulates freedom of contractual relations in the milk and milk products sector. In this constitutional justice case, the petitioner impugned the provisions of

[12] See, for example, Ruling of 20 December 2017, Constitutional Court of the Republic of Lithuania.

[13] See, for example, Ruling of 21 December 2006, Constitutional Court of the Republic of Lithuania.

[14] Ruling of 4 December 2008, Constitutional Court of the Republic of Lithuania.

[15] Decision of 20 December 2017, Constitutional Court of the Republic of Lithuania.

the law that had imposed restrictions on the contracting parties to agree on factors for the purchase price of raw milk other than those provided for in the law and the prohibition to reduce the cost by more than three percentage points without the permission of the state institution.

Having held that European Union law is also a source of interpretation of the Constitution (in certain areas), there is no constitutional basis for interpreting the Constitution in those areas differently from how those areas are regulated under EU law (at least for now). Only after receiving the ruling of the CJEU did the Constitutional Court decide that *inter alia*, the impugned legal regulation governing trade in milk due to its adoption procedure conflicted with the Constitution.[16]

Another example of the application of EU law in constitutional law is the invocation of EU law in constitutional proceedings. The reliance on EU law, the jurisprudence of the CJEU interpreting it, and their significant influence on constitutional jurisprudence may be illustrated in a few numbers. For example, in the last almost 10 years, i.e. from 2015 to 2024, the Constitutional Court *expressis verbis* relied on the Charter of Fundamental Rights of the European Union (Charter), CJEU jurisprudence, and applied them in 15 constitutional justice cases related to the following areas: protection of human dignity, private and family life, rights and interests of the child, non-discrimination, freedom of thought, conscience and religion, the spelling of people's names and surnames in documents, the issuance of a residence permit in the case of family reunification, the legal status of asylum seekers, social security, economic activity, the access to justice, legal assistance in criminal proceedings, restrictions on the implementation of fundamental rights and other areas.

Among the decisions mentioned, three rulings of the Constitutional Court warrant particular attention, as they illustrate the substantial influence of European Union law—including the Charter of Fundamental Rights—and the jurisprudence of the Court of Justice of the European Union on the development of Lithuanian constitutional doctrine.

In its ruling of 11 January 2019, the Constitutional Court addressed the issue of granting a temporary residence permit in Lithuania to a foreign national based on family reunification. The case concerned a family formed through a same-sex marriage registered in a foreign jurisdiction (Denmark). In this decision, the Court interpreted the constitutional concept of "family" in a gender-neutral manner, thereby establishing a legal basis for facilitating the free movement of persons under the family reunification principle, as European Union law required. This interpretation was notably informed by the Court's extensive engagement with the Treaty on the Functioning of the European Union, the Charter of Fundamental Rights of the European Union, and the jurisprudence of the Court of Justice of the European Union. The challenged provision of the Law on the Legal Status of Foreigners—allowing for the issuance of a temporary residence permit in cases of family reunification when the spouse or registered partner is a citizen of Lithuania or holds a residence permit in the country—was found to be compatible with the Constitution.

[16] Ruling of 6 February 2020, Constitutional Court of the Republic of Lithuania.

In its ruling of 7 June 2023, the Constitutional Court examined the constitutionality of the procedure for issuing temporary accommodation to asylum seekers during a mass influx of foreigners in cases of emergency, state of emergency, or state of war. The applicant, detained after illegally crossing the Lithuanian border, submitted an asylum request but was placed in temporary accommodation for six months without the right to move freely within Lithuania. The applicant argued that this amounted to detention, as the legal regulation restricted freedom without a court decision, lacked procedural guarantees, and did not allow for judicial review, thereby violating the Constitution. The Constitutional Court upheld the applicant's concerns. In its decision, it found that the Law on the Legal Status of Foreigners, which restricted asylum seekers' freedom of movement for up to six months, violated Article 20 of the Constitution, which guarantees the inviolability of personal liberty. Due to its intensity and duration, this restriction was deemed equivalent to detention, requiring adherence to constitutional safeguards, as supported by CJEU case law. In the ruling above, the Constitutional Court relied on EU law related to the legal status of asylum seekers, including requirements for their temporary accommodation and restrictions on their freedom. One of the sources of EU law in these areas was Article 18 of the Charter, establishing the right to asylum.

On 5 July 2023, the Constitutional Court addressed[17] a legal regulation regarding when the name and/or surname of a Lithuanian citizen could be written in Latin letters (without diacritical marks) in documents confirming personal identity or civil status records. The regulation in question provided specific circumstances where a citizen's name could be written in non-Lithuanian characters, disregarding the official opinion of the State Lithuanian Language Commission (VLKK). This raised concerns about compliance with the requirements of Article 14 of the Constitution, which mandates the legislator to determine regulations for writing names and surnames in personal documents. However, the Constitutional Court rejected the applicant's objections, affirming that the legal provisions allowing the use of Latin letters (without diacritical marks) in certain instances did not conflict with the Constitution. The Court's reasoning marked a development in its stance compared to previous decisions, which emphasized using the state language in public life. The Court's position was influenced by Article 7 of the Charter of Fundamental Rights ("Right to private and family life") and the jurisprudence of the CJEU, which seeks to safeguard fundamental rights in the context of naming conventions. Additionally, in the Runevič-Vardyn case, the CJEU observed that while EU member states have competence in regulating the entry of names in civil status records, they must exercise this competence in compliance with EU law, particularly the provisions of Article 21 of the Treaty on the Functioning of the European Union concerning the freedom of movement and residence of all EU citizens within the member states.[18]

The three reviewed examples of the jurisprudence of the Constitutional Court confirm the significant influence of EU law and the practice of the CJEU interpreting

[17] Ruling of 5 July 2023, Constitutional Court of the Republic of Lithuania.

[18] Ruling of 12 May 2011, *Malgožata Runevič-Vardyn et al. against Vilnius city municipality administration*, Court of Justice of the European Union, C 391/09, EU:C:2011:291.

it. It can be seen that these sources are used in the interpretation and application of the Constitution in areas where Lithuania shares or entrusts the competence of state institutions to the European Union (and also other sources of Lithuanian ordinary law). In this way, the Constitution and the constitutional jurisprudence developed on its basis, case by case, seems to keep opening up to EU law while ensuring the commitment to implement the requirements of European Union law properly.

3.5 Constitutional Protection of the Lithuania's EU-Membership Obligation

Regarding membership in the EU, the obligations arising therefrom, and the relationship between EU law and the provisions of the national Constitution, one more fundamental constitutional principle—the principle of the geopolitical orientation of the State of Lithuania—should be noted. The Constitutional Court develops it in its jurisprudence.[19] It implies the Republic of Lithuania's membership in the European Union (and NATO) and the necessity to fulfil the respective international obligations related to this membership. Such geopolitical orientation of the State of Lithuania is based upon the recognised and protected universal democratic constitutional values common with the values of other European (and North American) states.[20]

The country's geopolitical orientation guides the European integration chosen by the Republic of Lithuania, and as such, the obligation to fulfil EU membership requirements is constitutionally protected.[21] Such protection is determined by the close connection between the principle of the geopolitical orientation of the Lithuanian state and fundamental constitutional values, which are particularly protected and enshrined in Article 1 of the Constitution—the independence of the state, democracy, as well as the natural nature of human rights and freedoms. These values form the basis of the Constitution as a social contract, the nation's everyday life and the state of Lithuania itself is based on it. No one can deny the provisions of the Constitution, which establish these fundamental constitutional values, because that would mean denying the essence of the Constitution itself.

As early as 2014, the Constitutional Court of Lithuania formulated a doctrine on the limits of constitutional amendment. Central to this doctrine is the self-imposed constraint that amendments negating Lithuania's obligations under EU law are impermissible unless the state withdraws from the European Union.[22] Such a withdrawal would also require a referendum, given that accession to the EU was approved through this democratic process. Therefore, in the opinion of E. Jarašiūnas, membership in the

[19] Ruling of 7 July 2011, Constitutional Court of the Republic of Lithuania.

[20] Jočienė 2023.

[21] Žalimas 2020, pp. 54–58.

[22] Ruling of 24 January 2014, Constitutional Court of the Republic of Lithuania.

European Union, as a constitutional value, can be regarded—alongside other fundamental constitutional values forming the protected so-called constitutional core—as a foundational element of the constitutional system. Its loss would lead to a fundamental transformation of the entire constitutional order.[23]

3.6 Conclusions

Lithuania's membership in the European Union should be understood within the context of all constitutional values. Both the general constitutional principles governing Lithuania's international cooperation and the specific constitutional foundations of Lithuania's EU membership are essential to understanding EU membership as a constitutional value and obligation in Lithuania.

When interpreting the Constitution in light of the principle of its integrity, it is crucial to ensure that the balance of constitutional values is maintained. Solutions must be found to ensure that no value is overlooked or unduly restricted at the intersection of Lithuania's full EU membership as a constitutional value and other values protected by the Constitution.

Both the supremacy of the Constitution and the obligation to adhere to EU law are derived from the Constitution itself, which requires the Constitutional Court to uphold the sovereignty of the Constitution while also fulfilling the duties of EU membership undertaken by Lithuania. Consequently, the Constitutional Court is developing a responsible and cautious approach to Lithuania's EU membership as a constitutional value, ensuring the fulfilment of related obligations and safeguarding this value.

References

Birmontienė T (2020) Konstitucinė teisė ir tarptautinė bei Europos Sąjungos teisė: kas diktuoja teisės sistemų sąveikos ribas? [Constitutional law and international and European Union law: who dictates the limits of the interaction between the legal systems] In: XXI amžiaus iššūkiai tarptautinei teisei. Liber Amicorum Sauliui Katuokai. MRU, Vilnius, pp 72–101

Birmontienė T (2023) Konstitucinė doktrina ir Konstitucijos interpretavimo (ne)laisvė [Constitutional Doctrine and the (Non)Freedom of the Interpretation of the Constitution]. In: Konstitucinė justicija Lietuvoje: trys veiklos dešimtmečiai: recenzuotų mokslinių straipsnių rinkinys. Vilniaus universiteto leidykla, pp 24–43. https://doi.org/10.15388/KJL.2023.2

Jarašiūnas E (2018) Lietuvos Respublikos visateisė narystė Europos Sąjungoje kaip konstitucinė vertybė [Full membership of the Republic of Lithuania in the European Union as a constitutional value]. Jurisprudencija 25(1):8–37 https://doi.org/10.13165/JUR-18-25-1-01

Jarukaitis I (2006) Adoption of the Third Constitutional Act and Its Impact on National Constitutional System. Teisė 60:22–37

Jočienė D (2023) From national constitutional identity to European integration: the relationship between the national Constitution and European Union law. https://lrkt.lt/data/public/uploads/2022/09/rapport_jociene_en.pdf. Accessed 2 May 2025

[23] Jarašiūnas 2018, p. 10.

Kūris E (2024) Brussels in Strasbourg: Theoretical Reflections on the Impact of European Union Law on the Case-Law of the European Court of Human Rights. Teisė 131:8-22 https://doi.org/10.15388/Teise.2024.131.1

Žalimas D (2020) Tarptautinė teisė konstitucinėje paradigmoje: grėsmė konstitucijos viršenybei? [International law in Constitutional Paradigm: the danger for the Supremacy of the Constitution?] In: XXI amžiaus iššūkiai tarptautinei teisei. Liber Amicorum Sauliui Katuokai. MRU, Vilnius, pp 72–101. https://doi.org/10.13165/LA.2020.06.01

Tomas Davulis is a doctor of law, a professor at the Law Faculty of Vilnius University and a Justice of the Constitutional Court of the Republic of Lithuania. All opinions expressed herein are personal to the author.

Chapter 4
Values of the European Union in the Face of Crises: Protected, Challenged, Modified?

Indrė Isokaitė-Valužė and Haroldas Šinkūnas

Contents

Abstract The chapter explores the impact of crises on the values of the European Union with the aim to comprehensively assess different aspects and basic trends of this effect on the implementation of European Union values and to discuss their sufficiency, taking their nature and role into account. This is being achieved, initially, researching the development and establishment of European Union values in European Union law and evaluating their nature, role and functions. Further, addressing the impact of crises in general, our focus is on the migration crisis (cases of the Mediterranean migration crisis and "instrumentalised" migration from Belarus) and the security crisis (Russia's war in Ukraine). Finally, the research deals with the possibilities of and challenges to the enforcement of these values and assesses their vitality. Systematic and structural research of the evolution, nature, contents of European Union values and their resilience to threats leads to insights on crisis-related developments, and some reservations on the sufficiency of European Union values is expressed. The conclusions reflect comprehensive insights on the challenges related with the conceptual and procedural aspects of how the researched values are defined, perceived and safeguarded, differences between the value in question and the type

I. Isokaitė-Valužė (✉) · H. Šinkūnas
Faculty of Law, Vilnius University, Vilnius, Lithuania
e-mail: indre.isokaite@tf.vu.lt

H. Šinkūnas
e-mail: haroldas.sinkunas@tf.vu.lt

I. Isokaitė-Valužė and H. Šinkūnas (eds.), *The European Union 2004-2024*,
https://doi.org/10.1007/978-94-6265-718-2_4

of crisis and possible options to strengthen the role of European Union values and increase their resilience to threats.

Keywords European Union · European Union values · Crises · Migration · Security · War in Ukraine · Solidarity · Human rights

4.1 Introduction

"Crisis" is a word which has been heard loudly and repeatedly during recent years in particular, and the last two decades as well: the list of economic crisis, migration crisis, public health crisis, democracy (rule of law) crises has been supplemented or even overshadowed by a security crisis. These emergencies were (and remain) different in nature, scale and States affected. However, each posed a great challenge to the European Union (the EU or Union) and its values. Each tested the objectives related to the Union as a European Project or a European idea and the expectations of the Member States. The EU itself emerged after a great world crisis—a war—and Russia's aggression against Ukraine has brought the world into a new era of insecurity.

Crises are cyclical, they challenge the foundations of each organisation, demand response and usually mobilise efforts, but may foster tensions as well. During difficult times values should serve as guidelines which highlight the path to be followed, imply the reason to take action or indicate measures to reach aims. In a certain sense, a value implies an aim in itself. Nonetheless, decades-long new developments test the validity of values and question their contents and hierarchy in a new environment. Moreover, the moment of the establishment of the organization and defining its values explicitly do not necessarily coincide as was the case of the EU and the initial limit of the organisation's competence is also not a final determination. The Union, established as a coal and steel community focused on economic aims, has developed into the EU, dealing with a significant number of issues, including human rights and foreign and security policy.

The aim of this chapter is to research the impact of crises on EU values in general and a few of them in particular with a focus on their nature, development and role in order to determine the sufficiency of EU values and the capability of retaining their importance as well as resilience to crises. This purpose is to be achieved through the following tasks: (1) to overview the emergence of EU values in EU law and their development with an emphasis on their nature, role, functions and relevance; (2) to determine basic patterns of how crises affect EU values in general; (3) to explore the impact of two particular crises—the migration crisis (Mediterranean migration crisis and "instrumentalised" migration from Belarus) and security crisis (Russia's war in Ukraine)—on EU values and (4) to discuss the enforcement of these values for the ultimate aim to assess whether existing EU values are capable and sufficient to withstand threats and to provide some insights for the future.

The chapter is therefore structured corresponding to the tasks set. In the first section EU values are researched as guidelines and framework, tracing their development and assessing the impact of threats on them. The second section provides a look into several areas (migration with a focus on solidarity and security (the war in Ukraine) highlighting unity). The third section aims at the analysis of the enforcement of EU values and their sufficiency.

Due to the fundamental impact of the crises on the EU and its values and an exceptional relevance of these transformations, a rather extensive body of research has been created on this broad issue in legal doctrine in general.[1] This chapter, however, mostly aims at considering the capability and sufficiency of existing EU values to respond to threats with the focus on their nature, development, role and enforcement comprehensively and systematically. The main research source is legal doctrine, in addition, EU treaties and studies (reports)[2] are referred to among other sources.

The chapter uses the following methods of scientific research. Systematic analysis is used in order to overview the landscape of major recent crises experienced by the EU and their effect on EU values. Comprehensive analysis is needed to explore intersections and the interrelation of different elements relevant for the research, for example, conceptual and procedural aspects of EU values and their enforcement. A chronological approach is taken in tracing the emergence and evolution of the values in EU law. Similarities and differences of situations (e.g. response to migration crisis and security crisis) are researched by comparison. Among other research methods a deductive approach or inductive logic is applied at times, for example, in making assumptions on the validity of a case-based conclusion also for other cases or, *vice versa*, applying a general finding to a particular case.

4.2 Values of the European Union as Guidelines and Framework

4.2.1 Nature and Development of the EU Values

The EU declares the following values it is founded on: respect for human dignity, freedom, democracy, equality, the rule of law and respect for human rights, including the rights of persons belonging to minorities. The Treaty of Lisbon (2007)[3] created a full legal personality of the EU and explicitly listed the values.[4]

---

[1] For example, research by Hällström 2020.

[2] For example, a study by the European Union 2022.

[3] Treaty of Lisbon amending the Treaty on EU and the Treaty establishing the European Community entered into force on 1 December 2009. OJ C 306, 17.12.2007, pp. 1–271.

[4] Currently Article 2 of the Treaty on EU (consolidated version). OJ 2016 C 202, pp. 15–45.

However, at the beginning "there was no values driven vocation".[5] The Treaty of Rome (1957)[6] which established the European Economic Community, aimed at integration and economic growth and laid foundations of an 'ever closer union,' paved the way to the subsequent treaties, on the basis of which the EU grew, its fields of competence expanded, institutional mechanisms developed and the EU values were ultimately established. Although the Treaty of Rome listed mainly economic and social aims related with a common market (economic and social progress, including balanced trade, fair competition, improving citizens' living and working conditions), it also reflected the ideas of peace and liberty and referred to the principles of the United Nations (UN) Charter.[7] The Treaty of Maastricht (1992)[8] created the EU, there was no reference to values, however, they were implied in the principles of the Union.[9] This did not change with the Treaty of Amsterdam (1997):[10] in addition to the EU principles direct reference to values and human rights was still outside the EU's agenda.[11] The Treaty of Nice (2001)[12] reformed the institutional structure of the EU and prepared for the accession of ten countries which remains the largest ever EU enlargement until today, however, still without any emphasis on the values. The Treaty of Lisbon not only listed the EU values but also declared their promotion as the Union's aim.[13]

The explicit establishment of the EU values, in no case contesting the relevance thereof, should not be overestimated in terms of tracing the emergence of the guiding ideas and founding principles of the EU without which the Union could have not been created. The EU is "a project driven by values" and such is EU membership—about the choice of values not less than economic growth.[14] Even before being listed explicitly, the values (or at least the ideas representing them) were implied in the

[5] Weatherill 2016, p. 393.

[6] Treaty establishing the European Economic Community entered into force on 1 January 1958. OJ C 224, 31.8.1992, pp. 6–79.

[7] 1945, 1 UNTS XVI.

[8] Treaty on EU entered into force on 1 November 1993. OJ C 191, 29.7.1992, pp. 1–112.

[9] The Preamble declared the importance of the principles of liberty, democracy, the rule of law, and respect for human rights, and Article F(2) stated that the EU shall respect the fundamental rights.

[10] Treaty of Amsterdam Amending Treaty on EU entered into force on 1 May 1999.

[11] Treaty of Amsterdam amended the Treaty on EU (Article F): the Union is founded on the principles of "liberty, democracy, respect for human rights and fundamental freedoms, and the rule of law, principles which are common to the Member States".

[12] Treaty of Nice amending the Treaty on European Union, the Treaties establishing the European Communities and certain related acts entered into force on 1 February 2003. OJ C 80, 10.3.2001, pp. 1–87.

[13] Under the Treaty of Lisbon, the Treaty on EU was supplemented: "The Union is founded on the values of respect for human dignity, freedom, democracy, equality, the rule of law and respect for human rights, including the rights of persons belonging to minorities. These values are common to the Member States in a society in which pluralism, non-discrimination, tolerance, justice, solidarity and equality between women and men prevail" (currently Article 2 of the Treaty on EU (consolidated version)). "The Union's aim is to promote peace, its values and the well-being of its peoples" (currently Article 3, para 1 of the Treaty on EU (consolidated version)).

[14] Weatherill 2016, p. 393.

principles and aims of the EU and also at least partly derived from or inspired by the constitutional traditions of its Member States, which share the same values not only as European democracies but also as the members of the major international regional organizations such as the Council of Europe[15] and NATO.[16] Still, there is an obvious difference between being implied in principles or aims and being established explicitly and covered by a mechanism for protection and enforcement.[17]

Human dignity is not only a human right, a value, but a basis for and a source from which other fundamental rights are derived. It is firmly established in the EU Charter of Fundamental Rights:[18] "human dignity is inviolable. It must be respected and protected",[19] as well as fundamental rights which form part of EU law and so are enforceable. Democracy is a key principle of the EU governance and the form availing the protection of human rights: in the words of the European Court of Human Rights (ECtHR), it "appears to be the only political model contemplated by the Convention and, accordingly, the only one compatible with it".[20] The contribution to the protection of human rights and the United Nations principles[21] is among the aims of the EU acting externally. Democracy, the rule of law, the universality and indivisibility of human rights and fundamental freedoms, respect for human dignity, equality and solidarity, and respect for the principles of the UN Charter and international law are the principles guiding EU external action.[22] Equality is a main condition in enjoying human rights and in the EU also creates equal possibilities to benefit from what the Union offers to its citizens. The rule of law encompasses perhaps the longest list of elements, including equality, supremacy of law, accountability, *etc.*

EU values in terms of their essence and meaning represent the ideas that should keep together and integrate Member States and certain communalities which could be recognized by Member States as reflecting their constitutional traditions and general principles. The interrelation among these elements is well reflected in EU law: "fundamental rights, as guaranteed by the European Convention for the Protection of Human Rights and Fundamental Freedoms and as they result from the constitutional

[15] The Preamble of the Statute of the Council of Europe (Council of Europe. Statute of the Council of Europe. ETS 1) declares States' "devotion to the spiritual and moral values which are the common heritage of their peoples and the true source of individual freedom, political liberty and the rule of law, principles which form the basis of all genuine democracy."

[16] The Preamble of the North Atlantic Treaty (UNTS 34, p. 243) declares determination "to safeguard the freedom, common heritage and civilisation of their peoples, founded on the principles of democracy, individual liberty and the rule of law."

[17] See Sect. 4.4.

[18] OJ C 326, 26.10.2012, pp. 391–407.

[19] Article 1.

[20] ECtHR judgement of 30 January 1998 in case *United Communist Party of Turkey and Others v. Turkey*, para 45. "Convention" refers to the European Convention on Human Rights. Council of Europe Treaty Series 005, Council of Europe, 1950.

[21] Article 2 of the UN Charter establishes sovereign equality of States, *pacta sunt servanda* and good faith, peaceful dispute settlement, prohibition of the use of force, cooperation for the aims of and assistance to the United Nations, non-intervention into domestic affairs.

[22] Treaty on EU (consolidated version), Article 21.

traditions common to the Member States, shall constitute general principles of the Union's law".[23] According to the Court of Justice of the EU (CJEU), EU values "are common to all Member States; therefore, they define the core of the EU identity as a common legal order".[24]

Legal doctrine suggests that "discourse, narratives and collective histories have been instrumental in creating a value-based narrative for the EU".[25] In addition to ideological aspect of the perceived communality, some authors propose also historical and geopolitical unity[26] and others say that reflections of a common identity may be understood as shared by EU citizens as an "emotional community".[27] Values and emotions also guide humans in their response to threats: "humans possess intentions, motivations, emotions, values that shape their perception of risks and opportunities and how they make decisions".[28]

EU values characterize the EU, reflect its identity and ground legitimacy, build a framework for internal policies and guide external action, foster integration, reflect the power and essence of the EU. Much is enshrined in and implied by values: they reflect ideas, aims, beliefs that are perceived by the EU, its Member States and reflected in the EU Community or EU citizen's minds, they also show interdependence and trust. Moreover, as the CJEU stressed, "Article 2 of the TEU is not just a set of policy guidelines or intentions; it enshrines the fundamental values, which are at the heart of the very identity of the EU, and that these values are expressed in concrete legal principles which establish legally binding obligations on the EU Member States".[29]

EU values as to their legal expression mainly fall under the umbrella of human rights, there is an obvious interconnection among the values, also some coincidence. In terms of their contents they are not equal though. For example, if, to compare a few of them, the protection of fundamental rights is governed by a separate mechanism, human dignity is a source of human rights and a separate fundamental right and democracy is a political form of governance. Thus as ideas, EU values are rather similar and contribute to each other. However, they are also different as regards specifics when it comes to the subjects and addressees, the level or field of implementation and resilience to crises, which is always a game-changer.

---

[23] Treaty on EU (consolidated version), Article 6, para 3.

[24] Jarukaitis 2024, p. 26.

[25] Hällström 2020, p. 3.

[26] Chopin and Macek 2022, p. 4.

[27] "[E]motional community concept, might enlighten the substantive content of the EU's foreign policy, hence its shared normative framework <…> if combined with collective memory, might also tell us the foundations of the EU's emotional narrative in collective identity construction". Gürkan 2024, p. 639.

[28] Bełdyga 2023, p. 75.

[29] Jarukaitis 2024, p. 26.

4.2.2 Impact of Threats on EU Values

Political, security, diplomacy, economic, migration, public health and other crises, differing in nature, scale or even location, affect the EU and its Member States as well as their citizens—the European Community. On the one hand, the existence of the impact of the crises on values could be presumed, on the other hand, it is not that unequivocal, explicit or the same in each case.

The impact in question was acknowledged already by the founders of the EU: Jean Monnet said that "Europe would be built through crises, and that it would be the sum of their solutions".[30] The evolution of the EU and the crises it has faced in recent decades confirm that this acknowledgement remains valid. A crisis of EU values was diagnosed many times in legal doctrine contesting the ability of the EU (its institutions) to cope with them and to uphold EU values. For example, researchers state that the EU "is experiencing a crisis of values, as some Member States are openly flouting the basic principles of EU law"[31] and consider that this could be regarded as a political crisis and a legal crisis. Others indicate "an external and an internal crisis of values"[32] of the EU as a community of values. Monetary union, common market, common asylum area, EU membership and expansion were challenged by different threats.

Crises are cyclical and thus remind us of limitedness in time which is characteristic to mechanisms and institutions, despite the dream of guiding values being perpetual. The Treaty of Lisbon was referred to by W. Munchau as "a pre-crisis treaty for a post-crisis world".[33] The values crisis has been threatening not only the EU, but the whole world recently. In addition to the fourth year of Russia's war against Ukraine (open aggression, although the war started in 2014 after Crimea's occupation) all of Europe has been concerned if not shocked by the position of the USA, suspending support for Ukraine, questioning the future of NATO and established world order.[34] The world seems to turn to a new era of breaking rules, changing a decade-long established balance of powers and, what is raising the greatest concern, departing from the values of the EU and the foundations of the international world order in general. All these developments witness that nothing is forever and nothing can be taken for granted. This may be said about values as well: they are vulnerable to crises and need to be safeguarded.

A crisis, naturally, threatens the establishment and the usual order of functioning. Values and crises, which underpin the formation of the EU identity, are both complicated concepts in terms of the many different implications they have, including the

[30] Calleja and Rusche 2024, p. 17.

[31] Scheppele *et al.* 2020, p. 118.

[32] Groussot and Karageorgiou 2023, p. 30.

[33] Munchau, cited by Hällström 2020, p. 1.

[34] Reuters. Three weeks that changed the world: How Trump turned against Ukraine and Europe. https://www.reuters.com/investigations/3-weeks-that-changed-world-how-trump-turned-against-ukraine-europe-2025-03-10/. Accessed 2 February 2025.

complexity of their nature, consequences and related expectations. There is a potential enshrined in the values: threats may weaken the values and at the same time foster resilience to the attacks thereby encouraging will to safeguard the values which in their turn also imply background of and guidelines for action. The causes of crises are also relevant, speaking of the abilities of the Union and its Member States, to respond to crises, to maintain common policies or stick to values despite a changing environment. Crises many be of a different nature and origin, they may be internal and external, regional and global, long-lasting or fragmented, and these differences may have a different impact on each particular value. For example, it is proposed that "economic insecurity has a direct impact on values and beliefs".[35] Crises may also emerge from failure to uphold established values, lack of their implementation or distrust, but may also be stipulated by global or regional developments.

The relation between values and risks may be defined not merely as between a challenge and an opportunity, but also as between a threat and a new risk. Shocks may foster unity, however, they also increase tensions in finding consensus on how to respond to threats. Therefore, and in the words of I. Jarukaitis, "these crises act as both centrifugal and centripetal forces in the EU".[36]

Not EU values as mere treaty provisions alone, but the environment of their application and invocation by the EU, Member States and their perception by a European Community, is what brings and also tests the vitality of EU values. The effects of a crisis may touch a particular State (some States) or a State may misuse or even oppose national interests or sovereignty to EU values. So different elements combine in a value–crisis relation.

Threats test the unity and coherence of the Union and the European Community, and the EU values and aims make the EU more than merely a sum of Member States; there is a need of interconnection and interaction. Compliance with EU values is a condition for EU accession and an instrument of integration as they call for a sincere cooperation and mutual trust. Despite the primary aim for an economic union, EU membership is also a choice of values and obligation to act in line with them. Among them there is a "need to remain geopolitically united, to protect itself from authoritarian and even totalitarian temptation, to replace the law of the strongest with law and equality between States, to prefer peaceful settlements over conflicts between States, and to champion a vision of inter-State relations as a positive-sum game <…>".[37] Although there is a discussion on the EU's direction towards more unity or fragmentation, in any case the role of solidarity is correctly emphasized as related with social justice, focusing on essential common aims, however, not providing a clear answer as regards its implementation and enforceability.

[35] Algan *et al.* 2017, p. 316.

[36] "On the one hand, they encourage the European Union and its Member States to join forces to find common solutions at EU level in order to counter systemic threats. On the other hand, they inevitably highlight disagreements on how, to what extent and by what means to tackle the above-mentioned threats". Jarukaitis 2024, p. 24.

[37] Chopin and Macek 2022, p. 4.

4.3 A Look into Several Areas

4.3.1 Asylum: Testing Solidarity

Migration crises are specific as there is a human story beyond each asylum seeker and certain interests permeate the policies adopted by international organisations and States. Migration routes, causes, scale and nature have been changing, however, migration remains a global issue. The experience of the EU highlights two migration crises to be addressed in this subsection: the Mediterranean refugee crisis (2015) and the illegal migration crisis at the EU Eastern borders (2021) known as a hybrid attack from Belarus.

The right to asylum is directly established in the EU law[38] and the EU forms a Common European Asylum System, however, the afore-mentioned crises have questioned solidarity as never before and raised concerns as regards human rights. The concept of asylum is based on humanity, however, irregular and massive influxes of migrants too often put human dignity at stake.

Although the EU is aimed at benefitting from interdependence and combining efforts to deal with challenges, it is particularly difficult to ensure this communality and burden-sharing when it comes to asylum. Migration influxes are hardly amenable to even distribution of asylum seekers across the EU common asylum area. In addition, there are also other implications: issues related to States' resources to deal with irregular and huge flows of migrants, the nature of the migration influxes (legal, illegal, hybrid, *etc.*) and communities' attitudes towards the asylum seekers.

Although solidarity is not directly listed among the EU values it is among the guiding principles of asylum in the EU. Interesting to note that solidarity, freedom and equality were also referred to in the Millennium Declaration adopted by the UN General Assembly (2000) as "essential to international relations in the twenty-first century" and is defined through the idea of sharing and contributing: "global challenges must be managed in a way that distributes the costs and burdens fairly in accordance with basic principles of equity and social justice".[39] A. Von Bogdandy in his recent research emphasized that solidarity "is rooted in Schuman's declaration (and thus the depths of European integration). Second, it strengthens the distinctiveness of republicanism in European society with regard to redistribution and social cohesion".[40]

Although solidarity does not mean absolute equality in burden-sharing, the idea of making the asylum area common was hardly compatible with the well-known migration trends and statistics witnessing that the majority of refugees are hosted by a neighbouring country or several neighbouring countries.[41] Both above mentioned

---

[38] Article 18 of the EU Charter of Fundamental Rights.

[39] United Nations. General Assembly resolution A/RES/55/2 of 8 September 2000.

[40] Von Bogdandy 2024, p. 8.

[41] About 69% are hosted by (a) neighbouring state(s). UNHCR. Refugee Agency. Refugee data finder. https://www.unhcr.org/refugee-statistics. Accessed 2 February 2025.

migration crises confirmed this assumption. Migrants "instrumentalised" by Belarus reached the borders of mainly Lithuania, Latvia and Poland (also migrants aided by Russia gathered at the Finland border)[42] and in the Mediterranean refugee crisis Italy, Malta, Greece and Spain took a greater part of the burden addressing huge influxes of migrants coming from Syria, Afghanistan, as well as Nigeria, Pakistan, Somalia, *etc.*[43]

Challenges arising from huge influxes of migrants were followed by proceedings instituted against certain South European States before the ECtHR, where a number of violations of the prohibition of torture, inhuman or degrading treatment, right to liberty and security of a person, right to a fair trial, right to respect for private and family life, right to an effective remedy and prohibition of collective expulsion of aliens were established. The ECtHR was solid in stating that the crisis was no excuse for non-compliance with human rights standards due to the absolute nature of certain human rights in question. The ECtHR acknowledged that it was aware of and did not underestimate the burden posed by influxes of asylum seekers on the States which form the Union's external borders and that was "particularly aware of the difficulties related to the phenomenon of migration by sea, involving for States additional complications in controlling the borders in southern Europe",[44] however, States' obligations as regards the prohibition of torture and inhuman treatment remained valid to the full extent.[45] Similar insights were shared in legal doctrine, e.g. noticing that the EU system then was suffering "from the cardinal error of blocking legal and secure access to Europe for those in need of international protection".[46]

The influx of migrants aided (pushed) by Belarus to the external borders of the EU placed Lithuania, Latvia and Poland in a complicated situation requiring protection of national security, EU borders and complying with human rights obligations, including an underlying principle of *non-refoulement*. Such irregular massive migrant flows fostered certain national measures which were criticised by human rights defenders and proceedings have been instituted by such migrants before the ECtHR claiming refusal to enter as "pushbacks".[47]

Both cases were an example of crises which tested solidarity and unity of the Member States and also encouraged some developments within the EU asylum

---

[42] European Commission. Commission steps up support for Member States to strengthen EU security and counter the weaponisation of migration. https://ec.europa.eu/commission/presscorner/detail/en/ip_24_6251. Accessed 2 February 2025.

[43] Directorate-General for External Policies (2015) Migrants in the Mediterranean: protecting human rights https://www.europarl.europa.eu/RegData/etudes/STUD/2015/535005/EXPO_STU(2015)535005_EN.pdf. Accessed 2 February 2025, pp. 9, 13.

[44] ECtHR judgment of 23 February 2012 in the case *Hirsi Jamaa and others v. Italy*, para 122.

[45] Collective expulsion of aliens in such cases was recognised as a violation of Article 3 of the European Convention on Human Rights and Article 4 of Protocol 4 usually among other articles.

[46] Bendel 2017, p. 44.

[47] In February 2025 there were over 30 cases regarding "pushbacks" at the Belarusian borders from summer 2021 to summer 2023 pending before the ECtHR against Latvia, Lithuania and Poland. ECtHR Press Release: Grand Chamber hearing concerning alleged "pushbacks" at the Lithuanian-Belarusian border, 12 February 2025.

system. There was a need of making the asylum mechanism more flexible in dealing with irregular and (or) huge flows of migrants and differentiating their nature, i.e. cases of true asylum seekers and cases related with illegal migration and human smuggling.

The reform proposed in 2020 was to reflect a comprehensive approach to migration and asylum policy based on increasing solidarity and flexibility, aimed at efficient asylum and return procedures and strengthened partnerships with third countries.[48] The Pact on Migration and Asylum is presented by the EU as "remaining grounded in our European values".[49] In response to "instrumentalised" migration, financial, operational and diplomatic efforts were taken, as well as some legal measures foreseen.[50]

The EU reform also reflects developments on a global level. A need for a comprehensive approach to migration and strengthened cooperation is elaborated in the Global Compact for Safe, Orderly and Regular Migration (2018).[51] This agreement (although a non-legally binding) also emphasizes the importance of solidarity and presents the balance among States' sovereignty and migration governance on an international level, including some flexibility for States to select policy options to address specifics of the migration situations they face.

The situations presented raised discussion on solidarity being selective and double standards applied, i.e. depending on the crisis and the country in question. In general, surveys usually indicate unwillingness to accept immigrants due to security or identity related concerns. For example, E. Wiącek proposed that "the 'rediscovery' of ethnicity over the last decade in Europe has been accompanied by a shift in the system of values"[52] and addressed a certain reservation to multiculturalism.[53] Such a case-based approach was also confirmed in the case of war refugees from Ukraine, when Poland, Lithuania and other European States demonstrated a high degree of solidarity with the Ukrainian people welcoming war refugees fleeing from Russia's aggression, thereby also emphasizing unity.

[48] European Commission. Common European Asylum System (2025). https://home-affairs.ec.europa.eu/policies/migration-and-asylum/common-european-asylum-system_en. Accessed 2 February 2025.

[49] European Commission (2024) Pact on Migration and Asylum. https://home-affairs.ec.europa.eu/policies/migration-and-asylum/pact-migration-and-asylum_en. Accessed 2 February 2025.

[50] European Commission. Commission steps up support for Member States to strengthen EU security and counter the weaponisation of migration.

[51] United Nations (2018) UN General Assembly Resolution A/RES/73/195. Global Compact for Safe, Orderly and Regular Migration.

[52] Wiącek 2019, p. 162.

[53] "In its Eurosceptical attitude and skepticism towards multiculturalism, Poland is not the only one: similar tendencies can be seen in France, Austria, Germany and Hungary". *Ibid.*, p. 163.

4.3.2 Security: Strengthening Unity

In the field of common foreign security policy, the Union is guided by the EU values and the principles of the UN Charter. This field is also an example of EU competence development which plays an important role in response to Russia's aggression against Ukraine as it reveals the importance of unity and a value-based approach.

Institutional mechanisms in the area of common foreign security policy emerged together with explicit listing of the EU values in the Treaty of Lisbon.[54] The pursuing of common policies and actions in the EU shall be aimed at "a high degree of cooperation in all fields of international relations, in order to safeguard its values, fundamental interests, security, independence and integrity".[55]

Shortly after the beginning of Russia's aggression against Ukraine in 2022, the EU and Member States had not only condemned the aggression, but had been seeking Russia's accountability and providing political, humanitarian, military and financial support for Ukraine and its people.[56] "Everything what has been done so far seeking to use frozen Russian assets for funding Ukraine's victory and reconstruction or looking for creative legal solutions for lifting personal immunities of Russia's political and military leadership while establishing a Special Tribunal for the crime of aggression against Ukraine are illustrative examples of the international community being willing to create new legal mechanisms by adapting international law so that it continues to safeguard one of its main principles—responsibility for breaches of international law".[57] The Union and its Member States' united action representing Europe's voice in this new global development is of fundamental importance.

The Union's response was exceptional in terms of adopting unprecedented sanctions. These sanctions cover a wide range of individual, economic, diplomatic and other measures adopted in respect to Russia, ranging from closing European air space to suspending Kremlin-based disinformation channels.[58] It is quite unique that such sanctions, which normally should be applied by the UN Security Council, have been and are further imposed by the EU.

Russia's aggression reminds us that key values cannot be sacrificed when faced with historic challenges. In this case "the reinvigorated feeling of common belonging and solidarity <…> provide an opportunity to present a united front when it comes to the fundamental values that characterize the European model and the European project itself, by reducing the political space afforded to illiberal and Europhobic narratives".[59] War in Ukraine has clearly called for united action by Member States

[54] It established the EU's diplomatic arm, the European External Action Service under the authority of the High Representative of the Union for Foreign Affairs and Security Policy.

[55] Treaty on EU (consolidated version), Article 21, para 2a.

[56] European Union. EU support for Ukraine (2025). https://european-union.europa.eu/priorities-and-actions/eu-support-ukraine_en. Accessed 2 February 2025.

[57] Isokaitė-Valužė and Grigaitė-Daugirdė 2024, p. 24.

[58] European Council. EU sanctions against Russia explained (2025). https://www.consilium.europa.eu/en/policies/sanctions-against-russia-explained/. Accessed 2 February 2025.

[59] Chopin and Macek 2022, p. 17.

and increasing power of the EU in international relations. Member States have been demonstrating more courage than before or at least they better understand the importance of investment in security and stability and protection of democracy against threats from authoritarian regimes.

4.4 Enforcement of EU Values and Assessment of Their Sufficiency

The preceding research which has revealed that the concept of EU values is surrounded by numerous issues related with their nature, contents, role and resilience to threats, naturally leads to the importance of exploring the enforcement of EU values. The ease of making EU values work hardly can be presumed, as S. Weatherill puts it, "commitment to values is contested terrain".[60]

The enforcement of EU values is not only a procedural issue, but also has a conceptual, moral (in other words, ideological or immaterial) side. Although, in general, the values are of the EU, they are mainly to be realised by the Member States and safeguarded by the Union.

As regards the procedure, there is a mechanism for the enforcement of EU values established in EU Law (Treaty on EU). EU institutions are entrusted to take respective actions when there is a risk of breach of values and when a breach already occurs. The first case is aimed at preventive measures: the EU institutions (European Parliament, European Commission, European Council) may determine "that there is a clear risk of a serious breach by a Member State of the values referred to in Article 2",[61] the Member State shall address the European Council which takes a decision.[62] The second case is already related with sanctions: the European Council may "determine the existence of a serious and persistent breach by a Member State of the values".[63] Such determination may lead to the "suspension of certain of the rights of the EU Member State (including the voting rights of the representative of the government of that Member State in the Council)".[64] The decision on suspension is taken by the European Council and after the Member State is invited to submit observations.

The fact that this mechanism has been invoked only in respect of two states (Hungary and Poland) so far and the procedure itself gives rise to doubts as regards the effectiveness of the tools that the EU possesses for the enforcement of EU values.

[60] Weatherill 2016, p. 416.

[61] Article 7, para 1.

[62] A high majority is required – of at least 4/5 Member States.

[63] European Council shall act by unanimity on a proposal by one third of the Member States or by the European Commission and after obtaining the consent of the European Parliament. Article 7, para 2.

[64] Article 7, para 3.

Although the EU declares it strengthens the mechanisms to enforce values,[65] the Union's failure to protect these values and make them work was expressed in legal doctrine. For example, D. Kochenov argued that "the ability of EU institutions to monitor and assess compliance with basic EU values virtually disappeared"[66] and that the invocation of Article 2 of the Treaty on EU "could also raise arguments that the 'values on which the Union is built' are illusory in a number of respects".[67]

The experience of activating the mechanism in question against Hungary[68] and Poland[69] revealed shortcomings and was hardly efficient. Research has addressed this ineffectiveness, for example, it was concluded by M. Kawczyńska (who examined the case of Poland) that "existing instruments have proved ineffective in terms of the comprehensive enforcement of EU fundamental values".[70] However, there are differences between these two cases, including the differing position of each of two States towards such key issues as the support for Ukraine (Poland has been continuously demonstrating political and proving humanitarian, financial and other support, however, Hungary many times attempted to block the Union's support for Ukraine initiatives). "The erosion of EU values and disregard of EU law by the Orbán government"[71] at the hearth of the Article 7 mechanism (launched in 2018 and revisited last time at the end of 2024) shows that EU institutions have taken established measures, including blocking access to EU funds, however, "Hungary did not notify any remedy to address the related rule-of-law concerns"[72] and has been continuously demonstrating unwillingness to contribute or even show intention to block decisions crucial to the Union and its values.

[65] European Parliament. Factsheets on the European Union (2025). The protection of Article 2 TEU values in the EU. https://www.europarl.europa.eu/factsheets/en/sheet/146/the-protection-of-article-2-teu-values-in-the-eu. Accessed 2 February 2025.

[66] Kochenov, cited by Nicola 2018, p. 135.

[67] Kochenov, cited by Kalaitzaki 2020, p. 65.

[68] This was the first time the Article 7 mechanism was activated (in 2018). Hungary raised concerns as regards the erosion of democracy, rule of law and fundamental rights due to certain actions in the field of elections, judiciary, human rights and freedoms, corruption, *etc.* European Parliament. Breaches of EU values: how the EU can act (infographic). https://www.europarl.europa.eu/topics/en/article/20180222STO98434/breaches-of-eu-values-how-the-eu-can-act-infographic. Accessed 2 February 2025.

[69] European Commission launched the procedure to determine whether Poland due to its controversial judicial reforms was in breach of core EU values in 2017 (infringement proceedings were instituted in 2015), however, this has not led to limiting Poland's rights (as sanctions). In March 2022, the European Parliament adopted a resolution on the rule of law in the EU regretting "the inability of the Council to make meaningful progress" in relation to the Article 7 process and with regards "to the threats to common European values in Poland and Hungary". Fella 2024, pp. 6, 22, 26.

[70] Kawczyńska 2020, p. 248.

[71] Wahl 2025.

[72] *Ibid.*

In addition to the above presented mechanism, the Union also possesses other means that may be invoked to protect EU values. Enforcement may be not only political, but also judicial.[73]

As the EU values are implied in the provisions on fundamental rights and other provisions of EU law, the following judicial mechanisms may also be used: infringement procedure and preliminary ruling procedure. Preliminary ruling procedures may be activated with the aim of asking the CJEU to ensure the uniform application of EU law and the respect for fundamental values at the domestic level. Individual violations by Member States may be subject to infringement procedure. Both "infringement proceedings or preliminary rulings are designed to ensure compliance with the fundamental values only when the Member States act within the scope of Union law".[74] Such cases comprise a rather significant scope, in particular, as the EU Charter of Fundamental Rights is part of binding EU law. The Court also protects the general principles which enshrine fundamental rights. However, "fundamental rights as general principles of EU law have rarely been used, and only recently with any positive effect".[75]

The enforcement of EU values may be explored in normal times and times of shock; the latter highlight the EU deficits to protect "values – what they stand for and as outright concepts".[76] In both cases the realisation of EU values should be explored starting from a conceptual approach and interrelation among the values. As mentioned before, human rights derive from human dignity and equality is a prerequisite in implementing human rights, freedom is linked to democracy and the latter together with the rule of law and human rights form the usual three-pillar background. Thus safeguarding human rights falls under the protection of fundamental rights and Member States are bound by both the EU Charter of Fundamental Rights and European Convention on Human Rights. The rule of law is aimed to safeguard fundamental rights, values and democracy and there is a specific mechanism established for the enforcement of the rule of law at the EU: the European Commission may invoke a three-stage framework to address systematic threats to the rule of law in Member States.[77]

Turning to the moral, immaterial or ideological side of the EU, values in terms of the ideas they represent and their realisation in the EU as a European Community, the task is even more complicated, however, not less meaningful. In this respect the issue of a European identity should be addressed in terms of certain communalities

---

[73] See, e.g. Jarukaitis 2024.

[74] European Commission. Communication from the Commission to the Council and the European Parliament on Article 7 of the Treaty on European Union. Respect for and promotion of the values on which the Union is based. COM(2003) 606 final.

[75] Kalaitzaki 2020, p. 53.

[76] "Political polarisation, economic challenges and fragmentation between member states have all served as moments during which there are apparent failures involved in upholding values." Hällström 2020, p. 3.

[77] European Commission. Rule of law framework (2025). https://commission.europa.eu/strategy-and-policy/policies/justice-and-fundamental-rights/upholding-rule-law/rule-law/rule-law-framework_en. Accessed 2 February 2025.

that EU values should mean for a European citizen. Surveys indicate the lack of a European identity: citizens identify themselves first of all with their State but not Europe or the Union.[78] In searching for reasons it is proposed that "identification with 'Europe' lacks the traits of a thick, ethnic identity".[79] The EU motto "united in diversity" reflects multiculturalism enshrined in historical heritage, cultural traditions and constitutional orders or the Member States. This lack of association of EU citizens with the EU should be addressed as capable of decreasing the meaning of the EU values and undermining their enforcement, subsequently, affecting the resilience to threats.

The above addressed communality of a "European family" should not be perceived limiting it to some specific, e.g. historical or cultural similarities, but should be understood in a broader sense. For example, S. Gürkan referred to an "emotional community concept" which "if combined with collective memory, might also tell us the foundations of the EU's emotional narrative in collective identity construction".[80] A lack of "deeply rooted European identities and loyalties" is indicated as a reason of the vulnerability to attacks also by other authors.[81]

Taking into account the conceptual expression of EU values and their list, the European identity could perhaps be strengthened by considering the search for communalities in such notions as religion, solidarity, humanity or unity. Some ambiguity as regards the exhaustiveness of the list of EU values is implied by the wording of Article 2 of the Treaty on EU: the first sentence lists values and the second sentence stipulates that "[t]hese values are common to the Member States in a society in which pluralism, non-discrimination, tolerance, justice, solidarity and equality between women and men prevail".

Common heritage or memory could be searched in the inheritance of Europe, religion, European Christianity: "cultural, religious and humanist inheritance of Europe" is referred to in the preamble of the Treaty on EU.[82] Referring to political mobilization of values, researchers refer to the "invocation of the Christian heritage of Europe to comfort a common culture pre-existing the nation-states"[83] as an example of a "call to identity, memory and communicative resources in a quest for legitimization (governing through values)".[84] The role of Christianity should be acknowledged, although there are difficulties in assimilating it with EU values. For example, T. Lähdesmäki makes reference to "balancing Christianity and secularism" and "the

---

[78] "Most people in Europe do not think of their political identity as primarily "European"". Weatherill 2016, p. 8.

[79] "It has remained secondary to identification with the nation(-state) for a very large majority of citizens." Schimmelfennig 2024, p. 3400.

[80] Gürkan 2024, p. 639.

[81] Schimmelfennig 2024, p. 3403.

[82] The preamble stipulates: "Drawing inspiration from the cultural, religious and humanist inheritance of Europe, from which have developed the universal values of the inviolable and inalienable rights of the human person, freedom, democracy, equality and the rule of law".

[83] Calligaro *et al.* 2016, p. 6.

[84] *Ibid.*

challenge of incorporating Christianity into the EU's value discourse".[85] The unique nature of the Union, focused on interdependence and coordinated action, may also call to consider solidarity which could reflect the expectations of the Union and the Member States. Some ambiguity implied in the relation between the Union's values and the general principles could indicate the need for considering such principles as justice to be listed separately among the values, although it is covered by the rule of law. Similarly, humanity could also be discussed. However, it is implied in human rights and human dignity.

In order to safeguard EU values, their recognition, trust in them, their role and potential they imply is needed. Enforcement of EU values is also related with different expectations of Member States and their perception by EU citizens as a European Community, as well as the EU in reaching its aims, including its power in a changing world. EU values may be implemented by Member States differently, at times even opposed to national interests or constitutional rules, and the balance of sharing competences between the EU and Member States is also relevant. EU values shall be implemented both, internally, within the EU, and externally, when the EU acts globally. For example, I. Jarukaitis indicates "the need for further changes to maintain the EU's viability and its importance in the modern world, as this is the only way to ensure respect for its fundamental values".[86]

The success of enforcement of EU values does not depend directly or solely on their definition and list, but also on the approach taken, in particular, in times of crises. A crisis experience is also what may strengthen communalities among European nations. It is proposed that "the degree to which political actors can mobilize exclusive national identities in a crisis hinges upon the degree of symmetry and commonality of the crisis experience".[87]

The Union itself has taken efforts to address the role of values in time of crises and how to safeguard them. In 2022 the report "EU values in times of crises: Strategic Crises Management in the EU"[88] was adopted, thereby once more highlighting their important role in how we perceive and respond to crises. Solidarity is indicated as "a guiding principle for strategic crisis management" and it is also explored "how ethical values can contribute to strategic crisis management".[89] Values influence the way of understanding risks and choosing means to respond to challenges.

The implementation of EU values could be explored in both a short term and a long term perspective, in the latter case acknowledging that the means for the enforcement of EU values should be reviewed in time taking into account the developments which may prove certain approaches to be no longer effective. For example, although the EU is correctly referred to as "a forum to manage interdependence",[90] there are different

[85] Lähdesmäki 2022, p. 182.

[86] Jarukaitis 2024, p. 29.

[87] Ferrara and Kriesi 2022, p. 1360.

[88] European Union (2022) European Group on Ethics in Science and New Technologies. Values in times of crisis – Strategic crisis management in the EU.

[89] *Ibid.*

[90] Weatherill 2016, p. 415.

ways to achieve that. Certain shift from an ever-closer union to differentiation was recognised. Differentiation should be examined in relation to solidarity, taking into account the balance of competences shared between the EU and Member States and a particular aim to be reached in a specific case. The possibility of a different scope of contribution by a Member State may demonstrate certain flexibility of the EU, however, should not prevail over the common aims, attaining which demands the commitment to the EU values and principles. In the words of R. Uitz, "differentiation, however, cannot and should not be used to excuse the wilful violation of the founding values of the Union or the foundation of the EU legal order, the primacy of EU law".[91] EU values are not merely a summary of the past, but are guidelines through the current challenges and the reason of a common future.

4.5 Conclusions

The EU values, namely, human dignity, freedom, democracy, equality, the rule of law and respect for human rights, were explicitly listed for the first time in the Treaty of Lisbon (2009), but have been implied by the principles of the Union established in the preceding treaties. EU values are different in terms of their contents and there is some overlap in and an interrelation among the notions they represent (e.g. human rights are derived from human dignity, the rule of law encompasses human rights, democracy, *etc.*). They reflect the ideas of certain commonalities of the Member States and guidelines to be followed as well as the framework for EU institutions to act. The protection of EU values is enshrined in the aims of the Union: these values characterise the EU, build its identity, ground its legitimacy, permeate governance and integrate Member States. The value-based narrative of the EU is grounded on a common past, similar histories, shared ideas, collective aims and memories. They have certain connections with the general principles and constitutional traditions of Member States. EU values form the background of EU law, are precondition for the accession to the EU, an instrument for European integration, serve as guidelines in the Union's external relations and underpin the importance of being protected in face of challenges.

Crises are cyclical, and accordingly EU values are periodically tested. Crises have an impact on EU values, which might have similarities and differences, may call for activating some specific procedures or foster conceptual developments as regards the perception of EU values in the European Community and trust in the EU and its institutions. Crises may indicate vulnerabilities of EU values or shortcomings of mechanisms to safeguard them, they may encourage will to protect the values and seek more unity, but also may raise tensions on how to respond to challenges. A crisis is often seen as an accelerator fostering resilience and initiating some developments to find ways to better protect values and make them sustainable. In this respect challenges strengthen the understanding of the role of EU values which in their turn

[91] Uitz 2022, p. 948.

reflect the reason crises are to be handled and form guidelines during difficult times. Although threats may pave a path to changes and transition, the response is usually limited in time, often subject to circumstances of uncertainty and surrounded by different expectations of Member States. Therefore, there is some ambiguity in a value-crisis relationship and specifics in each particular case.

Different stakeholders, levels, fields and time in implementing the EU values shall be acknowledged, but values stand out when faced with crises. Migration crises are always specific due to particularly human, social, economic, political, emotional and other implications they bring. Both, the Mediterranean migration crisis and "instrumentalised" migrants aided by Belarus and pushed to the borders of East European States tested solidarity of the Member States and proved that the asylum area of the EU was far from being common. These experiences fostered certain reforms of the EU migration and asylum policy aiming at more flexibility and responsibility as well as fairer burden-sharing. In addition, there is a need to be capable to respond to different types of migration influxes: States should have scope to protect the EU external borders and their security when faced with illegal or irregular migration, however, human rights obligations should always be complied with.

A security crisis in the framework of Russia's aggression against Ukraine reminds us that EU membership is a value-based choice, not only driven by economic implications. Providing Ukraine with political, humanitarian, financial and even military support, accepting war refugees and imposing unprecedented sanctions in respect to Russia, Member States not only demonstrated unity, humanity and solidarity with the Ukrainian people, but also strengthened trust in the values of the EU, in particular, newly perceived and revealed the importance of democracy and freedom in opposition to authoritarian threats.

EU values are interrelated but different in terms of their scope and respective mechanisms to implement them. Enforcement of EU values may be subject to political and judicial mechanisms. The procedure established in EU law is available to be activated by the EU institutions in case of a risk of breach of EU values and when the breach already has occurred. When the values are covered by EU law applied by a Member State, a preliminary ruling procedure or infringement procedure may be invoked as well. However, the conceptual, ideological (moral or immaterial) side of EU values is not less important than retaining their vitality. They should frame the Union, hold Member States together and bring their citizens closer, values should show the historical, economic and social context of their normativity. The enforcement of EU values may suffer due to lack of communalities usually perceived through a European identity. The EU value-based narrative is derived from common histories, memories, traditions or other common roots, in this respect several additional notions such as religion, Christian heritage, solidarity or unity might be considered as potentially be listed among the EU values. Some communalities may also rise from a crisis-based experience. One should not forget that the EU was created after the biggest crisis—war, currently facing crucial threats to Europe's security again, upholding EU values is a historical test and an opportunity.

References

Algan Y, Guriev S, Papaioannou E, Passari E (2017) The European Trust Crisis and the Rise of Populism. Brookings Papers on Economic Activity. Brookings Institution Press, pp 309–382

Bełdyga N (2023) The Role of Community Resilience Dimensions of Agency and Resources in Community Resilience to Crises and Uncertainty in Polish Border Communities. European Integration Studies 17:71–82. https://doi.org/10.5755/j01.eis.1.17.33991

Bendel P (2017) The EU "Refugee Crisis": Have We Lost Our Compass? In: Zenner H-P, Šelih A (eds) Human Rights and Refugees. Nationale Academie der Wissenschaften, Leopoldina, 415:39–46

Calleja D, Rusche T M (2024) Įvadas. In: ES teisei – 70 metų. Savo piliečių labui veikianti Sąjunga [Introduction. In: 70 Years of EU Law. Union acting for the benefit of its Citizens]. Publications Office of the European Union, Luxemburg, pp 15–32

Calligaro O, Coman R, Foret F, Heinderyckx F, Kudria T, Perez-Seoane A (2016) Values in the EU policies and discourse. A first assessment. CEVIPOL Working Papers 3:5–52. https://doi.org/10.3917/lcdc.163.0005

Chopin T, Macek L (2022) European Values a debate to be clarified, a struggle to be fought. Democracy & Citizenship Policy Paper, pp 1–17

European Union (2022) European Group on Ethics in Science and New Technologies. Values in times of crisis: Strategic crisis management in the EU. European Commission. Directorate-General for Research and Innovation. Luxembourg: Publications Office of the European Union, ISBN 978-92-76-55607-7, https://doi.org/10.2777/79910

Fella S (2024) Poland: The Law and Justice Government and relations with the EU, 2015–2023, House of Commons Library. https://researchbriefings.files.parliament.uk/documents/CBP-9868/CBP-9868.pdf. Accessed 2 February 2025

Ferrara F M, Kriesi H (2022) Crisis pressures and European integration. Journal of European Public Policy 29(9):1351–1373, https://doi.org/10.1080/13501763.2021.1966079

Groussot X, Karageorgiou E (2023) Solidarity and the Crisis of Values in the European Union. https://doi.org/10.2139/ssrn.4567824. Accessed 2 February 2025

Gürkan S (2024) Constructing an 'emotional community' in times of crisis: the EU's response to Russia's invasion of Ukraine in 2022. Journal of European Integration 46(5):635–659, https://doi.org/10.1080/07036337.2024.2360703

Hällström S (2020) Values and Crises of the European Union. Reflecting on the Narratives of Values and Crises in the State of the Union Addresses 2010 – 2020. Institute of European Democrats. https://www.iedonline.eu/publications/2020/geopolitics-values/values-and-crises-of-the-european-union-reflecting-on-the-narratives-of-values-and-crises-in-the-state-of-the-union-addresses-2010-2020-af-haellstroem. Accessed 2 February 2025

Isokaitė-Valužė I, Grigaitė-Daugirdė G (2024) Invocation of International (Treaty) Law Principles against an Aggressor State: Suspension, Restriction of Membership Rights, Expulsion? Kyiv-Mohyla Law & Politics Journal 10:19–50

Jarukaitis I (2024) The European Union as a Community of Values: The Importance of the Dialogue between the Court of Justice of the European Union and National Courts. Vilnius University, Vilnius, Teisė 131:23–43, https://doi.org/10.15388/Teise.2024.131.2

Kalaitzaki K (2020) EU Citizenship as a Means of Broadening the Application of EU Fundamental Rights: Developments and Limits. In: Cambien N et al (eds) European Citizenship under Stress: Social Justice, Brexit and other Challenges. Koninklijke Brill NV, Leiden, pp 44–66

Kawczyńska M (2020) Combating the constitutional crisis in Poland – Can the European Union provide an effective remedy? Hungarian Journal of Legal Studies 61(2):229–253, https://doi.org/10.1556/2052.2020.00269

Lähdesmäki T (2022) The role of Christianity in the European Union's heritage and history initiatives. Journal of European Studies 52(3–4):170–186, https://doi.org/10.1177/00472441221115571

Nicola G F (2018) Another view of the cathedral: What does the rule of law crisis tell us about democratizing the EU? Maastricht Journal of European and Comparative Law 25(2):133–138, https://doi.org/10.1177/1023263X18786382

Scheppele K L, Kochenov D V, Grabowska-Moroz B (2020) EU Values Are Law, after All: Enforcing EU Values through Systemic Infringement Actions by the European Commission and the Member States of the European Union. Yearbook of European Law 39(1):3–121, https://doi.org/10.1093/yel/yeaa012

Schimmelfennig F (2024) Crisis and polity formation in the European Union. Journal of European Public Policy 31(10):3396–3420, https://doi.org/10.1080/13501763.2024.2313107

Uitz R (2022) The Rule of Law in the EU: Crisis, Differentiation, Conditionality European Papers 7(2):929–948. ISSN 2499-8249 - https://doi.org/10.15166/2499-8249/587

Von Bogdandy A (2024) The European Renaissance of Republicanism: On the Future of EU Law in Light of Article 2 TEU. Max Planck Institute for Comparative Public Law & International Law (MPIL) Research Paper No. 2024-02

Wahl T (2025) Hungary: Rule-of-Law Developments in the Second Half of 2024. 6 February 2025 / Preprint Issue 4/2024

Weatherill S (2016) Law and Values in the European Union. Oxford University Press, Oxford

Wiącek E (2019) The Rhetoric of the "March of Independence" in Poland (2010–2017) as the Answer for the Policy of Multiculturalism in EU and the Refugee Crisis. Księgarnia Akademicka. Politeja 4(61):149–166. https://doi.org/10.12797/Politeja.16.2019.61.09

Indrė Isokaitė-Valužė is a doctor of law, an associate professor, and Advisor to the Dean for international development at the Law Faculty of Vilnius University.

Haroldas Šinkūnas is a doctor of law, a professor and the Dean of the Law Faculty of Vilnius University.

Chapter 5
The Legal Framework of the EU's Enlargement Under the Magnifying Glass: The 2003 Accession Treaty Before the EU Courts

Saulius Lukas Kalėda

Contents

Abstract The accession of ten new Member States to the EU on the 1st of May 2004 was but a culmination of far-reaching preparation efforts in the candidate countries, as well as complex multilateral negotiations, which resulted in the conclusion of the 2003 Accession Treaty, an elaborate legal instrument containing adaptations of EU law and transitional arrangements. Taking as a starting point the principle of immediate and full application of EU law in the new Member States, this chapter retraces and analyses some of the accession-related legal problems, which were addressed in the case law of the EU courts related to the interpretation of the 2003 Accession Treaty. These issues are grouped into two categories, concerning, respectively, the temporal and the material scope of EU law in the new Member States. The temporal

S. L. Kalėda (✉)
Faculty of Law, Vilnius University, Vilnius, Lithuania
e-mail: saulius.kaleda@tf.vu.lt

I. Isokaitė-Valužė and H. Šinkūnas (eds.), *The European Union 2004-2024*,
https://doi.org/10.1007/978-94-6265-718-2_5

issues raised in the post-accession litigation covered diverse matters such as the late publication of EU acts in the new Member States, the temporal scope of the Court's preliminary rulings jurisdiction and the judicial protection of the new Member States in the interim period. The substantive legal issues are related to a wide range of EU law areas stemming from the fundamental freedoms of the internal market to the application of State aid law in the new Member States. The common thread of those cases is their link to horizontal jurisprudential developments in EU law. The analysis of judgments of EU courts concerning the interpretation of the 2003 Accession Treaty shows that legal problems, which at first sight may appear to concern isolated issues related to enlargement, have influenced the EU court's case law on such fundamental aspects of EU law as the interpretation of the principle of legal certainty, the scope of fundamental market freedoms or the invocability of the Charter in infringement proceedings.

Keywords EU law · Enlargement · Accession negotiations · Application of EU law in new Member States · Temporal scope of EU law · Consequences of non-publication of EU acts · Free movement of workers · Free movement of capital · Existing State aid

5.1 Introduction

The political and legal consequences of the EU's historic enlargement in 2004 can hardly be overestimated. The accession in 2004 of Central and Eastern European countries, just as subsequent accessions in 2007 and 2013, which in a way remained in the shadow of the big bang enlargement, completed the process of reunification of a Europe divided for decades by the Iron Curtain. The enlargement to Central and Eastern European countries also marked a new stage in the evolution of the EU, laying down the foundations for its identity, as a unique legal and political system destined to restore unity in Europe by embracing the values of democracy, the rule of law and respect for fundamental rights.[1]

It is a symbolic coincidence that 2024, the twenty-year anniversary of enlargement, was also the year of commemoration of Czesław Miłosz, Polish writer and Nobel prize laureate born in Lithuania, alumnus of the Law Faculty of Vilnius University. Europe's reunification is a recurring team in Miłosz's works, in particular in his autobiographical essay, 'Native Europe', which revolves around the idea that Europe's identity would never be complete without its Eastern and Northern parts, its 'Septentrion'. While in his Nobel Lecture in 1980, Miłosz could still refer, in plural, to the existence of 'two Europes' and call himself "the poet of the 'Other Europe'", those references to a divided Europe would no longer hold true in 2004.

[1] As reflected in the third recital of the preamble to the TEU, which recalls the historic importance of the division of Europe, as well as in the joint declaration of Member States and acceding States, 'One Europe', annexed to the Final Act of the 2003 Accession Treaty.

Accession of ten new members to the EU on 1 May 2004 was the culmination of far-reaching preparation efforts in the candidate countries, as well as the result of complex multilateral negotiations, which led to the conclusion of an international treaty, the Treaty of Accession,[2] signed in Athens on 16 April 2003. The length and the elaborate structure of the 2003 Accession Treaty, while in some respects anachronistic,[3] reflect the complexity of political and legal issues that had to be discussed and resolved in order to pave the way for the Union of 25 members. Those issues, which span a large range of areas, contained in 31 negotiating chapters, gave rise to a net of transitional provisions, which on the date of accession merged into the already complex EU law edifice. Moreover, given its unprecedented scale, the enlargement was perceived as a potential challenge to the process of integration and even "to the constitutional fabric of the Union" itself.[4] Those concerns had to be addressed by the institutional provisions of the Accession Treaty and the ensuing institutional reforms enacted by the Nice and the Lisbon Treaties.

Some, or perhaps even most, of these issues raised in the context of the 2004 enlargement did not lead to legal disputes, thus, attesting to the robustness of solutions found during the accession negotiations. While transitional arrangements applied in 15 out of 31 chapters of the acquis,[5] as the following analysis attests, only few of them have led to litigation before the EU courts. However, some of them have raised

[2] Treaty between the Kingdom of Belgium, the Kingdom of Denmark, the Federal Republic of Germany, the Hellenic Republic, the Kingdom of Spain, the French Republic, Ireland, the Italian Republic, the Grand Duchy of Luxembourg, the Kingdom of the Netherlands, the Republic of Austria, the Portuguese Republic, the Republic of Finland, the Kingdom of Sweden, the United Kingdom of Great Britain and Northern Ireland (Member States of the European Union) and the Czech Republic, the Republic of Estonia, the Republic of Cyprus, the Republic of Latvia, the Republic of Lithuania, the Republic of Hungary, the Republic of Malta, the Republic of Poland, the Republic of Slovenia and the Slovak Republic on the accession of the Czech Republic, the Republic of Estonia, the Republic of Cyprus, the Republic of Latvia, the Republic of Lithuania, the Republic of Hungary, the Republic of Malta, the Republic of Poland, the Republic of Slovenia and the Slovak Republic to the European Union, signed in Athens on 16 April 2003 (OJ 2003 L 236, p. 17, hereafter 'the 2003 Accession Treaty'), which includes as its integral part the Act concerning the conditions of accession of the Czech Republic, the Republic of Estonia, the Republic of Cyprus, the Republic of Latvia, the Republic of Lithuania, the Republic of Hungary, the Republic of Malta, the Republic of Poland, the Republic of Slovenia and the Slovak Republic and the adjustments to the Treaties on which the European Union is founded (OJ 2003 L 236, p. 33; hereafter 'the 2003 Act of Accession').

[3] The division between the Accession Treaty and the Act of Accession is historically due to different accession procedures under the former EC Treaty and Euratom (which required the conclusion of an international agreement) and the ECSC Treaty (whereby the accession takes effect on the basis of the Council decision and the deposit of an act of accession by the acceding State). At the time of the 2004 enlargement, this two-pronged structure was no longer necessary, as the ECSC Treaty had already expired, but it was nevertheless maintained. The structure of the 2007 Accession Treaty is even more complex since it was concluded at the time of the ongoing ratifications of the Treaty establishing a Constitution for Europe, and had to take into account possible alternative outcomes of the ratification. See Łazowski 2007, p. 404.

[4] See Inglis 2004, p. 939.

[5] For an overview of these transitional arrangements, see Inglis 2004, p. 960.

substantial difficulties, which resonated in the case law of the EU courts in the years following the accession.

The purpose of this chapter is to retrace and analyse some of the accession-related problems addressed in litigation before the EU courts. While this may sound like a historical exercise, it is important to look back at the past difficulties in order to anticipate the forthcoming enlargements.[6] In this respect, twenty years allow us to fully assess the existence of any legal knots that had not been entirely resolved during the negotiations and had to be dealt with by the EU courts after accession. From the methodological viewpoint, this chapter relies on a comparative and contextual analysis of the jurisprudence of the EU courts. It is important to note that, regarding the temporal law of EU law in the new Member States, this jurisprudence is largely inspired by French and German legal theories concerning the application of law in time, which introduced the concept of 'immediate effect' (effet immédiat, Sofortwirkung) of the new rules to the existing situations that arose under the previous legal regime.[7] It should be said, as a caveat, that this analysis is not intended to comprehensively cover all accession-related legal issues, but instead focuses on specific problems that are of wider importance for the development of EU law. One major issue which is left beyond the ambit of the present analysis concerns the respect of EU values by the new Member States and the principle of non-regression, as consolidated by the Court in *Repubblika* and subsequent case law.[8] The latter case law, while closely related to the principles governing new accessions,[9] does not directly concern the interpretation of the 2003 Accession Treaty and, given its constitutional significance, would call for a separate analysis.[10]

5.2 The Principle of Immediate and Full Application of EU Law

The starting point for any legal analysis of accession instruments is the principle of immediate and full application of EU law to (and in) the new Member States. According to this principle, which has consistently guided the EU accessions since the very first enlargement, the new Member State is, subject to any transitional

[6] EU enlargement is an ongoing political process, which has again gained momentum recently: there are currently nine candidate countries for accession (Albania, Bosnia and Herzegovina, Georgia, Moldova, Montenegro, North Macedonia, Serbia, Turkey, Ukraine) and one potential candidate country (Kosovo).

[7] See Roubier 1960; Heukels 1990.

[8] CJEU, Case C-896/19, *Repubblika*, Judgment, 20 April 2021, ECLI:EU:C:2021:311, paras 63 to 65; CJEU, Joined Cases C-83/19, C-127/19, C-195/19, C-291/19, C-355/19 and C-397/19, *Asociația 'Forumul Judecătorilor din România' and Others*, ECLI:EU:C:2021:393, para 162; CJEU, Case C-791/19, *Commission v Poland (Disciplinary regime for judges)*, Judgment, 15 July 2021, ECLI:EU:C:2021:596, para 51.

[9] See Kalėda 2024, p. 256.

[10] See Łazowski 2022, p. 1803.

arrangements reflected in the accession treaty, obliged to implement and enforce the whole body of EU law from the first day of its membership.[11]

Given the broad scope of EU *acquis*, it was decided to encapsulate this obligation in a general clause contained in the accession treaties, instead of drawing a list of EU acts applicable at the time of accession. Hence, the very notion of *acquis* has accession related roots, as it made its first appearance in the EU terminology at the time of the 1973 accessions of Denmark, Ireland and the UK.[12] In the context of the 2004 enlargement, the obligation in question was reflected in the opening provisions of the 2003 Act of Accession. In particular, Article 2 of that Act provides that "from the date of accession, the provisions of the original Treaties and the acts adopted by the institutions … before accession shall be binding on the new Member States and shall apply in those States under the conditions laid down in those Treaties and in this Act". The following provisions of the Act mirror various elements of EU law: Article 3 concerns the implementation of the Schengen acquis, Article 4—the Economic and Monetary Union, Article 5—sui generis acts of EU law, Article 6—international agreements and conventions. Regarding the EU directives and decisions, these provisions are complemented by Article 53 of the Act of Accession, which states that "upon accession, the new Member States shall be considered as being addressees of directives and decisions" and "shall be considered as having received notification of such directives and decisions upon accession", as well as Article 54: "the new Member States shall put into effect the measures necessary for them to comply, from the date of accession, with the provisions of directives".

The principle of immediate and full application of EU law, as reflected in the 2003 Act of Accession, has duly found its way into the accession related case law of the EU courts. While interpreting Articles 2 and 10 of the Act, the Court recalled that they are based on the "principle that the provisions of EU law apply *ab initio* and *in toto* to new Member States".[13] The Court's accession related case law allows to infer several consequences of that principle. First, any derogations to the full application of EU law in the new Member State are considered as exceptions, which can only be allowed insofar as they are expressly laid down in the transitional provisions contained in the Accession Treaty. Furthermore, they must be interpreted strictly.[14] Secondly, the purpose of transitional derogations is to enable the implementation of EU law and, thus, to ensure that it can be fully applied in the new Member State after the end of any transitional period. As a consequence, for instance, the Court ruled out the possibility to interpret the derogating provisions laid down in the 2003 Act of

[11] See Kalėda 2004, p. 102.

[12] See Delcourt 2001, p. 829.

[13] See, for instance, CJEU, Case C-350/08, *Commission v Lithuania*, Judgment, 28 October 2010, ECLI:EU:C:2010:642, para 55, which refers to the case law developed during previous enlargements: CJEU, Case 258/81, *Metallurgiki Halyps v Commission*, Judgment, 9 December 1982, ECLI:EU:C:1982:422, para 8; CJEU, Case C-233/97, *KappAhl*, Judgment, 3 December 1998, ECLI:EU:C:1998:585, para 15; and CJEU, Case C-420/07, *Apostolides*, Judgment, 28 April 2009, ECLI:EU:C:2009:271, para 33.

[14] CJEU, Case 77/82, *Peskeloglou*, Judgment, 23 March 1983, ECLI:EU:C:1983:92, para 12, and CJEU, Case C-233/97, *KappAhl*, Judgment, 3 December 1998, ECLI:EU:C:1998:585, para 18.

Accession extensively, in a way which would have extended their application beyond explicitly envisaged transitional periods.[15] Thirdly, the principle of immediate effect implies that the starting point for the interpretation of the temporal scope of EU law in the new Member States is the date of their accession.[16] In accordance with the consistent case law of the Court regarding the temporal scope of new rules, in the absence of explicit derogations, new substantive rules must be considered as applying immediately to the future effects of a situation which arose under the old rule. Applying that principle in the context of new accessions, the Court held that, where the act of accession contains no specific provision on the temporal scope of application of a provision of EU law, that provision must be considered to be immediately applicable and binding as regards that Member State as from the date of its accession to the EU, so that it applies to the future effects of situations arising before accession.[17]

While the principle of immediate and full application of EU law forms part of a consistent body of case law, its application in the context of the 2004 enlargement gave rise to several controversies related to both elements of that principle: to the *immediate* effect of EU law in the new Member State (its temporal scope) and its *full* effect (its material scope).

5.3 Issues Related to the Temporal Scope of Application of EU Law in New Member States

5.3.1 Closing a Lacuna in the Judicial Protection Related to the Interim Period

From the institutional perspective, the new Member States become members of the EU on the date of accession and from that date they fully participate in the EU's decision-making processes. However, this conceptual construction is incomplete, as it does not take into account the inevitable interruption, which takes place between the end of accession negotiations (or rather the 'cut-off' date of negotiations) and the actual date of accession. This period, which is called an 'interim period', is regulated in the accession instruments, EU internal arrangements and an exchange of letters with the acceding States on an information and consultation procedure, so as to allow those States to take part in the activities of the EU institutions and express their

[15] See CJEU, Case C-127/17, *Commission v Poland*, Judgment, 21 March 2019, ECLI:EU:C:2019:236, para 103.

[16] For an analysis of the accession related intertemporal rules, see Kalėda 2004, p. 103.

[17] See CJEU, Case C-441/08, *Elektrownia Pątnów II*, Judgment, 12 November 2009, ECLI:EU:C:2009:698, para 32; CJEU, Case C-385/08, *Commission v Poland*, Judgment, 22 December 2010, not published, ECLI:EU:C:2010:801, para 29; CJEU, Case C-424/10 and C-425/10, Ziolkowski and Szeja, Judgment, 21 December 2011, ECLI:EU:C:2011:866, para 57, and CJEU, Case C-256/15, *Nemec*, Judgment, 15 December 2016, ECLI:EU:C:2016:954, para 25.

position with regard to the EU acts adopted after the end of negotiations, but before the date of accession.[18]

In the context of the 2004 enlargement, a substantial controversy arose as to the new Member States' right to judicial protection against the EU acts adopted during the interim period. The Court has ruled upon this issue in *Poland/Council*,[19] in which Poland sought the annulment of a Council Decision, adopted on 22 March 2004, thus, before the date of accession, adapting the Act of Accession as regards the payments to farmers under the common agricultural policy. The Polish Government was aware of the proposal to adopt such a decision and opposed it at all stages of the legislative process, by relying on the interim period mechanisms. However, not yet being a Member State, Poland could not have formally voted against it. Following the accession, Poland brought an action for an annulment, considering that the Council's act was not a mere adaptation of the Act of Accession, but a substantive alteration of the negotiated arrangements.

The Council contested the admissibility of that challenge arguing that the action was brought out of time. Hence, the preliminary issue in the case concerned the calculation of the time limit in an action for annulment brought by a new Member State against an act adopted before its accession. Poland, supported *inter alia* by Lithuania, argued that the starting date for the calculation of the time limit is the date of accession. Both new Member States contended that the observer status during the interim period did not effectively secure the interests of the acceding States, since it did not confer the right to vote in the Council. Therefore, it was crucial to ensure that after their accession the new Member States can effectively contest such acts in the EU courts. The Council, on its part, maintained that the time limit has started to flow from the 15th day after publication of the act, as provided in Article 230 EC (now Article 263 TFEU) and the Rules of Procedure of the Court. In particular, the Council argued that, in the absence of any special arrangements in the Act of Accession, the new Member States were subject to the same rules regarding the calculation of time limits as any other applicant.

Advocate General Poiares Maduro took the view that the time limit must flow from the date of accession. He observed that the lack of special arrangements in the Act of Accession reflects rather the fact that its authors had not thought about the shortfall in judicial protection of the new Member States.[20] The Advocate General observed

---

[18] Article 57 of the 2003 Act of Accession and exchange of letters annexed to the Final act of the 2003 Treaty of Accession on an information and consultation procedure for the adoption of certain decisions and other measures to be taken during the period preceding accession. A post-accession dispute before the court revealed an imperfection in the interim period arrangements which did not include the power of the Council to adopt temporary derogations to EU acts adopted in the interim period. This was taken into account in Article 55 of the 2005 Act of Accession. See CJEU, Case C-413/04, *Parliament v Council*, Judgment 28 November 2006, ECLI:EU:C:2006:741, para 76; and CJEU, Case C-414/04, *Parliament v Council*, Judgment, 28 November 2006, ECLI:EU:C:2006:742, para 53.

[19] CJEU, Case C-273/04, *Poland v Council*, Judgment, 23 October 2007, ECLI:EU:C:2007:622.

[20] CJEU, Case C-273/04, *Poland v Council*, Opinion of Advocate General Poiares Maduro, 21 June 2007, ECLI:EU:C:2007:361, para 38.

that, possibly, Poland could have brought the proceedings even before the date of accession, under the right of action conferred on any "legal person" (that complex question had been ultimately resolved only years later[21]), but considered that this would amount to a refusal of the status of a privileged applicant, compromising the judicial protection of the new Member States and, ultimately, undermining the principle of equality of the Member States.[22] The Court largely followed the reasoning of the Advocate General and confirmed that the *dies a quo* of the time limit for bringing proceedings by the new Member States is, in respect of the acts adopted and published in the interim period, the date of their accession.[23] This solution closed a lacuna in the legal arrangements governing the interim period, while at the same time significantly improving legal certainty and guaranteeing effective judicial protection of the new Member States.[24]

5.3.2 Controversies Regarding the Temporal Scope of the Court's Preliminary Rulings Jurisdiction

The interpretation of the temporal scope of EU law in the new Member States has a direct bearing on the Court's jurisdiction to rule on preliminary references submitted by the new Member States' courts after accession. This is due to the fact that the Court's preliminary rulings jurisdiction is restricted to the cases stemming from the disputes related to the application of EU law and, hence, in principle, to situations falling within the scope of EU law. However, in some exceptional cases, in particular, the so-called '*Dzodzi* line of cases', the Court has accepted its jurisdiction to rule on the interpretation of EU law, even though the dispute fell outside the proper scope of EU law, but its provisions were rendered applicable by virtue of national law.[25] The primary reason for the Court's acceptance of jurisdiction in such cases lay with the concern that the interpretation of national provisions making a renvoi to EU law could ultimately undermine the uniform application of that law in the cases falling within its scope of application. Similar justification could potentially apply in the context of enlargement. While preparing for accession, candidate countries were required to harmonise their law with EU law in a large number of areas. This obligation had its legal basis in the Europe Agreements concluded by the European Communities

[21] CJEU, Case C-872/19 P, *Venezuela v Council (Whether a third State is affected)*, Judgment, 22 June 2021, ECLI:EU:C:2021:507.

[22] CJEU, Case C-273/04, Poland v Council, Opinion of Advocate General Poiares Maduro, 21 June 2007, ECLI:EU:C:2007:361, paras 40, 48.

[23] CJEU, Case C 273/04, Poland v Council, Judgment, 23 October 2007, ECLI:EU:C:2007:622.

[24] See also CJEU, Case C-336/09 P, *Poland v Commission*, Judgment, 26 June 2012, ECLI:EU:C:2012:386. This solution was relevant for later accessions, see Łazowski 2012, p. 8.

[25] On the development of that case law, see Tridimas 2003, p. 9; Kalėda 2000, p. 1.

and their Member States with the Eastern and Central European countries.[26] Since harmonisation exercise took place in the new Member States even before their accession, their national courts faced numerous disputes related to the interpretation of national rules implementing EU law. Obviously, before the date of accession, the national courts of an acceding State could not refer preliminary questions to the Court. However, after that date, there seemed to be valid arguments for the Court to accept preliminary references coming from the new Member States' courts even where they related to the disputes concerning the application of national harmonised rules before accession. By accepting its jurisdiction the Court could have shown the openness towards new participants in the judicial dialogue, which constitutes the cornerstone of EU law and the principal tool for ensuring its uniform application.[27] Moreover, since the application of EU law posed a significant challenge to the national courts in the new Member States, the Court could have been expected to take a pragmatic view to the temporal scope of its jurisdiction.[28]

However, on one of the first occasions, in *Ynos*, the Court has firmly rejected the possibility to interpret EU law in a pre-accession dispute.[29] The case at hand concerned the interpretation of the Unfair Contractual Terms Directive[30] in the dispute stemming from an agency contract for the sale of immovable property entered into before accession. Hungary and the European Commission argued before the Court that the Directive is not applicable because all the facts of the case antedated Hungary's accession. However, several other Member States considered that the Court should accept the preliminary reference, given that the Hungarian courts were in any event obliged to take into account the Directive while interpreting their harmonised national law.[31] The Court declined its jurisdiction indicating, in a succinct reasoning, that the facts of the dispute in the main proceedings occurred prior to Hungary's accession. While the Court did not elaborate upon the reasons for taking a strict position, a possible justification for the Court's approach could be found in the lessons drawn from the 1995 enlargement. At that time, the Swedish Supreme Court did not follow the interpretation of EU law provided by the Court in two early post-accession cases, by relying on the fact that the cases concerned pre-accession disputes falling outside the temporal reach of EU law.[32]

---

[26] See, for instance, Title V, Chapter III (Articles 69 to 71) of Europe Agreement establishing an Association between the European Communities and their Member States, of the one part, and the Republic of Lithuania, of the other part (OJ L 51, 20.2.1998, p. 3).

[27] Półtorak 2008, p. 1380.

[28] Bobek 2008, p. 281.

[29] CJEU, Case C-302/04, *Ynos*, Judgment, 10 January 2006, ECLI:EU:C:2006:9, and see also CJEU, Case, C-168/06, *Ceramika Paradyż*, Order, 6 March 2007, not published, ECLI:EU:C:2007:139.

[30] Council Directive 93/13/EEC of 5 April 1993 on unfair terms in consumer contracts (OJ 1993 L 95, p. 29).

[31] See CJEU, Case C-280/06, *ETI and Others*, Opinion of Advocate General Kokott, 3 July 2007, ECLI: ECLI:EU:C:2007:404.

[32] See, in the context of the 1995 accession, CJEU, Case C-43/95, *Data Delecta Aktiebolag and Forsberg*, Judgment, 26 September 1996, ECLI:EU:C:1996:357 (and Opinion of Advocate General La

In its subsequent case law, the Court has confirmed the approach taken in its *Ynos* ruling. Thus, it is now settled case-law that the Court has jurisdiction to interpret EU law 'only as regards its application in a new Member State with effect from the date of that State's accession to the European Union', to the exclusion of any factual situations ante-dating the accession.[33] On the other hand, the Court has recognised its jurisdiction in cases where only part of the facts related to the period preceding the accession, while the factual situation giving rise to the dispute continued after accession and thus could be 'caught' by the application of EU law. For instance, the Court rejected Hungary's objection to its jurisdiction in a case concerning the interpretation of the freedom of movement of capital in relation to rights stemming from usufruct contracts concluded before Hungary's accession. Even though the rights in issue were created before accession, they continued to produce effects and were cancelled by the national legislation adopted nearly ten years after Hungary's accession.[34]

In the light of the now-established case law, the scope of a court's preliminary rulings jurisdiction in the context of new accessions depends on the distinction between legal situations that had become definitive before accession and those, which continued to produce effects after accession. That distinction is, in itself, a reflection of a wider principle, according to which "as a matter of principle, new rules apply immediately to the future effects of a situation which arose under the old rules".[35] The formula in question follows the classic description of immediate effect, which encompasses 'situations en cours et conséquences futures des faits passés' (pending situations and future consequences of the past facts).[36] As the later Court's case law shows, the demarcation between existing and established legal situations, while based on strong theoretical foundations, has proven to be a complex and casuistic exercise.[37]

Pergola, ECLI:EU:C:1996:212); and CJEU, Case C-122/96, *Saldanha and MTS Securities Corporation*, Judgment, 2 October 1997, ECLI:EU:C:1997:458 (and Opinion of Advocate General La Pergola, ECLI:EU:C:1997:228). The Court ruled, contrary to the Opinions of Advocate General La Pergola, that EU law applies to the *cautio iudicatum solvi* paid before accession, if the judicial proceedings continue after accession. Moreover, following the Court's ruling in *Data Delecta Aktiebolag and Forsberg*, the Swedish Supreme Court disagreed with the Court's interpretation of the scope ratione temporis of EU law.

[33] See, to that effect, CJEU, Case C-302/04, *Ynos*, Judgment, 10 January 2006, EU:C:2006:9, para 36 and the case-law cited.

[34] CJEU, Cases C-52/16 and C-113/16, *SEGRO and Horváth*, Judgment, 6 March 2018, ECLI:EU:C:2018:157, paras 38–39. As to the substance of this case, see Sect. 5.4.2. infra.

[35] CJEU, Case 270/84 *Licata*, Judgment, 10 July 1986, ECLI:EU:C:1986:304, para 31.

[36] See Roubier 1960, p. 364.

[37] See CJEU, Cases C-180/10 and C-181/10, *Słaby and Others*, Judgment, 15 September 2011, ECLI:EU:C:2011:589, para 27; CJEU, Case C-664/16, *Vădan*, Judgment, 21 November 2018, ECLI:EU:C:2018:933, para 34; CJEU, Joined Cases C-424/10 and C-425/10, *Ziolkowski and Szeja*, Judgment, 21 December 2011, ECLI:EU:C:2011:866, paras 56–63; CJEU, Case C-256/15, *Nemec*, Judgment, 15 December 2016, ECLI:EU:C:2016:954, paras 21–27; CJEU, Case C-96/08, *CIBA*, Judgment, 15 April 2010, ECLI:EU:C:2010:185, para 15; CJEU, Case C-364/17, *Varna Holideis*, Judgment, 27 June 2018, ECLI:EU:C:2018:500, para 18. The Court summarised its case law in

5.3.3 *Consequences of the Late Publication of EU Acts in New Official Languages*

One of the consequences of the principle of immediate and full application of EU law is the obligation of the EU institutions to publish all existing EU legislation in the new official languages of the EU by the date of accession. This obligation is reflected in Article 58 of the 2003 Act of Accession, which provides that the texts of the EU legal acts adopted before accession, drawn up by the EU institutions in the new official languages, "are authentic under the same conditions as the texts drawn up in the pre-existing eleven languages, and must be published in the Official Journal of the European Union if the texts in the present languages were so published". In the context of the 2004 enlargement, the EU institutions encountered some difficulties in fulfilling this obligation, so that not all official EU texts in the new languages were available on 1 May 2004.[38]

The lack of accessibility of official texts of EU legislation, especially, of directly applicable regulations in the area of customs law, have given rise to numerous legal disputes before the national courts, which ultimately referred the question to the Court. The need to clarify legal consequences of the failure to ensure accessibility of EU law on the first days after accession was not only a horizontal issue, but also a matter of constitutional importance, since it concerned the application of the principles of legal certainty, legality, equality, and, ultimately, the value of the rule of law.

That thorny issue was resolved in *Skoma-Lux*,[39] a preliminary reference submitted by a Czech court in a dispute between the importer and the national customs authority, regarding a fine imposed in respect of customs infringements allegedly committed shortly after accession. The applicant argued that the customs authority could not rely upon the EU legislation, which had not yet been properly published in the Czech language. Advocate General Kokott, while underlining the constitutional importance of the issue raised, observed that it concerned late publication of an EU regulation in certain official languages, rather than a complete lack of its publication. As a consequence, the validity of the regulation was not in issue. However, in the light of the principle of legal certainty, which requires that rules allow individuals to ascertain unequivocally their obligations, the unpublished rules could not be enforced against citizens in the new Member States. Thus, the Advocate General rejected the application of the 'constitutive' doctrine which would make the validity of EU acts dependent on their publication in all the official languages, but instead proposed a

CJEU, Case C-242/18, *UniCredit Leasing*, Judgment, 3 July 2019, ECLI:EU:C:2019:558, paras 31–35.

[38] The electronic editions of the Official Journal of the EU became authentic only from 1st July 2013 (see Council Regulation (EU) N° 216/2013 of 7 March 2013 on the electronic publication of the Official Journal of the European Union, OJ L 69, 13.3.2013, p. 1).

[39] CJEU, Case C-161/06, *Skoma-Lux*, Judgment, 11 December 2007, ECLI:EU:C:2007:773.

more limited consequence of 'unenforceability' of such acts.[40] The Court followed the same approach by holding that enforcement of EU provisions, which have not been published in the Official Journal of the European Union in the language of a new Member State, against individuals in that State, would be contrary to Article 58 of the 2003 Act of Accession and the principle of legal certainty. The Court observed that it is irrelevant that individuals in the new Member States could have learned of the EU legislation by other means, such as unofficial publications on the Internet. The Court also clarified that the lack of proper publication in the new languages did not put into question the validity or existence of an EU act, but only its 'enforceability'.[41]

The issue in question and the ruling in *Skoma-Lux* sparked an academic debate. Some authors stressed that the Court, while providing an acceptable solution, disregarded a more general and complex question.[42] For instance, the lack of publication could, arguably, be resolved differently in the areas of civil law and criminal law, since in the latter the solution must respect the general principle of *nullum crimen, nulla poena sine lege*.[43] Another controversial aspect of the ruling related to the recognition of financial consequences for the new Member States and the ensuing limitation of the temporal effect of the Court's interpretation, which is implicit in the ruling.[44] Some of those debated consequences were addressed in the subsequent case law. In particular, the Court later clarified that the rule stated in *Skoma-Lux* did not preclude enforcement against individuals of the national legislation implementing provisions of EU regulations in the area of customs union. In such situations the *Skoma-Lux* rule remained only of a residual application, limited to the cases where the national authorities intended to rely on EU provisions which were not implemented by the national rules.[45]

The Court's case law on the consequences of late publication of EU acts in the context of accession had a wider reach and shaped the general case law of the Court on the lack of publication and the lack of accessibility of directly applicable EU acts. According to that case law, an EU regulation cannot take effect unless it has been published in the Official Journal, and cannot be enforced against individuals in a Member State before they have the opportunity to make themselves acquainted via its proper publication.[46]

---

[40] CJEU, Case C-161/06, *Skoma-Lux*, Opinion of Advocate General Kokott, 18 September 2007, ECLI:EU:C:2007:525, notably paras 24 and 86.

[41] CJEU, Case C-161/06, *Skoma-Lux*, Judgment, 11 December 2007, ECLI:EU:C:2007:773, para 51. See also CJEU, Case C-410/09, *Polska Telefonia Cyfrowa*, Judgment, 12 May 2011, ECLI:EU:C:2011:294, paras 24–29.

[42] See Bobek 2008, p. 1621; Lasiński-Sulecki and Morawski 2008, p. 725.

[43] This was partly addressed by the Court: see para 73 of the judgment in *Skoma-Lux*.

[44] See Bobek 2008, p. 1622.

[45] See CJEU, Case C-146/11, *Pimix*, Judgment, 12 July 2012, ECLI:EU:C:2012:450, para 42.

[46] See CJEU, Case C-345/06, *Heinrich*, Judgment, 10 March 2009, ECLI:EU:C:2009:140, paras 42–43 and 62.

5.4 Issues Related to the Material Scope of Application of EU Law to the New Member States

5.4.1 Interpretation of Transitional Arrangements Regarding the Free Movement of Workers

The freedom of movement of citizens of the new Member States and their access to the labour market in the old Member States was one of the most debated political issues in the context of accession negotiations. The negotiations resulted in an elaborate net of transitional provisions, laid down in Annexes V to XIV to the 2003 Act of Accession, allowing the old Member States to limit or control, to differing degrees, the flows of migration from eight new Member States.[47] These transitional arrangements followed a three steps approach, spread over a seven-year period (2+3+2), during which the discretion of the old Member States to limit free movement of workers was gradually reduced.[48] The provisions in question were partly modelled on similar arrangements adopted on the occasion of the 1985 accession of Spain and Portugal, thus, allowing to draw some indications from the case law related to that accession.[49] However, to a large extent the 2004 arrangements raised new legal issues.

The Court had several opportunities to interpret transitional provisions of the 2003 Act of Accession concerning the free movement of workers. In *Commission/Germany*, the Commission alleged that Germany infringed on the freedom of movement of workers, first, by limiting the posting of workers by Polish undertakings and, secondly, by violating the standstill clause laid down in Paragraph 13 of Chapter 2 of Annex XII to the Act of Accession. The latter allegation invited the Court to interpret the standstill arrangement, which is a frequent transitional solution, not only in the context of accession. In general, such clauses prohibit the introduction of new legislative or administrative measures having the object or effect of creating more restrictive conditions than those applicable on the relevant date—which, in the present case, was the date of the signature of the 2003 Accession Treaty.[50] The new and complex issue raised by the case was whether the standstill clause precluded not only the adoption of restrictive legislative or administrative measures, but also, more generally, precluded any widening of the restrictions on access to the national labour market. In this case, Germany did not adopt any new restrictive measures, but merely reorganised geographic districts subject to the national labour market protection clause, with the effect that access to the German labour market has *de*

[47] Cyprus was not concerned by transitional arrangements regarding the free movement of workers. Malta negotiated the right to introduce safeguard measures against workers from the other 24 Member States.

[48] See Inglis 2004, p. 965; Adinolfi 2005, p. 485.

[49] See CJEU, Case C-113/89, *Rush Portuguesa*, Judgment, 27 March 1990, ECLI:EU:C:1990:142.

[50] CJEU, Case C-37/98, *Savas*, Judgment, 11 May 2000, ECLI:EU:C:2000:224, para 69, and CJEU, Case C-242/06, *Sahin*, Judgment, 17 September 2009, ECLI:EU:C:2009:554, para 63.

facto become more restricted for Polish workers. The Court rejected the Commission's claim that such a consequence was caught by the standstill clause and ruled that the alleged restriction is a mere consequence of a new factual situation which has developed in the labour market.[51]

Two further cases allowed the Court to interpret transitional arrangements regarding the free movement of workers in the light of their general objectives, that is, to prevent disturbances on the labour market of the 'old' Member States due to the immediate arrival of a large number of workers from the new Member States.[52]

First, in *Vicoplus*, the Court confirmed that the Netherlands could invoke those transitional provisions in order to continue to impose, during the seven-year transitional period, the obligation to have a work permit for workers hired out from a new Member State.[53] Furthermore, the Court set out three criteria for determining whether a worked was 'hired out' within the meaning of the Posting of Workers Directive.[54] These criteria concerned, first, the fact that the worker remains in the employ of the undertaking providing the service, no contract of employment being entered into with the user undertaking. Secondly, the movement of the worker to the host Member State must constitute the very purpose of the provision of services effected by the undertaking providing the services. Thirdly, the employee must carry out his tasks under the control and direction of the user undertaking.[55] Those three criteria allowed the Dutch courts to determine whether Polish workers were 'hired out' in the Netherlands, and therefore could be required to hold work permits during the transitional period, or whether they were rather 'posted'. The Court further developed these criteria in *Martin Meat*.[56]

Second, in *Prefeta*, the Court interpreted the transitional provisions on the free movement of workers laid down in the 2003 Act of Accession, in the context of the measures adopted by the United Kingdom (before Brexit), which precluded Polish nationals who had not worked for an uninterrupted period of 12 months from retaining their status of 'worker' if they were temporarily unable to work as the result of an illness or accident. Since the national provisions in question transposed Article 7(3) of Directive 2004/38, the Court was asked to clarify whether the United Kingdom was entitled to rely on the transitional arrangements in order to disapply that provision. The Court found that the United Kingdom could indeed derogate from Article 7(3) of Directive 2004/38, since it was necessary in order to give full effect to the transitional

---

[51] CJEU, Case C-546/07, *Commission v* Germany, Judgment, 21 January 2010, ECLI:EU:C:2010:25, para 64. The Court, however, upheld the first complaint raised by the Commission.

[52] See, CJEU, Cases C-307/09 to C-309/09, *Vicoplus and Others*, Judgment, 10 February 2011, ECLI:EU:C:2011:64, para 34.

[53] *Ibid.*, paras 40–41.

[54] Article 1(3)(c) of Directive 96/71/EC of the European Parliament and of the Council of 16 December 1996 concerning the posting of workers in the framework of the provision of services (OJ 1997 L 18, p. 1).

[55] CJEU, Cases C-307/09 to C-309/09, *Vicoplus and Others*, Judgment, 10 February 2011, ECLI:EU:C:2011:64, para 51.

[56] CJEU, Case C-586/13, *Martin Meat*, Judgment, 18 June 2015, ECLI:EU:C:2015:405, para 41.

provisions in the 2003 Act of Accession in situations where a migrant worker had ceased to work prior to completing 12 uninterrupted months of registered work in the United Kingdom. The Court observed that the transitional arrangements in question were intended to restrict the right of economically inactive nationals from new Member States to reside in the United Kingdom for the purpose of seeking work.[57]

Hence, the Court interpreted transitional arrangements concerning the freedom of movement of workers in such a way as to strike a balance between the achievement of their specific purpose, that is, to prevent disturbances on the labour market of the existing Member States, and of their general objective, that is, the facilitation of the full application of fundamental market freedoms after the expiry of the seven-year transitional period. The case law developed by the Court in the context of the 2003 enlargement informed the interpretation of similar arrangements adopted on the occasion of subsequent accessions.[58]

5.4.2 Post-accession Controversies Surrounding the Free Movement of Capital and the Acquisition of Agricultural Land

The freedom of movement of capital and, in particular, the acquisition of agricultural land in the new Member States was another horizontal issue addressed in the accession negotiations. On a smaller scale, it also played a role in the context of the 1995 enlargement, in relation to the acquisition of second residences.[59]

The transitional provisions, laid down in the relevant Annexes to the 2003 Act of Accession, allowed six new Member States (the Czech Republic, Estonia, Hungary, Latvia, Lithuania and Slovakia) to maintain, during a seven-year transitional period, the prohibitions on the acquisition of agricultural land by legal persons and by natural persons who are non-residents or non-nationals. The restrictions had to exist on the date of the signature of the Accession Treaty and were subject to a standstill clause. Moreover, the transitional periods could be extended by a further three years, by means of a Commission's decision, in case of a threat of serious disturbances on the agricultural land market of the Member States in question.[60] Poland succeeded in obtaining a similar transitional arrangement for a longer, twelve-year period.

---

[57] CJEU, Case C-618/16, *Prefeta*, Judgment, 13 September 2018, ECLI:EU:C:2018:719, paras 47–48.

[58] With respect to Croatia's accession, see CJEU, Case C-18/17, *Danieli & C. Officine Meccaniche and Others*, Judgment, 14 November 2018, ECLI:EU:C:2018:904.

[59] See with respect to Article 70 of the 1994 Act of Accession, CJEU, Case C-302/97, *Konle*, Judgment, 1 June 1999, ECLI:EU:C:1999:271; CJEU, Case C-300/01, Salzmann, 15 May 2003, ECLI:EU:C:2003:283. See Forman and Booss 1995, p. 118.

[60] Four new Member States applied and were granted such an extension: Hungary, Latvia, Lithuania and Slovakia.

Similar arrangements were negotiated and introduced in the context of 2007 and 2013 enlargements.[61]

While those provisions of the 2003 Act of Accession, in themselves, did not give rise to any significant controversies before the EU courts, their expiry has led to the adoption by Hungary of a new legislation, restrictive of a free movement of capital, which was subject to intensive litigation at the EU level and led to several important legal developments.

In the context of accession, Hungary benefited from a total ten-year transitional period authorising it to retain restrictions on the acquisition of agricultural land by non-resident EU citizens. Close to the end of that transitional period, almost ten years after accession, Hungary amended its legislation on agricultural land imposing a general prohibition on the creation of rights of usufruct over agricultural land, except between close relatives. Moreover, the new legislation prescribed the extinction of existing usufructuary rights except for those created between close relatives. The cancellation of the rights of usufruct was systematic and affected large numbers of Hungarian nationals as well as nationals of other Member States. In *SEGRO and Horváth*,[62] the Court held that the legislation, which extinguishes by operation of law the rights of usufruct held over agricultural land by nationals of other Member States, restricts free movement of capital guaranteed in Article 63 TFEU. Furthermore, the Court found that Hungary did not advance any objective reason capable of justifying such a restriction. In particular, while the stated reason for the adoption of the new legislation was to penalise the circumvention of restrictions on acquisition of agricultural land, the systematic cancellation of usufruct rights was disproportionate, since it did not enable the national courts to carry out a case-by-case examination in order to assess the evidence of any allegedly abusive or fraudulent conduct.

In a parallel infringement case, *Commission/Hungary (Usufruct over agricultural land)*,[63] the Commission has for the first time, alongside the violation of the fundamental freedoms of the internal market, invoked a violation of the Charter, namely, the right to property under its Article 17. The Commission argued that the cancellation of usufruct rights to agricultural land deprived the persons concerned of their property rights, without due justification nor fair compensation. The Court examined that plea and found that by cancelling the rights of usufruct related to agricultural land Hungary has not only infringed the fundamental freedom of movement of capital, but also violated the right to property. Thus, the Court declared that Hungary has failed to fulfil its obligations under Article 63 TFEU 'in conjunction' with Article 17 of the Charter. Even though the Court referred to the joint violation of both the fundamental freedom and the Charter and did not discuss whether the infringement

[61] The Accession Treaty 2005 provided for two transitional periods with regard to the acquisition of secondary residences and the acquisition of agricultural land, forests and forestry land. For restrictions on acquisition of agricultural land in the 2012 Accession Treaty, see Łazowski 2012, p. 29.

[62] CJEU, Cases C-52/16 and C-113/16, *SEGRO and Horváth*, Judgment, 6 March 2018, ECLI:EU:C:2018:157.

[63] CJEU, Case C-235/17, *Commission/Hungary (Usufruct over agricultural land)*, Judgment, 21 May 2019, ECLI:EU:C:2019:432.

could be based solely on the Charter,[64] the case was unprecedented and paved the way for wider developments concerning the invocability of the Charter in infringement proceedings.[65] In a subsequent related case, the Court confirmed the duty of the national courts hearing an action against a decision rejecting a request for reinstatement of the rights of usufruct, to order the competent administrative authority to reinstate the right.[66]

5.4.3 Interpreting the Notion of 'Existing State Aid'

The control of State aid in ten countries joining the EU was considered a problematic issue during the accession negotiations, in particular, in view of their past as centrally planned economies and their large public sector. While it was clearly understood that, from the date of accession, any State aid in the new Member States would be, with some limited transitional derogations,[67] subject to the application of EU State aid rules, the EU's concerns also related to the existence of aid granted in Central and Eastern European countries before accession.

In the EU State aid control system, the procedural regime applicable to State aid measures differs depending on whether the aid is 'new' or 'existing'. Whereas new aid may not be implemented until it is approved by the Commission (Article 108(3) TFEU), existing aid schemes are subject to constant review by the Commission pursuant to Article 108(1) TFEU. During earlier enlargements, with the notable exception of the accession of the EEA States in 1995,[68] all aid measures put into effect prior to accession were considered to be 'existing aid', just as aid granted prior to the entry into force of the TFEU in the respective Member States. This traditional solution was deemed unsatisfactory in the context of the 2004 enlargement. Instead, in 2002, the Commission outlined a more sophisticated scheme, whereby only measures approved by the national competition authorities in the candidate countries, and to which the Commission did not object via interim mechanism, could be regarded as 'existing aid'.[69] Thus, apart from those approved measures, as well as the measures explicitly listed in the Appendix agreed during the accession negotiations, any aid granted on or after 10 December 1994[70] and still applicable after accession was to

[64] This aspect was resolved in subsequent case law, see CJEU, Case C-66/18, *Commission v Hungary (Higher education)*, Judgment, 6 October 2020, ECLI:EU:C:2020:792.

[65] See Prete and Smulders 2021, p. 290; Morijn 2022, p. 1137.

[66] See CJEU, Case C-177/20, *Grossmania*, Judgment, 10 March 2022, ECLI:EU:C:2022:175.

[67] For an overview of those transitional arrangements, see Kuik 2004, p. 9.

[68] In accordance with Article 172(5) of the 1994 Accession Treaty, pre-accession aid granted during 1994 without having been notified to and approved by the EFTA Surveillance Authority, could not be considered as 'existing' State aid.

[69] European Commission, '2002 State Aid Scoreboard - Special edition on the candidate countries' (COM(2002)638). See also Schütterle 2003, p. 29; Di Bucci and Stobiecka 2008, p. 322.

[70] This date refers to the conclusions of the Essen European Council, of 9 December 1994, which outlined a strategy to prepare for the accession of the associated Central and Eastern European

be considered as 'new aid'.[71] Separate provisions related to aid in the agricultural sector.[72]

This arrangement, unprecedented in the EU's enlargement practice, was laid down in Chapter 3 of Annex IV to the 2003 Act of Accession, which provided that only the following three categories of pre-accession aid measures were to be regarded as existing aid: '(i) aid measures put into effect before 10 December 1994; (ii) aid measures listed in the Appendix to this Annex; (iii) aid measures which prior to the date of accession were assessed by the State aid monitoring authority of the new Member State and found to be compatible with the acquis, and to which the Commission did not raise an objection on the ground of serious doubts as to the compatibility of the measure with the common market'. The provisions in question applied without distinction to State aid schemes and to individual aid.

The EU Courts had their first opportunity to interpret these provisions in *Budapesti Erőmű/Commission*,[73] in the context of a State aid measure resulting from the power purchase agreements concluded in Hungary long before the date of its accession, but still applicable after that date. The applicant contested the Commission's jurisdiction on the grounds that the aid resulted from the agreements concluded before accession. The General Court rejected that argument indicating that Chapter 3 of Annex IV to the 2003 Act of Accession precisely dealt with the aid put into effect before the date of accession and still applicable after that date, which showed that such measures were caught by the EU State Aid Law. Since the measure in question was not listed in the Appendix to Annex IV to the 2003 Act of Accession, it was deemed to be new aid. Furthermore, while the applicant argued that a measure had not been regarded as State aid at the time of its introduction, the General Court indicated that it was clear from the wording of Chapter 3 of Annex IV that it also covered measures which subsequently became State aid, and that such measures must also be regarded as new aid. The General Court observed that it follows from Article 2 of the 2003 Act of Accession, that the EU rules in relation to State aid became mandatory in Hungary on the date of accession. Therefore, that date constituted the relevant date for the assessment whether the measure at issue constitutes State aid. Finally, the General

countries (Annex IV of the conclusions), including the requirement to align with the EU's competition and State aids policy. See Kuik 2004, p. 366. The date also had a particular relevance regarding Poland, as it marked the entry into force of the law on special economic zones and the grant of related State aid. See Schütterle 2003, p. 36.

[71] CJEU, Cases C-702/20 and C-17/21, *DOBELES HES*, Judgment, 12 January 2023, ECLI:EU:C:2023:1, para 101.

[72] See Chapter 4 of Annex IV to the 2003 Act of Accession. These provisions were interpreted in CJEU, Case C-111/10, Commission v Council, Judgment, 4 December 2013, EU:C:2013:785; CJEU, Case C-117/10, Commission v Council, Judgment, 4 December 2013, ECLI:EU:C:2013:786; CJEU, Case C-118/10, Commission v Council, Judgment, 4 December 2013, ECLI:EU:C:2013:787; and CJEU, Case C-121/10, Commission v Council, Judgment, 4 December 2013, EU:C:2013:784.

[73] See CJEU, Cases T-80/06 and T-182/09, *Budapesti Erőmű v Commission*, Judgment, 13 February 2012, ECLI:EU:T:2012:65.

Court confirmed the Commission's finding that the measure constitutes State aid and is incompatible with the internal market.[74]

In response to the applicant's argument invoking the principle of legitimate expectations, the General Court observed that the Europe Agreement with Hungary, which entered into force in 1994, that is to say, before the power purchase agreements were signed, already provided for measures of State aid control. Therefore, at the time when the power purchase agreements were concluded, Hungary was under an obligation to apply State aid rules analogous to those applicable under EU law. Interestingly, the latter reasoning would not hold true in a case originating from other acceding States, notably Lithuania, Latvia, Estonia or Slovenia, since the Europe Agreements with those countries entered into force later, in 1998. Hence, the reasoning of the General Court revealed a controversial aspect of the transitional measures concerning those Member States, for whom the setting of 10 December 1994 as a cut-off date might not seem entirely justified.[75]

The General Court reiterated similar findings in two later cases concerning the Hungarian electricity market.[76] While the reasoning of the Court appears to be strongly rooted in the wording of the 2003 Act of Accession, the resulting consequence for operators in Hungary has drawn critical remarks alleging discriminatory treatment of investors in new Member States and the protection of their legitimate expectations.[77] That being said, the General Court's findings were fully confirmed on appeal. Indeed, in its judgment on appeal, the Court hinted at the fact that any other conclusion would render the transitional arrangements contained in the Accession Treaty meaningless.[78]

The Court's solution was also consonant with the judgment in *Kremikovtzi*,[79] regarding restructuring aid grated prior to accession in Bulgaria. In that judgment, concerning similar transitional arrangements included in the 2005 Act of Accession, the Court held that State aid measures implemented by Bulgaria before accession but still applicable after accession are subject to the Commission's powers. Thus, the cases in question allowed the EU courts to clarify several complex questions concerning the application of the unprecedented arrangements governing the control of State aid in new Member States, in the light of the objectives of the 2003 and 2005 Acts of Accession.

Finally, more recently, the Court had an opportunity to clarify the temporal scope of EU State aid law in a new Member State, in *Commission/European Food and Others ('Micula case')*. This case was but one in a long-lasting saga concerning the

---

[74] *Ibid.*, paras 52–62 and the operative part.

[75] *Ibid.*, para 59. See for a similar argument Schütterle 2003, p. 29.

[76] CJEU, Case T-468/08, *Tisza Erőmű v Commission*, Judgment, 30 April 2014, ECLI:EU:T:2014:235; and CJEU, Case T-179/09, *Dunamenti Erőmű v Commission*, Judgment, 30 April 2014, ECLI:EU:T:2014:236.

[77] See Wollmann 2015, p. 289.

[78] CJEU, Case C-357/14 P, *Electrabel and Dunamenti Erőmű v Commission*, Judgment, 1 October 2015, ECLI:EU:C:2015:64265.

[79] CJEU, Case C-262/11, *Kremikovtzi*, Judgment, 29 November 2012, ECLI:EU:C:2012:760, para 52.

payment of compensation awarded by an arbitral tribunal in the arbitral proceedings concluded after Romania's accession, for the damage allegedly suffered by Swedish investors due to the repeal of the tax incentives scheme in Romania before its accession. The General Court concluded that the advantage ensuing from the right to obtain compensation was granted before Romania's accession to the European Union and, thus, the Commission lacked jurisdiction to assess the alleged State aid under Article 108 TFEU. On appeal, the Court quashed the judgment considering that the decisive temporal factor for establishing the date on which the right to receive State aid was conferred on its beneficiaries was the acquisition of a definitive right to receive that aid. In this case, the right to compensation was granted only by the arbitration award which was delivered after accession. Hence, the Commission was competent to adopt the decision at the issue under Article 108 TFEU.[80] Furthermore, the Court recalled that Articles 267 and 344 TFEU must be interpreted as precluding an arbitration clause contained in an intra-EU bilateral investment agreement.[81]

The latter pronouncement connects this case to the Court's constitutional case law resulting from *Achmea*.[82] That case law must be viewed in the context of bilateral investment treaties concluded between Western and Eastern European countries after the fall of the Iron Curtain in order to create a favourable climate for investment. The inclusion of investment arbitration clauses in those agreements was a way to strengthen investor protection, but also a sign of a lack of trust in the judicial system of those countries. The Court's constitutional pronouncement confirming incompatibility of such arbitration clauses in intra-EU agreements not only reaffirmed the principles of autonomy of EU law, effective judicial protection and mutual trust, but is also aimed at protecting the underlying values of rule of law and equality,[83] thus, ultimately, confirming that the divide between Eastern and Western European countries has become obsolete.

5.5 Conclusions

In the course of twenty years following the 2004 enlargement, the judicial interpretation of the elaborate legal instruments based on the 2003 Accession Treaty has led to several important developments of the EU courts' case law related to new accessions. The judgments resulting from post-accession disputes have clarified key issues related to the temporal scope of application of EU law in the new Member States: the judicial protection in the interim period, the consequences of late publication of EU acts in new languages and the temporal scope of the Court's preliminary rulings

---

[80] CJEU, Case C-638/19 P, *Commission v European Food and Others*, Judgment, 25 January 2022, ECLI:EU:C:2022:50, para 124.

[81] *Ibid.*, para 138.

[82] See CJEU, Case C-284/16, *Achmea*, Judgment, 6 March 2018, ECLI:EU:C:2018:158; CJEU, Case C-741/19, *Republic of Moldova*, Judgment, 2 September 2021, ECLI:EU:C:2021:655.

[83] See Lenaerts and Gutiérrez-Fons 2023, p. 1507.

jurisdiction. The case law also touched upon several important areas of substantive EU law, as illustrated by examples related to the freedom of movement of workers, the freedom of movement of capital and State aid control.

The common thread of those post-accession cases is their link to wider horizontal issues in EU law. Indeed, the analysis of accession-related cases shows that the problems, which could have appeared at the outset as isolated enlargement disputes, have influenced the general EU courts' case law developments on such fundamental issues as the principle of legal certainty, the interpretation of the fundamental market freedoms or the invocability of the Charter in infringement proceedings. Another common feature of the accession-related case law can be seen in the underlying objective of transitional arrangements contained in the Accession Treaty, which are aimed at ensuring the full and effective application of EU law to (and in) the new Member States and, thus, contributing to equality and mutual trust between the Member States.

References

Adinolfi A (2005) Free Movement and Access to Work of Citizens of the New Member States: The Transitional Measures. Common Market Law Review 42(2):469–498

Bobek M (2008) Learning to Talk: Preliminary Rulings, the Courts of the New Member States and the Court of Justice. Common Market Law Review 45(6):1611–1643

Delcourt Ch (2001) The Acquis Communautaire: Has the Concept Had Its Day? Common Market Law Review 38(4):829–870

Di Bucci V, Stobiecka-Kuik A (2008) The Temporal Application of the State Aid Rules, EC State Aid Law. Kluwer Law International, the Netherlands, pp 311–346

Forman J, Booss D (1995) Enlargement: Legal and Procedural Aspects. Common Market Law Review 32(1):95–130

Heukels T (1990) Intertemporales Gemeinschaftsrecht: Rückwirkung, Sofortwirkung und Rechtsschutz in der Rechtsprechung des Gerichtshofes der Europäischen Gemeinschaften. Nomos, Baden-Baden

Inglis K (2004) The Union's Fifth Accession Treaty: New Means to Make Enlargement Possible. Common Market Law Review 41(4):937–973

Kalėda SL (2000) Extension of the Preliminary Rulings Procedure Outside the Scope of Community Law: 'The Dzodzi Line of Cases'. European Integration Online Papers 11(4)

Kalėda SL (2004) Immediate Effect of Community Law in the New Member States: Is there a Place for a Consistent Doctrine? European Law Journal 10(1):102–122

Kalėda SL (2024) The Role of European Union Courts in Shaping the Legal Framework of Accession to the European Union. ERA Forum 25, pp 249–258

Kuik K (2004) State Aid and the 2004 Accession – Overview of Recent Developments. European State Aid Law Quarterly 3(3):9–15

Lasiński-Sulecki K, Morawski W (2008) Late Publication of EC Law in Languages of New Member States and its Effects: Obligations on Individuals Following the Court's Judgment in Skoma–Lux, Common Market Law Review 45(3):705–725

Łazowski A (2007) And Then They Were Twenty-Seven… A Legal Appraisal of the Sixth Accession Treaty. Common Market Law Review 44(2):401–430

Łazowski A (2012) European Union Do Not Worry, Croatia Is Behind You: A Commentary On The Seventh Accession Treaty. Croatian Yearbook of European Law & Policy 8(1):1–39

Łazowski A (2022) Strengthening the Rule of Law and the EU Pre-accession Policy: Repubblika v. Il-Prim Ministru. Common Market Law Review 59(6):1803–1822
Lenaerts K, Gutiérrez-Fons JA (2023) High Hopes: Autonomy and the Identity of the EU. European Papers 8(3):1495–1511
Morijn J (2022) Separate Charter Invocation as a New Enforcement Method: The Lex NGO Case. Common Market Law Review 59(4):1137–1168
Półtorak N (2008) Ratione Temporis Application of the Preliminary Rulings Procedure. Common Market Law Review 45(5):1357–1381
Prete L, Smulders B (2021) The Age of Maturity of Infringement Proceedings. Common Market Law Review 58(2):285–332
Roubier P (1960) Le droit transitoire (conflits de lois dans le temps). Dalloz-Sirey, Paris
Schütterle P (2003) Enlargement: Pre-Accession – State Aid after Accession. European State Aid Law Quarterly 2(1):29–38
Tridimas T (2003) Knocking on Heaven's Door: Fragmentation, Efficiency and Defiance in the Preliminary Reference Procedure. Common Market Law Review 40(1):9–50
Wollmann H (2015) Long-Term Power Purchase Agreements and Market Liberalization. European State Aid Law Quarterly 14(2):284–290

Saulius Lukas Kalėda is a Professor at the Law Faculty of Vilnius University and a Judge at the General Court of the European Union.

Chapter 6
Europeanization of National Constitutional Identity: 20 Years of Latvia in the European Union

Jānis Pleps, Kalvis Engīzers and Viktorija Soņeca

Contents

Abstract The Latvian legal system, including the *Satversme* (Constitution of Latvia), demonstrates a constructive alignment with the European Union law, recognizing it as an integral part of the national legal system and acknowledging its supremacy (primacy). Even Latvia's constitutional identity, as recognized by the Constitutional Court, does not conflict with European Union law but rather incorporates the European dimension as a key element of its constitutional identity. Over the past two decades, European Union membership and participation in European integration have become fundamental constitutional principles shaping Latvia's constitutional identity. The Europeanization of Latvia's constitutional framework serves to strengthen democracy and the rule of law while also providing an additional safeguard for maintaining national independence. As a core principle of Latvia's constitutional identity, European Union membership significantly influences the application of legal norms and legal reasoning. National legal norms must be interpreted in accordance

J. Pleps (✉)
University of Latvia, Riga, Latvia
e-mail: janis.pleps@lu.lv

K. Engīzers
Riga, Latvia
e-mail: kalvis.engizers@gmail.com

V. Soņeca
Riga Graduate School of Law, Riga, Latvia
e-mail: viktorija.soneca@gmail.com

I. Isokaitė-Valužė and H. Šinkūnas (eds.), *The European Union 2004-2024*,
https://doi.org/10.1007/978-94-6265-718-2_6

with European Union law, with due recognition of its supremacy. The values, constitutional principles, and norms that form Latvia's constitutional identity should be harmonized with European Union membership, ensuring coherence and avoiding any irreconcilable conflicts or fragmentation between the national legal system and European Union law.

Keywords Europeanization · *Satversme* (Constitution of Latvia) · European Union · Constitutional identity · Supremacy (primacy) of European Union law · Constitutional Court · Application of legal norms · Judicial dialogue

6.1 Introduction

On 20 September 2003, a referendum on joining the European Union was held. A total of 1,010,467 Latvian citizens participated (71.5% of all eligible voters), and 676,700 of them voted in favour (67% of all votes).[1] Based on the results of the referendum, the accession treaty was ratified by the *Saeima* (Parliament) on 30 October 2003,[2] and on 1 May 2004, the Republic of Latvia (Latvia) officially became a member of the European Union. Symbolically, this fulfilled Latvia's historical ambition to return to Europe after regaining independence following 50 years of Soviet occupation.[3] However, this was not the end of history. As Robert Schuman stated on 9 May 1950,

[1] *Par tautas nobalsošanas par Latvijas dalību Eiropas Savienībā rezultātiem: Centrālās vēlēšanu komisijas 2003.gada 6.oktobra lēmums* Nr.20 [On results of the referendum on Latvian membership in the European Union: decision No.20 of the Central Election Commission, 6 October 2003]. Latvijas Vēstnesis, 2003, Nr. 138. See: Taurēns and Feldmanis 2016, p. 171.

[2] *Par Līgumu starp Beļģijas Karalisti, Dānijas Karalisti, Vācijas Federatīvo Republiku, Grieķijas Republiku, Spānijas Karalisti, Francijas Republiku, Īriju, Itālijas Republiku, Luksemburgas Lielhercogisti, Nīderlandes Karalisti, Austrijas Republiku, Portugāles Republiku, Somijas Republiku, Zviedrijas Karalisti, Lielbritānijas un Ziemeļīrijas Apvienoto Karalisti (Eiropas Savienības dalībvalstīm) un Čehijas Republiku, Igaunijas Republiku, Kipras Republiku, Latvijas Republiku, Lietuvas Republiku, Ungārijas Republiku, Maltas Republiku, Polijas Republiku, Slovēnijas Republiku, Slovākijas Republiku par Čehijas Republikas, Igaunijas Republikas, Kipras Republikas, Latvijas Republikas, Lietuvas Republikas, Ungārijas Republikas, Maltas Republikas, Polijas Republikas, Slovēnijas Republikas un Slovākijas Republikas pievienošanos Eiropas Savienībai* [On the Treaty between the Kingdom of Belgium, the Kingdom of Denmark, the Federal Republic of Germany, the Hellenic Republic, the Kingdom of Spain, the French Republic, Ireland, the Italian Republic, the Grand Duchy of Luxembourg, the Kingdom of the Netherlands, the Republic of Austria, the Portuguese Republic, the Republic of Finland, the Kingdom of Sweden, the United Kingdom of Great Britain and Northern Ireland (Member States of the European Union) and the Czech Republic, the Republic of Estonia, the Republic of Cyprus, the Republic of Latvia, the Republic of Lithuania, the Republic of Hungary, the Republic of Malta, the Republic of Poland, the Republic of Slovenia, the Slovak Republic, concerning the accession of the Czech Republic, the Republic of Estonia, the Republic of Cyprus, the Republic of Latvia, the Republic of Lithuania, the Republic of Hungary, the Republic of Malta, the Republic of Poland, the Republic of Slovenia and the Slovak Republic to the European Union]. Latvijas Vēstnesis, 2003, Nr. 159.

[3] See more: Vīķe-Freiberga 2016.

"Europe will not be made all at once, or according to a single plan".[4] Twenty years of European Union membership, celebrated in May 2024, have been marked by various challenges and crises for both the European Union and its member states. European integration is still an ongoing process, and not everything that has happened can be described as a success story for the project of a united Europe. Nevertheless, joining the European Union twenty years ago was the right political decision—one that has significantly influenced Latvia and its society.

As expected, membership in the European Union significantly transformed the national legal system, integrating the application of European Union law into the daily work of the judiciary and civil servants. The Europeanization of the legal system required substantial changes in legal reasoning, the application of legal norms, and legal education. It also necessitated the reinterpretation of key constitutional concepts, such as state independence, sovereignty, and the supremacy of the constitution.

The *Satversme*[5] (Constitution of Latvia), adopted on 15 February 1922, and fully incorporated on 6 July 1993, must now be interpreted and applied within a European context, expanding the national perspective and recognizing both the European Union's legal framework as an integral part of the Latvian legal system and the supremacy (primacy) of European Union law.[6] This constitutional shift was achieved not only through formal amendments to the constitutional text but also through changes in legal practice and legal culture.

From the very beginning, the Constitutional Court of Latvia demonstrated a receptive and cooperative approach toward European Union law, a stance that was embraced within both legal practice and legal doctrine. Even the development of the concept of constitutional identity after 2012[7] did not disrupt Latvia's relationship with European Union law. For the Latvian legal system, the recognition of European values and European identity as fundamental components of national values and identity has become almost axiomatic.

The primary aim of this chapter is to analyse Europeanization as a crucial element of Latvia's constitutional identity over the past twenty years, exploring both the deeper political and sentimental motivations behind this process and its practical consequences. To achieve this, the authors will outline the key stages of the *Satversme*'s Europeanization, as well as its impact on the application of legal norms and legal methodology in preventing potential conflicts between national and

---

[4] Schuman 1950.

[5] The Constitution of the Republic of Latvia. https://likumi.lv/ta/en/en/id/57980-the-constitution-of-the-republic-of-latvia.

[6] The supremacy of the European Union law also is known as the primacy of European Union law. See further: Ziller 2022, p. 9.

[7] Konstitucionālo tiesību komisijas 2012.gada 17 septembra viedoklis "Par Latvijas konstitucionālajiem pamatiem un neaizskaramo Satversmes kodolu" [Opinion of the Constitutional Law Commission "On Constitutional Foundations of Latvia and the Inviolable Core of the *Satversme*", 17 September 2012]. https://blogi.lu.lv/tzpi/files/2017/03/17092012_Viedoklis_2.pdf. Accessed 1 February 2025. See also: Kusiņš 2024, p. 263.

European Union legal systems. Essential methods in this regard include the interpretation of national legal norms in accordance with European Union law and the judicial dialogue between Latvia's supreme courts (particularly the Constitutional Court) and the European Court of Justice (CJEU). This research is primarily focused on constitutional law and legal theory, drawing on relevant case law from the Constitutional Court and its treatment in legal doctrine.

6.2 Europeanization as a Part of the Constitutional Identity of Latvia

6.2.1 Transformation of the Legal System to the European Union

Membership in the European Union (at that time still the European Communities) was one of the strategic goals of Latvia following the restoration of independence.[8] This objective was reflected in the government's earliest political documents and strategies, shaping both foreign and domestic policy with the aim of achieving European Union membership as swiftly as possible.[9]

On the one hand, participation in European integration was driven by a sentimental desire to return to Europe after fifty years of Soviet occupation.[10] Robert Schuman's vision[11] of securing peace, stability, and prosperity in Europe through supranational institutions and closer state integration was appealing not only to Western Europe after World War II but also to Central and Eastern Europe following the Annus Mirabilis of 1989.[12] On the other hand, membership in the European Union—alongside accession to the North Atlantic Treaty Organization—was regarded as one of the most reliable long-term security guarantees for Latvia's restored independence.

Historical experience with Russia left little room for optimism regarding regional security and geopolitical stability. Given that Latvia regained independence during the collapse of the Soviet Union and a period of Russian weakness, there was a strong perception of the need to seize this unique historical opportunity and distance itself from Russia as much as possible.[13] The concept of the "Russian world" and Russia's geopolitical ambitions to maintain influence over former Soviet republics—limiting

[8] See further: Stiprais 2021.

[9] Taurēns and Feldmanis 2016, pp. 94–102; 126–134.

[10] Kalniete 2016, pp. 163–164.

[11] Schuman 1950.

[12] See further: Kershaw 2018.

[13] Taurēns and Feldmanis 2016, pp. 94–95; Rostoks 2020, pp. 37–38.

their ability to pursue independent foreign and security policies—demonstrate that Latvia and the other Baltic states fully recognized their limited options.[14]

The need to secure Latvia's restored independence in the long term and to distance itself from potential Russian influence and threats shaped the country's approach to European integration. Both society as a whole and the political and intellectual elites recognized the deeper significance and crucial importance of joining the European Union.[15]

From time to time, Latvia's political agenda has included discussions about positioning the country as a bridge between the European Union and Russia, remaining outside the European Union, or fostering closer cooperation with Russia based on historical ties from the Soviet occupation period. However, these political approaches never gained sufficient support to influence state policies and strategies. Geopolitical concerns also played a significant role in shaping discussions on European integration. Even though there was not overwhelming enthusiasm or optimism, few openly identified as Eurosceptics or campaigned against European Union membership. It was widely understood that remaining outside the European Union, given the context of potential Russian influence and threats, was not a viable option. Historically, European Union membership was seen as the only available path to long-term security and guarantees of independence—a goal that was ultimately achieved.

Integration into the European Union led to the Europeanization[16] of nearly all aspects of life, with a particular need to harmonize the legal system, necessitating comprehensive legal reforms.[17] Following the restoration of independence, Latvia's legal system had to undergo a fundamental transformation—from a socialist (Soviet) legal framework back to Western legal tradition and the continental European legal system. This transformation was further reinforced by the process of learning and practically adopting European Union law.[18] As the first Justices of the Constitutional Court noted, "Latvia must not only align the texts of its normative acts with the legal norms of the European Union but also embrace Western legal theory—namely, legal thinking. Only then will legislation, harmonized in substance, function in the same way as in the European Union. A unified legal understanding within the European tradition and legal culture is one of the preconditions for the proper functioning of the European Union."[19]

European Union membership required not only formal accession procedures and the harmonization of national legislation with European Union law but also a deeper understanding of the fundamental principles of European Union law and the *acquis*

---

[14] See further: Judgement of 10 July 2025 of the European Court of Human Rights in case Rodina and Borisova v Latvia, applications nos. 2623/16 and 2299/16, para. 111.

[15] Vīķe-Freiberga 2018, pp. 34–40.

[16] See further: Rollis 2020.

[17] Levits 2019a, pp. 822–866.

[18] See further: Kušners and Balode-Buraka 2020; Harbaceviča 2016.

[19] Dissenting Opinions of the Constitutional Court justices Aivars Endziņš, Juris Jelāgins and Anita Ušacka in case No.2000-03-01, para 5. https://www.satv.tiesa.gov.lv/wp-content/uploads/2000/03/2000-03-01_Atseviskas_domas_ENG.pdf. Accessed 1 February 2025.

communautaire. It also demanded the adoption of European legal methodology and reasoning traditions. This transformation affected not only legislators and civil servants but also the judiciary and legal practitioners, who had to adapt to the new legal and social reality in which European Union law became an integral part of the legal system. Consequently, it was necessary to reform legal education and provide continuous training for legal professionals to prepare them for the application of European Union law.[20]

6.2.2 *Europeanization of the* Satversme

Potential membership in the European Union raised concerns about the loss of national sovereignty and independent statehood, with fears of rapid European federalization.[21] These concerns were particularly significant in Latvia, which had only recently regained independence from the Soviet Union, and they played an important role in shaping public opinion as well as the perspectives of the political and legal elite.[22]

At the initiative of then-President Vaira Vīķe-Freiberga, special constitutional amendments were drafted to regulate Latvia's membership in the European Union, with a focus on securing national sovereignty.[23] An intensive dialogue with society was also organized to explore the potential benefits and risks of joining the European Union. The constitutional amendments took a technical approach, primarily outlining the procedure for accession and explicitly guaranteeing the right to withdraw from the European Union.[24] In both cases, the decision was placed in the hands of the people—any fundamental issues concerning European Union membership were to be

[20] Rezevska 2024, pp. 10–11. Compare: Kühn 2011, pp. 267–292.

[21] Albi 2005, pp. 24–35, 56–61.

[22] Working Group 2001.

[23] Discussion 2000.

[24] Main regulation concerning membership in the European Union was included in Article 68 of the *Satversme*: "[..] Upon entering into international agreements, Latvia, with the purpose of strengthening democracy, may delegate a part of its State institution competencies to international institutions. The *Saeima* may ratify international agreements in which a part of State institution competencies are delegated to international institutions in sittings in which at least two-thirds of the members of the *Saeima* participate, and a two-thirds majority vote of the members present is necessary for ratification. Membership of Latvia in the European Union shall be decided by a national referendum, which is proposed by the *Saeima*. Substantial changes in the terms regarding the membership of Latvia in the European Union shall be decided by a national referendum if such referendum is requested by at least one-half of the members of the *Saeima*."

Article 79 of the *Satversme* was amended prescribing that "decision regarding membership of Latvia in the European Union or substantial changes in the terms regarding such membership submitted for national referendum shall be deemed adopted if the number of voters is at least half of the number of electors as participated in the previous *Saeima* election and if the majority has voted in favour of the [..] membership of Latvia in the European Union or substantial changes in the terms regarding such membership." Amendments to the *Satversme* were adopted on 8 May 2003 and came into force on 8 June 2003.

decided by referendum. Based on the outcome of such a referendum, the *Saeima*, by a qualified (constitutional) majority, would have the authority to ratify international treaties providing for Latvia's accession to or withdrawal from the European Union.[25]

The working group responsible for drafting the constitutional amendments decided not to alter the fundamental principles of the *Satversme*, maintaining the position that European Union membership is compatible with Articles 1 and 2 of the *Satversme*, which enshrine state sovereignty and the sovereignty of the people. The working group argued that the core of national sovereignty and independence remained intact as long as the people retained the constitutional right to withdraw from the European Union—the ultimate power to make the final decision.[26] Moreover, European Union membership was not framed as a limitation, delegation, or sharing of sovereignty but rather as the transfer of specific state competencies to the European Union. Article 68 of the *Satversme* even stipulated that such supranational cooperation strengthens Latvian democracy.

This constitutional framework was strongly influenced by then-President of the Constitutional Court, Aivars Endziņš, who openly expressed his Euro-optimism and dismissed concerns that European Union membership could undermine Latvian statehood.[27] This Euro-optimistic approach was later endorsed by the Constitutional Court in its rulings. The Court defined Latvia's accession to the European Union as a process of "friendly openness" toward European integration, stating that European Union law has become an integral part of the Latvian legal system.[28] The Constitutional Court has since interpreted also the *Satversme* in a manner that takes European Union law into account, ensuring the avoidance of conflicts between the two legal systems.[29]

During discussions on potential constitutional amendments, proposals were made to explicitly enshrine Latvia's European Union membership as a fundamental constitutional principle. At the time Egils Levits, a Judge at the European Court of Human Rights, suggested introducing a new Article 2a in the *Satversme*, stating that "Latvia is a member state of the European Union." This provision would have served as a foundation for constitutional interpretation, embedding a European dimension within the *Satversme*.[30] Similar ideas were proposed by Professor Ineta Ziemele, who advocated for a more detailed reflection on the constitutional implications of European

---

[25] See further: Levits 2005, pp. 16–26.

[26] Working Group 2001. This position was later accepted by the Constitutional Court. See: Judgement of the Constitutional Court of the Republic of Latvia in case No.2008-35-01, 7 April 2009, para 16–17. https://www.satv.tiesa.gov.lv/web/viewer.html?file=/wp-content/uploads/2008/09/2008-35_01_ENG.pdf. Accessed 1 February 2025.

[27] Endziņš 2004.

[28] Judgment of the Constitutional Court of the Republic of Latvia in case No.2007-11-03, 17 January 2008, para 24.2. https://www.satv.tiesa.gov.lv/web/viewer.html?file=/wp-content/uploads/2007/05/2007-11-03_Spriedums_ENG.pdf. Accessed 1 February 2025.

[29] See further: Krūma and Statkus 2019.

[30] Levits 2019b, pp. 424–425.

Union membership.[31] Although these proposals were not formally adopted, they nonetheless influenced the interpretation of the *Satversme*.[32]

Following the adoption of constitutional amendments establishing the legal basis for European Union membership, Professor Ringolds Balodis rightly observed that the principle of European integration had been incorporated into the *Satversme*. The openness of the *Satversme* towards European integration is increasingly gaining outstanding importance as an additional fundamental constitutional principle.[33] This principle defines Latvia as a member state of the European Union and a participant in the broader European integration project. When the *Satversme* was later amended to include a new, more detailed preamble, it explicitly affirmed that Latvia's identity is rooted in European culture, values, and worldview, and that Latvia should contribute to the further development of a united Europe.[34]

Concerns about the potential federalization of Europe and the erosion of state independence and sovereignty provided the foundation for the rapid development of the concept of constitutional identity. Initially formulated in German legal thought and by the German Federal Constitutional Court as a means to limit the effects of globalization and European integration, this concept was quickly adopted by the constitutional courts of other European Union member states.[35] The Latvian Constitutional Court also embraced this opportunity to define the fundamental values and principles that are inviolable.[36] As the Court stated, "The State of Latvia is based on such fundamental values that, among others, include basic rights and fundamental freedoms, democracy, the sovereignty of the State and the people, the separation of powers, and the rule of law. The State has the duty to guarantee these values, and they cannot be infringed by introducing amendments to the *Satversme*."[37]

In Latvia, the development of constitutional identity was not primarily driven by concerns over European integration but rather by the necessity of strengthening and safeguarding national statehood and democracy against potential threats from Russia, which has sought to destabilize Latvia's political system.[38] From this perspective, Latvia's Europeanization and its membership in the European Union serve as additional safeguards for protecting national sovereignty and democratic governance.

---

[31] See further: Ziemele 2005, pp. 22–58.

[32] See further: Ziemele 2021.

[33] Balodis 2004, pp. 16–17.

[34] Levits 2020. It was supposed also by the Constitutional Court. See: Judgement of the Constitutional Court of the Republic of Latvia in case No.2020-39-02, 4 June 2021, para 14.2. https://www.satv.tiesa.gov.lv/wp-content/uploads/2020/08/2020-39-02_Judgement.pdf. Accessed 1 February 2025.

[35] See further: Osipova 2020a.

[36] See further: Osipova 2020b.

[37] Judgement of the Constitutional Court of the Republic of Latvia in case No.2008-35-01, 7 April 2009, para 17. https://www.satv.tiesa.gov.lv/web/viewer.html?file=/wp-content/uploads/2008/09/2008-35_01_ENG.pdf. Accessed 1 February 2025.

[38] Osipova 2020a, p. 40.

This understanding is reflected in the key elements of Latvia's constitutional identity, where European identity and inalienable membership in the European Union—along with participation in further European integration to create a more unified and effective Europe—are considered integral components. As was stated by Professor Timothy Snyder, "it is impossible to talk about stable, modern and sovereign states without Europe".[39]

This is not merely a symbolic or sentimental statement; Latvia's status as an independent, democratic republic based on the rule of law inherently includes its position as a member state of the European Union. Constitutional identity encompasses not only the fundamental values of national identity but also affirms Latvia's European Union membership as a principle of equal importance and significance. In interpreting the *Satversme*, this must be considered—Europeanization within the constitutional framework holds the same importance as state independence and sovereignty, the Latvian language as the state language, and the rule of law and fundamental human rights. This is a crucial conceptual and practical principle for ensuring a harmonious interpretation and application of European Union law, as well as for the deeper integration of European Union law into Latvia's national legal system.

6.3 Europeanization of the Thinking of Latvian Lawyers

The leading Latvian legal theorist and legal philosopher professor Daiga Rezevska defines a legal system as "the broadest issues related to law in the relevant country—all legal phenomena of the relevant society, including questions of law (also the system of laws) and institutional questions. The legal [system] encompasses all sources of law, all legal acts adopted (issued) or otherwise binding in the State, and all institutions somehow involved in the application of law (both court and administrative institutions), as well as the totality of legal relations that have been established and exist in this system."[40] The accession of Latvia to the European Union has had an impact on all these facets, but a more detailed overview is required regarding the interplay between the European Union legal order and the sources of law and legal institutions of the Latvian legal system.

Firstly, the European Union membership played a crucial role in forming how courts apply the law in the Latvian legal system today as it obliged them to disapply national law incompatible with European Union law. In 2004, at the onset of the European enlargement, Czech legal scholar Zdenek Kühn claimed that due to post-communist thinking and behavioural patterns "most new European judges are not thinking on the same wavelength as most of their Western counterparts. They adhere to many old-fashioned doctrines and narratives which would be more familiar to Western European judges in the 19th century than to judges in the early 21st

[39] Snyder 2021, p. 183.

[40] Rezevska 2024, p. 16.

century".[41] He argued that prior to the European enlargement the overly positivistic understanding of law of the national judges precluded decentralized judicial review diffused throughout all levels of the ordinary judiciary. "Instead, it was necessary to establish special constitutional tribunals in post-communist Europe".[42] While Zdenek Kühn might not have had Latvia in his mind while writing that, the situation in the Latvian legal system was similar at the time as it, too, was undergoing a transformation.

Just five years prior to Latvia's accession to the European Union, Egils Levits, then Justice at the European Court of Human Rights, warned that Latvian courts do not perform judicial review of national law even though this is their duty and human rights had been granted higher legal force than regular provisions of national law.[43] The newly established Constitutional Court which was a body of centralized judicial review was an exception. The Constitutional Court was a trailblazer and as such set the bar for other national courts. While the Constitutional Court dealt with issues relating to European Union integration and supremacy of European Union law as early as 2003, the first time it indirectly referred to the supremacy of European Union law as a part of the (dis)application of national law was in 2008 by referring to the consequences of Latvia's accession to the European Union.[44] By doing so, the Constitutional Court empowered other national courts to be more active in performing their tasks as European Union courts as established in the case-law of CJEU and national procedural laws.

The need to ensure supremacy of European Union law, alongside guidance provided by the Constitutional Court and work of legal scholars in the fields of legal theory and European Union law, was essential in strengthening judicial review in the Latvian legal system. Twenty years after Latvia's accession to the European Union, there is no doubt that in the Latvian legal system judicial review is an integral and mandatory part of the application of law and that it forms a core tenet of one of the legal methods used in the application of law, namely, the higher critique of legal norms.[45] Furthermore, Latvian legal theory has embraced European integration even further, by recognizing judgements of the CJEU as an independent source of law and, as such, "compulsory and binding" and applicable "independently to support the operative (holding) part of a legal decision".[46] This openness to European Union law and case law of CJEU in particular and the empowerment of national courts as European Union agents that come with it indicates that Latvia's accession to the

[41] Kühn 2004, p. 567.

[42] *Ibid.*, p. 566.

[43] Levits 1999, p. 9.

[44] Judgment of the Constitutional Court of the Republic of Latvia in case No.2007-11-03, 17 January 2008. https://www.satv.tiesa.gov.lv/web/viewer.html?file=/wp-content/uploads/2007/05/2007-11-03_Spriedums_ENG.pdf. Accessed 1 February 2025.

[45] Rezevska 2024, p. 82.

[46] *Ibid.*, pp. 72–73.

European Union has contributed to the broader trend of convergence of Common Law and Civil Law legal arrangements.[47]

Secondly, while the Latvian legal system and the European Union legal order are mutually intertwined, the latter is still an autonomous legal order. The use of methods of interpretation in European Union law differs from the use of methods of interpretation in national law. For example, in interpretation of European Union law, there are three methods of interpretation (literal, contextual and teleological[48]) and the literal method of interpretation is deemed to be dominant.[49] However, in the interpretation of Latvian national law there are four methods of interpretation (literal, systemic (contextual), historic, and teleological) and there is no hierarchy between them as all of them must be applied in each and every case. This example shows that the Latvian legal system is open to European Union law, it also accommodates the differences of the two legal orders.

Thirdly, Latvia's European Union membership had a significant impact on the work of the *Saeima*. The Rule of Order of the *Saeima* were amended as early as 2001 to establish the Commission of European Matters so that the *Saeima* could participate in European Union matters.[50] Furthermore, the Cabinet of Ministers amended the regulations on drafting legislative acts establishing the order for referring to relevant European Union legislation in draft national laws.[51] Nevertheless, it was the Constitutional Court that changed the game in this regard, too.

In 2019, the Constitutional Court passed a landmark judgement[52] recognizing the existence of the principle of good legislation as a legally binding norm. The Court held that when drafting new legislation, the legislator was obliged to ascertain whether, among other things, the envisaged legislation was in conformity with European Union law. Only by abiding by the requirements of the principle of good legislation, can the legislator ensure that the proposed legislation is sustainable. Failure to do so could result in the Court deciding the legislation in question to be unconstitutional and invalid. Furthermore, the Court emphasized the importance of the principle of sincere cooperation enshrined in Article 4(3) of the Treaty on European Union (TEU), claiming that this principle obliged the member states to abstain from activities that might impair the interests of the European Union and that it also precluded Latvia from adopting legislation that would impair the interests of the European Union in

[47] See further: Van Hoecke and Warrington 1998.

[48] See further: Lenaerts and Gutiérrez-Fons 2022, pp. 23–74.

[49] Ziemele and Čeiča 2024, p. 214.

[50] Rules of Order of *Saeima*. https://likumi.lv/ta/en/en/id/57517-rules-of-order-of-saeima. Accessed 1 February 2025.

[51] Regulations No 108 of 3 February 2009 of the Cabinet of Ministers "Regulations on Drafting Legislative Acts". https://likumi.lv/ta/id/187822-normativo-aktu-projektu-sagatavosanas-noteikumi. Accessed 1 February 2025.

[52] Judgement of the Latvian Constitutional Court in the case No. 2018-11-01, 6 March 2019, para 18.1 and 18.4. https://www.satv.tiesa.gov.lv/wp-content/uploads/2018/07/2018-11-01_Judgement.pdf. Accessed 1 February 2025.

the field of data protection in between the time of coming into force of General Data Protection regulation[53] and the moment it becomes applicable.

Lastly, Joseph H. H. Weiler and Doreen Lustig were right when they argued that "identity can be used or abused as part of political and constitutional reasoning", as "it resonates with a deep-seated yearning for the uniqueness of the human subject," which they "located [..] in the normative territory of human dignity".[54] The Latvian Constitutional Court is *de facto* using national constitutional identity by aligning it with the core values of the European Union as enshrined in Article 2 TEU. Namely, the Court has defined its role as to ensure that the application of European Union law strengthens Latvia as a democratic state based on the rule of law, and human dignity and freedom of every human being.[55] The dialogue between the Constitutional Court and the CJEU proves that.

6.4 Judicial Dialogue as an Instrument of European Integration

In every Member State, there is both a national legal system and a European Union legal order, highlighting the significance of the principle of the supremacy of European Union law.[56] The *Costa v Enel* ruling was the first judgment by the CJEU to establish the doctrine of supremacy,[57] a principle reaffirmed in various subsequent cases, particularly in *Simmenthal*,[58] which explicitly stated that national constitutional provisions are also subject to the supremacy of European Union law. Mentioned principle was reiterated more recently in the *Lin*[59] case emphasizing that "the principle of the supremacy of European Union law establishes the pre-eminence of European Union law over the law of the Member States. That principle therefore requires all Member State bodies to give full effect to the various European Union provisions,

[53] Regulation (EU) 2016/679 of the European Parliament and of the Council of 27 April 2016 on the protection of natural persons with regard to the processing of personal data and on the free movement of such data, and repealing Directive 95/46/EC (General Data Protection Regulation). https://eur-lex.europa.eu/eli/reg/2016/679/oj/eng; this regulation came into force on 25 May 2016, and became applicable on 25 May 2018.

[54] Lustig and Weiler 2018, p. 359.

[55] Judgement of the Latvian Constitutional Court in the case No.2018-18-01, 13 November 2021, para 15.2. https://www.satv.tiesa.gov.lv/wp-content/uploads/2018/08/2018-18-01_Judgement.pdf. Accessed 1 February 2025.

[56] See further: Fabbrini 2015.

[57] Judgment of the Court of Justice of the European Union of 15 July 1964 in case C-6/64 Costa v E.N.E.L., ECLI:EU:C:1964:66.

[58] Judgment of the Court of Justice of the European Union of 9 March 1978 in case C-106/77 Amministrazione delle finanze dello Stato v Simmenthal, ECLI:EU:C:1978:49.

[59] Judgment of the Court of Justice of the European Union of 24 July 2023 in case C-107/23 PPU Lin, ECLI:EU:C:2023:606.

and the law of the Member States may not undermine the effect accorded to those various provisions in the territory of those States".[60]

To date, the mentioned principle has not been codified in the European Union Treaties.[61] An attempt to explicitly include it was made in the Treaty establishing a Constitution for Europe[62]—signed in 2004 but never ratified—,[63] which stated in Article I-6 that "[t]he Constitution and law adopted by the institutions of the [European Union] in exercising competences conferred on it shall have supremacy over the law of the Member States."[64] However, the Treaty of Lisbon did not include the principle of supremacy. Instead, a non-binding Declaration No 17 regarding supremacy of European Union law was appended to the Lisbon Treaty.[65] This declaration references an opinion from the Council's Legal Service dated 22 June 2007, highlighting that the supremacy of European Union law "is a cornerstone principle of [European Union] law".[66] Moreover, the crucial significance of the principle of supremacy of European Union law was underscored in the European Parliament resolution of 21 November 2023 (2022/2143(INI)).[67]

In the national legal system the Constitutional Court of Latvia has emphasized, firstly, that Latvia must fulfil all obligations arising from European Union membership upon its accession to the European Union. Secondly, with the ratification of the Treaty on Latvia's Accession to the European Union, Latvia has recognized the openness of its legal system to European Union law. Therefore, in light of the supremacy of European Union law as stated in the second part of Article 68 of the *Satversme*, Latvia must consider European Union law as well as the interpretations provided by the case law of the CJEU when adopting and applying national legal provisions.[68] Thus, European Union legal acts and CJEU case law must be taken into account in the application of national law, ensuring that national legislation is interpreted in a

---

[60] *Ibid.*, para 128.

[61] Craig and De Búrca 2020, p. 314; Ziemele and Čeiča 2024, pp. 212–213.

[62] Treaty establishing a Constitution for Europe, OJ C 310, 16.12.2004, p. 1474.

[63] Draft treaty establishing a constitution for Europe (not ratified). https://www.europarl.europa.eu/about-parliament/en/in-the-past/the-parliament-and-the-treaties/draft-treaty-establishing-a-constitution-for-europe. Accessed 1 February 2025.

[64] Treaty establishing a Constitution for Europe, OJ C 310, 16.12.2004, pp. 1–474.

[65] Consolidated version of the Treaty on the Functioning of the European Union - DECLARATIONS annexed to the Final Act of the Intergovernmental Conference which adopted the Treaty of Lisbon, signed on 13 December 2007 - A. DECLARATIONS CONCERNING PROVISIONS OF THE TREATIES - 17. Declaration concerning primacy, OJ C 115, 9.5.2008, p. 344.

[66] *Ibid.*

[67] European Parliament resolution of 21 November 2023 on the implementation of the principle of primacy of EU law (2022/2143(INI)). https://www.europarl.europa.eu/doceo/document/TA-9-2023-0406_EN.html. Accessed 1 February 2025.

[68] Judgment of the Constitutional Court of the Republic of Latvia in case No.2018-18-01, 13 November 2021, para 15.2. https://www.satv.tiesa.gov.lv/wp-content/uploads/2018/08/2018-18-01_Judgement.pdf. Accessed 1 February 2025.

manner consistent with Latvia's obligations to the European Union.[69] To be precise, "provisions of Latvian law are to be interpreted in a way that removes conflicts with Latvia's obligations towards the [European Union], unless this touches upon the fundamental principles included in the *Satversme*".[70] These fundamental principles are defined by the Constitutional Court in case No. 2008-35-01[71] and developed as the concept of constitutional identity.[72]

Mentioned is an important aspect as national constitutional courts "are empowered to safeguard the inviolability of the constitutional principles essential for democracy and the rule of law within individual Member States."[73] At the same time, it should be recognized that the primary responsibility of the CJEU is to ensure consistency and uniformity in the interpretation of European Union law, thereby maintaining its coherence, full effect, and autonomy.[74] For the CJEU to fulfil its duties effectively, national courts should not possess the power to question the necessity or, in certain instances, the obligation to refer preliminary questions to the CJEU, as stated in Article 267 of the Treaty on the Functioning of the European Union (TFEU).[75]

Therefore, judicial dialogue plays a crucial role in fostering harmony and coherence between the two legal systems[76] as Article 19 TEU, which gives concrete expression to the value of the rule of law stated in Article 2 TEU, entrusts the responsibility for ensuring judicial review in the European Union legal order not only to the CJEU but also to national courts. Consequently, national courts, in collaboration with the CJEU, fulfil a duty entrusted to them jointly of ensuring that in the interpretation and application of the Treaties is observed.[77]

In Latvia, for instance, the Supreme Court frequently seeks preliminary rulings from the CJEU. Additionally, the Latvian Supreme Court actively incorporates the principle of the supremacy of European Union law into its case law. By doing so, the court reinforces the notion that European Union law holds supremacy over conflicting national legislation, thereby promoting legal uniformity and stability across member states. This commitment to adhering to European Union jurisprudence is essential

[69] Judgment of the Constitutional Court of the Republic of Latvia in case No.2007-11-03, 17 January 2008, para 24.2 and 25.4. https://www.satv.tiesa.gov.lv/web/viewer.html?file=/wp-content/uploads/2007/05/2007-11-03_Spriedums_ENG.pdf. Accessed 1 February 2025.

[70] *Ibid.*, para 25.4.

[71] Judgement of the Constitutional Court of the Republic of Latvia in case No.2008-35-01, 7 April 2009, para 17. https://www.satv.tiesa.gov.lv/web/viewer.html?file=/wp-content/uploads/2008/09/2008-35_01_ENG.pdf. Accessed 1 February 2025.

[72] Judgement of the Constitutional Court of the Republic of Latvia in case No.2020-39-02, 4 June 2021, para 14.1. and 14.2. https://www.satv.tiesa.gov.lv/wp-content/uploads/2020/08/2020-39-02_Judgement.pdf. Accessed 1 February 2025.

[73] See further: Habermas 2012.

[74] Opinion 1/17 of the Court of Justice of the European Union of 30.04.2019, ECLI:EU:C:2019:341, para 111.

[75] Ziemele 2019.

[76] Osipova 2022.

[77] Judgment of the Court of Justice of the European Union of 27 February 2018 in case C-64/16 Associação Sindical dos Juízes Portugueses, ECLI:EU:C:2018:117, para 32–33.

for safeguarding the rule of law and the effectiveness of the European Union law.[78] Moreover, the Constitutional Court is very active in utilizing the preliminary rulings mechanism and engaging in dialogue with the CJEU. It has not shied away from discussing national identity with the CJEU. In doing so, the Constitutional Court has highlighted the importance of the Latvian language in its collaboration with the CJEU.[79]

The Constitutional Court in Case No. 2020-33-01[80] assessed whether legal provisions restricting the right of private higher education institutions to implement study programs in foreign languages were compatible with Article 1 and the first three sentences of Article 105 of the *Satversme*. Considering the issue of a particular case, where the dispute in the main proceedings was brought by 20 members of the *Saeima* who questioned the validity of Article 5(1) and Article 56(3) of the Law on higher education institutions and point 49 of the transitional provisions of that law, the Constitutional Court asked preliminary questions to the CJEU to provide a preliminary ruling under Article 267 of the TFEU.

Answering to preliminary questions of the Constitutional Court, the CJEU, in the case of "Boriss Cilevičs and Others",[81] confirmed the compatibility of Latvian legislation which, in principle, obliges higher education institutions to provide teaching solely in the official language of that Member State, in so far as such legislation is justified on grounds related to the protection of its national identity.[82] The CJEU analysed the compatibility of the national legislation with Article 49 of the TFEU considering that higher education institutions fall within the scope of the freedom of establishment and that this article also covers the freedom to conduct a business protected in Article 16 of the Charter of Fundamental Rights (Charter). Because the restriction brought about by national legislation from the point of view of Article 49 TFEU also covers possible limitations of the exercise of the rights and freedoms laid down in Articles 15 to 17 of the Charter, the CJEU held that a separate examination of the freedom to conduct a business enshrined in Article 16 of the Charter is not necessary.[83]

The CJEU pointed out that all measures which prohibit, impede or render less attractive the exercise of the freedom guaranteed by Article 49 TFEU must be

---

[78] See, for example, judgement of 21 March 2024 of the Supreme Court in case No. C30532919, SKC-3/2024, ECLI:LV:AT:2024:0321.C30532919.10.S, and judgement of 5 November 2019 of the Supreme Court in case No. A420150416, SKA-226/2019 ECLI:LV:AT:2019:1105.A420150416.2.S.

[79] Judgement of 7 September 2022 of the Court of Justice of the European Union in case C-391/20, Boriss Cilevičs and Others, ECLI:EU:C:2022:638.

[80] Judgement of the Constitutional Court of the Republic of Latvia in case No. 2020-33-01, 9 February 2023. https://www.satv.tiesa.gov.lv/wp-content/uploads/2020/06/2020-33-01_Judgement.pdf. Accessed 1 February 2025.

[81] Judgement of 7 September 2022 of the Court of Justice of the European Union in case C-391/20, Boriss Cilevičs and Others, ECLI:EU:C:2022:638.

[82] *Ibid.*, para 87.

[83] *Ibid.*, para 56.

regarded as restrictions on the freedom of establishment.[84] In the present case, even if nationals of other Member States may establish themselves in Latvia and provide higher education courses, such a possibility is, in principle, conditioned by the obligation to provide those courses solely in the official language of that Member State. Moreover, the CJEU noted that an obligation of that kind is such as to render less attractive the establishment of those nationals in the Member State imposing that obligation, which therefore constitutes a restriction on the freedom guaranteed by Article 49 TFEU.[85] However, regarding the justification of the restriction to the freedom guaranteed in Article 49 TFEU, the CJEU stated that the objective of promoting and encouraging the use of one of the official languages of a Member State must be regarded as being a legitimate objective which, in principle, justifies a restriction on the obligations imposed by the freedom of establishment enshrined in Article 49 TFEU.[86] Additionally, the CJEU noted that it is true that Member States enjoy broad discretion in their choice of the measures capable of achieving the objectives of their policy of protecting the official language, since such a policy constitutes a manifestation of national identity for the purposes of Article 4(2) TEU. However, the fact remains that that discretion cannot justify a serious undermining of the rights which individuals derive from the provisions of the European Union treaties enshrining their fundamental freedoms.[87]

Following the CJEU's judgment, the Constitutional Court stated that it follows from the obligations assumed by Latvia with its membership in the European Union that the rights included in Article 105 of the *Satversme* must be specified in conjunction with the freedom to conduct a business, included in Article 16 of the Charter, and the freedom of establishment, included in Article 49 of the TFEU.[88] Moreover, the Constitutional Court pointed out that the Latvian language as the state language gives the Latvian state a certain—and specifically Latvian—national-cultural identity.[89] Taking into account the fact that the Latvian language is an integral part of the constitutional identity and the common language of communication and democratic participation of the society, as well as the fact that, in the conditions of globalisation, Latvia is the only place in the world where the existence and development of the Latvian language and, consequently, of the Latvian nation can be guaranteed, narrowing of the use of the Latvian language as the state language in the territory of the state is considered as a threat to the democratic state order. Thus, national law provides for strengthening of the official language protects the democratic state order.[90] Therefore, the Constitutional Court stated that provisions obliging higher

---

[84] *Ibid.*, paras 60–61.

[85] *Ibid.*, paras 62–63.

[86] *Ibid.*, para 70.

[87] *Ibid.*, para 83.

[88] Judgement of the Constitutional Court of the Republic of Latvia in case No. 2020-33-01, 9 February 2023, para 27.2. https://www.satv.tiesa.gov.lv/wp-content/uploads/2020/06/2020-33-01_Judgement.pdf. Accessed 1 February 2025.

[89] *Ibid.*, para 30.

[90] *Ibid.*

education institutions to use the national language in principle are an expression of the national identity of the Member States, which promote the use of the national language and ensure that this language is also used at the university level.

It should be acknowledged that the status of the Latvian language as the state language—a crucial and sensitive issue for Latvia and its society—has been strengthened through an effective dialogue between the Constitutional Court and the CJEU. From the perspective of European Union law, the CJEU recognizes the Latvian language as an essential element of Latvia's national constitutional identity, which must be protected. At the same time, the Constitutional Court has ensured the protection of the Latvian language in harmony with European Union law.

6.5 Conclusion

Participation in the European integration and membership in the European Union is element of the constitutional identity of Latvia. The so-called principle of European integration is a fundamental constitutional principle of Latvian legal system which ensures friendly openness of the Latvian legal system to European Union law and recognition of the supremacy of European Union law.

The European dimension of the *Satversme* ensures that the *Satversme* should be interpreted in harmony with European Union law. Still the European Union is based on values defined in Article 2 TEU, there should not be disharmony between membership in the European Union and other constitutional values, principles and norms, included in the constitutional identity of Latvia.

The judicial dialogue between supreme national courts, especially the Constitutional Court and the CJEU, is a correct and effective legal method which allows us to solve potential disagreements on matters of constitutional identity in harmonic and respectful way without judicial conflicts and constitutional crisis.

EU member states must adhere to the principle of supremacy of European Union law, including in matters of national identity, by utilizing the mechanism of preliminary rulings. This approach allows member states the flexibility to act independently while simultaneously ensuring compliance with EU law.

The accession of Latvia to the European Union and the euro-optimism of the Constitutional Court played a crucial role in empowering and authorizing other national courts to apply the law in accordance with Western legal tradition by performing judicial review and, thus, strengthening the rule of law in Latvia in general.

References

Albi A (2005) EU Enlargement and the Constitutions of Central and Eastern Europe. Cambridge University Press, Cambridge

Balodis R (2004) The Constitution of Latvia. Institut für Rechtspolitik an der Universität Trier, Trier
Craig P, De Búrca G (2020) EU Law: Text, Cases, and Materials, 7th edn. Oxford University Press, Oxford
Discussion (2000) Diskusija "Latvijas Republikas Satversme un Eiropas Savienība" [Discussion "The Satversme of the Republic of Latvia and the European Union"]. Likums un Tiesības 2(6):162–168
Endziņš A (2004) Eiropas Konstitūcijas līgums un Latvijas Republikas Satversme [The Treaty establishing Constitution for Europe and the *Satversme* of the Republic of Latvia]. Jurista Vārds 39:2–5
Fabbrini F (2015) After the OMT Case: The Supremacy of EU Law as the Guarantee of the Equality of the Member States. German Law Journal 16(4):1003–1023
Habermas J (2012) The Crisis of the European Union in the Light of a Constitutionalization of International Law. European Journal of International Law 23(2):335–348
Harbaceviča S (2016) Eiropas Savienības likumdošanas pārņemšana Latvijas likumdošanā un tiesībās [Reception of the European Union legislation in the Latvian legislation and legal system]. In: Kozlova K (ed) Atgriešanās Eiropā Latvijas prezidentu, premjerministru, ministru un diplomātu esejās. No starptautiskās atzīšanas līdz pirmajai prezidentūrai Eiropas Savienībā. 1990–2015 [The Re-emergence of the Latvian State in Europe from International Recognition to the first EU Presidency: 1990–2015. Essays by Latvian statesmen and diplomats]. Zinātne, Riga, pp 199–215
Kalniete S (2016) Kā trāpīt desmitniekā (How to hit the top ten). In: Kozlova K (ed) Atgriešanās Eiropā Latvijas prezidentu, premjerministru, ministru un diplomātu esejās. No starptautiskās atzīšanas līdz pirmajai prezidentūrai Eiropas Savienībā. 1990–2015 [The Re-emergence of the Latvian State in Europe from International Recognition to the first EU Presidency: 1990–2015. Essays by Latvian statesmen and diplomats]. Zinātne, Riga, pp 163–194
Kershaw I (2018) Roller-Coaster: Europe, 1950–2017. Penguin, London
Krūma K, Statkus S (2019) The Constitution of Latvia – A Bridge Between Traditions and Modernity. In: Albi A, Bardutzky S (eds) National Constitutions in European and Global Governance: Democracy, Rights, the Rule of Law. T. M. C. Asser Press, The Hague, pp 951–995
Kusiņš G (2024) Konstitucionālo tiesību pamati [Foundations of Constitutional Law]. In: Ziemele I, Osipova S (eds) Publiskās tiesības. Ievads [Public Law. Introduction]. Tiesu Namu Aģentūra, Riga, pp 250–282
Kušners E, Balode-Buraka E (2020) Behind the scenes: EU Accession Challenges. Baltic Yearbook of International Law, vol.19, 2020, pp.104–128
Kühn Z (2004) Worlds Apart: Western and Central European Judicial Culture at the Onset of the European Enlargement. The American Journal of Comparative Law 52(3):531–567
Kühn Z (2011) The Judiciary in Central and Eastern Europe. Mechanical Jurisprudence in Transformation? Martinus Nijhoff Publishers, Leiden/Boston
Lenaerts K, Gutiérrez-Fons J (2022) Eiropas Savienības Tiesas interpretācijas metodes [Methods of Interpretation of the Court of Justice of the European Union]. Tiesu namu aģentūra, Riga
Levits E (1999) Latvijas tiesiskā iekārta transformācijas procesā [The Latvian Legal System Under Transformation]. Likums un Tiesības 1:6–12
Levits E (2005) European Community Law within the Hierarchy of Legal Norms of Latvia. In: Jundzis T (ed) First Year in the European Union: Current Legal Issues. Baltic Center for Strategic Studies at the Latvian Academy of Science, Riga, pp 9–31
Levits E (2019a) Latvijas tiesību attīstība kopš 1990.gada – no padomju sistēmas uz modernu Eiropas Savienības dalībvalsts tiesību sistēmu [Development of Latvian Law from 1990 – from Soviet system to modern legal system of member state of the European Union]. In: Levits E (author) Valstsgriba. Idejas un domas Latvijai. 1985–2018 [The Will to have a State. Ideas and thoughts for Latvia, 1985–2018]. Latvijas Vēstnesis, pp 820–828

Levits E (2019b) Satversme un Eiropas Savienība [The *Satversme* and the European Union]. In: Levits E (author) Valstsgriba. Idejas un domas Latvijai. 1985–2018 [The Will to have a State. Ideas and thoughts for Latvia, 1985–2018]. Latvijas Vēstnesis, pp 421–427
Levits E (2020) Foreword. In: Auers D (ed) Latvia. Human Development Report 2019/2020. Europeanization of Latvia. Advanced Social and Political Research Institute of the University of Latvia, Riga, pp 3–4
Lustig D, Weiler JHH (2018) Judicial review in the contemporary world – Retrospective and prospective. International Journal of Constitutional Law 16(2):315–372
Osipova S (2020a) Tautas gars, pamatnorma un konstitucionālā identitāte [*Volksgeist*, *Grundnorm* and Constitutional Identity]. In: Osipova S (author) Nācija, valoda, tiesiska valsts: ceļā uz rītdienu [Nation, Language and Rule of Law: On the Way to Tomorrow]. Tiesu Namu Aģentūra, Riga, pp 35–42
Osipova S (2020b) Latvijas Republikas konstitucionālā identitāte Satversmes tiesas spriedumos [The Constitutional Identity of the Republic of Latvia in the judgments of the Constitutional Court]. In: Osipova S (author) Nācija, valoda, tiesiska valsts: ceļā uz rītdienu [Nation, Language and Rule of Law: On the Way to Tomorrow]. Tiesu Namu Aģentūra, Riga, pp 43–52
Osipova S (2022) Introductory speech by Ms Sanita Osipova, President of the Constitutional Court of the Republic of Latvia. In: EUnited in diversity: between common constitutional traditions and national identities. International conference, Riga, Latvia, 2–3 September 2021. Court of Justice of the European Union, Luxembourg, pp 19–20
Rezevska D (2024) General Principles of Law. Natural Rights, Legal Methods, and System Principles. Brill/Nijhoff, Leiden/Boston
Rollis I (2020) A short history of Europeanization concept. In: Auers D (ed) Latvia. Human Development Report 2019/2020. Europeanization of Latvia. Advanced Social and Political Research Institute of the University of Latvia, Riga, pp 11–13
Rostoks T (2020) Europeanization of Latvia's Foreign Policy. In: Auers D (ed) Latvia. Human Development Report 2019/2020. Europeanization of Latvia. Advanced Social and Political Research Institute of the University of Latvia, Riga, pp 35–43
Schuman R (1950) Schuman Declaration May 1950. https://european-union.europa.eu/principles-countries-history/history-eu/1945-59/schuman-declaration-may-1950_en. Accessed 1 February 2025
Snyder T (2021) Memory, Sovereignty and State. Some Reflections on 100 Years of Polish Independence. In: Kerski B, Koltan J (eds) Solidarity, Democracy, Europe. European Solidarity Centre, Gdańsk, pp 177–183
Stiprais E (2021) European integration. In: Drēģeris M (ed) A Century of Latvian Diplomacy. The First Hundred Years of Latvia's Diplomacy and Its Foreign Service (1919–2019) as Reflected in Essays by Diplomats. Zvaigzne ABC, Riga, pp 195–217
Taurēns J, Feldmanis I (2016) Latvijas ārpolitika un diplomātija 20.gadsimtā [Latvia's Foreign Policy and Diplomacy in the XXth century]. Jumava, Riga
Van Hoecke M, Warrington M (1998) Legal Cultures, Legal Paradigms and Legal Doctrine: Towards a New Model for Comparative Law. The International and Comparative Law Quarterly 47(3):495–536
Vīķe-Freiberga V (2016) Latvijas valsts garais ceļš, iekļaujoties Eiropas un transatlantiskajā apritē [The long road of the State of Latvia, joining the European and Transatlantic communities]. In: Kozlova K (ed) Atgriešanās Eiropā Latvijas prezidentu, premjerministru, ministru un diplomātu esejās. No starptautiskās atzīšanas līdz pirmajai prezidentūrai Eiropas Savienībā. 1990–2015 [The Re-emergence of the Latvian State in Europe from International Recognition to the first EU Presidency: 1990–2015. Essays by Latvian statesmen and diplomats]. Zinātne, Riga, pp 145–160
Vīķe-Freiberga V (2018) Latvia and the Latvians as Europeans in the Age of Globalisation. In: Stradiņš J (ed) Latvia and Latvians. Collection of scholarly articles in 2 volumes, Volume I. Latvian Academy of Science, Riga, pp 29–53

Working group (2001) Kādēļ Latvijas konstitūcijā nepieciešami labojumi. Darba grupas Satversmes grozījumu izstrādei piedāvātā projekta teorētiskais pamatojums [Why it is necessary to make amendments to the Constitution of Latvia. Theoretical background for the project of the constitutional amendments proposed by the Working Group for elaboration amendments to the *Satversme*]. Jurista Vārds 207, pp 1–3

Ziemele I (2005) Starptautiskās tiesības un cilvēktiesības Latvijā: abstrakcija vai realitāte [International Law and Human Rights in Latvia: abstraction or reality]. Tiesu Namu Aģentūra, Riga

Ziemele I (2019) Can Constitutional Courts delimit European Identity? Speech by the President of the Constitutional Court Ineta Ziemele at the conference "Constitutional EUdentity 2019 unity in diversity – common and particular values", 08.03.2019. https://www.satv.tiesa.gov.lv/en/runas-un-raksti/can-constitutional-courts-delimit-european-identity/. Accessed 1 February 2025

Ziemele I (2021) Latvija Eiropas Savienībā [Latvia in the European Union]. In: Ziemele I (ed) Cilvēktiesības Latvijā un pasaulē [Human Rights in Latvia and the World]. Tiesu Namu Aģentūra, Riga, pp 329–333

Ziemele I, Čeiča I (2024) Eiropas Savienības tiesību pamati [Foundations of European Union Law]. In: Ziemele I, Osipova S (eds) Publiskās tiesības. Ievads [Public Law. Introduction]. Tiesu Namu Aģentūra, Riga, pp 177–233

Ziller J (2022) The primacy of European Union law. https://www.europarl.europa.eu/RegData/etudes/STUD/2022/732474/IPOL_STU(2022)732474_EN.pdf. Accessed 1 February 2025

Jānis Pleps is an Associate Professor at the Faculty of Law, University of Latvia, and a Judge at the Supreme Court of Latvia.

Kalvis Engīzers is a lawyer, a former Lecturer at the Faculty of Law, University of Latvia, and a former Adviser to the Minister of Justice of Latvia.

Viktorija Soņeca is a Lecturer at the Riga Graduate School of Law, and an Adviser to the Supreme Court of Latvia.

Part III
European Integration: A Closer Look into Several Areas

Chapter 7
Impact of the Interpretation of the Principle of Effectiveness in the Case Law of the Court of Justice of the European Union on National Case Law

Danguolė Bublienė

Contents

Abstract Although the CJEU's interpretation of the content and meaning of the EU's principle of effectiveness still sparks debates in legal doctrine, it is already clear that the case law on this principle is too far gone to turn it back. This chapter does not intend to deny or criticize the CJEU's case law regarding this principle; instead, it assesses its impact on the practice of national courts. Due to the principle of procedural autonomy, EU law does not harmonize the rules of implementation in the consumer protection area. However, as demonstrated in this chapter, the content of the principle of effectiveness, as interpreted in the CJEU's case law, provides consumers with additional remedies, and influences both procedural and substantive legal norms. Assessment of the effectiveness of national rules is carried out not *in abstracto*, but *in concreto*, case by case, which makes it fragmented and haphazard. This undoubtedly impedes national courts' ability to apply EU law norms effectively and ensure that the execution of consumer rights is timely and effective.

Keywords EU law · Principle of effectiveness · CJEU case law · Interpretation of the principle of effectiveness · Consumer procedural rights · Consumer redress · National court practice

---

D. Bublienė (✉)
Faculty of Law, Vilnius University, Vilnius, Lithuania
e-mail: danguole.bubliene@tf.vu.lt

I. Isokaitė-Valužė and H. Šinkūnas (eds.), *The European Union 2004-2024*,
https://doi.org/10.1007/978-94-6265-718-2_7

7.1 Introduction

Nowadays, nobody questions the importance of the Court of Justice of the European Union (hereinafter—also the CJEU) in developing European Union (hereinafter—also EU) law and ensuring the rights of individuals it itself prescribes. Effectiveness is a fundamental principle, and important EU law application rules are created through its interpretation. It is challenging to label these rules a 'system', as they are rather a total sum of separate *rules*. Clearly, effectiveness gained an unrestricted potential in EU law, and turned into a highly developed, complex, and multifaceted use tool. Being a very dynamic principle, in just a few decades it transcended beyond its classic meaning of "practical effect"[1] and is no longer understood solely as a tool for effective judicial remedy or defence of individual rights, and (or) a constraint on national procedural autonomy. It is linked with other fundamental principles: EU law supremacy, direct effect, indirect effect or a duty of consistent interpretation, and Member State's responsibility for breaching EU law.

Legal doctrine is full of various, and sometimes even contradictory, metaphors to describe this principle, which is a testament to its significance and extraordinariness of its application: "a key pillar of a Union based on the rule of law",[2] "a pivotal cornerstone for the protection of individual rights",[3] "a meta-rule",[4] "a meta-norm" ("constitutional core of the EU legal order"),[5] "the very soul of legal rules",[6] an "anchor for creative solutions in the EU case law",[7] "the driver of constitutional evolution of Union system",[8] "a silent revolution" ("which constrains the fundamental national procedural autonomy in the application and enforcement of EU law originally agreed in the EU treaties"),[9] an "incantation [whose aim is to] trigger national compliance",[10] "an unruly horse",[11] a "fiction ungrounded in the EU Treaties",[12] a principle "under strain",[13] and the contemporary case law of the CJEU is often described as "a new stage of complexity and sophistication of the use of the principle".[14]

In legal doctrine, there are mixed debates about the legal nature, content, scope, limits, contextual results, and importance of this principle. Without engaging in a

---

[1] Mendez-Pinedo 2021, p. 12.

[2] Bonelli 2019, p. 35.

[3] Mendez-Pinedo 2021, p. 5.

[4] Mayr 2012, pp. 8–21.

[5] Roeben 2020, p. 31.

[6] Pescatore 1983, pp. 155–157.

[7] Gentile 2023, p. 128.

[8] Liakopoulos 2019, p. 22.

[9] Mendez-Pinedo 2021, pp. 5, 14.

[10] *Ibid.*, p. 24.

[11] Arnull 2011.

[12] Rasmussen, Ross and Sadl's criticism, see Mendez-Pinedo 2021, p. 27.

[13] Eliantonio 2019, pp. 255–265.

[14] Mendez-Pinedo 2021, p. 16.

deep analysis of both sceptical and optimistic perspectives, it is clear today that, as mentioned above, the interpretation of these principles in the case law of the CJEU has already produced a certain result (one might even say a powerful one) and turned into a reality to be reckoned with. At least for some authors, there is no way back.[15] The reality is that the CJEU uses and interprets this principle in various ways and contexts, leading to results that also vary in practice.

On the one hand, it is great that the CJEU offers a vast arsenal of legal arguments ("weapons") to be used by individuals who seek to defend their rights in national and European courts. On the other hand, it is a challenge for every practicing lawyer (including judges) not only to navigate the subtleties of this principle, but also to ensure its coherent application in their cases: first and foremost, to recognize it, to draw attention to it, to narrow down the problem and address it within the very important boundaries drawn by other common principles of EU law—EU law supremacy, national procedural autonomy, legal certainty and security, *res iudicata*, and others.

In this chapter, the principle of effectiveness is analysed only as a general principle and only insofar as it relates to the right to effective judicial remedy and its influence on the enforcement of consumer rights. Consumer law is the area where EU law undoubtedly creates rights for consumers. And not just any rights—rights of a mandatory nature. However, EU law only has limited power in their enforcement and the mandatory nature of such rights does not override the principle of EU Member States' procedural autonomy. EU consumer law directives connect the sanctions for breach of consumer rights with the sacred formula of "effective, proportionate, dissuasive", and leave the details to be determined by national law. In this regard, the Modernisation (or so-called 'Omnibus') directive[16] did not introduce any significant changes either. However, step by step, case by case, it appears that the development of the principle of effectiveness is undermining a standard of autonomy in Consumer Law area and even ushers in some confusion.

What content does the CJEU prescribe today to this principle in its case law while interpreting Consumer Law norms? To what extent does the interpretation of this principle influence rules regarding individual rights protection? Can this interpretation be effectively enforced solely through courts, without making necessary adjustments to the regulatory framework, especially considering the complexities of applying codified legal acts? These aspects will be further analysed in this chapter.

[15] *Ibid.*, p. 11.

[16] Directive (EU) 2019/2161 of the European Parliament and of the Council of 27 November 2019 amending Council Directive 93/13/EEC and Directives 98/6/EC, 2005/29/EC and 2011/83/EU of the European Parliament and of the Council as regards the better enforcement and modernisation of Union consumer protection rules.

7.2 The Content of the Principle of Effectiveness in the CJEU's Case Law While Interpreting EU Consumer Law

The beginning of interpreting the principle of effectiveness dates back to 1976 (*REWE* case[17]), and it was later developed in the *Johnston* case[18] and the jurisprudence that followed. Effectiveness means that national rules cannot preclude individuals (including consumers) from using the rights conferred to them by EU law (or make it excessively difficult). Today, the legal basis of this principle is considered to be a tandem of Art. 47 of the Charter of Fundamental Rights of the European Union, which guarantees the right to an effective remedy and to a fair trial, and Art. 19 of the Treaty on European Union, which outlines the competencies of the CJEU and national courts in enforcing EU law. Using Art. 47 of the Charter pulls the principle of effectiveness closer to the principle of effective judicial remedy. On the other hand, it appears that the principle of effectiveness has not gained greater certainty because of such tandem.

The principle of effectiveness was first developed in administrative law and its procedure. Admittedly, Consumer Law (and through it—private law) also did not avoid its influence, and the number of cases where it affects private law is growing. Based on this principle, national courts are already referring questions to the CJEU for preliminary rulings to clarify the content of EU law.

As N. Reich puts it, the principle of effectiveness not only obliges to create remedies *for* protection, but also to eliminate restrictions *to* protection.[19] This limited effect of the principle of effectiveness is based on the procedural autonomy that the EU Member States enjoy. For example, while interpreting the Unfair Terms Directive,[20] the CJEU on several occasions has stressed that, in principle, EU law does not harmonize the procedures applicable to examining whether a contractual term is unfair and that those procedures accordingly fall within the domestic legal system of the Member States, by the principle of procedural autonomy of those States; nevertheless, those procedures must be no less favourable than those governing similar domestic actions (principle of equivalence) and not make it impossible in practice or excessively difficult to exercise the rights conferred by EU law (principle of effectiveness).[21] However, it is evident from the case law of the CJEU that this limited effect

[17] CJEU, Case C-33/76, *Rewe-Zentralfinanz eG and Rewe-Zentral AG v Landwirtschaftskammer für das Saarland*, Judgement, 16 December 1976, ECLI:EU:C:1976:188.

[18] CJEU, Case C-222/84, *Marguerite Johnston v Chief Constable of the Royal Ulster Constabulary*, Judgement, 15 May 1986, ECLI:EU:C:1986:206.

[19] Reich 2014, p. 92.

[20] Council Directive 93/13/EEC of 5 April 1993 on unfair terms in consumer contracts.

[21] E.g., CJEU, Case C-600/19, *MA v Ibercaja Banco, SA*, Judgement, 17 May 2022, ECLI:EU:C:2022:394, para 39 and the case law cited; CJEU, Case C-407/18, *Addiko Bank*, Judgement, 26 June 2019, ECLI:EU:C:2019:537, para 45 and 46 and the case law cited; CJEU, Case C-156/21, *Hungary v European Parliament and the Council of the European Union*, Judgement, 16 February 2022, ECLI:EU:C:2022:97, para 129.

of application does not prevent the CJEU from delivering judgements impacting not only procedural but also substantive legal norms. Although the CJEU does not rule on the application of supplementary measures, and the wording used in requests for preliminary rulings (as well as the answers)—specifically, "the directive precludes a provision of national law which…"—does not provide for new remedies, that does not eliminate (or protect from) the effect of this principle to national substantive or procedural law in the area of consumer protection.

While interpreting the principle of effectiveness in the area of Consumer Law, the CJEU has developed quite a few new remedies that were not even hinted at in the letter of the directives. An absolute champion in this regard is the Unfair Contract Terms Directive,[22] whose application scope is gradually (and sometimes even surprisingly) extended by the CJEU. Although the CJEU acknowledged that the principle of effectiveness should not be expanded to the point where the national court would fully compensate for total inertia on the part of the consumer[23] (provided that the consumer can exercise effective remedies under reasonable circumstances[24]) it did issue a number of decisions where new remedies reinforced implementation of consumer rights. Many examples can be mentioned.

By intervening in the dispositive principle that prevails in private law (i.e. by restricting it), the CJEU empowered (and thereby obliged) national courts to qualify the contract as a consumer contract *ex officio*,[25] assess the fairness of its terms, evaluate the information provided to the consumer under the consumer credit rules, as well as ensure compliance with the obligation to assess the consumer's credit-worthiness,[26] and change consumer's chosen remedy if it is no longer possible to apply for it in separate proceedings.[27] Such obligations apply regardless of whether the consumer was represented by a lawyer, whether the consumer participated in proceedings, whether the case is still at the first instance or has already progressed beyond that, or whether the proceedings were summary or default.[28]

---

[22] Council Directive 93/13/EEC of 5 April 1993 on unfair terms in consumer contracts.

[23] CJEU, Case C-40/08, *Asturcom Telecomunicaciones SL v Cristina Rodríguez Nogueira*, Judgement, 6 October 2009, ECLI:EU:C:2009:615, para 47; CJEU, Case C-137/08, *VB Pénzügyi Lízing Zrt. v Ferenc Schneider*, Judgement, 9 November 2010, ECLI:EU:C:2010:659, para 56; CJEU, Case C-415/11, *Mohamed Aziz v Caixa d'Estalvis de Catalunya, Tarragona i Manresa (Catalunyacaixa)*, Judgement, 14 March 2013, ECLI:EU:C:2013:164, para 47; CJEU, Case C-472/11, *Banif Plus Bank Zrt v Csaba Csipai and Viktória Csipai*, Judgement, 21 February 2013, ECLI:EU:C:2013:88, para 24.

[24] CJEU, Case C-40/08, *Asturcom Telecomunicaciones SL v Cristina Rodríguez Nogueira*, Judgement, 6 October 2009, ECLI:EU:C:2009:615, paras 41–46.

[25] CJEU, Case C-497/13, *Froukje Faber v Autobedrijf Hazet Ochten BV*, Judgement, 4 June 2015, ECLI:EU:C:2015:357.

[26] CJEU, Case C-679/18, *OPR-Finance s. r. o. v GK*, Judgement, 5 March 2020, ECLI:EU:C:2020:167.

[27] CJEU, Case C-32/12, *Soledad Duarte Hueros v Autociba SA, Automóviles Citroën España SA*, Judgement, 3 October 2013, ECLI:EU:C:2013:637.

[28] CJEU, Case C-495/19, *Kancelaria Medius SA v RN*, Judgement, 4 June 2020, ECLI:EU:C:2020:431.

As the CJEU concluded, specific characteristics of court proceedings which take place under national law cannot constitute a factor which is liable to affect the legal protection from which consumers must benefit. Therefore, before issuing an order for payment to which a consumer can object, the court has to be able to assess the fairness of contract terms *ex officio*.[29] As time went by, while interpreting the regulation for a European order for payment procedure,[30] the CJEU ruled that the court must be able to request additional information (if necessary) to allow for the *ex officio* examination of potential unfairness of such terms.[31]

Fairly recently, the CJEU went even further in explaining the court's role in assessing the fairness of a term in the proceedings of an order for payment. In one of the cases, the CJEU[32] assessed whether the principle of effectiveness is not infringed where the court overseeing the enforcement of an order for payment cannot assess (either *ex officio* or at the consumer's request) the fairness of consumer credit contract terms due to a time-bar. Notably, in this case such an assessment has already been carried out by another court during the order for payment procedure, but there were grounds to believe that it was incomplete. The CJEU ruled[33] that a court's review of whether terms in a contract concluded between a consumer and a seller or supplier are unfair is consistent with the principle of effectiveness in the light of Directive 93/13 if, first, the consumer has been informed of the existence of that review and of the consequences of his or her inaction as regards the time-barring of the right to assert the possible unfairness of the contractual terms, and, secondly, the decision taken following that review contains a sufficient statement of reasons making it possible to identify the terms which were examined on that occasion and the reasons, even if set out in summary form, for the finding of the court that those terms are not unfair. A judicial decision which meets those requirements may have the effect of preventing a further review of whether the contractual terms are unfair in subsequent proceedings.

Further remedies of substantive rights were developed in instances where consumers purchased faulty items. In the *Weber/Putz*[34] case, the CJEU applied the principle of strict liability to a trader who sold a defective item and held that the consumer is entitled to compensation for costs related to the defective product, e.g., the cost of removing the defective tiles. This ruling prompted a review of the established practice of the right to reimbursement in Germany.

---

[29] CJEU, Case C-618/10, *Banco Espanol de Crédito SA v Joaquín Calderón Camino*, Judgement, 14 June 2012, ECLI:EU:C:2012:349.

[30] Regulation (EC) No 1896/2006 of the European Parliament and of the Council of 12 December 2006 creating a European order for payment procedure.

[31] CJEU, Joined Cases 453/18 and C-494/18, *Bondora AS v Carlos V. C. and XY*, Judgement, 19 December 2019, ECLI:EU:C:2019:1118.

[32] ECJ judgement of 29 February 2024, *Investcapital Ltd*, C-724/22.

[33] CJEU, Case C-724/22, *Investcapital Ltd*, Judgement, 29 February 2024, ECLI:EU:C:2024:182, paras 45 and 48.

[34] CJEU, Joined Cases C-65/09 and C-87/09, *Gebr. Weber GmbH v Jürgen Wittmer* (C-65/09) *and Ingrid Putz v Medianess Electronics GmbH* (C-87/09), *Bundesgerichtshof* (C-65/09) *and Amtsgericht Schorndorf* (C-87/09), Judgement, 16 June 2011, ECLI:EU:C:2011:396.

According to the case law of the CJEU there are numerous reasons why a remedy might be found to be ineffective, including: (i) a length of applicable periods, e.g., two weeks to lodge an objection to an order for payment was deemed too short,[35] whereas four weeks[36] sufficient, and two months (in the case of arbitration clause) reasonable;[37] (ii) paying high or discriminatory court fees and costs;[38] (iii) a set of different demands—a short term to lodge the objection (twenty days) and mandatory assistance of the lawyer;[39] (iv) demanding that objections must be thorough;[40] (v) a limitation period (either its short length or the unreasonable mechanism adopted to start the period running):[41] provided that they are established and known in advance, limitation periods of three to five years are sufficient to prepare and bring an effective action to enforce the restitutory effects of a finding that a contractual term was unfair (they are not, in themselves, incompatible with the principle of effectiveness, as long as it does not make it impossible or excessively difficult to exercise the rights in practice); connecting the start of the period of limitation with the occurrence of any payment made by the borrower may systematically deny the possibility of ever claiming repayments.

Analysis of the CJEU case law also reveals that the effectiveness of remedies can be affected by the rules allocating the costs relating to proceedings. Such an example requires the consumer to bear the costs of legal proceedings if he or she has not taken any steps prior to bringing proceedings against a seller or supplier.[42] In cases where the action of annulment of the contract is upheld fully, but the claim for restitutory damages is only partially upheld, ineffectiveness may be caused if costs relating to legal proceedings are tied to the amount of unduly paid sums which

[35] CJEU, Case C-618/10, *Banco Espanol de Crédito SA v Joaquín Calderón Camino*, Judgement, 14 June 2012, ECLI:EU:C:2012:349, para 54; CJEU, Case C-176/17, *Profi Credit Polska S.A. w Bielsku Białej v Mariusz Wawrzosek*, Judgement, 13 September 2018, ECLI:EU:C:2018:711, paras 65–66.

[36] CJEU, Case C-8/14, *BBVA SA v Pedro Peñalva López and others*, Judgement, 29 October 2015, ECLI:EU:C:2015:731.

[37] CJEU, Case C-40/08, *Asturcom Telecomunicaciones SL v Cristina Rodríguez Nogueira*, Judgement, 6 October 2009, ECLI:EU:C:2009:615.

[38] CJEU, Case C-176/17, *Profi Credit Polska S.A. w Bielsku Białej v Mariusz Wawrzosek*, Judgement, 13 September 2018, ECLI:EU:C:2018:711, paras 67–68. In this case, the debtor had to pay three-quarters of the court fees if he objected to the order for payment.

[39] CJEU, Case C-618/10, *Banco Espanol de Crédito SA v Joaquín Calderón Camino*, Judgement, 14 June 2012, ECLI:EU:C:2012:349, para 52.

[40] CJEU, Case C-176/17, *Profi Credit Polska S.A. w Bielsku Białej v Mariusz Wawrzosek*, Judgement, 13 September 2018, ECLI:EU:C:2018:711, paras 65–66.

[41] CJEU, Joined Cases C-776/19 and C-782/19, *VB and others v BNP Paribas Personal Finance SA, and AV and others v BNP Paribas Personal Finance SA, Procureur de la République*, Judgement, 10 June 2021, ECLI:EU:C:2021:470.

[42] CJEU, Case C-35/22, *CAJASUR Banco*, Judgement, 13 July 2023, ECLI:EU:C:2023:569; CJEU Case C- 215/21, *Servicios prescriptor y medios de pagos E.F.C. S.A.U*, Judgement, 22 September 2022, ECLI:EU:C:2022:773.

are refunded following a finding that a contractual term is void due to unfairness.[43] Compatibility with the principle of effectiveness has also been examined in a situation where the costs relating to proceedings incurred by the consumer were subject to a maximum limit.[44] The CJEU ruled that while Member States are allowed to set such limits, they must not deter consumers from starting legal proceedings. The limits have to be established in a way that ensures the consumer receives a reasonable and proportionate reimbursement, relative to the costs he or she would incur objectively if he or she were to initiate legal proceedings.

Legislation that prevents or restricts the granting of interim measures (such as suspending enforcement proceedings of obligations) where the consumer brings an action to declare a contract invalid due to an unfair contractual term has also been found incompatible with the principle of effectiveness.[45] The necessity to apply such measures arises from the fact that the consumer might pay more than the loan amount, and his or her financial situation might deteriorate due to the ongoing payments, leaving him or her without sufficient funds to initiate proceedings to obtain reimbursement of the sums to which he or she is entitled. Furthermore, the consumer's inability to pay the monthly instalments could lead the bank to initiate enforcement proceedings based on a loan agreement that may eventually be declared invalid.

According to the CJEU, legal action seeking to assess the fairness of contract terms can be brought even if the terms which it seeks to have prohibited have not been used in specific contracts.[46] In relation to individual and collective actions, the CJEU ruled that national law provisions prohibiting a court from adopting interim measures of its own motion, for as long as there is no final judgement in an ongoing collective action whose outcome may be applied to the individual action, are incompatible with the principle of effectiveness.[47] The same applies to the automatic suspension of an individual action pending a final judgement concerning an ongoing collective action.[48]

In order to determine whether a national procedural provision does not make the implementation of an EU-prescribed right excessively difficult or downright impossible, the CJEU considers the totality of circumstances—it assesses the relevance of such provision to the entirety of the proceedings, as well as the course and specificities of the proceedings in various national instances. Furthermore, the assessment of

---

[43] CJEU, Joined Cases C-224/19 and C-259/19, *CY v Caixabank SA and LG, PK v Banco Bilbao Vizcaya Argentaria SA*, Judgement, 16 July 2020, ECLI:EU:C:2020:578.

[44] CJEU, Case C-385/20, *EL and TP v Caixabank SA*, Judgement, 7 April 2022, ECLI:EU:C:2022:278.

[45] CJEU, Case C-287/22, *YQ, RJ v Getin Noble Bank S.A*, Judgement, 15 June 2023, ECLI:EU:C:2023:491.

[46] CJEU, Case C-472/10, *Nemzeti Fogyasztóvédelmi Hatóság v Invitel Távközlési Zrt*, Judgement, 26 April 2012, ECLI:EU:C:2012:242, para 37.

[47] CJEU, Joined Cases C-568/14 and C-570/14, *Ismael Fernández Oliva and others*, Judgement, 26 October 2016, ECLI:EU:C:2016:828.

[48] CJEU, Joined Cases C-381/14 and C-385/14, *Jorge Sales Sinués v Caixabank SA and Youssouf Drame Ba v Catalunya Caixa SA (Catalunya Banc SA)*, Judgement, 14 April 2016, ECLI:EU:C:2016:252.

the effectiveness of national provisions is carried out not *in abstracto*, but *in concreto*, on a case-by-case basis. Essentially (and it should be emphasized), this means that the development of remedies is haphazard and fragmented, as opposed to systemic. What does this imply for national courts?

7.3 The Impact That the CJEU Interpretation of the Principle of Effectiveness Has on the Jurisprudence of National Courts

Earlier provided examples of interpretation of the principle of effectiveness from the CJEU case law undoubtedly confirm that the principle of effectiveness has an impact on the scope of consumer rights that national courts must enforce, and thus, accordingly, has an impact on the national law that implements EU Consumer Law rules. For example, what does the CJEU's ruling that even in summary proceedings (where an order for payment is issued) national courts must assess the fairness of contract terms *ex officio* imply to national law? Given that an order for payment is a part of the simplified civil procedure and is issued without requiring evidence, such burden on courts implies a fundamental transformation (if not a negation altogether) of issuing an order for payment, and perhaps even calls into question its application to consumer disputes in general. Especially in the light of the recent above-mentioned ruling of the CJEU, that the court issuing an order for payment is required to examine the fairness of contractual terms and provide a sufficient statement of its reasons for such findings. Such obligation raises doubts as to whether an order for payment procedure (as a summary procedure) is feasible in consumer disputes at all. It is a paradox because an order for payment in most cases could be issued particularly in consumer disputes. And what does such a ruling mean to the national court? Undoubtedly, a national court that examines a consumer dispute must provide the exact same content of consumer rights and related remedies as the CJEU does.

Of course, the law is alive and reflects real life with all the changes that happen in society, therefore, its development through courts cannot be denied. Nevertheless, such an expansion of EU law compels national courts to be extremely attentive, proactive and maintain a close, ongoing dialogue with the CJEU. National courts are obliged to absorb the entirety of the CJEU jurisprudence. This means that they must not only identify issues related to the effectiveness of national law, but also (where necessary) raise appropriate legal arguments for a preliminary ruling; all of which should be preceded by continuous monitoring and a thorough analysis of the CJEU's case law. Given that the CJEU's case law covers a wide range of legal matters (i.e., areas of life), this might present a real challenge for national courts. Finally, national courts have to shoulder not only the analysis of the case law of the CJEU, but also of the ECHR and, in certain cases, even compare the two.

An unenthusiastic acceptance (as the Lithuanian example demonstrates) of the court's duty to assess the fairness of contract terms on its own motion confirms how difficult it is to turn interpretations of the CJEU practice into an alive and functioning tool. This institute was introduced[49] to EU law in 2000, and for the past 24 years it was supposed to be strengthening the enforcement of consumer rights. Its compatibility with national civil procedure law has not even been questioned in Lithuanian legal doctrine. The case law of Lithuania's Constitutional Court and court of cassation (the Supreme Court of Lithuania) also confirms that an active role of courts in consumer disputes organically fits in with civil procedure norms. And yet it was not enough to avoid mistakes—e.g., courts of first instance do not always fulfil their duty, and courts of appeal sometimes question the litigant's (consumer's) right to challenge the fairness of contract terms in the appeal instance. An amendment to the Civil Code (applicable since 13 June 2014), which directly (*expressis verbis*) obliged courts to assess the fairness of the contract terms, did not improve the situation a lot. Finally, as mentioned earlier, although the duty to act *ex officio* was initially developed in the area of unfair contract terms, the CJEU has extended it further to other institutes of consumer law. Therefore, even today it is still unclear how many lawyers in Lithuania are aware of the court's duty to assess *ex officio* whether the consumer received all the relevant information upon receiving consumer credit, or whether the assessment of the consumer's creditworthiness complied with requirements. The question is simple and straightforward—is the awareness (or lack thereof) in any way facilitated by the fragmented interpretation of EU law, which does not help to establish general rules (e.g., the court's duty to assess *ex officio* whether the consumer received all relevant information in *every* type of contract, not just in consumer credit contracts)?

To add more, sometimes it is unmistakably clear that even an active court may be unable to solve issues of remedies arising from interpreting the principle of effectiveness. One of the obvious examples is an already mentioned court's duty to assess the fairness of contract terms *ex officio* in an order for payment procedure. How should courts assess the fairness of the contract terms when a businessperson files for an order for payment today? The Supreme Court provided some 'recipes' in its overview of consumer credit regulation,[50] but following recent orders by the CJEU to provide arguments as to why the national court decided that certain terms are not unfair, these proposed solutions already fall short. Additionally, as it is widely known, a survey is neither case law nor a legislative tool. Thus, everything—including some subjective risks—falls in the hands of each judge. Will judges deal with this? It is more likely than not that they will, but the risk remains—how plausible it is for a particular judge to know everything and apply it adequately. It would be rather naïve to believe that with each case a judge can carry out a thorough analysis of the entirety of the CJEU's case law, assess its developments, prepare comparative analysis, and read all the academic articles that investigate challenges to implement the CJEU case law

[49] CJEU, Joined Cases C-240/98, C-241/98, C-242/98, C-243/98, C-244/98, *Océano Grupo Editorial SA v Roció Murciano Quintero and Salvat Editores SA v José M. Sánchez Alcón Prades, José Luis Copano Badillo, Mohammed Berroane and Emilio Viñas Feliú*, Judgement, 27 June 2000, ECLI:EU:C:2000:346.

[50] The Supreme Court of Lithuania. A survey of the specificities of consumer credit legal regulation and its application and interpretation in case law, 2020. https://www.lat.lt/lat-praktika/teismu-praktikos-apzvalgos/civiliniu-bylu-apzvalgos/67. Accessed 30 January 2025.

into national law. And this is not intended to question the competence of the judges, as some might superficially look at this problem. Will it be effective from a systemic point of view? Will legal certainty be ensured? It is doubtful. Even more doubts arise in continental law countries like Lithuania, where the Civil code and the Civil procedure code are codified. One of the features of codified legal acts is the interrelationship and systemic nature of their legal rules. It is difficult to establish such a system through sporadic case law. Therefore, before the principle of effectiveness is transposed to codified legal norms, its content developed by the CJEU case law cannot, in principle, ensure consumer rights timely and effectively.

7.4 Conclusions

There are no doubts, and it can be absolutely agreed with the opinion that the importance of the principle of an effective judicial remedy in the EU reflects the importance of courts in creating the EU legal order's moral face. This principle is clearly an element of the humanistic approach in which the legal community is based on individuals and their rights. This principle reflects the trust that liberal democracies have placed in courts to resolve conflicts. It reveals an intrinsic pacifistic European social relation whereby disagreements are resolved through judicial reasoning, and not in some other manner, such as violence or deception.[51]

But at the same time, it cannot be ignored that an ever-evolving principle that is developed day by day and (as we can see) and is wide open to broad interpretations should require a kind of "orderliness", a stricter and more responsible conception. A more detailed, clear and coherent (or at least more consistent) approach (though I hesitate to say 'theory') would be desirable for this multifaceted principle.

Even with the current fragmented interpretation of the principle of effectiveness, which shapes the practice of legal remedies (particularly given that this principle—often simultaneously—is examined from multiple perspectives),[52] the primary goal and task of the national court remains the same (and is extremely difficult)—to fully grasp the principle of effectiveness with all its nuances. This requires a coherent and detailed analysis of the CJEU case law, an assessment of its rationality and practicality for national law, especially an assessment of the need for systemic changes (perhaps even every such decision by the CJEU should prompt serious evaluation by the Ministry of Justice whether an intervention to the existing law is necessary). This calls for cooperation between everyone involved—academia, practice, legislation.

[51] See, e.g., Gentile 2023, pp. 128–143.

[52] (1) from a substantive and a formal/procedural point of view (twined with the equivalence principle regarding autonomy of national procedural laws); (2) as a tool of interpretation grounded in legal reasoning and functionalism in EU law; (3) as a legal principle fully independent in its meaning and scope but also as a principle integrated and limited by other fundamental principles of European law (i.e. primacy, protection of fundamental rights, classic principles of European/national criminal legal orders, legal certainty, and State liability for breaches of EU law). See, e.g., Mendez-Pinedo 2021, p. 27.

The principle of effectiveness itself demands this, so that the rights of individuals are protected in practice, function effectively and provide a sense of security to people.

References

Arnull A (2011) The Principle of Effective Judicial Protection in EU law: An Unruly Horse? European Law Review 1
Bonelli M (2019) Effective judicial protection in EU law: an evolving principle of a constitutional nature. Review of European Administrative Law 12(2)
Eliantonio M (2019) The principle of effectiveness: under strain? Review of European Administrative Law 12(2)
Gentile G (2023) Effective judicial protection: enforcement, judicial federalism and the politics of the EU law. European Law Open 2
Liakopoulos D (2019) Development and critics of effectiveness principle in EU international private law. https://doi.org/10.5007/2177-7055.2019v41n82p10
Mayr S (2012) Putting a Leash on the Court of Justice? Preconception in National Methodology v. Effect Utile as a Meta-Rule. European Journal of Legal Studies 5(2)
Mendez-Pinedo M E (2021) The principle of effectiveness of EU law: a difficult concept in legal scholarship. Juridical Tribune 11(1)
Pescatore P (1983) The Doctrine of direct effect: an infant disease of Community Law. European Law Review 8:155–157
Reich N (2014) The Principle of Effectiveness in General Principles of EU Civil Law, pp 89–129
Roeben V (2020) Judicial protection as a meta-norm in the EU judicial architecture. Hague Journal on the Rule of Law 12
Sadl U (2015) The role of Effet Utile in Preserving the Continuity and Authority of European Union Law: Evidence from the Citation Web of the Pre-accession Case-Law of the Court of Justice of the European Union. European Journal of Legal Studies 8(18)

Legislation

Civil Code of the Republic of Lithuania, 2020
The Supreme Court of Lithuania. A survey of the specificities of consumer credit legal regulation and its application and interpretation in case law, 2020. https://www.lat.lt/lat-praktika/teismu-praktikos-apzvalgos/civiliniu-bylu-apzvalgos/67. Accessed 30 January 2025
Directive (EU) 2019/2161 of the European Parliament and of the Council of 27 November 2019 amending Council Directive 93/13/EEC and Directives 98/6/EC, 2005/29/EC and 2011/83/EU of the European Parliament and of the Council as regards the better enforcement and modernisation of Union consumer protection rules
Directive 93/13/EEC of 5 April 1993 on unfair terms in consumer contracts
Regulation (EC) No 1896/2006 of the European Parliament and of the Council of 12 December 2006 creating a European order for payment procedure

Cases

CJEU, Case C-33/76, *Rewe-Zentralfinanz eG and Rewe-Zentral AG v Landwirtschaftskammer für das Saarland, Judgement*, 16 December 1976, ECLI:EU:C:1976:188
CJEU, Case C-222/84, *Marguerite Johnston v Chief Constable of the Royal Ulster Constabulary*, Judgement, 15 May 1986, ECLI:EU:C:1986:206
CJEU, Case C-40/08, *Asturcom Telecomunicaciones SL v Cristina Rodríguez Nogueira*, Judgement, 6 October 2009, ECLI:EU:C:2009:615
CJEU, Case C-137/08, *VB Pénzügyi Lízing Zrt. v Ferenc Schneider*, Judgement, 9 November 2010, ECLI:EU:C:2010:659
CJEU, Joined cases C-65/09 and C-87/09, *Gebr. Weber GmbH v Jürgen Wittmer* (C-65/09) *and Ingrid Putz v Medianess Electronics GmbH* (C-87/09), *Bundesgerichtshof* (C-65/09) *and Amtsgericht Schorndorf* (C-87/09), Judgement, 16 June 2011, ECLI:EU:C:2011:396
CJEU, Case C-618/10, *Banco Espanol de Crédito SA v Joaquín Calderón Camino*, Judgement, 14 June 2012, ECLI:EU:C:2012:349
CJEU, Case C-472/10, *Nemzeti Fogyasztóvédelmi Hatóság v Invitel Távközlési Zrt*, Judgement, 26 April 2012, ECLI:EU:C:2012:242
CJEU, Case C-472/11, *Banif Plus Bank Zrt v Csaba Csipai and Viktória Csipai*, Judgement, 21 February 2013, ECLI:EU:C:2013:88
CJEU, Case C-32/12, *Soledad Duarte Hueros v Autociba SA, Automóviles Citroën España SA*, Judgement, 3 October 2013, ECLI:EU:C:2013:637
CJEU, Case C-415/11, *Mohamed Aziz v Caixa d´Estalvis de Catalunya, Tarragona i Manresa (Catalunyacaixa)*, Judgement, 14 March 2013, ECLI:EU:C:2013:164
CJEU, Case C-497/13, *Froukje Faber v Autobedrijf Hazet Ochten BV*, Judgement, 4 June 2015, ECLI:EU:C:2015:357
CJEU, Case C-8/14, *BBVA SA v Pedro Peñalva López and others*, Judgement, 29 October 2015, ECLI:EU:C:2015:731
CJEU, Case C-377/14, *Ernst Georg Radlinger and Helena Radlingerová v Finway a.s*, Judgement, 21 April 2016, ECLI:EU:C:2016:283
CJEU, Joined Cases C-568/14 and C-570/14, *Ismael Fernández Oliva and others*, Judgement, 26 October 2016, ECLI:EU:C:2016:828
CJEU, Joined Cases C-381/14 and C-385/14, *Jorge Sales Sinués v Caixabank SA and Youssouf Drame Ba v Catalunya Caixa SA (Catalunya Banc SA)*, Judgement, 14 April 2016, ECLI:EU:C:2016:252
CJEU, Case C-176/17, *Profi Credit Polska S.A. w Bielsku Białej v Mariusz Wawrzosek*, Judgement, 13 September 2018, ECLI:EU:C:2018:711
CJEU, Case C-407/18, *Addiko Bank*, 26 June 2019, EU:C:2019:537
CJEU, Joined Cases C- 453/18 and C-494/18, *Bondora AS v Carlos V. C. and XY*, Judgement, 19 December 2019, ECLI:EU:C:2019:1118
CJEU, Case C-679/18, *OPR-Finance s. r. o. v GK*, Judgement, 5 March 2020, ECLI:EU:C:2020:167
CJEU, Case C-495/19, *Kancelaria Medius SA v RN*, Judgement, 4 June 2020, ECLI:EU:C:2020:431
CJEU, Joined Cases C-224/19 and C-259/19, *CY v Caixabank SA and LG, PK v Banco Bilbao Vizcaya Argentaria SA*, Judgement, 16 July 2020, ECLI:EU:C:2020:578
CJEU, Joined Cases C-240/98, C-241/98, C-242/98, C-243/98, C-244/98, *Océano Grupo Editorial SA v Roció Murciano Quintero and Salvat Editores SA v José M. Sánchez Alcón Prades, José Luis Copano Badillo, Mohammed Berroane and Emilio Viñas Feliú*, Judgement, 27 June 2000, ECLI:EU:C:2000:346
CJEU, Case C-156/21, *Hungary v European Parliament and the Council of the European Union*, Judgement, 16 February 2022, ECLI:EU:C:2022:97
CJEU, Case C-600/19, *MA v Ibercaja Banco, SA*, Judgement, 17 May 2022, ECLI:EU:C:2022:394
CJEU, Joined Cases C-776/19 and C-782/19, *VB and others v BNP Paribas Personal Finance SA, and AV and others v BNP Paribas Personal Finance SA, Procureur de la République*, Judgement, 10 June 2021, ECLI:EU:C:2021:470

CJEU, Case C-385/20, *EL and TP v Caixabank SA*, Judgement, 7 April 2022, ECLI:EU:C:2022:278
CJEU, Case C-35/22, *CAJASUR Banco*, Judgement, 13 July 2023, ECLI:EU:C:2023:569
CJEU Case C-215/21, *Servicios prescriptor y medios de pagos E.F.C. S.A.U*, Judgement, 22 September 2022, ECLI:EU:C:2022:773
CJEU, Case C-287/22, *YQ, RJ v Getin Noble Bank S.A*, Judgement, 15 June 2023, ECLI:EU:C:2023:491
CJEU, Case C-724/22, *Investcapital Ltd*, Judgement, 29 February 2024, ECLI:EU:C:2024:182

Danguolė Bublienė is a doctor of law, and an associate professor at the Law Faculty of Vilnius University. This chapter is based on the presentation delivered at the international scientific conference "The Republic of Lithuania in the European Union: twenty years of experience, challenges and growth" at Vilnius University on 24 May 2024.

Chapter 8
Hearing of a Child as a Reflection of the Influence of European Union Law on Polish Civil Procedural Law

Kinga Flaga-Gieruszyńska and Aleksandra Klich

Contents

Abstract The hearing of a child in Polish civil procedural law is a significant example of the impact of European Union law on national regulations. The principle of protecting children's rights, derived, among others, from the Charter of Fundamental Rights of the European Union (Article 24), obliges Member States to ensure that children are given the opportunity to express their views in matters affecting them. EU regulations in family and custody law, particularly those concerning child abduction and cross-border disputes, emphasize the obligation to hear children, highlighting the need to consider their well-being and perspectives in the decision-making process. The implementation of these standards has been reflected in the Polish Code of Civil Procedure, specifically in Articles 216(1) and 576(2). These provisions underline the right of a child to express their opinions in a manner appropriate to their age and maturity. The introduction of this practice strengthens the realization of the principle of the child's subjectivity, which is one of the cornerstones of the European approach to human rights protection. The influence of EU law is also evident in judicial practice, which increasingly prioritizes creating child-friendly conditions

K. Flaga-Gieruszyńska (✉)
University of Szczecin, Szczecin, Poland
e-mail: kinga.flaga-gieruszynska@usz.edu.pl

A. Klich
Faculty of Law, Vilnius University, Vilnius, Lithuania
e-mail: aleksandra.klich@tf.vu.lt

I. Isokaitė-Valužė and H. Šinkūnas (eds.), *The European Union 2004-2024*,
https://doi.org/10.1007/978-94-6265-718-2_8

for hearings. These changes underline the growing harmonization of Polish law with EU standards for the protection of children's rights.

Keywords Hearing of a child · Child-friendly justice · Subjectivity of the child · Polish civil procedural law · Children's rights · Charter of Fundamental Rights of the European Union · Family and custody law

8.1 Introduction

In the legal system of the European Union, the rights of the child are an important area of regulation in the area of human rights and freedoms. However, it should be emphasized that it is impossible to speak of ensuring the subjectivity of the child in substantive law without the introduction of adequate procedural guarantees, allowing the child to be heard in matters concerning his person and property. It is sometimes erroneously assumed that the child should be heard only in family and guardianship matters, but this is too narrow an assumption. The child is the subject of various rights and obligations, including property, so he should have the opportunity to express an opinion in any civil case whose outcome concerns the child's rights and obligations.

Within the framework of the harmonization of procedural law of the members of the European Union, the Polish legislation has taken steps to ensure the subjectivity of the child also on the grounds of civil proceedings. Not without significance in this area is the fact that the member states of the European Union are at the same time members of the Council of Europe, which has made activities for the rights of the child one of the fundamental goals of its law-making activity. As indicated in Article 52(3) of the EU Charter of Fundamental Rights[1] to the extent that this Charter contains rights that correspond to those guaranteed by the European Convention for the Protection of Human Rights and Fundamental Freedoms,[2] their meaning and scope are the same as those granted by this Convention. This provision does not prevent EU law from granting broader protection. It is understood that Article 52(3) CFR is intended to ensure the necessary consistency between the rights expressed therein and the corresponding rights guaranteed by the Convention in a manner that does not violate the autonomy of Union law. For example, taking into account the above-mentioned relationship between the provisions of the Convention on the right to a court and the principle of ensuring effective legal protection, which counts among the general principles of EU law, a court's action aimed at ensuring, in the possible forms available in national law, the enforcement of judgments of the ECtHR on the right to a court referred to in Article 6(1) of the Convention, is at the same time an action aimed at protecting the order of Union law encompassing the principle of effective legal protection, as stipulated in the second paragraph of Article 19(1)

[1] Official Journal of the EU. C 2010 No. 83, p. 389, hereinafter: CFR.

[2] Journal of Laws of 1993, no. 61, item 284.

of the TEU in conjunction with Article 47 of the Charter of Fundamental Rights.[3] In the doctrine, it has been argued that the purpose of the Charter was to highlight the significance of fundamental rights and present their content in a manner easily understandable to European citizens during a critical period when the European integration process faced a significant democratic deficit.[4] Consequently, it can be viewed, in our opinion, as having a more clarifying than innovative role. As previously mentioned, several rights enshrined in the Charter were already established and protected under primary and secondary EU law, as well as through the jurisprudence of the European Court of Justice.[5] Thus, the protection of procedural rights in the broadest sense, including the rights of the child as a subject of the proceedings, is a common value of the acquis of the two designated international organizations.

However, this study should focus on the legislative acquis of European Union law and the jurisprudence of the Court of Justice of the European Union, with particular emphasis on the procedural guarantees that the EU legislature seeks to provide for the child. This approach, for obvious reasons, is also reflected in Polish civil procedural law, which is gradually implementing solutions that guarantee the procedural subjectivity of the child.

It will be analysed not only the currently functioning solutions, but also the prospects for the development of procedural guarantees aimed at optimizing the participation of the child in civil proceedings, when the settlement will concern his rights and obligations. Consequently, the research hypothesis will be verified, according to which the hearing of the child is a fundamental instrument for the realization of the child's right to express his or her own views protected by European Union law. As a result, the judicial authority has a duty to respect the autonomy of the child's will in the course of the proceedings and in the ruling made by properly applying the hearing of the child, when this is possible given the child's age, maturity and health.

8.2 European Union Standards on the Subjectivity of the Child in Civil Proceedings

8.2.1 Charter of Fundamental Rights of the European Union (Article 24)

In the doctrine and judicature, the rights of the child are considered against the broader background of the protection of private and family life and the rights of the family of which the child is a member. Interestingly, the rights of the child considered in the context of family rights have not been declared unconditional by the Court of Justice.

---

[3] Order of the Supreme Court of 30 December 2021, I CSK 197/20, LEX No. 3314923.

[4] Besteliu and Brumar 2008, p. 88.

[5] Salomia 2012, p. 181.

This means that measures restricting their enjoyment are sometimes permitted, but the measures applied must not violate the essence of the protected fundamental right.[6] The grounds for admissibility, and thus the limits of protection of the rights of the child and the family, the Court of Justice determines by referring to the same determinants formulated in the Convention on the Rights of the Child,[7] as well as in the European Convention on Human Rights. The Charter follows the UNCRC in providing that the best interests of the child are to be "a primary consideration". From the perspective of the subject of this study, the key significance of Article 8(2) of the ECHR, which introduces formal and substantive criteria for restrictions, as well as formulates conditions relating to the manner of their implementation. The formal requirements of the ECHR relate to the right to impose restrictions only by law. The substantive criteria, on the other hand, relate to the introduction of measures motivated by one or more objectives that are legitimate in light of this legislation, and protection that is "necessary in a democratic society", i.e. that is justified by an overriding social need. It is not only the desirability of the measures introduced that weighs on their legality, but also their proportional alignment with the legitimate goal they serve to achieve.[8] However, these restrictions do not apply to rights of a procedural nature—both in civil and criminal proceedings. For the latter, an example of guarantee regulation is the Directive of the European Parliament and of the Council (EU) 2016/800 of 11 May 2016 on procedural guarantees for children who are suspects or defendants in criminal proceedings.[9] With regard to procedural safeguards, the only acceptable limitation is the characteristics or situation of the child that prevents him from being heard.

Central to the formation of the basis for the protection of children's rights is Article 24(1) of the CFR, which states that children have the right to such protection and care as is necessary for their well-being. The Charter states that "protection" is a "right" of the child. They are free to express their views. These opinions are taken into account in matters that affect them, according to their age and maturity. Consequently, every child has the right to express their views, which are then assessed to determine the extent of their consideration in decision-making. The subjects eligible under this provision are those who are under the age of 18, which is a continuation of the ideas expressed in the Convention on the Protection of the Rights of the Child. In this way, the EU legislator wants to guarantee the right to participate in the decision-making process to a person who is not yet emotionally and intellectually mature. The circumstance of the child's immaturity does not exempt authorities and institutions from the obligation to take into account the experience and views of the child in all matters that concern his person or property. Thus—unlike the material legal rights of the child, which may be subject to restrictions, as mentioned above—the right to be heard by the child is unconditional, making it impossible for public authorities

[6] Judgment of the Court of Justice of 11 July 2002, C-60/00, Mary Carpenter v Secretary of State for the Home Department, ECLI:EU:C:2002:434, para 40.

[7] UN Doc. E/CN.4/1989/48, paras 121–122; Alston 1994, p. 12.

[8] Majkowska-Szulc and Tomaszewska 2020a, b.

[9] Official Journal of Law 132, 21.5.2016, pp. 1–20.

and institutions to impose restrictions on it, other than those based on the child's age, maturity and state of health. It is worth to emphasize that children under the age of 18 may be capable of formulating views, even if they are not yet able to express them verbally. It is essential to recognize their expressions and respect them, while providing children with the opportunity to be heard. The child should also have "sufficient understanding" to be able to form his or her own opinions on the matter. It seems that it is not necessary to have "comprehensive knowledge of all aspects of the matter".[10]

As pointed out in the literature, in this way the category of the child's expression of opinions has been given a normative character, and, moreover, their right in this regard *expressis verbis* derives from legal regulations, according to which the views of the child are taken into account in all matters concerning him, in accordance with his age and maturity. The expression of the guarantee provided for on normative grounds is, for example, the provision of the opportunity to speak out in any legal proceedings, in accordance with the provisions of domestic law. The importance of the mentioned legal regulations cannot be overestimated not only in the normative layer, which has been pointed out, but above all in the social layer, relating to the construction of children's identity and the development of their skills of self-determination, as well as the formation of an attitude of growing in the conviction of their rights and duties.[11] Children's participation, like that of adults, should be understood in terms of sharing decisions. It is also considered a basic civil right. Only by participating in decision-making processes in the family, school and community do children learn about their rights, responsibilities. This, in turn, has a positive effect on respecting the decisions made.[12] Involving children in the decision-making process, including by guaranteeing their right to be heard, positively influences the formation of awareness that their freedom is limited by the rights and freedoms of others and that their actions may violate the rights of others.[13] Article 24(1) of the CFR presents an intriguing combination of what could broadly be described as children's rights to protection and empowerment, which frequently come into conflict. The integration of these two aspects within a single paragraph appears to be a deliberate attempt to strike a balance between the competing principles of paternalism and autonomy. Stating that a child has a "right" to such protection seems to carry more weight than merely urging that it be "ensured".[14] The children's approach should focus on integrating and incorporating their rights into the legal process, treating them as independent rights subjects and not just as passive recipients of care.[15] Recognizing children as active participants in legal proceedings strengthens their position in the legal system and ensures that they can exercise their rights. In addition, the right to express their opinions participating in the decision-making process fosters their sense

---

[10] Mal 2019, p. 240.

[11] Cała-Wacinkiewicz and Szwed 2022, pp. 114–115.

[12] Bosisio 2012, p. 144.

[13] Hart 1992, p. 5.

[14] Official Journal of EU 2010, C326, 391–407; McGlynn 2002, p. 397.

[15] Petrova 2018, p. 103.

of agency and responsibility for their own lives. Moreover, taking into account the child's voice allows more accurate and tailored decisions to be made, especially in family, guardianship or adoption matters. Children who realize the right to be heard also learn that their voice matters, which fosters the development of citizenship and social responsibility.

In summary, the Charter of Fundamental Rights of the European Union sets standards for the protection of the substantive and procedural rights of the child, establishing a starting point for the formation of detailed provisions both in the legal acts of the European Union and in the legal systems of individual member states. In the scope of this discussion, only those that are embedded in civil procedural law, which creates effective instruments for the child's ability to express his or her own views, will be highlighted. However, there is still a need to create further guidelines and good practices, especially in terms of assessing the EU's uniform obligations with regard to the rights of the child[16] and making sure that children are seen as individual rights-holders.[17] It is worth clarifying how the principles under Article 24 of the CFR are reflected in civil procedural law, especially in the context of a child's right to be heard and to have his or her views taken into account in accordance with his or her age and maturity. It is also possible to consider what procedural mechanisms exist in the various legal orders of EU member states to ensure the effective realization of this right. In addition, it would be useful to identify specific areas for further guidance and good practice, such as the harmonization of standards for hearing children in civil proceedings or the role of the child's procedural representatives, to ensure that children are seen as full rights-holders and not merely objects of protection. In conclusion, it is worth pointing out that children's participation in decision-making processes is crucial not only for their social development, but also for the effective realization of their rights. Involving children in decision-making—both at the family, school and community levels—shapes their sense of responsibility and, as indicated, their awareness of rights and responsibilities. In addition, it is worth noting that recognizing the child as a fully-fledged subject of rights, and not just an object of concern, has implications for the legal practice—both in terms of the right to be heard and to make decisions that affect their lives. Marking that a child has a "right" to protection, and not just an obligation to "provide" it, reinforces the child's status in the legal system and obliges state bodies to take concrete action. Therefore, it is worthwhile to analyse how legislation on children's rights can be implemented in practice, so that it realistically affects their legal and social situation.

8.2.2 EU Standards in Family and Custody Law Proceedings

The right to a child's hearing is regulated in European Union legislation relating to family and guardianship law in the broadest sense. This can be most clearly

[16] Stalford 2015, p. 229.

[17] Stalford *et al.* 2017, p. 5.

demonstrated by Council Regulation (EU) 2019/1111 of 25 June 2019 on jurisdiction, the recognition and enforcement of decisions in matrimonial matters and the matters of parental responsibility, and on international child abduction.[18] The EU legislation clearly indicates in the recitals of this regulation that the child's ability to freely express his or her views, as provided for in Article 24(1) of the CFR, plays an important role in the application of this regulation. Indeed, from this provision comes the legal obligation to take positive measures to ensure that the best interests and views of the child are taken into account when making placement decisions.[19] However, the regulation leaves the question of deciding who conducts the child's hearing and how the hearing is conducted to the national law and procedure in effect in the member states. Accordingly, the purpose of this legislation is not to determine who conducts the child's hearing—a judge in person or a properly trained specialist who then reports to the court—or where the child's hearing is conducted—in the courtroom or elsewhere or by other means. However, the EU legislator emphasizes that the hearing is a right of the child, but it cannot be treated as an absolute obligation, which is a break from the perception of procedural rights as rights of an absolute nature. It goes without saying that the right to a hearing must be evaluated with the child's welfare in mind. While it is clear from the case law of the Court of Justice that neither Article 24 CFR nor Council Regulation (EC) No 2201/2003 of 27 November 2003 concerning jurisdiction and the recognition and enforcement of judgments in matrimonial matters and the matters of parental responsibility, repealing Regulation (EC) No 1347/2000[20] do not provide that the court of the Member State of origin is obliged to take cognizance of the views of the child in every case in the form of a hearing, which means that the court retains a certain amount of discretion. The case law also provides that if the court decides to provide the child with an opportunity to be heard, it is obliged to adopt all measures necessary to conduct such a hearing, having regard to the best interests of the child and the circumstances of the particular case, in order to ensure the effectiveness of those provisions and to provide the child with a real and genuine opportunity to express his or her views. Hearing the child not only empowers the child by directly participating in the proceedings that affect him, but also better enables the judge or authority to assess the factual situation, which is a particularly difficult task in cross-border proceedings.[21] The child's right to be heard is considered an obligation, the observance of which in the European Union means ensuring that it is exercised by the judge of the country that issues the judgment, without any other country being able to control the actions of the judge of origin.[22] However, it is not specified how the child should be heard, so the cited regulation does

[18] Official Journal of Law 178, 2.7.2019, pp. 1–115.

[19] UN, Committee on the Rights of the Child (2013), General Comment No. 14 (2013) on the right to have his/her best interest taken as a primary consideration (Article 3 para 1), UN Doc. CRC/C/GC/14, 29 May 2013; UN, Committee on the Rights of the Child (2009), General Comment No. 12 (2009): The right of the child to be heard, UN Doc. CRC/C/GC/12, 20 July 2009, para 97.

[20] Official Journal of Law 338, 23.12.2003, pp. 1–29.

[21] Pretelli 2016, pp. 10–11.

[22] Rodríguez Pineau 2017, pp. 155–156.

not change the rules and practices of member states on hearing the child, but requires mutual recognition of legal systems.[23] Therefore, the court of a Member State should, to the fullest extent possible and always taking into account the best interests of the child, use all means available under national law, as well as specific instruments of international judicial cooperation, including, where appropriate, those provided for in Council Regulation (EC) No 1206/2001 of 28 May 2001 on cooperation between the courts of the Member States in the taking of evidence in civil or commercial matters.[24]

The child's right to be heard does not require that the court of a member state necessarily hold a hearing, but it does impose an obligation to ensure that procedures and legal conditions exist to allow the child to freely express his or her views and that those views are taken into account by the court. In other words, the legislation does not require that the child always be heard by a court of a member state, which leaves that court with a certain amount of discretion. Nevertheless, if that court decides to hear the child, the standards require that, taking into account the best interests of the child and the individual circumstances of each case, it must take all appropriate measures to bring about such a hearing, so that by giving the child a real and effective opportunity to express his or her views, the effectiveness (*effet utile*) of the aforementioned provisions is respected.[25] Article 24 of the CFR requires that legal procedures and conditions allowing children to express their opinions freely be made available to them, and that these opinions be obtained by the court.[26] As for the opportunity provided to the child to express his or her views, it should be up to the court of the Member State of origin to decide which method of hearing the child is appropriate. Therefore, it should not be possible to refuse recognition of a decision by another member state solely on the basis that the court of the member state of origin used a different method of hearing the child than the method that a court in the member state of recognition would have used. The Member State in which recognition is sought should not refuse recognition in cases where one of the exceptions justifying the non-application of that particular ground for refusal permitted under this Regulation applies. The effect of the application of such exceptions is that a court in the Member State of enforcement should not be able to refuse to enforce a judgment on the sole ground that the child was not given an opportunity to express his or her views, bearing in mind his or her welfare, if the proceedings concerned only the child's property, and provided that the provision of such an opportunity was not required by the subject matter of the proceedings or if there are compelling reasons that take into account, in particular, the urgency of the case. Such compelling grounds could, for example, relate to an imminent threat to the physical and mental integrity or life of the child, where additional delay could cause this threat to materialize. Consequently, the EU legislator seeks to indicate as precisely as possible the permissible restrictions on the

[23] Delgado Sáez 2019, p. 226.

[24] Official Journal of Law UE No 174, p. 1.

[25] Judgment of the Court of Justice of 22 December 2010, C-491/10 PPU, ZOTSiS 2010/12C/I-14247-14308, paras 65–67.

[26] CJEU, C-491/10 PPU, Joseba Adoni Aguirre Zarraga v Simone Pelz, 22 December 2010.

realization of the right to a hearing, focusing on criteria relating to the characteristics or situation of the child (for example, when it requires urgent intervention by state authorities).

According to Article 21 of Regulation 2019/1111, in exercising jurisdiction over matters of parental responsibility, the courts of Member States shall, in accordance with national law and procedure, ensure that a child who is capable of forming his or her views is given a real and effective opportunity to express his or her views, either directly or through a representative or an appropriate entity. The regulation emphasizes the obligation to hear the child in abduction proceedings, while reaffirming the EU institutions' desire to further strengthen the child's fundamental right to be heard.[27] Thus, this provision provides for both direct hearing (with the participation of the judicial authority) and indirect hearing (when the authority receives information about the child's views through specialized entities that communicate with the child). If the court, in accordance with national law and procedure, provides the child with the opportunity to express his views in accordance with this provision, the court shall give the child's views due weight in accordance with the child's age and maturity. Consequently, the implementation of the right to be heard by the child must not be merely formal, limited to the mere conduct of the hearing, but must take a real form, expressed in real influence on the content of the decision, if this is justified by the child's welfare.

The court that issued the judgment referred to in Article 42(1) of Regulation 2019/1111 shall, at the request of a party, issue a certificate regarding a judgment granting the right to personal contact with the child using the form in Annex V (Article 47(1)(a) of Regulation 2019/1111), as well as a judgment on the merits regarding custody of the child, providing for the return of the child, and issued in accordance with Article 29(6) of Regulation 2019/1111, using the form in Annex VI (Article 47(1)(b) of Regulation 2019/1111). Under the regulation in question, the court shall issue a certificate for privileged rulings only if the child has been given the opportunity to express his or her views (Article 47(3)(b) of the regulation). This restriction excludes the possibility of issuing a certificate if an act is carried out in violation of the basic rules of court proceedings in the Member State where recognition is sought. This amply demonstrates the importance of hearing the child in order to recognize that the proceedings were conducted in accordance with the standards of his subjectivity in procedural law.

Article 21 of the Regulation also applies to child return proceedings under the Convention on the Civil Aspects of International Child Abduction, done at The Hague on 25 October 1980.[28] However, the Hague Convention does not grant the child the right to decide for himself or herself where he or she will remain, so it is not sufficient for the abrogation of the obligation to order the child's return that the child expresses a preference to live in one country or the other. The provision of Article 13(2) of the Hague Convention, while allowing for the possibility of refusing to order the child's return, requires the child's objection while establishing that he or she has reached an

[27] Carpaneto 2019, p. 280.

[28] Journal of Laws of 1995, no. 108, item 528.

age and degree of maturity at which it is appropriate to take his or her opinion into account. The Hague Convention does not set any rigid age threshold at which it is appropriate to take the child's opinion into account. Nevertheless, while in the case of teenage children their sufficient maturity is usually not in doubt, the situation is different for younger children, especially those of preschool age. When assessing the child's maturity, it is necessary to examine whether the child is able to understand the purpose and consequences of returning to the country of permanent residence and provide reasons for his or her objection. The assessment in this regard is a matter for the court and does not require reference to an expert opinion in every case, although in borderline cases this measure may prove indispensable. An additional issue is the need to separate the child's own will, especially in the case of younger children, from the will of the parent in whose actual custody the child remains, and, if it is determined that the objection meets the requirements of Article 13(2) of the Hague Convention, the extent of the discretion given to the court as to the impact of the child's objection on the final decision on the case.[29] The doctrine also points to a threshold of 7 or 10 years as the age at which a child's objection can be taken into account in international practice, but taking into account the circumstances of the particular case.[30] On the other hand, in a ruling of the Polish Supreme Court, it was accepted that the expression of an opinion by a 5-year-old child has no legal significance due to his age, since he is not able to formulate his views.[31]

In summary, the provisions of European Union law that directly affect the realization of family and children's rights attach great importance to ensuring proper procedural guarantees of the subjectivity and autonomy of the child's will, the axis of which is the proper realization of the child's right to be heard, which includes the inclusion of rational views in the content of the judgment.

8.2.3 The Principle of the Child's Best Interests in EU Practice of Hearing

In doctrine, jurisprudence and, above all, in legislation, there are two basic concepts relating to securing the rights of the child—"the welfare of the child" and "the best interests of the child". This raises a fundamental problem as to the interrelation of these concepts and their interpretation for the purposes of specific cases.

Child welfare is often defined based on a system of specific values. S. Kolodziejski defined the welfare of the child as a set of values, both spiritual and material, which are necessary for the proper: (1) the physical development of the child, (2) the spiritual development of the child, and this in both its intellectual and moral aspects, (3) the proper preparation of the child to work for the good of society.[32] In another definition

[29] Order of the Supreme Court of 17 December 2020, I CSK 183/20, OSNC 2021, No. 6, item 45.
[30] Zalisko 2022, p. 193.
[31] Order of the Supreme Court of 19 December 2000, III CKN 1254/00, LEX No. 51867.
[32] Kołodziejski 1965, p. 30.

created by the doctrine of family law, the welfare of the child is defined as a complex of values of an intangible and material nature, necessary to ensure the proper physical and spiritual development of the child and to properly prepare him for work in accordance with his talents, while these values are determined by a wide variety of factors, the structure of which depends on the content of the applicable legal norm and the specific, currently existing situation of the child, assuming the convergence of the child's welfare, so understood, with the public interest.[33] At the same time, J. Ignaczewski stresses that when assessing the welfare of a child, objective conditions such as the age of the child, his gender, the characterological features of the parents, the mutual relationship of the parents to each other, to the child and to the parent's relatives cannot be overlooked. Subjective criteria, such as the sensitivity of the child, the mutual relations and bonds between parents and children, the child's sense of security, are also not insignificant.[34] M. Bieszczad pointed out that the good of the child as a general clause should be interpreted in a way that takes into account the positive, from the perspective of the social hierarchy of values, evaluation of the situation of the child. The social hierarchy of values should be an *ad casum* source for seeking social norms according to which the concept of the child's welfare should be valued.[35] In the Polish legal system, "the welfare of the child" as a constitutional value in its own right is an integral part of the broader value of "the welfare of the family",[36] as exemplified by Article 47 of the Polish Constitution, which stipulates that everyone has the right to legal protection of private life, family life, honour and good name, and to decide on his or her personal life. However, this issue is beyond the scope of this chapter. It is a manifestation of the general tendency of modern child welfare systems to be shaped taking into account two types, i.e. child protection-oriented and family welfare-oriented.[37]

In turn, referring to the concept of the child's interest, it should be pointed out that some representatives of the doctrine equate it with the child's welfare. In such a view, the welfare of the child should be understood primarily as personal interests, that is, concern for the child's physical and spiritual development and due preparation for work in accordance with his talents and in accordance with the interests of society, as well as the property interests of the minor, manifested in the proper management of his property, the proper allocation of the income flowing from it and leaving the substance of this property intact as far as possible.[38] However, some representatives of the doctrine clearly distinguish between these two concepts, pointing out that the interest of a subject should be understood as the sum of the elements of the state of affairs that concern the subject, and the legal interest consists in the subject's freedom to shape his situation in accordance with his subjective conviction. The welfare of the child in this view is the optimal arrangement of the elements of the state of affairs

[33] E.g. Stojanowska 1999, pp. 90–91.

[34] Ignaczewski 2009, p. 158.

[35] Bieszczad 2019, pp. 946–950.

[36] Banaszak and Jabłoński 1999, p. 132.

[37] Gilbert *et al.* 2011, p. 4.

[38] Marciniak 1975, p. 19.

pertaining to the subject that, from an objective point of view, are consistent with the subject's interest. Not every interest of the child deserves protection, but only one that is at the same time consistent with the objectively understood good of the minor.[39]

Of primary importance under European Union law is Article 24(2) of the CFR, which provides that in all actions concerning children, whether taken by public authorities or private institutions, the best interests of the child (as signalled, national legislatures sometimes use the concept of the best interests of the child) must be a primary consideration. Therefore, it is necessary to resolve how the term "best interests of the child" should be interpreted. In light of the considerations indicated, to consider that the best interests of the child are the optimized interests of the child, which is the same as the child's welfare. So, the law protects not every interest subjectively perceived by the child, but only such an interest as is valuable in an objective sense. Consequently, when speaking of the "best interests" of the child, it is necessary to speak not of a subjective belief in the optimality of a certain situation of the child, but of an objective state that is consistent with the child's welfare. Then we can talk about the state of identity of the concepts of the child's welfare and the child's best interests.

In the law of the European Union and the Council of Europe acquis, there is now a general consensus—including international law—in favour of the view that in all decisions concerning children, their welfare (or best interests understood in the same sense) must be paramount.[40] Certainly, European legislation cannot be created and promote children's rights without a clear and formal commitment to the UN Convention on the Rights of the Child, which contains the basic concepts of well-being and agency underlying the children's rights movement.[41] As indicated in the doctrine, in a properly functioning family, the child's welfare is in harmony with the interests of the parents. However, in the situation of their competition, the extreme understanding of the child's welfare, without verifying the legitimate interests of the parents, and therefore other members of the child's family, can lead to undesirable consequences. Family law does not eliminate the interest of parents as one of the premises for resolving cases of parent-child relations. If, in the final result, the protection of the child can be reconciled with the interests of the parents, the court should take their interests into account, even if the settlement would cause some temporary negative consequences for the child.[42] In this regard, the decisive issue is whether a fair balance is struck between the competing interests in the case—those of the child, both parents and public policy—while preserving the margin of discretion granted to states in such cases, given, however, that the best interests of the child are an overriding consideration. The interests of the child may, depending on their nature and seriousness, take precedence over those of the parents. The parents'

---

[39] Sokołowski 1996a, pp. 48–49; Sokołowski 1996b, p. 12.

[40] Judgment of the European Court of Human Rights, Grand Chamber, 6 July 2010, 41615/07, LEX No. 584577.

[41] Stalford 2005, p. 66.

[42] Wojtaszek-Mik 2022, p. 54 and the literature indicated therein.

interests, especially regarding regular contact with their children, nevertheless remain a factor to be considered in balancing the various interests present in the case.[43] Such an approach is crucial for interpreting the court's obligation to take into account the views of the child in the content of the decision, which will also affect the parents.

In Poland, the welfare of the child is a principle of the Polish legal system and one of the basic principles of Polish family law, to which all regulations in the sphere of relations between parents and children are subordinated.[44] There are no general provisions in the Polish Family and Guardianship Code[45] in which the principle of child welfare is separately articulated. However, reference to it is found in the regulations of all the most important institutions of this codification, including, in particular, those concerning parental authority, custody and contact with the child, adoption, the establishment of guardianship and custody. As the Polish Supreme Court emphasizes, at the root of every decision made on issues that may affect the interests of the child is the consideration of protecting the child's welfare. The Polish jurisprudence indicates that the concept of the child's welfare is a complex one. On the one hand, it encompasses the entire sphere of his most important personal matters, such as physical and spiritual development, proper education and upbringing, and preparation for adult life. On the other hand, it has a clear material dimension, which consists of the need to provide for the child's livelihood and the realization of goals of a personal nature, and in the case where he has property, also to take care of his property interests. The principle of the child's welfare has been recognized as a fundamental element of public policy. Consequently, the welfare of the child should be the basic premise of all authorities, courts and organizations and be taken into account in any proceedings concerning the child. The welfare of the child is a priority value that requires preferential treatment over the interests of others, including parents.[46] Thus, the Supreme Court equates the concept of "the welfare of the child" in Polish law with "the interests of the child" in EU, Council of Europe and convention acts.[47]

It should be agreed with the position that consideration of the interests of the child allows the competent public authorities or institutions to maintain the flexibility to assess and adapt protection to the individual case of the child. The aforementioned Article 24(2) of the CFR formulates an absolute legal obligation and applies to every individual decision of a public authority, especially the judiciary, not only in terms of factual findings, but above all in matters of law. The duties of the judicial authority in the application of the law are of particular importance here, since in all orders of states the courts are the bodies that ultimately decide the situation of the child. The implementation of the law through the prism of the overriding value of the interests of the child concerns both the sphere of the use of rules of procedure and

[43] Judgment of the European Court of Human Rights, Grand Chamber, 6 July 2010, 41615/07, LEX No. 584577.

[44] E.g., judgments of the Constitutional Court of 11.10.2011, K 16/10; of 21.01.2014, SK 5/12, Legalis.

[45] Consolidated text Journal of Laws of 2023, item 2809.

[46] Order of the Supreme Court of 2 June 2021, II CSKP 81/21, LEX No. 3219734.

[47] E.g. the Order of the Supreme Court of 20 October 2010, III CZP 72/10, OSNC 2011/5, item 60.

the interpretation of substantive law norms that constitute the substantive justification of decisions concerning children.[48]

In summary, the principle of the primacy of the child's welfare (or the best interests of the child) is both a constitutional, as well as a European and Convention interpretive principle of all legal norms governing the sphere of children's rights. At the same time, this principle is the axiological basis for the permissibility of state intervention in relations between parents and children. The Polish legislator in Articles 18 and 47 of the Polish Constitution[49] protects the family and respects the relationship between parents and children, however, in the event of the emergence of a conflict of values in these spheres, it unequivocally advocates the primacy of the child's welfare, which in some situations, especially in the case of conflict between parents, may order the restriction of the rights of one of the parents.[50] As a result, the welfare of the child, or the best interests of the child, is considered in acts of European Union and Polish law as a value that must be respected. Consideration of the welfare of the child appears not only on the legislative level, but also on the level of law application and interpretation. Even if a law in a particular case does not refer to this indefinite phrase, anyone who decides on or deals with a child's case is obliged to pay special attention to the child's welfare. These norms provide the basis for a universal obligation to respect the welfare of the child by all authorities, offices and persons.[51] This also applies to the judicial authorities, which are supposed to ensure that the child is treated as a subject of civil proceedings, using such instruments as listening to the child. It is impossible to imagine the realization of the idea of the child's welfare in the justice system without hearing the child's rational views.

8.3 Hearing of a Child in Polish Civil Proceedings

8.3.1 Legal Basis for Hearing a Child in Polish Civil Procedural Law

In the Polish legal system, the subjective treatment of the child, including on the grounds of procedural law, is reflected—still on the grounds of applying only the standards of the Council of Europe—in Article 72(1) of the Polish Constitution, according to which the Republic of Poland ensures the protection of children's rights. Everyone has the right to demand that public authorities protect the child from violence, cruelty, exploitation and demoralization. At the same time, in paragraph 3 of this provision, in the course of determining the rights of the child, public authorities and persons responsible for the child are obliged to listen to and, as far as possible,

[48] Majkowska-Szulc and Tomaszewska 2020a, b.

[49] Journal of Law of 1997, item 483.

[50] Order of the Supreme Court of 6 October 2021, I NSNc 357/21, OSNKN 2021/4, item 33.

[51] Smyczyński 2014, p. 56.

take into account the child's opinion. The primary purpose of this provision is not only to empower the child and provide adequate protection, but also to create a statutory framework that will provide such protection.[52]

From the perspective of Polish civil proceedings, the provisions of the Code of Civil Procedure are of particular importance.[53] According to the rules of Polish civil procedural law, civil cases are heard according to two modes—civil trial and non-trial. As a rule, the law transfers civil cases to be heard by trial, and when a case is to be heard by non-trial procedure, it transfers cases to this mode under special provisions (Article 13 § 1 of the Code of Civil Procedure). The non-trial procedure resolves key cases relating to the person of the child, including the entrustment of the exercise, limitation, suspension, deprivation and restoration of parental authority, and the establishment, limitation or prohibition of contact with the child, if they are not resolved in matrimonial proceedings.

To begin with, it should be emphasized that in the Polish legal system, the hearing of a child is not a means of evidence. This is due both to the location of this regulation outside the catalogue of means of evidence, and to the informalized nature of the conduct of this procedural action, deviating from the basic rules of evidence. It seems that the hearing is a source of knowledge of facts relevant to the case, similar in its nature to the so-called informational hearing of the parties or participants in the proceedings.

The legislation due to the peculiarities of each of these modes of Polish civil procedure, has introduced separate rules for hearing the child. In a civil trial, this is regulated by Article 216(1) of the Code of Civil Procedure. The court in cases involving the person of a minor child will hear the child if the child's mental development, state of health and degree of maturity allow it. Thus, in the civil process, the possibility of hearing the child about matters concerning his property is excluded. It is up to the court to assess the child's opinion and wishes, as expressed during the hearing, and should take into account the totality of the relations of each individual case. In other words, the fulfilment of these prerequisites must be evaluated by the court in light of the circumstances of the case in relation to the specific minor child. Since the child's hearing is a procedural act, both its conduct and omission are decided by the court, that is, by the court's panel, and not by its chairman.[54] As indicated in the doctrine, the Polish legislation does not provide for an indirect hearing. This term refers to a form of familiarization with the child's opinion and wishes not directly by the court, but through other entities (such as an opinion panel of court specialists, a psychologist or a guardian). This means that the so-called indirect hearing does not meet the requirements of Article 216(1) of the CCP. However, this does not exclude that in certain cases the court may become acquainted with the child's opinion through other entities, especially when the child's mental development, health or maturity prevents the use of Article 216(1) of the CCP.[55] The hearing

[52] Borysiak 2016, p. 1650.

[53] Consolidated text Journal of Law of 2024, item 1568.

[54] Supreme Court ruling of 13 December 2013, SNO 35/13, Legalis.

[55] Cieśliński 2024a.

of the child is voluntary, so if before the court the child refuses to participate in the hearing, the court will waive this act.

The hearing of the child is not exclusive of the nature of a formal activity irrelevant to the court's decision, because according to the circumstances, the child's mental development, state of health and degree of maturity, the court will take into account the child's opinion and reasonable wishes. At the same time, the legislation has rightly recognized that it is necessary to provide him with appropriate conditions that minimize his stress resulting from the situation of contact with the judicial body. For this reason, the child may be heard only once during the proceedings, unless significant circumstances come to light that require a second hearing. The re-hearing of the child shall be conducted by the same court, unless this is impossible or is prevented by the child's best interests. It is apt that unnecessary repetition of actions involving minors should be avoided. The deviations should be allowed only exceptionally, when it is necessary and, moreover, consistent with the welfare of the minor. If the hearing of the child is waived (including again, e.g., at the request of a party to the proceedings) no later than before the end of the proceedings, it shall be indicated in the minutes of the meeting or hearing for what reasons this activity was not carried out. Unjustified abandonment of the hearing of the child is a violation of procedural law, which practically always affects the outcome of the case, although it does not lead to the invalidity of civil proceedings due to deprivation of the opportunity to defend the rights of the child. On the other hand, in non-trial proceedings, the court in cases involving the person or property of the child will hear the child if his mental development, health and maturity allow it, taking into account, as far as possible, his reasonable wishes. The hearing is held outside the courtroom (Article 576 § 2 of the Code of Civil Procedure). The formalized nature of the hearing is accepted in the case law of Polish family courts. For example, in one of the rulings it was pointed out that the case of a minor expressed her opinion, admittedly only in a telephone conversation, but in the court's opinion a girl of 16 knows what she is saying, even if she says it only on the phone.[56] For this hearing, the provisions on hearing in a civil trial shall apply accordingly.

The appropriateness of hearing the child was emphasized by the Supreme Court, which stated that guided by expediency, taking into account the degree of maturity of the minor and the nature of the guardianship case, the competent court should familiarize itself with the position of the child, with a view to his welfare.[57] However, the position of the Supreme Court has emerged that the obligation to provide the child with an opportunity to be heard in any proceedings that affect him does not mean that the child in a case for the termination of parental authority over him is granted the status of a participant in the proceedings.[58] However, it is difficult to agree with this position, since in important matters of the child—and parental authority is undoubtedly one of these—the child should be the subject and not the object of

---

[56] Order of the District Court for the Capital City of Warsaw of 16 October 2018, VI Nsm 975/18, Legalis.

[57] Order of Supreme Court of 15 December 1998, I CKN 1122/98, Legalis.

[58] Order of Supreme Court of 16 December 1997, III CZP 63/97, Legalis.

the proceedings. Similarly, in adoption cases, the purpose of the hearing is to obtain information from the child regarding, for example, his relationship with the adopter, their mutual understanding and the level of adherence. Thus, the hearing can provide the court with information relevant to assessing whether the adoption and the type of adoption will be consistent with the welfare of the child, of decisive importance in determining whether the adoption can be ordered.[59] In the case of abandoning the hearing of the adoptee, the court should explain the reasons for this decision. This is necessary in order to assess the legitimacy of this decision and refute a possible charge of unjustified omission of the duty to hear the adoptee.[60] Consequently, it can be pointed out that an element of the child's subjectivity in civil proceedings will be both the right to be heard and the granting of the child the status of a participant in the proceedings. Regarding the latter element, there is still no clear position taken by some European Union member states.

This does not change the fact that the Polish legislation develops the institution of the hearing of the child, making it the basis for the implementation of procedural guarantees of the child's subjectivity, especially with regard to cases relating to relations between children and parents. In this way, the above-mentioned principle of protecting the welfare of the child can be fully realized.

8.3.2 *Procedure for Hearing of a Child*

As stipulated in Article 216(2) of the Code of Civil Procedure, the child's hearing shall be held in a closed session, which shall be held in suitably adapted premises at the seat of the court or, if the child's welfare so requires, outside the seat of the court. Thus, flexibility is left to judges in the choice of the hearing room, which should be adapted primarily to the age of the child. The hearing venue should be "friendly" and give the child a sense of security. Currently, in Polish civil procedural law, there is no possibility of a remote form of hearing a child.

In addition to the judge, only an expert psychologist may participate in the child's hearing if, due to the child's health, mental development or age, it is necessary to provide psychological assistance during the hearing or it is necessary to assist the judge in identifying the child's needs during the hearing. In order for the court to decide on the participation of a psychologist in the hearing, it is necessary to know the child's situation in advance. This can be done by means of a probation interview, or possibly by material provided by the parties (e.g. psychological opinions, medical documents, opinions on the student, etc.).[61] The legislation has determined that this activity may not involve a protocol officer, another expert (such as a doctor of another specialty), the parties and their attorneys, as well as other subjects of the proceedings (even public interest advocates). It is an oversight of the legislation that the provision

---

[59] Order of Supreme Court of 2 December 2011, III CSK 65/11, Legalis.

[60] Order of Supreme Court of 22 June 2012, V CSK 283/11, Legalis.

[61] Cieśliński 2024b.

does not provide for the participation of an interpreter, which is, after all, necessary in the situation of a child who does not speak Polish and yet introduces such a possibility in the implementing regulations, which is an obvious inconsistency of the legislation.

An official note is made of the course of the child's hearing. The legislation does not specify the detail of this note, but certainly the course of the hearing cannot remain a secret of the judge and the child, so it should be appropriately detailed. However, the note should not include content that the child has expressed a wish to omit. In addition, the course of the child's hearing shall not be recorded by means of a sound or image and sound recording device. This exclusion is conditioned by psychological considerations but results in the absence of any control over the course of this activity in the appellate instance, which is widely criticized in the doctrine of civil procedural law.[62] It seems that a good solution could be to introduce the recording of activities in a way that is imperceptible to the child. Nevertheless, the best interest of the child takes priority above all.

Detailed rules for conducting a hearing of a child in civil proceedings are set forth in the Ordinance of the Minister of Justice of 21 October 2024 on the manner of preparing and conducting a hearing of a child and the conditions to be met by the premises intended for holding such hearings.[63] As signalled earlier, in order to prepare the child's hearing, the court, on the basis of the case file, during the hearing or interview of the parent, guardian or person under whose custody the child remains, the guardian's interview or the opinion of an expert, shall determine: (1) whether the child's mental development, state of health and degree of maturity make it possible to conduct a hearing; (2) the way the child communicates with the environment and the way the child functions to the extent relevant to establishing contact with the child and conducting a hearing, including the timing of optimal cognitive activity; (3) whether there are special circumstances that justify the presence at the hearing of an expert psychologist. In determining the time and duration of the hearing on a day other than the date of the hearing, the court shall consider the age of the child, the child's state of health and the circumstances regarding the way the child functions. As indicated above, in the case of children who do not speak Polish, children who use Polish sign language, and children with special needs in communication, the court also takes into account the circumstance that the statements will require translation, or the fact that the child uses assistive and alternative communication. When planning the duration of the hearing, the court shall consider that there may be a need to order a break in the conducted hearing.

In notifying of the hearing, the court shall inform of the content of the provisions of the Code of Civil Procedure regarding the hearing of the child and how to document the hearing. The person who is to bring the child to the hearing shall be served by the court with a notice intended for the child, drawn up in a manner understandable to the child, which shall include an explanation of the purpose, manner and place of the hearing, and an instruction that, after arriving at the court and seeing the place of

---

[62] *Ibid.*

[63] Journal of Law of 2024, item 1579.

the hearing, the child will be able to make a decision on participation in the hearing. A child with autism spectrum disorders or intellectual disabilities shall be allowed to view the place of the hearing on the court premises at least two days before the date of the hearing, and the court shall be informed of this when notifying of the hearing. The person with whom the child has come to the hearing should be informed of the expected duration of the hearing and indicated where he can await its completion. If siblings are scheduled to be heard on the same day, the children's hearings shall be held consecutively. The child must be informed of the waiting place of the person with whom he has come to the hearing. Official attire shall not be used during the hearing.

Before the hearing begins, the judge allows the child to become familiar with the place of the hearing or reacquaint himself with the place, explains to the child in a manner that is understandable to him and appropriate to his needs the rules of the hearing and his right to refuse to participate in the hearing, and informs him of the purpose of the hearing, explaining to the child that he is not responsible for the content of the decision that will be made by the court. The judge also explains to the child the role of those participating in the hearing. The judge instructs the child that if he or she does not understand the questions being asked, does not know the answers to certain questions, needs clarification or supplementation, believes that he or she has been misunderstood, or has other needs, he or she should make this known. The judge agrees with the child on how he will signal the situations indicated in the first sentence. When listening: (1) use simple language, ask open-ended questions, avoid figurative statements and messages that contain judgments of those close to the child; (2) do not ask questions that suggest answers; (3) observe the child's reactions and emotions, including fear, anxiety, crying, nervousness, fatigue, weariness, frequency of deferral, and respond appropriately to the situation. If an expert psychologist participates in the hearing, he or she shall assist the judge, as necessary, in explaining in a child-appropriate manner the information that the judge must provide to the child. The expert psychologist shall provide the judge with assistance, as necessary, in formulating questions for the child, and shall observe the child's reactions and emotions, in particular fear, anxiety, crying or nervousness, fatigue and weariness, and shall indicate to the judge ways to support the child and how to respond to situations that obstruct the hearing. At the end of the hearing, the child should be asked if he has any questions for the judge. In addition, at the end of the hearing, the judge shall interview the child on a topic unrelated to the subject of the hearing, and if the hearing is attended by an expert psychologist, if appropriate, take steps to reduce the child's emotional tension associated with participation in the hearing.

The regulation also specifies detailed requirements relating to the appearance and equipment of the place where the hearing will take place. The place of the hearing shall be determined taking into account the needs of the child, taking into account children with special needs. For example, when hearing children who have mental disorders or developmental disorders, it shall be ensured that distractions in the form of bright colours, strong smells and loud sounds are reduced sufficiently to ensure the ability to concentrate and speak freely.

8.4 Perspectives on the Child's Subjectivity in Procedural Law

The future of hearing the child in civil proceedings is a topic of great interest in both legal and social contexts. In the legal systems of the European Union, there is an increasing emphasis on respecting the rights of the child, including his or her right to express his or her own opinions. Key European Union and national laws oblige states to ensure that the child has the opportunity to participate in decisions that affect him or her. In the future, greater standardization of hearing procedures should be sought through the introduction of uniform standards for hearing the child in all procedures involving the child's person and property, while the practice of taking the child's opinion into account must be further introduced. Thus, the courts should give more weight to the child's statements, as long as they are expressed freely and are in the child's best interest.

Both practitioners and legal theorists point to the need to professionalize the process of hearing a child. In this regard, it is necessary to develop training for judges and mediators in communicating with children and recognizing their emotional needs, as well as to make more specific rules for the participation of professionals (such as psychologists or family mediators) who can support the child during the hearing, taking care of the child's comfort and safety. Hearing a child must be done in a way that protects the child's emotional and psychological well-being.

Therefore, one of the crucial areas that can be influenced by the future of shaping the child's subjectivity in terms of procedural law is the development of new technologies. Recital 53 of Regulation No. 2019/1111 already indicates that, without prejudice to other EU instruments, if it is not possible to hear a party or hear a child in person, and if technical means are available, the court may consider conducting the hearing or hearing by videoconference or other communication technology, unless, in light of the particular circumstances of the case, the use of such technology would not be appropriate for the fair conduct of the proceedings. Thus, allowing the child to speak remotely to avoid the stress of being present in court is one possible solution, which the Polish legislature has not currently considered.

Today, Polish law lacks rigid age limits for hearing a child—the decision to do so depends on the court's discretion and the child's ability to understand the situation. In the future, it is worth considering the possibility of providing a professional, individual approach in taking into account the intellectual and emotional abilities and family situation of the child when deciding on a hearing. In Polish procedural law, this should be expressed primarily in providing for the use of special knowledge in determining, among other things, the ability to communicate with the child and the independence of opinions expressed by the child.

The problem in the Polish legal system seems to be the balance between the protection of the child's privacy and the openness of the proceedings. The hearing of the child is a delicate issue that requires reconciliation of different values subject to legal protection. The welfare of the child being the overriding value in this case, which does not exclude ensuring minimal protection of other subjects, e.g. in terms of procedural justice. For this reason, it is necessary to consider within the framework of future EU and Polish procedural regulations a solution that ensures a balance between limiting access to the information disclosed by the child only to the judge, the absence of the parties and their attorneys in order to prevent manipulation of the child or the exertion of pressure on the child by the parents, and ensuring the possibility of verifying the correctness of the conduct of the hearing in the framework of the analysis of the procedural material by the court of second instance, given its importance for the resolution of the case.

There is no doubt that the future of hearing the child in civil proceedings is moving toward greater consideration of the child's voice while ensuring maximum protection of the child's welfare. The key challenges are to ensure that the process is professionalized, to protect it from manipulation, and to further improve the conditions that allow the child to feel comfortable and safe. New technologies, specialized training and legislative developments can play an important role in further shaping the process.

8.5 Conclusion

European Union law, particularly with regard to the protection of the substantive and procedural rights of the child, has had a significant impact on the development of Polish civil procedural law. The implementation of EU legislation, such as Article 24 of the Charter of Fundamental Rights of the European Union, has led to a more explicit consideration of the child's right to be heard in Polish civil proceedings, both in civil trial and non-trial proceedings. In accordance with the standards formed within the framework of the *acquis communautaire* of the European Union and the Council of Europe, Polish law increasingly treats the child as a subject rather than an object of proceedings. The hearing of the child, as an expression of his autonomy and respect for his dignity, has acquired the status of a fundamental procedural right. At the same time, efforts are being made to unify the standards for hearing the child in EU member states, which is reflected in Polish law. Amendments to the Polish Code of Civil Procedure, taking into account the needs and welfare of the child, are also the result of the implementation of EU legal solutions. An example is Article 216(1) of the CCP, which imposes an obligation on the court to hear the child if his mental development, state of health and degree of maturity allow it.

There is no doubt that EU regulations such as Brussels II bis[64] (now replaced by Brussels II ter) have contributed to strengthening mechanisms for the protection of children's rights in cross-border matters, including custody, contact and the exercise of parental responsibility. Hearing the child has become a key element in these cases,

---

[64] Council of the European Union (2003), Council Regulation (EC) No. 2201/2003 of 27 November 2003 concerning jurisdiction and the recognition and enforcement of judgments in matrimonial matters and the matters of parental responsibility, repealing Regulation (EC) No 1347/2000, OJ 2003 L 338 (Brussels II bis).

forcing Polish courts to adapt their procedures to EU requirements. Both regulations apply to all decisions related to parental responsibility. In addition, the rules on jurisdiction, which are mostly based on the child's habitual place of residence, are explicitly structured with the child's best interests in mind. It is also noteworthy that special attention has been paid to the need to respect the views of the child.[65] Although there are still many solutions to be implemented, an example of which is the use of means of remote communication, which the Polish legislator in the current state of the law has excluded with regard to the hearing of the child.

In summary, European Union law is clearly shaping the direction of changes in Polish civil procedural law, contributing to strengthening children's rights and ensuring their fuller protection in court proceedings. The child's hearing is not only an implementation of EU standards, but also a practical step towards increasing children's participation in decision-making processes that directly affect their lives. The future realization of the right to a child's hearing is conditioned by the fact that European Union law imposes an obligation to continuously improve the system for the protection of children's rights. Further amendments to the Polish procedural law can be expected, which will introduce more precise regulations on the hearing of the child. In practice, Polish courts are increasingly taking into account the opinion of the child as a key factor in making decisions in family cases. This process is conducive to strengthening the protection of children's rights and the realization of their best interests.

References

Alston P (1994) The best interests principle: Towards a reconciliation of culture and human rights. International Journal of Law and the Family 8:1–15

Banaszak B, Jabłoński M (1999) In: Boć J (ed) Konstytucje Rzeczypospolitej Polskiej oraz komentarz do Konstytucji RP z 1997 roku [Constitutions of the Republic of Poland and Commentary to the 1997 Constitution of the Republic of Poland]. Wrocław

Besteliu R M, Brumar C (2008) Protecţia internaţională a drepturilor omului, Note de curs, Ed a IV-a revizuită [International Protection of Human Rights, Course Notes, 4th revised edition]. Universul Juridic, Bucharest

Bieszczad M (2019) Dobro dziecka jako klauzula generalna – ustalenie znaczenia pojęcia dobra dziecka w XXI w. [Child welfare as a general clause – establishing the meaning of the concept of child welfare in the 21st century]. Monitor Prawniczy No. 17

Borysiak W (2016) Komentarz do art. 72, Nb 2 [Commentary on Article 72, Side Number 2]. In: Safjan M, Bosek L (eds) Konstytucja RP, t. I. Komentarz. Art. 1-86 [Constitution of the Republic of Poland, vol. I. Commentary. Articles 1-86]. Warsaw

Bosisio R (2012) Children's Right to Be Heard. What Children Think. International Journal of Children's Rights, No. 20

Cała-Wacinkiewicz E, Szwed E (2022) Prawa dzieci do wyrażania własnych poglądów a prawa rodziców do wychowywania dzieci zgodnie z własnymi przekonaniami - uwarunkowania prawnomiędzynarodowe [Children's rights to express their own views versus parents' rights

[65] European Union Agency for Fundamental Rights and Council of Europe 2015, p. 79.

to raise their children in accordance with their own beliefs - international legal considerations]. Studia Prawnicze KUL, No. 1

Carpaneto L (2019) Impact of the best interests of the child on the Brussels II ter Regulation In: Bergamini E, Ragni C (eds) Fundamental Rights and Best Interests of the Child in Transnational Families. Intersentia, Antwerp

Cieśliński M (2024a) Komentarz do art. 216(1), Nb A.6 [Commentary to Article 216(1), Side Number A.6]. In: Rylski P, Olaś A (eds). Kodeks postępowania cywilnego Komentarz. [Code of Civil Procedure. Commentary]. Warsaw

Cieśliński M (2024b) Komentarz do art. 216(2), Nb C.14 [Commentary to Article 216(2), Side Number C.14]. In: Rylski P, Olaś A (eds) Kodeks postępowania cywilnego Komentarz. [Code of Civil Procedure. Commentary]. Warsaw

Delgado Sáez J (2019) The Right of the Child to be Heard in Parental Responsibility Proceedings, In: Boele-Woelki K, Martiny D (eds) Plurality and Diversity of Family Relations in Europe. European Family Law. Intersentia, Antwerp

European Union Agency for Fundamental Rights and Council of Europe (2015) Handbook on European law relating to the rights of the child, https://fra.europa.eu/en/publication/2015/handbook-european-law-relating-rights-child. Accessed 29 January 2025

Gilbert N, Parton N, Skivenes M (2011) Child protection systems: International trends and orientations. New York

Hart R (1992) Children's Participation. From Tokenism to Participation. Florence

Ignaczewski J (2009) Pochodzenie dziecka i władza rodzicielska po nowelizacji. Art. 61[9]–113[6] KRO. Komentarz [The origin of the child and parental authority after the amendment. Art. 61[9]–113[6] of the Family and Guardianship Code. Commentary]. Warsaw

Kołodziejski S (1965) Dobro wspólnych małoletnich dzieci – jako przesłanka odmowy orzeczenia rozwodu [The welfare of minor children as grounds for refusing to grant a divorce]. Palestra No. 9

Majkowska-Szulc S, Tomaszewska M (2020) Komentarz do art. 24, Nb I. 8 [Commentary on Article 24, Side Number I. 8]. In: Wróbel A (ed) Karta Praw Podstawowych Unii Europejskiej Komentarz [Charter of Fundamental Rights of the European Union. Commentary]. Warsaw

Majkowska-Szulc S, Tomaszewska M (2020) Komentarz do art. 24, Nb IV.7 [Commentary on Article 24, Side Number IV.7]. In: Wróbel A (ed) Karta Praw Podstawowych Unii Europejskiej Komentarz. [Charter of Fundamental Rights of the European Union. Commentary].Warsaw

Mal Ch (2019) Maturity and the Child's Right to be Heard in Family Law Proceedings: Article 12 UNCRC and Case Law of the ECtHR Compared In: Boel-Wielki K, Martiny D (eds) Plurality and Diversity of Family Relations in Europe. European Family Law

Marciniak J (1975) Treść i sprawowanie opieki nad małoletnim [Content and exercise of parental authority over a minor]. Warsaw

McGlynn C (2002) Rights for Children? The Potential Impact of the European Union Charter of Fundamental Rights. European Public Law 8(3)

Petrova T (2018) The twofold approach to children's freedom of movement rights under European law: Can 'children's equilibrium' guide the interpretation of the post-Brexit rights of UK children residing in the EU? Croatian Yearbook of European Law & Policy 14

Pretelli I (2016) Child Abduction and Return Proceedings In: Recasting the Brussels IIa Regulation, Workshop 8 November 2016 Compilation of briefings No. 17, https://www.eumonitor.eu/9353000/1/j9vvik7m1c3gyxp/vk8mjcu4rcvg?d=08-05-2018#:~:text=Compilation%20of%20briefings%20for%20the%20JURI%20Committee. Accessed 29 January 2025

Rodríguez Pineau E (2017) La refundición del Reglamento Bruselas II bis: de nuevo sobre la función del Derecho internacional privado europeo [The recast of the Brussels IIa Regulation: once again on the role of European private international law]. Revista Española De Derecho Internacional 69

Salomia O M (2012) The role of the European Union Charter of Fundamental Rights in the new European context. Lex ET Scientia International Journal, No. XIX(2)

Smyczyński T (ed) (2014) System Prawa Prywatnego [System of Private Law], t. 11. Prawo rodzinne i opiekuńcze. Warsaw

Sokołowski T (1996a) Skutki prawne rozwodu [Legal effects of divorce]. Poznań

Sokołowski T (1996b) Władza rodzicielska nad dorastającym dzieckiem [Parental authority over an adolescent child]. Poznań

Stalford H (2005) Constitutionalising Equality in The European Union: A Children's Rights perspective. International Journal of Discrimination and the Law 8

Stalford H (2015) The CRC in Litigation under EU Law In: Liefaard T, Doek JE (eds) Litigating the Rights of the Child: The UN Convention on the Rights of the Child in Domestic and International Jurisprudence. Springer

Stalford H, Hollingsworth K, Gilmore S (2017) Introducing Children's Rights Judgments In: Stalford H, Hollingsworth K, Gilmore S (eds) Rewriting Children's Rights Judgments: From Academic Vision to New Practice. Hart Publishing

Stojanowska W (1999) Dobro dziecka jako instrument wykładni norm konwencji o prawach dziecka oraz prawa polskiego i jako dyrektywa jego stosowania [The welfare of the child as an instrument for interpreting the norms of the Convention on the Rights of the Child and Polish law, and as a guideline for its application]. In: Smyczyński T (ed) Konwencja o prawach dziecka. Analiza i wykładnia [Convention on the Rights of the Child. Analysis and interpretation]. Poznań

Wojtaszek-Mik E (2022) Dobro dziecka a odmowa jego wydania na podstawie art. 13 ust. 1 lit. b Konwencji haskiej dotyczącej cywilnych aspektów uprowadzenia dziecka za granicę [The best interests of the child and refusal to surrender the child pursuant to Article 13(1)(b) of The Hague Convention on the Civil Aspects of International Child Abduction]. Prawo w Działaniu, No. 50

Zalisko M (2022) In: Gołaczyński J (ed) Jurysdykcja, uznawanie i wykonywanie orzeczeń w sprawach małżeńskich i w sprawach dotyczących odpowiedzialności rodzicielskiej oraz w sprawie uprowadzenia dziecka za granicę [Jurisdiction, recognition, and enforcement of judgments in matrimonial matters, matters of parental responsibility, and matters of child abduction]. Komentarz do Rozporządzenia Rady UE 2019/1111 [Commentary on EU Council Regulation 2019/1111]. Warsaw

Kinga Flaga-Gieruszyńska is a Dr. Hab., a Professor of the University of Szczecin, and a Vice-Rector for Organization at the University of Szczecin.

Aleksandra Klich is a Dr., and a Visiting Senior Lecturer at the Law Faculty of Vilnius University.

Chapter 9
Amendments in the Legal Acts Dealing with Criminal Offences in Lithuania: Impact and Insights for the Future

Ligita Gasparėnienė and Rita Remeikienė

Contents

Abstract This chapter examines the relationship between economic conditions, legislative amendments and crime trends, contributing to the understanding of the causes of crime and the socio-economic factors influencing it. Crime imposes significant social costs, hindering socio-economic development at all levels. Although crime trends vary over time and across regions, many patterns co-vary internationally despite differences in political and socio-economic conditions or crime policies. Macro-level variations and similarities in crime trends have been explained through diverse frameworks, with cross-national and longitudinal research on crime rates gaining importance. Focusing on Lithuania, this study utilises national statistical data and other sources to explore how amendments to legal acts on criminal offences affect crime trends. It addresses the central question: can economic conditions and legislative changes explain crime trends across time and place? The results showed that economic conditions and legislative amendments in Lithuania significantly, though unevenly, impact crime trends. Effective legislative strategies require

L. Gasparėnienė (✉) · R. Remeikienė
Faculty of Law, Vilnius University, Vilnius, Lithuania
e-mail: ligita.gaspareniene@tf.vu.lt

R. Remeikienė
e-mail: rita.remeikiene@tf.vu.lt

I. Isokaitė-Valužė and H. Šinkūnas (eds.), *The European Union 2004-2024*,
https://doi.org/10.1007/978-94-6265-718-2_9

a thorough analysis of social and economic factors and alignment with broader policies tackling social inequality, unemployment, and other factors driving criminal behaviour, ensuring meaningful contributions to public safety, social cohesion, and justice.

Keywords Crime trends · Criminal law · Economy · EU directives regulation · Legislative amendments · Legislative frameworks · Lithuania's law

9.1 Introduction

Crime is a pervasive issue that significantly impacts the stability and development of societies. It imposes substantial social and economic costs, distorting progress and affecting communities on multiple levels.[1] While crime trends vary across time and regions, certain patterns often align internationally,[2] regardless of differing political systems, socio-economic conditions, or crime policies.[3] These macro-level similarities and variations have been explored through longitudinal and cross-national research,[4] which has emerged as a crucial field for understanding global crime dynamics.[5]

This study examines Lithuania's unique context to assess the influence of legislative amendments on crime trends. By utilizing national statistical data and other relevant sources, it evaluates the effectiveness of legal reforms and their broader societal implications. The research also highlights the critical role of economic factors in shaping crime patterns,[6] as socio-economic inequalities and unemployment often act as catalysts for criminal behaviour.[7]

Through an analysis of changes in Lithuania's legal framework, particularly in response to EU directives and international obligations, this chapter contributes to the broader discourse on the interplay between legislative measures, socio-economic factors, and crime trends. It aims to provide valuable insights for policymakers, emphasizing strategies that align legal reforms with broader social policies to promote equity and public safety.

---

[1] Cohen and Bowles 2010, pp. 143–162.

[2] Eisner 2009, pp. 40–59.

[3] Tonry 2016, pp. 1–37.

[4] Eisner 2014, pp. 289–386.

[5] Lehti and Sirén 2020, pp. 245–263.

[6] Baumer et al. 2018, pp. 39–61.

[7] Rosenfeld and Messner 2013, pp. 68–97.

9.2 Reform of Lithuanian Criminal Law

Lithuanian criminal law has undergone significant reforms since the restoration of independence in 1990, with a major milestone marked by Lithuania's accession to the European Union in 2004.[8] These changes align with both the country's transition to democracy and its integration into the international legal community.[9] Over the decades, the legal system has evolved to move away from its Soviet legal heritage, adopting a modern framework based on democratic principles. These reforms reflect the country's efforts to safeguard human rights, uphold the rule of law, and harmonize its national legislation with international and European Union standards. Below are the key legal acts and amendments that have shaped Lithuanian criminal law:

1. **1991 Criminal Code Reform**. Following independence, Lithuania initially adapted the Soviet-era Criminal Code of 1961 to remove ideological influences and ensure compliance with the democratic principles outlined in the Constitution.[10] These reforms encompassed the decriminalisation of certain offences, reflecting a shift towards a more liberal legal philosophy, and the incorporation of robust legal safeguards to protect human rights and fundamental freedoms.
2. **2000 Criminal Code**. The adoption of Lithuania's new Criminal Code in 2000 marked a critical milestone in the modernisation of its legal system, replacing the outdated Soviet-era framework with a contemporary model aligned with democratic principles and international human rights standards.[11] A significant feature of this reform was the clear distinction drawn between crimes and misdemeanours, which facilitated a more nuanced and proportionate legal approach to offences. This was further reinforced by the introduction of the proportionality principle in sentencing, ensuring that penalties were tailored to the gravity of the offence and its specific circumstances, thus promoting fairness and justice. Another noteworthy innovation was the incorporation of restorative justice mechanisms, reflecting Lithuania's adherence to international commitments such as the International Covenant on Civil and Political Rights.[12] Restorative practices aimed to repair the harm caused by criminal acts through inclusive processes that engaged victims, offenders, and the wider community, fostering reconciliation

[8] Treaty concerning the Accession of the Czech Republic, the Republic of Estonia, the Republic of Cyprus, the Republic of Latvia, the Republic of Lithuania, the Republic of Hungary, the Republic of Malta, the Republic of Poland, the Republic of Slovenia and the Slovak Republic to the European Union, signed 16 April 2003, entered into force 1 May 2004. https://eur-lex.europa.eu/legal-content/EN/TXT/?uri=OJ:L:2003:236:TOC. Accessed 5 January 2025.

[9] Constitution of the Republic of Lithuania, adopted on 25 October 1992 (English version). https://e-seimas.lrs.lt/portal/legalAct/lt/TAD/TAIS.21892?jfwid=-g0zrzp4le. Accessed 29 January 2025.

[10] Constitution of Lithuania 1992, see footnote 9 above.

[11] Criminal Code of the Republic of Lithuania, adopted on 26 September 2000, No. VIII-1968, entered into force on 1 May 2003 (English version). https://e-seimas.lrs.lt/portal/legalAct/lt/TAD/TAIS.111555?jfwid=-g0zrzp4le. Accessed 14 April 2025.

[12] International Covenant on Civil and Political Rights, adopted by the UN General Assembly on 16 December 1966, entered into force 23 March 1976. https://www.ohchr.org/en/instruments-mechanisms/instruments/international-covenant-civil-and-political-rights. Accessed 8 April 2025.

and reducing recidivism. These comprehensive changes underscored Lithuania's dedication to building a criminal justice system that prioritises human rights, equity, and effective governance.

3. **Post-2004 Amendments**. Following Lithuania's accession to the European Union in 2004, the nation undertook extensive amendments to its Criminal Code to ensure alignment with EU legal standards and obligations. A primary focus of these reforms was the enhancement of measures to combat organised crime, human trafficking, and terrorism.[13] Furthermore, significant advancements were made in protecting victims' rights, particularly those of minors, reflecting the provisions outlined in Directive 2012/29/EU.[14] Reforms also addressed emerging challenges in environmental crime and financial fraud.[15] These amendments underscored Lithuania's commitment to integrating EU legal principles while addressing contemporary issues in criminal justice and upholding high standards of victim protection and crime prevention.
4. **Recent Amendments**. Recent amendments to Lithuania's Criminal Code have been shaped by the evolving challenges posed by technological advancements and societal shifts. Enhanced regulations on cybercrime, in alignment with the Budapest Convention on Cybercrime,[16] address the growing threat of digital offences, ensuring a robust legal framework for combating cybercriminal activities. Additionally, stronger penalties for hate crimes and domestic violence reflect a national commitment to protecting vulnerable individuals and fostering a more inclusive society.[17] The reforms also place greater emphasis on alternative sanctions, reducing the reliance on imprisonment and promoting rehabilitation, in accordance with Directive (EU) 2019/1937.[18] These updates demonstrate Lithuania's proactive approach to modernising its legal system to meet contemporary demands while maintaining a focus on justice and human rights.

The evolution of Lithuanian criminal law has been firmly grounded in core principles and international obligations, reflecting a commitment to modern legal standards and global cooperation. Central to these reforms is the principle of the rule of law,

---

[13] Council Framework Decision 2002/475/JHA of 13 June 2002 on combating terrorism, OJ L 164, 22.6.2002, p. 3–7. https://eur-lex.europa.eu/legal-content/EN/TXT/?uri=CELEX%3A32002F0475. Accessed 11 April 2025.

[14] Directive 2012/29/EU of the European Parliament and of the Council of 25 October 2012 establishing minimum standards on the rights, support and protection of victims of crime, and replacing Council Framework Decision 2001/220/JHA, OJ L 315, 14.11.2012, pp. 57–73.

[15] Directive 2008/99/EC of the European Parliament and of the Council of 19 November 2008 on the protection of the environment through criminal law, OJ L 328, 6.12.2008, pp. 28–37.

[16] Council of Europe, Convention on Cybercrime, Budapest, 23 November 2001, ETS No. 185. https://www.coe.int/en/web/conventions/full-list?module=treaty-detail&treatynum=185. Accessed 19 October 2024.

[17] Information Technology and Communications Department under the Ministry of the Interior of the Republic of Lithuania, Crime Statistics 2022, 2023. https://osp.stat.gov.lt/en/nusikalstamumas-ir-baudziamoji-teisena1. Accessed 12 April 2025.

[18] Directive (EU) 2019/1937 of the European Parliament and of the Council of 23 October 2019 on the protection of persons who report breaches of Union law, OJ L 305, 26.11.2019, pp. 17–56.

which demands that all legal actions are predictable, transparent, and grounded in established legal frameworks. This includes the principle of proportionality, ensuring that penalties are carefully calibrated to correspond with the severity and circumstances of each offence, in line with Article 7 of the European Convention on Human Rights. Furthermore, the protection and promotion of human rights have been integral to Lithuania's legal development, with reforms designed to uphold the rights and freedoms enshrined in the EU Charter of Fundamental Rights.[19]

Equally significant has been Lithuania's dedication to integrating international legal norms into its criminal justice system. This includes implementing obligations under key global treaties, such as the United Nations Convention against Corruption, which establishes comprehensive measures to prevent, detect, and combat corruption in both the public and private sectors.[20] These foundational principles and commitments reflect Lithuania's resolve to create a criminal justice system that not only addresses domestic concerns but also aligns seamlessly with international legal and ethical standards, ensuring justice, fairness, and respect for human dignity in a globalised context.

The evolution of Lithuanian criminal law demonstrates a consistent effort to modernize the legal framework, uphold individual rights, and address emerging challenges. The incorporation of EU directives and international conventions illustrates Lithuania's commitment to an effective and democratic criminal justice system.[21] See Table 9.1.

The reforms in Lithuanian criminal law from 1992 to 2024 represent a significant evolution from a Soviet-era legal framework to a modern, democratic system aligned with international standards. These changes reflect Lithuania's commitment to addressing contemporary challenges such as organised crime, human trafficking, and financial fraud, while also emphasising the protection of human rights and the promotion of restorative justice. The gradual incorporation of EU directives and international conventions has ensured a robust legal system capable of safeguarding societal equity and individual dignity. Collectively, these reforms demonstrate Lithuania's proactive approach to fostering a fair, effective, and adaptable criminal justice system.

The reforms in Lithuanian criminal law were guided by key principles that prioritised fairness, human rights, and rehabilitation. The rule of law ensured penalties aligned with the severity of crimes, fostering fairness and transparency, as exemplified by the 2000 Criminal Code's focus on proportionality in sentencing. Emphasis on human rights protection permeated the reforms, introducing standards for victim protection in line with the EU Charter of Fundamental Rights and

---

[19] Charter of Fundamental Rights of the European Union, proclaimed at Nice on 7 December 2000, OJ C 364, 18.12.2000, pp. 1–22.

[20] United Nations, Convention against Corruption, adopted by the UN General Assembly resolution 58/4 of 31 October 2003, entered into force 14 December 2005, UN Treaty Series, vol. 2349, p. 41. https://treaties.un.org/doc/Publication/UNTS/Volume%202349/v2349.pdf. Accessed 10 December 2024.

[21] Council of Europe, Rule of Law Checklist, European Commission for Democracy through Law (Venice Commission), Strasbourg, 2021. https://www.venice.coe.int/webforms/documents/default.aspx?pdffile=CDL-AD(2016)007-e. Accessed 12 April 2025.

Table 9.1 Chronology of Lithuanian criminal law reforms (1992–2024)

Year	Reform	Description	Source
1992	Transition from Soviet Criminal Law	Eliminated Soviet ideological influences and aligned the legal framework with democratic values	*Constitution of the Republic of Lithuania (1992)*[22]
2000	Adoption of a New Criminal Code	Replaced the Soviet-era Criminal Code with a modernised framework	*Criminal Code of the Republic of Lithuania (2000)*[23]
2002	EU Accession and Harmonisation	Amendments to harmonise with EU directives addressing organised crime and victims' rights	*Council Framework Decision 2002/475/JHA*[24]
2015	Strengthened Hate Crime Legislation	Introduced stricter penalties and clearer definitions for hate crimes	*Council of Europe, Recommendations on Hate Crime (2015)*[25]
2016	Introduction of Electronic Monitoring	Implemented electronic monitoring as an alternative to imprisonment	*Council of Europe (2016)*[26]
2017	Enhanced Anti-Human Trafficking Laws	Strengthened protections for trafficking victims, particularly minors	*Directive 2011/36/EU*[27]

(continued)

[22] Constitution of Lithuania 1992, see footnote 9 above.

[23] Criminal Code of the Republic of Lithuania 2000, see footnote 11 above.

[24] Council Framework Decision 2002/475/JHA, see footnote 13 above.

[25] Council of Europe, ECRI General Policy Recommendation No. 15 on Combating Hate Speech, adopted on 8 December 2015, European Commission against Racism and Intolerance (ECRI), Strasbourg. https://rm.coe.int/ecri-general-policy-recommendation-no-15-on-combating-hate-speech/16808b5b01. Accessed 13 April 2025.

[26] Council of Europe, Standards and Ethics in Electronic Monitoring, Strasbourg, 2016. https://rm.coe.int/handbook-standards-ethics-in-electronic-monitoring-eng/16806ab9b0. Accessed 28 January 2025.

[27] Directive 2011/36/EU of the European Parliament and of the Council of 5 April 2011 on preventing and combating trafficking in human beings and protecting its victims, and replacing Council Framework Decision 2002/629/JHA, OJ L 101, 15.4.2011, pp. 1–11.

Table 9.1 (continued)

Year	Reform	Description	Source
2019	Measures Against Money Laundering	Tightened measures against money laundering and financial fraud	*Directive 2018/843/EU*[28]
2022	Domestic Violence and Hate Crime Reforms	Introduced harsher penalties for domestic violence and hate crimes	*Ministry of the Interior of the Republic of Lithuania (2022)*
2022	Adjustments to Economic and Financial Crimes	Raised thresholds for criminal liability in property and financial offences	*Ministry of Justice of Lithuania, Report on Criminal Law Amendments (2022)*
2024	Comprehensive Updates to Criminal Liability	Systematised penalties for corporate entities and expanded alternative sanctions	*Criminal Code Reform, Lithuania (2024)*[29]

Source The authors

[28] Directive (EU) 2018/843 of the European Parliament and of the Council of 30 May 2018 amending Directive (EU) 2015/849 on the prevention of the use of the financial system for the purposes of money laundering or terrorist financing, and amending Directives 2009/138/EC and 2013/36/EU, OJ L 156, 19.6.2018, pp. 43–74.

[29] Government of the Republic of Lithuania, Explanatory Note on Amendments to the Criminal Code [Aiškinamasis raštas dėl Baudžiamojo kodekso pakeitimų, Lt.], 2024. https://lrv.lt/media/viesa/saugykla/2024/3/q3-74fz8yds.pdf. Accessed 12 April 2025.

enhancing safeguards against hate crimes and domestic violence to promote equity and dignity. Additionally, the shift towards restorative justice encouraged rehabilitative approaches, including practices like electronic monitoring, reducing the reliance on imprisonment and promoting reintegration into society.

By integrating these principles and international provisions, Lithuania has progressively built a criminal justice system that balances the dual objectives of maintaining societal order and upholding individual rights. The reforms reflect a thoughtful convergence of domestic priorities and international commitments, enabling Lithuania to navigate the complexities of a globalised legal environment.

9.3 Motivation for Legislative Changes

The evolution of Lithuania's legal framework has been significantly influenced by various factors, including rising crime rates, public pressure, international obligations, and socio-economic transformations. Notably, the integration of European Union (EU) directives has played a crucial role in shaping national legislation, particularly in areas concerning criminal justice and legal protection.

The main EU directives that significantly influenced Lithuania's criminal law include:

- **Directive 2011/36/EU[30] on combating human trafficking**. Establishes minimum standards for defining offences and penalties related to human trafficking and provides measures for victim protection and assistance.
- **Directive 2011/93/EU[31] on combating sexual abuse and child pornography**. Introduces criminal measures against sexual exploitation of children, child prostitution, and child pornography, including minimum penalties and preventive actions.
- **Directive 2014/42/EU[32] on the confiscation of criminal assets**. Sets rules for the freezing and confiscation of criminally acquired assets to prevent criminal organisations from benefiting from illegal gains.
- **Directive 2013/40/EU[33] on attacks against information systems**. Criminalises unlawful access, system interference, and data interference, with specific sanctions for such offences.

[30] Directive 2011/36/EU, see footnote 27 above.

[31] Directive 2011/93/EU of the European Parliament and of the Council of 13 December 2011 on combating the sexual abuse and sexual exploitation of children and child pornography, and replacing Council Framework Decision 2004/68/JHA, OJ L 335, 17.12.2011, pp. 1–14.

[32] Directive 2014/42/EU of the European Parliament and of the Council of 3 April 2014 on the freezing and confiscation of instrumentalities and proceeds of crime in the European Union, OJ L 127, 29.4.2014, pp. 39–50.

[33] Directive 2013/40/EU of the European Parliament and of the Council of 12 August 2013 on attacks against information systems and replacing Council Framework Decision 2005/222/JHA, OJ L 218, 14.8.2013, pp. 8–14.

- **Directive 2008/99/EC[34] on environmental protection through criminal law**. Requires Member States to impose criminal sanctions for certain environmental law violations to enhance environmental protection.

These directives have been integrated into Lithuania's Criminal Code, aligning national legislation with EU requirements and strengthening the legal framework to combat these crimes.

In response to increasing crime rates, Lithuania has implemented legislative amendments aimed at enhancing public safety and aligning with EU standards. For instance, the adoption of the Law on the Prevention of Organized Crime reflects efforts to address complex criminal activities and comply with EU directives on combating organized crime.[35] This legislation underscores the country's commitment to harmonizing its legal system with broader European frameworks.

Public pressure has also been a catalyst for legal reforms, especially concerning environmental protection. Significant environmental incidents have prompted the enactment of stricter regulations to ensure compliance with EU environmental directives. These measures aim to uphold the precautionary and preventive principles, as well as the "polluter pays" principle, thereby enhancing environmental governance.[36] Strengthened legal protection mechanisms for the rights of environmental human rights defenders is an urgent need to achieve the Sustainable Development Goals and the environmental rule of law.[37] Proedrou and Pournara[38] have highlighted that climate change is increasingly framed as ecocide, with a focus on the role of the capitalist system and anthropocentric ethics in perpetuating environmental and social injustices. While the criminalisation of ecocide may not guarantee a rapid phase-out of fossil fuels, it holds potential as a significant tool for strengthening climate policy by facilitating cases before the International Criminal Court and promoting the adoption of national legislation. Proedrou and Pournara[39] argue that green criminology offers a valuable perspective by framing actions contributing to climate change as criminal behaviour rather than merely business practices subject to reform or eco-modernisation. This perspective highlights the necessity of legislative innovations in Lithuania to align with international efforts to strengthen environmental protection measures, address ecological harm, and foster valuable discussions that contribute to improved legal regulation and more effective environmental protection. In Lithuania, the "polluter pays" principle is applied across various economic sectors, particularly

---

[34] Directive 2008/99/EC, see footnote 15 above.

[35] Republic of Lithuania, Law on the Prevention of Organised Crime, No. XIII-3068, adopted on 23 June 2020, entered into force on 1 July 2020. https://e-seimas.lrs.lt/portal/legalAct/lt/TAD/f225c030b6a911ea9a12d0dada3ca61b. Accessed 12 April 2025.

[36] The Annual Legal Review 2022, presented at the Constitutional Court of the Republic of Lithuania, 22 February 2023. https://www.mruni.eu/en/news/the-annual-law-review-presented-constitutional-court/. Accessed 12 April 2025.

[37] Oral 2024, pp. 393–421.

[38] Proedrou and Pournara 2024a, pp. 1–14.

[39] Proedrou and Pournara 2024b, pp. 1–19.

those with a direct impact on the environment. The main sectors subject to this principle include:

- **Industry and energy**. Companies emitting pollutants into the air, water, or soil are required to pay pollution taxes and invest in environmental protection measures. For example, thermal power plants and manufacturing enterprises.
- **Agriculture**. This sector is associated with the use of fertilisers and pesticides, livestock waste management, and water pollution. Farmers must comply with environmental regulations and may face taxes or fines for pollution.
- **Transport**. Road transport operators pay fees for emissions, while freight carriers are taxed for fuel-related pollution. The use of less polluting vehicles is also encouraged.
- **Waste management**. Companies generating significant waste or managing it (e.g., waste incineration plants) are taxed based on pollution levels.
- **Construction sector**. Developers must compensate for environmental impacts such as damage to soil, forests, or biodiversity caused during construction.
- **Oil and gas sector**. Companies involved in oil or gas extraction, processing, and transportation are obligated to pay pollution taxes for emissions.
- **Water supply and wastewater management**. Wastewater treatment facilities are charged for discharging untreated or insufficiently treated wastewater into water bodies.

These sectors must adhere to the "polluter pays" principle by paying pollution taxes, implementing pollution reduction measures, and compensating for environmental damage. In Lithuania, this principle is regulated by legislation related to environmental protection and the use of natural resources.

International obligations, particularly those arising from EU membership, have necessitated the transposition of EU legal acts into Lithuania's national legal system. This process, while essential for legal harmonization, has presented challenges due to the complexities involved in integrating EU laws with national legislation. Addressing these challenges requires a deep understanding of the origins and objectives of EU directives to ensure effective implementation.[40] Socio-economic transformations have further influenced legislative changes. The transition to a market economy and shifts in social dynamics have led to reforms in various legal sectors, including labour law and social policy. These reforms aim to align national laws with EU standards, facilitating smoother integration into the European single market and promoting social cohesion.[41]

Lithuania has already undergone a significant stage in its economic development by transitioning from a centralised (planned) economy to a market economy. This transition facilitated the country's integration into international markets, creating

[40] European Commission (2023) Country report non-discrimination: Transposition and implementation at national level of Council Directives 2000/43 and 2000/78: Lithuania 2023. Publications Office of the European Union. https://op.europa.eu/en/publication-detail/-/publication/22599516-8a8a-11ee-99ba-01aa75ed71a1/language-en. Accessed 4 December 2024.

[41] The Annual Legal Review 2022, see footnote 36 above.

opportunities for economic growth and competitiveness. However, today, economic transformation continues, with a focus on transitioning towards a sustainable and circular economy, which not only promotes the conservation of natural resources but also aims to establish a more efficient production and consumption system.

The constitutions of European states reflect diverse approaches to sustainability; however, the Lithuanian Constitutional Court treats it as an intergenerational social contract. Lithuania's legal system highlights the potential of green public procurement to foster sustainable development by allowing for error correction and ensuring compliance with environmental requirements. In the field of international investment, sustainability principles are often confined to models, underscoring the need for greater investor accountability and mandatory legal mechanisms. Ensuring sustainability also faces challenges in the area of data protection, where a balance must be struck between environmental goals and individual privacy rights.[42]

In the context of sustainable work, there is a call to clearly define principles of sustainable labour and implement stricter legal mechanisms to safeguard workers' rights. Private law also plays a significant role in promoting sustainability, for example, through the use of long-lasting products and the inclusion of sustainability clauses in commercial contracts. In Lithuania, environmental offences are predominantly addressed through administrative and civil remedies, emphasising the need for broader application of criminal liability in this domain.[43]

The essence of a circular economy is to ensure that products and materials are used for as long as possible, waste is recycled, and natural resources are preserved. This requires fundamental changes not only in business and production sectors but also in the legal system. The shift from a linear to a circular economy in Lithuania poses certain challenges for criminal law. The main challenges include:[44]

1. **Updating Legal Regulations**. Current legislation may be insufficient to regulate new circular economy models. There is a need to review and update criminal laws to encompass new offences related to circular economy processes, such as illegal waste recycling, hazardous waste management, or theft of secondary raw materials.
2. **Establishing Responsibility**. A circular economy involves many different actors across various stages of production, consumption, and recycling. This complicates the process of determining responsibility for potential offences, such as environmental pollution or illegal waste handling.
3. **Emergence of New Offences**. The transition to a circular economy may lead to the emergence of new offences, such as fraud involving recycling certificates, illegal export or import of secondary raw materials, or intellectual property violations linked to the design of recycled products.
4. **International Cooperation**. The circular economy often includes international processes, such as the export and import of waste for recycling. This necessitates

---

[42] Bartolacelli and Sagatienė 2023.

[43] *Ibid.*

[44] Camplani 2021, p. 263.

stronger collaboration among international law enforcement agencies to combat cross-border crimes related to illegal waste transport or secondary raw material trade.

5. **Raising Public Awareness**. To prevent crimes associated with the circular economy, it is essential to increase public awareness of lawful waste management and recycling practices, promote responsible consumption, and encourage reporting of potential violations.

Criminal law in Lithuania must adapt to this new economic direction to ensure that the principles of the circular economy are implemented not only in theory but also in practice. To successfully transition to a circular economy while ensuring effective enforcement of criminal law, it is essential to continuously monitor emerging challenges, adjust the legal framework accordingly, and enhance the capabilities of law enforcement institutions.

Comparatively, other EU member states have experienced similar influences on their legal systems. The harmonization of laws across the EU underscores the collective effort to address common challenges such as crime, environmental protection, and socio-economic development. Lithuania's legislative changes reflect a broader trend within the EU, where member states adapt their legal frameworks in response to both internal dynamics and external obligations.

Lithuania's legislative amendments are the result of a confluence of factors, including rising crime rates, public advocacy, international commitments, and socio-economic changes. The influence of EU law, particularly through directives regulating crime and legal protection, has been instrumental in this process, ensuring that national legislation aligns with European standards and effectively addresses contemporary challenges. Changes in Lithuanian legislation were driven by a combination of interconnected factors, reflecting both internal challenges and external obligations. Table 9.2 illustrates how these factors can be analysed.

The factors outlined above highlight the multifaceted motivations behind the amendments to Lithuania's legal acts. These changes demonstrate a proactive approach to addressing internal challenges such as rising crime rates and public demands, while simultaneously fulfilling external obligations, particularly those arising from EU membership. This interplay between domestic priorities and international requirements underscores the dynamic nature of legislative development in a rapidly evolving socio-economic and geopolitical landscape.

9.4 Evaluation of the Impact of the Amendments

The amendments to Lithuania's legal acts dealing with criminal offences have produced a multifaceted impact on crime rates, legal procedures, and societal attitudes. A comprehensive analysis of both quantitative data and qualitative studies offers a deeper understanding of these effects.

Table 9.2 Factors motivating changes in Lithuania's legal acts

Factors	Motivations	Examples/Impacts
Rising Crime Rates	Addressing public safety concerns and combating organised crime effectively	Adoption of the Law on the Prevention of Organised Crime
Public Pressure and Societal Concerns	Responding to societal advocacy for stronger regulations, particularly in environmental protection and social policy	Stricter environmental laws implementing EU directives; labour law reforms for workplace protections
International Obligations	Aligning national legal framework with EU directives and membership requirements	Transposition of EU laws on environmental protection, data sharing, and fair trials
Socio-Economic Transformations	Adapting laws to support the transition to a market-oriented economy and evolving social dynamics	Legal updates in labour, trade, and social policies to align with the European single market
Global and Regional Trends	Adapting to broader trends like climate change, migration, and technological advancements	Implementation of GDPR-inspired data privacy regulations and climate-focused legal reforms

Source The authors

Statistical evidence suggests that recent legal reforms have contributed to a notable decline in crime rates. According to data from the Lithuanian State Data Agency,[45] 45,000 criminal offences were recorded in 2023, representing a 10% decrease compared to 2022. This reduction was particularly evident in theft-related crimes, which decreased by 15%, and violent crimes, which saw an 8% decline. Additionally, instances of smuggling dropped by 20% in the same period, highlighting improved efficiency in law enforcement operations.[46] These figures indicate that legislative amendments have had a tangible impact on reducing certain types of crime.

Reforms targeting specific offences have also demonstrated varying levels of success. For instance, the decriminalisation of small quantities of drugs, introduced in 2022, led to a 5% reduction in drug-related criminal cases. This suggests that the shift towards less punitive measures may have helped to address some underlying issues contributing to such crimes.[47] However, contrasting evidence indicates that earlier legislative changes in 2017, which introduced stricter penalties for drug possession, led to a doubling of drug-related cases. This raises questions about the effectiveness of punitive versus rehabilitative approaches. Qualitative research provides further insights into how these legal amendments have been implemented

[45] Lithuanian State Data Agency, Crime Statistics 2023 (Nusikalstamumo statistika, Lt.), Vilnius, 2024. https://osp.stat.gov.lt/statistiniu-rodikliu-analize?hash=6bb6b1d3-3c5e-4b17-b5c2-92ad2d0b94a4#/. Accessed 12 April 2025.

[46] Lithuanian State Data Agency, see footnote 45 above.

[47] *Ibid.*

and perceived by stakeholders. Operational improvements were accompanied by updates to legal frameworks, which facilitated a more streamlined approach to criminal investigations.[48]

Despite these positive developments, challenges remain in ensuring consistent application of amended laws. Studies highlight that ambiguities in the interpretation of legal provisions and discrepancies in their enforcement continue to hinder the uniform implementation of reforms.[49] This suggests a need for further clarity and guidance to support legal practitioners in applying the revised legislation effectively.

Lithuania's legal amendments have also been assessed in a broader international context. Comparative analyses indicate that these reforms align with European Union standards, particularly in areas such as human rights and the abolition of the death penalty. Lithuania's 1998 decision to abolish capital punishment remains a landmark achievement, reflecting compliance with the requirements of the European Council and the European Union.[50] However, in areas such as combating organised crime, experts argue that additional measures are required to match the best practices of other EU member states. Theoretical perspectives on criminal law reforms further emphasise the significance of these amendments in aligning Lithuania's legal system with contemporary trends in Western jurisprudence. The introduction of a new Criminal Code has been recognised as a substantial advancement, although practical challenges persist, requiring ongoing adjustments to ensure its efficacy.

Nevertheless, certain limitations in the existing body of research should be addressed. Most studies focus on the immediate effects of legal amendments, while the long-term impact on crime trends and systemic changes remains underexplored. Additionally, while national statistics provide an overview of crime rates, there is a lack of region-specific analyses that could reveal variations influenced by socio-economic factors.[51]

After regaining independence in 1990, Lithuania faced economic hardships and social transformation, which led to an increase in crime rates. In 1991, approximately 50,000 criminal offences were recorded, and by 1995, this figure had risen to over 80,000.[52] By the end of the decade, crime levels began to stabilise, although they remained high.[53]

During the period between 2001 and 2010, Lithuania's accession to the European Union in 2004 strengthened law enforcement institutions and improved economic conditions, contributing to a decline in crime. In 2003, around 70,000 criminal

[48] Kiškis 2006.

[49] *Ibid.*

[50] Council of the European Union, EU Guidelines on the Death Penalty, Brussels, 29 June 1998. https://www.refworld.org/policy/legalguidance/eu/1998/en/49523. Accessed 29 January 2025.

[51] Lithuanian State Data Agency, see footnote 45 above.

[52] Lithuanian State Data Agency, Crime and Criminal Justice Statistics, Official Statistics Portal, 2024. https://osp.stat.gov.lt/nusikalstamumas-ir-baudziamoji-teisena. Accessed 29 January 2025.

[53] Ministry of the Interior of the Republic of Lithuania (2022). Annual Report 2022. Available at https://vrm.lrv.lt/uploads/vrm/documents/files/00000_VRM_2022%20m_veiklos_ataskaita_skelbti.pdf?utm_source=chatgpt.com.

Table 9.3 Trends in recorded criminal offences in Lithuania (1991–2024)

Year	Description
1991	Approximately 50,000 criminal offences were recorded in Lithuania following economic and social challenges
1995	The number of recorded offences peaked at over 80,000 due to economic difficulties and social transformation
2003	About 70,000 criminal offences were recorded, reflecting a gradual decline in crime rates
2010	The number of offences decreased to 60,000 as law enforcement efforts and economic conditions improved
2015	Approximately 55,000 offences were recorded, continuing the downward trend in crime rates
2020	Crime numbers dropped further to about 46,000, though cybercrime showed upward trends
2021	The lowest number of offences in independent Lithuania's history was recorded—42,525 offences
2022	Crime increased by 7.5% to 45,710 offences, though serious violent crimes remained at historic lows

Source The authors using data from the Official Statistics Portal and the Informatics and Communication Department

offences were recorded, decreasing to 60,000 by 2010.[54] This period also saw a noticeable reduction in property crimes, particularly thefts.[55] Between 2011 and 2020, the downward trend in crime rates continued. In 2015, approximately 55,000 criminal offences were registered, decreasing to 46,000 by 2020.[56] However, certain types of crime, such as cybercrime, showed an upward trend during this time.[57]

In 2021, Lithuania recorded approximately 42,000 criminal offences, the lowest number since independence.[58] However, in 2022, the number of offences rose by 7.5%, reaching 45,710.[59] Violent crimes, such as homicides, remained at historically low levels, with only 76 homicides recorded in 2021.[60] These data indicate that while overall crime rates are declining, specific categories of crime continue to pose challenges. Table 9.3 summarises the trends in recorded criminal offences in Lithuania from 1991 to 2024, highlighting significant changes and providing sources for the data. It illustrates the evolution of crime rates alongside key socio-economic and legal developments.

The data in the table demonstrate how socio-economic transitions, such as EU accession and improvements in law enforcement, significantly influenced crime

[54] Official Statistics Portal 2024, see footnote 52 above.

[55] Ministry of the Interior of the Republic of Lithuania (2022), see footnote 53 above.

[56] Official Statistics Portal 2024, see footnote 52 above.

[57] Ministry of the Interior of the Republic of Lithuania (2022), see footnote 53 above.

[58] Official Statistics Portal 2024, see footnote 52 above.

[59] *Ibid.*

[60] Ministry of the Interior of the Republic of Lithuania (2022), see footnote 53 above.

rates. While the overall trend shows a steady decline in recorded offences, certain categories, such as cybercrime, continue to challenge law enforcement.

The amendments to Lithuania's legal acts dealing with criminal offences have had a significant impact on the country's criminal justice system. While the reforms have contributed to reductions in crime rates and improved efficiency in law enforcement, challenges related to implementation and regional disparities persist. Moreover, the evolving nature of crime, particularly the rise in cybercrime, underscores the need for continued evaluation and adaptation of the legal framework to meet new challenges. These findings highlight the importance of a dynamic approach to legislative reform, ensuring that Lithuania's legal system remains both effective and responsive to societal needs.

9.5 Comparison with Other Baltic and Nordic Countries

Lithuania's legal amendments addressing criminal offences reflect broader European Union trends, yet they reveal distinct characteristics when compared to other EU countries, particularly the Baltic states and Nordic countries. Examining these similarities and differences provides valuable insights into potential legislative advancements Lithuania could adopt in the future. As of 2021, Lithuania had one of the highest incarceration rates in the EU, with 220 prisoners per 100,000 inhabitants. This rate was significantly higher than the EU average of 106 prisoners per 100,000 people. In contrast, Nordic countries such as Finland and Sweden reported much lower incarceration rates, with 51 and 73 prisoners per 100,000 inhabitants, respectively.[61]

Lithuania's legislative framework is closely aligned with EU directives, particularly regarding human rights and the rule of law. The abolition of the death penalty in 1998 positioned Lithuania in compliance with the European Convention on Human Rights, a milestone shared with most EU countries.[62] Similarly, Lithuania has adopted EU-wide standards in combating cross-border crimes, such as trafficking and cybercrime, which reflect a commitment to international cooperation.

Despite these commonalities, Lithuania's implementation timeline often lags behind some Western European nations. For instance, while the General Data Protection Regulation was implemented uniformly across the EU, Lithuania faced initial challenges in harmonising its cybersecurity laws with broader EU frameworks, whereas Nordic countries like Denmark and Sweden had pre-existing robust systems in place.[63]

Lithuania shares many legislative trends with its Baltic neighbours, Latvia and Estonia, particularly in reforms aimed at modernising criminal justice systems.

[61] Statista. Incarceration rate in European countries in 2022. https://www.statista.com/statistics/957501/incarceration-rate-in-europe/. Accessed 29 January 2025.

[62] European Council 1998, https://aei.pitt.edu/54469/1/cpr_344.pdf.

[63] European Commission. GDPR Implementation Report, 2023. https://commission.europa.eu/index_en. Accessed 16 April 2025.

All three countries have introduced restorative justice measures and alternative sentencing to reduce incarceration rates, mirroring EU objectives. However, Estonia has been a regional leader in digitalising its legal processes, integrating e-justice platforms that streamline judicial efficiency. Lithuania, while progressing, still lags behind Estonia in implementing fully digitalised court systems.[64]

Moreover, Latvia has adopted stricter anti-corruption measures, resulting in greater transparency and more effective prosecution of economic crimes. Lithuania could consider adapting similar provisions to strengthen its efforts against financial crime and enhance public trust in governance.[65]

The Nordic countries, known for their progressive legal systems, offer a wealth of potential legislative adaptations for Lithuania. Sweden and Finland, for example, have successfully implemented restorative justice models for juvenile offenders, focusing on rehabilitation rather than punishment. Lithuania has made strides in this area but could benefit from further integrating such practices, particularly for reducing recidivism among young offenders.[66] Another notable trend in the Nordic region is the emphasis on addressing the root causes of crime, such as social inequality and mental health issues. Norway's comprehensive approach, which combines criminal justice reforms with strong welfare policies, has contributed to one of the lowest recidivism rates in Europe. The Finnish experience demonstrates that fines for environmental crimes are often suboptimal, meaning they are lower than the optimal level required to ensure effective deterrence. In Lithuania, as in Finland, questions arise regarding the systematic assessment of environmental damage and illicit gains, and their inclusion in sentencing decisions. In Finland, it has been observed that low fines, insufficient confiscation of illicit gains, and inefficient use of law enforcement resources reduce the deterrent effect. Lindqvist et al.[67] point out that suboptimal fines and a low probability of detecting offences result, indicating that the current legal practice fails to ensure adequate crime prevention. In Lithuania, it is worth examining whether the applied methods sufficiently consider environmental restoration costs and striving for greater effectiveness in fines and preventive measures, as suggested in the Finnish analysis. Lithuania could adapt similar integrated approaches, particularly in addressing domestic violence and substance abuse, which remain significant challenges.[68]

To further modernise its legal system, Lithuania could benefit from adopting successful practices from other European nations. These strategies aim to enhance judicial efficiency, promote rehabilitation, improve transparency, and address the root

---

[64] OECD. E-Justice in the Baltic States: Progress and Challenges. https://www.oecd.org/. Accessed 16 April 2025.

[65] Transparency International, Corruption Perceptions Index 2023, Berlin, 2024. https://www.transparency.org/en/cpi/2023/index. Accessed 16 April 2025.

[66] United Nations Office on Drugs and Crime (UNODC), Global Prison Population and Trends: A Focus on Rehabilitation, 2023. https://www.unodc.org/documents/data-and-analysis/briefs/Prison_brief_2024.pdf. Accessed 29 January 2025.

[67] Lindqvist et al. 2024, pp. 75–200.

[68] Council of Europe, *5th General Report on GREVIO's Activities*, Strasbourg, 2023. https://rm.coe.int/5th-general-report-on-grevio-s-activities/1680b1f78f. Accessed 29 January 2025.

Table 9.4 Future directions for Lithuania's legal framework

Strategy	Description	Inspiration
Enhanced Digitalisation	Leveraging e-justice systems to streamline judicial processes and improve transparency in court systems	Estonia
Broader Use of Restorative Justice	Expanding rehabilitation programs for juveniles and low-risk offenders, focusing on reducing recidivism	Nordic countries (e.g., Sweden, Finland)
Comprehensive Anti-Corruption Reforms	Adopting stricter measures to combat corruption, ensuring greater accountability and transparency	Latvia
Integrated Social Policies	Implementing holistic approaches to address crime's root causes, such as social inequality and mental health issues	Norway

Source The author using data from Estonia's e-justice system,[69] Nordic juvenile justice reforms,[70] Latvia's anti-corruption measures,[71] and Norway's integrated social policies[72]

causes of crime. Table 9.4 summarises these potential directions and the countries from which Lithuania can draw inspiration.

By aligning with best practices from neighbouring and Nordic countries, Lithuania can continue to modernise its legal system while addressing unique domestic challenges. The high incarceration rate in Lithuania, coupled with potential recidivism challenges, indicates a need for reforms in the criminal justice system. Adopting practices from countries with lower incarceration and recidivism rates, such as Finland and Sweden, could be beneficial. Implementing restorative justice programs, enhancing rehabilitation efforts, and focusing on crime prevention strategies may help reduce both incarceration and recidivism rates in Lithuania. Lithuania's legal amendments largely align with EU standards, particularly in upholding human rights and combating cross-border crime. However, the implementation of certain reforms, such as cybersecurity and digitalisation, lags behind countries like Estonia and the Nordic nations, which have established robust systems early on. Our Baltic neighbours provide relevant examples, such as Latvia's stringent anti-corruption measures and Estonia's e-justice system, which Lithuania could emulate to enhance transparency and efficiency.

[69] European Commission, 2023 Rule of Law Report: Country Chapter on the rule of law situation in Estonia, Brussels, 5 July 2023. https://commission.europa.eu/system/files/2023-07/18_1_52573_coun_chap_estonia_en.pdf. Accessed 29 January 2025.

[70] Lappi-Seppälä 2016, pp. 155–190.

[71] Transparency International 2023, see footnote 65 above.

[72] Council of Europe 2023, see footnote 68 above.

Drawing inspiration from the Nordic model, Lithuania could further develop restorative justice practices, particularly for juvenile offenders, and adopt integrated social policies to address underlying factors of crime, such as social inequality and mental health. These adaptations would not only modernise Lithuania's legal framework but also position it as a regional leader in criminal justice reform.

9.6 Trends in the Development of Criminal Policy

Lithuania's criminal policy has evolved significantly over the past three decades, transitioning from a punitive-focused approach in the 1990s to a more balanced framework that integrates preventive measures with stricter penalties. This evolution reflects the country's efforts to align with European legal standards while addressing unique societal and criminal challenges.

In the early years following independence, Lithuania faced a surge in organised crime and violent offences due to economic instability and social transformation. In response, the government implemented harsh penalties as a primary deterrent. During the 1990s, sentences for serious crimes, particularly for organised criminal groups and drug-related offences, were significantly increased.[73] However, this retributive focus led to overcrowded prisons and failed to address the root causes of crime, such as poverty and unemployment.

By the early 2000s, recognising the limitations of punitive measures, Lithuania began integrating preventive strategies into its criminal policy. The adoption of alternative sentencing measures, such as probation and community service, aimed to reduce incarceration rates and rehabilitate offenders. At the same time, preventive policing initiatives were introduced to engage communities in crime prevention, particularly in urban areas with high crime rates.[74] Significant legal amendments during this period included the introduction of restorative justice programmes, particularly for juveniles, focusing on mediation between offenders and victims, as well as anti-corruption campaigns that combined stricter penalties with public awareness initiatives to reduce fraud and misuse of public funds.

In recent years, legislative reforms in Lithuania have sought to balance stricter penalties for severe crimes with preventive measures aimed at reducing crime rates and recidivism. For instance, the Anti-Corruption Law introduced harsher penalties for public sector corruption while simultaneously enhancing whistle-blower protections to encourage reporting.[75] Similarly, reforms in drug-related offences targeted major trafficking operations with severe sanctions while focusing on rehabilitation for minor offenders. Legal amendments have also increased sentences for domestic violence and sexual offences, reflecting a zero-tolerance approach,

---

[73] Official Statistics Portal 2024, see footnote 52 above.

[74] Ministry of the Interior of the Republic of Lithuania (2022), see footnote 53 above.

[75] Transparency International, Corruption Perceptions Index 2023, Berlin, 2024. https://www.transparency.org/en/cpi/2023/index. Accessed 16 April 2025.

paired with increased funding for victim support programmes and public education campaigns.[76] Youth crime prevention initiatives, such as community-based programmes targeting at-risk youth, have combined mentorship with education and skills training, showing promise in reducing juvenile delinquency and recidivism.[77] Cybercrime legislation has also been strengthened, with stricter penalties for online fraud and hacking, accompanied by preventive measures such as cybersecurity education and collaboration with EU agencies.[78]

The effectiveness of Lithuania's blended approach has been mixed. Stricter penalties for violent and corruption-related offences have led to increased deterrence, with a measurable decline in homicide rates and high-profile corruption cases. Preventive initiatives targeting youth and low-risk offenders have contributed to lower recidivism rates in these groups.[79] However, Lithuania continues to struggle with high incarceration rates compared to the EU average, suggesting that preventive measures have not fully counterbalanced the reliance on punitive approaches. Additionally, inconsistent funding and resource allocation for preventive programmes limit their long-term impact.

To enhance the balance between prevention and punishment, Lithuania could expand restorative justice initiatives, particularly for non-violent offenders, to reduce incarceration rates. Strengthened funding for community-based prevention programmes focusing on youth engagement and education could further improve outcomes. Developing integrated support systems for victims of crime would also ensure a more holistic approach to justice. By refining its criminal policy, Lithuania can build a legal framework that not only deters crime but also addresses its underlying causes, fostering a safer and more equitable society.

9.7 Challenges and Insights for the Future

Lithuania's legal system faces a range of challenges in addressing criminal offences, many of which stem from the evolving nature of crime, advancements in technology, and societal changes. While significant progress has been made in recent decades, several areas require attention to ensure that the system remains effective and adaptive to modern demands.

One pressing challenge is the rise of cybercrime, which poses significant difficulties for the Lithuanian legal system. Crimes such as online fraud, identity theft, and data breaches are growing in frequency and complexity. Current laws, though relatively robust, struggle to keep up with the rapidly evolving digital landscape.

[76] Council of Europe 2023, see footnote 68 above.

[77] UNODC. Juvenile Justice Reforms in Europe. https://www.unodc.org/. Accessed 16 April 2025.

[78] European Commission. GDPR Implementation Report, 2023. https://commission.europa.eu/index_en. Accessed 16 April 2025.

[79] Official Statistics Portal 2024, see footnote 52 above.

Moreover, the system faces a shortage of skilled investigators and limited technological resources to combat these crimes effectively. Strengthening international cooperation, particularly within the European Union, and investing in advanced digital tools could enhance Lithuania's ability to respond to these threats.

The country's high incarceration rate also remains a critical issue. Despite the introduction of alternative sentencing measures such as probation and community service, imprisonment is still disproportionately relied upon, leading to overcrowded prisons and insufficient focus on rehabilitation. This overreliance undermines efforts to reduce recidivism and reintegrate offenders into society. Expanding restorative justice initiatives and prioritising rehabilitation programmes could alleviate these issues and create a more balanced approach.

Social inequality represents another key factor contributing to criminal activity, particularly in economically disadvantaged regions. Crimes such as theft and drug-related offences are often closely linked to poverty and lack of social opportunities. The legal system alone cannot address these underlying causes; a more integrated approach that combines legal reforms with targeted social policies is essential. Education, employment programmes, and support services for at-risk populations would not only reduce crime rates but also foster long-term social cohesion.

Victim support services in Lithuania, while established, are unevenly distributed and underfunded. Victims of violent crimes, including domestic violence and sexual offences, often lack access to comprehensive legal and psychological support, particularly in rural areas. Improving funding for these services and creating a standardised national framework would ensure that all victims receive adequate care and protection.

Rabbi[80] conducted a study which identified environmental crimes such as pollution, illegal waste disposal, trade in protected species, and the destruction of natural resources as significant issues within the EU. The study revealed that the intensity of these crimes is influenced by population growth, poverty, and regional disparities. To effectively address these challenges, an integrated approach is essential focusing on education and awareness-raising, strengthening corporate accountability, and fostering international cooperation through unified regulations and technological solutions.[81] Lithuania also faces challenges in fully aligning with evolving EU directives, particularly in areas such as environmental crime and human trafficking. While progress has been made, gaps in implementation and enforcement limit the effectiveness of these directives. Strengthening legal provisions in these areas, particularly by addressing environmental offences in line with the EU Green Deal, would align Lithuania's legal framework with broader European goals.

Looking ahead, Lithuania has an opportunity to modernise its legal system further by focusing on technological integration and community engagement. Developing digital platforms for case management, inspired by Estonia's advanced e-governance

---

[80] Rabbi 2024.

[81] *Ibid.*

systems, could reduce delays and improve transparency in judicial processes. Additionally, fostering trust between law enforcement and local communities through enhanced community policing efforts could improve crime prevention and reporting.

By addressing these challenges and building on existing strengths, Lithuania can create a more resilient and adaptable legal system. This requires a balance between innovation and social responsibility, ensuring that the legal framework not only deters crime but also promotes justice and inclusivity in a rapidly changing world.

9.8 Conclusion

The reform of Lithuania's criminal law reflects a consistent transition from its Soviet legacy to a modern legal system based on democratic principles and aligned with international and European Union legal standards. This evolution has strengthened the protection of fundamental human rights, enhanced the effectiveness of the justice system, and enabled adaptability to emerging social and technological challenges. However, the reforms have highlighted critical issues and areas for improvement that require ongoing attention.

The modernisation of criminal law has significantly contributed to the reduction in crime rates, particularly following the adoption of the new Criminal Code in 2000 and the integration of EU legal directives. Initiatives such as restorative justice programmes and alternative sentencing have successfully balanced crime prevention with social reintegration. Nonetheless, Lithuania continues to grapple with high incarceration rates, indicating a need for greater investment in alternatives to imprisonment and more focused efforts to reduce reoffending.

Technological advancements and the rise of cybercrime present new challenges for Lithuania's legal system. Limited resources and a shortage of skilled professionals hinder the country's ability to effectively address crimes such as online fraud and data breaches. Strengthening technological capabilities and fostering international cooperation will be essential to combat these increasingly sophisticated threats.

Social inequality, particularly in economically disadvantaged regions, remains a significant driver of criminal activity. Issues such as poverty and limited access to social services contribute to crimes like theft and drug use. Addressing these challenges requires an integrated approach that combines legal measures with social policies, including education, employment initiatives, and support for vulnerable groups, to foster long-term social cohesion and reduce crime rates.

The transposition of international and EU legal acts into national law remains a complex but critical process for Lithuania. Ensuring full harmonisation requires a deeper understanding of the objectives and contexts of these legal instruments, alongside enhanced implementation. Additionally, Lithuania could benefit from adopting successful practices from neighbouring countries, such as Estonia's advancements in digitalising the legal system and Latvia's stringent anti-corruption measures, as well as Nordic approaches to restorative justice and social policy integration.

As societal needs and technological landscapes evolve, Lithuania's criminal justice system must continue to develop preventative measures and embrace innovation. Greater focus on youth crime prevention, investment in legal system digitalisation, and equitable access to high-quality justice services nationwide are recommended. These steps would not only address existing issues more effectively but also foster a fairer and more socially responsible society.

References

Bartolacelli A, Sagatienė D (eds) (2023) Law and Sustainability: Perspectives for Lithuania and Beyond. Księgarnia Akademicka, Kraków. https://books.akademicka.pl/publishing/catalog/view/540/1745/2180. Accessed 29 November 2024

Baumer E P, Vélez M B, Rosenfeld R (2018) Bringing crime trends back into criminology: A critical assessment of the literature and a blueprint for future inquiry. Annual Review of Criminology 1:39–61. https://doi.org/10.1146/annurev-criminol-032317-092339

Camplani F (2021) Environmental Criminal Law towards Circular Economy. Business Law and Management (BLM2): International Conference on Advanced Marketing (ICAM4), An International Joint e-Conference-2021, Department of Marketing Management, Faculty of Commerce and Management Studies, University of Kelaniya, Sri Lanka, p 263

Cohen M A, Bowles R (2010) Estimating Costs of Crime. In: Piquero A, Weisburd D (eds) Handbook of Quantitative Criminology. Springer, New York, NY, pp 143–162. https://doi.org/10.1007/978-0-387-77650-7_8

Eisner M (2009) The uses of violence: An examination of some cross-cutting issues. International Journal of Conflict and Violence 3(1):40–59. https://doi.org/10.4119/ijcv-2792

Eisner M (2014) Long-term historical trends in violent crime. Crime and Justice 43(1):289–386. https://doi.org/10.1086/652229

Kiškis A (2006) Crime in Lithuania: What Has Legal Reform Changed? [Nusikalstamumas Lietuvoje: ką pakeitė teisės reforma?]. Jurisprudencija 81(3). https://ojs.mruni.eu/ojs/jurisprudence/article/view/2896. Accessed 12 December 2024

Lappi-Seppälä T (2016) Youth justice and youth sanctions in four Nordic states. In: Jensen FL, Jepsen J (eds) Juvenile Justice in Global Perspective. Routledge, pp 155–190

Lehti M, Sirén R (2020) Trends in homicide and violent crime in Finland, 1750–2020. Scandinavian Journal of Criminology 21(3):245–263

Lindqvist R, Lombardini C, Suvantola L et al. (2024) The deterrence effect of criminal sanctions against environmental crime in Finland: An application of the rational choice model of crime. European Journal of Law and Economics 58(2):75–200. https://doi.org/10.1007/s10657-024-09818-8

Oral E (2024) The environmental rule of law and the protection of human rights defenders: Law, society, technology, and markets. International Environmental Agreements 24:393–421. https://doi.org/10.1007/s10784-024-09645-x

Proedrou F, Pournara M (2024a) Exploring representations of climate change as ecocide: Implications for climate policy. Climate Policy 24(1):1–14. https://doi.org/10.1080/14693062.2024.2368859

Proedrou F, Pournara M (2024b) A limited green criminological turn in the EU approach to climate change? Mapping representations of climate change as ecocide. Journal of European Integration 46(1):1–19. https://doi.org/10.1080/07036337.2024.2440875

Rabbi MF (2024) Unveiling environmental crime trends and intensity in the EU countries through a sustainability lens. European Journal of Criminal Policy and Research. https://doi.org/10.1007/s10610-024-09607-8

Rosenfeld R, Messner SF (2013) Understanding the economic context of crime in capitalist societies. In: Understanding the economic context of crime in capitalist societies. SAGE Publications Ltd, pp 68–97. https://doi.org/10.4135/9781446270097
Tonry M (2016) Crime and justice in America: 1975–2025. University of Chicago Press, Chicago, pp 1–37

Ligita Gasparėnienė is a senior researcher at the Law Faculty of Vilnius University.

Rita Remeikienė is a senior researcher at the Law Faculty of Vilnius University.

Chapter 10
Application of the Principle of Proportionality: Criminal Law Aspects in the Case Law of the Constitutional Court of the Republic of Lithuania and the Court of Justice of the European Union

Gintaras Goda and Lina Beliūnienė

Contents

Abstract While assessing the proportionality of measures in the field of personal data gathered by intelligence services surveillance, the Court of Justice of the European Union (CJEU) and the Constitutional Court of the Republic of Lithuania attach the same significance to this principle as one of elements of rule of law in the interpretation of the Charter of Fundamental Rights of the European Union and other relevant pieces of the European Union legislation and the Constitution, respectively. Both courts use the general notion of proportionality that national measures undertaken must be proportionate to their objectives. However, the practice of both courts affirms that application of this principle in their practice is to some extent specific. According to the analysed case-law, not all structural components of the typical proportionality test are used by the courts. Based on comparative analysis, the chapter overviews

G. Goda
Faculty of Law, Vilnius University, Vilnius, Lithuania
e-mail: gintaras.goda@tf.vu.lt

L. Beliūnienė (✉)
Institute of Law at the Lithuanian Centre for Social Sciences, Constitutional Court of the Republic of Lithuania, Vilnius, Lithuania
e-mail: lina.beliuniene@lrkt.lt

I. Isokaitė-Valužė and H. Šinkūnas (eds.), *The European Union 2004-2024*,
https://doi.org/10.1007/978-94-6265-718-2_10

this and the other most important developments in the recent case law of the CJEU and the Lithuanian Constitutional Court in the field of surveillance by intelligence services, and reveals specifics of the application of the principle of proportionality in cases of other clashes between individual rights and public interests: right to family life and public security, right to property and prevention of crimes, as well right to acquire and possess weapons and public security or public order. The chapter also suggests a possible direction for the future interrelation of jurisprudences.

Keywords Proportionality principle · Right to private and family life · Surveillance by intelligence services · Public security · Prevention of crimes · Extended confiscation · Lithuanian Constitutional Court · European Court of Justice

10.1 Introduction

The contextual element of the rule of law—the principle of proportionality—originally developed by the German Federal Constitutional Court, as a judicial tool to examine limitations of fundamental rights, become an integral part of global constitutionalism. However, this check of national measures is practiced in different ways in various national, international or supranational courts[1] and due to this reason, its application is a continuous object of interest for scientists and practitioners despite the existing extensive literature on proportionality analysis. National literature comprises such aspects as recognition and development of the principle of proportionality in European Union (EU) administrative law,[2] comparisons of the case law made by the European Court of Justice (CJEU) with the relevant case law made by the European Court of Human Rights (ECtHR),[3] some criminal law reflections in the CJEU case law,[4] as well as other issues focusing on criminal law at the national level examining, for example, proportionality of personal freedom and interests of security due to criminal intelligence activities.[5]

Specifics of application of the principle of proportionality at the international level was identified in the recent times of Covid-19 (i.e. taking into account the possibility to deviate from international obligations to the extent strictly required by the exigencies of the public health situation),[6] however, application of proportionality is relevant also in such spheres as collection of data and surveillance. These

[1] Steiner et al. 2020, pp. 1–2.
[2] Danėlienė 2012.
[3] Leonaitė 2013.
[4] For example, see Prapiestytė 2024.
[5] For example, see Gutauskas 2019, 2022.
[6] Ondřejek and Horák 2024.

spheres are recognised as a particular challenge to the rule of law in the international arena. This was confirmed in the Rule of Law Checklist[7] created by the European Commission for Democracy through Law which is the Council of Europe's advisory body on constitutional matters. Later it was confirmed by the European Union Agency for Fundamental Rights. According to its updated report 'Surveillance by intelligence services: Fundamental rights safeguards and remedies in the EU' of 2023, enhanced security measures should be enshrined in a strong fundamental rights framework, where the necessity and proportionality of surveillance measures are regularly assessed.[8] Thus, comprehensive analysis of application of proportionality at the crossroads of constitutional, international and criminal law is of special interest.

In addition to challenges of developing an objective standard (in the context of criminal sentencing also[9]), criticism of proportionality concerning non-existence of unambiguous rules on what would constitute proportionate or disproportionate[10] are often examined especially in case of national courts and the ECtHR. Scholars link the use of proportionality with interpretation and balancing activities: interpretation is achieved by balancing of interests and values, balancing is made by interpreting, and interpretative activity has an evaluative character.[11] The authors put an emphasis on different factors important for proportionality analysis: the role of proportionality in constitutional review and punitiveness in criminal punishment may turn out to be very different phenomena, driven by different principal actors and causal factors, and of different orders of salience.[12]

The jurisprudence of the CJEU which gets relatively less attention is also significant in this context. It is relevant because the EU law sets limits which cannot be exceeded by any measures (including those in the sphere of criminal law) imposed by the Member States in so far as they relate to the exercise of fundamental freedoms.[13] The CJEU consistently uses the principle of proportionality in its case-law. National courts including the Lithuanian Constitutional Court also consistently uses

[7] Council of Europe. European Commission for Democracy through Law (Venice Commission) (2016) Rule of Law Checklist. Adopted by at its 106th Plenary Session (Venice, 11–12 March 2016), p. 49. https://www.venice.coe.int/images/SITE%20IMAGES/Publications/Rule_of_Law_Check_List.pdf. Accessed 25 January 2025.

[8] European Union Agency for Fundamental Rights (FRA) report (2023) Surveillance by Intelligence Services: Fundamental Rights safeguards and Remedies in the EU. https://fra.europa.eu/en/publication/2023/surveillance-update?page=4#read-online. Accessed 25 January 2025.

[9] For example, see Ristroph 2005, p. 3.

[10] Lang 2020, p. 129.

[11] Perlingieri 2018.

[12] Bomhoff 2016, p. 20.

[13] Consolidated versions of the Treaty on European Union and the Treaty on the Functioning of the European Union, Official Journal of the European Union OJ C 202 7 June 2016. https://eur-lex.europa.eu/legal-content/EN/TXT/HTML/?uri=OJ:C:2016:202:FULL. Accessed 25 January 2025. Charter of Fundamental Rights of the European Union OJ C 202, 7.6.2016, https://eur-lex.europa.eu/legal-content/EN/TXT/?uri=CELEX:12016P/TXT. Accessed 25 January 2025.

the principle of proportionality and, as in the other states, most refer to the Charter in the areas of migration, data protection and criminal law.[14]

The authors of the chapter aim to analyse the judicial practice of application of the proportionality principle by the Lithuanian Constitutional Court and the CJEU, and to compare them by identifying their similar elements, as well their specifics. Due to this, in this chapter it is presumed that as the EU law including the Charter of Fundamental Rights of the European Union (Charter) and the case law of the CJEU are regarded as a source of the application and interpretation of Lithuanian law, including the Constitution,[15] application of the principle of proportionality in the Lithuanian Constitutional Court has similarities with that of the CJEU, as well as its specifics, dependent on national context and other circumstances important for the case.

Bearing in mind the typical three steps of the proportionality test comprising necessity, suitability, and proportionality in the narrower sense (or balancing), specifically, this chapter overviews the application of proportionality in recent cases and reveals the experience of both courts gained when two legal interests compete. These cases are related to situations, firstly, during the application of criminal intelligence (non-publicly obtained) measures, i.e. the state official's right to privacy and prevention of crimes. Secondly, concerning application of proportionality in case of other clashes between the right of sentenced persons to family life and public security, as well as right to property and prevention of crimes and right to acquire and possess weapons and public security or public order. All these issues are considered in the light of arguments presented by both analysed courts in their decisions.

10.2 Essence of the Content of the Principle of Proportionality in the Relevant EU Legislation and the Constitution

In the framework of principles and guiding ideas with immense scope and importance to EU law, the Charter also obligates to observe the principle of proportionality. Although the Charter foresees application of the proportionality principle not only to the Member States, but also to acts of the EU, the object of this chapter is its application to national measures. Thus, regarding criminal offences and penalties it

---

[14] Charter of Fundamental Rights is the EU's Bill of Human Rights. Charter's untapped potential, nationally. https://fra.europa.eu/en/publications-and-resources/infographics/charters-untapped-potential-nationally. Accessed 25 January 2025.

[15] *Inter alia*, the Lithuanian Constitutional Court's rulings of 11 January 2019 (TAR, 2019, No. 439. https://lrkt.lt/en/court-acts/search/170/ta1915/content. Accessed 25 January 2025) and 18 April 2019 (TAR, 2019, No. 6411. https://lrkt.lt/en/court-acts/search/170/ta1938/content. Accessed 25 January 2025). Similarly, the Constitutional Court stated concerning the Convention of Human Rights and Fundamental Freedoms of 1950 and the case law of the ECtHR (for example, the Constitutional Court's ruling of 8 May 2000 (*Valstybės žinios*, 2000, No. 39-1105. https://lrkt.lt/en/court-acts/search/170/ta1160/content. Accessed 25 January 2025)).

is relevant that para 3 of Article 49 ("Principles of legality and proportionality of criminal offences and penalties") requires that "The severity of penalties must not be disproportionate to the criminal offence".[16] This Paragraph, as it is explained by the authority of the Praesidium of the Convention which drafted the Charter, "states the general principle of proportionality between penalties and criminal offences which is enshrined in the common constitutional traditions of the Member States and in the case-law of the Court of Justice of the Communities".[17] Thus, this regulation constitutes restriction on the power to punish.

In the broader human rights context, the principle of proportionality is treated as limitation of restrictions on the exercise of the fundamental rights and freedoms recognised by the Charter. This principle is explicitly revealed in the context of Article 52 ("Scope and interpretation of rights and principles"). According to its para 1, "Any limitation on the exercise of the rights and freedoms recognised by this Charter must be provided for by law and respect the essence of those rights and freedoms. Subject to the principle of proportionality, limitations may be made only if they are necessary and genuinely meet objectives of general interest recognised by the Union or the need to protect the rights and freedoms of others". Paying regard to the fact that the most fundamental rights are not absolute and to the complex formulation of the afore-mentioned paragraph, this principle could be approached in the light of all arrangements established for the limitation of rights, i.e. necessity of measure, together with such requirements of limitation on the exercise of the rights and freedoms as limitation by law and non-violation of the essence of those rights and freedoms. This was confirmed by the CJEU in the context of arrangements for the limitation of rights revealing that "those restrictions in fact correspond to objectives of general interest pursued by the Community and do not constitute, with regard to the aim pursued, disproportionate and unreasonable interference undermining the very substance of those rights' (judgment of 13 April 2000, Case C-292/97, paragraph 45 of the grounds)".[18] However, it is also important that the concept of the essence of fundamental rights could be incorporated into a proportionality assessment and as the limit on the limitations that may be imposed on the exercise of the fundamental right it is also of an autonomous nature.[19] In addition, under the principle of proportionality, limitations "must apply only in so far as is strictly necessary and the legislation which entails the limitations in question must lay down clear and precise rules governing the scope and application of those limitations".[20]

---

[16] See footnote 14 above.

[17] European Union (2007) Explanations relating to the Charter of Fundamental Rights, OJ C 303. https://eur-lex.europa.eu/LexUriServ/LexUriServ.do?uri=OJ:C:2007:303:0017:0035:en:PDF. Accessed 25 January 2025.

[18] *Ibid.*

[19] Lenaerts 2019, p. 788.

[20] CJEU (Grand Chamber), C-118/22 NG v Direktor na Glavna direktsia 'Natsionalna politsia' pri Ministerstvo na vatreshnite raboti, 30 January 2024. EU:C:2024:97, para 39. https://eur-lex.europa.eu/legal-content/EN/TXT/?uri=CELEX:62022CJ0118. Accessed 25 January 2025.

According to explanations originally prepared under the authority of the Praesidium of the Convention which drafted the Charter, "The reference to general interests recognised by the Union covers both the objectives mentioned in Article 3 of the Treaty on European Union and other interests protected by specific provisions of the Treaties such as Article 4(1) of the Treaty on European Union and Articles 35(3), 36 and 346 of the Treaty on the Functioning of the European Union".[21]

The objectives mentioned in Article 3 of the Treaty on European Union[22] which are relevant to the analysed issues of criminal law and human rights include, *inter alia*, offering its citizens an area of freedom, security and justice without internal frontiers, in which the free movement of persons is ensured in conjunction with appropriate measures with respect to external border controls, asylum, immigration and the prevention and combating of crime. Other interests protected by specific provisions of the Treaties such as Article 4(1) of the Treaty on European Union and Articles 35(3), 36 and 346 of the Treaty on the Functioning of the European Union,[23] *inter alia*, are: competences not conferred upon the Union in the Treaties remain with the Member States; the provisions of Articles 34 and 35 shall not preclude prohibitions or restrictions on imports, exports or goods in transit justified on grounds of public morality, public policy or public security.

In addition, according to Article 52(3) of the Charter, the necessary consistency between the rights contained in the Charter and the corresponding rights guaranteed in the Convention of Human Rights and Fundamental Freedoms of 1950 (ECHR) is to be guaranteed;[24] this does not prevent EU law providing more extensive protection.

Overall, similar to the analysis of proportionality used in the case law of the ECtHR, the CJEU tries to answer these questions: "(i) does the measure pursue a legitimate goal; (ii) is it suitable to attain that goal; (iii) is it the least restrictive measure available in order to achieve the aim equally well as the measure chosen; and (iv) have the competing interests been balanced correctly?"[25] Like the ECtHR, the CJEU employs a balancing-based, non-structured analysis of proportionality; the elements of a typical three-tiered proportionality test, including the element of a least restrictive alternative are employed in a complex manner, i.e. together with other circumstances relevant to a particular case.[26]

[21] See footnote 17 above.

[22] See footnote 13 above.

[23] See footnote 13 above.

[24] CJEU (Grand Chamber), Joined Cases C-511/18, C-512/18 and C-520/18 La Quadrature du Net and Others v Premier ministre and Others, 6 October 2020 EU:C:2020:791. https://eur-lex.europa.eu/legal-content/en/TXT/?uri=CELEX:62018CJ0511. Accessed 25 January 2025.

[25] Kellerbauer et al. 2024, p. 611.

[26] Leonaitė 2013, p. 362.

The norms of EU law are a constituent part of the legal system of Lithuania.[27] It is also important that the Lithuanian Constitution[28] does not explicitly embody the principle of proportionality. However, in the context of human rights it is important that the Constitution enshrines conditions for limitation of implementation of constitutional rights and freedoms which, as explained by the Constitutional Court in its official constitutional doctrine, comprise a few requirements. According to the Constitution, it is allowed to limit the implementation of constitutional rights and freedoms of a person if the following conditions are followed: the limitations are established by means of a law; the limitations are necessary in a democratic society in order to protect the rights and freedoms of other persons, the values consolidated in the Constitution, as well as constitutionally important objectives; the limitations do not deny the nature and essence of rights or freedoms; and the constitutional principle of proportionality is observed.[29] These conditions in their essence are similar to that enshrined in EU law. It is interesting that these conditions were revealed in the practice of the Constitutional Court while considering constitutionality of legal regulation on criminal intelligence activities, telecommunications, and criminal law and procedure (the enumerated spheres are especially relevant in this chapter). In addition, this practice reveals that prevention of crimes and their investigation was explicitly treated as a constant function of the state and a constitutionally important objective.[30]

Public interests or constitutionally important objectives in Lithuania which could limit implementation of human rights are objectives consolidated in general terms by the Constitution, guaranteeing the particular human right. According to the Constitution, such objectives are arranged as follows, for example: from the necessity to guarantee public order (para 2 of Article 24, para 4 of Article 26 and para 2 of Article 36), necessity to apprehend a criminal (para 2 of Article 24), and necessity to protect the security of the State or society (para 4 of Article 26, para 2 of Article 32 and para 2 of Article 36), to the necessity to protect the health or morals of people (para 2 of Article 24, para 3 of Article 25, para 2 of Article 32 and para 2 of Article 36). Their sequence according to the text in all these articles is not the same, however, they could be treated as being close to those set out in the Articles 8–11 of the ECHR remembering that the constitutional human rights catalogue was prepared on the basis of international human rights standards, including the ECHR.

---

[27] Law on Supplementing the Constitution of the Republic of Lithuania with the Constitutional Act "On the Membership of the Republic of Lithuania in the European Union" and Supplementing Article 150 of the Constitution of the Republic of Lithuania. *Valstybės žinios*, 2004, No. 111-4123. https://lrkt.lt/en/about-the-court/legal-information/the-constitution/192. Accessed 25 January 2025.

[28] Constitution of the Republic of Lithuania (1992). *Valstybės žinios*, 1992, No. 33-1014. https://lrkt.lt/en/about-the-court/legal-information/the-constitution/192. Accessed 25 January 2025.

[29] Constitutional Court's rulings of 8 May (*Valstybės žinios*, 2000, No. 39-1105. https://lrkt.lt/en/court-acts/search/170/ta1160/content. Accessed 25 January 2025) and 19 September 2002 (*Valstybės žinios*, 2002, No. 93-4000. https://lrkt.lt/en/court-acts/search/170/ta1210/content. Accessed 25 January 2025).

[30] Constitutional Court's ruling of 19 September 2002. See footnote 29 above.

In the beginning of its activities the Constitutional Court addressed the principle of proportionality for the first time with reference to the jurisprudence of the ECtHR,[31] and later, it is concluded, that it moved towards the authentic constitutional doctrine.[32] The principle of proportionality, as one of the elements of the constitutional principle of a state under the rule of law, means that the measures provided for by law must be in line with legitimate objectives important to society, that these measures must be necessary in order to reach the said objectives, and that these measures must not restrict the rights or freedoms of a person clearly more than necessary in order to reach the said objectives,[33] including that these measures must not deny the essence of the rights or freedoms.[34]

The requirement of the constitutional principle of proportionality that human rights and freedoms not be limited by law more than necessary in order to reach the legitimate objectives that are important to society, *inter alia*, implies a requirement for the legislator to establish such legal regulation that would create preconditions to sufficiently individualise the limitations of human rights and freedoms. The legal regulation limiting the rights and freedoms of a person, which is provided for by law, must be such that would create preconditions to assess as much as possible the individual position of each person and, by taking account of all the important circumstances, to individualise respectively the concrete measures that are applicable to and limit the rights of a concrete person.[35]

Specifically, concerning criminal sanctions, the main requirement for the state while establishing the liability and sanctions to be applied to persons is that these sanctions must be proportionate to the committed violation of law.[36] In the context of establishment of criminal liability for criminal deeds, and ensuring of security

---

[31] Constitutional Court's ruling of 18 April 1996, *Valstybės žinios*, 1996, No. 36-915. https://lrkt.lt/en/court-acts/search/170/ta1002/content. Accessed 25 January 2025.

[32] National report prepared by the Constitutional Court of the Republic of Lithuania, XVIIth Congress of the Conference of European Constitutional Courts. Role of the Constitutional Courts in Upholding and Applying the Constitutional Principles, p. 35. https://www.confeuconstco.org/reports/rep-xvii/lituanie_EN.pdf. Accessed 25 January 2025.

[33] *Inter alia*, Constitutional Court's ruling of 11 December 2009, *Valstybės žinios*, 2009, No. 148-6632. https://lrkt.lt/en/court-acts/search/170/ta1295/content. Accessed 25 January 2025.

[34] The preventive measures which are aimed at restricting and reducing crime, are, as a rule, linked with a particular limitation on the implementation of human rights and freedoms, by which, it should be stressed, the essence of these rights and freedoms may not be denied. Constitutional Court's ruling of 29 December 2004, *Valstybės žinios*, 2005, No. 1-7. https://lrkt.lt/en/court-acts/search/170/ta1281/content. Accessed 25 January 2025.

[35] *Inter alia*, Constitutional Court's rulings of 7 July 2011 (*Valstybės žinios*, 2011, No. 84-4106. https://lrkt.lt/en/court-acts/search/170/ta1107/content. Accessed 25 January 2025), 17 February 2016 (TAR, 2016, No. 2985. https://lrkt.lt/en/court-acts/search/170/ta1602/content. Accessed 25 January 2025), 22 September 2022 (TAR, 2022, No. 19372. https://lrkt.lt/lt/teismo-aktai/paieska/135/ta2728/content. Accessed 25 January 2025), and 4 June 2024 (TAR, 2024, No. 10188. https://lrkt.lt/lt/teismo-aktai/paieska/135/ta3007/content. Accessed 25 January 2025).

[36] Constitutional Court's ruling of 16 January 2006, *Valstybės žinios*, 2006, No. 7-254. https://lrkt.lt/en/court-acts/search/170/ta1364/content. Accessed 25 January 2025.

of each person and all society from criminal attempts, the requirement of differentiated legal regulation and legal liability for corresponding criminal deeds also applies. When regulating the relations linked with the establishment of this liability, the legislator enjoys broad discretion; he, *inter alia*, may, while taking account of the nature, danger (gravity), scale and other signs of the criminal deeds, consolidates differentiated legal regulation and establishes different legal liability for corresponding criminal deeds. However, this discretion of the legislature is not absolute: the legislature must pay heed to the norms and principles of the Constitution, *inter alia*, the imperatives of regularity and inner consistency of the legal system, which arise from the Constitution.[37]

Therefore, the essence of the content of the principle of proportionality in the relevant EU legislation and the Constitution could be shortly summarized as a requirement to use only (1) what is necessary to achieve the objective, (2) what is appropriate to achieve the objective, and (3) what is not too strict.[38] However, further analysis shows that the courts do not use all of these structural components of the proportionality test.

10.3 Aspects of Application of the Principle of Proportionality in Case of a Clash Between the Right to Private Life and the Public Interest of Prevention of Crimes

Application of the principle of proportionality is relevant in the electronic communications sector. The analysed situation is related to the traffic and location data retained by providers of electronic communications services and made available to authorities in charge of criminal proceedings and subsequent use of those data in an investigation into misconduct in office. In this context both analysed courts considered two cases concerning two EU directives, i.e. Directive 2002/58 of the European Parliament and of the Council of 12 July 2002 concerning the processing of personal data and the protection of privacy in the electronic communications sector (Directive on privacy and electronic communications), as amended by Directive 2009/136/EC of the European Parliament and of the Council of 25 November 2009 (Directive 2002/58)[39] and Directive 2016/680 of the European Parliament and of the Council of 27 April 2016 on the protection of natural persons with regard to the processing

[37] *Ibid.*

[38] Goda 2014, p. 41.

[39] Directive 2002/58/EC of the European Parliament and of the Council of 12 July 2002 concerning the processing of personal data and the protection of privacy in the electronic communications sector (Directive on privacy and electronic communications) Official Journal L 201, 31/07/2002. https://eur-lex.europa.eu/legal-content/EN/TXT/HTML/?uri=CELEX:32002L0058. Accessed 25 January 2025.

of personal data by competent authorities for the purposes of the prevention, investigation, detection or prosecution of criminal offences or the execution of criminal penalties, and on the free movement of such data, and repealing Council Framework Decision 2008/977/JHA (Directive 2016/680).[40]

The CJEU had the possibility to explain the provisions of the Directive 2002/58/EC in its judgment of 7 September 2023 Case C-162/22 *A.G. v. Lietuvos Respublikos generalinė prokuratūra* on the basis of request for a preliminary ruling from the Lithuanian Supreme Administrative Court concerning the use of criminal intelligence information in investigating misconduct in office of a corrupt nature.[41] At the national level information gathered in accordance with the provisions of the Law on Criminal Intelligence had been used to assess whether the appellant in the main proceedings had engaged in misconduct in office and had been dismissed from the position in state service. The appellant before the Supreme Administrative Court of Lithuania claimed that access by the intelligence bodies, in connection with a criminal intelligence operation, to traffic data and the actual content of electronic communications constituted such a serious interference with fundamental rights that, having regard to the provisions of Directive 2002/58 and the Charter, such access could be granted only for the purpose of combating serious crime. However, Article 19(3) of the Law on Criminal Intelligence provides that such data may be used to investigate not only serious criminal offences, but also disciplinary misconduct or misconduct in office related to acts of corruption. In this case the referring court, relying on the previous CJEU case law, remind that, so far as concerns the objective of preventing, investigating, detecting and prosecuting criminal offences, in accordance with the principle of proportionality, only action to combat serious crime and measures to prevent serious threats to public security are capable of justifying serious interference with the fundamental rights enshrined in Articles 7 and 8 of the Charter ("Respect for private and family life" and "Protection of personal data", respectively), such as the interference entailed by the retention of traffic and location data, whether the retention be general and indiscriminate or targeted.

Thus, the request expressly concerned the interpretation of Article 15(1) of Directive 2002/58 which enshrines the possibility for the Member States to introduce exceptions to the obligation of ensuring the confidentiality of personal data, where such a restriction constitutes a necessary, appropriate and proportionate measure within a democratic society to safeguard national security, defence and public security, and the prevention, investigation, detection and prosecution of criminal offences or of unauthorised use of the electronic communication system; to that end, Member

[40] Directive 2016/680 of the European Parliament and of the Council of 27 April 2016 on the protection of natural persons with regard to the processing of personal data by competent authorities for the purposes of the prevention, investigation, detection or prosecution of criminal offences or the execution of criminal penalties, and on the free movement of such data, and repealing Council Framework Decision 2008/977/JHA. OJ L 119, 4.5.2016. https://eur-lex.europa.eu/eli/dir/2016/680/oj/eng. Accessed 25 January 2025.

[41] CJEU, Case C-162/22 A.G. v. Lietuvos Respublikos generalinė prokuratūra, 7 September 2023, EU:C:2023:631. https://eur-lex.europa.eu/legal-content/EN/TXT/PDF/?uri=CELEX:62022CJ0162. Accessed 25 January 2025.

States may, *inter alia*, adopt legislative measures providing for the retention of data for a limited period justified on one of those grounds. The request was made as follows: "Must the Article 15(1), read in conjunction with Articles 7, 8, 11 and 52(1) of the [Charter], be interpreted as prohibiting the competent public authorities from using data retained by providers of electronic communications services which may provide information on the data of, and communications made by, a user of a means of electronic communications, in investigations into corruption-related misconduct in office, irrespective of whether access to those data has been granted, in the particular case, for the purposes of combating serious crime and preventing serious threats to public security?"

The CJEU ruled that Article 15(1) of Directive 2002/58/EC, read in the light of the afore-mentioned articles of the Charter, must be interpreted as precluding the use, in connection with investigations into corruption-related misconduct in office, of personal data relating to electronic communications which have been retained, pursuant to a legislative measure adopted under that provision, by providers of electronic communications services and which have subsequently been made available, pursuant to that measure, to the competent authorities for the purpose of combating serious crime. Therefore, the CJEU judgment means that the disputed legal regulation of the Law on Criminal Intelligence is in agreement with the public prosecutor's office that such data used to investigate disciplinary misconduct or misconduct in office could be treated as non-compliant with EU law.[42] However, the Lithuanian Constitutional Court in its previous ruling of 18 April 2019[43] had made different conclusions while assessing the constitutionality of Article 19(3) of the Law on Criminal Intelligence. The Constitutional Court acknowledged that the disputed provision of this law (together with other related laws), according to which the secretly gathered criminal intelligence information is collected on criminal acts of corruption, declassified and used for the purposes of the disciplinary investigation, were not in conflict with the Constitution.

Concerning the principle of proportionality it is important that the Supreme Administrative Court of Lithuania, the petitioner in that ruling, grounded its doubts, *inter alia*, on the fact that the use of criminal intelligence information to bring persons to official liability is not a necessary and proportionate state measure to achieve the purpose of that liability; in this case, the balance among the values enshrined in the Constitution—the public interest in ensuring order in state service and public confidence in the state service system and in safeguarding the constitutional rights of persons to respect for private life and the right to enter state service—had not been maintained.

While assessing the established limitations to the protection of the private life of state officials, the Constitutional Court revealed certain aspects of the duty of the state to take measures to prevent corruption and the abuse of power in state service. The Constitutional Court held that the right of a person to privacy, including the right to respect for private life and for its inviolability, as well as the right to the inviolability

[42] Tamavičiūtė 2023, pp. 253–254.

[43] Constitutional Court's ruling of 18 April 2019. See footnote 15 above.

of personal correspondence, telephone conversations, and other communications, is not absolute. Under the Constitution, *inter alia*, Article 22 thereof, and the constitutional principle of a state under the rule of law, any person, thus, including a state servant (official), committing criminal or other acts that are contrary to law, for instance, misconduct in office, must be aware that such actions will trigger an appropriate reaction from authorised state institutions, meaning that a violation of the law (whether being committed or already committed) may lead to coercive measures lawfully and reasonably enforced by the state, where those coercive measures will have a certain effect on the conduct of that person, and interfere with his/her private life. It was also emphasised in this ruling that the Constitution, *inter alia*, the provision of para 3 of Article 5 thereof that state institutions serve the people, the provision of para 1 of Article 33 thereof that citizens have the right to enter state service on equal terms, the constitutional concept of state service, and the constitutional principles of transparency and publicity of state service give rise to the duty of the state to take all possible measures to prevent corruption and the abuse of power in state service restricting the exercise of the right to the protection of private life or the right to enter state service.

According to the assessment of the Constitutional Court, the impugned legal regulation, consolidated in para 3 of Article 19 of the Law on Criminal Intelligence is justified by constitutionally important objectives pursued by the state, such as ensuring proper functioning of state service, its transparency and publicity, as well as preventing corruption and acts of a corrupt nature in state service. The Constitutional Court stated that this is a necessary and proportionate measure in a democratic society in order to achieve the objective of official liability in accordance with the Constitution, i.e. to create the preconditions for the proper application of official liability, as a public form of control over officials of a democratic state and of their accountability to society, for acts incompatible with the requirements, arising from the Constitution, for state service as a system and for state officials. After providing for the possibility of declassifying criminal intelligence information about an act with the characteristics of a corrupt criminal act and using it for the investigation of misconduct in office of a corrupt nature, the right to the protection of private life, enshrined in Article 22 of the Constitution, and the right to enter state service, enshrined in para 1 of Article 33 thereof, are not restricted more than is permitted by the Constitution, since the essence of these rights has not been denied.

These arguments used by the Constitutional Court lead to the conclusion that the Court went through every applicable step of the proportionality test (necessity, suitability, and proportionality in the narrower sense), however, without showing the way how it reached its decision that the afore-mentioned rights in this situation were not restricted more than it is permitted by the Constitution, i.e. the Court only shortly justified its position with the fact about non-denying of the essence of these rights.

Moreover, according to the ruling of the Constitutional Court, the use of declassified criminal intelligence information for the investigation of disciplinary offences was allowed only with such further guarantees as, for example: the relevant state authorities, upon receiving declassified criminal intelligence information, must protect the rights of the person about whom it has been collected (to ensure the presumption of innocence), ensure the protection of such information from, *inter alia*, unjustified dissemination (distribution), and guarantee that such information will be used only for the specific purpose specified in the law, namely, for the purpose of investigating misconduct in public office of corrupt character. Thus, it means that the Lithuanian courts when implementing justice should verify all circumstances regarding the collection, keeping and use of such information, including the necessity and proportionality of use of such information for the investigation of disciplinary offences.

The enumerated guarantees could be treated as a reflection of the jurisprudence formulated by the ECtHR in its respective cases cited in the ruling of 18 April 2019 of the Constitutional Court. Although the Constitutional Court in its analysed ruling did not rely on the case law of the CJEU, after reviewing the requirements set out in the EU legislation (including Directive (EU) 2016/680), the Constitutional Court noted that the authorised state authorities, both when collecting criminal intelligence information and when using it, must take all possible measures to ensure the standards of human rights in the field of protection of personal data as set out in the EU legislation and/or the legislation of Lithuania implementing it.

On the basis of the Lithuanian request, the CJEU conclusion concerning interpretation of Article 15(1) of Directive 2002/58 was reached also while using a proportionality analysis. It comprised such major issues as: (1) evaluation whether a legislative measure adopted corresponds, genuinely and strictly, to public interest objectives; (2) evaluation whether a legislative measure is proportionate to the seriousness of the interference that it entails.

The CJEU analysed the importance of objectives that are capable of justifying a limitation of rights and obligations, and held that the list of objectives set out in the first sentence of Article 15(1) of that directive is exhaustive, as a result of which a legislative measure adopted under that provision must correspond, genuinely and strictly, to one of those objectives.[44] The CJEU grounded its position on a hierarchy amongst the objectives, in accordance with the principle of proportionality (the sequence, like in the text of the aforementioned article, is such: objective of safeguarding national security, objectives of combating crime in general, even serious crime, and of safeguarding public security).

The CJEU recalled that the question whether the Member States may justify a limitation on the rights and obligations laid down, *inter alia*, in Articles 5, 6 and 9 of Directive 2002/58 must be assessed by measuring the seriousness of the interference entailed by such a limitation and by verifying that the importance of the public interest objective pursued by that limitation is proportionate to that seriousness (para 37).[45] The importance of the objective pursued by access to data must be greater than that of the objective which justified retention. These arguments were applied

---

[44] See also CJEU, Case C-140/20 Commissioner of An Garda Síochána and Others, 5 April 2022, EU:C:2022:258, para 41. https://curia.europa.eu/juris/liste.jsf?num=C-140/20. Accessed 25 January 2025.

[45] See also CJEU (Grand Chamber), Joined Cases C-511/18, C-512/18 and C-520/18 La Quadrature du Net and Others v. Premier ministre and Others, 6 October 2020 EU:C:2020:791, para 131. See footnote 24 above.

to the subsequent use of traffic and location data retained by providers of electronic communications services. Once they have been retained and made available to the competent authorities for the purpose of combating serious crime, such data cannot be transmitted to other authorities and used in order to achieve objectives, such as, in the present case, combating corruption-related misconduct in office, which are of lesser importance in the hierarchy of objectives of public interest than the objective of combating serious crime and preventing serious threats to public security. To authorise, in that situation, access to retained data and the use thereof would be contrary to that hierarchy of public interest objectives (para 41).[46]

Therefore, the CJEU concluded that while it is true that internal investigations into disciplinary misconduct or misconduct in office related to acts of corruption may play an important role in the fight against such acts, a legislative measure providing for such investigations does not correspond, genuinely and strictly, to the objective of the prosecution and punishment of criminal offences, referred to in the first sentence of Article 15(1) of Directive 2002/58, which covers only criminal prosecutions (para 43).

Comparing two analysed decisions adopted by the CJEU and the Lithuanian Constitutional Court it is important to notice that the specifics of the Constitutional Court's decision is in the national discretion concentrating on the great significance attached to the prevention of corruption. Its significance is equated to constitutionally important objective in a democracy governed by the rule of law and promoting its progress.

10.4 Aspects of Application of the Principle of Proportionality in the Case of Other Clashes Between Individual Rights and Public Interests

There are several more recent rulings related to criminal law aspects the Constitutional Court used to consider whether the impugned legal regulation was not in contradiction, *inter alia*, with the constitutional principle of proportionality. These rulings are grounded on the EU legislation including the respective case law of the CJEU and illustrate how the Constitutional Court applied all steps of the proportionality test, except cases when the Constitutional Court found a violation in one of steps of this test and do not proceed any further in verifying the remaining elements.

The latter situation emerges from the Ruling of 4 June 2024 of the Constitutional Court.[47] The Court recognised the provisions of the Code of the Enforcement of Sentences, insofar as it did not grant sentenced persons serving a life sentence the right to short-term trips from the place of serving the sentence, to be in conflict with

[46] See also CJEU, Case C 140/20 Commissioner of An Garda Síochána and Others, para 99. See footnote 44 above.

[47] Constitutional Court's ruling of 4 June 2024, TAR, 2024, No. 10188. https://lrkt.lt/lt/teismo-aktai/paieska/135/ta3007/content. Accessed 25 January 2025.

the Constitution. Due to the fact that, according to the impugned legal regulation, this right is granted to sentenced persons serving a fixed-term sentence of the deprivation of liberty, such a legal regulation, in the opinion of the petitioner, constituted, *inter alia*, a violation of para 2 of Article 21 of the Constitution, which establishes that human dignity is protected by law.

The Constitutional Court affirmed the doubts of the petitioner. It was held that the legislature had failed to ensure the proper protection of the dignity of these sentenced persons in accordance with dignity protected under paras 2 and 3 of Article 21 of the Constitution (and the protection of which is inseparable from the protection of their personal and family life), as well as had disproportionately limited the right to the protection of personal and family life, which is guaranteed under para 4 of Article 22 of the Constitution.

This conclusion was made relying on, *inter alia*, Articles 4 and 7 of the Charter ("Respect for private and family life" and "Prohibition of torture and inhuman or degrading treatment or punishment" respectively) and Articles 3 and 8 of the ECHR ("Prohibition of torture" and "Right to respect for private and family life", respectively) and its case law formulated by the ECtHR. Although according to the Constitution, a person's right to privacy, including the right to respect for private and family life, is not absolute, the Constitutional Court noted that the right of the sentenced persons to respect for their family life, regardless of the length of their sentence, should not be unduly limited. Under the Constitution as well as under the ECHR, the refusal to allow a sentenced person to attend the funeral (or otherwise to say goodbye) of his or her relative amounts to an interference with the respect for the individual's private and family life. Although the interference in question was provided for in the legislation and pursued legitimate aims, the Constitutional Court made it possible to understand that such a limitation was not necessary in a democratic society, i.e. it was disproportionate to the aim pursued.

Summarising the above-mentioned provisions of the EU law, as well as the jurisprudence of the ECtHR, the Constitutional Court pointed out that the aim of the sentences of imprisonment for a fixed term and life imprisonment is to re-educate the convicted person, to return him or her to free society (the principle of re-socialisation of convicted persons). Therefore, irrespective of the length of the sentence, the dignity of all convicted persons serving such sentences should be respected, and their right to respect for their family life should not be unduly restricted. In this context, the Constitutional Court also noted that the right to leave the place of imprisonment for a short period of time for important reasons (on account of the death or an incurable illness of a close relative or other humane reasons), which promotes the re-socialisation of sentenced persons, should be granted to all sentenced persons serving a prison sentence, provided that they fulfil the conditions for the grant of such a right, which should be assessed by the competent national authorities on a case by case basis. The Constitutional Court noted that, under the Constitution, *inter alia*, paras 2 and 3 of Article 21 and para 4 of Article 22 thereof, when regulating the relationships connected with the enforcement of sentences, among others, when establishing the conditions for serving a sentence of the deprivation of liberty, the legislature must ensure the dignity of sentenced persons, the protection of which is inseparable from the protection of their personal and family life; the conditions for serving a sentence of the deprivation of liberty must be such that all persons deprived of their liberty, regardless of the duration of the sentence of the deprivation of liberty imposed on them, are treated humanely and are not humiliated, and these conditions must not unjustifiably limit the right of sentenced persons to personal and family life. Thus, the Constitutional Court in this ruling especially verified the first element of proportionality, relying on the practice of the ECtHR, and did not explicitly proceed any further in verifying the remaining elements of proportionality comprising the proportionality test.

The second example in this context—the ruling of 12 October 2023 of the Lithuanian Constitutional Court.[48] It affirmed compliance of the impugned legal regulation to the principle of proportionality while grounding its position on the EU legislation and case law of the CJEU. The Constitutional Court examined the constitutionality of provisions of Article 72^3 of the Criminal Code, under which the extended confiscation of property is the taking into ownership of the state of the property of the offender or part thereof disproportionate to the legitimate income of the offender, where there are grounds for believing that the property has been obtained by criminal means, and such confiscation of property is imposed when the offender fails, in the course of criminal proceedings, to provide proof of the lawfulness of the acquisition of the property. This legal regulation was declared to be constitutional including from the point of its proportionality.

The petitioner which was subjected to such a legal measure as extended confiscation of property, i.e. the sum of money referred to in the judgment of conviction, based its doubts concerning the compliance of the impugned legal regulation with Article 23 of the Constitution (ensuring protection of the right to property) principally on the fact that the extended confiscation of property is a disproportionate criminal measure to the objective pursued. The Constitutional Court dismissed these doubts. In view of the fact that, under Article 23 of the Constitution, the right of ownership is not absolute, the Constitutional Court also paid regard to the general principle of law that no one can take advantage of his or her own illegal act and to the aim of ensuring of effective protection of the whole of society against criminal acts. In this context, the legislature may also establish such legal measures whereby the property acquired by criminal means may be taken into ownership by the state from a person who has committed a criminal act for property benefit in order to prevent any person from having an incentive to continue to commit criminal acts and to continue to receive property benefit from it. A person who has acquired property by criminal means, i.e. in a manner that is conflict with the requirements stemming from the Constitution, *inter alia*, the principles of lawfulness and fairness, cannot expect that his or her property acquired in this way will be protected in accordance with Article 23 of the Constitution.

---

[48] Constitutional Court's ruling of 12 October 2023. TAR, 2023, No. 20188. https://lrkt.lt/lt/teismo-aktai/paieska/135/ta2908/content. Accessed 25 January 2025.

In assessing the constitutionality of the impugned legal regulation, the Constitutional Court held that the impugned legal regulation aimed to achieve the constitutionally justifiable objective—to implement the obligation of the state arising from, *inter alia*, the constitutional principles of a state under the rule of law and justice, to protect each person and all society against criminal attempts, to restore justice and legal order based on constitutional values, to guarantee the public interest in preventing new crimes, and to restrict and reduce crime, as well as to reduce the damage caused by them to the state and society. Under the impugned legal regulation, not all the property held by the offender, which does not correspond to the legitimate income of the offender, is taken into ownership of the state, but only the property acquired and held (or transferred to other persons) within a defined period of time, i.e. during the commission of the said less serious, serious or grave intentional crime, after the commission of the said crime, or within the period of five years preceding its commission, and only such a part of the property that exceeds the legitimate income by more than 250 MSLs is taken into ownership of the state. Since the impugned legal regulation clearly defines the most serious crimes for committing which persons are subject to the extended confiscation of property, as well as the amount of property acquired during the specified period that is subject to the extended confiscation of property, the Constitutional Court held that there were no grounds for stating that such a legal measure is not proportionate to the said constitutionally justifiable objective pursued or that the consolidated legal regulation disproportionately restricts the ownership rights of a person, which are protected under Article 23 of the Constitution.

It is consistent that the impugned national legal regulation which was inspired by the legislation of the EU was examined paying regard *inter alia* to the relevant case law of the CJEU related to interpreting of the EU legislation on confiscation of crime-related proceeds, instrumentalities and property, namely the relevant Council Framework Decision 2005/212/JHA of 24 February 2005,[49] as well Directive 2014/42/EU of the European Parliament and of the Council of 3 April 2014 on the freezing and confiscation of instrumentalities and proceeds of crime in the European Union.[50] According to Article 5 of the latter Directive, Member States shall adopt the necessary measures to enable the confiscation, either in whole or in part, of property belonging to a person convicted of a criminal offence which is liable to give rise, directly or indirectly, to economic benefit, where a court, on the basis of the circumstances of the case, including the specific facts and available evidence, such as that the value of the property is disproportionate to the lawful income of the convicted person, is satisfied that the property in question is derived from criminal conduct. The Constitutional Court grounded its conclusions also on the decision of 21 October 2021 of the CJEU in Joined Cases C-845/19 and C-863/*19 Okrazhna prokuratura – Varna Criminal*

[49] Council Framework Decision 2005/212/JHA of 24 February 2005 on Confiscation of Crime-Related Proceeds, Instrumentalities and Property OJ L 68, 15.3.2005. https://eur-lex.europa.eu/eli/dec_framw/2005/212/oj/eng. Accessed 25 January 2025.

[50] Directive 2014/42/EU of the European Parliament and of the Council of 3 April 2014 on the freezing and confiscation of instrumentalities and proceeds of crime in the European Union OJ L 127, 29.4.2014. https://eur-lex.europa.eu/eli/dir/2014/42/oj/eng. Accessed 25 January 2025.

proceedings v. DR,[51] in which it interpreted the provisions of the Directive, including its Article 5. The CJEU concluded that Directive 2014/42 must be interpreted as meaning that it not only provides for the confiscation of property constituting an economic benefit derived from the criminal offence in respect of which the perpetrator has been convicted, but also provides for the confiscation of property belonging to that perpetrator in respect of which the national court hearing the case is satisfied that it derives from other criminal conduct, in compliance with the defined safeguards and on condition that the offence in respect of which its perpetrator has been convicted is among those listed in provisions of that directive and that that offence is liable to give rise, directly or indirectly, to economic benefit within the meaning of the same directive.

In case of the third practical example, the constitutional principle of proportionality was the main tool for recognising unconstitutionality of the impugned legal regulation in the ruling of 15 March 2023 of the Lithuanian Constitutional Court.[52] It examined the provisions of the Law on the Control of Weapons and Ammunition under which a natural person who, by an effective court judgment, has been declared guilty of an intentional violent crime for whose commission the greatest punishment provided for by the Criminal Code exceeds six years of the deprivation of liberty is not considered to be a person of good repute for an indefinite period of time and permanently forfeits the right to acquire and possess specific weapons and their ammunition. The impugned provision was found to be in conflict with the constitutional principle of a state under the rule of law, insofar as the preconditions for an indefinite limitation on the right of a person having committed an intentional violent crime to acquire and possess weapons and their ammunition had been created by taking into consideration only the maximum term of the deprivation of liberty provided for in the Criminal Code for such a crime, irrespective of the length of time elapsed after the commission of the crime and irrespective of whether such a person, by acquiring and holding weapons and their ammunition, would pose a threat to public security or public order.

In this ruling the Constitutional Court emphasised constitutional limitations on a wide discretion of the legislature due to the situation emerged as, under the impugned legal regulation, not only the persons who have committed certain particularly dangerous crimes for which the most severe penalties are provided for are permanently deprived of the right to acquire and hold certain weapons and their ammunition. Therefore, the legislature disregarded the requirements stemming from the constitutional principle of proportionality and thus also disregarded the constitutional principle of a state under the rule of law. Respectively, the Constitutional Court specified in the ruling what legal regulation in this area would be in line with the Constitution, among others, the constitutional principle of proportionality. In

[51] CJEU, Joined Cases C 845/19 and C 863/19 Okrazhna prokuratura – Varna Criminal proceedings v. DR, 21 October 2021, EU:C:2021:864.

[52] Constitutional Court's ruling of 15 March 2023 TAR, 2023, No. 26122. https://lrkt.lt/en/court-acts/search/170/ta2839/content. Accessed 25 January 2025.

implementing its duty to establish the conditions and procedure for issuing and withdrawing permits to acquire weapons and ammunition in order to create preconditions for ensuring public order and public security, to protect human rights and freedoms, the legislature may lay down such measures for limiting the right to acquire and possess weapons and ammunition under the conditions and in accordance with the procedure laid down by law whereby the persons convicted for commission of a criminal act would not be issued permits to acquire weapons and ammunition for a certain period of time specified by the legislature and the issued permits would be withdrawn. However, such a legal regulation must make it possible to assess, as far as possible, the individual situation of each person and taking into account all the relevant circumstances. In this case the legislature may not to issue a permit for the acquisition of weapons and ammunition to a person who has committed a criminal act and who, even after the expiry of the time limit prescribed by the legislature, continues to pose a danger to public security or public order. Also such a legal regulation under which the persons who have committed certain particularly dangerous crimes for which the most severe penalties are provided for would never be issued permits to acquire certain weapons and ammunition would also meet the Constitution, among others, the constitutional principle of proportionality.

In the context of constitutional requirement of individualisation of the limitations of the human rights and freedoms as a part of proportionality test it is important that this requirement was relevant for constituting unconstitutionality of legal regulation adopted in response to the mass influx of migrants faced by the State of Lithuania in 2021. In its ruling of 4 June 2023 on the temporary accommodation of an asylum seeker during an extraordinary situation, a state of emergency, or a state of war declared due to the mass influx of foreigners the Constitutional Court held that the accommodation of all asylum seekers in designated places without giving them the right to move freely within the territory of Lithuania, which could last up to six months, due to the intensity of the limitation of the liberty of the person and the duration of its application, could amount to the person's detention. Although the legislature pursued legitimate objectives and therefore could establish such a legal regulation restricting the liberty of a person, in this case it did not comply with the constitutional requirement not to restrict the rights of a person beyond what is necessary for the attainment of a legitimate objective and, in deciding on the application of a measure limiting the liberty of a person, to assess the individual situation of each person as far as possible and to individualise the specific applicable measures limiting the liberty of a person: no preconditions were created for an individual assessment of each person's situation, among others, of the real threat posed by him or her to values protected by the Constitution, the interests of the state and society, which were intended to be protected by such a legal regulation, and no preconditions were created for the application of alternative measures that were less restrictive of the liberty of a person, which may have been applicable in the case of his or her detention. The legislature also had failed to observe the constitutional requirement to provide for the possibility of verifying the lawfulness and reasonableness of such limitation before a court. These conclusions of the Constitutional Court, among others, were based on international standards for measures applicable to asylum seekers, including those developed by EU law and the CJEU.

To sum up, a set of analysed cases considered by the Lithuanian Constitutional Court grounded on the respective EU legislation including the jurisprudence of the CJEU confirms that the application of the principle of proportionality, as in the case of the CJEU, is dependent on all the relevant circumstances of the case. Paying regard to them, the Constitutional Court uses only the first element from the proportionality test (i.e. necessity) if it finds its violation primarily. This is in line with the case law of the CJEU.[53] However, the Constitutional Court sometimes uses non explicit analysis of proportionality sensu stricto. Thus, it is suggested that the national court, as well the CJEU, "provides comprehensive reasoning demonstrating that it has taken account of and explored the various options available by asking how the competing interests in the case would be affected if another route had been pursued".[54] This could be done in order to avoid such a pitfall that "a court descends into judicial policy making rather than fulfilling its role of neutral arbiter".[55]

10.5 Conclusions

Overview of application of proportionality carried out in the analysed practice of the Lithuanian Constitutional Court and the European Union Court of Justice related to the criminal law aspects confirms the great significance afforded to proportionality as a judicial tool for resolving clashes between the promotion of public interests and the protection of human rights. It is one of important factors determining the conclusion in the case.

Since application of the principle of proportionality in both analysed courts pay regard to all the relevant circumstances in the case, it is flexible and there is no one standard of review. Both courts use not all structural components of the typical proportionality test (for example, in case when they find a violation in the first steps of this test), however, in principle, they ensure the general notion of proportionality meaning that national measures undertaken must be proportionate to their objectives.

The identified specifics in application of the proportionality test leads to the conclusion that the positions of the CJEU in its judgment of 7 September 2023 and the Lithuanian Constitutional Court's in its ruling of 18 April 2019 concerning use of personal data gathered by surveillance of intelligence services could not be treated as examples of the divergent judicial application of proportionality. On the one hand, both courts made their value assessments sensitive to supranational and national legislation, respectively. On the other hand, possible direction for future interrelation of jurisprudences—more frequent judicial dialogue with the CJEU through the

[53] In addition, according to Koen Lenaerts, both the EU and national courts should apply the "respect-for-the-essence test" before undertaking the balancing. Lenaerts 2019, p. 779.

[54] Kellerbauer et al. 2024, p. 612.

[55] *Ibid.*

national requests concerning application of the EU legislation—could be suggested for the Lithuanian Constitutional Court as it referred to the CJEU only twice.

References

Bomhoff J (2016) Beyond Proportionality: Thinking Comparatively About Constitutional Review and Punitiveness. LSE Law, Society and Economy Working Papers 12/2016. https://ssrn.com/abstract=2800345. Accessed 25 January 2025

Danėlienė I (2012) The Principle of Proportionality in Administrative Law [Proporcingumo principas administracinėje teisėje]. Doctoral Dissertation, Social Sciences, Law (01 S). Vilnius University, Vilnius. https://www.tf.vu.lt/wp-content/uploads/2016/08/Ingrida-Dan%C4%97lien%C4%97_Proporcingumo-principas-administracin%C4%97je-teis%C4%97je.pdf. Accessed 25 January 2025

Goda G (2014) Priorities in Terms of Values in Criminal Procedure [Vertybiniai prioritetai baudžiamajame procese]. Registrų centras, Vilnius

Gutauskas A (2019) Criminal Intelligence and the Privacy of Human Life [Kriminalinė žvalgyba ir privatus žmogaus gyvenimas]. Teisė 113:8–26. https://etalpykla.lituanistika.lt/fedora/objects/LT-LDB-0001:J.04~2019~1584868269825/datastreams/DS.002.0.01.ARTIC/content. Accessed 25 January 2025

Gutauskas A (2022) Application of Measures Adopted in the Law on Criminal Intelligence and Protection of Human Rights in Contemporary Modern Life [Kriminalinės žvalgybos įstatyme įtvirtintų priemonių taikymas ir žmogaus teisių apsauga šiuolaikiniame moderniame gyvenime]. In: Sudavičius B (ed) On the Road with the Constitution Kelyje su Konstitucija]. Vilnius University, Vilnius, pp 53–71. https://etalpykla.lituanistika.lt/fedora/objects/LT-LDB-0001:J.04~2022~1693574037974/datastreams/DS.002.0.01.ARTIC/content. Accessed 25 January 2025

Kellerbauer M, Klamert M, Tomkin J (eds) (2024) The EU Treaties and the Charter of Fundamental Rights: A Commentary (2024), 2nd edn., Volume I, Treaty on European Union and Charter of Fundamental Rights of the European Union. Oxford University Press

Lang A (2020) Proportionality Analysis by the German Federal Constitutional Court. In: Kremnitzer M, Steiner T, Lang A (eds) Proportionality in Action: Comparative and Empirical Perspectives on the Judicial Practice. Cambridge University Press

Lenaerts K (2019) Limits on Limitations: The Essence of Fundamental Rights in the EU. German Law Journal 20(6):779–793. https://www.cambridge.org/core/journals/german-law-journal/article/limits-on-limitations-the-essence-of-fundamental-rights-in-the-eu/3071D1A8FB881031F8E3F6D5799959BD. Accessed 25 January 2025

Leonaitė E (2013) Principle of Proportionality in the Case Law of the European Court of Human Rights [Proporcingumo principas Europos Žmogaus Teisių Teismo jurisprudencijoje]. Doctoral Dissertation, Social Sciences, Law (01 S). Vilnius University, Vilnius. https://www.tf.vu.lt/wp-content/uploads/2016/08/Erika-Leonait%C4%97_Proporcingumo-principas-Europos-%C5%BDmogaus-Teisi%C5%B3-Teismo-jurisprudencijoje.pdf. Accessed 25 January 2025

Ondřejek P, Horák F (2024) Proportionality during Times of Crisis: Precautionary Application of Proportionality Analysis in the Judicial Review of Emergency Measures. European Constitutional Law Review 20(1):27–51. https://www.cambridge.org/core/journals/european-constitutional-law-review/article/proportionality-during-times-of-crisis-precautionary-application-of-proportionality-analysis-in-the-judicial-review-of-emergency-measures/62C4F195CB89FA3F1CA8D27A77EACCF0. Accessed 25 January 2025

Perlingieri G (2018) Reasonableness and Balancing in Recent Interpretation by the Italian Constitutional Court. The Italian Law Journal 4(2):385–420. https://theitalianlawjournal.it/data/uploads/4-italj-2-2018/4-italj-2-2018-full-issue.pdf. Accessed 25 January 2025

Prapiestytė D (2024) Reflections of Criminal Law in the Jurisprudence of the European Court of Justice [Baudžiamosios teisės atspindžiai Europos Sąjungos Teisingumo Teismo jurisprudencijoje]. In: Lithuanian criminal justice law: Experience and future [Lietuvos baudžiamosios justicijos teisė: patirtis ir ateitis]. Vilnius University, Vilnius, pp 179–198. https://www.zurnalai.vu.lt/open-series/article/view/38056/35667. Accessed 25 January 2025

Ristroph A (2005) Proportionality as a Principle of Limited Government. Duke Law Journal 55, Utah Legal Studies Paper No. 05-19. https://ssrn.com/abstract=851624. Accessed 25 January 2025

Steiner T, Lang A, Kremnitzer M (2020) Introduction. In: Kremnitzer M, Steiner T, Lang A (eds) Proportionality in Action: Comparative and Empirical Perspectives on the Judicial Practice. Cambridge University Press

Tamavičiūtė V (2023) Preliminary Rulings of the CJEU in 2023 Based on Questions Referred by Lithuanian Courts [2023 m. ESTT prejudiciniai sprendimai pagal Lietuvos teismų perduotus klausimus]. In: The Lithuanian law 2023 [Lietuvos teisė 2023. Esminiai pokyčiai]. Mykolas Romeris University, Vilnius, pp 235–263. https://cris.mruni.eu/server/api/core/bitstreams/343f1092-50a2-42f2-b308-4d421f7016e7/content. Accessed 25 January 2025

Gintaras Goda is doctor of law, professor of practice at the Law Faculty of Vilnius University, President of the Constitutional Court of the Republic of Lithuania.

Lina Beliūnienė is doctor of law, assistant to the President of the Constitutional Court of the Republic of Lithuania, research fellow of the Institute of Law at the Lithuanian Centre for Social Sciences.

Chapter 11
Jurisdiction of the Court of Justice of the European Union in the Field of the Common Foreign and Security Policy and the Principle of Rule of Law

Irmantas Jarukaitis

Contents

Abstract Article 2 of the Treaty on European Union (TEU) establishes fundamental values of the European Union (EU) and the rule of law is one of them. For its part, Article 19 para 1 of the TEU establishes the primary objective of the Court of Justice (CJEU, the Court)—to ensure the respect for the principle of rule of law within the European Union. This provision consolidates the jurisprudence of the CJEU initiated by the *Les Verts* judgement and secures the central place of the Court in fulfilling this task within the EU judicial system. Still the EU primary law establishes various derogations to the general jurisdiction of the CJEU. One of the most extensive derogations is established in Article 275 of the Treaty on the Functioning of the European Union (TFEU) in the field of the Common Foreign and Security Policy (CFSP). Thus, the aim of the chapter is to provide for an outline of the jurisprudence of the CJEU as regards its jurisdiction in the CFSP field and its impact on the overall EU constitutional architecture. In order to do that, first, the special character and place of the CFSP in the EU constitutional architecture will be discussed. Then the recent case law of the CJEU in this field will be analysed. The analysis will focus on the efforts of the CJEU to find the right balance between the wording of the EU primary law and the need to ensure the unity, effectiveness of EU law and respect for the rule of law. It will provide an insight into the impact of this jurisprudence on the overall balance of powers between EU political institutions and the CJEU as well as the CJEU and national courts.

I. Jarukaitis (✉)
Faculty of Law, Vilnius University, Vilnius, Lithuania
e-mail: irmantas.jarukaitis@tf.vu.lt

I. Isokaitė-Valužė and H. Šinkūnas (eds.), *The European Union 2004-2024*,
https://doi.org/10.1007/978-94-6265-718-2_11

Keywords Values of the European Union · The principle of rule of law · The right to effective judicial protection · Jurisdiction of the Court of Justice of the European Union · Derogations · Common Foreign and Security Policy

11.1 Introduction

Since the beginning of the European integration process, one of the most common characterisations of the European Communities, later—the EU is that of the "Community/Union of law" (in French, *communauté/l'Union de droit*). Such a characterisation aims at emphasising different aspects of the nature and functioning of the EU.[1] One of the fundamental aspects of such a qualification is that the EU integration process itself, differently from various previous attempts to create an "integrated" Europe,[2] is based on law. Indeed, EU law and its development are also among the fundamental preconditions for integration and, at the same time, a means to achieving it (integration through law).[3] Needless to say, in such a context the principle of rule of law is of paramount importance. With its seminal judgement in the *Les Verts* case[4] delivered in 1986, the CJEU placed the principle of rule of law and one of its components, the principle of effective judicial protection, at the heart of the EU constitutional architecture.

However, when the Maastricht Treaty came into force in 1993, the role of the CJEU in the context of two newly introduced "intergovernmental" pillars was either non-existent or very limited. Whereas the later primary law amendments by the Amsterdam, Nice and Lisbon Treaties gradually "communitarised" the former third pillar—the Police and Judicial Co-operation in Criminal Matters (PJCC), which after the entry into force of the Lisbon Treaty was fully subjected to the Community method as the Area of Freedom, Security and Justice (AFSJ), the other "stronghold" (the CFSP) retained its specific nature. Thus, as a general rule, even after the entry into force of the Lisbon Treaty in 2009, the CFSP rests immune from CJEU jurisdiction,

---

[1] Jarukaitis 2023, pp. 47–48.

[2] What is meant here, is that the history of Europe is, to a great extent, the history of wars, including two world wars that happened in the 20th century.

[3] A vivid reflection of this statement is the CJEU case law examples, where such integrating character of EU law is recognised *expressis verbis*. For example, in para 50 of the opinion of 14 December 1991 on *Draft agreement between the Community, on the one hand, and the countries of the European Free Trade Association, on the other, relating to the creation of the European Economic Area,* 1/91, EU:C:1991:490, the CJEU noted that "the Court of Justice has to secure observance of a particular legal order and *to foster its development* with a view to achieving the objectives set out in particular in Articles 2, 8a and 102a of the EEC Treaty and *to attaining a European Union among the Member States*, as is stated in the Solemn Declaration of Stuttgart of 19 June 1983 (section 2.5) referred to in the first recital in the preamble to the Single European Act. *In that context, free trade and competition are merely means of achieving those objectives*" [emphasis by the author].

[4] CJEU, C-294/83 *Les Verts*, Judgement, 23 April 1986, ECLI:EU:C:1986:166, para 23.

although Article 24 para 1, second subparagraph of the TEU[5] and Article 275 of the TFEU[6] provide for two exceptions to this general derogation: the first is related to the distribution of public powers between the CFSP and the rest of EU competences and the second concerns the judicial control of the EU restrictive measures adopted against natural or legal persons.

Needless to say, this specific legal landscape created a tension between the imperative of effective judicial protection (and, with it, the unity, consistency and effectiveness of the EU legal order) on the one hand and the will of the EU Member States to keep the CFSP activities away from the scrutiny of the CJEU. Not surprisingly, it generated quite a lot of litigation giving the CJEU plenty of opportunities to search for a delicate balance between the two. Besides, back in 2013 the CJEU signalled that such a limitation of the CJEU's jurisdiction was problematic from the point of view of the EU's future accession to the European Convention of Human Rights (ECHR).[7] That consideration as well as correspondence between Article 6 of the ECHR and Article 47 of the EU Charter of Fundamental Rights (the Charter) prompted the CJEU to explore the jurisprudence of the European Court of Human Rights (the ECtHR) in order to ensure a coherence of the approaches of the CJEU and the ECtHR as regards the standards of effective judicial protection in this area.

Thus, the aim of the chapter is to provide an outline of the jurisprudence of the CJEU as regards its jurisdiction in the CFSP field and its impact on the overall EU constitutional architecture. In order to do that, first, the short analysis of the special character and place of the CFSP in the EU constitutional architecture will be provided. Then the recent case law of the CJEU in this field culminating in recent judgements *KS and KD*[8] and *Neves 77*[9] will be discussed. The research will focus on the efforts of the CJEU to find the right balance between the wording of the EU primary law and the need to ensure the unity, effectiveness of EU law and respect for the rule of law. As will be discussed further, this jurisprudence was developed using two traditional

---

[5] Article 24, para 1, second subparagraph, TEU stipulates that the Court of Justice of the European Union shall not have jurisdiction with respect to these provisions, with the exception of its jurisdiction to monitor compliance with Article 40 of this Treaty and to review the legality of certain decisions as provided for by the second paragraph of Article 275 of the Treaty on the Functioning of the European Union.

[6] Article 275 TFEU provides that "The Court of Justice of the European Union shall not have jurisdiction with respect to the provisions relating to the common foreign and security policy nor with respect to acts adopted on the basis of those provisions. However, the Court shall have jurisdiction to monitor compliance with Article 40 of the Treaty on European Union and to rule on proceedings, brought in accordance with the conditions laid down in the fourth paragraph of Article 263 of this Treaty, reviewing the legality of decisions providing for restrictive measures against natural or legal persons adopted by the Council on the basis of Chapter 2 of Title V of the Treaty on European Union".

[7] CJEU, 2/13 *Accession of the European Union to the European Convention for the Protection of Human Rights and Fundamental Freedoms*, Opinion, 18 December 2014, ECLI:EU:C:2014:2454.

[8] CJEU, joined cases C-29/22 P and C-44/22 P *KS and KD v Council and Others*, Judgement, 10 September 2024, ECLI:EU:C:2024:725.

[9] CJEU, case C-351/22, *Neves 77 Solutions SRL*, Judgement, 10 September 2024, ECLI:EU:C:2024:723.

tools of the EU judicial toolkit—the preliminary rulings procedure and direct action procedure before the EU courts. These two procedural paths predetermine different issues to be tackled in relation to the jurisdiction of the CJEU in the CFSP field. On the one hand, in case of direct actions, the central issues relate, first, to the definition of a 'proper' measure, which comes within the scope of the CFSP derogation, and then, the definition of the boundaries of exceptions to that derogation. Thus, primarily these cases touch upon the question of horizontal balance of powers between EU political institutions and the CJEU. In cases dealt with by national courts, the picture is more complex in a sense that an additional question regarding the division of powers between the CJEU and national courts arises. Finally, some conclusions are proposed on the basis of the undertaken research.

11.2 Specific Features of the CFSP in the Context of the CJEU Jurisdiction

The Maastricht Treaty, signed in 1992 by then twelve Member States, was the biggest *formal*[10] "quantum leap" of the integration process over forty years.[11] It marked the transformation of the European Communities into the European Union, reflecting its deeper, political aspirations.

On the one hand, the Maastricht Treaty enhanced the supranational nature of the so-called first pillar (the European Communities). Among other things, it introduced EU citizenship, laid the basis for a gradual introduction of a single currency, strengthened the powers of the European Parliament (for example, by introducing the so-called co-decision legislative procedure) and the Commission, and expanded the use of the qualified majority vote in the Council.

Still, some authors treated developments introduced by the Maastricht as a constitutional *volte face*, because, despite its more intense supranational nature, the EU was still based on the Member States as its constitutional foundation.[12] This statement was particularly true because the Maastricht Treaty introduced two new pillars—the PJCC and the CFSP, which, different from the first pillar, were based on methods

[10] The term 'formal' is used to emphasize that here we speak only about formal changes of EU primary law. However, one must not forget about the incremental constitutional developments resulting from the jurisprudence of the CJEU during this period.

[11] It should be recalled that the draft Treaty establishing the European Defence Community was "on the table" back in 1952, but was rejected by the National Assembly of France. Thus, it took forty years to go back to this idea.

[12] As noted by Prof. Besselink, "From a Community turning away from and beyond the Member States, depriving them of their sovereign essence, the Treaty acknowledged that the Union was based on the Member States. Instead of going beyond them, the Member States were made the constitutional foundation; moreover, their different identities had to be respected rather than overcome. The supranational vision of the 1950s had to come to terms with the political reality that Member States were not going to be superseded by the European Community or Union": Besselink 2010, p. 41.

of traditional intergovernmental cooperation, meaning that the Community method was not applicable to those pillars.

This aspect is also important in the context of the jurisdiction of the CJEU. As mentioned above, the *Les Verts* judgement was delivered back in 1986, that is, at the time when only the European Communities existed. However, given the intergovernmental nature of the PJCC and the CFSP, the CJEU's powers in those two pillars were almost absent.[13] Although the CJEU's jurisdiction was gradually expanded in the PJCC field by the Treaty of Amsterdam,[14] the CFSP remained unaffected both by the Treaty of Amsterdam and the Treaty of Nice. In fact, before the Lisbon Treaty, only Article 46 of the EU Treaty conferred very limited jurisdiction to the CJEU in the CFSP field.[15]

The next stage of reflections on the absence of the CJEU's powers in the CFSP field coincided with the general discussion on the nature and further development of the EU undertaken by the Convention on the Future of the European Union in 2001-2003. The Convention produced the (unsuccessful) Treaty establishing a Constitution for Europe (the EU Constitutional Treaty), which, after the failure to ratify it by all the Member States, was later transformed into the Lisbon Treaty. The principal framework to address this question was the Discussion Circle on the Court of Justice which, among other things, reflected upon the Supplementary Report on the question of judicial control relating to the common foreign and security policy (the Report).[16]

The content of the Report revealed the vast choice of options: maintaining the *status quo*; extending the CJEU's powers by giving the national courts the possibility to use the preliminary ruling procedure in order to *interpret* the CFSP measures; expansion of the possibility of litigation by private persons against the CFSP measures which may affect persons *other than from an economic point of view* (for example, visa bans), including actions for damages; giving the EU institutions and Member States the right to seek the annulment of the CFSP measures on the grounds that they were taken in violation of the Constitution or of a rule of international law by which the EU or all the Member States have agreed to be bound; extension of the Court's jurisdiction to CFSP matters on the same conditions as those that were applicable in the former first pillar. The Report also showed that, beyond the *status quo*, members of the Circle were divided by which option to choose. Although during later discussions there were several suggestions calling for a strengthened legal protection in the CFSP

[13] The only provision related to the PJCC could be found in Article K3 of the TEU, which envisaged conferring the jurisdiction to the CJEU to interpret international conventions concluded among the EU Member States.

[14] Article 35 of the TEU provided limited powers to interpret the PJCC measures and to rule on their validity.

[15] After the entry into force of the Nice Treaty, see Arts 46 and 47 of the TEU. See as well, for example, CJEU, case C-170/96 *Commission v Council*, Judgement, 12 May 1998, ECLI:EU:C:1998:219; CJEU, case C-91/05 *Commission v Council*, Judgement, 20 May 2008, ECLI:EU:C:2008:288.

[16] https://data.consilium.europa.eu/doc/document/CV-689-2003-REV-1/en/pdf. Accessed 8 March 2025.

field, the final result—Article III-376 of the EU Constitutional Treaty[17]—basically reflected the *status quo* and was, with some linguistic differences, brought over to the Lisbon Treaty.

One may ask a question, why, despite the obvious political will to further "constitutionalise" the EU primary law, including making the Charter legally binding, the proposals to expand the CJEU's jurisdiction in the CFSP field did not prosper? The answer may be found in the specific features of the CFSP, which still reflects the traits of intergovernmental cooperation.[18] As provided in Article 24 para 1 of the TEU, the CFSP is subject to specific rules and procedures. First, in this field the main role is played by the European Council and the Council.[19] Decisions as a rule are taken by unanimity. Besides, according to Article 41 of the TEU, specific rules apply to the financing of the CFSP activities. Even more important, it is the nature of the activities carried out and decisions adopted in the CFSP field. According to Article 24 para 1 of the TEU, the adoption of legislative acts in the CFSP field is excluded. The contents of Chapter Two of the TEU show that the CFSP matters are, as rule, political, they have an operational character. From that perspective, the EU pursues its objectives through a set of broadly defined actions, which are mainly of political and an executive nature. CFSP measures are primarily intended to govern EU institutions, bodies, the Member States and, as a rule, they are not intended to create rights or obligations for private parties. All these features led the Advocate General Michal Bobek to label a general derogation to the CJEU's jurisdiction in the CFSP field a "content-based exceptionalism",[20] because the above-mentioned specificities make those CFSP measures, by their nature, hardly amenable to judicial review.

Still, it should be underlined that these specific features are subject to several important limitations. First, the CFSP is not excluded from the field of application of EU fundamental values and principles. On the contrary, the wording of Article

---

[17] "The Court of Justice of the European Union shall not have jurisdiction with respect to Articles I-40 and I-41 and the provisions of Chapter II of Title V concerning the common foreign and security policy and Article III-293 insofar as it concerns the common foreign and security policy. However, the Court shall have jurisdiction to monitor compliance with Article III-308 and to rule on proceedings, brought in accordance with the conditions laid down in Article III-365(4), reviewing the legality of European decisions providing for restrictive measures against natural or legal persons adopted by the Council on the basis of Chapter II of Title V".

[18] See the Declaration No 13 concerning the common foreign and security policy, attached to the Lisbon Treaty.

[19] Namely the Council adopts decisions and regulations, imposing restrictive measures.

[20] CJEU, Advocate General *Michal Bobek*, case C-14/19 P *European Union Satellite Centre v KF*, Opinion, 19 March 2020, ECLI:EU:C:2020:220, para 74.

3 para 5,[21] Article 21 para 1,[22] Article 23 of the TEU[23] confirms the thesis that the CFSP activities are subjected to the same EU fundamental values and principles.[24] Besides, Article 51 para 1 of the Charter does not establish any exceptions as regards its field of application to the CFSP activities. Finally, even with the above-mentioned specific features present, under the Lisbon Treaty, the CFSP became part of the same EU legal order. This conclusion is very important, because it means that the general rules of public international law as regards, for example, the mechanisms of dispute settlement, sanctioning and enforcement[25] are not applicable to the CFSP activities in the context of the relationships between the EU institutions and the Member States.[26] Even though being *lex imperfecta*,[27] the CFSP remains part of EU law. As will be discussed further, all these features are important when it comes to proper interpretation of Article 24 of the TEU and Article 275 of the TFEU.

11.3 Jurisdiction of the CJEU in the CFSP Field: Recent Jurisprudence of the Court

The rule of law features as one of the fundamental values of the EU enshrined in Article 2 of the TEU. The CJEU makes it clear in its jurisprudence that the principle of rule of law is one of the most fundamental legal principles of the EU legal order. The Court emphasises the imperative nature of the principle, which is confirmed,

---

[21] "In its relations with the wider world, the Union shall uphold and promote its values and interests and contribute to the protection of its citizens. It shall contribute to peace, security, the sustainable development of the Earth, solidarity and mutual respect among peoples, free and fair trade, eradication of poverty and the protection of human rights, in particular the rights of the child, as well as to the strict observance and the development of international law, including respect for the principles of the United Nations Charter".

[22] "The Union's action on the international scene shall be guided by the principles which have inspired its own creation, development and enlargement, and which it seeks to advance in the wider world: democracy, the rule of law, the universality and indivisibility of human rights and fundamental freedoms, respect for human dignity, the principles of equality and solidarity, and respect for the principles of the United Nations Charter and international law".

[23] "The Union's action on the international scene, pursuant to this Chapter, shall be guided by the principles, shall pursue the objectives of, and be conducted in accordance with, the general provisions laid down in Chapter 1".

[24] See, for example, CJEU, case C-72/15 *Rosneft*, Judgement, 28 March 2017, ECLI:EU:C:2017:236, para 72; CJEU, case C-134/19 P *Bank Refah Kargaran*, Judgement, 6 October 2020, ECLI:EU:C:2020:793, para 35; CJEU, case C-29/22 P and C-44/22 P *KS and KD v Council and others*, Judgement, 10 September 2024, ECLI:EU:C:2024:725, para 68.

[25] CJEU, Advocate General *Nils Wahl*, case C-455/14 P *H v Council and Others*, Opinion, 7 April 2016, ECLI:EU:C:2016:212, paras 45–50.

[26] See, for example, Article 344 of the TFEU: "Member States undertake not to submit a dispute concerning the interpretation or application of the Treaties to any method of settlement other than those provided for therein".

[27] CJEU, Advocate General *Nils Wahl*, case C-455/14 P *H v Council and Others*, Opinion, 7 April 2016, ECLI:EU:C:2016:212, para 45.

among the other aspects, by the fact that it may not be simply "set aside" by the EU Member States by invoking the national identity clause, established in Article 4 para 2 of the TEU.[28]

When it comes to the principle of effective judicial protection, which is a corollary of the principle of rule of law,[29] Article 19 para 1 of the TEU provides that the Court of Justice of the European Union comprises the Court of Justice, the General Court, and specialised courts. This Court ensures that the interpretation and application of treaties *comply with the law* (in French, *elle assure le respect du droit*). For their part, Member States have the obligation to provide the remedies necessary to ensure effective judicial protection in areas falling within Union law (in French, *une protection juridictionelle effective dans les domaines couverts par le droit de l'Union*). This provision of the TEU introduced by the Lisbon Treaty is a general reflection of the CJEU jurisprudence on completeness[30] and complementarity[31] of judicial remedies at the EU and national level, started back in 1986 in its *Les Verts* judgement.[32] The idea of this vast and consistent jurisprudence is very clear—all

[28] See, for example, CJEU, case C-156/21 *Hungary v European Parliament and Council*, Judgement, 16 February 2022, ECLI:EU:C:2022:97, paras 232–234; case C-157/21 *Poland v European Parliament and Council*, Judgement, 16 February 2022, ECLI:EU:C:2022:98, paras 264–266.

[29] See, for example, CJEU, case C-362/14 *Maximillian Schrems v Data Protection Commissioner*, 6 October 2015, ECLI:EU:C:2015:650, para 95.

[30] See for example, CJEU, case C-550/09 *E and F*, 29 June 2010, EU:C:2010:382, paras 44–46: "the European Union is based on the rule of law and the acts of its institutions are subject to review by the Court of their compatibility with EU law and, in particular, with the Treaty on the Functioning of the European Union and the general principles of law. The Treaty on the Functioning of the European Union has established a complete system of legal remedies and procedures designed to confer on the judicature of the European Union jurisdiction to review the legality of acts of the institutions of the European Union [...] It follows that, in proceedings before the national courts, every party has the right to plead before the court hearing the case the illegality of the provisions contained in legislative acts of the European Union which serve as the basis for a decision or act of national law relied upon against him and to prompt that court, which does not have jurisdiction itself to make a finding of such illegality, to put that question to the Court by means of a reference for a preliminary ruling [...] The recognition of that right presupposes, however, that the party in question had no right of direct action under Article 263 TFEU by which it could challenge provisions, the consequences of which it is suffering without having been able to seek their annulment".

[31] See, for example, CJEU, case C-72/15 *Rosneft*, Judgement, 28 March 2017, ECLI:EU:C:2017:236, para 66: "The review of the legality of acts of the Union that the Court is to ensure under the Treaties relies, in accordance with settled case-law, on two complementary judicial procedures. The FEU Treaty has established, by Articles 263 and 277, on the one hand, and Article 267, on the other, *a complete system of legal remedies and procedures designed to ensure judicial review of the legality of European Union acts, and has entrusted such review to the Courts of the European Union*."

[32] As the Court stated, "the Community is based on the rule of law, inasmuch as neither its Member States nor its institutions can avoid review of the conformity of their acts with the basic constitutional charter, the EC Treaty, which established a complete system of legal remedies and procedures designed to enable the Court of Justice to review the legality of acts of the institutions": CJEU, case C-294/83 *Les Verts v Parliament,* 23 April 1986, ECLI:EU:C:1986:166, para 23.

EU legal acts producing legal effects may be subjected to the judicial scrutiny of the CJEU as regards their compliance with EU law requirements.[33]

Still, even after the entry into force of the Lisbon Treaty, the EU primary law establishes several derogations to this general principle. While some of them are rather marginal (for example, see Article 7 of the TEU and Article 269 para 1 of the TFEU;[34] Article 276 of the TFEU[35]), the general derogation from the jurisdiction of the CJEU in the CFSP field pursuant to Article 24 para 1 of the TEU and Article 275 para 1 of the TFEU is really a broad one. It reflects, in essence, the remaining intergovernmental nature of this field of activities of the EU, predetermined, among other things, by the above-mentioned wish to ensure a specific institutional balance.[36]

Given its broad nature and far-reaching consequences to litigants, it is not surprising that this derogation was subjected to quite frequent litigation before the CJEU and (indirectly) national courts. The jurisprudence of the CJEU developed so far,[37] may be classified into several broad categories. First of all, the question may arise, whether a challenged measure[38] comes within the scope of application of the CFSP provisions, that is to say, whether it falls within the derogation of Article 275 para 1 of the TFEU. As explained by the Advocate General *Michal Bobek* in his Opinion in *European Union Satellite Centre v KF* case, in order to be considered a "CFSP measure", coming within the scope of application of the abovementioned derogation, the CJEU practice requires that a measure be both *formally* (i.e., be adopted under the basis of the CFSP provisions) and *substantially* (in terms of its contents) related to the CFSP field.[39] Such an approach is based on the idea, that

---

[33] See, for example, CJEU, case C-439/13 P *Elitaliana Spa v Eulex Kosovo*, Judgement, 12 November 2015, ECLI:EU:C:2015:753, para 67.

[34] Article 269 para 1 of the TFEU provides that "The Court of Justice shall have jurisdiction to decide on the legality of an act adopted by the European Council or by the Council pursuant to Article 7 of the Treaty on European Union solely at the request of the Member State concerned by a determination of the European Council or of the Council and ***in respect solely of the procedural stipulations contained in that Article***" [emphasis added]. Given the importance of the principle of rule of law and effective judicial protection in the EU institutional setup, it is no coincidence that the CJEU interprets this limitation narrowly: see, for example, CJEU, case C-650/18 *Hungary v Parliament*, Judgement, 3 June 2021, EU:C:2021:426.

[35] Article 276 of the TFEU provides that 'In exercising its powers regarding the provisions of Chapters 4 and 5 of Title V of Part Three relating to the area of freedom, security and justice, the Court of Justice of the European Union ***shall have no jurisdiction to review the validity or proportionality of operations carried out by the police or other law-enforcement services of a Member State or the exercise of the responsibilities incumbent upon Member States with regard to the maintenance of law and order and the safeguarding of internal security'*** [emphasis added].

[36] See, for example, Heliskoski 2018, pp. 2–5.

[37] Attention should be brought to the fact that a substantial number of further mentioned cases were decided by the Grand Chamber of the Court, thus showing a sensitivity of the issues raised.

[38] In the context of the Article the term 'challenged measure' is understood in a wide sense, including indirect challenges, for example, in the context of claims for damages.

[39] CJEU, Advocate General *Michal Bobek*, case C-14/19 P *European Union Satellite Centre v KF*, Opinion, 19 March 2020, ECLI:EU:C:2020:220, para 61.

each derogation, especially the one limiting the fundamental principle of law, should be interpreted narrowly.[40]

For example, in the *Elitaliana SpA v Eulex Kosovo* case a dispute revolved around a call for tenders for helicopter support for the Eulex Mission in Kosovo. Different from the General Court, which accepted the plea of inadmissibility raised by Eulex Kosovo that it did not have jurisdiction given that the measures at issue had been adopted on the basis of the provisions relating to the CFSP, the CJEU pointed out that the Eulex Kosovo Mission was civilian in nature and the expenditure relating to the helicopter support service for the Eulex Kosovo Mission was to be allocated to the EU budget. Thus, the measure at issue (the contract), whose annulment was pleaded under the basis of the *EU public procurement rules*, which gave rise to expenditure to be charged to the EU budget, was not considered a 'true' CFSP measure in order to exclude the CJEU's jurisdiction to *interpret and apply the provisions of the Financial Regulation* with regard to public procurement.[41]

Similarly, in cases *H* v *Council and Others*[42] and the above-mentioned *European Union Satellite Centre v KF*,[43] the CJEU, although admitting that the challenged measures were formally adopted in the CFSP field, pointed out that Article 24 of the TEU and Article 275 of the TFEU must be interpreted restrictively and the scope of the derogation which they establish cannot be considered so extensive as to exclude the jurisdiction of the EU judicature to review *acts of staff management*. Besides, in the *H* v *Council and Others* judgement the Court made it clear that if, from a substantial point of view, a challenged measure has a dual nature, i.e., an aspect falling within the CFSP, and an aspect not related to that field, the derogation would not apply.[44]

As regards the procedural aspects, in the *Mauritius*[45] and *Tanzania*[46] judgments the CJEU ruled that it had jurisdiction to evaluate whether international agreements were concluded in compliance with the *procedure established in* Article *218 TFEU* (i.e., not a CFSP provision), although from the *substantial point of view* their content came within the scope of application of the CFSP.

Thus, this double requirement, developed to qualify as a true CFSP measure is consistent with the idea that the derogation of Article 275 para 1 of the TFEU should be treated as an exception. Although the wording of the above-mentioned provision might give the impression that those two requirements should be treated

[40] See, for example, CJEU, case C-658/11 *Parliament* v *Council*, 24 June 2014, EU:C:2014:2025, para 70.

[41] CJEU, case C-439/13 P *Elitaliana SpA v Eulex Kosovo*, Judgment, 12 November 2015, ECLI:EU:C:2015:753, paras 47–50.

[42] CJEU, case C-455/14 P *H* v *Council and Others*, Judgment, 19 July 2016, EU:C:2016:569, paras 39–40, 54–55.

[43] CJEU, case C-14/19 P *European Union Satellite Centre v KF*, Judgment, 25 June 2020, ECLI:EU:C:2020:492, para 66.

[44] CJEU, case C-455/14 P *H* v *Council and Others*, Judgment, 19 July 2016, EU:C:2016:569, paras 54–55.

[45] CJEU, case C-658/11 *Parliament v Council*, Judgment, 24 June 2014, ECLI: EU:C:2014:2025.

[46] CJEU, case C-263/14 *Parliament v Council*, Judgment, 14 June 2016, ECLI: EU:C:2016:435.

as separate,[47] the jurisprudence of the CJEU leaves no doubt that such a literal interpretation wouldn't be in line with the fundamental principles of the EU. Besides, it is fully compatible with the above-described rationale of the specific features of the CFSP and guaranties that only measures which *directly* concern the definition, implementation or execution of the CFSP *policy* is caught by the derogation.

Further, once established that a challenged measure falls into the category of a CFSP measure, the question may arise whether one or two exceptions to the derogation of Article 275 para 1 of the TFEU are applicable. So far, depending on the questions arising in a particular case, two strands of jurisprudence of the CJEU may be identified. First, the questions of the jurisdiction of the CJEU may arise in the course of proceedings before national courts where *national measures* adopted in order to implement EU law are challenged. In this type of situation, one of the issues is a distribution of powers between the CJEU and national courts and their interplay. Second, in the case of direct actions, the main object of discussion is a proper definition of the scope of application of exceptions to the derogation of Article 275 para 1 of the TFEU.

In the context of preliminary rulings procedure under Article 267 of the TFEU, two judgments of the Grand Chamber of the Court, *Rosneft*[48] and the recently adopted *Neves 77*,[49] merit particular attention. These cases are a good example of the complementarity of a decentralised judicial protection system in the EU and the importance of a dialogue between the CJEU and national courts in order to ensure the rule of law. The *Rosneft* case concerned the restrictive measures adopted by the Council and implementing measures adopted by United Kingdom institutions against a Russian company in the context of Russian aggression against Ukraine in 2014. In response to those acts of Russia, the Council adopted a set of restrictive measures under the CFSP, including Decision 2014/512[50] and, within the scope of application of the TFEU, Regulation No 833/2014.[51] As of 8 September 2014, both Decision 2014/512 and Regulation No 833/2014 specifically mentioned *Rosneft* as an entity that is subject to some of the restrictions imposed by those acts. *Rosneft* brought actions against the restrictive measures both before the EU and the UK courts. Before the General Court it sought directly the annulment of the contested acts. In addition, *Rosneft* brought an application for judicial review before the High Court of Justice (England & Wales), Queen's Bench Division. In this context, it claimed that both the restrictive measures adopted by the Council and the national implementing measures were invalid.

---

[47] "The Court of Justice of the European Union shall not have jurisdiction with respect to *the provisions* relating to the common foreign and security policy ***nor*** with respect to acts adopted *on the basis* of those provisions" [emphasis added].

[48] CJEU, case C-72/15 *Rosneft*, Judgement, 28 March 2017, ECLI:EU:C:2017:236.

[49] CJEU, case C-351/22 *Neves 77 Solutions SRL*, Judgement, 10 September 2024, ECLI:EU:C:2024:723.

[50] Council Decision 2014/512/CFSP of 31 July 2014 concerning restrictive measures in view of Russia's actions destabilising the situation in Ukraine. OJ L 229, 31.7.2014, pp. 13–17.

[51] Council Regulation (EU) No 833/2014 of 31 July 2014 concerning restrictive measures in view of Russia's actions destabilising the situation in Ukraine. OJ L 229, 31.7.2014, pp. 1–11.

Thus, *ratione materiae*, the object of the litigation before a national court was *individual restrictive measures*, besides, the contested EU legal act was also directed against the applicant. The referring court was mindful of the *Foto-Frost* judgment[52] of the CJEU and noted that it didn't have a jurisdiction to rule on the validity of those EU acts. It pointed out that, on the one hand, the contested measures were adopted in the CFSP field, but, on the other hand, those measures had a serious impact on the applicant and that the principle of effective judicial protection was at stake. Thus, it posed preliminary questions both, as regards the jurisdiction of the CJEU as well as the validity of the relevant EU rules and, in case of their legality, their proper interpretation. It should be pointed out at the outset that, on the one hand, the *object* of the litigation was individual restrictive measures adopted against a moral person. On the other hand, *the wording* of Article 275 para 2 of the TFEU mentions only "proceedings, brought in accordance with the conditions laid down *in the fourth paragraph of Article 263 of this Treaty*, reviewing the legality of decisions providing for restrictive measures against natural or legal persons adopted by the Council on the basis of Chapter 2 of Title V of the Treaty on European Union" and is silent on the preliminary rulings procedure under Article 267 of the TFEU. Therefore, the main issue as regards the jurisdiction of the CJEU was of more a procedural rather than of a substantial nature.

Some of the EU Member States and the Council intervened before the Court and pleaded that it lacked jurisdiction to give a preliminary ruling on the validity of Decision 2014/512. Both Advocate General Wathelet[53] and the CJEU disagreed. The Court insisted on the need to ensure a complete legal system of remedies and underlined the complementarity of judicial proceedings under Articles 263 and 267 of the TFEU.[54] It noted that requests for preliminary rulings on the validity of EU measures serve in essence the same function as direct actions before EU courts, namely, they ensure effective judicial protection within the EU. Further, while admitting that the Charter cannot confer jurisdiction to the Court where the EU primary law excludes it, the CJEU relied on Article 47 of the Charter as reaffirmation of the principle of effective judicial protection in order to support the conclusion that the derogation to the Court's jurisdiction in the field of the CFSP should be interpreted strictly. Therefore, it concluded that the restrictive interpretation of EU primary law, excluding its jurisdiction to rule on the validity of EU legal acts when they relate to restrictive measures against natural or legal persons, would be inconsistent with the system of effective judicial protection established by EU primary law. Besides, not surprisingly, the CJEU rejected the argument that in this type of situations national courts alone could ensure the same level of protection. Here, the Court relied on its *Foto-Frost* judgment and insisted on its exclusive competence to rule on the validity of EU legal

[52] CJEU, case C-314/85 *Foto-Frost v Hauptzollamt Lübeck-Ost*, Judgement, 22 October 1987, ECLI:EU:C:1987:452.

[53] CJEU, Advocate General *Melchior Wathelet*, case C-72/15 *Rosneft*, Opinion, 31 May 216, ECLI:EU:C:2016:381.

[54] Besides, in para 62 of the Judgement the CJEU pointed out that regarding its jurisdiction to monitor compliance with Article 40 of the TEU, the Treaties do not make provision for any particular means by which such judicial monitoring is to be carried out.

acts in order to ensure the uniformity, coherence, legal certainty and the effectiveness of the EU legal order.[55]

To sum up, the result of the *Rosneft* case was such that the exception of Article 275 para 2 of the TFEU as regards the restrictive measures against natural or legal persons was extended *procedurally*, i.e., to situations when national courts face challenges of validity of CFSP measures and there is a necessity to trigger the preliminary rulings procedure. Thus, on the one hand, there was a necessity to ensure the effective judicial protection of litigants' rights and, on the other, the uniformity, coherence and the effectives of the EU legal order.

This jurisprudence was further developed in a recent *Neves 77* case,[56] which, from the point of view of the jurisdiction of the Court, was more complex and complicated. The preliminary reference concerning the interpretation of the general CFSP act—the above-mentioned Decision 2014/512—was brought before the CJEU by the Romanian court in the context of a national litigation in which a Romanian company challenged a fine and an order of confiscation which were imposed by national authorities for an alleged violation of the sanctions regime, established at the EU level and implemented at the national level. It should be noted that the challenged national administrative act found the violation of both provisions of Decision 2014/512 and the order of the government implementing that CFSP decision. Although it may seem that the main difference between the *Rosneft* and *Neves 77* cases stem from the fact that in the latter case the preliminary questions posed by a national court related to the *interpretation* rather than validity of EU legal rules, this difference is not very relevant.[57] The main aspect of the case was the fact that in this particular situation the CFSP decision was not followed by the adoption of a regulation under Article 215 of the TFEU which would give full effects of EU law including its primacy and direct effect in the Member States. Thus, from the point of view of the jurisdiction of the Court, the main question was the following: does the CJEU has a jurisdiction to interpret *a general* CFSP measure, although it's not 'incorporated' by a subsequent regulation adopted by the Council on the basis of Article 215 of the TFEU? Again, although the views of the intervening parties differed, the Court, partially building on the *Rosneft* judgement, answered that question positively. It recalled the two exceptions of Article 275 para 2 of the TFEU and, as regards measures adopted on the basis of provisions relating to the CFSP, pointed out that *it is the individual nature* of those measures which permits access to the EU Courts. However, it was clear that the interpretation of EU law sought by a national court (Article 2(2)(a) of Decision 2014/512) concerned a measure of *general scope*, thus, this exception to the derogation was not applicable. However, the Court stressed that its jurisdiction is in no way restricted with respect to a regulation, adopted on the basis of Article 215

[55] See paras 77–80 of the *Rosneft* judgement.

[56] CJEU, case C-351/22, *Neves 77 Solutions SRL*, Judgement, 10 September 2024, ECLI:EU:C:2024:723.

[57] It should be noted that when deciding on the validity of a legal act a court must interpret it (unless validity is challenged on purely procedural, not substantive arguments), thus, as a rule, a decision on validity is at the same time a decision, interpreting such a legal act.

of the TFEU, which gives effect to the positions adopted by the EU in the context of the CFSP, because such regulations are EU acts adopted on the basis of the TFEU and in respect to which the EU courts have full jurisdiction. In this case there was no dispute that no regulation incorporating Decision 2014/512 was adopted. The CJEU noted that with respect to its jurisdiction to monitor compliance with Article 40 of the TEU, the EU primary law does not make provision for any particular means by which such judicial monitoring is to be carried out, thus, it is the Court's responsibility to ensure that implementation of the CFSP by the Council does not impinge upon the application of the procedures and the extent of the respective powers of the institutions laid down by the EU law for the exercise of the EU's competences. Further, the Court stressed that Article 215 of the TFEU serves as a bridge between the objectives of the TEU in matters of the CFSP and the actions of the EU involving restrictive measures falling within the scope of the TFEU, thus, the Council *has the obligation* stemming from EU primary law to adopt necessary measures on the basis of Article 215 para 1 of the TFEU in order to give a full effect to a CFSP measure.[58] Accordingly, the Council cannot circumvent the Court's jurisdiction regarding a regulation under that article by not adopting such a measure, because otherwise such inaction would limit the right of judicial protection of the private parties. Therefore, the Court concluded that it had jurisdiction to give a preliminary ruling on the interpretation of a measure of general scope contained in an act adopted in the context of the CFSP, where the Council should have implemented that measure, which served as a basis for national sanctions imposed on a natural or legal person, by a regulation adopted under Article 215 of the TFEU.[59]

As may be seen from those arguments, the Court based its jurisdiction to interpret a CFSP measure of general scope on the existence of a legislative omission on the part of the Council which had a negative impact on both the access of private parties to justice and the jurisdiction of the Court. When it comes to the substantive part of the judgment interpreting various provisions of EU law, attention should be brought to the fact that the Court interpreted Article 17 of the Charter, thus once again confirming the thesis that the Charter is fully applicable in the CFSP field.

To conclude, both the *Rosneft* and *Neves 77* judgements serve as examples of extensive interpretation of the scope of jurisdiction of the Court in the CFSP field. Such direction is completely understandable because it ensures both the effective judicial protection of litigants' rights and the uniformity, coherence and effectiveness of EU law. Besides, such an interpretation does not go beyond the perimeter of the exceptions laid down in Article 275 para 2 of the TFEU and is more predetermined by procedural considerations, because *ratione materiae* both cases are related to *individual restrictive measures* (or sanctions imposed because of disrespect of those measures).

---

[58] In that regard, the Court pointed to a clear content of Article 215 para 1 of the TFEU: the words 'shall adopt', in contrast to the words 'may adopt' used in para 2 of the article.

[59] As regards the case at issue, the CJEU pointed out the fact that the prohibition established by the CFSP measure was intended to restrict the ability of economic operators to carry out transactions that come within the scope of the TFEU. Accordingly, it could be enforced at EU level only where it is followed by the adoption of a regulation under Article 215 TFEU.

Turning to direct actions under Article 263 of the TFEU, first, it should be noted that the jurisprudence of the CJEU envisaging such a right in the context of the CFSP restrictive measures predates the Lisbon Treaty, by which it was explicitly added as an exception to the derogation in Article 275 para 2 of the TFEU. The Court recognised the right of the parties to challenge those measures in the *Kadi* judgement[60] even in the context of implementation of the United Nation Security Council (UN SC) resolutions. It should be emphasised that namely in this case the jurisdiction of the EU courts was questioned from a very particular angle. It was argued by some litigants that a challenged EU regulation was implementing the UN SC resolutions, therefore, the provisions of that regulation were not amenable to judicial review because of the primacy of those resolutions over EU law. The CJEU didn't agree with this approach and underlined that the obligations imposed by an international agreement cannot have the effect of prejudicing the constitutional principles of EU primary law, which include the principle that all EU legal acts must respect fundamental rights, that respect constituting a condition of their lawfulness which it is for the Court to review in the framework of the complete system of legal remedies established by the Treaty.[61] Thus, one may say that the exception to the derogation, established in Article 275 para 2 of the TFEU by the Lisbon Treaty, is a reflection of the *Kadi* judgement.

Once the Lisbon Treaty came into force, there were no further challenges to the jurisdiction of the EU courts as regards direct actions against individual restrictive measures by private parties. These restrictive measures may be classified into three categories: (1) measures implementing collective sanctions, introduced at the international level (imposed by the UN SC); (2) measures taken by the EU beyond those that were imposed by the UN SC; (3) autonomous measures adopted by the EU.[62] The specific decision-making process should be mentioned as well. First, the Council adopts (by unanimity) a (political) decision in the framework of the CFSP[63] and then it adopts (by qualified majority) a regulation in order to formulate the exact scope and content of particular restrictive measures. While the Council decisions are binding only on EU institutions and Member States, regulations, as usual, are directly applicable and are binding to private parties at the national level.[64]

Needless to say, as indicated in Article 275 para 2 of the TFEU, actions challenging restrictive measures, must respect the requirements of Article 263 para 4 of the TFEU. It means that litigants must be directly and individually concerned by a challenged measure.[65] The jurisprudence of the EU courts developed so far shows

---

[60] CJEU, joined cases C-402/05 P and C-415/05 P *Kadi and Al Barakaat International Foundation v Council and Commission*, Judgement, 3 September 2008, ECLI:EU:C:2008:461.

[61] See para 285 of the Judgement.

[62] Happold and Bogdanova 2024, pp. 5–6.

[63] Using Article 29 of the TEU as a legal basis for adoption of such acts.

[64] Kellerbauer et al. 2019, pp. 1635–1636.

[65] See, for example, CJEU, case C-872/19 P *Bolivarian Republic of Venezuela v Council*, Judgement, 22 June 2021, ECLI:EU:C:2021:507, para 61; CJEU, case C-348/20 P *Nord Stream 2 AG v European Parliament and Council*, Judgement, 12 July 2022, ECLI:EU:C:2022:548, paras 74, 156–158.

that litigants invoke different grounds, both substantial and procedural, in order to prove the illegality of contested measures, for example, the lack of the competence of the EU or the Council to adopt those measures;[66] a violation of the obligation to state reasons;[67] a violation of the rights of defence or effective judicial protection;[68] a violation of the right to property;[69] a violation of the freedom to conduct business;[70] a violation of the freedom of expression and information.[71] Given the fact that the practice of the use of restrictive measures by the EU as part of its external policies increased drastically in recent years, it is not surprising that this type of cases forms a noticeable part of the workload of the EU courts.[72]

Later, prompted by the actions of litigants, the CJEU further developed its jurisprudence, going beyond direct challenges of annulment of individual restrictive measures.

In the *Bank Refah* case the Court was called upon to rule on its jurisdiction in a situation where a plaintiff claimed damages for a harm allegedly caused by *individual restrictive measures* taken in decisions adopted pursuant to the CFSP.[73] In that case, the General Court ruled that such an action in the field of the CFSP fell outside the EU courts' jurisdiction.[74] Once again, the Court disagreed with such a restrictive interpretation of jurisdiction of the EU courts and followed the approach proposed by Advocate General Gerard Hogan.[75] On the one hand, the CJEU acknowledged that Article 275 of the TFEU does not explicitly mention its jurisdiction to rule on a harm allegedly caused by restrictive measures taken in CFSP decisions.[76] However, it repeated the necessity to interpret the derogation of Article 275 of the TFEU narrowly, pointed to the autonomous nature of actions for damages and the necessity to ensure the judicial protection of individuals' rights.[77] The Court underlined that its jurisdiction is not limited with respect to actions of damages in so far as it concerns

[66] See, for example, paras 158–236 of the *Kadi* judgement; para 88 of the *Rosneft* judgement; CJEU, case T-125/22 *RT France v Council*, Judgement, 27 July 2022, ECLI:EU:T:2022:483, para 52.

[67] See, for example, CJEU, case C-530/17 P *Mykola Yanovych Azarov v Council*, Judgement, 19 December 2018, ECLI:EU:C:2018:1031, paras 22, 30.

[68] See, for example paras 80–84 of the *RT France v Council* judgement.

[69] See, for example, CJEU, case T-720/14 *Arkady Romanovich Rotenberg v Council*, Judgement, 30 November 2016, ECLI:EU:T:2016:689, paras 166–173.

[70] See, for example, para 222 of the *RT France v Council* judgement.

[71] See, for example, paras 131–140 of the *RT France v Council* judgement.

[72] For example, according to the statistics provided by the CJEU, 116 cases related to restrictive measures were pending before the General Court making it the fifth most abundant category of cases: Annual Report 2023 of the Court of Justice of the European Union, p. 17: https://curia.europa.eu/jcms/upload/docs/application/pdf/2024-04/ra_pan_2023_en.pdf. Accessed 16 March 2025.

[73] CJEU, case C-134/19 P *Bank Refah Kargaran*, Judgement, 6 October 2020, ECLI:EU:C:2020:793.

[74] See paras 30–32 of the *Bank Refah* judgment.

[75] CJEU, Advocate General *Gerard Hogan*, case C-134/19 P *Bank Refah Kargaran v Council of the European Union*, Opinion, 28 May 2020, ECLI:EU:C:2020:396.

[76] Para 31 of the *Bank Refah* judgement.

[77] Paras 32–33 of the *Bank Refah* judgement.

restrictive measures provided for by regulations based on Article 215 of the TFEU.[78] Given the fact that Article 215 of the TFEU serves as a bridge between the objectives of the TEU in the CFSP matters and the actions of the EU involving economic measures falling within the scope of the TFEU, the CJEU emphasised the need to ensure the coherence of the EU judicial protection system by accepting its jurisdiction in actions for damages for the harm allegedly caused by restrictive measures provided for in CFSP decisions.[79] Thus, the Court took a step further, however, the subject matter of a dispute maintained a link with an individual restrictive measure.

The next major development of the jurisprudence of the CJEU is, without any doubt, its recent judgment in the case of *KS and KD v Council and others.*[80] The case concerned a claim for damages from the EU for the alleged harm inflicted on the family members of disappeared persons in the Kosovo conflict on the ground that the EU Rule of Law Mission in Kosovo, established by Joint Action 2008/124/CFSP, did not investigate the crimes in a proper manner and thus violated certain fundamental rights. Thus, the main novelty of the case stemmed from the fact that, different from the cases discussed above, the object of this case had nothing to do with individual restrictive measures, nor with proper delimitation of competences under Article 40 of the TEU. The General Court dismissed the action by the order on the ground that it manifestly lacked jurisdiction in this case, because the conduct in question fell within the scope of political or strategic decisions within the CFSP field.[81]

Once again, the CJEU disagreed. On the one hand, it rejected the argument that the General Court incorrectly interpreted Article 47 of the Charter and disregarded the jurisprudence of the CJEU concerning the complete system of legal remedies and protection of fundamental rights within the EU.[82] The Court confirmed that both the general principles of the EU and the Charter are applicable in the CFSP field.[83] However, it emphasised that Article 24 of the TEU establishes a clear limitation to the jurisdiction of the CJEU,[84] whereas provisions of the Charter may not be interpreted as conferring jurisdiction to the Court when provisions of the primary law exclude it.[85] Still, the Court underlined that such a limitation of its jurisdiction may be reconciled both with the ECHR and the Charter. Given the necessity to interpret Article 47 of the Charter and Arts 6 and 13 of the ECHR consistently, the Court relied

[78] Para 37 of the *Bank Refah* judgement.

[79] Paras 38–39 of the *Bank Refah* judgement.

[80] CJEU, joined cases C-29/22 P and C-44/22 P *KS and KD v Council and Others*, Judgement, 10 September 2024, ECLI:EU:C:2024:725.

[81] Paras 28–33 of the *KS and KD* judgement.

[82] Basically, that was the main line of reasoning of Advocate General Tamara Capeta, who proposed to accept the existence of the jurisdiction of the CJEU on the basis of the imperative to ensure effective protection of fundamental rights: CJEU, Advocate General *Tamara Ćapeta*, joined cases C-29/22 P and C-44/22 P *KS and KD v Council and Others*, Opinion, 23 November 2023, ECLI:EU:C:2023:901.

[83] Paras 66–68 of the *KS and KD* judgement.

[84] Para 69 of the *KS and KD* judgement.

[85] Para 71 of the *KS and KD* judgement.

on the jurisprudence of the ECtHR in which the latter Court accepted constitutional limitations of jurisdiction of national courts in the context of international relations.[86]

On the other hand, the CJEU accepted as valid the arguments of the appellants that the General Court misinterpreted the jurisprudence of the CJEU as regards the definition of a "true" CFSP measure, and accordingly the scope of the derogation. Relying on its earlier discussed case law, the Court stressed that the jurisdiction of the EU courts may be based on the fact that the acts or omissions of the EU are not *directly related to the political or strategic choices made in the context of the CFSP, and in particular the Common Security and Defence Policy (CSDP).*[87] According to the Court, this kind of delimitation of its jurisdiction reflects the *raison d'être* of the specific features of the CFSP and ensures a fine balance between the *effet utile* of specific provisions in the CFSP field and the need to ensure the right to an effective remedy. Finally, the Court undertook the analysis of the particular case in order to determine whether the General Court was right to conclude that the acts or omissions covered by the action could be qualified as "political or strategic issues which concerned definition and implementation of the CFSP". The outcome of this analysis was such that certain parts of the action were declared as not falling within the scope of the derogation.[88]

The arguments of the Court in this case show that it decided to focus on the policy dimension of the contested acts or omissions and overall objectives of the specific features of the CFSP which served as a basis for the introduction of the derogation to the Courts' jurisdiction. If a measure is a part of a broader policy decision, the derogation would apply. However, if it boils down to the everyday operation level, such measure would not be treated as a "true" CFSP measure to which the derogation is applicable, thus, the CJEU would have jurisdiction. Such delimitation clearly

---

[86] See para 78 of the *KS and KD* judgement referring to the judgements of the ECtHR of 14 December 2006, *Markovic and Others v Italy*, CE:ECHR:2006:1214JUD000139803, paras 93 and 99, and of 14 September 2022, *H.F. and Others v France*, CE:ECHR:2022:0914JUD002438419, para 281.

[87] Para 116 of the *KS and KD* judgement.

[88] More precisely, in para 137 of the *KS and KD* judgement the Court declared that it had jurisdiction regarding a breach of Articles 2 and 3 ECHR and of Articles 2 and 4 of the Charter, committed by Eulex Kosovo, on account of the insufficient investigation of the disappearance and killing of their family members, owing to that mission's lack of appropriate personnel to perform its executive mandate, a breach found by the review panel on 11 November 2015 in respect of KS and on 19 October 2016 in respect of KD; a breach of Article 6(1) and Article 13 ECHR and of Article 47 of the Charter, owing to the absence of provisions for legal aid for qualifying applicants in proceedings before the review panel and to the establishment of that panel without the power to enforce its decisions or a remedy for breaches of human rights committed by Eulex Kosovo; the failure to take remedial action to remedy some or all of the breaches referred to in the first and second indents, despite the fact that the findings of the review panel were allegedly brought to the European Union's attention by the Head of Eulex Kosovo on 29 April 2016; the misuse or abuse of executive power by the Council and the EEAS on 12 October 2017 by their assertions that Eulex Kosovo had done the best that it could to investigate the crimes at issue of which members of the families of KS and KD were victims and that the review panel was not intended to be a judicial body; the misuse or abuse of executive or public power for failing to ensure that the case of KD, concerning a war crime, be subject to a legally sound review by Eulex Kosovo and/or the Specialist Prosecutor's Office for investigation and prosecution before the Kosovo Specialist Chamber.

mirrors the idea of specific nature of the CFSP and its limits: as a rule, broad policy decisions do not affect individuals or their legal position directly, whereas individual decisions taken in the context of that policy might cause consequences affecting individuals. Not surprisingly, several commentators suggested[89] that with *KS and KD* judgement the Court employed for the first time the political question doctrine which, developed by some national jurisdictions,[90] was already invoked back in the *Kadi* case[91] and discussed by different authors in the context of EU law for some time.[92] Such an approach allows not to empty the essence of the derogation provided by the Masters of the Treaties, but, at the same time, to ensure the effective judicial protection of individual rights within the EU. Of course, this case was only the first step and it's obvious to envisage that further actions before the Court will give plenty of opportunities to further elaborate the test of *"acts or omission that are directly related to the political or strategic choices in the context of the CFSP"*. Besides, one may not overlook broader implications of this judgment concerning the prospective accession of the EU to the ECHR. Although in its Opinion 2/13 the CJEU clearly indicated that the limitations of its jurisdiction in the CFSP field create an obstacle to the EU's accession to the ECHR from the point of view of the EU constitutional architecture,[93] *KS and KD* judgement at least diminishes this obstacle by aligning approaches of the CJEU and the ECtHR as regards acceptable limitations of the right to judicial protection in this particular field.

11.4 Conclusions

The jurisprudence of the CJEU concerning the scope of its jurisdiction in the CFSP field reflects the willingness to search for a balance between, on the one hand, the specific features of the CFSP characterised by its intergovernmental and political nature of decision-making and the imperative of respect of the rule of law as a fundamental EU value and to ensure effective judicial protection within the EU on

---

[89] See, for example, Havani 2024; Sarmiento and Sanchez 2024; Vandenbosch 2024.

[90] See, for example, Political Question Doctrine 2016, pp. 723–744; Bradley and Posner 2023, pp. 1031–1090.

[91] It should be noted that the „political question" doctrine was (unsuccessfully) invoked for the first time already in the *Kadi* case: CJEU, Advocate General *Miguel Poiares Maduro*, joined cases C-402/05 P and C-415/05 P *Kadi and Al Barakaat International Foundation v Council and Commission*, Opinion, 16 January 2008, ECLI:EU:C:2008:11, paras 33–35.

[92] See, for example, Butler 2018, pp. 329–354; Mercescu and Doroga 2021, pp. 16–30.

[93] In paras 254–257 of the Opinion the Court pointed out that according to the draft accession agreement, the ECtHR would be empowered to rule on the compatibility with the ECHR of the CFSP measures, including those whose legality the CJEU could not review. It recalled that, according to its case-law, the jurisdiction to carry out a judicial review of acts, actions or omissions on the part of the EU, including in the light of fundamental rights, cannot be conferred exclusively on an international court which is outside the institutional and judicial framework of the EU. Thus, the draft agreement envisaged failed to have regard to the specific characteristics of EU law with regard to the judicial review of the CFSP measures.

the other. Still, the CJEU makes it clear that despite the specific features of the CFSP, it forms part of EU law, and thus, fundamental EU values and the Charter are fully applicable in this field. This is one of the reasons why the case-law developed so far demonstrates a clear direction of restrictive interpretation of the scope of the application of the derogation established in Article 275 para 1 of the TFEU. One may say that the Court ‘squeezes’ the scope of application of that derogation from two sides. First, it interprets strictly the notion of the CFSP measure. Second, it interprets extensively the exceptions to that derogation provided in Article 275 para 2 of the TFEU. Such a trend is seen both in the context of procedural limitations, as witnessed in the *Rosneft* judgement, and in terms of the substantive object of litigation. While earlier cases exhibited a direct or at least indirect link with an individual restrictive measure, explicitly mentioned in Article 275 para 2 of the TFEU, the *KS and KD* judgement severs that link by establishing a qualitatively new criterion defining the limits of jurisdiction of the Court in the CFSP. Still, even this judgement does not depart from the main rationale of this derogation—the jurisprudence of the Court, generated so far, focuses on protection of individual rights and does not touch upon the legality of general policy decisions.

References

Books, Articles, etc.

Besselink L F M (2010) National and Constitutional Identity Before and After Lisbon. Utrecht Law Review 6(3):41

Bradley C A, Posner E A (2023) The Real Political Question Doctrine. Stanford Law Review 75

Butler G (2018) In Search of the Political Question Doctrine in EU Law. Legal Issues of Economic Integration 45(4)

Happold M, Bogdanova I (2024) Report on the limitations of the current EU restrictive measures (sanctions) regimes. University of Luxembourg

Havani A N (2024) An EU external relations political question doctrine that suffers no human rights exception: Joined cases C-299/22 P and C-44/22 P KS and KD on the Court’s jurisdiction in the CFSP matters. European Law Blog https://www.europeanlawblog.eu/pub/kwd8041a/release/2. Accessed 16 March 2025

Heliskoski J (2018) Made in Luxembourg: The Fabrication of the Law on Jurisdiction of the Court of Justice of the European Union in the Field of Common Foreign and Security Policy. Europe and the World: A Law Review. UCL Press 2(1)

Jarukaitis I (2023) Cooperation Between Lithuanian Administrative Courts and the Court of Justice of the European Union in the Development of European Union Law: Constructive Dialogue. In: Žaltauskaitė-Žalimienė S, Treigė M (eds) European Union Law and Lithuanian Administrative Justice. Vilnius University Press, Vilnius

Kellerbauer M, Klamert M, Tomkin J (2019) The EU Treaties and the Charter of Fundamental Rights: A Commentary. Oxford University Press, Oxford

Mercescu A, Doroga S (2021) Should the European Court of Justice Develop A Political Question Doctrine? International Comparative Jurisprudence 7(1)

Political Question Doctrine (Harvard Law Review) (2016) Political Questions, Public Rights, and Sovereign Immunity. Harvard Law Review, 2016, Vol 130

Sarmiento D, Sanchez S I (2024) Insight: "KS and Neves 77: Paving the Way to the EU's accession to the ECHR". EU Law Live https://eulawlive.com/insight-ks-and-neves-77-paving-the-way-to-the-eus-accession-to-the-echr/. Accessed 16 March 2025

Vandenbosch S (2024) The Political Question Doctrine Under Close Control: What the European Court of Human Rights and the Court of Justice of the European Union Tell Us About the Changing Contours of Judicial Review in Europe. VerfBlog, 2024/10/30, https://verfassungsblog.de/the-political-question-doctrine-under-close-control/, https://doi.org/10.59704/7f65cbb649e92df6. Accessed 16 March 2025

Judgements, Opinions of the CJEU, Opinions of Advocates General

Judgement of 23 April 1986, *Les Verts*, 294/83, ECLI:EU:C:1986:166

Judgement of 22 October 1987, *Foto-Frost v Hauptzollamt Lübeck-Ost*, C-314/85, ECLI:EU:C:1987:452

Opinion of 14 December 1991, *Draft agreement between the Community, on the one hand, and the countries of the European Free Trade Association, on the other, relating to the creation of the European Economic Area,* 1/91, EU:C:1991:490

Judgement of 12 May 1998, *Commission v Council*, C-170/96, ECLI:EU:C:1998:219

Opinion of the Advocate General *Miguel Poiares Maduro* of 16 January 2008, *Kadi and Al Barakaat International Foundation v Council and Commission*, joined cases C-402/05 P and C-415/05 P, ECLI:EU:C:2008:11

Judgement of 20 May 2008, *Commission v Council*, C-91/05, ECLI:EU:C:2008:288

Judgement of 3 September 2008, *Kadi and Al Barakaat International Foundation v Council and Commission*, joined Cases C-402/05 P and C-415/05 P, ECLI:EU:C:2008:461

Judgement of 29 June 2010, *E and F*, C-550/09 EU:C:2010:382

Judgement of 24 June 2014, *Parliament* v *Council*, C-658/11 EU:C:2014:2025

Opinion of the CJEU of 18 December 2014, *Accession of the European Union to the European Convention for the Protection of Human Rights and Fundamental Freedoms*, 2/13, ECLI:EU:C:2014:2454

Judgement of 6 October 2015, *Maximillian Schrems v Data Protection Commissioner*, C-362/14, ECLI:EU:C:2015:650

Judgement of 12 November 2015, *Elitaliana Spa v Eulex Kosovo*, C-439/13 P, ECLI:EU:C:2015:753

Opinion of the Advocate General *Nils Wahl* of 7 April 2016, *H v Council and Others*, C-455/14 P, ECLI:EU:C:2016:212

Opinion of the Advocate General *Melchior Wathelet* of 31 May 216, *Rosneft*, C-72/15, ECLI:EU:C:2016:381

Judgment of 14 June 2016, *Parliament v Council,* C-263/14, ECLI: EU:C:2016:435

Judgment of 19 July 2016, *H* v *Council and Others*, C-455/14 P, EU:C:2016:569

Judgement of the General Court of 30 November 2016, *Arkady Romanovich Rotenberg v Council*, T-720/14, ECLI:EU:T:2016:689

Judgement of 28 March 2017, *Rosneft*, C-72/15 ECLI:EU:C:2017:236

Judgement of 19 December 2018, *Mykola Yanovych Azarov v Council*, C-530/17 P, ECLI:EU:C:2018:1031

Opinion of the Advocate General *Michal Bobek* of 19 March 2020, *European Union Satellite Centre v KF*, C-14/19 P, ECLI:EU:C:2020:220

Opinion of the Advocate General *Gerard Hogan* of 28 May 2020, *Bank Refah Kargaran v Council of the European Union*, C-134/19 P ECLI:EU:C:2020:396

Judgement of 25 June 2020, *European Union Satellite Centre v KF*, C-14/19 P, ECLI:EU:C:2020:492

Judgement of 3 June 2021, *Hungary v Parliament*, C-650/18, EU:C:2021:426

Judgement of 6 October 2020, *Bank Refah Kargaran*, C-134/19 P, ECLI:EU:C:2020:793
Judgement of 22 June 2021, *Bolivarian Republic of Venezuela v Council*, C-872/19 P, ECLI:EU:C:2021:507
Judgement of 16 February 2022, *Hungary v European Parliament and Council*, C-156/21 ECLI:EU:C:2022:97
Judgement 16 February 2022, *Poland v European Parliament and Council*, Judgement, C-157/21, ECLI:EU:C:2022:98
Judgement of 12 July 2022, *Nord Stream 2 AG v European Parliament and Council*, C-348/20 P, ECLI:EU:C:2022:548
Judgement of 27 July 2022 of the General Court, *RT France v Council*, Judgement, T-125/22 ECLI:EU:T:2022:483
Opinion of the Advocate General *Tamara Ćapeta* of 23 November 2023, *KS and KD v Council and Others*, joined cases C-29/22 P and C-44/22 P, ECLI:EU:C:2023:901
Judgement of 10 September 2024, *KS and KD v Council and Others*, joined cases C-29/22 P and C-44/22 P, ECLI:EU:C:2024:725
Judgement of 10 September 2024, *Neves 77 Solutions SRL*, Case C-351/22, ECLI:EU:C:2024:723

Irmantas Jarukaitis is a doctor of law, a professor at the Law Faculty of Vilnius University and a Judge (President of the IVth Chamber) of the Court of Justice of the European Union. All views expressed in the chapter are personal.

Chapter 12
Development and Challenges of the European Union's External Relations

Stefan Kadelbach

Contents

Abstract Foreign relations policies of the European Union are under the continuous challenge to balance out the objectives of the internal market, the EU's constitutional principles and the pursuit of legitimate geopolitical interests. This trilemma is a result of political history, as is the relationship between its components that have been modified repeatedly after paradigm shifts in international relations in general. Presently, the EU is under pressure to react on a new geopolitical constellation. So far, the framework of the Founding Treaties, as it has been reformed moderately in various steps, has proved flexible enough to cope with new developments such as, for instance, its enlargement in 2004 and the recent reorientation in the Common Security and Defence Policy. In the next round of enlargement at the latest, however, some principal changes in the Treaties' institutional architecture will be inevitable.

Keywords Accession · Association · Common Commercial Policy · Common Foreign and Security Policy · External relations of the European Union

---

S. Kadelbach (✉)
Goethe University Frankfurt am Main, Frankfurt am Main, Germany
e-mail: s.kadelbach@jur.uni-frankfurt.de

I. Isokaitė-Valužė and H. Šinkūnas (eds.), *The European Union 2004-2024*,
https://doi.org/10.1007/978-94-6265-718-2_12

12.1 Introduction

This chapter will deal with the relationship between different objectives of external relations of the EU and the question of how to balance them out. It starts from the assumption that EU foreign relations operate in a trilemma between the economic interests of the common market, geopolitical objectives and the promotion of the EU's constitutional principles and values. To elaborate on how external policies aim at reconciling these at times antagonistic forces, I will proceed in three steps. First, I should like to take a look back at the times in which the present Treaty framework came about (Sect. 12.2) Secondly, I will try to assess what the present balance of interest and value-oriented foreign relations of the EU is by looking into the main areas of external policies which are put in place under the so-called Community method (Sect. 12.3) Some more observations will address the Common Foreign and Security Policy which follows other rules (Sect. 12.4), before I conclude (Sect. 12.5).

12.2 History

After the failure of the European Political and Defence Communities in the 1950s and the *Fouchet* Plans in the early 1960s,[1] EU foreign policy was, for a long time, ancillary to the goal of the Common Market as envisaged in the Rome Treaties. External competencies were expressly foreseen in the fields of Common Commercial Policy and in the association policy, the latter partly oriented towards development in states with "traditional ties" to then EEC Member States, i.e. their former colonies,[2] and partly towards enlargement.

It was in the early 1970s that external relations were expressly re-introduced into the EEC (later EC) framework under the name of European Political Co-operation (EPC), in an epoch of détente, rising awareness of energy dependence of third states, the breakdown of the original Bretton Woods system and the first steps towards what is today the G7.[3] It was also in these days that the European Court of Justice (ECJ) began to develop its so-called ERTA jurisprudence that recognized implicit external competencies where the EC had legislative powers to act internally.[4] However, the understanding of political cooperation in the areas of external relations was that it would primarily serve the economic interests of the EC and its member states. The Single European Act, a reform Treaty of 1986, shortly alluded to this state of affairs in its preamble.[5]

---

[1] Loth 2014, pp. 41 *et seq.*, 100 *et seq.*; Patel 2020, pp. 61 *et seq.*

[2] Gozzi 2021, ch. X.

[3] Judt 2005, pp. 453 *et seq.*

[4] ECJ, Case 22/70, *Commission of the European Communities v Council of the European Communities* [1971] ECR 263; for further jurisprudence Kadelbach 2020.

[5] Single European Act, signed 17 February 1986, OJ 1987 L 169/1.

An explicit change in paradigm began in the wake of the Maastricht Treaty in 1992 when the EPC became the Common Foreign and Security Policy (CFSP) and was formally integrated in a more differentiated way into the Founding Treaties, shortly after the fall of the iron curtain.[6] One of the motives may have been to have the foreign policy of the reunited Germany closely integrated into the institutional framework of the EU, but also the wish to be better prepared for the new political landscape in Europe.[7] The 2004 enlargement that was on the agenda of the newly created EU from the beginning required intensive consultation and cooperation. All this took place in a geopolitical landscape within a unique atmosphere of international cooperation, which resulted in the end of the blockade in the UN Security Council, the founding of the World Trade Organization WTO and the accession of Russia and other former Soviet republics to various international treaty systems. The TEU is reminiscent of this epoch in Article 21 (1) where it sets out its value orientation at the beginning and underlines the EU's ambition to act as a "soft power", as it has been often said in the past years.[8]

There is no need to convince anyone that these days are over. Today, we live in an epoch of systemic competition between the so-called West on the one hand and rising powers, such as China, or states in fear of decline like Russia and their followers on the other. The aggressive war in Ukraine demonstrates the existential dimensions this conflict has assumed. The Treaty framework, however, is still the same as before. Is the EU prepared to adapt its policies to these new circumstances?

On its face, it appears feasible for the EU under the Treaties to re-define the EU's external orientation. Article 21 TEU speaks of "principles" as a general term, when it refers to its "values", but also allows for the safeguarding of "fundamental interests" and "security" as "objectives" to be pursued while respecting the "principles" (Article 21 (3) TEU). Article 22 TEU speaks of "strategic interests and objectives" the EU "shall identify". Hence, it appears that different weights may be put on the two (principles and interests), without, however, giving up on its principles and values.[9]

The need to seek a balance between the three tenets of EU foreign relations, i.e. the external dimension of the common market, promotion of constitutional values and safeguard of geopolitical interest, may, for instance, play a role in the choice of partners for informal or treaty relations, but also in the definition of conditions on which agreements may grant preferences to third states. The objective to secure supply chains and to counter economic coercion by third actors may become increasingly important factors in that equation. Let us take a look at how the equilibrium is sought in practice.

---

[6] Treaty on European Union, signed 7 February 1992, OJ 1992 C 191/1.

[7] Loth 2014, pp. 288 *et seq.*

[8] Moser 2020.

[9] Plohmann 2024; Soldatos 2024.

12.3 Trade, Association, Development and Enlargement

12.3.1 Common Commercial Policy

The Common Commercial Policy (CCP) has always had a foreign relations dimension, but it was only with the Lisbon Treaty that the seemingly technical area of international trade has become an integral part. The reformed TEU framework did not only extend foreign trade to the full WTO programme and beyond (i.e. investment protection, see Article 207 TFEU), it also provided for an explicit new orientation of the CCP and its integration into general external policies of the EU, underlined by the consistency requirement in Articles 205 TFEU, 21 (3) TEU. In connection with Article 21 TEU, the ambition is also that the CCP is supposed to be value-oriented.[10] By adding trade policies to the areas in which ordinary legislative procedure with enhanced participation of the European Parliament applies, the field has been politicised considerably compared to the pre-Lisbon era.

Thus, trade agreements are not purely trade-related, but follow a "Trade-Plus" strategy.[11] The obligation to hold commercial relations in keeping with the EU's principles and interests already plays out in the current generation of trade agreements such as those with Singapore and Vietnam on trade and investment,[12] and it influences ongoing negotiations with other ASEAN States like Indonesia[13] or the never-ending story on trade talks with India.[14] Other examples are Latin American states with which such agreements have been concluded or are in the process of ratification, such as Chile.[15] The project of a Comprehensive Investment Agreement project with China is atypical in that it primarily covers investment, but negotiations were suspended in 2021 after the situation of the Uyghurs caused considerable human rights concerns.[16]

---

[10] Speech by President of the European Commission U. von der Leyen before the European Parliament of 27 November 2019, as cited by Mildner 2021, p. 399.

[11] Overview at European Council, EU Trade Agreements, https://policy.trade.ec.europa.eu. Accessed 25 January 2025.

[12] Investment Protection Agreement and Free Trade Agreement between the EU and the Republic of Viet Nam, signed 30 June 2019, OJ 2019 L 175/1 and OJ 2020 L 186/3, respectively; Investment Protection Agreement and Free Trade Agreement between the EU and the Republic of Singapore, signed 19 and 20 October 2018, OJ 2018 L 279/1 and OJ 2019 L 294/3, respectively.

[13] Negotiation rounds that have started in July 2016 are still ongoing, documentation found on the Commission's website on trade policies, https://policy.trade.ec.europa.eu/eu-trade-relationships-country-and-region/countries-and-regions/indonesia/eu-indonesia-agreement_en. Accessed 25 January 2025.

[14] New negotiations began in June 2022, see Commission, EU and India kick-start ambitious trade agenda, press release of 17 June 2022, https://policy.trade.ec.europa.eu/news/eu-and-india-kick-start-ambitious-trade-agenda-2022-06-17_en. Accessed 25 January 2025.

[15] Interim Agreement on Trade and Advanced Framework Agreement between the EU and Chile, signed 13 Dec 2023, OJ L 2025/67 and 2024/1759 (not yet in force), respectively.

[16] McElwee 2023.

The Founding Treaties are flexible enough to go beyond and to strive for the deepening of relations with like-minded states, as a new generation of global trade and association agreements do. This like-mindedness does not only extend to market-economy, but also to common geopolitical interests and common constitutional principles. The agreements with South Korea or the Comprehensive Economic and Trade Agreement (CETA) with Canada are perhaps prototypes in that respect,[17] new treaties with other partners like New Zealand and Australia (envisaged) might follow these examples.[18] Treaty relations of such dimensions almost necessarily trigger political controversy in domestic politics of the state parties since they touch sensible questions of labour standards, environmental protection, or food safety. The parties are democracies after all. This potential of conflict entails difficulties in concluding such comprehensive treaties, as we have seen in the context of the Transatlantic Trade and Investment Partnership (TTIP) with the United Sates[19] and CETA.[20] The risk is that such agreements fail, with geopolitical repercussions that are hard to assess, but the chance is that deeper relations of that type with like-minded societies become internal affairs within the respective states and create more awareness of the need to cooperate more closely.

Some words are necessary with respect to the status of the EU within the WTO, in EU terms also a matter of the CCP. Apparently, in spite of all deficiencies, the WTO is the common denominator of states with competing interests and political systems. Presently, the WTO system is the only basis for trade relations with the two antagonistic superpowers in the world, at least when it comes to the international economy, i.e. the US and China. These three actors, China, the US and the EU, are the parties that are the most frequent respondents in trade disputes within the WTO framework,[21] and there is potential for more to come, taking into account the adversarial climate caused by conflict over export subsidies, copyright claims, trade defence measures, sanctions regimes and, most recently, arbitrary tariffs that entail countervailing responses. Also, high politics have their impact, if we think of the complaint raised by the EU against China because of sanctions against Lithuania in

---

[17] Free Trade Agreement between the EU and its Member States and the Republic of Korea, signed 6 October 2010, OJ 2011 L 127/6; Comprehensive Economic and Trade Agreement between Canada and the EU and its Member States, signed 30 October 2016, OJ 2017 L 11/23.

[18] Cf. the existing Free Trade Agreement between the EU and New Zealand, signed 9 July 2023, OJ L 2024/866. For Australia, see negotiating directives, Council of the EU, Doc 7663/18 ADD 1 DCL 1, 25 June 2018.

[19] See Art. 3 of Council Decision 6052/19 of 9 April 2019 that declares TTIP negotiating directives obsolete.

[20] For court proceedings resulting from CETA see ECJ, Opinion 1/17 of 30 April 2019, ECLI:EU:C:2019:341; German Federal Constitutional Court, Case 2 BvR 1368/16, Judgment of 9 February 2022, 160 Entscheidungen des Bundesverfassungsgerichts 208, English version found at https://bundesverfassungsgericht.de/shareddocs/entscheidungen/en/2022/02/rs20220209_2bvr136816en.html. Accessed 25 January 2025.

[21] See the overview on the WTO website, https://www.wto.org/english/tratop_e/dispu_e/dispu_by_country_e.htm. Accessed 25 January 2025.

the wake of its Taiwan policy.[22] The dispute settlement system within the WTO, as we all know, is not fully in place so the EU and others seek new enforcement tools and plurilateral solutions for violations of international trade law. Even though many of the dysfunctional features of current trade law are due to US idiosyncrasies, the picture mirrors the present situation of international relations. Good or bad, at least there, the EU appears as a third player that is not necessarily a party in the US/China controversy.

What could be added are some remarks about the initiatives of the EU to use the competence given under Article 207 TFEU to adapt its policies to the new circumstances and to offset each of the three tenets described above. In this vein, the geopolitical approach of the current Commission can, for instance, be seen in the enlarged kit of trade defence instruments in the last few years. Two examples can be mentioned:

- The EU introduced an anti-coercion instrument in 2023 that acts as a deterrent if countries restrict trade to try to force a change in EU policies.[23] This tool allows the EU to resolve conflicts through negotiations and to launch countermeasures as a last resort. Why this instrument is necessary appears in the example of trade restrictions imposed by China on Lithuania after the latter had announced that it was in the process of improving trade relations with Taiwan in June 2021.[24]
- Furthermore, the EU passed the Foreign Subsidies Regulation,[25] which the former Vice President of the European Commission Vestager describes as "a piece in the geopolitical puzzle", in order to protect the internal market from distortions that have become more likely in recent years, since export subsidies gained prominence as a policy tool around the world and sometimes as a means to gain market positions.[26]

Both instruments are based on Article 207 TFEU and reinforce the observation that multilateral organizations such as the WTO have become less capable to address the issues of international trade nowadays, not the least since the WTO dispute settlement mechanism has been considerably weakened. The European Commission is

[22] WTO, China – Measures Concerning Trade in Goods and Services, Request for Consultations by the European Union, WT/DS610/1, 31 January 2022.

[23] Regulation (EU) 2023/2675 of the European Parliament and of the Council of 22 November 2023 on the protection of the Union and its Members States from economic coercion by third countries, OJ L 2023/2675.

[24] European Parliament, Anti-coercion instrument: The EU's new weapon to protect trade, 20 September 2023, https://www.europarl.europa.eu/topics/en/article/20230915STO05214/anti-coercion-instrument-the-eu-s-new-weapon-to-protect-trade. Accessed 25 January 2025.

[25] Regulation (EU) 2022/2560 of the European Parliament and of the Council of 14 December 2022 on foreign subsidies distorting the internal market.

[26] Keynote of European Commission Vice President M Vestager for the Concurrences Conference on the Foreign Subsidies Regulation: "Foreign Subsidies – a piece in the geopolitical puzzle", 6 March 2023, Keynote of EVP Vestager for the Concurrences Conference.

continuing to propose new instruments to strengthen economic security and adopted new initiatives in January 2024.[27]

12.3.2 Association and Development

The second traditional area of external relations of the EU is association policies. The term is vague and can be filled with various contents, and it does not come as a surprise that the Article on association (Article 217) does not appear as one of the categories of Union competence in Articles 2 to 6 TFEU. Association agreements are often based on additional powers such as the CCP. Thus, association appears in different types, which are also of interest in terms of different ways to balance out the objectives of foreign relations as described earlier.

First, like development cooperation (Article 208 TFEU), association can serve the purpose to fulfil the EU's obligation to pursue "integration of all countries into the world economy" (Article 21 (2) lit e TEU). The Cotonou Treaty with 79 countries from Africa, the Caribbean and the Pacific[28] (today organized in the OACPS) and its successor, the Samoa Agreement of 15 November 2023 and its regional protocols,[29] set up the framework for economic relations with ACP states. The construction is that the association treaty provides the roof for European Partnership Agreements to be concluded under its auspices.[30] The system as a whole covers not only preferential trade and development, but also democracy and human rights, sustainable growth, climate change, peace and security, and migration, with a shift towards the latter subject matters: The official websites of EU institutions praise the Samoa agreement as the basis for cooperation in these "priority areas". However, this rhetoric is overshadowed by the fact that a profound reorientation is currently taking place in Africa where the influence of the former colonial powers, in particular France, is on the retreat and the European approach competes with Chinese policies to satisfy interest in commodities in return for seemingly generous loan agreements or Russian assertive action to secure gains from raw materials accompanied by activities of privately organized military companies linked to the Russian State that support elites of doubtful legitimacy. Again, as in CCP and multilateral trade, association and development have become a battlefield of competing systems.

---

[27] European Commission, Press Release "Commission proposes new initiatives to strengthen economic security", 24 January 2024, https://ec.europa.eu/commission/presscorner/detail/en/IP_24_363. Accessed 25 January 2025.

[28] Partnership agreement between the members of the African, Caribbean and Pacific group of states and the EC and its member states, signed Cotonou 23 June 2000, OJ 2000 L 317/3.

[29] Partnership agreement between the EU and its Member States and the Members of the Organization of African, Caribbean and Pacific States, signed Apia, Samoa 15 November 2023, OJ L 2023/2862.

[30] For an example, see the Economic Partnership Agreement with Kenya, signed 8 Dec 2020, OJ L 2024/1658.

Secondly, association is a term to express closer ties with trade and economic areas in other parts of the world. We already mentioned ASEAN; the efforts to establish cooperation with the trade areas of Mercosur and the Andean Pact have been going on for quite some time.[31] By a similar token, Comprehensive and Enhanced Partnership Agreements are concluded or envisaged with states in the Caucasus (Armenia, Azerbaijan second generation, on hold since 2019) and Central Asia (Kazakhstan, in preparation are treaties with Kyrgyzstan and Uzbekistan).[32] Here, trade interests (less than the "plus") are dominant.

Thirdly, association agreements are a tool of neighbourhood policy, even though the concept as such as it was laid down in Article 8 TEU has failed dramatically. Treaties with states in the Mediterranean area, i.e. North Africa and the Middle East come into that category; geopolitics and the idea to surround the EU with a ring of connected partners towards the South and the East, with the initial idea to include Russia and Ukraine, has been a strong motive for this type of treaty relations.[33]

And fourthly, and perhaps most importantly, association may express special relations with closely connected like-minded states in the sense referred to above, as it has been done with EEA, Switzerland and the UK.[34] One may also mention other states with whom treaty relations have entered a new stage compared with former types of trade agreements, such as Canada, South Korea, New Zealand, and one day Australia or Japan.

12.3.3 Enlargement

Enlargement is probably the field with the most complicated relationship between interests of the common market and other external policies. If we look at the past 20 years, tensions of that kind have not always been clearly visible. Back in 2004, it was the wish of the then eight new members to be integrated in the West, both for political and economic reasons. The so-called Eastern enlargement is usually described as a success, despite some scepticism at the time.[35] Economic key numbers for Lithuania, for example, show that the average gross domestic product per capita increased from 53% of the EU average to 88%, and Lithuania has become second on the list of countries with the most favourable conditions for foreign direct investment (after

[31] For Members of Andean see Trade Agreement between the European Union and its Member States and Colombia and Peru, signed 26 June 2012, OJ L 2024/2804 (Ecuador acceded later); on Mercosur see Torres Jarrín and Aramayo 2023.

[32] For an overview, see the Commission's website on EU Trade agreements, https://policy.trade.ec.europa.eu/eu-trade-relationships-country-and-region/negotiations-and-agreements_en. Accessed 25 January 2025.

[33] Kotzur 2022.

[34] Agreement on the European Economic Area, signed 2 May 1992, OJ 1994 L 1/3 (Iceland, Liechtenstein and Norway); on the impasse of negotiations with Switzerland about a new framework agreement see Epiney 2022; for EU/UK relations after Brexit see Radunz and Riedel 2024.

[35] Loth 2014, pp. 348 *et seq.*

Estonia and before Poland ranking third), which indicates the potential for further growth.[36]

The other and perhaps more important part of the story is the transformation of state institutions and societies in the countries formerly under the influence of Soviet rule. Let me only stress that the willingness to find compromises between the national interest of societies that have regained their independence and common European interests as they are pursued in the EU is not equally strong in all of the countries that have acceded in 2004 or, in the cases of Bulgaria and Romania, in 2007. These tensions have an impact on the CFSP, as we all know. I will come back to this point shortly.

What are the prospects for further enlargement? Presently, there are nine countries with a more or less legally defined candidate status, six from the area west of the Balkans (Albania, Bosnia and Herzegovina, Kosovo, Montenegro, North Macedonia, Serbia), plus Moldova, Georgia (on conditions), Ukraine and the special case of Turkey (negotiations frozen since 2016).[37]

The substantial legal requirements of accession are well known, they are spelled out in the so-called value clause (Article 49 read together with Article 2 TEU) and the Copenhagen Criteria of 1993.[38] On the other hand, there are obvious implications on geopolitics. German Chancellor *Scholz* only recently stressed during a visit of his colleague from Montenegro, *Spajić*, that there would be no "purely geopolitical decision" in the course of further enlargement, and fidelity to principles like the rule of law were not negotiable. On this occasion he stressed that Montenegro's chances were good, but also mentioned in the same vein that this country supported the EU course with respect to Russia.[39]

The statement fits with the traditional German position that enlargement must come with conditionality and consolidation, but this has always been hard to defend. The accession of Greece, for which Germany gave in to French wishes and over-ruled together with it the Commission's recommendation to postpone accession, was an example.[40] To be sure, geopolitics cannot be a sufficient motive in itself for such matters. Accession is an expression of self-determination, and it is perhaps not necessary to remind ourselves here of *Kant*'s insight that people may never be used as a means to an end.[41] However, it is no coincidence that the enlargement process has been revitalized (20 years after the declaration of Thessaloniki)[42] in the wake of the Russian attack against Ukraine. As Russia is seeking influence in South East Europe,

---

[36] Mihm 2024.

[37] For a recent step in the EU's enlargement strategy Regulation (EU) 2024/1449 of the European Parliament and the Council of 14 May 2024 on establishing the Reform and Growth Facility for the Western Balkans, OJ L 2024/1449.

[38] European Council in Copenhagen, 21–22 June 1993, Presidential Conclusions, Council Doc 180/1/93, no. 7.

[39] Lohse 2024.

[40] Lippert 2021, p. 455 f.

[41] Kant 1795/1968, p. 196 f.

[42] EU Western Balkans Summit Thessaloniki, Declaration of 21 June 2003, Council Doc 10229/03.

appeals to act are increasingly urgent. Thus, it is no audacious prophecy to foresee that there must be compromises, as there have been in the past, as regards progress in fields like anti-corruption, combatting organised crime, money laundering and the like.[43]

Many see the risk of conflict being imported, thus threatening Europe's security, i.e. by accepting Serbia in spite of unresolved tension with Kosovo or Ukraine and Moldova while Russia has ambitions to annex these countries. However, as former Estonian Prime Minister and today High Representative for Foreign Affairs and Security Policy of the EU *Kaja Kallas* stated, leaving these countries in a "grey zone" is widely considered to be even more dangerous.[44] That is true for both sides, the EU and the candidate states.

One of the more general, but related reservations to enlargement is the structure of the EU itself. And indeed, it is hardly conceivable to expand the EU to 35 or 36 members and to uphold the unanimity principle.[45] That there is a constant temptation to seek gains from veto buyouts can be demonstrated by the example of the decision in the beginning with negotiations with Ukraine on accession to the EU.[46] That takes us to my last point, the CFSP.

12.4 Common Foreign and Security Policy

As was said in the beginning, the CFSP follows other procedural rules than the policies dealt with so far. That the Founding Treaties stem from a different epoch is particularly true of the CFSP. It responds to the needs of the geopolitical constellation after the Cold War which was characterized by mostly non-international conflicts far away in the global South, terrorism as the most serious threat to international security, a more or less well-functioning Security Council of the United Nations, and regional security systems acting under its mandate. The CFSP has developed from a vehicle of economic interests into an instrument of coordination between allies in a difficult, but distant environment. It is questionable whether the EU, with this Treaty framework, is still in a position to follow its policies adequately. The question is closely linked to the desirability of more European sovereignty.[47]

Soon after the Russian attack against Ukraine, there was widespread satisfaction that the CFSP mechanisms appeared to work also in time of serious crisis. Various sanction packages were set up, the European Peace Facility created only shortly before was doubled in volume to finance delivery and replenishment of both lethal and non-lethal weapons by the member states as well as the training of Ukrainian soldiers, and a new Strategic Compass, at the Versailles summit in March 2022, was

[43] Cf. Chaltiel 2024, p. 193; but also see Jovanović 2024, p. 215.

[44] Kallas 2024, p. 29.

[45] Marti 2024.

[46] Van der Burchard 2023.

[47] Holterhus and Weber 2024.

agreed upon.[48] Today, the initial enthusiasm has become weaker. Military support has proved insufficient, the United States has changed its policies, and some political actors profit from the fear of an extension of the war. Furthermore, the weaknesses of European defence capacities have become apparent on all counts, be it the number of troops, their equipment, or the readiness in some Member States to provide more financial resources.

Apart from political will, for future deepening of integration and enlargement, two structural questions are of interest. The first question concerns the posture of the EU's CFSP vis-à-vis NATO, more so since the US today appears to be less reliable than it used to be. Lithuania, as other states these days, celebrates 20 years of membership in both organisations. For most East and Central European States, when it comes to external security, for obvious reasons the prevalent interest is in NATO, and the TEU, in Article 42 (2) and (7), takes this into account. For the time being, the CFSP will remain NATO's "little brother". This has also been the stance taken by German governments ever since, and in the past, Germany has supported both memberships if acceding states so wished. Recent changes in the political landscape will necessitate a reorientation also in that regard.

With respect to an EU candidate state that sees itself in serious tensions or even in an ongoing war and can therefore not become a NATO member, the problem arises whether the defence clause in Article 42 (7) TEU applies to its situation as well. There is some debate on interpretation, but in my view the better arguments, taken from the drafting history as well as the structure of the clause, militate for a reading according to which it, as a treaty obligation, applies only after the European Council has decided to enter the stage of a Common Defence (as distinguished from Defence Policy, Article 42 (2) TEU), which it has not yet done. Even though France invoked the clause after the Bataclan terrorist assaults in 2015, the reaction of third states leaves room for the interpretation that they did not treat the case as self-defence in the sense of the Treaty.[49] Thus, the fear that EU member states could be entangled into an armed conflict against their intentions is not a matter of law, irrespective of the answer to the further question whether or not the obligation would be of a legal or merely a political nature.

The second and more pressing issue for the time to come is the problem of transformation of the EU's institutional structures designed for peacetime into an organization that is resilient towards external threats. The unanimity requirement was mentioned earlier. That integration is not very deep in that field also shows in the fact that large portions of the EU budget are designed for agriculture and other civilian purposes, and it is still the member states that finance common defence policy (Article 41 (2) TEU); a twin problem, as it were, is that the CFSP is not accountable to the European Parliament.[50] Europe must do more for its security, and it has to do it in a more integrated manner. It remains to be seen if increasing awareness of the military

---

[48] Informal Meeting of the Heads of State or Government, Versailles Declaration 10–11 March 2022; for the context see Moser 2024; Hoffmeister 2024.

[49] Perakis 2024, pp. 147 *et seq.*

[50] For recent criticism see former French Minister of Defence Goulard 2024.

threat, political pressure and unprecedented efforts to mobilize financial resources for defence will yield results in that respect. First steps have been taken that presuppose a readiness to integrate the defence sector into industrial policy (Article 173 TFEU), to read the term "operative expenditure" in the sense of Article 41 (2) TEU more widely as not to preclude financing of military equipment via the EU budget, and to make use of the emergency clause of Article 122 TFEU to raise financial resources to that end.[51]

12.5 Conclusions

Obviously, the EU has begun to respond to the necessities of a world of multilateralism based on rules towards a geopolitical power game that comes with existential threats. The new paradigm of the Commission is called open strategic autonomy, which means that the EU still follows its principles as defined in the Treaties, but prepares itself to defend its interests from a more powerful position.[52]

What can we make of this? I suggest three conclusions:

First, several fields of the EU's external relations policies have become more and more interrelated. To what I have said so far, I could add the fields of industrial policy and its security dimensions, but also climate change and energy, both of which are components of the green transition which is (still) a mainstream policy of the EU.

Secondly, the logical consequence should be to harmonize procedures, including those valid in areas which operate in an intergovernmental manner.

Third, the success of the East enlargement tells us, that in the long run, enlargement helps not only the acceding states, but also makes the EU stronger, both in terms of visibility of its principles and in pursuance of its external interests.

To project these lessons into the future, the balance in pursuing "interests" (Article 21 TEU) and upholding standards (Article 2 TEU), i.e. the solution of the typical foreign affairs dilemma between universalism and particularism, must be found in a new "European communitarianism", if only to resist external pressure and to respond to existential necessity.

Acknowledgments The chapter is based on my speech held at the conference on the occasion of the 20th anniversary of the membership of Lithuania in the EU at Vilnius, 24 May 2024. The author is grateful to Thomas Siurkus for his input and comments on an earlier version of the manuscript. Internet sources cited herein were last accessed on 25 January 2025.

---

[51] Cf. Commission, High Representative of the Union for Foreign Affairs and Security Policy, Joint White Paper for European Defence Readiness 2030, 19 March 2025, JOIN (2015) 120 final.

[52] See Lumet 2022.

References

Chaltiel F (2024) La dynamique de l'élargissement de l'Union européenne [The dynamics of European Union enlargement]. Revue de l'Union européenne 677:193
Epiney A (2022) Les implications de l'échec des négociations d'un accord-cadre entre la Suisse et l'Union européenne [The implications of the failure of negotiations on a framework agreement between Switzerland and the EU]. Cahiers fribourgeois de droit européen no 30, Fribourg
Gozzi G (2021) Eredità Coloniale e Costruzione dell'Europa [Colonial Legacy and the Construction of Europe]. Il Mulino, Milan
Goulard S (2024) L'Europe enfla si bien qu'elle creva [Europe's enlarging so well that it's creaking]. Tallandier, Paris
Hoffmeister F (2024) Higher, faster, further: Recent legal developments in the European Union's Common Security and Defence Policy under the 2022 Strategic Compass. In: Kadelbach S, Hofmann R (eds) The Common Security and Defence Policy of the EU. Nomos, Baden-Baden, pp 55–87
Holterhus TP, Weber F (2024) Orte und Bedeutungsebenen von Souveränität [Places and levels of meaning of sovereignty] In: Holterhus TP, Weber F (eds) Handbuch Europäische Souveränität. Mohr Siebeck, Tübingen, pp 1–45
Jovanović M (2024) L'UE et les Balkans occidentaux: entre mots et maux. Revue de l'Union européenne 677:215–223
Judt T (2005) Postwar. A History of Europe since 1945. Pimlico Random House, London
Kadelbach S (2020) ERTA Case. In: Max Planck Encyclopedia of Public International Law. Oxford University Press
Kallas K (2024) Grey Zones are Potential Sources of War, Interview. European Voices 01/2024, pp 24–29
Kant I (1795/1968) Zum ewigen Frieden. Ein philosophischer Entwurf. In: Weischedel W (ed) Immanuel Kant Werkausgabe, vol XI. Insel, Frankfurt am Main, pp 193–251
Kotzur M (2022) Europäische Nachbarschaftspolitik [European Neighbourhood Policy]. In: von Arnauld A, Bungenberg M (eds) Europäische Außenbeziehungen, 2nd edn. Nomos, Baden-Baden, pp 401–437
Lippert B (2021) Die Bundesrepublik Deutschland und die Erweiterung der Europäischen Union [The Federal Republic of Germany and the Enlargement of the European Union]. In: Böttger K, Jopp M (eds) Handbuch zur deutschen Europapolitik, 2nd edn. Nomos, Baden-Baden, pp 447–462
Lohse E (2024) Scholz macht Montenegro Hoffnung auf EU-Beitritt. Frankfurter Allgemeine Zeitung, 30 Apr 2024, p 4
Loth W (2014) Europas Einigung. Eine unvollendete Geschichte [European Unification: An Unfinished Story]. Campus, Frankfurt am Main/New York
Lumet S (2022) The Double Integration Doctrine, an interview with Sabine Weyand. Géopolitique 31 Jan 2022, https://geopolitique.eu/en/2022/01/31/the-double-integration-doctrine-sabine-weyand/. Accessed 25 January 2025
Marti G (2024) Plongée au cœur du rapport "naviguer en haute mer: réforme et enlargissement de l'UE au XXIe siècle". Revue trimestrielle de droit européen, pp 95–106
McElwee L (2023) The Rise and Demise of the EU-China Investment Agreement. Center of International and Strategic Studies Briefs, Washington DC
Mihm A (2024) Eine Erfolgsgeschichte mit Schönheitsfehlern [A success story with flaws]. Frankfurter Allgemeine Zeitung, 30 Apr 2024, p 18
Mildner S A (2021) Deutsche Interessen in der europäischen Handelspolitik [German interests in European Trade Policy]. In: Böttger K, Jopp M (eds) Handbuch zur deutschen Europapolitik, 2nd edn. Nomos, Baden-Baden, pp 399–425
Moser C (2020) Hard Power Europe? Zeitschrift für ausländisches öffentliches Recht und Völkerrecht 80:1–12

Moser C (2024) The impact of the war in Ukraine on the EU's Common Security and Defence Policy. In: Kadelbach S, Hofmann R (eds) The Common Security and Defence Policy of the EU. Nomos, Baden-Baden, pp 23–54

Patel K P (2020) Project Europe. A History. Cambridge University Press

Perakis M (2024) The Common Security and Defence Policy of the EU – A Greek Perspective. In: Kadelbach S, Hofmann R (eds) The Common Security and Defence Policy of the EU. Nomos, Baden-Baden, pp 133–156

Plohmann M (2024) Die Interessen der Union im EU-Außenverfassungsrecht [The interests of the Union in EU foreign relations law]. Mohr Siebeck, Tübingen

Radunz A, Riedel R (2024) Differentiated Integration beyond Brexit – Revisiting cleavage perspective in Times of Multiple Crises. Routledge, London/New York

Soldatos P (2024) Essai sur l'impératif d'une stratégie géopolitique de l'Union européenne, à la lumière de la guerre en Ukraine et au-delà. Revue de l'Union européenne 679:344–353

Torres Jarrín M, Aramayo L (2023) EU-Mercosur Interregionalism. Springer Nature, Cham

Van der Burchard H (2023) Scholz gets Orbán out of the room to open Ukraine's membership talks. Politico, 15 Dec 2023, https://www.politico.eu/article/olaf-scholz-gets-viktor-orban-out-the-room-to-approve-ukraine-accession-talks/. Accessed 25 January 2025

Stefan Kadelbach is a professor for Public International Law and European Union Law at Goethe University Frankfurt am Main and the Dean of the Faculty of Law.

Chapter 13
The Impact of the Judgements of the Court of Justice of the European Union in the Protection of the Rule of Law During Constitutional Crisis in Poland

Ewa Michałkiewicz-Kądziela

Contents

Abstract The Court of Justice of the European Union is a judicial body whose decisions play an important role and have an impact on the legal systems of the Member States and their functioning. It is the decisions of the Court that ensure European Union law is effective and consistent in all the Member States of the European Union. Due to emerging global challenges that constitute a denial of traditional democratic values, and as a result create space for the development of populism and illiberal forms of democracy, the chapter will focus on indicating what role the Court of Justice of the EU currently plays in protecting the fundamental principle of the rule of law. In order to be able to answer this pressing question, the case of the constitutional crisis that began in Poland in 2015 and continues to this day will be analysed. This example will be used to discuss how a Member State violated the treaty (and constitutional) rule of law. Then, the individual actions taken by the Court of Justice of the European Union and the judgments it issued to restore the rule of law in Poland will be described and finally, their effectiveness will be assessed.

E. Michałkiewicz-Kądziela (✉)
Faculty of Law and Administration, University of Szczecin, Szczecin, Poland
e-mail: ewa.michalkiewicz-kadziela@usz.edu.pl

I. Isokaitė-Valužė and H. Šinkūnas (eds.), *The European Union 2004-2024*,
https://doi.org/10.1007/978-94-6265-718-2_13

Keywords Court of Justice of the European Union · Rule of law · Constitutional crisis · Judicial system · Supreme Court · Judges' independence

13.1 Introduction

The Court of Justice of the European Union is one of the bodies of the European Union (EU) that plays a key role in ensuring the uniform interpretation of EU law and its observance in all Member States and institutions of the European Union. Its establishment is closely linked to the development of the European integration process, the aim of which was to create a common market and then deepen political and economic cooperation between European countries. Established by the Treaties of Rome in 1957, its task was to interpret the treaties, rule on the conformity of actions taken by member states with Community law, and resolve disputes arising between states and institutions of the European Economic Community.[1]

Initially, the Court was assigned a relatively small range of cases, but over time, as the European Communities began to develop, this catalogue gradually began to grow. Subsequent enlargements, the adoption of new treaties, the transformation of the Communities into the European Union and new areas of activity of this international organization led to the growth of the Court's importance and the extension of its competences to new policy fields. Over time, as a result of the adoption of new treaties, changes also occurred in the structure and functioning of the Court, which was to ensure the unification of the judicial system of the European Union and the improvement of its functioning.[2] The greatest influence on the current shape of the Court and its position was undoubtedly exerted by the Treaty of Lisbon, which not only gave the Court new competences in the field of ruling on the protection of human rights, but also extended its scope of control over other bodies of the European Union.

Today, the Court of Justice of the European Union is seen as one of the most important international judicial bodies, and its rulings affect the functioning of the Member States and their legal systems. Its main task, which is to ensure the effectiveness and coherence of European Union law, has therefore contributed to the transformation of the Court's case law into a tool that is to have a real impact on the shaping of national legislative processes, as well as on the interpretations of legal provisions made by national judicial bodies.

The impact of the Court of Justice of the European Union is unquestionable, but global changes that challenge traditional democratic values and create opportunities for the development of populism and illiberal forms of democracy force us to reflect on what the current role of the Court is and what tools it has at its disposal to protect the Member States of the European Union from contemporary threats. In order to answer these pressing questions, the case of the constitutional crisis that began in Poland in 2015 and continues to this day will be analysed. This example will be

[1] Charzewski 2017, p. 53.

[2] Helios and Jedlecka 2018, p. 25.

used to discuss how a Member State violated the treaty (also the constitutional) rule of law. Then, the individual actions taken by the Court of Justice of the European Union and the judgments it issued in order to restore the rule of law in Poland will be described and finally, their effectiveness will be assessed.

13.2 The Rule of Law and the Case of Poland

The rule of law is a universal concept and a one of the main pillars of democratic states. It appeared in ancient philosophy, when Aristotle came to the conclusion that the rule of law is making a decision by the law and on the ground of law, not by man.[3] The modern embodiment of this idea is the assumption that "government officials and citizens are bound by and abide by the law".[4] In its original form, the rule of law was based on three pillars: absolute supremacy of the law (the law has a dominant influence on the actions taken by the authorities and prevails over their arbitrary decisions), equality for all before the law (every person must be treated in the same way before the court, regardless of their position) and an independent judiciary (it is a guarantor of the realization of human rights and the obligations of the authorities).[5] The list of elements that make up the rule of law has now been enriched, especially through the interpretative activity of international organizations. To this list we can therefore add, among others: legality, legal certainty, separation of powers (European Union),[6] prevention of abuse the powers, access to justice (Council of Europe),[7] or human rights (United Nations).[8]

There is no doubt that the rule of law is an extremely important basis for the existence and functioning of democratic states (though not only),[9] as well as for the operation of international organizations. Despite the fact that at present the catalogue of elements of the rule of law is not always uniformly perceived (and sometimes its broad understanding is even criticized),[10] the adoption of the minimum content of the rule of law (both at the national and international level) for the purposes of this study will be sufficient. This will then enable an assessment of whether Poland has violated the rule of law, and if so, to what extent.

---

[3] Stein 2019, p. 187.

[4] Tamanaha 2012, p. 233.

[5] Dicey 1982, pp. 120–122.

[6] What is the rule of law? https://commission.europa.eu/strategy-and-policy/policies/justice-and-fundamental-rights/upholding-rule-law/rule-law/what-rule-law_en. Accessed 2 February 2025.

[7] Rule of law. https://www.venice.coe.int/WebForms/pages/?p=02_Rule_of_law&lang=EN. Accessed 2 February 2025.

[8] The Rule of Law and Transitional Justice in Conflict and Post-Conflict Societies: Report of the Secretary-General, UN SC, UN Doc. S/2004/616 at 4. https://digitallibrary.un.org/record/527647?v=pdf. Accessed 2 February 2025; What is the rule of law? https://www.un.org/ruleoflaw/what-is-the-rule-of-law/. Accessed 2 February 2025.

[9] Tamanaha 2012, p. 235.

[10] *Ibid.*, pp. 233–234.

13.2.1 The Meaning of the Rule of Law in the European Union

The rule of law has not been expressed directly in treaty law, which is why the European Union had to deal with allegations of a lack of definition of this concept.[11] However, it is generally accepted that the rule of law in European Union law should be interpreted from Article 2 of the Treaty on European Union, where it is hidden under the concept of the "state of law" and is supported by other values that support its implementation. The inclusion of this principle in primary law not only indicates its special place in European Community law, but also gives it a key role in the process of developing integration from the very beginning of the creation of the communities.[12]

The literature on the subject notes that the content of the EU rule of law principle is supplemented by subsequent articles of the Treaty on European Union (including Article 19, Article 22), or the provisions of the Charter of Fundamental Rights of the European Union (Article 47).[13] Also helpful in this respect are the interpretations of the concept of "the rule of law", which were made by EU bodies—the European Commission[14] or the Court of Justice of the European Union.[15] It is indicated that in the Community sense, the rule of law principle refers to all public authorities that are obliged to act within the limits defined by law and in accordance with values such as democracy, freedom, human rights, or access to independent and impartial courts.[16] Respect for the rule of law by the Member States is essential for the functioning of the European Union, primarily in terms of running the common internal market, implementing the principle of mutual trust and the effective application of Union law throughout the European Union.

In order to protect the rule of law uniformly in all Member States, the European Union has created a protection plan based on three actions: actions to promote and deepen knowledge about the rule of law; the creation of annual reports on the state of the rule of law in individual European Union countries; initiation of the procedure under Article 7 of the Treaty on European Union.[17] This comprehensive strategy is therefore based on taking preventive actions to raise awareness of the importance of the rule of law for the functioning of the European Union and democratic states. Then, on taking monitoring actions to track down any violations in order to eliminate them immediately. And finally, on sanctioning actions aimed at forcing the Member

[11] Maria Pankowska (2019) Jedna wypowiedź, cztery fałsze. Waszczykowski zabłądził ws. UE i praworządności. https://oko.press/co-waszczykowski-wie-o-ue-i-praworzadnosci-jedna-wypowiedz-cztery-falsze. Accessed 2 February 2025.

[12] Rule of law. https://europeanmovement.eu/policy/rule-of-law/. Accessed 2 February 2025.

[13] Pech 2022, pp. 108–109.

[14] Taborowski 2019, pp. 20–21.

[15] C -294/83 Parti écologiste 'Les Verts' v European Parliament, Judgment 1988, EU:C:1986:166.

[16] Węcławska-Misiurek 2021, pp. 16–17.

[17] Rule of law. https://eur-lex.europa.eu/legal-content/EN/TXT/?uri=LEGISSUM:rule_of_law. Accessed 2 February 2025.

State to introduce appropriate reforms aimed at restoring compliance with European Union law.

13.2.2 *The Meaning of the Rule of Law in the Polish Legal System*

In the Polish legal system, the equivalent of "the rule of law" can be found in the Constitution of the Republic of Poland of 2 April 1997[18] in Article 2, which states that "The Republic of Poland shall be a democratic state ruled by law and implementing the principles of social justice". Terminological differences result primarily from conceptual differences between the Anglo-Saxon "the rule of law" and the German "principle of state ruled by law", which has been implemented into Polish constitutional law.[19] Nevertheless, it is worth noting that despite different names, both principles are based on similar pillars.[20]

Placing the principle of the democratic state ruled of law at the very beginning of the most important legal act in the state indicates its extremely important nature.[21] The principle in question consists of three elements: the democratic state, the rule of law and the principle of social justice. Similar to the Treaty on European Union, in the Polish constitution one can look in vain for a legal definition of this principle, and the meanings attributed to it by constitutional law and legal theory are often of a completely different nature.[22]

Decoding the content of the principle of Article 2 of the Constitution of the Republic of Poland, although not easy, is possible thanks to the achievements of the doctrine of constitutional law and the case law of the Constitutional Tribunal,[23] as well as the interpretations of the Court of Justice of the European Union. The Constitutional Tribunal found that the principle of a democratic state of law is a set of "various values expressed directly or indirectly in the Constitution, concerning law, the political system of the state and the relations between the state and the individual".[24] This set is not closed, therefore the principles listed by the Constitutional Tribunal, which are components of the rule of law (such as, for example: the principle of citizens' trust in the state, the principle of non-retroactivity of law, the principle of balance of powers, the principle of judicial independence) are only examples, and the catalogue itself may be extended.[25] In this case, however, the Constitutional

---

[18] Dz.U. z 1997 r. nr 78, poz. 483.

[19] Garlicki 2014, pp. 328–329.

[20] Sozański 2014, pp. 30–31.

[21] Bałaban 2018, p. 54.

[22] Gmerek 2016, pp. 77–78.

[23] Sozański 2014, p. 29.

[24] Judgment of the Constitutional Tribunal of 25 November 1997, file reference K 26/97, OTK 5-6/1997, para 64.

[25] Miętek 2019, pp. 81–83.

Tribunal is accused of inconsistency in the scope of the concepts used in its rulings, which often leads to interpretational chaos in the already complicated interpretation of the "democratic state of law".

The need to respect the rule of law and to be guided by the principle of the supremacy of law over the will of the authorities results not only from the provisions of the Polish Constitution, but also from the provisions of the Treaty on European Union. The phrase "state ruled by law" used in both acts should be interpreted similarly, giving it the same meaning as minimal content of the rule of law. Therefore, it should be recognized that the minimum scope of guarantees of this principle is the necessity for states to comply with three elements: absolute supremacy of the law, equality for all before the law and an independent judiciary, and it is in relation to them that the analysis of the Polish case of violation of the rule of law will be made.

13.2.3 Poland's Violation of the Rule of Law

The beginning of the constitutional crisis in Poland dates back to the end of 2015, when the Sejm of the 7th term made legislative changes in such a way that it became possible to elect two judges of the Constitutional Tribunal, who in principle should have been elected by the Sejm of the next term.[26] When the 8th term of the Sejm took power, it invalidated the resolutions on the election of judges of the Constitutional Tribunal, not only in terms of the two incorrect appointments, but also in terms of the three remaining judges who were correctly appointed to serve as judges of the Constitutional Tribunal by the 7th term of the Sejm.[27] This situation has resulted in the fact that to this day, the Constitutional Tribunal has three incorrectly filled judicial positions, and the President of the Republic of Poland refuses to swear in three properly appointed judges of the Constitutional Tribunal and to allow them to perform their duties.

The way to partially resolve the dispute was to amend the laws on the structure and functioning of the Constitutional Tribunal. However, the introduction of these acts into the Polish legal system complicated the situation of the Tribunal even more. The new legal acts not only introduced new functions previously unknown to the Constitution of the Republic of Poland, but also complicated the rules for electing new judges of the Constitutional Tribunal in such a way that certain doubts arose concerning not only the effectiveness of appointing the new President of the Constitutional Tribunal, but also the correctness of appointing subsequent judges of the Constitutional Tribunal.[28] The current functioning of the Constitutional Tribunal also raises certain concerns, especially in the case of appointing the same or similar benches of judges to hear cases of a political nature.[29]

---

[26] Radziewicz 2020, pp. 3–4.

[27] Małdziński 2019, p. 30.

[28] Ziółkowski 2019, pp. 2–3.

[29] Romanowicz 2022, pp. 74–90.

Irregularities in the appointment of judges to the Constitutional Tribunal and the other issues raised above entail enormous consequences for the entire Polish legal system. Firstly, it is pointed out that the authority of the Constitutional Tribunal has fallen, as it once enjoyed great respect and public trust, and is now perceived rather as a politicised body. Secondly, there are concerns about the independence of adjudicating panels and the impartiality of individual judges, particularly in the context of rulings issued by them in cases of political importance. Thirdly, there are justified concerns that panels of judges adjudicating with the participation of incorrectly appointed judges cannot be recognised as independent and impartial courts within the meaning of international law, including European law. Moreover, some authors claim that the improper appointment of several judges of the Constitutional Tribunal affects the legality of the appointment of the entire composition of the Constitutional Tribunal, and consequently they deny legitimacy to the actions of the Constitutional Tribunal as such.[30] A situation in which this right was used by the authorities in an instrumental manner and leads to an imbalance in the powers, and subsequently to deprivation of the right to an independent and impartial court, cannot be understood otherwise than as a violation of the elementary pillars of the rule of law.

The constitutional crisis in Poland deepened further due to the amendment of the Act on the National Council of the Judiciary of 8 December 2017.[31] This act introduced new rules for electing members of the National Council of the Judiciary. Fifteen members elected from among judges of the Supreme Court, common courts, administrative courts and military courts had previously been nominated by the judicial community. However, the amendment of the Act entrusted this competence to the Sejm. On the basis of this change, a legal dispute arose concerning whether the representation of the judicial community should be chosen by representatives of the Sejm, especially since the Constitution of the Republic of Poland clearly indicates in other provisions how many and which members of the National Council of the Judiciary the Sejm has the right to elect. The adoption of the position that the adopted legal solutions were unconstitutional led to questioning the legitimacy of the National Council of the Judiciary established in its new form.[32] All procedures in which the National Council of the Judiciary participated were defective, which had an impact on the issue of the legality of promoting and appointing new judges (this concerned not only the common courts, but also the Supreme Court). At present, it is considered that several thousand judges were appointed in an incorrect promotion procedure or in the appointment of assessors.

The problem with the unconstitutionality of the composition of the National Council of the Judiciary is so serious, complicated and extensive that there is no simple solution that could reverse the negative effects of the reforms carried out, especially since the violation of the law has persisted for such a long time. The change in the way the members of the National Council of the Judiciary function and are appointed has led to a risky situation, where other authorities can exert real

---

[30] Sadurski 2018.

[31] Dz.U. 2018 poz. 3.

[32] Skotnicki 2020, p. 48.

influence on the judiciary. First of all, the principle of the balance of powers has been disturbed, and secondly, the effect of this has been the inability to guarantee access to an independent and impartial court. Moreover, in the international context, this situation has led to a disturbance of the principle of equality in the law, due to the fact that natural and legal persons in different countries of the European Union had different access to an independent and impartial court. This undoubtedly proves the violation of the fundamental principles that make up the principle of the rule of law.

Another case of violation of the rule of law by Poland were the changes that affected the structure and principles of operation of the Supreme Court. The Act of 8 December 2017[33] established two new chambers in the Supreme Court—the Chamber of Extraordinary Control and Public Affairs and the Disciplinary Chamber (currently known as the Chamber of Professional Liability). The new chambers were staffed with the participation of the already reformed National Council of the Judiciary, which resulted in their being defective from the very beginning. Additionally, the scope of competences of both new chambers, especially the Disciplinary Chamber, was assessed negatively. It received tools that could serve to interfere too far with judicial independence. In addition, the Disciplinary Chamber was excluded from the supervision of the First President of the Supreme Court, had a separate budget and administrative services. Moreover, the remuneration of judges appointed to the Disciplinary Chamber was 40% higher than the remuneration of other judges of the Supreme Court.[34] The new act also introduced the institution of the Disciplinary Spokesman for Judges of Common Courts, who was to be appointed by the Minister of Justice. New rules for establishing disciplinary courts for judges were also presented.

In this case, the violation of the rule of law consisted, first, in the lack of ensuring access to an independent and impartial court. The judges who took up positions in a procedure involving the unconstitutionally staffed National Council of the Judiciary are judges appointed in a flawed procedure, and therefore their participation in adjudication will result in the entire proceedings being flawed. Second, in the disruption of the separation of powers by granting the executive power too much influence on the functioning of the judiciary. The possibility of the Minister of Justice interfering in disciplinary proceedings of judges by independently appointing a disciplinary spokesman aroused deep opposition from the legal community.

The last controversial change to mention in terms of protecting the rule of law in Poland was the change in the retirement age of Supreme Court judges. The aforementioned 2017 Supreme Court Act lowered the retirement age from 70 to 65, which meant that judges who were still active over the age of 65 were sent into retirement if they were not reappointed after the reform came into force. This not only meant a violation of the principle of non-retroactivity of the law, as the new provisions were to apply to all judges, not only those appointed under the new law, but also the possibility of the executive power controlling the composition of the Supreme Court, as the new act did not provide any specific guidelines for the President of

[33] Dz.U. 2018 poz. 5.

[34] Wróbel 2019, pp. 17–31.

the Republic of Poland to follow when considering judges' applications to extend their employment.[35] In this way, 27 of the 72 active judges of the Supreme Court were forced to retire, including the person who held the position of First President of the Supreme Court (interruption of the term of office during its duration; at the very end the First President of the Supreme Court could finish the whole term).[36] These changes were considered in the doctrine as far-reaching interference in the independence of the judiciary by the legislative and executive authorities,[37] which constituted a violation of the principle of a democratic state of law.

The constitutional crisis in Poland began in 2015 with the case of the incorrect election of judges of the Constitutional Tribunal, but over the years it has deepened, encompassing new areas of the Polish justice system. Significant changes have been made not only in the structure of the Supreme Court or in the rules for appointing members of the National Council of the Judiciary, but also certain changes affecting the common courts have been introduced, which are difficult to reconcile with the principle of a democratic state of law. In all cases, allegations were made primarily related to the violation of the separation and balance of powers and the lack of guaranteeing access to an independent court. The cases described above clearly constituted a violation of the rule of law, not only in its domestic understanding, but also in the understanding given to this concept in the legal system of the European Union.

13.3 Court of Justice of the European Union—Rulings in the Case of Poland

The changes made to the Polish legal system in the area of judicial power were closely monitored by the European Union, not only because of the threat they posed to Polish democracy, but also because of the threats they posed to the system of European law and the functioning of the entire European Union. However, when Poland's actions actually began to violate the rule of law, the EU institutions initiated appropriate procedures. Ultimately, this led to the European Commission, acting as the "guardian of the treaties", filing several complaints against Poland for consideration before the Court of Justice of the European Union.

Initially, the Court had to answer the question of whether it was competent to hear complaints concerning matters related to the administration of justice, because these are the exclusive competences of the Member States—they exercise full control over their legal systems and the organisation of the administration of justice. However, the Court decided that adjudicating in this area was entirely possible, because it would not

[35] Świątkowski 2018, pp. 5–12.

[36] Oświadczenie Komisji Europejskiej dotyczące wyroku Trybunału Sprawiedliwości Unii Europejskiej w sprawie polskiej ustawy o Sądzie Najwyższym z dnia 24 czerwca 2019 r. https://ec.europa.eu/commission/presscorner/detail/pl/STATEMENT_19_3376. Accessed 18 January 2024.

[37] Grajewski 2018, pp. 609–620.

interfere in the internal issues of the court system, but would only check whether the Member State was fulfilling its obligations under European Union law. This means that the Member State has full freedom in shaping its own administration of justice, but must do so in such a way as to comply with EU law and the fundamental values and principles of the European Union. When a state fails to fulfil its obligations, the Court has the competence to take action.

In matters concerning the Polish justice system, the Court of Justice of the European Union has adjudicated cases concerning the Constitutional Tribunal, the National Council of the Judiciary, the new chambers of the Supreme Court, and the lowering of the retirement age of Supreme Court judges. These rulings were very important from the point of view of protecting the rule of law, and the Tribunal itself played an extremely important role in this respect. Currently, it is the implementation of its rulings that is seen as the only chance to restore the rule of law in Poland.

13.3.1 Constitutional Tribunal

On 17 July 2023, the European Commission filed an application with the Court of Justice of the European Union[38] alleging that:

- The case law of the Constitutional Tribunal (judgment of 7 October 2021, K 3/21 and judgment of 14 July 2021, K 7/20) led to Poland's violation of its treaty obligations. In the aforementioned judgments, the Polish Constitutional Tribunal made an "erroneous, narrow interpretation of the Constitution of the Republic of Poland, clearly ignoring the case law of the CJEU"[39] in relation to the provision of Article 19 para 1, second subparagraph, TEU (the requirement of effective judicial protection by an independent, impartial court previously established by law);
- The mentioned judgments of the Polish Constitutional Tribunal violate fundamental principles such as: the principle of primacy of Community law, the principle of autonomy, the principle of effectiveness and uniform application of EU law, as well as the principle of binding effect of judgments of the Court of Justice of the European Union. In the content of the judgments, the Constitutional Tribunal rejects the above-mentioned treaty principles and orders all bodies in Poland to refrain from applying them;[40]
- Poland has flagrantly violated constitutional law and European Union law through the irregular appointment of judges to the Constitutional Tribunal in December 2015 and the irregularities in the procedure for appointing the President of the

[38] C-448/23 European Commission v Republic of Poland, in progress.

[39] Action brought on 17 July 2023 – European Commission v Poland, Case C-448/23 https://curia.europa.eu/juris/document/document.jsf;jsessionid=AE56BE951DC33898350F63194F611D29?text=&docid=276732&pageIndex=0&doclang=PL&mode=req&dir=&occ=first&part=1&cid=2930265. Accessed 15 February 2025.

[40] *Ibid.*

Constitutional Tribunal. In the complainant's opinion, the Polish Constitutional Tribunal has for these reasons ceased to meet the requirements of an independent, impartial and statutorily constituted court, which violates the requirements of Article 19 para 1, second subparagraph, TEU in conjunction with Article 47 of the Charter of Fundamental Rights of the European Union.[41]

Although this case has not yet been heard by the Court of Justice of the European Union, it is nevertheless expected that a similar line of case law to that in the cases against Romania will probably be followed.[42] Namely, the Court of Justice of the European Union has indicated that neither Article 2 of the Treaty on European Union nor the second subparagraph of Article 19(1) TEU precludes national law or practice from obliging ordinary courts to implement decisions of constitutional courts. However, such an obligation cannot arise where national law is not capable of guaranteeing the independence of the constitutional court. In such a situation, EU law requires national courts to set aside such national law or practice, since a constitutional court that is not independent will not effectively provide the adequate judicial protection required by the second subparagraph of Article 19(1) TEU.[43]

13.3.2 National Council of the Judiciary

The Court of Justice of the European Union also intervened in the matter of legislative changes affecting the National Council of the Judiciary. The case was examined in the form of preliminary questions submitted by the Polish Supreme Court, focusing on clarifying the issue of whether the Disciplinary Chamber of the Supreme Court, which consists solely of judges appointed with the participation of the new National Council of the Judiciary, can be considered an independent and impartial court. The Court of Justice of the European Union found that the preliminary questions submitted by the Supreme Court may become the subject of a ruling, because the manner of functioning of the National Council of the Judiciary can be assessed in the context of the application of EU law. This is particularly so because the issue of the independence of the judiciary has an extremely significant impact on the effectiveness of the application of EU law, and a threat to the principle of the independence of courts poses a risk to the functioning of the entire legal system of the European Union, not just a Member State.[44]

In this judgment, the Court of Justice defined the criteria on the basis of which it can be assessed whether the new National Council of the Judiciary is a body independent of the legislative and executive powers. Thus, the Court of Justice found that attention should be paid to:

---

[41] *Ibid.*

[42] C-357/19 Euro Box Promotion and Others v Inspecţia Judiciară, Judgment 2021, ECLI:EU:C:2021:1034; C-430/21 – RS, Judgment 2022, ECLI:EU:C:2022:99.

[43] *Ibid.*

[44] Safjan 2020, p. 5.

- the fact that the term of office of the members of the previous National Council of the Judiciary was shortened, despite constitutional guarantees;[45]
- the circumstances in the previous legal regulations in which 15 members of the National Council of the Judiciary were elected by the judicial community—currently they are elected by the Sejm, which appoints a total of 19 out of 25 members of the new National Council of the Judiciary. Moreover, as many as 23 out of 25 members of the new National Council of the Judiciary are elected on political grounds, which negatively affects the independence of this body;[46]
- the possibility of certain irregularities in the procedure for appointing certain members of the National Council of the Judiciary in its new form;[47]
- the state of implementation by the new National Council of the Judiciary of its constitutional task of safeguarding the independence of courts and judges, and the state of implementation of obligations arising from primary and derivative EU law;[48]
- the appeal procedure against resolutions of the National Council of the Judiciary on the appointment of a judge of the Supreme Court to the office;[49]
- all other circumstances that will be considered relevant when answering the question about the independence of the National Council of the Judiciary.[50]

The Court noted that the occurrence of one of these factors individually does not have to unequivocally prove that the National Council of the Judiciary is dependent on the legislative and executive authorities. Nevertheless, the occurrence of several of the above-mentioned criteria, in any configurations, may lead to the conclusion that the National Council of the Judiciary does not have the necessary attribute of independence.[51]

Its ground-breaking judgment also states that any court in Poland may assess the independence of the National Council of the Judiciary established in its new form, while attorneys of the parties may challenge judgments issued with the participation of judges appointed in the procedure in which the new National Council of the Judiciary participated.[52] The consequences of this state of affairs are extremely serious not only for the Polish legal system, but also for the entire EU legal order. Therefore, the Court of Justice of the European Union has clearly stated that immediate corrective action is necessary.

---

[45] Bogdanowicz P, Co oznacza dla Polski wyrok TSUE w sprawie KRS i Izby Dyscyplinarnej? ForumIdei, Fundacja im. Stefana Batorego, https://www.batory.org.pl/upload/files/Programy%20operacyjne/Forum%20Idei/Co%20oznacza%20wyrok%20TSUE.pdf. Accessed 30 January 2025.

[46] *Ibid.*

[47] *Ibid.*

[48] *Ibid.*

[49] *Ibid.*

[50] *Ibid.*

[51] Banaszczyk and Baszczeska 2020, p. 144.

[52] Bogdanowicz P, Co oznacza dla Polski wyrok TSUE w sprawie KRS i Izby Dyscyplinarnej? ForumIdei, Fundacja im. Stefana Batorego, https://www.batory.org.pl/upload/files/Programy%20operacyjne/Forum%20Idei/Co%20oznacza%20wyrok%20TSUE.pdf. Accessed 30 January 2025.

13.3.3 Supreme Court

Another ruling that played a significant role in protecting the rule of law concerned the disciplinary court system for judges. The Supreme Court Act of 2017 established two new chambers, including the Disciplinary Chamber. Its structure (structure, rules of appointment, remuneration) and the powers granted to it raised legal doubts about the independence of this chamber from the very beginning. The case was examined on the basis of a complaint filed against Poland by the European Commission. In the complaint, the Commission accused Poland of:

- allowing for a situation in which the content of court rulings could be considered a disciplinary offence;
- failing to ensure the independence and impartiality of the Disciplinary Chamber of the Supreme Court, which is responsible for reviewing decisions issued in disciplinary proceedings against judges;
- failing to ensure that judges of common courts have their cases heard by a court established under the Act by granting the President who directs the work of the Disciplinary Chamber of the Supreme Court the power to appoint the composition of disciplinary courts in the first instance at his discretion;
- failing to ensure that judges of common courts have their cases heard within a reasonable time by granting the Minister of Justice the power to appoint the Disciplinary Commissioner of the Minister of Justice, nor did it ensure the right to defence, allowing disciplinary proceedings to be conducted despite the justified absence of the judge or his defence counsel;
- limiting the possibility of referring preliminary questions by national courts to the Court of Justice of the European Union.[53]

By introducing these legislative changes to Polish law, Poland, according to the European Commission, violated the EU obligations arising from Article 19 para 1, second subparagraph, TEU and Article 267, second and third subparagraphs, TFEU.[54]

On 15 July 2021, the Court of Justice of the European Union accepted the allegations formulated in the complaint by the European Commission and issued a ruling, finding that the fundamental assumptions shaping the new system of disciplinary justice of judges of common courts are contrary to European Union law. In its judgment, the Court found that the newly established chamber of the Supreme Court does not have the attribute of independence, and the statutory provisions allow for influencing the content of judgments issued by judges. In addition, the Court noted that the competences granted to the President of the Disciplinary Chamber to independently shape the composition of the disciplinary court lead to a situation in which disciplinary cases of judges may be examined by an entity that is not a court within

[53] Action brought on 25 October 2019 – European Commission v. Republic of Poland (Case C-791/19).

[54] Wróblewski 2021, p. 626.

the meaning of national and EU law. The Court also negatively assessed the provisions on the basis of which judges may be held disciplinary liable for submitting a question for a preliminary ruling to the Court of Justice of the European Union. The Court found these provisions to be contrary to EU law, which grants judges of national courts the right, and sometimes even the obligation, to submit preliminary questions in the process of applying European Union law.[55]

13.3.4 Lowering the Retirement Age of Supreme Court Judges

The last of the judgments of the Court of Justice of the European Union under review concerns the issue of lowering the retirement age of Supreme Court judges. This case was considered by the Court on the basis of a complaint filed by the European Commission, in which the Commission requested a finding that Poland had violated EU law (Article 19(1) second subparagraph of the TEU in conjunction with Article 47 of the Charter of Fundamental Rights of the European Union) by applying the provisions on the new, lowered retirement age to serving Supreme Court judges (appointed before 3 April 2018). In addition, the European Commission noted that another failure to comply with EU obligations consisted in granting the President of the Republic of Poland complete freedom to decide to extend the active service of judges of that court after they had reached the newly determined retirement age.[56] The Commission further stressed that the Supreme Court is the body entrusted with the task of interpreting and applying European Union law and therefore should be guaranteed appropriate protection in the context of maintaining independence from other authorities.[57]

The Court of Justice of the European Union, despite the fact that the contested provisions were repealed by Poland on 1 January 2019, decided to continue the proceedings due to the fact that the Commission maintained its complaint and the legislative changes introduced by the Polish side occurred after the deadline set by the Court in the interim injunction. It also noted that despite the fact that the organisation of the justice system falls within the competence of the Member States, they are obliged to exercise this competence in accordance with the obligations arising from European Union law. Hence, the Court has the competence to hear this case.

In the judgment the Court agreed with the European Commission, arguing that the legislative changes that led to the lowering of the retirement age of Supreme Court judges are contrary to EU law and violate the principle of the irremovability of judges, which in turn constitutes a violation of the principle of judicial independence. The Court pointed out that the Supreme Court is a body that sometimes rules in its

---

[55] C-791/19 European Commission v Republic of Poland, Judgment 2021, ECLI:EU:C:2021:596.

[56] C-618/19 European Commission v Republic of Poland Judgment 2019, ECLI:EU:C:2019:531, para 1.

[57] *Ibid.*, para 32.

cases on issues related to the application of EU law and its interpretation. This means that the provisions organizing the structure and organization of the functioning of the Supreme Court should guarantee the requirements of effective judicial protection. Providing this protection is only possible when the court is independent. However, in the case of the Polish Supreme Court, its independence raises serious doubts. In order for a given body to be considered independent, there must be certain specific guarantees, such as the irremovability of a judge.

This principle is not absolute, but any departure from it should meet the requirement of proportionality and be justified by legal considerations. According to the Tribunal, the provisions introduced by the Supreme Court Act of 2017, even if they were intended to adjust the retirement age of judges to the general principles of the pension system in Poland, did not meet the requirements of proportionality. First of all, because retirement was not voluntary, but also because the act in question did not provide for transitional provisions that would protect active judges from forced retirement at the time of entry into force of the provisions. Therefore, the principles adopted by the legislator for changing the retirement age of Supreme Court judges did not guarantee judicial independence.

13.4 Conclusions

From the very beginning of its establishment, the Court of Justice of the European Union has been assigned an extremely important role, but one burdened with many challenges. One of the biggest challenges it has faced is the situation in which some Member States have begun to succumb to populist influences and have begun to violate their obligations under EU law. So how has the Court dealt with this crisis in the case of Poland and what were the results of the actions it has taken and if have these actions proven effective?

The rule of law crisis in Poland resulted in the Court issuing a series of judgments that not only referred to the situation of judicial reforms, but also specified in detail how the concept of the rule of law should be understood in the legal order of the European Union. The Court clearly emphasized that this principle applies in the EU legal order and is derived from Article 2 TEU, and is developed in Article 19 TEU, which must be read in conjunction with Article 47 of the Charter of Fundamental Rights of the European Union. On the basis of Article 19 TEU, the courts of the Member States are entrusted with the obligation to ensure the application of EU law and the guarantee of all rights derived therefrom. One of the principles implementing the rule of law is access to an independent court and the possibility of using national remedies guaranteeing such access—it is the state that is obliged to create a system of remedies and procedures that will ensure effective judicial review.

The Court also took the opportunity to recall that the European Union is a unique and autonomous legal order,[58] established by the Treaties. To protect it, a judicial

[58] Krzysztofik 2020, p. 247.

system was established to ensure a coherent and uniform interpretation of EU law, which is possible thanks to the dialogue between the Court of Justice of the European Union and national courts in the form of preliminary questions.

In addition, the Court of Justice of the European Union dispelled emerging doubts as to the competence to adjudicate in cases concerning the administration of justice. The Court pointed out that, in fact, the competence to shape the administration of justice belongs solely to the Member States, however, in connection with the fact that the courts of the Member States also play the role of EU courts (and therefore participate in the application of EU law), the Court has the competence to examine whether, in the process of shaping the administration of justice, the Member States fulfil their obligations arising from EU law. In its case law, it also took into account such national regulations that are contrary to EU law and the rule of law, e.g. improper filling of judicial positions made in breach of national and EU law, leading to the judicial body ceasing to meet the requirements of an independent, impartial court established by law; failure to ensure appropriate court procedures aimed at guaranteeing the exercise of rights granted by EU law; lowering the retirement age of a judge and applying these rules to an active judge whose appointment occurred before the entry into force of new statutory regulations.

From a theoretical point of view, the actions of the Court of Justice of the European Union have therefore led to the clarification of what the rule of law is in the EU sense, what regulations concerning the national organisation of the judicial system may be in conflict with it and what categories of cases fall within the jurisdiction of the Court of Justice. The case law of the Court of Justice in this area is extremely important and sets out the basic principles for the future that should be applied by the European Union countries when shaping their judicial systems independently. Thanks to such a detailed analysis of Polish cases and the clear explanations provided by the Court of Justice, shaping judicial systems in accordance with the rule of law should no longer be a challenge for the Member States.

Despite the great substantive significance of the judgments of the Court of Justice of the European Union, unfortunately their real effectiveness was not very high. However, this was not due to the lack of substantive value of these judgments, but to the objection of the Polish authorities as to their merits and the refusal to execute them (Poland refused to execute the judgments and to comply with some of the interim measures imposed in these judgments by the Court of Justice of the EU).[59] Such actions of the Polish authorities meant that not only did the violations of the rule of law not cease, but the state of constitutional crisis deepened with the passage of time. Only the enrichment of the judgments of the Court of Justice with financial sanctions brought certain, although insignificant results. For example, in the case of Poland's failure to apply an interim measure in the form of suspending certain national provisions violating the rule of law (the case of the Disciplinary Chamber of the Supreme Court), the Court of Justice imposed on Poland a penalty of EUR 1 million for each day of delay, but when Poland partially fulfilled the recommendations, this penalty was reduced by half. Since the Polish authorities refused to pay the

[59] Pech 2022.

daily penalty payment, the European Commission decided to enforce the arrears by offsetting them against the funds due to Poland from various claims on the European Union.[60]

Currently, after the parliamentary elections in October 2023, the new government is trying to implement the judgments of the Court of Justice, seeing them, rightly, as a way to restore the rule of law in Poland. Nevertheless, the road to this seems to be very long, considering the fact that some of the statutory changes are blocked by the President of the Republic of Poland, who denies the validity of the judgments of the Court of Justice. The composition of the Constitutional Tribunal and some elements of its functioning still require changes. The National Council of the Judiciary is also still operating in Poland, the composition of which was established on the basis of a new act from 2017, which is unconstitutional in nature. In addition, the issue of the Supreme Court chamber responsible for disciplinary procedures applied to judges remains unresolved. Despite the liquidation of the Disciplinary Chamber of the Supreme Court, in its place in July 2022 the Professional Liability Chamber was established, which has competences similar to the Disciplinary Chamber, and at the same time took over the structural and systemic defect from the Disciplinary Chamber. This means that despite the liquidation of the Disciplinary Chamber, the violation of the rule of law has not ceased, because only the name of this body has changed, and not its actual role and competences assigned to it.

The case of Poland shows that despite the fact that the Court used its competences and responded adequately to the violations that occurred, issuing judgments and applying interim measures, the effectiveness of the actions it took was not high. By deciding not to execute the judgments of the Court of Justice of the European Union, a Member State deprived them of a certain significance. This situation showed that in order to ensure the enforceability of the judgments of the CJEU, it must be supported by certain sanctioning measures or tools. The previous system based on mutual trust and respect for EU law and the position of the Court of Justice of the European Union does not exist in the event that the authorities of a Member State cease to be guided by common democratic values.

References

Bałaban A (2018) Granice interpretacji zasady demokratycznego państwa prawnego [The boundaries of the interpretation of the rule of law]. Ruch Prawniczy, Ekonomiczny i Socjologiczny 80:53–59

Banaszczyk Z, Baszczeska J (2020) Czy konsekwencją wyroku TSUE z 19.11.2019 r. w sprawach połączonych C-585/18, C-624/18, C-625/18 powinna być w jakimkolwiek zakresie debata nad pierwszeństwem prawa unijnego przed prawem polskim? [Should the consequence of the judgment of the CJEU of 19 November 2019 in joined cases C-585/18, C-624/18, C-625/18 be to any extent a debate on the primacy of EU law over Polish law?]. Palestra 5:142–153

[60] Katarzyna Żaczkiewicz-Zborska, TSUE: Polska zapłaci 320 mln euro za wadliwą reformę sądów z 2019 r. https://www.prawo.pl/prawnicy-sady/kara-dla-polski-za-wady-reformy-sadow-z-2019-r,531336.html. Accessed 5 February 2025.

Charzewski P (2017) Rola Trybunału Sprawiedliwości Unii Europejskiej w wykładni prawa w dobie multicentryzmu. In: Jabłoński P, Kaczor J, Pichlak M (eds) Prawo i polityka w sferze publicznej: perspektywa wewnętrzna. E-Wydawnictwo [The role of the Court of Justice of the European Union in interpreting the law in the era of multicentrism]. Prawnicza i Ekonomiczna Biblioteka Cyfrowa. Wydział Prawa, Administracji i Ekonomii Uniwersytetu Wrocławskiego, pp 53–71

Dicey A V (1982) Introduction To The Study Of The Law Of The Constitution. Liberty Classics, Indianapolis

Garlicki L (2014) Klauzula demokratycznego państwa prawa. Studies in Law: Research Materials 2:327–332

Gmerek K (2016) Krytyka prawa przez autorów tekstów prasowych w kontekście zasady demokratycznego państwa prawnego [Criticism of the law by authors of press texts in the context of the principle of a democratic state of law]. Acta Iuris Stetinensis 14:75–85

Grajewski K (2018) Przedterminowe zakończenie kadencji Pierwszego Prezesa Sądu Najwyższego w świetle art. 12 § 1 oraz art. 111 §1 i §4 nowej ustawy o Sądzie Najwyższym [Early termination of the term of office of the First President of the Supreme Court in light of Article 12 § 1 and Article 111 § 1 and § 4 of the new Act on the Supreme Court]. Gdańskie Studia Prawnicze XL:609–620

Helios J, Jedlecka W (2018) Wykładnia prawa Unii Europejskiej ze stanowiska teorii prawa [Interpreting European Union law from the perspective of legal theory]. E-Wydawnictwo. Prawnicza i Ekonomiczna Biblioteka Cyfrowa. Wydział Prawa, Administracji i Ekonomii Uniwersytetu Wrocławskiego

Krzysztofik E (2020) The definition of national court within the meaning of European Union law. Considerations in the context of the Polish reform of the judicial system. Teka Komisji Prawniczej PAN Oddział w Lublinie XIII, 1:247–264

Małdziński M (2019) Kryzys wokół Trybunału Konstytucyjnego w latach 2015–2018 [The crisis of the Constitutional Tribunal in 2015–2018]. Warsaw

Miętek A (2019) Zasada demokratycznego państwa prawnego w orzecznictwie Trybunału Konstytucyjnego [The principle of a democratic state of law in the case law of the Constitutional Tribunal]. Dialogi polityczne III RP 11:75–85

Pech L (2022) The Rule of Law as a Well-Established and Well-Defined Principle of EU Law. Hague Journal on the Rule of Law 14:107–138

Radziewicz P (2020) Kryzys konstytucyjny i paradygmatyczna zmiana konstytucji [Constitutional crisis and paradigmatic change of constitution]. Państwo i Prawo 10:3–24

Romanowicz M (2022) Instrumentalizacja Prawa a kryzys konstytucyjny – refleksja na gruncie kilku aktualnych ustaleń Profesora Piotra Winczorka [Instrumentalization of Law and the Constitutional Crisis – a Reflection on the Ground of Several Current Findings by Professor Piotr Winczorek]. Archiwum Filozofii Prawa i Filozofii Społecznej 3:74–90

Sadurski W (2018) Poland's Constitutional Breakdown. Oxford University Press

Safjan M (2020) Prawo do skutecznej ochrony sądowej – refleksje dotyczące wyroku TSUE z 19.11.2019 r. w sprawach połączonych C-585/18, C-624/18, C-625/18 [The right to effective judicial protection – reflections on the judgment of the ECJ of 19 November 2019 in joined cases C-585/18, C-624/18, C-625/18]. Palestra 5:5–27

Skotnicki K (2020) Problem konstytucyjności składu obecnej Krajowej Rady Sądownictwa w Polsce [The problem of the constitutionality of the composition of the current National Council of the Judiciary in Poland]. Acta Universitatis Lodziensis 93:47–59

Sozański J (2014) Zasada demokratycznego państwa prawnego w polskiej praktyce prawnej [The principle of a democratic state of law in Polish legal practice]. KNUV 42:28–40

Stein R (2019) What Exactly is the Rule of Law? Scholarship Repository University of Minnesota Law School 57:185–201

Świątkowski A (2018) Prawny spór o zgodność z Konstytucją RP regulacji i ich następstw osiągnięcia „wieku emerytalnego" przez sędziów Sądu Najwyższego [Legal dispute over the conformity with the Constitution of the Republic of Poland of the regulations and their consequences regarding the achievement of "retirement age" by judges of the Supreme Court]. Palestra 10:5–12

Taborowski M (2019) Mechanizmy ochrony praworządności państw członkowskich w prawie Unii Europejskiej. Studium przebudzenia systemu ponadnarodowego [Mechanisms for the Protection of the Rule of Law of Member States in European Union Law. A Study of the Awakening of the Supranational System]. Wolters Kluwer

Tamanaha B Z (2012) The History and Elements of the Rule of Law. Singapore Journal of Legal Studies: 232–247

Węcławska-Misiurek M (2021) Znaczenie zasady państwa prawnego w prawie Unii Europejskiej i polskim prawie konstytucyjnym w kontekście zasady wzajemnego zaufania [The importance of the rule of law in European Union law and Polish constitutional law in the context of the principle of mutual trust]. International Journal of Legal Studies 1:13–24

Wróbel W (2019) Izba Dyscyplinarna jako sąd wyjątkowy w rozumieniu art. 175 ust. 2 Konstytucji RP [The Disciplinary Chamber as an exceptional court within the meaning of Article 175 section 2 of the Constitution of the Republic of Poland]. Palestra 1–2:17–31

Wróblewski M (2021) Polskie regulacje dyscyplinarne dotyczące sędziów przed TSUE – sprawa C-791/19 (Izba Dyscyplinarna SN) oraz postępowanie wszczęte przez Komisję Europejską w sprawie tzw. ustawy kagańcowej [Polish disciplinary regulations concerning judges before the CJEU – case C-791/19 (Disciplinary Chamber of the Supreme Court) and the proceedings initiated by the European Commission regarding the so-called Muzzle Act]. In: Barcz J, Grzelak A, Szyndlauer R (eds) Problem praworządności w Polsce w świetle orzecznictwa Trybunału Sprawiedliwości UE (2018–2020). Warsaw, pp 625–669

Ziółkowski M (2019) Przywracanie praworządności w TK po kryzysie konstytucyjnym: wybór i powołanie Prezesa TK [Restoring the rule of law in the Constitutional Tribunal after the constitutional crisis: election and appointment of the President of the Constitutional Tribunal]. Archiwum Osiatyńskich, Warsaw

Ewa Michałkiewicz-Kądziela is a dr., an assistant professor, and Vice-Dean for International Cooperation at the Faculty of Law and Administration of the University of Szczecin.

Chapter 14
Judicial Review of Administrative Decisions by the Court of Justice of the European Union and by Lithuanian Courts

Rimvydas Norkus

Contents

Abstract This contribution seeks to highlight certain aspects of judicial review exercised by the Court of Justice of the European Union in order to compare them with the judicial review exercised by Lithuanian courts. These aspects will mainly cover the standard of judicial review (limited v unlimited review), the competence of the respective courts, as well as procedural aspects which can affect practical exercise of this review. As both the EU courts and national courts can be called upon to apply the same provisions of EU law (for instance, in competition law cases), and, moreover, national authorities can sometimes refer their cases to Union institutions, the differences in the exercise of judicial review and in procedural rules might lead to different outcomes depending on whether the administrative decision was taken by a national or by a Union authority and subject to review by national or by EU courts. I will therefore examine whether, in light of the principles of equivalence and effectiveness, some convergence may be desirable.

R. Norkus (✉)
Court of Justice of the European Union, Luxembourg, Luxembourg
e-mail: Rimvydas.Norkus@curia.europa.eu

I. Isokaitė-Valužė and H. Šinkūnas (eds.), *The European Union 2004-2024*,
https://doi.org/10.1007/978-94-6265-718-2_14

Keywords Judicial review · Standard of review · Manifest error · Complex economic assessment · Convergence · Equivalence and effectiveness

14.1 Introduction

The power of the judiciary to review the decisions of the executive is an essential aspect of any legal system based on the rule of law. Judicial review permits applicants to challenge administrative, legislative and judicial decisions for errors of fact and law. The question that immediately arises is: to what extent is a court entitled to put itself into the role of the decision maker and to examine where it went wrong? In other words, to what extent does the decision maker have the *right* to go *wrong*?

In relation to administrative decisions, on the one hand, it is clearly unconstitutional, for a court to intervene in policy decisions that have been entrusted to the executive. Indeed, a court's role is to ensure respect of the law, not to engage in political decisions. On the other hand, a court exercising judicial review must be able to intervene where an administrative body makes a decision based on fundamental errors of fact or law. Between those two extremes, there is a sliding scale of where a court can intervene, which is defined by the applicable *standard of review.*

However, the *standard of review* applied by a court is just one aspect that will determine the bounds of its review. Indeed, a series of other factors also define the boundaries of the court's review. The judicial review conducted by a court also depends on the procedural framework and legal tradition in which that court exercises its powers. Indeed, rules on standing and time limits, and even more fundamentally, the very understanding of what a judge's role should be and how active a role he or she should play in defining the dispute, are all factors that influence judicial review. In the European Union, these factors vary to different extents across the Member States, which all have rich legal traditions, sculpted by the state's history.

While the Court of Justice of the European Union ("CJEU")[1] is responsible for hearing challenges to the acts of the EU institutions, most EU law is implemented by the Member States. Therefore, national courts also bear the burden of hearing challenges to acts taken in application of EU law. This shared burden becomes most apparent where the EU courts and national courts are called upon to apply the same provisions of EU law, as is the case in relation to competition law. National authorities can even refer cases that come within their jurisdiction to the Commission.[2] In addition, findings of national competition authorities act as prima facie evidence of

[1] I will use "CJEU" or "EU Courts" to refer to the institution as a whole, which includes the Court of Justice ("ECJ") and the General Court.

[2] See to that effect ECJ, Joined Cases C-611/22 P and C-625/22 P *Illumina and Grail v Commission*, Judgment, 3 September 2024, ECLI:EU:C:2024:677; General Court, T-587/22 *Crown Holdings and Crown Cork & Seal Deutschland v Commission*, Judgment, 2 October 2024, ECLI: EU:T:2024:66 and General Court, T-589/22, *Silgan Holdings and Others v Commission*, Judgement, 2 October 2024 ECLI: EU:T:2024:662.

an infringement before all national courts.[3] Therefore, within the EU, the same set of facts could lead to decisions that are subject to review before several different jurisdictions, different standards of reviews, different procedural particularities, and could then, possibly lead to different outcomes. This may justify convergence in the level of scrutiny that is applied in the review of decisions made in application of EU law.

The Lithuanian administrative courts provide a particularly insightful study into the extent of possible convergence of judicial review at EU and at national level, but also into its limits. The Supreme Administrative Court, having begun operating on the 1 January 2001, is a "young" court and its case law has developed alongside, and mostly in harmony with, that of the CJEU. Twenty years after Lithuania's accession to the Union, one can observe the heavy influence that EU case law has had on administrative proceedings. Nevertheless, some aspects of judicial review conducted by national courts simply must differ, by virtue of their operation at the national, and not international, level.

In order to draw practical and coherent comparisons between the judicial review conducted by the EU courts and that which is conducted by the Lithuanian courts, I will first set out the basic framework and rules that govern the judicial review carried out by the CJEU (Sect. 14.2). I will then set out the basic features of the judicial review conducted by the Lithuanian administrative courts (Sect. 14.3). I will then compare these two parallel systems of judicial review (Sect. 14.4), which will allow me to arrive at a brief conclusion (Sect. 14.5).

14.2 Judicial Review at European Union Level

Unlike national executive powers, EU institutions have no inherent powers and may only exercise those which the Treaties have conferred on them. Given that these powers have been interpreted broadly and that the EU has competence in a vast array of areas, the potential scope of EU action is significant. Therefore, it is of utmost importance that the CJEU ensures that the EU institutions act only within the remit of their conferred powers and that their decisions are subject to sufficient scrutiny. Moreover, robust review by the courts can help to assuage, to a certain extent, concern that the EU institutions lack the same high level of democratic legitimacy that exists at the national level.[4]

---

[3] Article 9 of Directive 2014/104/EU of the European Parliament and of the Council of 26 November 2014 on certain rules governing actions for damages under national law for infringements of the competition law provisions of the Member States and of the European Union, OJ 2014 L 349, p. 1.

[4] Craig 2018, p. 483, in which he states "much discourse on the legitimacy of the EU and on accountability of its decisions. Imbuing the manifest error test with greater fore, and thereby bolstering substantive review, is one way in which to enhance accountability of those who made the initial decision…".

14.2.1 Legal Basis for EU Administrative Law

Article 263 of the Treaty on the Functioning of the European Union ("TFEU") acts as the central mechanism for judicial review of EU action by permitting applicants to directly challenge and seek the annulment of acts of the EU institutions. Article 263 does not grant the EU courts the power to replace the decision-maker and only provides for a mere review of the legality of the contested act. Indeed, when conducting a review under Article 263, "the EU Courts may in no circumstances substitute their own reasoning for that of the author of the contested act".[5]

Article 263 sets out which EU acts may be challenged, who is entitled to bring such actions, within what timeframe, and on which four grounds of review annulment may be sought. Certain institutions automatically have standing to challenge EU acts.[6] Private parties, on the other hand, must show that they are directly and individually concerned by the contested act, which can prove difficult to overcome.[7] The ECJ justifies such a high threshold for establishing *locus standi* on the basis that Article 263 is just one available avenue in "a complete system of legal remedies and procedures designed to permit the Court of Justice to review the legality of measures adopted by the institutions".[8] Indeed, applicants can also challenge the validity of an EU act indirectly through the preliminary reference procedure.[9]

Nevertheless, Article 263 plays a central role in judicial review by the EU courts and the General Court, having jurisdiction to hear all direct actions brought by private parties,[10] is the key actor of EU administrative law.

Article 278 TFEU provides that while actions brought before the EU courts do not have suspensory effect, the courts may order the suspension of the contested act. Furthermore, under Article 279, the courts are afforded the rather vague power to "prescribe any necessary interim measures" in "any cases before" them. However,

---

[5] ECJ, Case C-70/23 P, *Westfälische Drahtindustrie v Commission*, Judgment, 4 July 2024, ECLI:EU:C:2024:580, para 38.

[6] Article 263 distinguishes between privileged applicants, semi-privileged applicants, and non-privileged applicants. Privileged applicants are automatically entitled to seek the annulment of EU acts: Member States, the European Parliament, the Council, and the Commission. Semi-privileged applicants are entitled to seek the annulment of EU acts where it is necessary to protect their interests: the Court of Auditors, by the European Central Bank, and by the Committee of the Regions.

[7] The Lisbon Treaty removed the requirement of individual concern in relation to "regulatory acts that do not entail implementing measure". For a discussion on the impact of this amendment, see Albors-Lorens 2012, p. 518.

[8] ECJ, Case 294/83, *Parti Écologiste 'Les Verts' v European Parliament*, Judgment, 23 April 1986, ECR 1339, para 23.

[9] Article 269 TFEU provides that Member States can challenge the legality of decisions taken by the European Council or by the Council under Article 7 TEU. Article 277 TFEU permits the indirect challenge of an EU act via the plea of illegality.

[10] The General Court also hears direct actions brought by Member States against the Commission, and other direct actions, which are set out by the Treaties.

the Court exercises this power sparingly and will rarely order interim measures.[11] They will only be granted where "it is established that such an order is justified, prima facie, in fact and in law, and that it is urgent in so far as, in order to avoid serious and irreparable harm to the applicant's interests, it must be made and produce its effects before a decision is reached in the main action".[12] Further, the relief granted will only be prohibitive in nature. Indeed, EU courts cannot force an institution to take a particular action, even after the annulment of a contested act, a fact which the General Court frequently recalls.[13] As will be discussed below, this exists in contrast to many national systems, in which it is more common for a court to order an administrative body to act,[14] and moreover, in contrast to what the CJEU considers to be a necessary power for national courts to exercise in certain circumstances.[15]

Where the courts annul a contested act, the act will generally be declared void *ab initio*, subject to some exceptions.[16] The General Court will ground such a finding on one of the four grounds of review of Article 263, which have remained unchanged since the Treaty establishing the European Coal and Steel Community. They are: lack of competence, infringement of an essential procedural requirement, infringement of the treaties or of any rule of law relating to their application, or misuse of powers. However, while the text of Article 263 sets out the scope of review, it remains silent on the *standard of review* that is to be applied, thus leaving this task to the courts.[17]

[11] As of 2 February 2023, the General Court granted the interim measures sought (in full or in part) in only 81 out of 850 orders since its creation, or a rate of 9.5%. See Lefèvre and Nõmm 2023, p. 1001, footnote 7.

[12] See General Court, Case T-257/24 R, *Mazepin v Council*, Order of the Vice-President, 19 July 2024, not published, EU:T:2024:507, para 17; ECJ, C-162/15 P-R, *Evonik Degussa* v *Commission*, Order of the Vice-President, 2 March 2016, para 21 and the case-law cited.

[13] For a recent example, see General Court, Case T-1093/23, *AH v Commission*, Judgment, 22 January 2025, EU:T:2025:50, para. 50, which states, "the EU judicature cannot, without encroaching on the prerogatives of the administrative authority, order an EU institution to take the measures necessary for the enforcement of a judgment by which a decision is annulled".

[14] For example, in the common law, "a writ of mandamus" ordered by a court orders the performance of a specific act.

[15] ECJ, Case C–556/17, *Torubarov*, Judgment, 29 July 2019, ECLI:EU:C:2019:626, para 74.

[16] Article 264(2) TFEU allows the Courts to limit the effects of annulment where necessary. For example, in ECJ, Case 81/72 *Commission v Council*, Judgement, 5 June 1973, ECR 575, in order to "avoid discontinuity in the system of remuneration", the Court held that the articles declared void should remain applicable until the Council passed a new regulation.

[17] ECJ, Case C-83/98 P, *France v Ladbroke Racing and Commission*, Opinion of Advocate General Cosmas, 23 November 1999, EU:C:1999:577, at footnote 4: "… the Community judicature has the power to remain master of its tasks, defining itself the depth to which its investigation will go on each occasion".

14.2.2 The Standard of Judicial Review in EU Law

The standard of review can be understood as the extent of deference a court will allow the decision-maker. As former judge of the ECJ, Mr. Rosas, points out, in EU law, the standard of review is not "a term of art" that is set out by the treaties, nor does it have a "neat and precise delimitation from neighbouring concepts such as the question of admissibility, the principle of proportionality, or the notion of reasonableness".[18] Furthermore, the courts may apply the standard of review with varying degrees of intensity depending on a number of factors such as the breadth of discretion conferred on the deciding body, the complexity of the area, the political nature of the decision[19] or the impact of the decision on the rights of individuals. Generally speaking, the more the discretion afforded to the decision-maker resembles a pure policy decision, the less scope remains for the Court to intervene; the narrower the power afforded to the decision-maker, the more the Court can intervene.

Thus, at one extreme of the scale, where the EU courts find that an institution has a broad discretion that is of a political nature and they will declare that the contested decision is not amenable to judicial review.[20] On the other end of the scale, the Court does not defer to the institutions in relation to the interpretation of law. Article 19 of the Treaty on the European Union ("TEU") provides that the CJEU "shall ensure that in the interpretation and application of the Treaties the law is observed". Furthermore, the ECJ established relatively early on that national courts do not have jurisdiction to declare acts of the EU institutions invalid.[21] Therefore, the CJEU enjoys a monopoly on the interpretation of EU law and on the assessment of the legality of EU acts, which ensures the uniformity and coherence of Union law.[22]

Most decisions taken by the institutions exist in the middle ground between being completely at their discretion, and being a matter that is subject to the full review of the courts. Where a decision is amenable to judicial review, the courts will either conduct a "comprehensive review", which allows the Court to substitute its assessment for that of the administrative body, or a "limited review", in which the Court is limited to assessing whether there has been manifest error in assessment. The distinction between these two types of review developed within the context of the Court's review of competition decisions. The courts initially exhibited great reluctance to carry out

---

[18] Rosas 2019, para 5.

[19] See Case C-40/03 P, *Rica Foods v Commission*, Opinion of AG Léger, 17 February 2005, EU:C:2005:93 at point 45 to 49.

[20] For example, as the Court found in relation to a decision of the Parliament on how to deal with a petition (ECJ, Case C-261/13, *Schönberger v Parliament*, Judgment, 9 December 2014, ECLI:EU:C:2014:2423, para 24); or in relation to the power of the Commission to initiate infringement proceedings against a Member State (ECJ, Case 247/87, *Star Fruit v Commission*, Judgment, 14 February 1989, ECLI: ECLI:EU:C:1989:58).

[21] See ECJ, Case 314/85, *Foto-Frost v Hauptzollamt Lübeck-Ost*, Judgment, 22 October 1987. ECLI: ECLI:EU:C:1987:452, para 20.

[22] Rosas 2019, para 42.

extensive review where "limited review" applied, followed by a tendency towards more intense review,[23] especially in relation to complex economic assessments.

14.2.2.1 Limited Review v Comprehensive Review

The Court first made explicit reference to the distinction between the "comprehensive review", which applies "as a general rule" and a "limited" review, which applies as an exception, in its judgment in *Remia*.[24] However, these two distinct levels of review can be traced back to the Treaty establishing the European Coal and Steel Community ("ECSC Treaty"),[25] which prevented the Court from reviewing the economic evaluation on which the High Authority based its decision, except in the event of misuse of powers or manifest failure to observe the provisions of the ECSC Treaty.[26] Therefore, although the initial Treaty did not provide for a "general" standard of review, it was clear that the courts were to apply a "lighter" standard in relation to decisions involving economic matters. While reference to a lighter standard did not appear in any other treaty thereafter, the concept was enshrined in the case law of the Court as early as 1966, in the landmark judgment in *Consten and Grundig*.[27] In that case, the Court laid the foundation for limited review in finding that, where the Commission's power implies complex evaluations on economic matters, the Court would be limited to "an examination of the relevance of the facts and of the legal consequences, which the Commission deduces therefrom".[28]

As the case law developed, it became clear that there are two main scenarios in which the courts will conduct a limited review: either where the EU legislature has granted discretion on the administrative body to make a policy decision, or where the administrative decision is based on complex scientific, economic or technical assessments.[29] Indeed, the Court has found that the EU legislature "must be allowed

---

[23] "It is clear that while retaining the established grounds of review the EU Courts, and more especially the [General Court], have been applying these with greater intensity than hitherto, in some cases at least", Craig 2018, p. 452.

[24] ECJ, Case 42/84, *Remia and Others v Commission*, Judgment, 11 July 1985, EU:C:1985:327, para 34. See Castillo de la Torre and Gippini Fournier 2024, p. 380. For a recent example, see General Court, Case T-3/22, *ZHLPK v Commission*, Judgment, 11 September 2024, not published, EU:T:2024:616, para 138.

[25] Signed in Paris on 18 April 1951, entry into force 23 July 1952.

[26] Article 33 ECSC Treaty states: "The Court may not, however, examine the evaluation of the situation, resulting from economic facts or circumstances, in the light of which the High Authority took its decisions or made its recommendations, save where the High Authority is alleged to have misused its powers or to have manifestly failed to observe the provision of this Treaty or any rule of law relating to its application." For further discussion see Kalintiri 2016, para 1288.

[27] ECJ, Joined Cases 56 and 58/64, *Etablissements Consten and Grundig-Verkaufs v Commission*, Judgment, 13 July 1966, ECLI:EU:C:1966:41.

[28] *Ibid.*

[29] ECJ, Joined Cases C-71/23 P and C-82/23 P, *France v CWS Powder Coatings and Others* and *Commission v CWS Powder Coatings and Others*, Opinion of Advocate General Ćapeta, 6 February 2025, ECLI:EU:C:2025:65 point 72 and 73. See also ECJ, Joined Cases C-517/19 P and C-518/19

a broad discretion in areas which involve political, economic and social choices … and in which it is called upon to undertake complex assessments".[30]

The underlying reason for granting broad discretion and limiting judicial review in relation to complex areas may be explained by the natural tendency of any judge to be cautious when dealing with complex issues, such as those of an economic, environmental or medical nature, the understanding of which require more than just legal expertise.[31] This could lead one to the conclusion that the courts always exercise comprehensive review when policy choices and complex technical assessment are not involved. However, there have been occasions on which the Court has conferred broad discretion on administrative bodies despite the lack of any apparent complexity of the decision taken.[32] In its judgment in *Pharma Mar*,[33] the Court extended the European Medicines Agency's (EMA) broad discretion in conducting complex technical assessments to include defining the criteria necessary to establish the impartiality and independence of its experts for the evaluation of the quality, safety and efficacy of medicinal products,[34] despite the fact that these criteria seem neither technical nor complex and the Court does not seem to be in a worse position than EMA to appreciate the independence of its experts.

Indeed, to continue with this example, had the Court categorised the definition of those criteria as a question of law, it could have stepped into the role of the decision-maker, and substituted its judgment for that of the administrative body. After all, substitution of judgment for questions of law is considered to be "a cornerstone of judicial review in the EU".[35] Moreover, this ability is consistent with the EU courts' monopoly on interpretation of EU law, and more generally, with the rule that exists in many continental legal systems, "iura novit curia",[36] whereby the court is deemed to know the law. Nevertheless, by leaving the definition of those criteria to the EMA, the Court restricted itself to a limited review.

P, *Alvarez y Bejarano and Others v Commission*, Opinion of Advocate General Priit Pikamae, 21 October 2020, ECLI:EU:C:2020:848, para 38.

[30] ECJ, Case C-732/18 P, *Rosneft and Others v Council*, Judgment, 17 September 2020, not published, ECLI:EU:C:2020:727, para 91.

[31] Or, as succinctly put by Advocate General Ćapeta at point 86 of her Opinion of 6 February 2025 (see no. 29), "The courts are not scientists and cannot become scientists".

[32] Craig outlines several examples of where the Court has characterised the definition of certain concepts as amounting to discretion afforded on the administrative body by the Treaties, where, arguably, they could have just as easily been categorised questions of interpretation of the law. See Craig 2018, p. 444.

[33] ECJ, Joined Cases C-6/21 P and C-16/21 P, *Germany v Pharma Mar and Commission*, Judgment, 22 June 2023, ECLI:EU:C:2023:502, para 52.

[34] *Ibid.*

[35] Craig 2018, p. 444.

[36] Also, "*jura novit curia*", "*curia novit legem*", and so forth. For a discussion on how this rule works in practice at national and EU level, and even in common law systems in which it does not traditionally exist, see ECJ, Joined cases C-430/93 and C-431/93, *van Schijndel and van Veen v SPF*, Opinion of Mr Advocate General Jacobs, 15 June 1995 ECLI:EU:C:1995:185, points 33 to 42.

Within the remit of a limited review, the Court "must confine itself to checking that the rules on procedure and the statement of reasons have been complied with, that the facts are materially correct and that there has been no manifest error of assessment or misuse of powers".[37] Beyond the basic observance of procedural rules and the grounds of "misuse of powers" (which is rarely successful[38] and difficult to establish[39]), the key aspect of limited review thus turns on the definition that is accorded to "manifest error". The EU courts have applied this test with varying levels of intensity across the different areas of EU action over the years.

The term "manifest" was defined in earlier case law of the Court as referring to the failure to observe legal provisions as arising "from an obvious error in evaluation".[40] As Craig observes, this early case law suggests that the Court would only interfere in cases of "extreme and obvious forms of substantive error".[41] Indeed, he supports this statement by pointing out the fact that the courts would previously carry out their assessment in just "one or two brief paragraphs".[42] As any EU competition law practitioner will be acutely aware, this is in stark contrast to modern judgments of the General Court, which can easily span over one hundred pages. Clearly, the courts are willing to engage in rather high levels of review in the field of competition law. While the "manifest error" test will still be applied with a lighter touch in fields where the EU institutions are afforded broad, general powers which require the balancing of competing interests (for example in relation to the Common Agricultural Policy),[43] the level of scrutiny applied in relation to complex economic assessments has greatly increased over the years.

14.2.2.2 The Evolution of Complex Technical and Economic Evaluations

The concept of highly technical and complex economic matters was initially frequently relied on by the courts to refuse to carry out thorough review of the decisions of EU institutions. However, the Court has become increasingly prepared to entertain arguments that the decision maker got it wrong in relation to complex

[37] For a recent example, see General Court, Case T-146/22, *Ryanair v Commission (KLM II; COVID-19)*, Judgment, 7 February 2024, ECLI:EU:T:2024:68, para 59.

[38] Craig 2018, p. 467.

[39] The EU Courts has consistently held that "a decision is vitiated by misuse of powers only if it appears, on the basis of objective, relevant and consistent evidence, to have been taken for purposes other than those stated". This is quite clearly a very high threshold to overcome, considering the difficult nature of proving the intention of the decision-maker. For a recent example, see General Court, Case T-440/21, *TM v BCE*, Judgment, 14 December 2022, not published, ECLI:EU:T:2022:800, para 82.

[40] Court of First Instance, Case T-156/98, *RJB Mining v Commission*, Judgment, 31 January 2001, ECLI:EU:T:2001:29, para 87.

[41] Craig 2018, p. 480.

[42] *Ibid.*

[43] *Ibid.*

economic assessments. While Kalintiri points out the elusive yet omnipresent nature of this notion in competition law, she nonetheless provides some helpful examples of what the courts have found to be "complex".[44] Indeed, in relation to competition law, which relies heavily on economic theories, it can be difficult to clearly define where the role of the competition authority ends and where the role of the Court begins. Initially, the Court engaged in only "light" review of decisions of the Commission in relation to competition infringements. However, the Commission began exercising its powers with greater intensity and frequency, and, according to some, began to rely on "hazardous legal or economic theories".[45]

In addition, academics and practitioners alike began to criticise "the Commission's perceived unparalleled role as investigator, prosecutor and judge" in competition cases.[46] Thus, the year 2002 marked an undeniable turning point in the Court's approach to judicial review of merger control decisions, a year which the former president of the General Court, Mr. da Cruz Vilaça referred to as an "annus horribilis"[47] for the Commission. The Court of First Instance annulled three of the Commission's decisions on merger control,[48] including in the case *Tetra Laval*,[49] which was upheld on appeal to the ECJ. The Court confirmed in that case that whilst "the Commission has a margin of discretion with regard to economic matters, that does not mean that the Community Courts must refrain from reviewing the Commission's interpretation of information of an economic nature".[50]

The Court went on to find that, in addition to the standard test for manifest error, it must:

> inter alia, establish not only whether the evidence relied on is factually accurate, reliable and consistent but also whether that evidence contains all the relevant information which must be taken into account in order to assess a complex situation and whether it is capable of substantiating the conclusions drawn from it.[51]

The Court thus committed to a more thorough assessment of the decisions of the EU institutions, even when conducting a "limited" review. This standard went on to become the "standard formula for marginal review".[52] Nevertheless, this "standard"

---

[44] "To name but a few, the definition of the relevant market, a conclusion that an undertaking holds a dominant position, a finding that a conduct amounts to an abuse of dominance, the weighing-up exercise under Article 101(3) TFEU, and ascertaining that a concentration 'would significantly impede effective competition' in the common market are all examples of assessments that, according to EU Courts, call for limited review". Kalintiri 2016, para 1290.

[45] da Cruz Vilaça 2018, p. 176.

[46] Vesterdorf 2003, p. 143.

[47] da Cruz Vilaça 2018, p. 176.

[48] Court of First Instance, Case T-342/99, *Airtours v Commission*, Judgment, 6 June 2002, ECLI:EU:T:2002:146; Court of First Instance, Court of First Instance, Case T-77/02, *Schneider v Commission*, Judgment, 22 October 2002, ECLI:EU:T:2002:255.

[49] Case T-5/02, *Tetra Laval*, Judgment, 25 October 2002, ECLI:EU:T:2002:264.

[50] ECJ, Case C-12/03 P, *Commission v Tetra Laval*, Judgment, 15 February 2005, ECLI:EU:C:2005:87, para 39.

[51] *Ibid.*

[52] Kalintiri 2016, para 1289.

formula can be applied with varying levels of intensity, with the courts appearing to be more searching in certain areas, such as where the protection of fundamental rights are concerned.[53]

The difference in the *comprehensive* and *limited* standards of reviews is demonstrated in practice in the case law on State aid. As stated above, the EU courts will conduct a comprehensive review on points of law. The Court has found that "State aid" is a legal concept which must be interpreted on the basis of objective factors.[54] Furthermore, the Court found that the Commission does not have "broad discretion" in relation to the classification of a measure as "State aid".[55] Therefore, the EU Courts will conduct a comprehensive review as to whether the conditions laid down in Article 107(1) have been satisfied in order to assert the existence of State aid.[56] Nevertheless, if the Court considers that the Commission carried out complex or technical appraisals in coming to its finding of State aid, judicial review will be limited.[57]

14.2.3 Standard Jurisdiction v Unlimited Jurisdiction Under Article 261 TFEU

The review of legality under Article 263 is supplemented by the *unlimited* jurisdiction to cancel, reduce or increase fines that can be granted upon the courts under Article 261. This Article provides that regulations adopted by the European Parliament and the Council, or by the Council alone, may confer *unlimited jurisdiction* on the courts in relation to the review of penalties imposed under the relevant regulation. This empowers the Court to step into the shoes of the decision-maker and replace the EU institution's judgment with its own, even by relying on new evidence and facts which post-date the imposition of the fine.[58] The fines that garner the most publicity are those imposed by the Commission on undertakings in violation of competition law rules,[59]

---

[53] See, for example, ECJ, Joined Cases C-584/10 P, C-593/10 P and C-595/10 P, *European Commission v Kadi*, Judgment, 18 July 2013, ECLI:ECLI:EU:C:2013:518.

[54] See, *inter alia*, ECJ, Case C-486/15 P, *Commission v France and Orange*, Judgment, 30 November 2016, ECLI:EU:C:2016:912, para 87; ECJ, Case C-374/17, *A-Brauerei*, Opinion of Advocate General Saugmandsgaard Øe, 19 September 2018, ECLI:EU:C:2018:1024.

[55] ECJ, Case C-487/06 P, *British Aggregates v Commission*, Judgment, 22 December 2008, ECLI:EU:C:2008:757, para 112.

[56] General Court, Case T-121/15, *Fortischem v Commission*, Judgment, 24 September 2019, ECLI:EU:T:2019:684, para 62.

[57] General Court, Case T-423/14, *Larko v Commission*, Judgment, 1 February 2018, ECLI:EU:T:2018:57, para 59: "It is, however, for the Court to decide whether that is the case".

[58] Castillo de la Torre and Gippini Fournier 2024, p. 269.

[59] For example, on the 24 October 2024, the CJEU upheld the annulment by the General Court of the Commission's decision to fine Intel €1.06 billion, see https://www.theguardian.com/technology/2024/oct/24/intel-legal-battle-against-eu-880m-fine-competition. Accessed 12 February 2025. See also, on the 10 September 2024, the CJEU upheld a fine of 2.4 billion Euro imposed on Google

under Council Regulation 2003/1.[60] Article 31 of that regulation empowers the Court to "substitute its own appraisal for that of the Commission and, consequently, to cancel, reduce or increase the fine or periodic penalty payment imposed".[61]

Article 261 TFEU clearly confers vast powers on the courts in relation to the review of penalties. However, the unlimited power of the General Court is, of course, subject to the respect of general principles of EU law such as those of "adequate reasoning, proportionality, the individualisation of penalties and equal treatment".[62] Moreover, the Court has found that the jurisdiction is not exercised *ex officio* and the proceedings are *inter partes*, and thus, the Court must "examine all submissions on issues of fact and law" in relation to the fine.[63] Furthermore, the fine imposed by the General Court must be related to the amount of the initial fine imposed by the Commission, and cannot constitute a new fine that is legally distinct from the original.[64] Nevertheless, on appeal to the ECJ, the General Court's decision made in exercise of its unlimited jurisdiction will be subject to light review.

14.3 Judicial Review of Administrative Decisions by National Courts

In the decentralised system of implementation of Union law where national administrative authorities are expressly obliged to apply EU rules,[65] national courts, in cooperation with the Court of Justice, play an essential part in ensuring effective judicial protection in the fields covered by Union law. Recourse to the EU Courts or to national jurisdictions is a logical consequence of the adoption of decisions by EU institutions or by national administrative authorities.[66] In the latter case, national courts act within their own constitutional framework, apply their own procedural rules, exercise their own standard of judicial review and enforce their decisions within their own institutional setting.

---

by the Commission, see https://www.bbc.com/news/articles/cjw3e1pn741o. Accessed 12 February 2025.

[60] Council Regulation (EC) No 1/2003 of 16 December 2002 on the implementation of the rules on competition laid down in Articles 81 and 82 of the Treaty, OJ L 1, p. 1.

[61] ECJ, Case C-697/19 P, *Sony Corporation and Sony Electronics v Commission*, Judgment, 16 June 2022, ECLI:EU:C:2022:478, para 177 and cited case law.

[62] ECJ, Case C-440/19 P, *Pometon / Commission*, Judgment, 18 March 2021, ECLI: ECLI:EU:C:2021:214, para 160; ECJ, Case C-42/21 P, *Lietuvos geležinkeliai v Commission*, Judgment, 12 January 2023 ECLI: EU:C:2023:12, para 154.

[63] ECJ, Case C-42/21 P, *Lietuvos geležinkeliai v Commission*, Opinion of Advocate General Rantos, 7 July 2022, ECLI: ECLI:EU:C:2022:537, para 152.

[64] See no. 5, *Westfälische Drahtindustrie*, paras 40–41; ECJ, Case C-698/19 P, *Sony Optiarc and Sony Optiarc America v Commission*, Judgment, 16 June 2022, ECLI: EU:C:2022:480, para 92.

[65] See for instance, Article 3(1) of the Regulation 1/2003 (see no. 60).

[66] Case T-589/22, *Silgan*, (no. 2) para 54.

The relationship between national procedural law and Union law is governed by the principle of procedural autonomy, subject to observance of the principles of equivalence and effectiveness.[67] The CJEU specified that with regard, in particular, to the right of access to a tribunal, for a "tribunal" to be able to hear a dispute concerning rights and obligations arising under EU law in accordance with Article 47 of the Charter, it must have the power to consider all questions of fact and law that are relevant to the case before it.[68] This is the minimum common ground for judicial protection to be considered "effective". By setting this as the minimum scope of judicial review, the CJEU also acknowledges its own limits in the exercise of complex assessment and does not require national courts to conduct a more extensive review than that carried out by the CJEU in similar cases.[69] The question of whether a more extensive review can, nevertheless, be carried out is a matter to be dealt with by national law.

There has been nothing to suggest, in either the case law or legal commentary, that, generally speaking, in Lithuania, the protection of the rights which individuals derive from EU law does not satisfy the requirements of equivalence and effectiveness. Lithuanian courts effectively uphold such rights against the decisions of national administrative authorities and even against national legislative measures.[70] At the same time, some particularities of the judicial review exercised by Lithuanian courts (particularly those of a normative nature) may give the impression that the standard of judicial review differs significantly from that exercised by EU courts. However, the case law of the Lithuanian administrative courts is largely inspired by that of the EU courts, and therefore, these differences are limited. Before demonstrating this through a comparison of a few chosen elements, I will first outline some basic features of the system of judicial review in Lithuania.

[67] See ECJ, Case C-261/21, *F. Hoffmann-La Roche and Others*, Judgment, 21 December 2021, ECLI:EU:C:2021:1037, para 44: "Provided there are EU rules on the matter, it is, in accordance with the principle of procedural autonomy, for the national legal order of each Member State to establish procedural rules for those remedies, on condition, however, that those rules are not, in situations governed by EU law, less favourable than in similar domestic situations (principle of equivalence) and that they do not make it impossible in practice or excessively difficult to exercise the rights conferred by EU law (principle of effectiveness)".

[68] ECJ, Case C-199/11, *Otis and Others*, Judgment, 6 November 2012, ECLI:EU:C:2012:684, para 49.

[69] ECJ, Case C-120/97, *Upjohn*, Judgment, 21 January 1999, ECLI:EU:C:1999:14, para 35.

[70] A good illustration of the effectiveness of judicial protection before Lithuanian courts is provided in ECJ, Case C-72/22 PPU *Valstybės sienos apsaugos tarnyba*, Judgment, 30 June 2022, ECLI:EU:C:2022:505, in which the legislation limiting the right to lodge an application for international protection and automatic detention of asylum applicants who crossed the state border unlawfully was challenged.

14.3.1 Two-Tiered System of Judicial Review in Lithuania

Judicial review of administrative decisions in Lithuania is carried out by the administrative courts. These courts operate with two degrees of jurisdiction. On the first level, the cases are heard by the regional administrative courts. The parties can appeal these decisions to the Supreme Administrative Court, which is the last instance court. An appeal can be brought to challenge the alleged errors of fact and law of the first instance court. Unlike in civil and criminal cases, further appeal to the Supreme Court on points of law is not possible. Thus, the Supreme Administrative Court, as the court of last instance, is obliged to submit questions on the interpretation of EU law to the Court of Justice under Article 267 TFEU. It is also responsible for the unification of the case law in administrative matters.

In many areas of public administration, such as in tax disputes, land disputes, disputes over entries in public registries, an internal review mechanism or pre-trial appeal procedure can be prescribed by law. The applicants can also have recourse to a non-compulsory pre-trial appeal before an independent Administrative Disputes Commission, the decisions of which can be contested before the administrative courts. These pre-trial mechanisms justify having only two levels of jurisdiction, as compared to the three levels that exist in civil and criminal matters.

14.3.2 Procedural Framework for Judicial Review in Lithuanian Law

The Law on Administrative Proceedings of 1999[71] sets out the procedure to be followed in administrative cases. That law was amended in 2016[72] with the main objectives being to streamline proceedings, to provide a legal basis for digitalisation, and to facilitate the treatment of large groups of cases by introducing group actions and test cases.[73]

The standing requirements for bringing an action before the administrative courts are less stringent than those set out under Article 263, para 4 TFEU. The notions of direct and individual concern do not exist in Lithuanian administrative proceedings. Instead, access to the courts is based on the constitutional law principle of effective judicial protection[74] and is expressed in administrative procedural law as the right

[71] Lietuvos Respublikos administracinių bylų teisenos įstatymas [Law on Administrative Proceedings], published in official gazette Žin.1999, No 13-308.

[72] Lietuvos Respublikos administracinių bylų teisenos įstatymas [Law on Administrative Proceedings], published in the electronic registry of legal acts 2016-16849. https://e-seimas.lrs.lt/portal/legalAct/lt/TAD/TAIS.72290/asr?positionInSearchResults=0&searchModelUUID=6be60438-f2ab-4175-9171-4386c0f7e1c1. Accessed 12 February 2025.

[73] Inspired by the German model of "Musterverfahren" set out under Section 93a of the German Code of Administrative Court Procedure.

[74] See Andrijauskaitė 2021; Bareikytė et al. 2023; Spruogis and Vainiutė 2022.

of every interested party to apply to the courts, in accordance with the procedure laid down by law, in order to defend a right or interest that has been infringed or contested.[75] By specifying that the right to apply to a court belongs to an *interested party* the legislator intended to confer this right only on persons seeking the protection of their own rights or interests and thus excluded *actio popularis* from the scope of judicial protection.[76] In certain cases specified by law, recourse to the courts can be made by public prosecutors or other authorised bodies which act in the protection of the public interest.[77]

An action may be brought within one month from the date of publication of the contested act or notification of it to the interested party, unless a special law provides otherwise. This is more restrictive than the two months provided under Article 263. Omissions, however, can be challenged within two months from the expiry of the time limits for resolving the matter.

Except for in specific cases provided for by law,[78] the initiation of proceedings has no suspensory effect on the contested act. However, the administrative court can order "measures for securing the claim" on the conditions that the applicant establishes a prima facie case for the validity of the claim and that the absence of the requested measures would be likely to cause serious and irreparable damage. It is quite clear that the conditions for ordering these measures are very similar to interim measures ordered by EU courts. However, Lithuanian administrative courts are granted broader powers as to the choice of appropriate measures which are not restricted to measures of a suspensory or prohibitive character. In fact, the law specifically provides that the courts may also take measures where it is necessary to temporarily regulate a situation relating to a disputed legal relationship.[79] The courts previously lacked this power and the legislator made the deliberate choice to introduce it in the amended Law on Administrative Proceedings 2016, in order to reinforce the protection of individual rights pending the outcome of the court's decision.[80] The administrative courts are, however, very cautious when adopting this type of measure. The majority of interim measures are limited to suspending the contested act or prohibiting certain actions, such as the return of a migrant pending the court's decision.

---

[75] Article 5 of the Law on Administrative Proceedings.

[76] See to that effect, for example, the decision of the Lithuanian Constitutional Court of 8 April 2020 in the case KT70-A-S65/2020. https://lrkt.lt/data/public/uploads/2020/04/2020-04-08_kt70-a-s65-nuasmeninta.pdf. Accessed 12 February 2025.

[77] Article 5(3) of the Law on Administrative Proceedings.

[78] Automatic suspensory effects are attached, for example, to the action for an annulment of a decision of the tax authority imposing a penalty (Law on Tax Administration, 13 April 2004 No IX-2112, Article 152(6)), but not to a comparable decision of the competition authority (Law on Competition, 23 March 1999 No VIII-1099, Article 33(2)).

[79] Article 70 of the Law on Administrative Proceedings.

[80] The explanatory memorandum accompanying the draft law of the amendments of the Law of Administrative Proceedings mentions the example of ordering the correction of the data in the register pending the dispute. [Aiškinamasis raštas dėl Lietuvos Respublikos administracinių bylų teisenos įstatymo Nr. VIII-1029 pakeitimo įstatymo projekto], para 11. https://e-seimas.lrs.lt/portal/legalAct/lt/TAK/de7df5a2d6e111e49a8e8a8aa8141086?jfwid=-fjix91p14. Accessed 12 February 2025.

The annulment of the contested act will result in the act being considered void *ab initio*[81] and the situation that existed prior to its adoption will be restored. However, this does not lead to the automatic restoration of the legal force of the act that was in force prior to the annulment.[82]

14.4 Parallel Systems of Judicial Review: A Comparison

Having outlined the basic features of the judicial review of the EU and Lithuanian courts, I will now move on to a comparison of these two jurisdictions. First, I will compare the basic provisions which set out the scope of judicial review. Second, I will turn to consider the broader picture of the procedural context, the orders which the courts may take and the expectations of the role of the judge at national and international level. Finally, I will summarise the main aspects of comparison.

14.4.1 The Statutory Standard of Judicial Review in Lithuanian and EU Law

The scope of judicial review exercised by Lithuanian administrative courts is set out under Article 3 of the Law on Administrative Proceedings, which states that "[t]he court shall not assess the contested administrative act and action (or omission) in terms of political or economic expediency, but only whether, in a particular case, a law or other legal act has been infringed, whether the public administrative body has exceeded its powers, and whether the act or action (or omission) complies with the aims and objectives for which the body was established and given its powers." This provision is comparable to Article 263 TFEU, in that they both determine what can and cannot be subject to review by administrative courts.

Article 3 includes all legal issues but expressly excludes questions not amenable to judicial review, such as political or economic considerations. In any relation to legal issues, it is obvious for Lithuanian courts that limited review by no means extends to questions of law. By relying on the principle of *iura novit curia*, Lithuanian administrative courts can even perform the legal re-qualification of an administrative act which imposes a sanction on an individual, provided the factual elements remain the same and the right to be heard and procedural fairness were observed during the examination of the case.[83]

However, in relation to the exclusion of political or economic considerations, from early on in its case law, the Supreme Administrative Court had to clarify its

[81] Raižys 2005.

[82] Article 94 of the Law on Administrative Proceedings.

[83] Supreme Administrative Court of Lithuania, administrative case No. eA-362-968/2024, Resolution, 7 February 2024. https://www.infolex.lt/tp/2225657. Accessed 12 February 2025.

extent and contain the attempts of the administrative authorities to restrict review where, despite those authorities enjoying a certain amount of discretion, judicial review could not be entirely excluded due to the legal nature of the question. Such concepts are common in competition cases, such as the definition of the relevant market or the assessment of a dominant position. By relying on the case law of the CJEU concerning the scope of limited judicial review, the Supreme Administrative Court held that this type of review does not amount to an assessment of economic expediency prohibited by Article 3 of the Law on Administrative Proceedings.[84]

Lithuanian administrative courts recognise administrative discretion in complex matters in similar terms to the EU Courts. Thus, in a case concerning an abuse of dominant position, the Supreme Administrative Court held that the definition of the relevant market is a complex economic question. Therefore, while assessing the findings of the Competition Council, the court must only examine whether the Council complied with the procedural rules, whether all its conclusions were reasoned, whether there had been distortion of fact, whether a manifest error of assessment had been made, and whether there had been an abuse of powers.[85] The courts accord even broader discretion in relation to regulatory acts that develop or implement economic policy.[86] However, much like the case law of the ECJ following its judgment in *Tetra Laval*,[87] which established a more thorough review of factual elements in areas where the decision-maker conducted a complex technical or scientific appraisal, a similar trend can be observed in the case law of the Lithuanian administrative courts. Indeed, those courts are more willing to conduct a thorough examination of factual elements in areas in which an administrative authority enjoys broad discretion.[88]

With regard to the unlimited jurisdiction that can be granted to the EU courts under Article 261 TFEU, the Lithuanian statute does not provide for the same vast powers. Indeed, the latter do not have the power to increase fines. This would be seen as *reformatio in peius* and probably contradictory to the principle of effective judicial

---

[84] Supreme Administrative Court, administrative case No. A7-2203/2006 *TEO LT v Ryšių reguliavimo tarnyba*, Judgment, 18 December 2006; administrative case No. A502-34/2009 *Libra Vitalis v Competition Council*, Judgment, 16 October 2009.

[85] Supreme Administrative Court, 8 December 2008, administrative case No. A248-715/2008 *Mažeikių nafta v Competition Council*, Judgment, 8 December 2008.

[86] Judgment of the Constitutional Court, 31 May 2006. https://lrkt.lt/lt/teismo-aktai/paieska/135/ta213/content. Accessed 12 February 2025.

[87] See no. 50, *Tetra Laval*, para 39.

[88] See for instance the judgment of the Supreme Administrative Court in the *Mažeikių nafta* case, in which a thorough analysis of factual elements underlying market definition was conducted: Supreme Administrative Court, administrative case No. A248-715/2008 *Mažeikių nafta v Competition Council*, Judgment, 8 December 2008. https://www.lvat.lt/data/public/uploads/2018/01/d1_lvat_biuletenis_16.pdf. Accessed 12 February 2025. See also to that effect, judgment in E-Turas after reference to the CJEU (ECJ, Case C-74/14, *Eturas and Others*, Judgment, 21 January 2016, ECLI:EU:C:2016:42) as an example of thorough factual assessment of the Competition Council's findings: Supreme Administrative Court, administrative case No. A97-858/2016 *Eturas v Competition Council*, Judgment, 2 May 2016. https://www.infolex.lt/tp/1278767. Accessed 12 February 2025.

protection. While recognising the broad discretion of administrative authorities when imposing penalties, in particular in relation to the violation of competition rules, the administrative courts apply the same grid of analysis that they apply in the assessment of other discretionary decisions. The Supreme Administrative Court highlighted that it is for the applicant to provide evidence which would allow it to conclude that the Competition Council, in imposing the fine and setting the amount of the fine, has not exercised its discretion properly.[89] However, it should be noted that while the CJEU is granted broad powers in the exercise of its unlimited jurisdiction, the scope of this power is still subject to debate.[90] Indeed, the ECJ has not yet ruled on whether the Courts can raise the fine where an application to that effect has not been made, contrary to the principle of *reformation in peius*.[91]

14.4.2 Procedural Framework and Practical Considerations of Judicial Review at EU and National Level

The procedural context in which courts operate is an important factor which affects how those courts conduct judicial review.[92] If the judicial proceedings are driven by the applicant's initiative and the review is strictly limited to the grounds of appeal they formulated and pleaded before the court, the outcome of the case will be almost entirely dictated by the parties' autonomy. The situation is different where courts are invested with the power to compensate for some procedural omissions of the parties, in particular to raise certain pleas *ex officio*, to examine factual elements not relied on by the parties or to conduct a legal re-qualification of their pleas. The powers the courts enjoy vis-à-vis administrative authorities also shape the scope and the intensity of what is examined in the course of judicial proceedings.

The Lithuanian Law on Administrative Proceedings provides the administrative courts with the power not only to annul the contested act, but also to order the administrative authority that adopted it to remedy the infringement or comply with any other court order.[93] This power can be clearly contrasted with the powers exercised by EU courts, which, according to settled case law, cannot order any injunctions or directions to EU institutions or agencies.[94] According to the Article 266 TFEU,

[89] *Ibid.*

[90] ECJ, Case C-367/22, *Air Canada v Commission*, Opinion of Advocate General Rantos, 5 September 2024, ECLI:EU:C:2024:702, para 184.

[91] See ECJ, Cases C-293/13 P and C-294/13, *Fresh Del Monte Produce v Commission* and *Commission v Fresh Del Monte Produce*, Opinion of Advocate General Kokott, 11 December 2014, ECLI: ECLI:EU:C:2014:2439, para. 273, in which she argues that there is no prohibition on *reformation in peius* in respect of the exercise of the EU Court's unlimited jurisdiction and that the courts are, in principle, empowered to increase the fine, regardless of the forms of order sought by the parties.

[92] On the impact of procedural elements on the scope of the judicial review, see Nehl 2019, p. 164.

[93] Article 88 of the Law on Administrative Proceedings.

[94] General Court, Case T-134/20, *Huhtamaki v Commission*, Judgment, 2 March 2022, ECLI:EU:T:2022:100, para 18.

it is for the institution whose act has been declared void itself to take the necessary measures to comply with the judgment of the Court of Justice. In addition, that article does not establish an autonomous remedy by which the enforcement of the Court's judgment can be obtained.[95] Non-compliance with the judgment can simply result in an action for damages under Article 268 TFEU or in a new action for annulment. It follows that under Article 263 TFEU, the powers of EU courts are strictly limited to the annulment of the contested act. In addition, they cannot substitute their own reasoning for that of the author of the contested act[96] and cannot add any grounds to those included in that act.[97]

While the Supreme Administrative Court also asserts that the administrative court may not take a decision which falls within the competences of a public administrative body,[98] this statement is more difficult to reconcile with the extensive powers set out in the Law on Administrative Proceedings which allow the courts to order administrative authorities to take a specific action. In the early case law of the Lithuanian administrative courts, recourse to this remedy was relatively frequent. The courts not only ordered the administrative body to re-examine the question after the administrative act had been quashed, but also ordered which type of decision it had to take.[99] However, the more recent case law draws a slightly different picture, demonstrating that the courts are more cautious with regard to ordering substantive measures that could be regarded as encroaching on the jurisdiction of an administrative authority. While it is true that, in annulment decisions, the administrative courts still sometimes apply the standard formula and order the re-examination of the question, such an order essentially adds nothing to its normative content, as the obligation to take all the measures to comply with the judgment derives from the legislation itself.[100] On rare occasion, in cases of failure to act, the courts may set a precise time limit for compliance with the judgment, in order to ensure the effective protection of the violated rights at issue.[101] Any other order is categorised as "exceptional" by the

---

[95] ECJ, Case C-138/23 P, *British Airways v Commission*, Order, 27 October 2023, ECLI:EU:C:2023:821, para 35.

[96] ECJ, Case C-246/11 P, *Portugal v Commission*, Judgment, 28 February 2013, not published, ECLI:EU:C:2013:118 para 85 and the case-law cited.

[97] ECJ, Case C-456/18 P, *Hungary v Commission*, Judgment, 4 June 2020, ECLI:EU:C:2020:421, para 73.

[98] Supreme Administrative Court, administrative case No. A-1123-602/2016, Judgment, 21 November 2016; administrative case No. eA-362-968/2024, Judgment, 7 February 2024. https://www.infolex.lt/tp/2225657. Accessed 12 February 2025.

[99] See for instance, Supreme Administrative Court, No. A525-3043/2012, Judgment, 28 December 2012.

[100] "A final court decision and order is binding on all state institutions, officials and civil servants, companies, institutions, organisations, other natural and legal persons and must be enforced throughout the territory of the Republic of Lithuania", Article 3(2) of the Law on Administrative Proceedings.

[101] Supreme Administrative Court, administrative case No. AS602-82/2012, Judgment, 13 January 2012.

Supreme Administrative Court[102] and is virtually not used in practice. Therefore, in exercising the (broad) statutory powers to issue orders on administrative authorities, the administrative courts respect the principle of the separation of powers and do not exhibit the intention to take unrestricted liberty to encroach on the jurisdiction of the executive. At the same time, the CJEU itself interpreted the principle of effective judicial protection under Article 47 of the Charter as requiring national courts, in certain circumstances, to vary a decision of the administrative or quasi-judicial body that does not comply with its previous judgment and to substitute its own decision for it, disapplying as necessary the national law that would prohibit it from proceeding this way.[103] The broad powers bestowed on the Lithuanian administrative courts are consistent with this line of case law and therefore ensure compliance with effective judicial protection as defined under Union law.

Unlike in Lithuanian law, the scope of the judicial review exercised by the EU Courts is, in general, limited to what the applicant has set out in the application for annulment. The case law of the EU courts has consistently held that it is for the applicant to establish the subject-matter of the proceedings brought before them by setting out the form of order sought and the pleas in law on which he or she relies in the application. The EU courts may not depart from those claims and pleas, since to do otherwise would be to give judgment *ultra petita* and to exceed the limits of their powers.[104] Consequently, even where there has been a manifest infringement of a substantive right or a general principle of law, such as the principle of proportionality, the EU courts may only take this into account as a means to justify annulment if it was expressly pleaded in the application.[105] The only exceptions to this are so-called "procedural pleas", such as lack of competence on the part of the institution,[106] infringement of an essential procedural requirement,[107] or breach of the duty to state reasons,[108] which are all subject to *ex officio* review by the CJEU.

On the normative level, procedure before Lithuanian administrative courts is quite different to that of the EU courts. Although the main objective of administrative proceedings consists in protecting individual rights, Lithuanian case law and legal commentary have long recognised a certain public interest[109] in administrative

[102] See the thematic analysis of the jurisprudence of Supreme Administrative Court in applying the Law on Public Administration, 2016. https://www.lvat.lt/data/public/uploads/2018/01/biuletenis_30-apibendrinimas.pdf. Accessed 12 February 2025.

[103] See no. 15, *Torubarov*, para 74.

[104] ECJ, Case C-224/12 P *Commission v The Netherlands and ING Groep*, Judgment, 3 April 2014 ECLI:EU:C:2014:213, para 97.

[105] Nehl 2019, p. 165. ECJ, Case C-272/12 P *Commission v Ireland and Others*, Judgment, 10 December 2013, ECLI:EU:C:2013:812, para 36.

[106] ECJ, Case C-577/15 P, *SV Capital v ABE*, Judgment, 14 December 2016, ECLI:EU:C:2016:947, para 32.

[107] General Court, T-240/10, *Hungary v Commission*, Judgment, 13 December 2013, para 70.

[108] Court of First Instance, T-44/00, *Mannesmannröhren-Werke v Commission*, 8 July 2004, para 210.

[109] The Constitutional Court has repeatedly held that the public interest recognised by the State and protected by law is one of the most important conditions for the existence and development of

proceedings because of the relative weakness of certain applicants vis-à-vis public authorities and the general necessity to ensure the respect of the principle of legality in public administration.[110] To restore this imbalance, the Law on Administrative Proceedings prescribes an active role for administrative judges by stipulating that "where necessary, the court shall investigate *ex officio* the circumstances of the case which are relevant for its fair resolution. The court shall determine the scope of such investigation and shall not be bound by the requests of the parties to the administrative proceedings."[111] In addition, the court is authorised to act *ultra petita* if required by the public interest or where the rights and interests of the State and of persons protected by law would be substantially prejudiced if the complaint were not exceeded. In any event, the administrative court "shall not be bound by the wording of the claim made".[112] According to the case law, the active role of the court in administrative proceedings implies that not only can the circumstances of the case as alleged by the parties be examined and evaluated, but also whichever circumstances the court considers relevant to the case before it.[113]

Nevertheless, despite the administrative courts' statutory powers, the procedure remains, for the most part, parties-driven. Although the Supreme Administrative Court often reiterates the active role played by the administrative judge, the dominant case law reflects respect for the principle of *non ultra petita*. According to settled case law, the administrative court is not entitled to change the cause of action or the subject-matter of the claim on its own initiative, and may not normally go beyond the limits of the claim during the proceedings.[114] Further, the active role of the court and its duty to assist the parties to exercise their procedural rights cannot be interpreted as an obligation to act in favour of the applicant. Such an active approach in favour of one of the parties would violate the principles of the adversarial nature of proceedings and the impartiality of the court.[115] The court should not itself decide on the subject matter of the complaint, as this could also give rise to reasonable doubt as to the impartiality of the court and violate the principles of adversarial procedure and disposition.[116] In the rare cases in which the court carries out an *ex*

society itself (Ruling of the Constitutional Court of 13 May 2005). This interest is not defined as such but is considered to be understood as that which is objectively significant, necessary and valuable for the public or a part of it (Supreme Administrative Court, case No A3-11/2004, Judgment, 23 January 2004). Environmental protection, consumer protection, public security could be considered as examples where, depending on the circumstances of the case, public interest may feature.

[110] See the thematic analysis of the jurisprudence of the Supreme Administrative Court in Public Interest Litigation, 2009. https://lvat.lt/data/public/uploads/2018/01/16_apibendrinimas.pdf. Accessed 12 February 2025.

[111] Article 10 (1) of the Law on Administrative Proceedings.

[112] Article 80 (2) of the Law on Administrative Proceedings.

[113] Supreme Administrative Court, No. A575-88/2012, Judgment, 18 May 2012.

[114] See, for instance, Supreme Administrative Court, case eA-662-502/2021, Judgment, 1 April 2021.

[115] See, for instance, Supreme Administrative Court, case A7-757/2002, Judgment, 14 August 2002.

[116] See, for instance, Supreme Administrative Court, case AS403-317/2006, Judgment, 5 October 2006.

officio examination, it justifies this on the basis of a particular public interest which would be significantly prejudiced if the proceedings were limited to the pleas in law relied on by the applicant. Naturally, the right of the parties to submit observations on the plea raised of the court's motion is respected[117] in the same manner as before EU courts.[118] More frequently, however, the Supreme Administrative Court rejects arguments asserting an alleged error committed by a first instance court because there was no public interest involved and therefore no ground for exceeding the limit of the claim.[119]

At the same time, Lithuanian administrative courts are more "generous" in the application of the principle *iura novit curia* than the EU courts. They adhere to the maxim *da mihi factum, dabo tibi jus* and underline systematically that there is no obligation on the claimant to indicate the legal basis of their action, nor indicate a specific legal provision violated by the adoption of contested act. After assessing the facts, the court chooses the applicable legal rules to the established facts.[120] This principle is also recognised in the case law of the Court of Justice, which specifically allows the appropriate legal characterisation of the facts alleged by the claimant and does not consider that by doing so the General Court rules *ultra petita*.[121] Its application is, however, much more broad in the case law of the Lithuanian administrative courts, which are not bound by the legal qualification of the grounds for annulment to the same extent as the EU courts and which can therefore research the violated legal provision themselves. Indeed, whereas the EU courts consider the simple evocation of a violation of certain principles as insufficiently substantiated and therefore inadmissible,[122] Lithuanian courts consider this sufficient and proceed on the basis of *iura novit curia* to the assessment of its possible violation.[123] This difference in approach can easily be explained by the fact that, unlike in proceedings before EU courts, representation by a professional lawyer is not compulsory in Lithuanian administrative proceedings. Either way, in order to ensure procedural fairness and to avoid surprise judgments, the right of the parties to comment on the

[117] See, for instance, Supreme Administrative Court, case eA-650-525/2022, Judgment, 14 December 2022.

[118] General Court, Case T-341/17, *British Airways v Commission*, Judgment, 30 March 2022, ECLI:EU:T:2022:182, para 177.

[119] See, for instance, Supreme Administrative Court, case A-550-602/2024, Judgment, 13 November 2024.

[120] See, for instance, Supreme Administrative Court, case eA-961-662/2022, Judgment, 3 November 2022.

[121] ECJ, Case C-301/19 P, *Commission v Printeos*, Judgment, 20 January 2021, ECLI:EU:C:2021:39, para 54.

[122] For a recent example, General Court, Case T-221/23, *WS v EUIPO*, Judgment, 13 November 2024, ECLI:EU:T:2024:820 para 34.

[123] "Although the applicant did not explicitly identify the principle infringed, he did indicate the circumstances of the unlawfulness of the decision in that respect. There is no requirement for the applicant to state the legal basis of the complaint when bringing an action before the Court of First Instance; the Court decides on the lawfulness of the law applied by the public authority and the procedures followed, which is a consequence of the principle of iura novit curia". Supreme Administrative Court, case A-735-602/2019, Judgment, 13 November 2019.

legal re-qualification of the applicant's pleas must be respected in the same manner as in the case of a plea raised on the court's motion.

14.4.3 Overview of Comparison

The analysis of the above points of comparison demonstrate no significant differences in the judicial review carried out by the EU courts and by Lithuanian administrative courts. Despite the trend of Europeanisation of national procedural frameworks, there is no common objective to ensure that the result of judicial review be the same irrespective of the judicial authority conducting the review. The system of judicial review in Lithuania guarantees the possibility to consider all the relevant questions of fact and law on two levels of jurisdiction, by the regional administrative courts at first instance and, on appeal, the Supreme Administrative Court. By this complete system of review, the effectiveness of the judicial review is fully observed. Much like the EU courts, the Lithuanian courts defer the assessment of complex technical or economic matters to the discretion of the administrative authorities and only exercise limited review in respect of those decisions. However, judicial review conducted by Lithuanian courts in regard to complex matters has intensified in a similar manner as that of the EU courts.

Lithuanian administrative courts enjoy broad procedural powers as regards the investigation of the case. In addition, they are far less restricted than the EU courts in their choice of orders and directions to the administrative authorities, at least on a normative level. In practice, these powers are exercised with respect for the prerogatives of the executive and only when duly justified by the circumstances of the case.

Furthermore, the absence of compulsory legal representation before Lithuanian administrative courts leads to less formalistic application of procedural rules than before EU courts. In particular, the principle *iura novit curia* removes all limits to the legal qualification of the factual circumstances invoked by the parties. The procedural fairness and the right to comment on all changes in the subject of the litigation conducted on the initiative of the court is, however, respected by Lithuanian courts in the same manner as by EU courts.

14.5 Conclusions

The scope and standard of judicial review constitute essential elements in the assessment and protection of the rights which individuals derive from Union law. However, the precise contours of the scope and standard of review are influenced by more than just the statutory provisions which set them out and they must be understood within the context of the entire legal system. Indeed, constitutional principles, legislative constraints and powers, the applicable rules of procedure and the understanding of the role of the judge in a specific legal tradition are all factors which influence a court's power of review.

The fundamental differences in these factors which exist between member states and the EU lead to natural and inevitable differences in judicial review. This is understandable and even desirable, as the different jurisdictions do not always exercise exactly the same role. Despite these fundamental features, and while on paper it may seem that the Lithuanian courts are empowered to exercise a much more rigorous judicial review than the EU courts in certain circumstances, the Lithuanian administrative courts take much inspiration from the EU courts. Therefore, in practical terms, these differences are limited. Indeed, a judicial body remains "judge of its own jurisdiction",[124] and therefore the courts have significant power to define the bounds of their own review. The Lithuanian administrative courts demonstrate the possibility of the courts to take inspiration from other jurisdictions in order to ensure consistent protection of the rights provided under EU law while respecting the principles of equivalence and effectiveness and, also, the national legal context in which it exists.

I would like to thank Síofra Collins, a lawyer at the Court of Justice, for her assistance and revision of the text.

References

Albors-Lorens A (2012) Remedies against EU Institutions after Lisbon. Cambridge Law Journal 71:3:507

Andrijauskaitė A (2021) Administrative Procedure and Judicial Review in Lithuania. In: Della Cananea G, Andenas M (eds) Judicial Review of Administration in Europe. Online edition, Oxford Academic https://doi.org/10.1093/oso/9780198867609.003.0012. Accessed 11 February 2025

Bareikytė S, Deviatnikovaitė I, Jacevič B, Paužaitė Kulvinskienė J (2023) Administrative Courts in Lithuania: History, Evolution, the Present, and Perspectives. Miscellanea Historico-Juridica, XXII: 2. https://miscellanea.uwb.edu.pl/article/view/777. Accessed 11 February 2025

Castillo de la Torre F, Gippini Fournier E (2024) Chapter 6: Scope and intensity of judicial review. In: Castillo de la Torre F, Gippini Fournier E (eds) Evidence, Proof and Judicial Review in EU Competition Law. Edward Elgar Publishing. https://doi.org/10.4337/9781839108686.00014. Accessed 11 February 2025

Craig P (2018) Law, Fact, and Discretion, EU Administrative Law. Oxford Academic. https://doi.org/10.1093/oso/9780198831655.003.0017. Accessed 11 February 2025

da Cruz Vilaça J L (2018) The intensity of judicial review in complex economic matters – recent competition law judgments of the Court of Justice of the EU. Journal of Antitrust Enforcement 6:2:173–188. https://doi.org/10.1093/jaenfo/jny003. Accessed 11 February 2025

Kalintiri A (2016) What's in a Name? The Marginal Standard of Review of "Complex Economic Assessments" in EU Competition. Common Market Law Review 53:5:1283–1316. https://doi.org/10.54648/cola2016116. Accessed 11 February 2025

Lefèvre S, Nõmm I (2023) The availability of interim measures before the General Court: Striking the right balance between the presumption of legality and the right to provisional protection.

[124] Rosas 2019, para 5.

Common Market Law Review 56:4:999–1026. https://doi.org/10.54648/cola2023072. Accessed 11 February 2025
Nehl HP (2019) Judicial Review of Complex Socio-Economic, Technical, and Scientific Assessments in the European Union. In: Mendes J (ed) EU Executive Discretion and the Limits of Law. Oxford University Press, 157–197
Raižys D (2005) Administracinių teismų sprendimų vykdymo problemos [The Problems of the Execution of Judgments of Administrative Courts]. Jurisprudencija 69:61
Rosas A (2019) Standard of Review: Court of Justice of the European Union (CJEU) In: Max Planck Encyclopedias of International Law. Oxford Public International Law. https://opil.ouplaw.com/display/10.1093/law-mpeipro/e3495.013.3495/law-mpeipro-e3495?prd=OPIL. Accessed 11 February 2025
Spruogis E, Vainiutė M (2022) Administraciniai teismai. Lietuvos konstitucinė teisė [Administrative Courts. Constitutional Law of Lithuania]. Mykolo Romerio universitetas. https://cris.mruni.eu/server/api/core/bitstreams/4a0e6465-20bb-4c16-b0ce-87994192b302/content. Accessed 11 February 2025
Vesterdorf B (2003) Certain Reflections on Recent Judgments Reviewing Commission Merger Control Decisions. In: Hoskins M, Robinson W (eds) A True European: Essays for Judge David Edward. Hart Publishing, 117–144. https://doi.org/10.5040/9781472562890.ch-010. Accessed 11 February 2025

Rimvydas Norkus is Advocate General at the Court of Justice of the European Union.

Chapter 15
Development of Criminal Law in Latvia in the Last 20 Years—The Impact and Expression of EU Law

Kristīne Strada-Rozenberga, Ārija Meikališa and Jānis Rozenbergs

Contents

Abstract The current chapter is dedicated to the assessment of the impact and expression of EU law in the development of substantive and procedural criminal law in Latvia over the last 20 years. The authors acknowledge that EU law has played an important role in the development of Latvian criminal law (both in substantive and procedural aspects), meanwhile there is no reason to unequivocally recognise that EU law has been the most frequent or decisive reason for amendments and changes in Latvian criminal legislation or the practice of its application. Describing the impact of EU law on the Latvian criminal justice system, the authors consider the main areas of its influence. In the area of substantive law, the focus is predominantly on criminalisation of offences as a consequence of EU requirements or recommendations, extension of the scope of certain criminal offences, as well as confiscation of instrumentalities and proceeds of crime. Two strands of influence are considered in relation to criminal procedural law: (1) cooperation (e.g., the European arrest warrant) and

K. Strada-Rozenberga (✉) · Ā. Meikališa · J. Rozenbergs
University of Latvia, Riga, Latvia
e-mail: strada@lu.lv

Ā. Meikališa
e-mail: arija.meikalisa@lu.lv

J. Rozenbergs
e-mail: janis.rozenbergs@lu.lv

I. Isokaitė-Valužė and H. Šinkūnas (eds.), *The European Union 2004-2024*,
https://doi.org/10.1007/978-94-6265-718-2_15

joint work (EPPO) in the EU criminal justice area; (2) the impact of EU law on the legal framework of so-called domestic or local criminal procedure.

Keywords Substantive criminal law · Procedural criminal law · Criminal procedure · Latvian legislation · Procedural guarantees · EPPO · European arrest warrant · Victim · Presumption of innocence · Right to information · Proceeds of crime

15.1 Introduction

After joining the European Union (EU) in May 2004, for the past 20 years Latvia's legal space has been inextricably linked to that of the EU. Current events and issues in the EU undoubtedly have an impact on the situation in Latvia. However, not all areas of law have been equally impacted during these 20 years or even today. There are spheres where the influence of EU law was felt much earlier and more strongly, while the range of issues regulated by criminal law for a long time was affected to a relatively small extent. Nevertheless, over time, both substantive and procedural criminal law has been significantly influenced by EU law. The purpose of this article is to present the authors' perspective on the impact of EU law on development of criminal law and criminal procedure in Latvia, drawing general observations and conclusions regarding the extent to which EU law has influenced the development of Latvian criminal law, whether it has been the main reason for changes and amendments to legal norms, and what recent developments it has brought to the practice of law enforcement in Latvia. The general conclusions are based on an analysis which considers the evolvement of Latvian criminal law legislation, trends and developments in the practice of its application, as well as the views expressed in Latvian doctrine over the last 20 years. The conclusions of the article contain appraisal of the authors' initial hypothesis that the EU has had a significant impact on the development of Latvian criminal law and criminal procedure, comparing it against the point of view that the introduction and application of EU legal norms do not constitute the dominant factor determining the development of Latvian criminal justice.

The point of departure is a general overview of the impact exerted by EU law on substantive and procedural criminal law of Latvia. It is followed by a slightly more detailed inquiry, supplemented by some illustrative examples, considering how the impact of EU legal norms in the criminal sphere has specifically manifested itself in substantive law and criminal procedure law.

15.2 Impact of EU Law on Development of Latvian Criminal Law and Criminal Procedure Law in the Last 20 Years—A General Overview

Substantive and procedural criminal law in Latvia is regulated by codified normative acts. The Criminal Law[1] (CL) was adopted on 17 June 1998 and entered into force on 1 April 1999, replacing the Criminal Code of 1961 inherited from the Soviet occupation period.[2] The Criminal Procedure Law[3] (CPL) was adopted on 21 April 2005 and entered into force on 1 October 2005, replacing the 1961 Latvian Criminal Procedure Code,[4] which, likewise, was a legacy of the Soviet occupation period.[5] Both laws have been substantially amended over time, hence, the versions currently in force differ significantly from those adopted by the Latvian Parliament (*Saeima*) in 1998 and 2005. The following section contains a general overview characterising the development of substantive law, followed by consideration of procedural law, focusing on the impact of EU rules.

According to Indra Aizupe, Director of the Criminal Justice Department of the Ministry of Justice of the Republic of Latvia, Latvian criminal law does not live in isolation from the common European and international trends influenced by global crime. At the same time, criminal justice is influenced by national needs. The rapid development of technology, the free movement of persons and the ability of organised crime entities to find new ways of committing transgressions compel law enforcers, policy makers and legislators to respond ever more rapidly to the challenges of the modern world.[6]

Since the adoption of the CL in 1998 until January 2025, the Latvian legislature has amended this law 82 times. In the General Part of the CL, which lays down the basic principles of criminal law, only 22 articles out of 95 have not been amended, while in the Special Part of the CL only a single article has not been subject to amendments. The numerous revisions of the CL reveal that most of them were made, first of all, to implement and transpose the requirements of the European Union and international law (e.g., money counterfeiting, gender equality, prohibition of discrimination, prevention of prostitution, combating terrorism, etc.), secondly, to clarify and adapt terminology to other legislation, thirdly, to ensure the protection of children's rights, fourthly, to implement changes in the penal system, fifthly, to introduce new criminal law institutes, and finally, as a result of the legislator's legal

[1] Criminal Law. https://likumi.lv/ta/id/88966-kriminallikums. Accessed 1 March 2025.

[2] Latvian Criminal Code. https://likumi.lv/ta/id/318953-latvijas-kriminalkodekss. Accessed 1 March 2025.

[3] Criminal Procedure Law. https://likumi.lv/ta/id/107820-kriminalprocesa-likums. Accessed 1 March 2025.

[4] Latvian Criminal Procedure Code. https://likumi.lv/ta/id/90971-latvijas-kriminalprocesa-kodekss. Accessed 1 March 2025.

[5] In greater detail see Liholaja and Strada-Rozenberga 2017, pp. 217, 227–228.

[6] Aizupe 2024, p. 24.

creativity.[7] Thus, the CL amendments of 13 December 2012 introduced a "reform of criminal penalties policy", whilst the amendments of 17 December 2020, which were generally aimed at "improving the criminal penalties system", initiated a reform of juvenile criminal liability, *inter alia*, by introducing differences in application and commutation of penalties. The CL has also been supplemented with new chapters—Chapter VIII(1) on coercive measures applicable to legal persons and Chapter VIII(2) on special confiscation of property.[8]

Concurrently, the CL incorporates legal provisions deriving from a total of 25 EU directives. The most important areas where amendments and additions have been made to the CL on the basis of the EU law requirements are money laundering, liability for breach of EU sanctions, human trafficking, sexual abuse of children, and fraud affecting EU interests.

The next subject of general overview concerning the impact of EU law is procedural criminal law. The new CPL was awaited with high expectations for a modern, comprehensible and long-term regulation of criminal procedural relations. However, these expectations were not fulfilled and the CPL, just like the CL, has become one of the most frequently amended laws in Latvia.

In the nearly 20 years since adoption of the CPL, the Latvian Parliament has passed more than 50 laws amending this law. The reasons for the amendments have been analysed several times in the literature. Initially, three main reasons for amending the CPL were identified: (1) implementation of EU norms; (2) correction of inaccuracies and shortcomings; (3) reaction to current developments identified in law enforcement practice.[9] Subsequently, three more were added: (1) compliance with the judgments of the Constitutional Court of Latvia (Constitutional Court), which ruled on the unconstitutionality of the provisions of the CCL; (2) compliance with general development trends (e.g. transition to e-addresses, or implementation of the legal policy goal of simplifying and speeding up criminal proceedings); (3) systemic efforts to revise criminal law and procedure.[10]

Patently, the implementation of EU standards is consistently recognised as one of the reasons for amending the CPL. The amendments to the norms of the Latvian CPL have appeared both by introducing the positions of the EU framework decisions, and later—the norms of the directives. Actually, more than a quarter of the laws amending the CPL in their justification include references to the transposition of EU frameworks, directives, or the enforcement of EU regulations. It should be noted, however, that in nearly all of these cases the decision to amend the CPL also had additional reasons. Nevertheless, there are grounds for concluding that, overall, the proportion of changes to the CPL influenced by EU legislation is not the highest, while still being significant. Moreover, it cannot be overlooked that the impact of EU rules has varied for different parts of the CPL. For example, the transposition of EU rules was clearly the main reason for the amendments to Part C of the CPL,

---

[7] Liholaja et al. 2009.

[8] Vīnkalna 2024, pp. 232–233.

[9] For greater detail see Meikališa 2015, p. 142.

[10] Meikališa 2021, pp. 273–274.

which concerns international cooperation in criminal matters. However, as regards Part A (General Provisions) and Part B (Pre-trial Criminal Proceedings and Court Proceedings in Criminal Cases) of the CPL, which are essentially applicable to criminal proceedings conducted in Latvia, the proportion of amendments to the CPL influenced by EU rules is not the highest, but it still occupies a sufficiently important place.[11]

Furthermore, it is worth mentioning that in recent years, in addition to issuing of directives, the EU has also been characterised by adoption of regulations in the field of criminal procedure. The direct applicability of regulations does not require their provisions to be transposed into national law. However, ensuring the appropriate application of regulations may, nevertheless, require amendments to national law. For example, the following are prominent examples of directly applicable regulations currently in force in Latvia, the full functioning of which also required amendments to the CCP: (1) Council Regulation (EU) 2017/1939[12] and (2) Regulation (EU) 2018/1805 of the European Parliament and of the Council.[13]

It can therefore be concluded that, in chronological order, starting with framework decisions, then—directives and, finally, regulations, EU law has gradually but significantly influenced the provisions of the CL and the CPL in Latvia. It is noteworthy that Latvia has been quite disciplined in fulfilling its obligations to comply with EU norms, both in terms of the deadlines for transposition and the content of the norms. This is evidenced by the relatively low number of infringement cases brought against Latvia for compliance with EU criminal law standards. While there have been cases (some of which will be mentioned below), the number is not significant and low compared to other countries.

To briefly address the impact of EU law on national criminal law practice, which is beyond the scope of this chapter, it must be admitted that referrals from Latvian courts to the ECJ for preliminary rulings are not very frequent. In total, less than 10 cases can be identified. The best-known examples are Case C-182/15, in which the ECJ ruled on the interpretation of Articles 18 and 21 TFEU,[14] where the question for a preliminary ruling was referred by the Latvian Supreme Court; Case C-3/20,[15] in which the CJEU, answering a question for a preliminary ruling from the Latvian court, gave a preliminary ruling on Articles 11(a), 17 and 22 of the Protocol (No. 7) on Privileges and Immunities of the European Union. Article 17, para 1; and Joined Cases C-767/22, C-49/23 and C-161/23,[16] in which, in response to a preliminary

[11] In greater detail see Meikališa and Strada-Rozenberga 2019, p. 43.

[12] Council Regulation (EU) 2017/1939 of 12 October 2017 implementing enhanced cooperation on the establishment of the European Public Prosecutor's Office ("the EPPO"), OJ L 283. http://data.europa.eu/eli/reg/2017/1939/oj.

[13] Regulation (EU) 2018/1805 of the European Parliament and of the Council of 14 November 2018 on the mutual recognition of freezing orders and confiscation orders, OJ L 303. http://data.europa.eu/eli/reg/2018/1805/oj.

[14] CJEU, Case C-182/15 *Petruhhin*, Judgment, 6 September 2016, EU:C:2016:630.

[15] CJEU, Case C-3/20 *LR Ģenerālprokuratūra*, Judgment, 30 November 2021, EU:C:2021:969.

[16] CJEU, Joined Cases C-767/22, C-49/23 and C-161/23 *1Dream OÜ and Others v Latvijas Republikas Saeima*, Judgment, 4 October 2024, EU:C:2024:823.

question from the Constitutional Court of Latvia, the CJEU gave the interpretation of Article 47 of the Charter of Fundamental Rights of the European Union, Council Framework Decision 2005/212/JHA, Directive 2014/42/EU and the principle of the primacy of EU law.

Latvian courts also use a review of EU law (framework decisions, directives, regulations), both those that apply directly to criminal law and those that apply to other sectors (framework decisions, directives, regulations), in the reasoning for their decisions in criminal cases. Thus, using a simple keyword search, the anonymised database of court decisions for 2024 yields several dozen decisions in criminal matters which contain references to EU rules.

The above shows that EU law has played a role both in the development of criminal law and in its application in practice. The impact of EU law on substantive and procedural law will be examined in greater detail below.

15.3 Development of Latvian Criminal Law under the Influence of EU Law

As it has already been pointed out above, the most extensive amendments to the CL have not been adopted to implement EU directives, but the influence of EU law on the development of Latvian criminal law cannot be overlooked. The following section will provide a concise insight into the key amendments to the CL which implemented the requirements of the EU directives.

In order to implement the requirements of Directive 2009/52/EC,[17] which affected only one provision of the CL—Article 280 “Violation of Provisions Regarding Employment of Persons” was reworded. Prior to these amendments, the CL did not provide for the criminalisation of the employment of persons who are not entitled to reside in the Republic of Latvia; Article 280 of the CL previously stipulated imposition of a criminal penalty for the violation of restrictions or rules concerning the employment of a person provided by law, if committed by an employer, and if committed repeatedly within one year. However, under Article 9 of the Directive, Member States shall ensure that a breach of the prohibition of illegal employment is a criminal offence if it is committed intentionally in all the following circumstances:

a. the infringement is continuing or persistent;
b. the infringement is committed while illegally employing a significant number of illegally staying third-country nationals;
c. the offence is committed under particularly exploitative working conditions;
d. the offence is committed by an employer who, although not having previously been charged with or convicted of an offence under Framework Decision 2002/629/JHA, uses the work or services of an illegally staying third-country national knowing that he/she is a victim of trafficking in human beings:

[17] Amendments to the Criminal Law of 16 June 2011. https://likumi.lv/ta/id/232251-grozijumi-kriminallikuma. Accessed 1 March 2025.

e. the offence relates to the illegal employment of minors.

The amendments to the CL of 16 June 2011 make it a criminal offence for an employer to employ a person who is not entitled to reside in the Republic of Latvia, if the employer employs a minor, employs more than five persons, employs a person under particularly exploitative working conditions, or knowingly employs a victim of human trafficking. Consequently, this provision of the law is currently intended to deter employers from such unlawful conduct and to reduce the opportunities for third-country nationals to work illegally in the Republic of Latvia.[18] It is also interesting to note that since 2011, i.e. in 14 years, only a few criminal proceedings have been initiated for the offence under this provision of the CL.[19]

Turning next to the measures provided by criminal law against trafficking in human beings, it should be noted that trafficking in human beings has been included as an independent criminal offence in the CL since 2002,[20] when, in compliance with the United Nations Convention against Transnational Organized Crime[21] and the Protocol to Prevent, Suppress and Punish Trafficking in Persons Especially Women and Children, supplementing the United Nations Convention against Transnational Organized Crime,[22] two new provisions were added to the CL: Article 154(1) of the CL criminalized trafficking in human beings, and Article 154(2) of the CL defined trafficking in human beings. However, an assessment of the compatibility of this regulation with Directive 2011/36/EU[23] has identified a number of clarifications that need to be made to these provisions. The amendments to the CL adopted on 13 December 2012[24] were mainly focused on penalty policy issues and affected a wide range of CL provisions, however, before the adoption of the draft law in the third reading, it was decided to make some changes to the transposition of Directive 2011/36/EU in the CL.

In particular, respecting Article 8 of the Directive, which stipulates that Member States shall, in accordance with the fundamental principles of their legal systems, take the necessary measures to ensure that the competent national authorities are entitled not to prosecute or impose sanctions on victims of trafficking in human

[18] For greater detail see Preliminary Impact Assessment Report on the Draft Law "Amendments to the Criminal Law" of 16 June 2011 (annotation). https://titania.saeima.lv/LIVS10/SaeimaLIVS10.nsf/0/13C70EC70F7C490DC2257842004D34F0?OpenDocument. Accessed 1 March 2025.

[19] https://www.ic.iem.gov.lv/lv/kriminala-statistika. Accessed 1 March 2025.

[20] Amendments to the Criminal Law of 24 April 2002. https://likumi.lv/ta/id/61914-grozijumi-kriminallikuma. Accessed 1 March 2025.

[21] United Nations Convention against Transnational Organized Crime, opened for signature 15 November 2000, vol. 2225, entered into force 29 September 2003, UNTOC.

[22] Protocol to Prevent, Suppress and Punish Trafficking in Persons, Especially Women and Children, Supplementing the United Nations Convention Against Transnational Organized Crime, opened for signature 15 November 2000, vol. 2237, entered into force 25 December 2003.

[23] Directive 2011/36/EU of the European Parliament and of the Council of 5 April 2011 on preventing and combating trafficking in human beings and protecting its victims, and replacing Council Framework Decision 2002/629/JHA, OJ L 101. http://data.europa.eu/eli/dir/2011/36/oj.

[24] Amendments to the Criminal Law of 25 April 2022. https://likumi.lv/ta/id/61914-grozijumi-kriminallikuma. Accessed 1 March 2025.

beings for engaging in criminal activities which they have been forced to commit, it was decided to add a new provision to the general part of the CL (CL 58(6)), which provides for the possibility of exempting a person from criminal liability, if he/she committed a criminal offence at a time when he/she was subjected to trafficking in human beings and was forced to do so.

At the same time, the third reading of the draft law also included amendments to the CL, which clarified and expanded the concept of trafficking in human beings (Article 154(2) CL) and clarified the descriptions of the constituent elements of criminal offences related to trafficking in human beings (Article 154(1) CL), but these should rather be regarded as editorial clarifications.

Directive 2011/93/EU[25] was transposed into the CL by the amendments of 15 May 2014 to the CL.[26] The Directive sets minimum standards on the constituent elements and sanctions for offences involving sexual abuse, sexual exploitation of children and child pornography. According to Articles 159 and 160 of the CL, criminal liability for unnatural sexual intercourse or gratification of sexual desires is incurred when the acts are committed by means of violence, threats or taking advantage of the victim's state of helplessness, whereas in practice a person may be forced to perform such acts without physical violence or the threat thereof. The Directive criminalises, among other things, engaging in sexual activity with a child through coercion or abuse of a recognised position of trust, authority or influence over the child. Similarly, the Council of Europe Convention on preventing and combating violence against women and domestic violence of 11 May 2011[27] underlines that any sexual act committed without consent is punishable, even in cases where the victim of the abuse has not physically resisted. In the light of the above, it was concluded that the Latvian criminal law framework was too narrow[28] and, accordingly, the provisions of the CL criminalizing rape, forcible sexual gratification and fornication (Articles 159, 160, 162 of the CL) were clarified by differentiating the gravity of liability depending on whether these sexual offences are committed against an adult who has reached the age of 18, or against a person who has not yet attained the age of sixteen years, or against a person under the age of 16. The amendments broadened the scope of these sexual offences to include acts involving violence or threats, as well as acts committed without the consent of the victim through the use of trust, authority or other influence over the victim.

---

[25] Directive 2011/93/EU of the European Parliament and of the Council of 13 December 2011 on combating the sexual abuse and sexual exploitation of children and child pornography, and replacing Council Framework Decision 2004/68/JHA, OJ L 335. http://data.europa.eu/eli/dir/2011/93/oj.

[26] Amendments to the Criminal Law of 15 May 2014. https://likumi.lv/ta/id/290-grozijumi-kriminallikuma. Accessed 1 March 2025.

[27] Council of Europe Convention on preventing and combating violence against women and domestic violence, opened for signature 11 May 2011, 210, entered into force 1 August 2014.

[28] In greater detail see Preliminary Impact Assessment Report on the Draft Law "Amendments to the Criminal Law" of 15 May 2014 (annotation). https://titania.saeima.lv/LIVS11/SaeimaLIVS11.nsf/0/A27D6DE7097B3AB1C2257BB10021A54D?OpenDocument. Accessed 1 March 2025.

Directive 2014/42/EU[29] was implemented in CL by amendments of 22 June 2017,[30] while harmonising CL with international conventions.[31] Article 4 of the Directive stipulates that Member States shall take the necessary measures to enable the confiscation, either in whole or in part, of instrumentalities and proceeds or property the value of which corresponds to such instrumentalities or proceeds, subject to a final conviction for a criminal offence, which may also result from proceedings *in absentia*. As provided for in the Directive, proceeds of crime can include any property, including property that has been wholly or partly transformed or converted into other property, and property that has been combined with property obtained from legitimate sources, up to the estimated value of the combined proceeds of crime. They may include proceeds or other benefits arising from the proceeds of crime or from the property into or with which those proceeds have been transformed or converted or with which they have been merged. Furthermore, Articles 5 and 6 of the Directive provide for the introduction of extended confiscation and confiscation from a third party into Member States' legal systems.

Accordingly, the 22 June 2017 amendments to the CL supplemented the law with a new chapter "Special Confiscation of Property", stipulating that special confiscation of property is the compulsory forfeiture without consideration of property acquired criminally or the object of commission of a criminal offence or property related to a criminal offence. Special confiscation of property is not a criminal sanction but a means of coercive influence under criminal law.

The concept of directly and indirectly acquired criminal property has been defined, and the law provides for extended confiscation of criminally acquired property. At the same time, it should be noted that such legal institutes were previously defined in the Latvian Criminal Procedure Law, however, Latvian legislator decided to include this regulation in the source of substantive criminal law—the CL, while supplementing and clarifying this regulation in line with the requirements of the Directive.

Just as the European Parliament is constantly innovating, Latvian officials and legislators are constantly working to harmonise Latvian criminal law with EU legislation. In this context, two legislative initiatives have not yet been adopted by the Parliament as of January 2025, but are in the drafting stage.

In January 2025, the Cabinet of Ministers approved the draft law "Amendments to the CL" (project ID 24-TA-2018),[32] prepared by the Ministry of Justice, for further

---

[29] Directive 2014/42/EU of the European Parliament and of the Council of 3 April 2014 on the freezing and confiscation of instrumentalities and proceeds of crime in the European Union, OJ L 127. http://data.europa.eu/eli/dir/2014/42/oj.

[30] Amendments to the Criminal Law of 22 June 2017. https://likumi.lv/ta/id/292016-grozijumi-kriminallikuma. Accessed 1 March 2025.

[31] UNTOC, above no. 22; United Nations Convention against illicit traffic in narcotic drugs and psychotropic substances, opened for signature 20 December 1988, vol. 1582, entered into force 11 November 1990; Council of Europe Convention on Laundering, Search, Seizure and Confiscation of the Proceeds from Crime and on the Financing of Terrorism, opened for signature 16 May 2005, 198, entered into force 1 May 2008.

[32] Draft Law "Amendments to the Criminal Law". https://tapportals.mk.gov.lv/structuralizer/data/nodes/3e67e5f7-8375-4f28-9bcb-855cb84191e0/preview. Accessed 1 March 2025.

submission to the Parliament in order to align the CL with the requirements of Directive (EU) 2024/1226.[33] The Directive ensures harmonisation in the area of infringements of EU restrictive measures by setting minimum rules concerning offences and penalties for infringements of EU restrictive measures, i.e., approximating definitions of offences, ensuring effective, dissuasive and proportionate forms and levels of penalties, facilitating national and cross-border investigations and prosecutions. In general, the Latvian legislation, as formulated in the CL, already meets the requirements of the Directive, since Article 84 of the CL provides for criminal liability for violation of sanctions imposed by the United Nations, the European Union and other international organisations or national sanctions imposed by the Republic of Latvia, thus, a person can already be held criminally liable under the Latvian legislation for all possible types of restrictive measures of the European Union listed in Article 3(1)(a)–(i) of the Directive, which are deemed criminal offences in the Member States.

In this case, the changes to the CL are not intended to introduce a new offence or to clarify the description of the offence, but instead to take advantage of the possibility provided by the Directive to decriminalise some of the activities that have been criminalised so far. In particular, Article 3(2) of the Directive gives the Member States a discretion to provide that the conduct with funds, economic resources, goods, services, transactions or activities of a value of less than 10,000 euro does not constitute a criminal offence. Consequently, given the existing geopolitical complexity of the situation concerning the sanction-related offences, as well as the significant lack of investigative resources and the identified risks of timely investigations in all the initiated criminal proceedings, it was concluded that it was not proportionate to criminalise more formal and minor sanction-related offences for which only administrative liability could be imposed using the discretion granted by the Directive.[34] Therefore, the proposed amendments provide for criminal liability in a separate norm to be invoked for violation of EU sanctions, which is manifested by the acquisition, sale or transfer of goods subject to sanctions across the customs border of the Republic of Latvia, or provision of brokerage services, or any other prohibited activities with these goods, if the value of these goods exceeds 10,000 euro. The same acts with lower-value goods should be punishable administratively without criminal liability, whereas, for reasons of national security, the criminalisation of breaches of EU sanctions involving goods of strategic importance, firearms and their essential components, ammunition, goods or technology for military purposes will be imposed regardless of the value of the goods.[35]

---

[33] Directive (EU) 2024/1226 of the European Parliament and of the Council of 24 April 2024 on the definition of criminal offences and penalties for the violation of Union restrictive measures and amending Directive (EU) 2018/1673, OJ L, 2024/1226. http://data.europa.eu/eli/dir/2024/1226/oj.

[34] In greater detail see Preliminary Impact Assessment Report on the Draft Law "Amendments to the Criminal Law" (annotation). https://tapportals.mk.gov.lv/annotation/4c6881ab-0c1b-4476-adb4-a4083fdd33d3. Accessed 1 March 2025.

[35] In greater detail see Minutes of the 14th Saeima's Legal Commission's 11 February 2025 meeting, No. 141.1.9/3-8-14/25. https://titania.saeima.lv/LIVS/SaeimasNotikumi.nsf/0/154cc9802d1d67d1c2258c29003f2f64/$FILE/PR_2025_02_11_1000_JK.pdf. Accessed 1 March 2025.

The second legislative initiative that has not yet reached the Parliament in January 2025, being in the drafting stage at the Ministry of Justice, is the issue of amendments to certain articles of the CL to ensure compliance with Directive 2017/1371.[36] In particular, the representatives of the European Public Prosecutor's Office (EPPO) at the meeting of the Coordination Council for the Protection of the European Union's Financial Interests on 28 November 2024 raised the issue concerning the incompatibility of Article 210 of the CL, which criminalises the fraudulent obtaining and use of credit and other loans, and Article 220 of the CL, which criminalises the absconding of property, with the requirements of this Directive. The representative of the EPPO pointed out that the scope of the Directive is broader than the current provisions of the CL. Although the infringement procedure INFR(2021)2231 against Latvia was terminated by the European Commission on 24 April 2024, recognising that the Directive had been correctly transposed at national level,[37] the European Public Prosecutor's Office encounters difficulties in applying the rules of the CL.[38] In particular, the provision of Article 210 of the CL (Fraudulent Obtaining and Use of Credit and Other Loans), effective as of January 2025, stipulates criminal liability for knowingly making false statements in order to obtain a subsidy, grant, credit or other loan or during the use of a subsidy, grant, credit or other loan, if this has caused substantial damage. Article 3(2)(a) of the Directive provides that the following shall be regarded as fraud affecting the Union's financial interests in respect of non-procurement-related expenditure, any act or omission relating to:

- the use or presentation of false, incorrect or incomplete statements or documents, which has as its effect the misappropriation or wrongful retention of funds or assets from the Union budget or budgets managed by the Union, or on its behalf;
- non-disclosure of information in violation of a specific obligation, with the same effect; or
- the misapplication of such funds or assets for purposes other than those for which they were originally granted.

It follows from Article 3(2)(a) of the Directive that fraud is not solely an active act—submission of inaccurate, incomplete information or documents, which corresponds to the active act of knowingly making false statements provided for in Article 210 of CL, but also an omission—failure to disclose information, which is not covered by the disposition of Article 210 of CL. As pointed out by the EPPO, in practice, there are cases when, during the implementation of a project, some essential information

[36] Directive (EU) 2017/1371 of the European Parliament and of the Council of 5 July 2017 on the fight against fraud to the Union's financial interests by means of criminal law, L 198. http://data.europa.eu/eli/dir/2017/1371/oj.

[37] European Commission. Infringement decisions https://ec.europa.eu/atwork/applying-eu-law/infringements-proceedings/infringement_decisions/?lang_code=en&langCode=EN&version=v1&typeOfSearch=byDecision&refId=INFR(2021)2231&page=1&size=10&order=desc&sortColumns=decisionDate. Accessed 1 March 2025.

[38] Minutes of the Coordination Council for the Protection of the European Union's Financial Interests 26 November 2014 meeting, No. 2/2024. https://www.fm.gov.lv/lv/media/19885/download?attachment. Accessed 1 March 2025.

is withheld and this is done intentionally, and in a situation where this withheld or undisclosed information would have been known to the supervisory authorities of EU funding mechanisms, it is likely that EU funds would have been recovered from the beneficiary, or not granted at all. Moreover, the EPPO indicates that the subject matter of the offence under Article 210 of the CL needs to be broadened. Currently, the terms “subsidies” and “grants” may not cover all possible types of EU funding, such as financial instruments, so it would be desirable to use a universal term in the CL that would cover all types of EU funding.

However, the maximum penalty of short-term imprisonment of up to three months provided for in Article 220 of the CL (Concealment of Property), which criminalizes the alienation, damage, destruction, squandering, concealment or other defalcation of property or means of payment for the purpose of evading payment of a debt or other obligation, may not be in line with the Directive. It would not be sufficient to comply with the requirement laid down in Article 3(3) that Member States must provide for a maximum term of imprisonment of at least four years for the offences referred to in Article 3(2)(a) of the Directive, where the damage or benefit caused by the offence is more than 100,000 euro. Consequently, a second part is currently being considered for this Article of the CL, envisaging increased liability for these acts when committed on a large scale and imposing a maximum penalty of up to four years’ imprisonment.

15.4 Development of Latvian Criminal Procedure Law under the Influence of EU Law

In describing the impact of EU law on Latvian criminal procedure law, just like in other EU countries, two main directions can be identified: (1) the introduction and improvement of instruments for cooperation and joint action; and (2) the so-called domestic or local influence on the process. Regarding the latter, two further trends can be established: (1) strengthening the protection of those involved in criminal proceedings; and (2) increasing the effectiveness of certain procedural measures.[39]

15.4.1 Developing Latvian Criminal Procedural Law in the Context of EU Criminal Justice Cooperation

The impact of EU law on the development of criminal procedure has largely been linked to the question of how to work effectively within a single area—the European Union. Chronologically, the first measure was the introduction of cooperation instruments based on the principle of mutual recognition. This was followed by the

[39] See also Dundurs 2011, p. 14; Strada-Rozenberga 2012, pp. 423–435; Meikališa and Strada-Rozenberga 2019, pp. 41–58.

introduction of institutions that were based not only on cooperation, but also on working together.

The introduction of instruments based on the principle of mutual recognition is chronologically first of all linked to the European arrest warrant, which was introduced in the EU through the Council Framework Decision of 13 June 2002 on the European arrest warrant and the surrender procedures between Member States,[40] and established in Latvia by means of the Latvian Criminal Code, which was in force until October 2005. This instrument was one of the first EU legal instruments to be introduced through amendments to the Latvian Criminal Procedure Code, which entered into force on 30 June 2004.[41] Later, Latvia introduced a number of instruments to strengthen cooperation under the EU Framework Decisions. In 2008, two laws[42] amending the CPL entered into force, implementing the requirements of three Framework Decisions,[43] *inter alia*, by introducing such cooperation instruments as orders freezing property or evidence. In 2009, a law[44] was adopted implementing the Council Framework Decision 2006/783/JHA of 6 October 2006 on the application of the principle of mutual recognition to confiscation orders.[45] In 2012, a law amending the CPL[46] implemented the provisions of five EU Framework Decisions.[47]

---

[40] Council Framework Decision of 13 June 2002 on the European arrest warrant and the surrender procedures between Member States - Statements made by certain Member States on the adoption of the Framework Decision, IO L 190. https://eur-lex.europa.eu/legal-content/GA/TXT/?uri=CELEX%3A32002F0584. Accessed 1 March 2025.

[41] Amendments to the Latvian Criminal Procedure Code. https://likumi.lv/ta/id/90027-grozijumi-latvijas-kriminalprocesa-kodeksa. Accessed 1 March 2025; in greater detail see Feldmane 2015, p. 131.

[42] Amendments to the Criminal Procedure Law of 22 November 2007. https://likumi.lv/ta/id/167760-grozijumi-kriminalprocesa-likuma. Accessed 1 March 2025; Amendments to the Criminal Procedure Law of 29 June 2008. https://likumi.lv/ta/id/178193-grozijumi-kriminalprocesa-likuma. Accessed 1 March 2025.

[43] Council Framework Decision 2003/577/JHA of 22 July 2003 on the execution in the European Union of orders freezing property or evidence, *OJ L 196*. https://eur-lex.europa.eu/legal-content/EN/TXT/?uri=CELEX%3A02003F0577-20030802; Council Framework Decision 2005/212/JHA of 24 February 2005 on Confiscation of Crime-Related Proceeds, Instrumentalities and Property, *OJ L 68*. https://eur-lex.europa.eu/legal-content/EN/TXT/?uri=CELEX:32005F0212; Council Framework Decision 2005/214/JHA of 24 February 2005 on the application of the principle of mutual recognition to financial penalties, *OJ L 76*. https://eur-lex.europa.eu/legal-content/EN/TXT/?uri=CELEX:02005F0214-20090328.

[44] Amendments to the Criminal Procedure Law of 11 June 2009. https://likumi.lv/ta/id/194030-grozijumi-kriminalprocesa-likuma. Accessed 1 March 2025.

[45] Council Framework Decision 2006/783/JHA of 6 October 2006 on the application of the principle of mutual recognition to confiscation orders, *OJ L 328*. https://eur-lex.europa.eu/legal-content/LV/TXT/?uri=CELEX%3A02006F0783-20090328&qid=1740740935715.

[46] Amendments to the Criminal Procedure Law of 24 May 2012. https://likumi.lv/ta/id/249047-grozijumi-kriminalprocesa-likuma. Accessed 1 March 2025; Amendments to the Criminal Procedure Law of 20 December 2012. https://likumi.lv/ta/id/253953-grozijumi-kriminalprocesa-likuma. Accessed 1 March 2025.

[47] Council Framework Decision 2008/909/JHA of 27 November 2008 on the application of the principle of mutual recognition to judgments in criminal matters imposing custodial sentences or measures involving deprivation of liberty for the purpose of their enforcement in the European

Further strengthening of cooperation instruments is already linked to the implementation of EU directives, and in recent years—to ensuring the effective functioning of EU regulations. The later examples include the European Protection Order (Directive 2011/99/EU[48]), which was incorporated into the CPL in February 2015 when the relevant amendments to the CPL[49] came into force, and European Investigation Order (Directive 2014/41/EU[50]), which was incorporated into the CPL in April 2017.[51] At the same time, it should be recognised that the impact of EU law in the subsequent period is not so much to introduce new instruments but rather to improve the effectiveness of the existing ones.

A good example of this is Directive 2014/42/EU[52] or Regulation 2018/1805 on the mutual recognition of freezing orders and confiscation orders.[53]

The legal framework for cooperation in the EU area in the provisions of the CPL has not always been stable and unchanging. For example, while the European investigation order has not undergone any changes since its introduction in 2017, the legal framework for the European arrest warrant has been amended several times. Since the entry into force of the CPL in October 2005, 15 laws have been amended

Union, *OJ L 327*. http://data.europa.eu/eli/dec_framw/2008/909/2009-03-28; Council Framework Decision 2008/947/JHA of 27 November 2008 on the application of the principle of mutual recognition to judgments and probation decisions with a view to the supervision of probation measures and alternative sanctions, *OJ L 337*. http://data.europa.eu/eli/dec_framw/2008/947/2009-03-28; Council Framework Decision 2009/299/JHA of 26 February 2009 amending Framework Decisions 2002/584/JHA, 2005/214/JHA, 2006/783/JHA, 2008/909/JHA and 2008/947/JHA, thereby enhancing the procedural rights of persons and fostering the application of the principle of mutual recognition to decisions rendered in the absence of the person concerned at the trial, *OJ L 81*. http://data.europa.eu/eli/dec_framw/2009/299/oj; Council Framework Decision 2009/829/JHA of 23 October 2009 on the application, between Member States of the European Union, of the principle of mutual recognition to decisions on supervision measures as an alternative to provisional detention, *OJ L 294*. http://data.europa.eu/eli/dec_framw/2009/829/oj; Council Framework Decision 2009/948/JHA of 30 November 2009 on prevention and settlement of conflicts of exercise of jurisdiction in criminal proceedings, *OJ L 328*. http://data.europa.eu/eli/dec_framw/2009/948/oj.

[48] Directive 2011/99/EU of the European Parliament and of the Council of 13 December 2011 on the European protection order, OJ L 338. http://data.europa.eu/eli/dir/2011/99/oj.

[49] Amendments to the Criminal Procedure Law of 29 January 2015. https://www.vestnesis.lv/ta/id/272127-grozijumi-kriminalprocesa-likuma. Accessed 1 March 2025.

[50] Directive 2014/41/EU of the European Parliament and of the Council of 3 April 2014 regarding the European Investigation Order in criminal matters, *OJ L 130*. https://eur-lex.europa.eu/legal-content/LV/TXT/?uri=CELEX:02014L0041-20140501.

[51] Amendments to the Criminal Procedure Law of 30 March 2017. https://www.vestnesis.lv/op/2017/75.5. Accessed 1 March 2025.

[52] Directive 2014/42/EU of the European Parliament and of the Council of 3 April 2014 on the freezing and confiscation of instrumentalities and proceeds of crime in the European Union, *OJ L 127*. https://eur-lex.europa.eu/legal-content/EN/TXT/?uri=CELEX:02014L0042-20140519.

[53] Regulation (EU) 2018/1805 of the European Parliament and of the Council of 14 November 2018 on the mutual recognition of freezing orders and confiscation orders PE/38/2018/REV/1, OJ L 303. http://data.europa.eu/eli/reg/2018/1805/oj.

regarding the legal framework of the European arrest warrant (both its transmission to EU countries and its execution in Latvia).[54]

Cooperation instruments based on the principle of mutual recognition are not only enshrined in law, but also applied in practice. For example, in his report for 2023, the Prosecutor General points out that "in autumn 2023, in the context of the Council of the European Union's 10th round of mutual evaluation, Latvia was evaluated on issues related to application of the European Investigation Order, which analysed the transposition of European Union acts into national legislation and problems of practical application. Following the evaluation, positive feedback was received concerning the work of the Prosecutor General's Office, and the Latvian Prosecutor's Office is viewed as a model to other EU countries in terms of the proactive, open and constructive use and enforcement of the mutual recognition instrument by the central authority".[55]

It can be said that the cooperation instruments that have been introduced have been put into practice. For example, according to the Prosecutor General's report for 2023, 50 European arrest warrants were received from abroad (the highest number was from Germany (18), Lithuania (6) and Estonia (6)), 48 European arrest warrants were sent to other EU countries (the highest number was to Germany (19), Netherlands (9), Lithuania (4) and Estonia (4)).[56] Compared to 2022, the number of European arrest warrants received for execution is increasing, as in 2022, 36 European arrest warrants were received from abroad (mostly from Germany (13), Lithuania (9) and Estonia (5)). However, the volume of European arrest warrants sent for execution in 2023 is decreasing, as in 2022, 76 European arrest warrants were sent to other EU countries for execution (mainly to Germany (38), the Netherlands (9), Spain (7) and

[54] Amendments to the Criminal Procedure Law of 22 November 2007. https://likumi.lv/ta/id/167760-grozijumi-kriminalprocesa-likuma; Amendments to the Criminal Procedure Law of 29 June 2008. https://likumi.lv/ta/id/178193-grozijumi-kriminalprocesa-likuma; Amendments to the Criminal Procedure Law of 12 March 2009. https://likumi.lv/ta/id/190010-grozijumi-kriminalprocesa-likuma; Amendments to the Criminal Procedure Law of 11 June 2009. https://likumi.lv/ta/id/194030-grozijumi-kriminalprocesa-likuma; Amendments to the Criminal Procedure Law of 21 October 2010. https://likumi.lv/ta/id/220967-grozijumi-kriminalprocesa-likuma; Amendments to the Criminal Procedure Law of 24 May 2012. https://likumi.lv/ta/id/249047-grozijumi-kriminalprocesa-likuma https://likumi.lv/ta/id/253953-grozijumi-kriminalprocesa-likuma; Amendments to the Criminal Procedure Law of 20 December 2012. https://likumi.lv/ta/id/253953-grozijumi-kriminalprocesa-likuma; Amendments to the Criminal Procedure Law of 23 May 2013. https://likumi.lv/ta/id/257425-grozijumi-kriminalprocesa-likuma; Amendments to the Criminal Procedure Law of 19 December 2013. https://likumi.lv/ta/id/263447-grozijumi-kriminalprocesa-likuma; Amendments to the Criminal Procedure Law of 18 February 2016. https://likumi.lv/ta/id/280784-grozijumi-kriminalprocesa-likuma; Amendments to the Criminal Procedure Law of 30 March 2017. https://likumi.lv/ta/id/290109-grozijumi-kriminalprocesa-likuma; Amendments to the Criminal Procedure Law of 20 June 2018. https://likumi.lv/ta/id/300107-grozijumi-kriminalprocesa-likuma; Amendments to the Criminal Procedure Law of 7 January 2021. https://likumi.lv/ta/id/320345-grozijumi-kriminalprocesa-likuma; Amendments to the Criminal Procedure Law of 6 October 2022. https://likumi.lv/ta/id/336542-grozijumi-kriminalprocesa-likuma; Amendments to the Criminal Procedure Law of 19 September 2024. https://likumi.lv/ta/id/355473-grozijumi-kriminalprocesa-likuma.

[55] Prosecutor General 2024, p. 52.

[56] *Ibid.*, pp. 44, 49.

Lithuania (5)).[57] The trends cannot be described as permanent, for example, in 2021, 58 European Arrest Decisions were received (most from Germany—25, Estonia—7 and Poland—5 decisions, respectively), while 42 European Arrest Decisions were sent for execution (most to Germany (15), the Netherlands (11), Ireland (5)).[58]

To conclude the review of cooperation in the EU criminal justice area, a form of higher-level cooperation should be briefly considered—it is no longer an example of co-working, but a joint working institution—the EPPO. The EPPO started its activities in Latvia in 2021, when amendments to the CPL came into force, including direct references to Regulation 2017/1939 and the powers of the EPPO in the text of the law.[59] An updated annotation (Initial Impact Report) is available for these amendments to the law. This document meticulously analyses the launch of the EPPO and the content of the amendments to the CPL.[60] Some changes concerning the competence of the EPPO have been introduced in 2022,[61] and their explanation is included in the extended annotation of the draft law.[62]

With regard to the practical functioning of the EPPO in Latvia, it can be noted that the EPPO has made a relatively successful start in Latvia. According to publicly available information characterising the situation at the beginning of 2024 (information for 2024 is not yet available at the time of writing) "[…] 40 criminal proceedings had been opened in Latvia concerning irregularities, of which 33 were under active investigation. The total financial loss constituted 65.3 million euro, of which 41.3 million euro relates to VAT fraud, while the loss in EU fund fraud cases was around 24 million euro. The recovered funds currently amount to around 10 million euro. The EPPO has managed to recover around 6 million euro in Latvia. This amount is made up of funds recovered through judgments or voluntarily returned sums. In Latvia, 16 new criminal proceedings were initiated in 2023, with a total incurred loss of around 42 million euro. The largest losses were due to VAT fraud. Five persons were prosecuted last year. Latvia's figures show that the EPPO has referred five criminal cases to court in two and a half years. Two are pending and three have resulted in convictions".[63]

Taking into account all of the above, it can be said that Latvia has been relatively successful in its work in the area of mutual cooperation in the field of EU criminal

---

[57] Prosecutor General 2023, pp. 182, 185.

[58] Prosecutor General 2022, p. 231.

[59] Amendments to the Criminal Procedure Law of 7 January 2021. https://likumi.lv/ta/id/320345-grozijumi-kriminalprocesa-likuma. Accessed 1 March 2025.

[60] Updated annotation of the Draft Law "Amendments to the Criminal Law" of 7 January 2021. https://likumi.lv/wwwraksti/LIKUMI/PAPILDINATAS_ANOTACIJAS/PAPILDIN_ANOT_GROZ_KPL_774_200121.DOCX. Accessed 1 March 2025.

[61] Amendments to the Criminal Procedure Law of 6 October 2022. https://likumi.lv/ta/id/336542-grozijumi-kriminalprocesa-likuma. Accessed 1 March 2025.

[62] Updated annotation of the Draft Law "Amendments to the Criminal Law" of 6 October 2022. https://likumi.lv/wwwraksti/LIKUMI/PAPILDINATAS_ANOTACIJAS/TMPAPILDIN_ANOT_GROZ_KPL_1323_211122.DOCX. Accessed 1 March 2025.

[63] Jurista Vārds 2024, p. 4; see also Prosecutor General 2024, p. 59; European Public Prosecutor's Office 2024, pp. 38–39.

justice and it is foreseeable that this course of action will be continued, developed and strengthened.

15.4.2 The Impact of EU Law on the Regulation of Domestic Criminal Procedure of Latvia

With regard to the impact of EU law on the so-called domestic—national or local criminal procedural framework, as already indicated, two directions can be distinguished. To place them in chronological order, the first is the strengthening of procedural guarantees for participants in proceedings, while the second is the rationalisation of certain criminal procedural solutions. On the other hand, in terms of impact, improving procedural safeguards prevails.

One example of EU action that has influenced the amendments to the provisions of the Criminal Procedure Code with a view to making certain criminal justice institutions more effective, is the legal framework for the freezing and confiscation of proceeds from crime, instruments of crime, etc., as well as the interests of persons involved in these matters. The objective of streamlining criminal proceedings for certain types of offences has, undoubtedly, also been the focus of other directives (e.g., Directive 2011/36/EU[64] or Directive 2011/92/EU[65]), for example, by providing that criminal proceedings for certain types of offences should be conducted regardless of the victim's wishes and even in cases when the victim withdraws his or her application. However, the provisions of these directives cannot be considered to have influenced the development of the CPL, as they did not require any amendments to the CPL, whose previous provisions were in line with the directives.[66]

Hence, it is useful to take a closer look at the development of the procedural safeguards system. The introduction of a common system of minimum guarantees in the EU area was undeniably necessary to introduce and ensure the effective application of instruments based on the principle of mutual recognition, but its impact surpasses mutual cooperation, as it also affects the so-called domestic or local criminal proceedings without an element of cooperation. Furthermore, it must be noted—"application of the minimum procedural guarantees to certain participants of the proceedings follow both from those EU directives, which have been adopted for the purpose of reinforcing the principle of mutual recognition, as, for example, Directives 2010/

[64] Directive 2011/36/EU of the European Parliament and of the Council of 5 April 2011 on preventing and combating trafficking in human beings and protecting its victims, and replacing Council Framework Decision 2002/629/JHA, OJ L 101. http://data.europa.eu/eli/dir/2011/36/oj.

[65] Directive 2011/92/EU of the European Parliament and of the Council of 13 December 2011 on the assessment of the effects of certain public and private projects on the environment (codification) Text with EEA relevance, *OJ L 26*. http://data.europa.eu/eli/dir/2011/92/oj.

[66] Meikališa and Strada-Rozenberga 2019, p. 48.

64/EU,[67] 2012/13/EU,[68] 2012/29/EU,[69] (EU) 2016/1919,[70] (EU) 2016/343,[71] (EU) 2016/800,[72] as well as those that are aimed at effectively combatting certain offences and the need for specific protection for the victims of these offences, as Directives 2011/36/EU[73] and 2011/92/EU.[74] The reinforcement of the procedural guarantees, predominantly, applies to two groups of persons – persons, who have the right to defence, and victims".[75]

Undeniably, the provisions of the directives are of importance in the context of strengthening procedural guarantees. Particularly considering the impact of directives on the development of the CPL, which has been especially active in the period between 2010 and 2020, it should be noted that the CPL currently incorporates the legal provisions of more than 10 EU directives.

The norms of EU directives aimed at ensuring and strengthening the minimum rights of participants in criminal proceedings could be divided into two groups—(1) those applicable to any participant in criminal proceedings who meets the respective

[67] Directive 2010/64/EU of the European Parliament and of the Council of 20 October 2010 on the right to interpretation and translation in criminal proceedings, *OJ L 280*. http://data.europa.eu/eli/dir/2010/64/oj.

[68] Directive 2012/13/EU of the European Parliament and of the Council of 22 May 2012 on the right to information in criminal proceedings, *OJ L 142*. http://data.europa.eu/eli/dir/2012/13/oj.

[69] Directive 2012/29/EU of the European Parliament and of the Council of 25 October 2012 establishing minimum standards on the rights, support and protection of victims of crime, and replacing Council Framework Decision 2001/220/JHA, *OJ L 315*. http://data.europa.eu/eli/dir/2012/29/oj.

[70] Directive (EU) 2016/1919 of the European Parliament and of the Council of 26 October 2016 on legal aid for suspects and accused persons in criminal proceedings and for requested persons in European arrest warrant proceedings, *OJ L 297*. http://data.europa.eu/eli/dir/2016/1919/oj.

[71] Directive (EU) 2016/343 of the European Parliament and of the Council of 9 March 2016 on the strengthening of certain aspects of the presumption of innocence and of the right to be present at the trial in criminal proceedings, *OJ L 65*. http://data.europa.eu/eli/dir/2016/343/oj.

[72] Directive (EU) 2016/800 of the European Parliament and of the Council of 11 May 2016 on procedural safeguards for children who are suspects or accused persons in criminal proceedings, *OJ L 132*. http://data.europa.eu/eli/dir/2016/800/oj.

[73] Directive 2011/36/EU of the European Parliament and of the Council of 5 April 2011 on preventing and combating trafficking in human beings and protecting its victims, and replacing Council Framework Decision 2002/629/JHA, *OJ L 101*. http://data.europa.eu/eli/dir/2011/36/oj.

[74] Directive 2011/92/EU of the European Parliament and of the Council of 13 December 2011 on the assessment of the effects of certain public and private projects on the environment (codification) Text with EEA relevance, *OJ L 26*. http://data.europa.eu/eli/dir/2011/92/oj.

[75] Meikališa and Strada-Rozenberga 2019, p. 48.

status, for example, a victim of a crime or a suspect, the accused person (e.g., Directives 2010/64/EU, 2012/13/EU, 2012/29/EU, 2013/48/EU,[76] (EU) 2016/343,[77] (EU) 2016/1919); and (2) those applicable to a specially selected group of participants in proceedings who, due to certain characteristics (set of characteristics), require special protection (for example, Directive 2011/36/EU,[78] 2011/92/EU,[79] 2012/29/EU[80]). The latter group can be further classified into three subgroups: (1) victims of criminal offences who enjoy specific protection, taking into account the criminal offence that they have been the target of and/or they special condition, etc.; (2) children with various procedural statuses; and (3) persons, who have been deprived of liberty during the proceedings. In view of the scope of the current chapter and its limitations, the focus will remain on the procedural safeguarding of victims in need of specific protection.[81]

From the point of view of content, two mutually related types of guarantees should be distinguished, which are characterised by different aims and purposes: (1) safeguards to ensure participation in criminal proceedings and measures to ensure their effectiveness; and (2) guarantees of adequate treatment.

Looking at the impact of EU law on Latvia, there is reason to believe that there was no need for substantial changes to the CPL with regard to the participation guarantees themselves, since in most cases the persons concerned (victims and defendants) have had more extensive and active participation rights in criminal proceedings in Latvia for decades. Similarly, the rights such as the right to a lawyer are provided for a wide range of participants (even witnesses) and at a very early stage (from the very beginning of the proceedings). There are only a few exceptions to this. For example, by implementing the requirements of Directive 2016/19/EU,[82] in 2018 a new party to criminal proceedings was introduced to the CPL—a person who has committed

---

[76] Directive 2013/48/EU of the European Parliament and of the Council of 22 October 2013 on the right of access to a lawyer in criminal proceedings and in European arrest warrant proceedings, and on the right to have a third party informed upon deprivation of liberty and to communicate with third persons and with consular authorities while deprived of liberty, *OJ L 294*. http://data.europa.eu/eli/dir/2013/48/oj.

[77] Directive (EU) 2016/343 of the European Parliament and of the Council of 9 March 2016 on the strengthening of certain aspects of the presumption of innocence and of the right to be present at the trial in criminal proceedings, *OJ L 65*. http://data.europa.eu/eli/dir/2016/343/oj.

[78] Directive 2011/36/EU of the European Parliament and of the Council of 5 April 2011 on preventing and combating trafficking in human beings and protecting its victims, and replacing Council Framework Decision 2002/629/JHA, *OJ L 101*. http://data.europa.eu/eli/dir/2011/36/oj.

[79] Directive 2011/92/EU of the European Parliament and of the Council of 13 December 2011 on the assessment of the effects of certain public and private projects on the environment (codification) Text with EEA relevance, *OJ L 26*. http://data.europa.eu/eli/dir/2011/92/oj.

[80] Directive 2012/29/EU of the European Parliament and of the Council of 25 October 2012 establishing minimum standards on the rights, support and protection of victims of crime, and replacing Council Framework Decision 2001/220/JHA, *OJ L 315*. http://data.europa.eu/eli/dir/2012/29/oj.

[81] For greater detail see Meikališa and Strada-Rozenberga 2019, p. 48.

[82] Directive (EU) 2016/1919 of the European Parliament and of the Council of 26 October 2016 on legal aid for suspects and accused persons in criminal proceedings and for requested persons in European arrest warrant proceedings, *OJ L 297*. http://data.europa.eu/eli/dir/2016/1919/oj.

an act that meets the elements of a criminal offence under the CL, but cannot be held criminally liable due to his or her minority. Such person has been included in the group of persons entitled to defence.[83] A special participant in criminal proceedings in Latvia is also worth mentioning—the owner of the property affected by criminal proceedings (i.e., a person who has been deprived of possession of the property or whose possession has been restricted in the course of criminal proceedings, but who is not a person entitled to a defence). This status has been introduced, and its regulation changed several times (see Article 111(1) of the CPL), mainly due to the problems identified in local doctrine and practice, but the influence of EU directives cannot be discounted, in particular the position expressed in Directive 2014/42/EU[84] on the need to ensure effective procedural protection of persons whose interests are affected in the course of confiscation.[85] It is also likely that the proper application of Regulation (EU) 2018/1805[86] will bring some new elements to the system of legal safeguards for this participant in criminal proceedings.

The situation is somewhat different when it comes to measures intended to ensure the effectiveness of participation. For example, the right to information, which should not be recognised as an end in itself but as a means to the effective exercise of other rights, is one of the most frequently raised issues, both from the perspective of development of the norms contained in the CPL and in practice. The most frequent discussion comprising legislative process, application of criminal procedural norms, as well as constitutional review, is concerned with the availability of information to a person whose detention is being considered, as well as in the application of non-conviction-based confiscation in criminal proceedings which is separate from the main proceedings. The direct impact of the EU law provisions has so far been most manifest in development of the provisions of the CPL relating to detention of persons. The situation regarding the decision to detain a person has changed in recent decades. This process has been gradual and by no means straightforward. For example, in 2013 the relevant right of access was formulated with the proviso that "access to the relevant material shall be possible to the extent that such access does not jeopardise the fundamental rights of others, the public interest and the achievement of the purpose of the criminal proceedings", and this proviso remained in place until 2022.[87] Significantly, the legislator's action was justified precisely by the need to comply with EU standards. In the supplementary remarks to the draft law amending

[83] Amendments to the Criminal Procedure Law of 27 September 2018. https://likumi.lv/ta/id/302152-grozijumi-kriminalprocesa-likuma. Accessed 1 March 2025.

[84] Directive 2014/42/EU of the European Parliament and of the Council of 3 April 2014 on the freezing and confiscation of instrumentalities and proceeds of crime in the European Union, *OJ L 127*. http://data.europa.eu/eli/dir/2014/42/oj.

[85] For greater detail see, for instance, Meikališa and Strada-Rozenberga 2017a, pp. 12–21; Meikališa and Strada-Rozenberga 2017b, pp. 32–33.

[86] Regulation (EU) 2018/1805 of the European Parliament and of the Council of 14 November 2018 on the mutual recognition of freezing orders and confiscation orders PE/38/2018/REV/1, OJ L 303. http://data.europa.eu/eli/reg/2018/1805/oj.

[87] Amendments to the Criminal Procedure Law of 6 October 2022. https://likumi.lv/ta/id/336542-grozijumi-kriminalprocesa-likuma. Accessed 1 March 2025.

the relevant provisions,[88] it is stated that "the amendments are intended to implement [...] the requirements of Directive 2012/13/EU on the right to information in criminal proceedings [...] in an appropriate manner, as well as to remedy the shortcomings in the implementation of Directive 2012/13/EU identified in the European Commission's formal notification of 23 September 2021 in infringement proceedings No. 2021/2100".

To conclude the general overview of the EU provisions and the legal framework of the so-called local or domestic criminal procedure, it should be noted that the most significant amendments to the provisions of the CPL in Latvia were necessary in order to introduce procedural rights and other provisions concerning the treatment of certain participants in the proceedings. A striking example of this is the case of certain groups of participants in proceedings, which are particularly protected and which were not known in the CPL prior to the introduction of the guidelines.

For instance, several amendments have been made to the CPL to strengthen the protection of children as a special category of participants in criminal proceedings. Among the most prominent of these are the 2018 amendments to the CPL,[89] which added to Article 12 of the CPL (Guarantee of Human Rights) a provision stating that it was a fundamental principle of criminal procedure that criminal proceedings involving a minor shall be conducted with due regard to the minor's age, maturity and any special needs. This resulted in adopting an obligation for the person conducting the proceedings to request an individual assessment report for each minor who has the right of defence, the rule that a minor shall be remanded in custody only in cases of extreme necessity, after considering the application of other security measures, as well as other amendments to the law strengthening the rights of a minor who has the right of defence.[90]

In accordance with the requirements of the directives, a specific participant—a specially protected victim, has been included, as previously, except for certain nuances concerning a victim who is a minor, no specific aspects were recognised in the protection of certain victims in Latvia,[91] and other changes have been made.[92] The status of a victim with special procedural protection was introduced in 2016,[93] with several later changes.[94] As of the beginning of 2016, such status is to be granted to persons who are: (1) minors; (2) persons who, due to a mental or other health disorder,

[88] Updated annotation of the Draft Law "Amendments to the Criminal Law" of 6 October 2022, p. 28. https://likumi.lv/wwwraksti/LIKUMI/PAPILDINATAS_ANOTACIJAS/TMPAPILDIN_ANOT_GROZ_KPL_1323_211122.DOCX. Accessed 1 March 2025.

[89] Amendments to the Criminal Procedure Law of 27 September 2018. https://likumi.lv/ta/id/302152-grozijumi-kriminalprocesa-likuma. Accessed 1 March 2025.

[90] For greater detail see Meikališa 2021, pp. 261–262.

[91] In greater detail see Meikališa 2014, pp. 4–19; Meikališa and Strada-Rozenberga 2019, p. 51.

[92] In greater detail see Meikališa and Strada-Rozenberga 2019, pp. 51–52.

[93] Amendments to the Criminal Procedure Law of 18 February 2016. https://likumi.lv/ta/id/280784-grozijumi-kriminalprocesa-likuma. Accessed 1 March 2025.

[94] Amendments to the Criminal Procedure Law of 27 September 2018. https://likumi.lv/ta/id/302152-grozijumi-kriminalprocesa-likuma; Amendments to the Criminal Procedure Law of 15 June 2023. https://likumi.lv/ta/id/343147-grozijumi-kriminalprocesa-likuma. Accessed 1 March 2025.

are unable to exercise their procedural rights; (3) persons who have been victims of an offence against their moral or sexual integrity or of trafficking in human beings; (4) a person who has been the victim of an offence involving violence or threats of violence committed by a relative, former spouse or person with whom the victim has had an unregistered marital relationship; (5) a person who may have suffered serious bodily injury or mental disorder as a result of an offence; (6) a person who has been the victim of an offence allegedly committed for racial, national, ethnic or religious reasons. It is further provided that the decision of the authority conducting the proceedings shall also recognise as particularly vulnerable a victim who is not specially referred to but who is particularly vulnerable as a result of the harm caused by the offence and who is not protected against repeated threats, intimidation or retaliation. In addition to the rights that must be ensured to any victim, a victim who fulfils this status has specific rights, for example, to have a confidant present during questioning, and to be informed of the release of the arrested or convicted person.[95]

In the context of the impact assessment of EU directives, the amendments to the CPL made to implement Directive 2016/343/EU[96] cannot be omitted. These amendments provided, *inter alia*, for the inclusion in the CPL of guidelines on the consequences of statements by public figures that violate the presumption of innocence. It is stipulated that if a public official other than a person involved in criminal proceedings has made a public statement about the guilt of a person in violation of the presumption of innocence, the person presiding over the proceedings shall, on the basis of a reasoned application by the person concerned, publicly inform about the violation of the principle of presumption of innocence and send a copy of the application to the body that may decide on the responsibility of the public official for consideration. Explicit references to the right to silence of a person entitled to defence have been included, as well as amendments to the legal regulation on obtaining/providing samples for comparative research, introducing the position that a person is not obliged to provide samples, the creation of which does not depend on his or her will. However, the position that there is an obligation to provide samples that exist independently of the person's will has been maintained. The rules on compulsory examinations have also been clarified.[97]

Admittedly, the aspect that has attracted the greatest public interest is the disclaimer on statements by officials not involved in criminal proceedings about a person's guilt. However, there are only a few publicly known cases in which the relevant provision of the CPL has been used. For example, in early 2024, a judge made a public statement about a violation of the presumption of innocence by the Prosecutor General. According to the judge, the violation consisted in the fact that the Prosecutor General, when questioned by a journalist about an acquittal by a court of first instance, stated that he believed it to be incorrect and that the judgment

---

[95] In greater detail see Meikališa 2021, pp. 248–249.

[96] Directive (EU) 2016/343 of the European Parliament and of the Council of 9 March 2016 on the strengthening of certain aspects of the presumption of innocence and of the right to be present at the trial in criminal proceedings, *OJ L 65*. http://data.europa.eu/eli/dir/2016/343/oj.

[97] Meikališa 2021, p. 261.

should be a conviction and with an appropriate sentence.[98] The State Prosecutor's Office filed a protest against the judge's public statement. According to the Prosecutor's Office, the judge's conduct in informing the public about the violation of the principle of the presumption of innocence does not comply with Article 19(4) of the CPL and Directive (EU) 2016/343 and the Prosecutor General, as the head of the public prosecutor's office, in answering questions of public interest, actually provided objective information on the progress of the criminal proceedings, i.e. he pointed out the instance that the Prosecutor's Office considered to be a miscarriage of justice and the protests that the Prosecutor's Office would file against the court's decision in order to achieve a fair settlement of the criminal procedural relations. In response to a reporter's question about the fairness of the Court's decision, the Prosecutor General expressed the Prosecution's vision of the final decision in this criminal case.[99] The Court rejected the appeal, whilst agreeing that the Prosecutor General had violated the presumption of innocence.[100] In July 2024, there was a similar judicial declaration that the Prosecutor General had violated the presumption of innocence.[101] Unfortunately, there is no information available on whether and, if so, by whom and in what way these notifications would have been followed up.

Interestingly, this measure, introduced in Latvia to ensure respect for the presumption of innocence on the basis of compliance with the Directive, has also been the subject of attention by the European Court of Human Rights. In Rimšēvičs v. Latvia (application No. 31634/18), the European Court of Human Rights concluded that "[...] various procedures for acknowledging or putting an end to the infringement of the presumption of innocence in the context of criminal proceedings together with civil-law remedies have been considered to be effective within the meaning of the Convention [...]. In the present case, such acknowledgement could be obtained through the use of section 19(4) of the Criminal Procedure Law. The Court therefore considers that a complaint under that provision together with a civil claim for compensation under the Civil Law can be considered an effective domestic remedy for an alleged breach of the presumption of innocence in the circumstances of the present case".[102]

In the view of the authors, the Court's finding that the statutory provisions of the CPL are sufficiently effective could be extended to other provisions of the CPL that strengthen procedural safeguards. The provisions of the CPL itself, although incomplete and imprecise in places, can be judged to be generally in line with EU standards. Another question, which is beyond the scope of this chapter, is how effective these

---

[98] https://www.tiesas.lv/aktualitates/rigas-pilsetas-tiesas-tiesnesa-martina-tupureina-publisks-pazinojums-par-igora-kuzmuka-nevainiguma-P-13003. Accessed 1 March 2025.

[99] https://www.prokuratura.lv/lv/aktualitates/2024/aktualitates/prokuratura-iesniedz-protestu-par-rigas-pilsetas-tiesas-tiesnesa-martina-tupureina-ricibu-publisku-informesanu-par-personas-nevainiguma-prezumpcijas-principa-parkapumu-3199. Accessed 1 March 2025.

[100] https://www.delfi.lv/161/criminal/120030482/tiesa-noraida-prokuraturas-protestu-par-stukana-veikto-nevainiguma-prezumpcijas-parkapsanu. Accessed 1 March 2025.

[101] https://www.tiesas.lv/aktualitates/tiesa-informe-par-nevainiguma-prezumpcijas-principa-parkapumu-no-amata-atstadinata-tiesu-izpilditaja-13096. Accessed 1 March 2025.

[102] ECtHR, *Rimšēvičs v. Latvia*, Decision, 10 October 2023, 31634/18, para 53.

safeguards are in practice. Here, the problems, while not enormous, may be greater than in the text of the law.

15.5 Conclusions

EU law has undoubtedly influenced the development of Latvian criminal law over the past 20 years. However, there is no reason to believe that the influence of EU law has been the main reason for the many changes in criminal law and criminal procedure. Integration into the EU criminal justice area often has not required changes to national legislation, as the legal framework already met the requirements set by the EU. It should also be recognised that the development of the so-called national or domestic criminal procedural legal framework has rather been influenced by local or other circumstances, such as the requirements of various international institutions or global trends. However, the impact of EU law should not be underestimated.

When describing the impact of EU law on Latvian criminal law, the main areas of influence in substantive criminal law are prevention of money laundering, the scope of confiscation of criminally acquired property, and offences against the financial interests of the EU.

Regarding procedural criminal law, it is recognised that the EU has had a significant impact on the legal framework and its application in practice,—in institutional matters, as well as introduction and strengthening of procedural safeguards.

The EU has exerted a significant impact on institutional issues, including the introduction of the European arrest warrant and creation of the EPPO. In the area of procedural safeguards, introduction and strengthening of the protection of vulnerable persons involved in criminal proceedings and development of certain aspects of the rights of participants in criminal proceedings cannot be underestimated.

A striking example is extending the presumption of innocence to cover both restrictions on public statements and protection of the public image of the accused. Furthermore, enforcement of wider access to case files as an element of a fair trial has also been of particular importance.

To conclude, the impact of EU law in the field of criminal law and criminal procedure thus far has been considerable, and it can be expected that EU legislation will retain its influence in the foreseeable future.

References

Aizupe I (2014) Krimināllikums un nākotnes perspektīva [Criminal Law and future perspective]. Jurista Vārds 1333:24–28

Dundurs Z (2011) Eiropas Savienības procesuālās tiesības kriminālprocesā [European Union procedural rights in criminal proceedings]. Jurista Vārds 680:14–18

European Public Prosecutor's Office (2024) EPPO Annual Report 2023. https://www.eppo.europa.eu/sites/default/files/2024-03/EPPO_Annual_Report_2023.pdf. Accessed 1 March 2025

Feldmane E (2015) Eiropas Savienības regulējuma krimināltiesībās ietekme uz Kriminālprocesa likuma regulējuma attīstību [The impact of European Union criminal law regulation on the development of the Criminal Procedure Law]. In: Kriminālprocesa likumam – 10. Pagātnes mācības un nākotnes izaicinājumi. Latvijas Vēstnesis, Riga, pp. 128–140

Jurista Vārds (2024) Iepazīstina ar EPPO 2023. gada darba rezultātiem [Presenting the EPPO's 2023 work results]. Jurista Vārds 1329:4

Liholaja V, Bērziņa B, Mekons K, Rupeiks J, Zalužinska L (2009) Study "Criminal law – developments in European and national law, the relationship between Pillars I and III, best practice in implementation methods". https://www.tm.gov.lv/sites/tm/files/2020-01/Documents/lv_documents_petijumi_kriminaltiesibas2.doc. Accessed 1 March 2025

Liholaja V, Strada-Rozenberga K (2017) Criminal Law and Procedure. In: Kerikmäe T, Joamets K, Pleps J, Rodiņa A, Berkmanas T, Gruodytė E (eds) The Law of the Baltic States. Springer, Cham, pp 217–237

Meikališa Ā (2014) Victims in Criminal Procedure: A Review of Latvian Criminal Procedure Norms through the Prism of Minimal EU Standards. Journal of the University of Latvia. Law 6:4–19

Meikališa Ā (2015) Kriminālprocesa likumam 10–fakti, vērtējumi, prognozes [The 10th Anniversary of the Criminal Law– Facts, Assessments, Forecasts]. In: Meikališa Ā, Strada-Rozenberga K (eds) Kriminālprocess. Raksti 2010–2015. Latvijas Vēstnesis, Riga, pp 95–150

Meikališa Ā (2021) Kriminālprocesa likuma grozījumu 2015–2021 vispārīgs apskats, secinājumi un prognozes [General overview, conclusions, and forecasts of the amendments to the Criminal Procedure Law 2015–2021]. In: Meikališa Ā, Strada-Rozenberga K (eds) Kriminālprocess. Raksti 2015–2020. Latvijas Universitātes Akadēmiskais apgāds, Riga, pp 245–280

Meikališa Ā, Strada-Rozenberga K (2017a) Pārmaiņu laiks kriminālprocesā turpinās – 2017. gada grozījumi [Time of change in criminal proceedings continues – 2017 Amendments]. Jurista Vārds 996:12–21

Meikališa Ā, Strada-Rozenberga K (2017b) Pārmaiņu laiks kriminālprocesā turpinās – 2017. gada grozījumi [Time of change in criminal proceedings continues – 2017 Amendments]. Jurista Vārds 997:28–36

Meikališa Ā, Strada-Rozenberga K (2019) Impact of Directives of European Parliament and of Council on Development of Latvian Criminal Procedure Law: General Overview and Procedural Protection of Victims with Specific Protection Needs. Journal of the University of Latvia. Law 12:41–58

Prosecutor General (2022) Report of the Prosecutor General of the Republic of Latvia on achievements of 2021 and priorities for 2022. https://prokuratura.lv/media/Normativie_akti/Zinojums.pdf. Accessed 1 March 2025

Prosecutor General (2023) Report of the Prosecutor General of the Republic of Latvia on the achievements of 2022 and priorities for 2023. https://www.prokuratura.lv/media/Normativie_akti/generalprokurora_zinojums_2022_01_03.pdf. Accessed 1 March 2025

Prosecutor General (2024) Report of the Prosecutor General of the Republic of Latvia on the achievements of 2023 and priorities for 2024. https://www.prokuratura.lv/media/gallery/Gener%C4%81lprokurora_zinojums_2023.pdf. Accessed 1 March 2025

Strada-Rozenberga K (2012) EU Criminal Justice – Development Trends and Impact in Latvia. In: Collection of research papers in conjunction with the International Scientific Conference "The Quality of Legal Acts and its importance in Contemporary Legal Space". UL Press, Riga, pp 423–435

Vīnkalna E (2024) Development tendences of the Criminal law. In: 82nd International Scientific Conference of the University of Latvia "Legislation and Its Outcome in Latvia: Lessons from the Past, Current Trends, Problems and Solutions". UL Press, Riga, pp 232–233

Part IV
The Future of the European Union: Thinking Ahead

Chapter 16
Small and Medium-Sized Central European Member States vs. EU Reform

Magdalena Bainczyk

Contents

Abstract The process of the next constitutional reform of the European Union (EU), of which the publication of the report of the German–French working group (2023), as well as the adoption by the European Parliament of the proposal to amend the EU's treaty basis in November 2023, was an important milestone, as announced by the old-new President of the European Commission, U. von der Leyen will be continued. The directions of this reform indicated in multiple EU documents, including also the current practice of applying EU law, call for an in-depth reflection on the present status of medium and small-sized Member States from Central Europe and the consequences of the proposed solutions for them. Having in mind the title of the volume "The European Union 2004–2024: Twenty Years of Legal Experience, Challenges and Growth after Unprecedented EU Enlargement", the chapter will be definitely focused on experiences and challenges from the perspective of Member States which acceded to the EU respectively in 2004, 2007 and 2013, and which belong to small and medium-sized countries and are located in Central Europe. The overall assessment of 20 years of membership is positive, although the process of integration of these countries has been completed neither at the economic level, reaching 51% of the EU average real GDP, nor at the institutional level, i.e. the omission of representatives of these countries from key positions in the EU. The proposed avenues of economic

M. Bainczyk (✉)
The Institute for Western Affairs, Poznań, Poland
e-mail: bainczyk@iz.poznan.pl

Andrzej Frycz Modrzewski University, Kraków, Poland

I. Isokaitė-Valužė and H. Šinkūnas (eds.), *The European Union 2004-2024*,
https://doi.org/10.1007/978-94-6265-718-2_16

development for the EU as a whole, as well as the proposed constitutional reform put forward by the Commission, the European Parliament, as well as the largest EU states, may widen the persisting gap between Central and Western Europe. However, without the elimination of this imbalance, an economic leap for the EU as a whole, its resilience, including against military threats, and further enlargement are out of the question.

Keywords Central Europe · EU reform · European peripheries · EU institutional framework · Three Seas Initiative · Small Member States · Medium-sized Member States

On questions of equality and justice, even though it is very difficult to discover the truth about them, nevertheless it is easier to hit upon it than to persuade people that have the power to get an advantage to agree to it; equality and justice are always sought by the weaker party, but those that have the upper hand pay no attention to them.[1]

16.1 Introduction

The aim of this chapter is to identify the present economic and social situation of small and medium-sized Central European Member States, their position in the institutional framework of the EU and its consequences for the policy-making-process. The chapter moreover examines the most dire consequences of the reforms proposed by the European Parliament, the European Commission and the French-German group, with special focus on the situation and problems of those Member States. The author will likewise attempt to design a possible path for future development of the above-mentioned Member States within the EU.

As the European Union has been defined as a *Rechtsgemeinschaft*[2] (English—*community of law*), also a "community based on rule of law, of a constitutional guarantee stemming from the EC Treaty as an autonomous legal system which is not to be prejudiced by an international agreement"[3] in the chapter, it applies mainly a legal dogmatic method, based on the treaties, EU acts, and documents prepared by EU institutions and a few Members States. Relevant academic literature will be included to adequately interpret the legal instruments and documents. Second, the chapter will consider economic data to understand better the position of given states in the EU. Third, some perspectives from literature and the political ideas of Staniszkis will be considered to outline the afore-mentioned development of Central Europe.

---

[1] Aristotle 4 BC.

[2] Zuleeg 1995, p. 9.

[3] CJEU, Case C-402/05 P and C-415/05 P, Judgment, 3 September 2008, ECLI:EU:C:2008:461, para 316.

The following considerations acquire a certain added value as both the EU institutions[4] and leaders of some Member States[5] pledge to revisit the process of EU enlargement, stymied after 2013. Currently, in the context of Russia's aggression against Ukraine, the new potential Member States include Ukraine, granted official candidate status, as well as the Western Balkan states, Moldova and Georgia. All of these countries belong to the small and eventually medium-sized countries (Ukraine) of Central and Eastern Europe.

16.2 Small and Medium-Sized Central European Member States—A Tentative Definition

With regard to the topic of the chapter, it is appropriate to define the concept of Central Europe and, subsequently, the small and medium-sized Member States from this region. It should be noted that such topics are the subject of a lively public debate, hence references to both literature and academic discourse.

The division into Western and Eastern Europe, "invented", as Wolff points out, by the West as early as the Enlightenment, persists to this day.[6] The division was cemented by the cold war, as evidenced by the 1984 essay by T. Venclova (Lithuania) titled "Poetry as Atonement": "The poetry of Eastern Europe comes no doubt closer to realism. Anyone who has compared Western poetry with authentic poetry written in totalitarian countries has probably experienced the peculiar sensation that these are not variants of the same art, but rather two different kinds of art. What in the West is merely entertainment or at best a confession on the Freudian couch, in the East it remains a matter of life and not infrequently death."[7] Roughly at that time, Kundera (Czechoslovakia, Czech Republic) published his seminal essay "The Tragedy of Central Europe", where he challenged the dichotomy, claiming that after 1945 we saw the emergence of Western Europe, Eastern Europe, as well as Central Europe, whose predicament is the most complicated.[8]

The term "Central Europe" is rooted in the intellectual legacy of the states located between Russia and Germany, but not only there. An interesting concept of *Mitteleuropa* (English—Central Europe) emerged in the early twentieth century. Coined by the German thinker Naumann,[9] it presupposes that the reception of German culture and German economic solutions will, on the one hand, ensure the prosperity of

[4] European Parliament resolution of 22 November 2023 on proposals of the European Parliament for the amendment of the Treaties (2022/2051(INL)), para 2.

[5] Scholz 2023, p. 4; Report of the Franco-German Working Group on the EU Institutional Reform, Paris-Berlin. 18 September 2023, p 11. https://institutdelors.eu/wp-content/uploads/2023/12/20230919-Group-of-Twelve-REPORT.pdf. Accessed 30 January 2025.

[6] Wolff 1994.

[7] Venclova 2002, p. 61.

[8] Kundera 1984.

[9] Naumann 1915.

the buffer zone between Germany and Russia, and on the other hand, guarantee Germany's influence and control in the region. Its creator is the patron of the German political foundation associated with the FDP, which, through its offices in Germany, but also in Prague, Sofia, Belgrade, and Bucharest, can put its patron's assumptions, of course not in the first line regarding the Mitteleuropa doctrine, into practice (Die Friedrich-Naumann-Stiftung für die Freiheit).[10] In the early twenty-first century, German intellectuals, too, recognised the very existence of Central Europe, departing in this way from the entrenched Eastern policy (German *Ostpolitik*). In 2005, the eminent German historian Schlögel wrote: "'Central Europe' – the term itself is already a provocation targeted at the wall which is present in our heads. From a Central European perspective, something that seemed immovable begins to move; from a Central European perspective, something that looks so natural becomes artificial. Isn't Central Europe older, more strongly bound together than the transformations after 1914, 1938 and the end of the war? […] Ultimately, the Central European perspective not only opens up the possibility of speculation, but also provides a glimpse of reality."[11]

Writer and former President of Czechoslovakia and then the Czech Republic V. Havel, one of the best recognised intellectuals of Central Europe, observed: "No list of specific features of Central European literature and culture misses one especially important one: a heightened sensitivity to danger and an extraordinary sense of the phenomenon of fear. This is perfectly understandable: in a territory with such a complex and convoluted history, culturally, ethnically, socially, or politically intricate, in the lands where the most diverse catastrophes in Europe are usually born or end, these very dimensions of human existence are naturally acutely perceived and sensed".[12] The countries of Central Europe no doubt share the sometimes very tragic historical background, which is reflected in the current state of their socio-economic development, the geopolitical situation, and the related sense of threat and fear, but also of realism, which varies from country to country and which is necessary for survival. It does not mean that these states form a political community, like e.g. the Low Countries.

In scholarly literature, Orzelska-Stączek, having analysed successive stages of the formation of the notion of Central Europe, observes that in the strictest sense, the term applies to the area of the Three Seas Initiative.[13] This Initiative is a platform of regional collaboration established in 2016 in Dubrovnik (Croatia). It unites 13 EU Member States who pool efforts to strengthen the infrastructural unity along the North–South axis.[14] In turn, Central Europe in its broadest sense covers a bigger area, including apart from the above states also the Western Balkans as well as Ukraine, Moldova, and a part of former Central and Eastern Europe still under Russian rule.

[10] Die Friedrich-Naumann-Stiftung für die Freiheit. Namensgeber. https://www.freiheit.org/de/friedrich-naumann-unser-namensgeber. Accessed 24 January 2025.

[11] Schlögel 2005, p. 15.

[12] Havel 2011, p. 352.

[13] Critically Staniszkis 2017.

[14] Three Seas Story. https://3seas.eu/about/threeseasstory. Accessed 20 January 2025.

According to the author, the presence of Russian soldiers has become decisive for defining the eastern frontiers of Central Europe, whereas the scale of Russia's military action and the level of violations will remain deeply ingrained in the public memory, influencing the perception of Central Europe and its identity.[15]

Bajda shows that despite a large number of small states globally, they are not the object of comprehensive scholarly studies, which is responsible for an absence of their generally accepted definition. Focusing on the EU Member States, the author opts for a simplified definition based on geographic criteria, i.e. the number of inhabitants and the area of a given country. According to this author, small European states are those with no more than 10 m inhabitants and a territory of up to 80,000 km^2, i.e. less than 50% of the average area of EU Member States.[16] According to the statistics for 2024,[17] in Central Europe these are Croatia, Czechia (with a slightly bigger population), Estonia, Lithuania, Latvia, Slovakia, Slovenia, and Hungary (with a bigger area). In support of this criterion, one can also invoke the population criterion for the allocation of votes in the Council until the relevant provisions of the Lisbon Treaty enter into force, as well as the allocation of seats in the European Parliament. Thus, Bulgaria and Romania can be counted among the medium-sized states of the region, while Poland is a debatable case, due to both its large area and population, which diverge sharply from those of the other states of the region. Poland is therefore deemed a medium or even large Member State. The number of seats allocated to Poland in the European Parliament is a staggering 53, while the second most populous country, Romania, has 33 MEPs.[18] Poland is, however, linked to these countries by a number of parameters defining its situation and position in the process of European integration and is therefore classified in this chapter as a medium-sized country. This classification is supported by a similar qualification of Poland and other Central European member states, e.g. within the framework of German foreign policy, which is still based on an East–West divide (German *Ostpolitik*).[19]

16.2.1 20 Years of EU Membership—A Glass Half Full

In pragmatic terms, Bajda observed that the goal of the states of Central Europe was to gain membership in European and transatlantic organisations, which was a natural reaction and goal after the fall of Communism, responsible for an immense open grey zone susceptible to rivalry of various ideas. Besides, as Bajda notes: "over the years the promise of membership in the European community mobilised candidates to

[15] Orzelska-Stączek 2022, p. 150.

[16] Bajda 2018, p. 57.

[17] Facts and figures on the European Union, https://european-union.europa.eu/principles-countries-history/facts-and-figures-european-union_en. Accessed 13 January 2025.

[18] Distribution of seats in the European Parliament. Seats per country for the 2024 elections. https://www.europarl.europa.eu/infographic/meps-seats/index_en.html. Accessed 20 December 2024.

[19] Bainczyk 2023, p. 193.

adopt Union regulations, open their markets for goods and services and, primarily to solve disputes between them with peaceful measures".[20] The great expectations raised by the accession of the Member States have only been partially fulfilled, judging by the economic and social status of these countries. Significant progress has been widely reported, with an average increase in GDP per capita of 11%. Still, when we compare Central and Eastern European economies with Western European economies, the figures are not so unequivocally positive. In their 2024 report "Glass half full. Searching for new sources for economic growth", Popławski and Baniak share the commonplace contention that the twenty years of Central European countries' membership in the EU have been a great economic success and the pace of economic growth has been relatively high, but observe at the same time that the project of integration of Central Europe is left unfinished and EU membership is no longer a panacea for all ills in the face of gradual loss of competitiveness of the EU on the global market.[21] It is most revealing to compare real GDP per capita in selected countries as a percentage of the EU average in 2003, i.e. the year before most countries joined the EU, in 2013 and 2023. The average growth of real GDP per capita in the Central European countries over 20 years was 11%, but income only reached 51% of the EU average GDP per capita in 2023.[22] One of the key ventures of the EU is an operational internal market, but this has not been fully realised in Central Europe along the North–South axis, not least because of the gravitation towards Western European partners more abundant in capital and knowledge. In most countries of the region, Germany remains the largest partner, while the economic links between the Member States remain insufficient.[23] This can be seen, for example, on shop shelves. In Poland, one hardly encounters Hungarian or Romanian products. One factor which hinders the completion of the internal market and thus the overcoming of the development disparity is the infrastructural deficiencies along the North–South axis.[24] One example of infrastructural backwardness is the time it takes to travel the 2500 km between Goteborg (Sweden) and Barcelona (Spain) and between Tallinn (Estonia) and Constanta (Romania). In 2019, travel time between Sweden and Spain was approximately 24 h by car and similarly by train. Correspondingly, along the Estonia-Romania route, travel time was 32 h by car and 3 days by train.[25] It should be mentioned that to date no investment has been completed that would fundamentally change transport links on the North–South axis, with the exception of Via Carpatia.[26] The latter is still being built thanks to the commitment of the participating states in the 3SI. In 2022, then-president of the Polish Bank Gospodarki Krajowej, Daszyńska-Muzyczka noted that as much as 650 billion EUR

[20] Bajda 2023, p. 11.

[21] Draghi 2024a, p. 7.

[22] Popławski and Baniak 2024, p. 9.

[23] Bainczyk 2023, p. 197.

[24] Brzezinski and Koranyi 2014, p. 1; Crandall 2024, p. 73.

[25] Spotdata 2019, p. 20.

[26] Via Carpatia. https://trojmorze.isppan.waw.pl/wybrane-projekty-priorytetowe/via-carpatia/. Accessed 3 January 2025.

is needed as an investment in the logistical, energy, and digital infrastructure in the region.[27] Attempting to close this North–South gap, from Estonia to Greece, is the Three Seas Initiative, which focuses on enhancing the transport, energy and digital infrastructure in the region. These three core objectives were significantly expanded at the 3SI summit in Vilnius in 2024 to include among others: the region's cyber resilience and cybersecurity, the resilience of dual-use infrastructure and a socially just and environmentally sustainable transition towards a climate neutral and resilient economy.[28]

At the same time, Central European states have been forced to change their public spending priorities, now largely allocated to ensuring public security. Nine out of eleven Central European states have exceeded the NATO threshold of 2% on defence spending, and among the 32 members of the Alliance, the top five states with the highest defence outlays relative to their GDP are: Poland 4.12%, Estonia 3.43%, and Latvia 3.15%.[29]

Bridging the infrastructure gap is a prerequisite for the successful implementation of the internal market on the East–West axis, for increasing the military resilience of the countries of Central Europe and thus of the EU as a whole, as well as for the success of the future EU membership of Ukraine or Moldova.[30]

Will the next two decades help to close the gaps between the EU Member States that joined the EU in 2004, 2007, and 2013? This depends on a variety of factors, which cannot be discussed *in extenso* here. These certainly include decisions taken by EU institutions in multiple areas which directly or otherwise impact the widening or closing of the gap between Member States. Examples of such decisions of the EU institutions for Central Europe include the European Commission's departure from the stringent state aid regulations. This was in response to the crisis caused by the Covid pandemic, but the recovery from this crisis, thanks to inter alia state aid, placed the less prosperous Central European states at a disadvantage. Between 2021 and 2023, companies from just two EU Member States, France and Germany, received 55% of the total state aid granted in the EU, while the volume of state aid granted in Central European countries amounted to 11%.[31] Another decision, with even more far-reaching and probably negative consequences is the fast decarbonisation of the EU's economy, which may mean partial deindustrialisation for at least some of the Central European Member States.[32] Other negative examples include the model of EU research and development policy, the engine of growth of the economy in Central Europe and the entire EU. In this area, Central European Member States have neither

---

[27] Szczyt Trójmorza w Rydze. Prezes BGK: okazja do rozmów o rozwoju infrastruktury w regionie, 2022. https://polskieradio24.pl/artykul/2983753,szczyt-trojmorza-w-rydze-prezes-bgk-okazja-do-rozmow-o-rozwoju-infrastruktury-w-regionie. Accessed 17 January 2025.

[28] Joint Declaration of the Ninth Summit of the Three Seas Initiative Vilnius, Lithuania, 11 April 2024, paras 18–21. https://media.voog.com/0000/0046/4166/files/Declaration.pdf. Accessed 10 December 2024.

[29] Falkenek 2024.

[30] Sebe 2024, p. 173.

[31] Popławski and Baniak 2024, p. 23.

[32] *Ibid.*, p. 21.

the facilities nor the public and private resources to compete with R&D centres in Western Europe. The relevant linkages between Central European countries are also fragile. The Draghi Report, according to which the research and development policy is to be one of the engines of the EU economy, proposes centralization of research at the European level and creation of supranational centres of excellence,[33] yet does not set out specific measures to close the gaps between Western Europe and the Central European Member States.[34] These concerns are justified in light of the position of the Central European Member States both in terms of ability to finance research and innovation and participation in EU programmes supporting research and innovation. Popławski and Baniak indicate that the Central European countries collectively secured €3.2 billion, or about 4.7% of the total Horizon 2020 budget, for 17% of all grants (c. 5900 out of c. 35,400 grants).[35]

The above examples confirm Staniszkis' still valid theory of the relationship between developed centres and backward peripheries. In light of the researcher's views, the most advanced economies and companies impose on the peripheries the procedures and institutions corresponding to their own stage of development. This, however, does not always support the development of the backward states, which are compelled to leapfrog certain stages of development. This, in turn, prevents them from reaping the benefits of innovative solutions.[36]

However, do the countries of Central Europe stand a chance of having their specific conditions taken into account in the current as well as in the proposed institutional framework?

16.3 Some Remarks on the Position of Small and Medium-Sized Member States in the EU's Institutional Framework

The position of small Member States has been analysed closely since the onset of European integration, first of all in reference to the decision-making process in the Council and to the number of commissioners.[37] This important historical aspect will be omitted in this chapter, and the impetus for these considerations was provided by the recent elections to the European Parliament of June 2024 and the subsequent appointments for key EU offices, which concluded only in November 2024. Under the provisions of the EU Treaty indicated below and in line with the established treaty practice, these offices include: President of the European Council, President of the European Commission, High Representative for Foreign and Security Policy, and President of the European Parliament. While in principle these offices should be

[33] Draghi 2024b, p. 245.

[34] *Ibid.*, p. 255.

[35] Popławski and Baniak 2024, p. 39.

[36] Staniszkis 2006, p. 161.

[37] Żurawski vel Grajewski 2023, p. 33.

exercised in a supranational manner, in the interest of the EU as a whole rather than to benefit the nationality of the office holder, only in the case of the President of the European Commission does such an obligation arise explicitly from the second and third sentences of Article 17(3) TEU. However, in view of the nature of the EU as an international organisation, its formation as a two-tier democracy (Article 10(1) and (2) TEU), as well as the specific provisions, the nationality of the office holders is relevant. In addition, knowledge of the realities of a particular part of the EU should not hinder, but actually help, the proper formulation of the so-called "general interest of the EU" (Article 17(1) sentence 1 TEU).

It is relevant to recall here the principle of equality of Member States before the Treaties, as well as the specific provisions of the procedure for the election of these offices. The principle of equality of States before the Treaties, in Article 4(2), first sentence, of the TEU, was introduced into EU law for the first time by the Lisbon Treaty, but it had previously been provided for in the Treaty establishing a Constitution for Europe, significant in the interest of small Member States in the context of abandoning the principle of unanimity in the Council's decision-making process.[38] The principle of the equality of states undoubtedly derives from the principle of the sovereign equality of states in Article 2(1) of the UN Charter, yet Haratsch points out another important factor in the context of the EU's constitutional evolution: the principle of the equality of constituent parts is likewise a major constitutional principle of the federal state.[39] Some commentators, however, take the view that Article 4(2), first sentence, of the TEU is addressed exclusively to the EU, and in particular does not apply to the cooperation of the large Member States in the run-up to decision-making processes, as long as the principle of horizontal loyalty is respected in accordance with Article 4(3) of the TEU.[40] No doubt, the principle of equality of states before Treaties as the overarching principle of the EU's operation, should be applied by the EU's institutions participating in the nominating procedure concerning key offices: by the European Council electing its President (Article 15(5) TEU), by the European Council and the European Parliament in the procedure for the nomination of the European Commission (Article 17(7) TEU), by the European Council in the procedure for the election of the High Representative for Foreign and Security Policy, and by the European Parliament not only in the election of the President of Parliament and its officers (Article 14(4) TEU), but also of other parliamentary bodies.

Given the above, the safeguard for the constitutional position of small and medium-sized Member States in the EU should be based on both the principle of equality before the Treaties, enshrined in the Treaty itself, and the aforementioned principle of loyal cooperation applied horizontally, i.e. also between Member States, which are obliged to cooperate, respect, show solidarity, and trust each other in a spirit

[38] Franzius 2023, paras 20–22.

[39] Haratsch 2020, p. 472.

[40] Franzius 2023, paras 20–22.

of loyalty. Kahl notes that the doctrine of the specific legal consequences of (horizontal) loyalty between Member States towards the Union has not yet been definitively established.[41] Undoubtedly, this doctrine should also extend to the selection process for key EU offices.

Specific provisions related to the selection procedure include Article 17(5), second sentence, of the TEU, which provides that "The members of the Commission shall be chosen from among the nationals of the Member States on the basis of a system of strictly equal rotation between the Member States, reflecting the demographic and geographical range of all the Member States". One should heed here the term "strictly equal rotation between the Member States". While it is true that this requirement refers to the situation of a reduction in the number of members of the Commission to two-thirds, it was echoed in general terms in Declaration No. 6, annexed to the Final Act of the Intergovernmental Conference which adopted the Treaty of Lisbon. According to the Declaration, "In choosing the persons called upon to hold the offices of President of the European Council, President of the Commission and High Representative of the Union for Foreign Affairs and Security Policy, due account is to be taken of the need to respect the geographical and demographic diversity of the Union and its Member States".[42]

In light of the above, a question arises whether the principle of the equality of states before the treaties and that of the respect for the geographical and demographic diversity of the Union and its Member States were respected in the selection of candidates for the key positions in the EU. This question can be answered by examining the elections to key EU offices so far, taking into account the nationality of the elected candidates. The reference period will be 2009–2029, i.e. after the accession of Bulgaria and Romania to the EU, when the number of small and medium-sized Central European countries reached 10 and increased to 11 in 2013. It should also be mentioned that on 1 December 2009, the provisions of the Lisbon Treaty, which included both the principle of equality of states before the treaties and the above-mentioned declaration, entered into force. 2029 is the date of the next elections to the European Parliament, which will be followed by another shuffling of personnel packages.

Table 16.1 will show the nationality of the persons holding the office of, respectively, President of the European Council (Article 15(5) and (6) TEU), President of the European Commission (Article 17(6) and (7) TEU), High Representative for Foreign and Security Policy (Article 18 TEU), and President of the European Parliament. As far as the President of the European Parliament is concerned, he was not mentioned in Declaration No. 6, as according to Article 14(4) it is the European Parliament that elects the President and its officers from among its members. However, this position was listed as one of the elements of the personnel package negotiated after the June

[41] Kahl 2022, para 179.

[42] A. Declarations concerning provisions of the treaties, 6. Declaration on Article 15(5) and (6), Article 17(6) and (7) and Article 18 of the Treaty on European Union. OJ C 202, 7.6.2016, p. 338.

Table 16.1 Nationality of the President of the EC, High Representative, President of the European Commission, and EP President from 2009 to 2029

Years	President of the European Council	President of the European Commission	High Representative	President of the European Parliament
2009–2014	H. Van Rompuy Belgium	J. M. Barroso Portugal	C. Ashton United Kingdom	2009–2012 Poland 2012–2014 FRG 2014 Italy
2014–2019	D. Tusk Poland	J.-C. Juncker Luxembourg	F. Mogherini Italy	2014–2017 FRG 2017–2019 Italy
2019–2024	C. Michel Belgium	U. v. Leyen FRG	J. Borell Spain	2019–2022 Italy 2022–2024 Malta
2024–2029?	A. Costa Portugal	U. v. Leyen FRG	K. Kallas Estonia	2024-Malta

Source The author

2024 elections,[43] and the European Parliament itself as an EU institution is bound by the principle of sovereign equality states before the Treaties.

Given the current number of Member States, the 11 "new" Central European Member States account for 40% of all EU Member States, but the number of their citizens in key EU offices does not in any way correspond to their percentage share. Out of a total of 20 terms of office between 2009 and 2024 (President of the European Council, President of the European Commission, High Representative for Foreign Policy, and President of the European Parliament), the countries in question have only filled the above-mentioned EU offices 3 times (Poland twice and Estonia once), so their share is 15%; if Poland is excluded as a large country, this share drops to 5%. By contrast, never has a citizen of a Central European state held office of the President of the Commission. Importantly, small and medium-sized Central European states are not alone here. Another striking feature is the complete absence of the "northern" EU countries, i.e. Sweden, Finland and Denmark as well as Ireland; the exception was the election in 2009 of C. Ashton (UK) as High Representative for Foreign and Security Policy. In view of the above, the geographical diversity stipulated by Declaration No. 6 and Article 17(5), second sentence, of the TEU is clearly not respected. The list of terms of office included is dominated by the founding states of the European Communities, which filled 11 out of 20 terms of office.

The unfavourable assessment of the situation from the point of view of the Central European Member States is exacerbated by the analysis made in 2020 by Haratsch with regard to the observance of the principle of equality of Member States before the Treaties as regards their continued operation. The author notes that the principle of equality of States before the Treaties has been fully preserved only in the Court of Auditors (Article 285 (2) TFEU) and Court of Justice of the EU. Under Article 19(2), first sentence, of the TEU, the Court of Justice shall consist of one judge from

[43] Baccini 2024.

each Member State, the General Court shall include at least one judge per Member State. The above principle does not hold, however, for the Advocates-General.[44]

One frequently quoted example of the inclusion of small Member States in EU decision-making processes is the principle of degressive proportionality in determining the number of seats allocated to them. At the same time, it should be remembered that in the 720-seat European Parliament, where voting takes place according to party affiliation, there are only two Central Europeans among the leaders of all parties in the Parliament: Morawiecki (Chairman of the European Conservatists and Reformists Party) and Tyszka (Co-Chairman of the Europe of Sovereign Nations), both form Poland.[45] No citizen of a Central European Member State is president of the three European parties supporting the 2024 Commission, i.e. the European People's Party, the Progressive Alliance of Socialists and Democrats in the European Parliament, and the Greens/EFS. Bearing in mind the fragmentation of votes allocated to small Central European countries among European political parties, all 11 of these countries have 207 seats in the 720-seat European Parliament for the 2024–2029 term. This low number of EP seats, combined with the vast parliamentary experience of representatives of Western European countries, often backed by a very large apparatus of national political parties, means that the voice of this part of the EU may not be heard when crucial decisions are made about the future of the organisation. This is shown, for example, by the handling of the work on the report that served as the basis for the November 2023 European Parliament resolution on amendments to the current treaties. The work in question took place within the Committee on Constitutional Affairs (AFCO). Six MEPs-rapporteurs were selected to draft the report on proposals of the European Parliament for the amendment of the Treaties. As many as four of them were from the FRG: Simon (EPP), Bischoff (S&D), Scholz (GUE/NGL), and Freund (Group of the Greens/European Free Alliance). The two others were Verhofstadt (Belgium, Renew Europe) and Saryusz-Wolski (Polska, ECR).[46] It is true that under the Treaties MEPs belong to European parties and are supposed to represent EU citizens rather than Member States, but the absence of representatives of small Central European countries in this important committee, whose work led to the enactment of the post-2023 Treaty, is striking. It should also be mentioned that Saryusz-Wolski did not sign the report prepared by the AFCO rapporteurs' group. According to the transparency information on the work of the committee, 13 external actors were consulted between August 2022 and December 2023, none representing Central Europe.[47] In view of the above, the information that no alternative proposal

[44] Haratsch 2020, p. 473.

[45] Links to the parties available via the political groups of the European Parliament. https://www.europarl.europa.eu/about-parliament/en/organisation-and-rules/organisation/political-groups. Accessed 14 January 2025.

[46] Report A9-0337/2023 on proposals of the European Parliament for the amendment of the Treaties (2022/2051(INL)).

[47] Transparency. Meetings with interest representatives published in line with the Rules of Procedure. https://oeil.secure.europarl.europa.eu/oeil/en/procedure-file?reference=2022/2051(INL)#section8. Accessed 16 December 2024.

for EU reforms authored at least in part by MEPs from Central European states has been put forth, seems redundant.

Last but not least the Draghi report, which was prepared in collaboration with hundreds of experts from both university centres, think tanks and business, was produced with hardly any input from such circles in Central Europe.[48] As already mentioned, this undoubtedly translated into its main assumptions, only partially recognising the economic, but also research and investment gap between Western and Central Europe.

With regard to the EU's institutional framework, there are objective reasons for the introduction of rules deviating from the principle of equality of states before the treaties. Haratsch mentions here; efficiency, a general function of the institution concerned or on the basis of the specific function of the decisions to be made by a body.[49] However the author comes to the following conclusion: "If one attempts to draw a final conclusion, it must be noted that there are many deviations from the equality of the Member States in the institutions and bodies of the Union".[50] Nevertheless the EU is still based on a two-tier democracy with an intergovernmental element. In a situation where supranational institutions are dominated by citizens of the 'old' Member States, intergovernmental institutions sometimes remain the only option to articulate the interests of the smaller and institutionally weaker Central European States. However, it should be stressed that the process of centralisation of power in the EU, involving the strengthening of supranational institutions such as the European Commission and the European Parliament, abolishing at the same time unanimity in the Council of the European Union, and in view of the aforementioned developments, may contribute to a further weakening of the abovementioned possibility.

Due to the limited length of the chapter and because of the institutional model adopted in the EU, our analysis, taking the perspective of small and medium-sized Central European Member States, will focus on the political guidelines of the European Commission, which, pursuant to Article 17(2) TEU, has the exclusive legislative initiative. Therefore, political guidelines constitute a roadmap for EU's legislation for a five-year period; it is EU law, in line with the concept of the community of law, that is the key instrument of integration, inevitably defining its direction. None of the guidelines of the Commission Presidents of the period 2009–2024 included among their priorities *expressis verbis* the levelling of economic and social asymmetries between the then old and new Member States. J.C. Juncker's political guidelines of 2014 proved more promising than those of 2009, at least on two counts. The new President of the European Commission observed that "the Union and our citizens now need to digest the addition of 13 Member States in the past ten years. The EU needs to take a break from enlargement so that we can consolidate what has been achieved among the 28".[51] Unfortunately, the document lacked detailed proposals

[48] Draghi 2024a, p. 3.

[49] Haratsch 2020, p. 493.

[50] *Ibid.*, p. 500.

[51] Juncker 2014, p. 12.

on how this consolidation should be carried out, and the argument about the need for it served to postpone discussion of further EU enlargement. Moreover, J.C. Juncker expressed clear support for Ukraine, attacked by Russia at the time, but again this did not result in proposals for even general measures to improve the EU's resilience to the Russian threat. However, at that time, the consolidation of the new members with the Community has unfortunately not been linked to the question of the EU's resilience as such. It is worth mentioning that just this year a report was published by the Atlantic Council, entitled "Completing Europe. From the North–South Corridor to Energy, Transportation, and Telecommunications Union".

It is true that significant resources were earmarked for cohesion policy. Popławski and Baniak notes, that Central European countries received nearly 45% (€243 billion, out of a total of €547 billion) of the EU structural and investment funds (ESIF) allocated in all 28 Member States under the 2014–2020 Multiannual Financial Framework.[52] It seems however that insufficient mechanisms were built into the EU's economic and social development programming to effectively close the gaps between Western and Central Europe. This was also because the countries themselves tended to adopt a passive basis of only authorising goals put forward by the EU institutions, even though EU development was already slowing down at the time.[53]

16.4 Future Reform of the EU and Small and Medium-Sized Member States

This part of the chapter will focus on two documents, different in nature but similar in content, which are vital for the process of EU reform which began in 2019.[54] It seems that the European Parliament resolution of 22 November 2023 on proposals of the European Parliament for the amendment of the Treaties is so far the only point of reference for a further discussion about EU reform.[55] At the very beginning it is important to recall the above comments on the procedure for preparing this document, as well as the fact that no Member State or group of Member States has exercised its competence to submit such a proposal (Article 48 (2) TEU).

In line with the motto of an ever-closer EU (Article 1 (2), the European Parliament proposes a further extension of the competences of the EU as such (Resolution, paras 13–15, also other detailed amendments), simultaneously with reinforcement of the European Parliament (Resolution, i.e. paras 3, 5, 6, 10, 12), a reduction of the competences of the Council (Resolution, i.e. paras 3, 6, 10) and its role as an intergovernmental institution in the institutional framework of the EU by increasing the number of areas where actions are decided by qualified majority voting and through the ordinary legislative procedure. Leaving aside a question of a deep systemic reform

[52] Popławski and Baniak 2024, p. 32.

[53] Draghi 2024a, Figure 3 GDP evolution, p. 12.

[54] Von der Leyen 2019.

[55] Bainczyk 2024a.

of the EU, caused by an eventual introduction of the above-mentioned amendments, and having in mind the developments described above, the proposed amendments may be a matter of concern for Central European Member States of the EU. The European Parliament proposes also to reduce the number of Commissioners or the Members of the Executive to 15 while respecting Article 17 (5) TEU. From the point of view of the institutional experiences of Central European Member States to date, the question of a new election system for the Commission may be also questionable. It has been stated that Commissioners shall be chosen by the Commission President on the basis of political preferences, whilst ensuring geographic and demographic balance. As shown above, the geographic and demographic balance was not implemented in the period of 2009–2024. The proposed institutional changes may therefore lead to further marginalization of the interests of Central European Member States.

The second document is a paper prepared by French and German experts at the initiative of the two governments. It is part of a long tradition of shaping the political system of the Communities and then the EU by these two countries,[56] which was also reflected in the Franco-German non-paper of 2019. In terms of the institutional reform, the Franco-German group's proposals do not differ significantly from those of the European Parliament, although the notion of a hybrid political system has been used, which is still intended to include intergovernmental elements. Examples of common approach are, for example: extension of the EU competences, reduction in the number of Commissioners, introduction of the lead candidate system long advocated by U. von der Leyen and also a full implementation "in all remaining policies" of a qualified majority voting in the Council combined, except for in CFSP, with the ordinary legislative procedure. The authors of the Franco-German report made, perhaps not entirely realistically, the assumption of an enlargement of the EU by three or even eight new Member States, they presented some solutions as regards the functioning of the Council designed especially (*sic!*) for small and medium-sized Member States: firstly "the trio format should be extended to a quintet of five presidencies, each spanning half of an institutional cycle. (…). In an enlarged EU, it would also ensure that each quintet has at least one larger Member State with greater administrative capacity and experience as this would enhance horizontal relations between Member States" (Report, p. 21). Secondly "Smaller to medium-sized Member States fear domination by the larger ones, as they can organise blocking minorities much more easily. The share of Member States and the population they represent should thus be adjusted. For instance, from the current system of 55% of Member states representing 65% of the EU population, it could be changed to 60% of Member States representing 60% of the population" (Report, p. 25). It should be noted that, firstly in the case of small and medium-sized Member States, it is not necessarily only about the negative aspect of blocking certain legislative initiatives, but the time has finally come for trying to push through their own proposals.

The future EU structure of the 'four circles' is discussed extensively in Chapter III of the Report, in which the authors present various scenarios for implementing proposed amendments. On the one hand, the structure is supposed to facilitate an

[56] Bainczyk 2024b, p. 88.

enlargement process. In this case enlargement will mean placing 10 new countries in the outer circles (No. 3 and No. 4). On the other hand, the 'four circles' allow to 'push out' Member States that do not accept the centralisation of power by the EU institutions—cf. "External differentiation could become relevant for the future of the (enlarged) EU if individual Member States either block necessary treaty reforms and consequently negotiate new opt-outs, or even prefer a less committed status regarding European integration. In these cases, a special association status with the EU could be envisioned" (Report, p. 39). The proposal of the authors of the Report is not novel, as these visions of differentiated integration are well known in literature.[57] As early as 1989, Chancellor Kohl's advisors presented the concept of a Europe of concentric circles.[58] The real crux of this proposal is circle 2, which is intended as an alternative for countries that do not accept further centralisation of competences at the level of the EU institutions. Circle 1 are the Eurozone countries, which in the future will transfer further competences to the EU and form a centralised EU state; circle 2 are countries that do not want further, deeper integration, but will pursue common political objectives with the EU and will be subject to systemic control by EU institutions; circle 3 are associated countries participating in the internal market, not represented in EU institutions, but subject to their control, including the CJ EU; circle 4 are countries undertaking closer political cooperation and included in the free trade area. Such a scenario has been so far often perceived in Central Europe as a marginalization and a threat to the European ambitions of those States. Given the experience of the last 20 years and the continued de facto differentiation in the status of Member States within the EU, perhaps it is time to use this differentiation creatively for the benefit of all Member States.

16.5 Conclusions

Completing "an ever closer union" (preamble to the TEU, Article 1 TEU), encounters a very prosaic obstacle in the form of the still existing significant, and historically determined, diversity of living conditions in the Member States[59] and, consequently, of the priorities of their societies. The failure of the EU institutions to take these determinants into account in the medium to long term will not contribute to the creation of a European nation and the deepening of the integration process, but may result in Central European Member States being pushed to the periphery of the EU. At the same time, even the slow changes in Western European societies, which become apparent in the results of national elections, do not ensure a change in the priorities of the Western European states, which could contribute to closing the socio-economic-institutional gap between Western and Central Europe. From the perspective of the

[57] Dahrendorf 1976.

[58] Mertes and Prill 1989.

[59] Cf. Living standards across the EU: consumption per inhabitant—all small and medium-sized Central European states are below the EU base line.

Central European Member States, in view of the declared assumptions of EU reform by the European Parliament, the European Commission and some Member States, which aims at increasing the centralisation of EU governance, also at the level of executive institutions, several scenarios of development are outlined, which may or may not be alternative to each other. These are, for example: (1) The formulation of EU reform proposals that would allow the effective implementation of the principle of equality of Member States and the principle of loyal cooperation and the representation of the interests of all Member States within the existing institutional framework, thus reducing the imbalance between Western and Central Europe; (2) The use of the mechanism of differentiated integration, in order to reduce the political, economic and social imbalance between the countries of Central Europe and those of Western Europe, in order to actively, once the gap has been closed, contribute to the future of the EU. It is also possible to envisage scenario 3, involving the continued inaction of small and medium-sized EU Member States, both in terms of EU reform itself and the implementation of key EU policies. This passivity may be due to a profit and loss calculation that has so far favoured support for deeper integration as designed by EU institutions. In addition to the obvious economic benefits, Bajda included here e.g. the shifting relations between states into a more conciliated approach, the readiness of organisations like the EU to take over the administrative or operational role, accumulation of knowledge from various areas from economic, which allows making more rational decisions, last but not least gaining additional guarantees of security.[60]

Scenario 3 is not a good one, not only for the small and medium-sized countries themselves. Still, it is a probable one given past experience, as the passivity of the Central European Member States may perpetrate the status quo. On the other hand, the closing of development gaps is, on balance, profitable for the so-called "old" Member States, as it strengthens the entire EU, also as a global player, and is a prerequisite for further successful EU enlargement. The 2009–2024 period, however, does not bode well for Scenario 1, as neither the European Commission's policy documents nor the most recent document on the reform of the EU economy, The Draghi Report, take into account the perspective of the Central European Member States.

One thing is certain: implementing the scenarios of activity of the Central European countries, favourable for the EU as a whole as they allow for a fuller realisation of the EU's objectives under Article 3(1) TEU (values, peace, prosperity), is not possible without the involvement of the countries of the region. This involvement, preferably coordinated, is impossible without the transformation of political elites, as Staniszkis pointed out back in 2006, so that they can exercise "power capable of harmonising interests and procedures within globalised, networked economies and public governance structures." Of particular relevance in the context of the chapter's topic, the political class in Central European states, in order to close any gaps, must be able to bring the standards that correspond to the interests of the communities they represent into the web of relationships at the EU level.[61]

---

[60] Bajda 2023, p. 117.

[61] Staniszkis 2006, p. 199.

Despite subjective and objective constraints, Central Europe, in the name of the common European good, should be willing to do so. In his excellent essay entitled "Our Central European Fears", which remains acutely topical in spite of being written in 1990, Havel argues: "Fear of our own incompetence can evoke new competency; fear of God or of our own conscience can evoke courage; fear of defeat can make us prevail. Fear of freedom can be the very thing that will ultimately teach us to create a freedom of real value. And fear of the future could be exactly what we need to bring about a better future".[62]

References

Aristotle (4 BC) Politics, Book VI, 1318 b4

Baccini F (2024) EU nomination process kicks off. Leaders of the Twenty-Seven in Brussels to reach an agreement as early as today, 17.06.2024. https://www.eunews.it/en/2024/06/17/eu-nomination-process-kicks-off-leaders-of-the-twenty-seven-in-brussels-to-reach-an-agreement-as-early-as-today/. Accessed 12 January 2025

Bainczyk M (2023) Germany's policy towards the Central European countries. In: Bajda P (ed) Small states within the European Union Challenges – dilemmas – strategies, Wydawnictwo Akademii Wymiaru Sprawiedliwości, Warsaw, pp 187–211

Bainczyk M (2024a) Francusko-niemieckie propozycje reformy UE. Utracona demokracja i konkurencyjność Europy Środkowej? [Franco-German proposals for EU reform. Lost democracy and the competitiveness for Central Europe?]. Biuletyn IZ 548, https://www.iz.poznan.pl/plik,pobierz,6484,29792ea1b76f4a74dbf843b903ee9b8b/Biuletyn%20Instytutu%20Zachodniegonr%20548.pdf. Accessed 12 January 2025

Bainczyk M (2024b) Od unijnego Staatenverbund do unijnego Bundesstaat. Władza w UE z perspektywy RFN [From Union Staatenverbund to Union Budesstaat. Power in the EU from the perspective of the Federal Republic Germany]. In: Biernat J Pieniążek M (eds) Dyskretny urok teorii [The discreet charm of theory]. Oficyna Wydawnicza AFM, Kraków, pp 79–95

Bajda P (2018) Małe państwo europejskie na arenie międzynarodowej. Polityka zagraniczna Republiki Słowackiej w latach 1993–2016 [A small European state on the international stage. The foreign policy of the Slovak Republic from 1993 to 2016]. Ośrodek Myśli Politycznej, Wydawnictwo Naukowe Uniwersytetu Kardynała Stefana Wyszyńskiego, Kraków-Warsaw

Bajda P (2023) Small European state – a specific actor in international relations. In: Bajda P (ed) Small states within the European Union: Challenges – dilemmas – strategies. Wydawnictwo Akademii Wymiaru Sprawiedliwości, Warsaw, pp 71–88

Brzezinski I, Koranyi D (2014) Completing Europe: The North-South Corridor, Atlantic Council, Washington. https://www.atlanticcouncil.org/wp-content/uploads/2024/07/Completing-Europe_Report.pdf. Accessed 10 December 2024

Crandall M (2024) The Three Seas Initiative and Estonia after the Outbreak of War in Ukraine. In: Orzelska-Stączek A (ed) The Three Seas Initiative. An original concept of regional cooperation in different approaches. Institute of Political Studies of the Polish Academy of Sciences, Warsaw, pp 73–84

Dahrendorf R (1976) A Third Europe? Third Jean Monnet Lecture by Professor Ralf Dahrendorf, Director of the London School of Economics, Florence, 26 November 1976. Archive of European Integration. https://aei.pitt.edu/11346/2/11346.pdf. Accessed 13 January 2025

[62] Havel 1990.

Draghi M (2024a) The future of European competitiveness. Part A | A competitiveness strategy for Europe. https://commission.europa.eu/document/download/97e481fd-2dc3-412d-be4c-f152a8232961_en?filename=The%20future%20of%20European%20competitiveness%20_%20A%20competitiveness%20strategy%20for%20Europe.pdf. Accessed 10 December 2024

Draghi M (2024b) The future of European competitiveness. Part B In-depth analysis and recommendations. https://commission.europa.eu/document/download/ec1409c1-d4b4-4882-8bdd-3519f86bbb92_en?filename=The%20future%20of%20European%20competitiveness_%20In-depth%20analysis%20and%20recommendations_0.pdf. Accessed 10 December 2024

Falkenek C (2024) Who's at 2 percent? Look how NATO allies have increased their defence spending since Russia's invasion of Ukraine. https://www.atlanticcouncil.org/blogs/econographics/whos-at-2-percent-look-how-nato-allies-have-increased-their-defense-spending-since-russias-invasion-of-ukraine/. Accessed 20 January 2025

Haratsch A (2020) Die Gleichheit der Mitgliedstaaten in den Institutionen und Entscheidungsverfahren der Europäischen Union – der rechtliche Rahmen [The equality of Member States in the institutions and decision-making processes of the European Union – the legal framework]. Europarecht, Nomos Verlag, Baden-Baden, pp 471–500

Havel V (1990) Address by Vaclav Havel President of the Czech and Slovak Federal Republic at the Salzburg Festival. Salzburg, 26 July 1990 https://www.muzeuminternetu.cz/offwebs/czech/352.htm. Accessed 29 January 2024

Havel V (2011) Siła bezsilnych i inne eseje. Agora SA, Warsaw

Juncker JC (2014) A New Start for Europe: My Agenda for Jobs, Growth, Fairness and Democratic Change. Political Guidelines for the next European Commission. Strasbourg, 15 July 2014, Jean-Claude Juncker. https://commission.europa.eu/system/files/2019-09/juncker-political-guidelines-speech_en.pdf. Accessed 1 February 2025

Kahl S (2022) EU-Vertrag (Lissabon) Art. 4 (Zuständigkeiten der Union, nationale Identität, loyale Zusammenarbeit) [Art. TEU (Lisbon) EU competences, national identity, loyal cooperation]. In: Calliess Ch, Ruffert M (eds) EUV/AEUV. Das Verfassungsrecht der Europäischen Union mit Europäischer Grundrechtcharta. Kommentar [Constitutional law of the European Union and EU Charter of Fundamental Rights. Commentary. C.H. Beck, Munich, paras 1–191

Kundera M (1984) The Tragedy of Central Europe (White E (transl.)). The New York Review of Books, April 26 issue. https://www.nybooks.com/articles/1984/04/26/the-tragedy-of-central-europe/?printpage=true. Accessed 20 January 2025

Franzius C (2023) EUV Art. 4 (Föderative Grundsätze) [Art. 4 TEU Federative Principles]. In: Pechstein M, Nowak C, Häde U (eds) Frankfurter Kommentar EUV/GRC/AEUV Bd. 1 [Frankfurt Commentary on TEU/EUCh/TFEU Vol. 1]. Mohr Siebeck, Tübingen, paras 1–178

Mertes M, Prill N J (1989) Der verhängnisvolle Irrtum eines Entweder-Oder. Eine Vision für Europa [The fatal fallacy of an either-or. A vision for Europe]. Frankfurter Allgemeine Zeitung, 19 July 1989, p. 8

Naumann F (1915) Mitteleuropa [Central Europe]. Verlag von Georg Reimer, Berlin

Orzelska-Stączek (2023) Europa Środkowa: nazwa regionu w świetle badań w ISP PAN [Central Europe: the name of the region in the light of research at the Institute of Political Studies of the Polish Academy of Sciences]. In: Stępniewski T (ed) Zrozumieć Europę od Haleckiego do Kłoczowskiego Środkową [Understanding Central Europe from Halecki to Kłoczowski]. Instytut Europy Środkowej, Lublin, pp 138–152

Popławski K, Baniak S (2024) A Glass Half Full. Searching for New Sources for Economic Growth. Ośrodek Studiów Wschodnich, Warsaw

Schlögel K (2005) Środek leży na wschodzie. Europa w stadium przejściowym [The centre lies in the East. Europe in transition]. Oficyna Naukowa, Warsaw

Scholz O (2023) Europe must turn its attention to the rest of the world, 9 Mai 2023, Speech by the Federal Chancellor in Strasbourg. https://www.bundesregierung.de/breg-en/news/speech-fc-eu-parliament-2189348. Accessed 31 January 2025

Sebe M (2024) The Three Seas Initiative: A Romanian Perspective from Riga to Bucharest. In: Orzelska-Stączek A (ed) The Three Seas Initiative. An original concept of regional cooperation

in different approaches. Institute of Political Studies of the Polish Academy of Sciences, Warsaw, pp 159–180
Spotdata (2019) Perspectives for infrastructural investments in the Three Seas region. A Special Report. https://3siif.eu/wp-content/uploads/2019/11/SpotData_Report_Three-Seas-region.pdf. Accessed 17 January 2025
Staniszkis J (2006) O władzy i bezsilności [About power and powerlessness]. Wydawnictwo Literackie, Kraków
Staniszkis J (2017) Europa Środkowa jest mitem [Central Europe is a myth]. https://teologiapolitycz na.pl/prof-jadwiga-staniszkis. Accessed 11 February 2025
Venclova T (2002) Poezja jako pokuta [Poetry as Atonement]. In: Venclova T (ed) Niezniszczalny rytm. Eseje o literaturze [The Unvanquished Rhythm. Essays on Literature]. Fundacja Pogranicze, Suwałki
Von der Leyen U (2019) A Union that strives for more. My agenda for Europe. By candidate for President of the European Commission. Ursula von der Leyen https://www.europarl.europa.eu/resources/library/media/20190716RES57231/20190716RES57231.pdf. Accessed 4 January 2025
Wolff L (1994) The Map of Civilization on the Mind of the Enlightenment. Stanford University Press
Zuleeg M (1995) Der rechtliche Zusammenhalt der Europäischen Gemeinschaft [The legal cohesion of the European Community]. In: Blomeyer W, Schachtschneider K A (eds) Die Europäische Union als Rechtsgemeinschaft [The European Union as a community of law]. Duncker&Humboldt, Berlin, pp 9–36
Żurawski vel Grajewski P (2023) Small states in the political system of the European Union. In: Bajda P (ed) Small states within the European Union Challenges – dilemmas – strategies. Wydawnictwo Akademii Wymiaru Sprawiedliwości, Warsaw, pp 33–70

Other Sources

Conference on the Future of Europe Franco-German non-paper on key questions and guidelines, https://www.politico.eu/wp-content/uploads/2019/11/Conference-on-the-Future-of-Europe.pdf. Accessed 30 January 2025
Declaration on Article 15(5) and (6), Article 17(6) and (7) and Article 18 of the Treaty on European Union. OJ C 202, 7.6.2016, p 338
Joint Declaration of the Ninth Summit of the Three Seas Initiative Vilnius, Lithuania, 11 April 2024. https://media.voog.com/0000/0046/4166/files/Declaration.pdf. Accessed 24 January 2025
Living standards across the EU: consumption per inhabitant https://european-union.europa.eu/principles-countries-history/facts-and-figures-european-union_en
Report of the Franco-German Working Group on the EU Institutional Reform, Paris-Berlin. 18 September 2023. https://institutdelors.eu/wp-content/uploads/2023/12/20230919-Group-of-Twelve-REPORT.pdf. Accessed 30 January 2025
Report A9-0337/2023 on proposals of the European Parliament for the amendment of the Treaties (2022/2051(INL)), 7.11.2023 Committee on Constitutional Affairs. https://www.europarl.europa.eu/doceo/document/A-9-2023-0337_EN.html. Accessed 16 December 2024
Three Seas Story (undated) https://3seas.eu/about/threeseasstory. Accessed 20 January 2025

Magdalena Bainczyk is a university professor, Ph.D. Habil., and chief legal analyst at the Institute for Western Affairs (Poznań), and professor of the Andrzej Frycz Modrzewski University (Kraków), Poland.

Chapter 17
20 Years Later: Lessons from Latvia's Accession to the European Union and Their Implications for Ukraine's European Union Membership

Edmunds Broks, Christoph Schewe, Arnis Buka and Lolita Buka

Contents

Abstract This chapter explores the European Union (EU) accession experiences of Latvia and Ukraine, analysing how Latvia's structured and politically supported path to EU membership offers both insights and contrasts to Ukraine's current trajectory. The study examines legal and institutional reforms undertaken by Latvia, particularly its constitutional and judicial transformations during the 1990s and early 2000s. In contrast, Ukraine's accession bid is shaped by ongoing war, geopolitical tensions,

E. Broks (✉) · A. Buka · L. Buka
Faculty of Law, University of Latvia, Riga, Latvia
e-mail: Edmunds.Broks@lu.lv

A. Buka
e-mail: Arnis.Buka@lu.lv

L. Buka
e-mail: Lolita.Buka@lu.lv

C. Schewe
University of Applied Sciences Kiel-Altenholz/Reinfeld, Altenholz, Germany
e-mail: Schewe@fhvd-sh.de

I. Isokaitė-Valužė and H. Šinkūnas (eds.), *The European Union 2004-2024*,
https://doi.org/10.1007/978-94-6265-718-2_17

and internal challenges such as corruption and judicial politicization. The chapter argues that while Latvia's experience provides useful lessons—particularly on how to align the national legal system with EU law—Ukraine's integration process will require a more flexible and politically adaptive approach from the EU. The chapter suggests that Ukraine's strategic significance may prompt a rethinking of traditional enlargement mechanisms, potentially leading to a new model of EU integration.

Keywords Accession to the EU · Candidate country · Copenhagen criteria · Article 49 Treaty of the EU · Acquis communautaire · Ukraine · Latvia · EU association agreements

17.1 Introduction

On 1 May 2024 Latvia along with 9 other EU Member States celebrated 20 years of EU membership. Today they are not *new* Member States anymore, however, their experiences of the accession process and the 2004 "Big Bang" enlargement are still vivid and well documented.[1] Three of these accession states, i.e., Latvia, Lithuania, and Estonia, had been incorporated into the USSR from 1945 to 1991, just as Ukraine had.[2] Due to their common past in Soviet structures, there may well be similarities, parallels or common problems in Ukraine's accession process that Latvia had experienced in the late 1990s. These experiences can be shared, mistakes avoided and best practices adopted and transposed. As both Latvia and Ukraine share historical parallels, transitioning from former Soviet republics to aspiring EU members, necessitating comprehensive political, economic, and legal reforms, Latvia's accession may offer valuable insights for Ukraine's current EU integration efforts.

However, when reflecting on experiences from over 20 years ago, one observes that the world, the EU, EU Member States and societies have changed considerably since then. Firstly, the world has become more fragmented and polarised.[3] Instead of the pursuit towards a frequently quoted "end of history",[4] we observe a worldwide polarisation accompanied by the formation of geopolitical blocs which follow confrontational approaches rather than seeking common solutions.[5] Secondly, the EU itself has undergone considerable changes. Quantitatively, the EU expanded from 15 to 28 Member States before Brexit reduced this number to 27. Furthermore, apart from the mere number of Member States, the number of EU citizens, and the size of the EU, there have been substantive changes regarding values, law and also the

[1] For the perspective of Estonia as one of the accession states, see e.g. Ministry of Foreign Affairs of Estonia (2018) Estonia's Way into the EU. https://eu.mfa.ee/wp-content/uploads/sites/19/2018/09/Estonias_way_into_the_EU.pdf. Accessed 12 January 2024.

[2] Extensively below in Sect. 17.2.1.

[3] Wagner 2024, p. 383.

[4] See e.g. Fukuyama 1992.

[5] See e.g. Münkler 2023.

heterogeneity of the Member States.[6] Today the differences among EU States extend beyond economic disparities and increasingly include diverging political orientations, shifting from socio-liberal to the conservative or even far-right positions.[7] While this might be seen as a usual development in democracies over time, a notable asymmetry has emerged in the transformation of previously shared attitudes. This divergence is particularly evident in the accession process, where Article 49 of the Treaty on European Union (TEU) references the values enshrined in Article 2. In recent years, Member States have displayed increasingly divergent interpretations of these values, leading to open disagreements, particularly concerning the rule of law, democracy, migration policies, and minority rights.[8]

It must also be noted at the outset that the Latvian experience of the accession process in the 1990s, although relevant for Ukraine due to some similarities with pre-accession Latvia (e.g., being post-Soviet, being relatively poorer than Western Europe and struggling to fight corruption as well as being in need of radically reforming judicial and administrative institutions), must be applied to Ukraine in 2024 rather cautiously. For one thing, Ukraine has not been encapsulated in the 1990s—it has grown and developed in its own way over decades and is quite a different creature from the Ukraine of the 1990s[9] and also from pre-accession Latvia. Moreover, the geopolitical context surrounding Ukraine's accession process is markedly different from that of Latvia, particularly given the ongoing Russian war of aggression and the associated security concerns that dominate Ukraine's European integration agenda. Additionally, Ukraine's economy, while still facing significant challenges, has diversified and modernized in ways that set it apart from the post-Soviet transition economies of the late 20th century. Also the scale and complexity of institutional reforms required in Ukraine, particularly with regard to anti-corruption measures, surpass those faced by Latvia at the time thus shaping a more intricate and demanding accession process for Ukraine today.

The structure of the chapter unfolds across three main subchapters. Section 17.2 examines the shared Soviet legacy and details the requirements of EU accession. Then Sect. 17.3 traces Ukraine's EU accession process, from the first cooperation agreement in 1994 to constitutional reforms and candidate status being granted in 2022, as well as the unique challenges that the country is currently facing. Sect. 17.4 turns to Latvia's accession experience, offering a chronology of its integration, legal reforms, and institutional transformations, particularly in its constitutional and judicial structures. Finally, conclusions are drawn from Latvia's accession process, contrasting Latvia's relatively smooth and politically supported EU accession in the 1990s with Ukraine's much more complicated and uncertain membership prospects today.

---

[6] Schewe and Blome 2021.

[7] Down and Han 2021, pp. 65–81.

[8] Cianetti et al. 2020, pp. 1–14.

[9] See e.g. Karatnycky 2024.

17.2 Historical Departure Points and the Accession Requirements

17.2.1 Shared Soviet Legacy

For both Latvia and Ukraine there is the shared historical legacy of being former USSR Republics (1945–1991). Even though the political system of the USSR underwent various changes over time and generalisations always bear inaccuracies, one may note that several defining characteristics remained relatively consistent and had lasting impacts. These were in particular the highly centralized decision-making structures in the USSR, dominated by the Communist Party, its Central Committee and foremost its Secretary General,[10] which allowed very minimal regional autonomy in the entire Soviet empire.

This centralized governance was also reflected in economic structures—centrally planned economies with emphasis on heavy industry, collective agriculture, and state ownership.[11] Legal and administrative systems, besides safeguarding governance, strived to achieve the ideological objectives of a totalitarian communist state.[12] Accordingly, the Soviet legal and administrative frameworks prioritised strict control over individuals and any kind of private enterprise.[13] In a more general way, one observes that laws were tools of governance rather than principles of justice, exemplified by the lack of an independent judiciary.[14] In line with the ideologically inspired political and legal system, the USSR in both Latvia and in Ukraine enforced cultural and educational policies which prioritized the dominance of the Russian language. In order to achieve uniformity, this often resulted in the suppression of local languages, cultures and national identities, in favour of cultivating a pan-Soviet citizen.[15]

This shared historical experience left similar structures and problems in the former USSR republics. Soviet heritage may have facilitated oligarch structures,[16] issues of corruption,[17] centralized governance culture,[18] and—particularly in the years following the collapse of the USSR—economic reliance on former USSR trade

---

[10] See e.g. Merl 2019, pp. 44, 47.

[11] With further references see: Schewe 2013; Schewe and Aliyev 2011, p. 568.

[12] Aust et al. 2020, p. 6.

[13] Goehrke 2010, pp. 133–136.

[14] The Venice Commission provides access to reports on a range of aspects relating to the rule of law, including the independence of courts and judges. See e.g. Venice Commission (Council of Europe) (n.d.) Documents by Country. https://www.venice.coe.int/WebForms/documents/by_country.aspx?lang=EN. Accessed 30 January 2025; Mälksoo 2016, pp. 3, 110.

[15] Mehnert 1981; Alexievich 2016.

[16] Kappeler et al. 2003; Fortescue 2009; Hildermeier 2017, p. 1145; Goehrke 2010, p. 139.

[17] Halbach 2020.

[18] Aust 2019, p. 104.

networks. Additionally, many former Soviet states, including Latvia and Ukraine, still need to cope with regional disparities and tensions related to minority rights.[19]

The transition from command to market economies first and foremost involved privatization in which the former Soviet republics were not equally successful.[20] Notwithstanding the general outcomes, this process was accompanied by significant challenges in both Latvia and Ukraine, including economic inequalities, high unemployment, massive emigration and the need to rebuild competitive industries. However, relatively early after (re)gaining independence, their further development went in considerably different directions.[21] While for Latvia EU and NATO membership were paramount priorities, Ukraine remained exposed and closely attached to Russia.[22]

17.2.2 Accession Requirements

The transition from a post-Soviet state to an EU Member State obviously requires profound political, economic, legal and institutional reforms. However, EU law and in particular Article 49 TEU, which is the only norm in EU primary law regulating accession,[23] deals with it in a very broad and perhaps even rudimentary[24] way:

> Any European State which respects the values referred to in Article 2 and is committed to promoting them may apply to become a member of the Union. The European Parliament and national Parliaments shall be notified of this application. The applicant State shall address its application to the Council, which shall act unanimously after consulting the Commission and after receiving the consent of the European Parliament, which shall act by a majority of its component members. The conditions of eligibility agreed upon by the European Council shall be taken into account.

[19] On the other hand, sometimes for the same reasons, the shared history, language proficiency and common experiences may foster cooperation, e.g., before the Russian attack on Ukraine, proficiency in the Russian language was seen as an asset and facilitator for communication. This, however, is not obvious anymore, as today the language has become a symbol of the common threat. Accordingly, inability to communicate in Russian is often considered as an advantage in order to uncouple from Russian influence and the Soviet past. On a range of aspects in Soviet daily life, see, e.g., Schlögel 2017; regarding Soviet cultural influence on the Baltic States. see, e.g., Angermann and Brüggemann 2018, p. 301.

[20] An OECD working paper written in 2004 in a diplomatic-optimistic style, sheds a light on the challenges facing some Asian states that formerly belonged to the USSR and that differ from the Eastern and Central European states that had joined the EU: Organisation for Economic Co-operation and Development (OECD) (2004) The Role of Multilateral and Regional Trade Disciplines in the Central Asian Countries. https://one.oecd.org/document/TD/TC/WP(2004)19/FINAL/en/pdf. Accessed 30 January 2025.

[21] On the different directions of State transformation after the collapse of the USSR, see Beichelt 2022; Pleines 2014, p. 52.

[22] Kappeler 2019.

[23] Kochenov and Janse 2022.

[24] Ohler 2021.

> The conditions of admission and the adjustments to the Treaties on which the Union is founded, which such admission entails, shall be the subject of an agreement between the Member States and the applicant State. This agreement shall be submitted for ratification by all the contracting States in accordance with their respective constitutional requirements.

Thus Article 49 TEU does not provide any precise guidelines for the process[25] but merely structures the accession into several phases, which—according to the subjective view on the process—may amount to either two[26] or three phases.[27] When considering three phases, one would count a first phase, which concerns the *application*—being dealt with in the first paragraph of Article 49 TEU. Those views distinguishing only two phases do not consider *application* as a separate phase and rather consider it as part of the second phase. The second is the *pre-candidate-phase*; while a third one is frequently labelled as the *accession-phase* as it primarily comprises accession negotiations (Article 49 (2) TEU).

Article 49 TEU only once explicitly refers to substantive law, namely to the values set out in Article 2 TEU. The Lisbon Treaty altered this provision and the last sentence now also states that: "*The conditions of eligibility agreed upon by the European Council shall be taken into account*" which opens the *pre-candidate-phase* to further substantive requirements. Thus, unlike Article 49 (1) TEU, which involves the EU's institutions and refers to the procedure of accessions, the second paragraph stipulates that "[...] *an agreement between the Member States and the applicant State*" may determine the substantive conditions of the accession.

Aside from adjusting procedures within the EU, the fifth enlargement with 12 states applying for EU membership created a general practical need to prepare these aspiring members to handle the political, legal and economic realities in the EU.[28] For this purpose, the *Copenhagen European Council,* which was addressing the upcoming accession, agreed in 1993 (and later reaffirmed in the Madrid European Council in 1995),[29] that applicant countries must meet certain requirements. It was only later that the *Copenhagen Criteria*—which had been applied during the fifth enlargement without being codified—were formally referred to in Article 49(1) of the TEU. They require states to possess stable institutions to guarantee democracy, the rule of law, human rights and respect for and protection of minorities. With regard to economic aspects, applicant states should have a functioning market economy, the capacity to withstand competitive pressure and market forces within the Union and to be able to meet obligations relating to the objectives of political, economic and monetary union.[30]

---

[25] Schewe et al. 2024.

[26] Terhechte 2017, para 21.

[27] Ohler 2021, paras 24–25.

[28] From the perspective of Estonia as one of the accession states, see Ministry of Foreign Affairs of Estonia (2018) Estonia's Way into the EU. Available at: https://eu.mfa.ee/wp-content/uploads/sites/19/2018/09/Estonias_way_into_the_EU.pdf. Accessed 12 January 2024.

[29] European Council (1993) Copenhagen Presidency conclusions, 1993, pp. 1–2. Available at: http://www.consilium.europa.eu/ueDocs/cms_Data/docs/pressData/de/ec/72924.pdf. Accessed 5 February 2025.

[30] See e.g. Hillion 2004.

Furthermore, candidates must adopt the *acquis communautaire*, i.e. effectively implement the rules, standards and policies that constitute the body of EU law. The scope of this latter requirement has continuously expanded and already in previous accessions the *acquis* comprised approximately 90.000 pages that had to be translated and incorporated into national legal systems.[31] This seemingly minor detail illustrates that practical requirements far exceed what one might initially expect when reading the minimalistic wording of Article 49 TEU.[32] Moreover, it demonstrates that, with the growing bulk of EU law—including case law of the Court of Justice of the European Union (CJEU)—meeting these requirements is becoming increasingly challenging for applicant states.[33]

17.3 Ukraine's Accession Process

17.3.1 Chronology of Ukraine's Accession

After gaining independence in 1991, Ukraine gradually developed closer ties with the EU, signing its first cooperation agreement[34] in 1994, much like Latvia. Over time, this partnership deepened, leading to the negotiation of the EU-Ukraine Association Agreement.[35] The signing of this agreement was delayed in 2013 when then-President Yanukovych, under pressure from Russia, refused to sign, sparking the Euromaidan protests and the Revolution of Dignity. Following his ousting in 2014, Ukraine keenly reaffirmed its pro-European course and finally signed the Agreement.

While the Association Agreement marked a significant step in Ukraine's European integration, it differed in a crucial aspect from the Association Agreements signed by Latvia and other Eastern European countries before their accession. Latvia's Association Agreement with the EU stated EU membership as a goal, setting a clear pathway for accession.[36] However, not all EU Association Agreements include such

[31] European Commission (2007) Translation: Where do we stand after completion of the fifth enlargement? MEMO/07/76, Brussels, 23 February 2007. https://ec.europa.eu/commission/presscorner/detail/de/MEMO_07_76. Accessed 12 January 2024.

[32] The reach of the Simmental decision illustrates the reach of the impact of EU law for member states. See: Beutel et al. 2022, pp. 123–142.

[33] European Commission (2005) *Guide to the Main Administrative Structures Required for Implementing the Acquis.* http://ec.europa.eu/enlargement/pdf/enlargement_process/accession_process/how_does_a_country_join_the_eu/negotiations_croatia_turkey/adminstructures_version_may05_35_ch_public_en.pdf. Accessed 5 February 2025.

[34] Partnership and Cooperation Agreement between the European Communities and their Member States, and Ukraine. OJ, 1998, L 49.

[35] Association Agreement between the European Union and its Member States, of the one part, and Ukraine of the other part, OJ, 2014, L 161; see e.g. Van der Loo et al. 2014.

[36] Article 1 as one of the aims of the treaty states: "to provide an appropriate framework for the gradual integration of Latvia into the European Union"—Europe Agreement Establishing an Association Between the European Communities and Their Member States, of the One Part, and

a provision, as they primarily aim to establish political and economic cooperation rather than guarantee future membership (e.g., the EU's Association Agreements with Morocco and Tunisia). Similar to the Morocco and Tunisia agreements, the Ukraine Association Agreement does not contain a clause stating EU accession as its objective.

However, Ukraine's Association Agreement altogether stands out from all other agreements of this type. Article 1 outlines a much broader and deeper political and economic integration than in any prior Association Agreement, stating that the agreement aims to "establish conditions for enhanced economic and trade relations leading towards Ukraine's gradual integration in the EU Internal Market". In addition, the agreement also aims to "promote gradual convergence in the area of foreign and security policy" and to "to complete the transition into a functioning market economy by means of, inter alia, the progressive approximation of its legislation to that of the Union".[37] The Association Agreement spans over 2000 pages in the Official Journal and has no less than 46 annexes detailing both institutional cooperation and providing for adoption of large parts of the EU's *acquis*. Thus, despite the lack of explicit membership prospects, as was the case for Latvia, Ukraine's agreement nonetheless includes an unprecedented level of integration without the promise of EU membership.

For its part Ukraine has continuously made efforts to solidify EU orientation in its internal law. For example, Ukraine's Constitution as amended in 2019, explicitly provides for the country's strategic course toward full EU membership, thus reinforcing its commitment to European integration. Also, the preamble of the Constitution affirms "the irreversibility of Ukraine's European and Euro-Atlantic path". Article 85 assigns the *Verkhovna Rada* the responsibility of shaping policies aligned with EU accession, while Article 102 designates the President as the guarantor of this course. Additionally, Article 116 tasks the Cabinet of Ministers with ensuring the state's strategic course towards full membership of Ukraine in the European Union.

Russia's full-scale invasion provided a significant impetus to accelerate Ukraine's accession—Ukraine submitted its application on February 28, 2022—just four days after Russia's invasion. As mentioned before, Article 49 of the TEU succinctly states that the applicant addresses its application to the Council,[38] which then acts unanimously after consulting the Commission and after receiving the consent of the European Parliament.[39] Accordingly the Council forwarded Ukraine's application to the European Commission, requesting it to draft an Opinion assessing Ukraine's ability to

---

the Republic of Latvia, of the Other Part, opened for signature 12 June 1995, *Official Journal of the European Communities*, L 403 (entered into force 1 February 1998).

[37] Association Agreement between the European Union and its Member States, of the one part, and Ukraine of the other part, OJ, 2014, L 161.

[38] The TFEU and the TEU refer simply to "the Council"—that is the Council of Ministers, not to be confused with the European Council, i.e., the meeting of the Heads of State and Government of the member states.

[39] Article 49 TEU provides that: "The conditions of eligibility agreed upon by the European Council shall be taken into account". The Article thus indicates that the requirements for accession are not uniformly set, but may be elaborated in accordance with the specifics of the situation.

meet the accession criteria.[40] The Commission subsequently provided Ukraine with two detailed questionnaires—one focused on political and economic criteria and the other addressing EU *acquis* chapters. Based on Ukraine's responses, the Commission issued a favourable Opinion on June 17, 2022, recommending that Ukraine be granted candidate status.[41] Shortly thereafter, the European Parliament also endorsed Ukraine.[42] With the Commission and the Parliament supporting Ukraine, the European Council conferred candidate status[43] on Ukraine during its meeting of 23 June 2022.[44]

17.3.2 Ukraine's EU Candidate Status

The European Council's decision to grant candidate status was documented in its 'Meeting Conclusion'. The exact legal status of this document is somewhat ambivalent. This document is not a legislative act under Article 288 of the Treaty on the Functioning of the European Union (TFEU). While the European Council is an EU institution, Article 15(1) TEU explicitly precludes it from exercising legislative functions. Moreover, under Article 263 TFEU, European Council acts are subject to judicial review by the CJEU only if they are "intended to produce legal effects vis-à-vis third parties". Similarly, the Commission's Opinion, framed as a "Communication to the European Parliament, the European Council, and the Council," lacks binding legal effects on third parties and is thus not subject to judicial review under Article 263 TFEU. The same legal status applies to the European Parliament's resolution endorsing Ukraine's candidacy.

As for any possible role of the CJEU in judicial review of any of the above-mentioned acts, it must first of all be noted that the CJEU evaluates legal effects of

[40] The Opinion evaluates not only Ukraine's compliance with the Copenhagen criteria but also its administrative capacity and efforts to implement the Association Agreement, including commitments under the Deep and Comprehensive Free Trade Area; see Eebel 2011; Darvas et al. 2024.

[41] European Commission (2022) Commission Opinion on Ukraine's Application for Membership of the European Union. COM(2022) 407 final, Brussels, 17 June 2022. https://neighbourhood-enlargement.ec.europa.eu/system/files/2022-06/Ukraine%20Opinion%20and%20Annex.pdf. Accessed 12 February 2025.

[42] European Parliament (2022) Resolution of 23 June 2022 on the Candidate Status of Ukraine, the Republic of Moldova, and Georgia (2022/2716(RSP)). (2023/C 32/01). https://eur-lex.europa.eu/legal-content/EN/TXT/PDF/?uri=CELEX:52022IP0249. Accessed 12 February 2025.

[43] The candidate country status has sparked legal and political debates on what, if any, legal implications the candidate country status actually carries or if it remains only a political gesture. This discussion is particularly relevant in assessing whether the European Council's decision could be subject to judicial review in the CJEU. See e.g. Kochenov and Janse 2022.

[44] European Council (2022) Conclusions of 23 and 24 June 2022. https://www.consilium.europa.eu/media/57442/2022-06-2324-euco-conclusions-en.pdf. Accessed 12 February 2025.

an act based on content, context, and institutional powers rather than the formal designation of an act.[45] In the case of candidate status, the decision does not impose binding legal obligations on the EU, its institutions, or the candidate country. Instead, it functions as a political commitment and a framework for future negotiations rather than an enforceable legal act. This seems to be in line with the CJEU's general reluctance to intervene in political decisions related to enlargement, as so far, the CJEU in its case-law has rarely addressed the concept of "candidate country" directly. For example, in *Korkmaz*, the General Court dismissed an application challenging Turkey's progress report without addressing the legal implications of candidate status.[46] Similarly, in *Spain v. Commission*, the CJEU interpreted a reference to 'candidate countries' in EU regulation as merely illustrative, thereby avoiding a substantive analysis of what candidate status entails.[47] These cases highlight the CJEU's reluctance to assign concrete legal effects to candidate status and suggest that any challenge to the European Council's decision would face significant hurdles.

Thus, all the above-mentioned instruments exemplify EU's reliance on "soft law"[48] in the accession process, which, while devoid of legally binding force, carries significant practical implications. First among these is that granting of candidate status serves as a potent demonstration of solidarity with Ukraine. This designation, representing a step closer to EU membership, uplifts the morale of Ukraine's armed forces and civilian population—a crucial psychological asset during wartime. Secondly, candidacy incentivizes Ukraine to embark on critical domestic reforms, addressing corruption, judicial independence, administrative efficiency, and other priority areas. The accession process exerts considerable pressure on the Ukrainian government from EU institutions, civil society, and the media to expedite these reforms. Thirdly, candidate status facilitates broader access to EU financial resources and support mechanisms.

The initial stages of the accession process, culminating in candidate status, also establish a framework for subsequent negotiations. The accession criteria, the Commission's questionnaire, and its Opinion collectively provide a preliminary roadmap of the requirements Ukraine must fulfil for EU membership. This roadmap is elaborated upon during the *acquis* screening process, where the Commission and candidate country conduct an in-depth review of EU legislation, offering a detailed understanding of the obligations entailed by membership.

While Article 49 TEU broadly outlines the procedural steps for candidacy, the process itself largely involves political decision-making rather than the creation of enforceable legal rights or obligations.[49] The stages—application submission,

---

[45] Court of Justice of the European Union (CJEU), *Hungary v Commission*, Judgment, 13 February 2014, Case C-31/13 P, para 55.

[46] General Court, *Korkmaz and Others v Commission*, Judgment, 30 March 2006, Case T-2/04.

[47] Court of Justice of the European Union (CJEU), *Spain v Commission*, Judgment, 17 January 2023, Case C-632/20 P, para 56.

[48] Snyder 1993; Peters 2011, pp. 423–424.

[49] Kochenov and Janse 2022.

Commission Opinion, European Parliament consent, and European Council Conclusions—are primarily political acts within an internal EU decision-making framework. General principles of law such as legitimate expectations, estoppel, or *venire contra factum proprium* are binding on EU institutions.[50] For instance, the Commission might be expected to refrain from imposing criteria or raising standards that were not previously stipulated or accepted as sufficient for Ukraine.

However, such arguments often hold limited practical sway, because the process for transitioning from a candidate to a member is negotiation and legal concepts such as *estoppel* are likely to be used only as bargaining chips. EU law does not confer a right to candidacy or a guaranteed membership to a candidate. Although the EU ever increasingly legalizes its operations, the pre-accession process remains fundamentally political, comprising formalized stages that hardly establish definitive legal rights or obligations. As a result, Ukraine's journey to EU membership will mostly depend on political talks rather than judicial decisions.

17.3.3 Challenges to Ukraine's Accession

The first obvious challenge for Ukraine is to fulfil the Copenhagen Criteria, i.e., political, economic, and *acquis*-related conditionalities. The political criterion, focused on the stability of institutions guaranteeing democracy, the rule of law, human rights, and the protection of minorities, may pose a formidable challenge for Ukraine. Adherence to the rule of law and judicial independence forms the bedrock of EU membership.[51] Accordingly, Ukraine's efforts to reform its judiciary, curb corruption, and enhance transparency constitute critical benchmarks of its readiness. Despite reforms, persistent issues related to politicization of Ukraine's courts and weak anti-corruption mechanisms underscore the need for further legal and institutional reforms.[52] Endemic corruption remains a considerable hurdle for Ukraine, frequently highlighted in the European Commission's progress reports and scholarly analyses.[53] Widespread corruption undermines public trust, deters foreign investment, and challenges the effective application of law. As the EU struggles to ensure adherence to the rule of law within existing member states—exemplified by the establishment of the Rule of Law Mechanism and conditionality frameworks[54]—Ukraine also is under increasing pressure to align its legal infrastructure with EU standards. While recent initiatives, including the establishment of specialized anti-corruption courts and the National Anti-Corruption Bureau of Ukraine, signal political will, the actual efficacy of these institutions requires ongoing scrutiny.[55]

---

[50] See e.g. Lenaerts and Gutiérrez-Fons 2010; Tridimas 2006.

[51] Kochenov 2008, pp. 47–51.

[52] Schimmelfennig 2008.

[53] Vachudova 2019.

[54] Pech and Scheppele 2017.

[55] Burlyuk 2017.

Another major challenge is the incorporation and effective implementation of *acquis*. Notably, the Association Agreement and the Deep and Comprehensive Free Trade Area Agreement between the EU and Ukraine have spurred significant legislative and regulatory reforms.[56] However, full alignment with the *acquis* requires both legislative harmonization and robust administrative capacity, which Ukraine is somewhat lacking. Institutional inefficiency and regulatory fragmentation may impede smooth transposition of EU norms, especially in complex sectors such as environmental protection and public procurement.[57]

The most formidable challenge—or rather an existential threat—is the ongoing war of Russian aggression. EU membership presupposes clear and undisputed territorial boundaries, effective governance over national territory, and some degree of stability in external relations.[58] The war has not only diverted significant governmental resources away from long-term reforms but has also created political and legal uncertainties regarding the state's territorial jurisdiction. While the EU acknowledges Ukraine's sovereignty and territorial integrity, any formal accession framework is likely to address conflict-resolution mechanisms and the broader regional security context.[59]

Finally, the EU's own enlargement fatigue and Russia-friendly EU members pose a considerable challenge to Ukraine's membership. Although the EU has reaffirmed its commitment to an enlargement policy oriented toward the Western Balkans and Eastern Europe, it is far from the keen enthusiasm of the 1990s when Latvia was bidding to join. Populist nationalism combined with periods of economic stagnation and growing Euroscepticism obviously constrain the political will necessary to realize further enlargement.[60] Ukraine must therefore navigate not only its domestic reform agenda but also the shifting contours of EU politics and public opinion.

Thus Ukraine's pursuit of EU membership involves a complex interplay of legal, political, and geopolitical factors that extend far beyond the formal requirements of Article 49 TEU and the Copenhagen Criteria. Efforts to strengthen the rule of law, intensify anti-corruption measures, and fully align with the *acquis* are central to the accession trajectory. The ongoing war coupled with the EU's own internal challenges, further complicates the process. The accession journey thus hinges on Ukraine's capacity to implement robust legal and institutional reforms while adapting to the evolving dynamics of European integration, and last but not least—not losing the war.

---

[56] Kovziridze et al. 2016.

[57] Magen 2007, pp. 355–359.

[58] See e.g. Tsygankov 2015.

[59] Lannon and Van Elsuwege 2020, pp. 241–264.

[60] Bechev 2011, pp. 89–92.

17.4 Latvia's Experience in Meeting Accession Requirements

17.4.1 Chronology of Latvia's Accession

Membership of the EU was a long-term political goal for Latvia right from 1991.[61] The reforms of the legal system that were implemented after the regaining of independence were also thoroughly conditioned by EU membership aspirations.[62] However, Latvia's path to EU membership was a complex legal and political process that evolved through several key agreements, gradually integrating the country into the EU's legal framework. As other former USSR republics, Latvia had to overcome ingrained soviet structures which obstructed its path towards EU accession. Accordingly, the accession process differed from the previous enlargements in order to facilitate that Latvia—as well as the other candidates—would meet the Copenhagen Criteria. For this purpose, several pre-accession steps had been established in order to safeguard the transition and approximation of national political, economic and legal structures.

The first major step was the Cooperation Agreement of 1992.[63] This agreement aimed to establish and develop trade relations between the parties, providing a foundation for economic cooperation. While it primarily focused on granting each party most-favoured-nation status in trade-related matters, it did not extensively regulate economic integration or legislative harmonization. However, its preamble included a reference to future agreements that would incorporate legal alignment, signalling Latvia's commitment to deeper integration with the EU.[64]

The next critical step was the Free Trade Agreement of 1994.[65] This agreement replaced the previous Cooperation Agreement and significantly expanded economic ties by promoting free movement of goods, competition policies, and trade-related payments. Importantly, Article 36 of the agreement explicitly emphasized the need for gradual legal harmonization, particularly in trade-related areas such as anti-dumping measures, competition law, customs legislation, technical regulations, and standards. This marked an important moment in Latvia's legal alignment with the EU, as it established a structured approach for adopting EU law.

---

[61] Eihmanis 2019.

[62] See e.g. Pleps 2024.

[63] Agreement between the Republic of Latvia and the European Economic Community on trade and commercial and economic cooperation [Līgums starp Latvijas Republiku un Eiropas Ekonomisko Kopienu par tirdzniecību un komerciālo un ekonomisko sadarbību], opened for signature 11 May 1993, *Ziņotājs* (entered into force 1 July 1995), Article 3.

[64] Harbaceviča 2003.

[65] Free Trade Agreement Between the Republic of Latvia and the Republic of Hungary, opened for signature 3 June 1993, *Latvijas Vēstnesis* (entered into force 1 July 1994).

The most important pre-accession treaty between Latvia and the EU was signed on June 12, 1995—the Association Agreement, also known as the Europe Agreement.[66] This agreement, which came into force in February 1998, not only replaced the Free Trade Agreement but also served as the legal foundation for Latvia's accession process.[67] Article 1(2) of the Agreement explicitly stated that one of its objectives was to provide a framework for Latvia's gradual integration into the European Union, marking a formal commitment to its EU membership aspirations. Thus, in contrast to Ukraine's experience, Latvia's Association Agreement was a predesigned step in a gradual integration strategy with membership as the eventual goal; whereas Ukraine's agreement does not include a membership promise and became a focal point of geopolitical struggle.

Latvia's Association Agreement was substantively similar to the EU treaties, particularly in areas of trade, legal approximation and institutional cooperation. However, the Association Agreement was rarely applied in Latvian courts, so its legal effect within the national system remained limited. A key distinction between the Association Agreement and the EU treaties was that the jurisprudence of the CJEU was not binding for the interpretation of provisions analogous to those found in EU primary law. This limitation arises from the nature of Association Agreements as international agreements under Article 217 TFEU. The CJEU has confirmed in its case-law (e.g., Case C-162/96, *Racke*,[68] and Case C-63/99, *Gloszczuk*[69]) that while Association Agreements pursue the objective of integration with the EU, they do not automatically confer the same legal effects as EU primary law; nor do they impose a general obligation to interpret their provisions in strict alignment with the EU treaties unless such alignment is expressly provided for in the agreement's text or required by its context or purpose.

Thus, Latvia's Association Agreement provided a legal framework for alignment but did not impose direct judicial oversight by the CJEU in the same way as the EU treaties do. Unsurprisingly, the Association Agreement was rarely applied in Latvian courts, and the case law of the CJEU was seldom used as guidance in interpreting the rules of the Association Agreement. Overall, before Latvia's accession to the EU, the understanding of EU law in Latvian legal practice was not well established, reflecting limited engagement with EU legal principles prior to membership.

---

[66] Europe Agreement Establishing an Association Between the European Communities and Their Member States, of the One Part, and the Republic of Latvia, of the Other Part, opened for signature 12 June 1995, *Official Journal of the European Communities*, L 403 (entered into force 1 February 1998).

[67] See Harbacevičа 2003.

[68] Court of Justice of the European Union, Gerhard Köbler v. Republik Österreich, Judgment, 30 September 2003, Case C-224/01.

[69] Court of Justice of the European Union, The Queen v. Secretary of State for the Home Department, ex parte: Wieslaw Gloszczuk and Elzbieta Gloszczuk, Judgment, 27 September 2001, Case C-63/99.

Following the signing of the Association Agreement, Latvia formally applied for EU membership on 27 October 1995.[70] During Latvia's accession process, the granting of candidate country status was less formalized compared to later enlargements. There was no single, explicit decision designating Latvia as a candidate country. However, the Helsinki European Council Conclusions[71] (1999) can be regarded as the first document of the European Council that confirmed Latvia's candidate country status, since it consistently used the term "candidate country" when referring to Latvia and other applicant states. For instance, the document stated: "The European Council reaffirms the inclusive nature of the accession process, which now comprises 13 candidate States within a single framework".[72] This *de facto* recognition indicated that Latvia indeed was considered a candidate country, despite the absence of a distinct formal decision on its status.

Accession negotiations began shortly after, in February 2000. The process covered 31 negotiation chapters, requiring reforms in legal structures, economic policies, and governance. Key areas included judicial independence, anti-corruption measures, and market liberalization.[73] For example, in 2000 an anti-corruption strategy was adopted by the Cabinet of Ministers which, among other things, emphasised the need to comply with EU law.[74] Subsequently in 2002 a law on Corruption Prevention and Combating Bureau came into force, establishing a dedicated anti-corruption agency.[75] Latvia had committed to the establishment of such an agency to prevent and combat corruption earlier during the accession negotiations.[76] Financial support from various financial instruments like the PHARE programme aided to align Latvia's legislation with EU law. By December 2002, all negotiation chapters were closed, paving the way for accession.[77]

[70] Ministry of Foreign Affairs of Latvia (n.d.) Latvija ceļā uz iestāšanos Eiropas Savienībā. Available at: https://www.mfa.gov.lv/lv/media/3149/download?attachment. Accessed 30 January 2025.

[71] European Council (1997) Presidency Conclusions – Helsinki European Council. 10–11 December 1999. Available at: https://www.europarl.europa.eu/summits/hel1_en.htm. Accessed 30 January 2025.

[72] European Council (1999) Presidency Conclusions – Helsinki European Council. 10-11 December 1999, para 4. https://www.europarl.europa.eu/summits/hel1_en.htm. Accessed 30 January 2025.

[73] Accession Criteria (Copenhagen Criteria), established by the European Council, 21-22 June 1993, *EUR-Lex*. https://eur-lex.europa.eu/legal-content/EN/TXT/?uri=LEGISSUM:e50010&frontOfficeSuffix=%2F. Accessed 30 January 2025.

[74] Korupcijas novēršanas koncepcija (Corruption Prevention Concept), approved by the Cabinet of Ministers on 8 August 2000. https://www.knab.gov.lv/lv/media/60/download?attachment. A ccessed 30 January 2025.

[75] Law on Corruption Prevention and Combating Bureau, adopted 18 April 2002, *Latvijas Vēstnesis* No. 65, entered into force 1 May 2002.

[76] Annotation to the Law on the Corruption Prevention and Combating Bureau, 2002, https://www.saeima.lv/L_Saeima7/lasa-LP1168_0.htm. Accessed 30 January 2025.

[77] Ministry of Foreign Affairs of Latvia (n.d.) Latvija ceļā uz iestāšanos Eiropas Savienībā. https://www.mfa.gov.lv/lv/media/3149/download?attachment. Accessed 30 January 2025.

Latvia signed the Accession Treaty on April 16, 2003, and in a referendum on September 20, 2003, 67% of voters supported EU membership.[78] Official accession followed on May 1, 2004, granting Latvia access to the EU single market, structural funds, and full participation in EU institutions. Subsequent integration efforts led to the adoption of the euro in 2014 and Latvia's entry into the Schengen Area in 2007 further enhancing its integration.[79]

17.4.2 Accession's Impact on Latvia's Legal System

17.4.2.1 Impact on Government and Legislative Process

It comes as no surprise that the influence of the EU on Latvian institutions and policy has been profound, going far beyond the rather technical adoption of *acquis*.[80] In EU affairs, the executive branch does not operate as a fully unified entity, as different ministers represent the country in the Council of the EU meetings depending on the policy area under discussion. As more ministries become involved in EU matters, the need for a well-structured and efficient coordination system becomes increasingly critical—both at the inter-ministerial level as well as within individual ministries.[81]

Before joining the EU, Latvia developed a structured institutional framework to manage the adoption and integration of EU law. A key institution in this process was the European Integration Bureau (*Eiropas integrācijas birojs*), established in 1995. It coordinated Latvia's EU accession efforts and facilitated negotiations. One of the Bureau's key functions was "to provide opinions on the compliance of regulatory acts with the requirements of the Europe Agreement and to submit proposals to state administration institutions on necessary amendments to regulatory acts to ensure their compliance with European Union law".[82] The Bureau also led public awareness campaigns and training in EU law for public officials. Overall, it played a central role in Latvia's EU accession by overseeing the alignment of national legislation with EU law and ensuring institutional capacities necessary for EU membership.

After Latvia's accession in 2004, the Bureau was dissolved and its responsibilities were transferred to the Ministry of Foreign Affairs and other institutions. However, Latvia's positive experience with the European Integration Bureau highlights the importance of establishing a single main institution with wide ranging competences to oversee the harmonization of national law with EU law. Such an institution not

---

[78] Providus (2003) 20. septembra referenduma oficiālie rezultāti. *Providus*, 8 October 2003. https://providus.lv/raksti/20-septembra-referenduma-oficialie-rezultati/. Accessed 30 January 2025.

[79] European Commission Representation in Latvia (n.d.) Latvija Eiropas Savienībā. https://latvia.representation.ec.europa.eu/par-mums/latvija-eiropas-savieniba_lv. Accessed 30 January 2025.

[80] Eihmanis 2019.

[81] Rometsch and Wessels 1996, p. 332.

[82] Eiropas integrācijas biroja nolikums (European Integration Bureau Regulation), *MK noteikumi* (Cabinet Regulations), *Latvijas Vēstnesis*, 23 September 1997, part 4.2.

only facilitates legal alignment during the accession process but also ensures that compliance with EU law becomes a routine part of the national legislative process. For example, in Latvia, a systematic requirement introduced by the Cabinet of Ministers has been in place since 2001, which requires ministries to include information in the annotation of any draft legislative act regarding their compliance with EU law.[83]

17.4.2.2 Impact on Latvian Constitutional Law

The adaptation of the national legal system for EU membership goes far beyond mere technical harmonization of norms or the allocation of governmental responsibilities. Latvia's experience demonstrates that upon joining the EU, the country must thoroughly assess the compatibility of its constitutional foundations and establish a constitutional framework for accession. Several options were discussed in the Latvian legal doctrine as to whether and how the Latvian Constitution should be amended due to EU membership.[84] In the end, Latvia amended two articles of its Constitution, Article 68, which concerns international agreements, was expanded with a provision stating that Latvia can delegate part of its sovereignty to international organizations. While Article 79, which regulates how referendums are held, was amended to include special rules for referendums related to Latvia's EU membership and potential substantial future changes to its membership terms. From Latvia's experience in this area, several key issues can be identified that could be relevant for Ukraine as it prepares to join the EU.

Perhaps the most crucial consideration is whether the Constitution should explicitly include EU-derived constitutional principles or only regulate accession procedures. The Latvian approach was that substantive constitutional amendments are unnecessary; instead, a reference to Latvia's EU membership process would provide a foundation for interpreting existing norms in line with EU law.[85] This approach ensures flexibility in adapting to evolving EU legal standards without requiring frequent constitutional revisions. Another key principle that Latvia adhered to in amending its constitution was to formulate amendments as concisely as possible. To minimize legal disruption, constitutional amendments should be limited both in scope and in wording. Even small changes can have far-reaching consequences, particularly in Latvia's succinct Constitution, which relies on precise interpretation techniques.[86]

Latvia tailored its constitutional amendments specifically to accommodate accession to the EU and NATO while ensuring they would not facilitate joining other

---

[83] See Kārtība, kādā aizpilda normatīvā akta projekta anotāciju (Procedure for Completing the Annotation of a Draft Legislative Act), *MK instrukcija* (Cabinet Instruction), *Latvijas Vēstnesis*, 28 August 2001.

[84] Levits 2000.

[85] Anonymous 2001; Pleps 2003.

[86] Anonymous 2001.

organizations like the Russia led Commonwealth of Independent States. The amendments were designed to allow sovereignty delegation only to organizations that align with Latvia's democratic values and international commitments, thereby preventing any legal framework that could enable integration into non-democratic or oppressive organizations.[87] This approach may be particularly relevant for Ukraine which experiences and is likely to continue to experience a certain amount of internal political division as to its preferred course.[88]

Furthermore, ensuring democratic legitimacy is crucial in the process of EU accession. Due to its major impact, EU accession requires the highest level of legitimacy, best ensured through a referendum. The formulation of the referendum question must be clear and unambiguous to ensure that voters fully understand the issue. Thus, Latvia chose not to vote directly on the constitutional amendments themselves, as they were somewhat complex due to legal nuances. Instead, the citizens were given the opportunity to answer a straightforward question: "Are you in favour of Latvia's membership in the European Union?"

After Latvia's accession to the European Union, the Constitution underwent further amendments in 2004.[89] These modifications were implemented particularly to harmonize Latvia's legal system with the substantive law of the European Union. Specifically, Article 98 was revised to enable Latvia to execute European Arrest Warrants concerning its own citizens, thereby aligning national legal provisions with EU judicial cooperation mechanisms. Additionally, Article 101 of the Constitution was supplemented to enshrine the right of EU citizens to participate in local elections in Latvia. This amendment was grounded in Article 22(1) TFEU (formerly Article 19 TEC), which stipulates that every EU citizen residing in a Member State of which they are not a national shall have the right to vote and to stand as a candidate in municipal elections under the same conditions as nationals of that state.[90] Some of these amendments to the Latvian Constitution needed to be further elaborated in specific laws, which are also part of Latvia's constitutional legal system.[91] A prominent example is the notion of referendum as the procedural mechanism through which Latvia joined the European Union. In this context, the most important legal act is the Law on National Referendums and Legislative Initiatives, which established detailed regulations on the procedure for holding referendums and who is entitled to initiate them.

[87] *Ibid.*

[88] However, 2019 amendments to Ukraine's Constitution, particularly Articles 85, 102 and 116 already attempt to solidify Ukraine's orientation towards the EU.

[89] Amendments to the Constitution of the Republic of Latvia, adopted 29 October 2004, *Latvijas Vēstnesis* No. 172, entered into force 9 November 2004.

[90] Krūma and Statkus 2019.

[91] Annotation to the Amendments to the Constitution of the Republic of Latvia, 2004. https://www.saeima.lv/Lapas/8Sae_Lprj/lasa-dd=LP0158_0.htm. Accessed 8 February 2025.

17.4.2.3 Impact on the Latvian Judicial System

It is the responsibility of national courts to enforce such foundational principles of EU law as direct effect and primacy of EU law established by the CJEU. Since the CJEU's ruling in *Van Gend & Loos*, individuals have had the right to directly invoke many provisions of EU law before national courts. Consequently, any national court, when handling a case involving EU legal norms, must apply these norms and acknowledge their supremacy over national legislation.[92] Therefore, upon accession to the EU, a country must establish a comprehensive legal framework that not only obligates national courts to uphold EU law but also provides clear procedural mechanisms for its effective implementation in judicial practice.[93]

To ensure the effective application of the EU law in Latvian courts, national procedural laws were amended to include brief, but explicit references to main legal principles of EU law.[94] This legislative strategy not only acknowledged the autonomous legal authority of EU law but also introduced practical guidelines to assist national courts in applying it within domestic proceedings. One of the key aspects of this approach was incorporating references to the preliminary ruling procedure into Latvian procedural laws. While the ultimate legal basis for preliminary rulings remains EU law itself, Latvian legislation was adapted to inform judges of their ability to refer cases to the CJEU. This is reflected in provisions such as Article 5.1 of the Civil Procedure Law, Article 104.1 of the Administrative Procedure Law, and Article 478(2) of the Criminal Procedure Law. For instance, Article 5.1 of the Civil Procedure Law states:

> In accordance with the legal norms of the European Union, a court shall make a request to the Court of Justice of the European Union regarding the interpretation or validity of legal norms for a preliminary ruling.[95]

This legislative framework serves a dual purpose. First, it ensures that Latvian judges, who were initially accustomed to operating solely within national legal boundaries, systematically engage with EU law. Second, it establishes a clear procedural link between national courts and the CJEU, fostering a more coherent and integrated judicial practice across the EU legal order. By embedding EU legal mechanisms within national law, Latvia has proactively facilitated judicial adaptation to

---

[92] For an in-depth analysis on legal adaptations, challenges and the role of national judges in ensuring compliance with EU legal principles see, e.g., Evas 2012.

[93] See e.g. Mazur 2024.

[94] Kerikmäe and Joamets 2017.

[95] For a more detailed discussion on the experience of Latvian courts in this context, see Buka and Broks 2021.

legal norms of the EU law.[96] This approach is not unique to Latvia—similar strategies have been employed by several other EU Member States seeking to enhance the efficiency and clarity of EU law application within their judicial systems.[97]

17.4.3 Legal Challenges Amid Broader EU Integration Issues

Latvia's legal dimension in the EU accession process was closely intertwined with its broader transition from the post-Soviet sphere and mindset to a European identity. Beyond the technical aspects of legal harmonization, the process also encompassed general economic changes as well as crucial reforms in areas such as anti-corruption measures,[98] judicial independence and minority rights.[99] After regaining independence in 1991 economic reforms initially focused on transitioning to a market economy. This included currency reform, price and trade liberalization, and above all large-scale privatization efforts. However, a second wave of reforms, occurring around the turn of the millennium, was directly tied to EU accession. This phase was centred on implementing EU regulations and ensuring that Latvia's economic system could function effectively within the EU's single market. Although not all the decisions were well received and popular,[100] the pre-accession period was an intense phase of structural transformation that laid the foundation for the country's successful development as an EU member state.[101]

As mentioned earlier, Latvia's accession to the EU significantly influenced its anti-corruption measures, as meeting EU standards required substantial reforms in governance, law enforcement, and public administration transparency. The EU's Copenhagen criteria mandated strong institutional safeguards against corruption, pushing Latvia to enhance its legal and institutional framework. In response, Latvia established the Corruption Prevention and Combating Bureau (KNAB) in 2002, an independent body tasked with investigating corruption, monitoring financing of

[96] Although the legislative framework is adequate, it should be noted that due to several reasons Latvian courts initially were relatively inactive in submitting preliminary rulings during the early years of EU membership. In fact, the Constitutional Court forwarded its first reference to the Court of Justice only in 2017—Satversmes tiesa (2017) Satversmes tiesa pirmo reizi pieņem lēmumu par jautājumu uzdošanu Eiropas Savienības Tiesai prejudiciāla nolēmuma pieņemšanai (For the first time, the Constitutional Court adopts a decision on referring questions for a preliminary ruling to the Court of Justice of the European Union). https://www.satv.tiesa.gov.lv/press-release/satversmes-tiesa-pirmo-reizi-pienem-lemumu-par-jautajumu-uzdosanu-eiropas-savienibas-tiesai-prejudiciala-nolemuma-pienemsanai/. Accessed 8 February 2025.

[97] See e.g. Bobek 2008.

[98] Rasnačs 1995.

[99] Kerikmäe et al. 2016.

[100] Fridrihsone 2010.

[101] Dombrovskis 2020, pp. 36-37.

political parties, and enforcing anti-bribery laws.[102] The EU's monitoring mechanisms and financial support facilitated the implementation of stricter regulations on public procurement, judicial integrity, and corporate governance. Additionally, Latvia adopted EU anti-corruption directives, aligning its legislation with broader European efforts to combat financial crimes and misuse of public funds.

Likewise, the Copenhagen criteria required Latvia to ensure independence, efficiency, and transparency of the judiciary, prompting significant institutional and legislative changes. A key milestone was the adoption of the Law on Judicial Power (likums "Par tiesu varu"),[103] which reinforced judicial independence by clearly defining the separation of powers and limiting political influence over the judiciary. Another major step was the establishment of the Judicial Council (Tieslietu padome), an autonomous body responsible for overseeing judicial appointments, ethical standards, and court administration in line with European best practices.[104] Furthermore, the Court Administration (Tiesu administrācija) was created to improve court efficiency, streamline case management, and ensure adequate financial and logistical support for the judiciary.[105]

EU-driven reforms also led to training programs for judges and legal professionals, ensuring they were equipped to interpret and apply EU law effectively. The establishment of the Administrative Court system in 2004 was another major step, allowing for specialized judicial review of government decisions, in line with European legal principles. These institutional reforms, influenced by EU recommendations, enhanced judicial transparency, efficiency, and professionalism, ultimately strengthening Latvia's legal framework and facilitating its smooth integration into the EU legal system.[106]

Latvia's EU accession process also significantly influenced minority rights protection, as compliance with the Copenhagen criteria required stronger legal safeguards. Under EU pressure, Latvia reformed its citizenship laws, easing naturalization for non-citizens and promoting social integration through bilingual education and anti-discrimination policies.

Thus, comparing Latvia's and Ukraine's EU accession processes, it seems that they both share common structural challenges but unfold in vastly different political and geopolitical contexts. Latvia's accession was part of a sharp post-Soviet transition, with EU membership seen as an absolute priority, ensuring a decisive and thorough approach to reforms. Legal harmonization, anti-corruption measures, and judicial

---

[102] Korupcijas novēršanas un apkarošanas biroja likums [Law on the Corruption Prevention and Combating Bureau], adopted 18 April 2002, *Latvijas Vēstnesis* No. 65, entered into force 1 May 2002.

[103] Par tiesu varu (Law on the Judiciary), adopted 15 December 1992, *Latvijas Vēstnesis* No. 1, entered into force 1 January 1993.

[104] Par Tieslietu padomi [On the Council for the Judiciary], *Tieslietu padome* (Council for the Judiciary). Available at: https://www.tieslietupadome.lv/lv/par-tieslietu-padomi. Accessed 30 January 2025.

[105] Tiesu administrācijas nolikums [Regulation on Court Administration], adopted 28 May 2004, *Latvijas Vēstnesis* No. 87, entered into force 1 June 2004.

[106] See Harbaceviča 2003.

independence were challenging but politically feasible due to the strong domestic consensus on European integration. Ukraine, on the other hand, faces a more turbulent and uncertain accession process, largely due to war, geopolitical tensions, and internal institutional weaknesses. Ukraine has demonstrated political will by creating anti-corruption bodies, however, systemic corruption, judicial politicization, and weak administrative capacity remain significant hurdles.

17.5 Conclusion

Almost fifty years of Soviet rule had deeply shaped the former USSR republics and imposed considerable obstacles for societies attempting to rebuild democratic institutions, transition to market economies and redefine their national identities. Latvia faced significant challenges in aligning its legal system with EU standards, requiring deep institutional reforms in areas such as judicial independence, constitutional adaptation and legislative harmonization. The necessity to embed EU law principles into national legislation, to establish coordination mechanisms across government bodies and to ensure courts effectively applied EU law posed additional complexities. However, Latvia has been rather successful in dealing with these challenges and now, 20 years after its accession, it is a confident Member State of the EU.

Unlike Latvia, which entered the EU when enlargement enjoyed broad political support from the old Member States, Ukraine faces a more sceptical EU, where economic concerns, geopolitical tensions and enlargement fatigue may well lead to a much more challenging accession process. However, Ukraine's strategic importance and resilience could also push the EU to rethink its traditional accession dynamics, leading to a different, possibly faster, but more complex integration process initially without full membership. Latvia's EU accession process was driven by an unwavering commitment to membership, making the statement "this is what the EU expects" an unbeatable argument in most Latvian policy discussions throughout the 1990s. Thus Latvia's political elite saw alignment with the EU as an unquestionable priority and approached reforms with an "overachiever" mindset. In contrast, Ukraine's path is shaped by its war experience, revolutionary history, and sheer size, giving it the confidence to be a tougher negotiator and potentially a more assertive EU Member State in the future.

These differences in the mindset are also inevitably reflected in the legal arrangements facilitating the accession. The main pre-accession legal instruments—the Association Agreements—differ significantly in the cases of Latvia and Ukraine. In Latvia's case, the Association Agreement was deliberately designed as a transitional step towards full EU membership. In contrast, Ukraine's agreement represents a model of integration without membership—a highly detailed and long-term legal framework without an explicit goal of EU accession. However, even if a clear political will in the current Member States for Ukraine's membership were to emerge, Latvia's experience highlights the substantial and complex transformation of the legal system that Ukraine would need to undergo.

References

Alexievich S (2016) Secondhand Time: The Last of the Soviets. Random House, New York

Angermann N, Brüggemann K (2018) Geschichte der baltischen Länder [History of the Baltic countries]. Reclam, Stuttgart

Anonymous (2001) Kādēļ Latvijas konstitūcijā nepieciešami labojumi [Why the Latvian Constitution needs amendments]. Jurista Vārds 14(207)

Aust M (2019) Im Schatten des Imperiums [In the shadow of the empire]. Beck, Munich

Aust M, Heineman-Grüder A, Nußberger A, Schmid U (2020) Osteuropa zwischen Mauerfall und Ukrainekrieg [Eastern Europe between the fall of the Berlin Wall and the war in Ukraine]. Suhrkamp, Berlin

Bechev D (2011) Constructing South East Europe: The Politics of Balkan Regional Cooperation. Palgrave Macmillan, Basingstoke

Beichelt T (2022) Zwischen Transformation und Posttransformation [Between transformation and post-transformation]. Aus Politik und Zeitgeschichte (ApuZ) 1–2:40

Beutel J, Broks E, Buka A, Schewe C (2022) Setting Aside National Rules that Conflict with EU Law: How *Simmenthal* Works in Germany and in Latvia. In: Amatucci C et al. (eds) New Legal Reality: Challenges and Perspectives II. University of Latvia Press, Riga

Bobek M (2008) Learning to Talk: Preliminary Rulings, the Courts of the New Member States and the Court of Justice. Common Market Law Review 45:1611–1643

Buka A, Broks E (2021) Application of the EU Law in Latvian Courts. Strani pravni život 65:569–584

Burlyuk O (2017) Enabling Legal Reforms in Ukraine: Internal and External Dimensions of the Rule of Law. Journal of European Integration 39(3):289–302

Cianetti L, Dawson J, Hanley S (eds) (2020) Rethinking "democratic backsliding" in Central and Eastern Europe – looking beyond Hungary and Poland. Routledge, London

Darvas Z M et al. (2024) Ukraine's Path to European Union Membership and Its Long-Term Implications. Bruegel Policy Brief 05/2024

Dombrovskis V (2020) Latvijas dalība Eiropas Savienībā – 15 gadi: bilance un perspektīvas [Latvia's EU membership - 15 years: balance sheet and prospects]. In: Steinbuka I (ed) Latvijas ceļš Eiropas Savienībā: 15, 30, 100. University of Latvia Press, Riga

Down I, Han K J (2021) Far right parties and 'Europe': societal polarization and the limits of EU issue contestation. Journal of European Integration 43:65–81. https://doi.org/10.1080/07036337.2020.1728263

Eebel V (2011) Relevance of Copenhagen Criteria in Actual Accession: Principles, Methods and Shortcomings of EU Pre-Accession Evaluation. Studies of Transition States and Societies 3(3):3–23

Eihmanis E (2019) Latvia and the European Union. Oxford Research Encyclopedia of Politics. https://doi.org/10.1093/acrefore/9780190228637.013.1039. Accessed 30 January 2025

Evas T (2012) Judicial Application of European Union Law in Post-Communist Countries: The Cases of Estonia and Latvia. Ashgate, Farnham

Fortescue S (2009) Russia's Oil Barons and Metal Magnates: Oligarchs and the State in Transition. Palgrave Macmillan, Basingstoke

Fridrihsone M (2010) Saldākās nozares rūgtais gals [The bitter end of the sweetest industry]. Providus, 30 September 2010. Available at: https://providus.lv/raksti/saldakas-nozares-rugtais-gals/. Accessed 30 January 2025

Fukuyama F (1992) The End of History and the Last Man. Free Press, New York

Goehrke C (2010) Russland – eine Strukturgeschichte [Russia - a structural history]. Ferdinand Schöningh, Paderborn

Halbach U (2020) Korruption und Korruptionsbekämpfung im Südkaukasus [Corruption and the fight against corruption in the South Caucasus]. SWP-Studie 2020/S 08. Stiftung Wissenschaft und Politik, Berlin. https://www.swp-berlin.org//10.18449/2020S08. Accessed 30 January 2025

Harbaceviča S (2003) Eiropas Savienības tiesību ieviešana Latvijā [Implementing European Union law for Latvia]. In: Alehno I (ed) Eiropas Savienības tiesību īstenošana Latvijā. Latvijas Vēstnesis, Riga
Hildermeier M (2017) Geschichte der Sowjetunion 1917–1991: Entstehung und Niedergang des ersten sozialistischen Staates [History of the Soviet Union 1917–1991: The emergence and decline of the first socialist state], 2nd edn. Verlag C.H. Beck, Munich
Hillion C (2004) The Copenhagen criteria and their progeny. In: Hillion C (ed) EU Enlargement: A Legal Approach. Hart Publishing, Oxford, pp 1–23
Kappeler A (2019) Kleine Geschichte der Ukraine [A brief history of Ukraine]. Auflage. C.H. Beck, Munich
Kappeler A, Kohut ZE, Sysyn FE, von Hagen M (eds) (2003) Culture, Nation, and Identity: The Ukrainian-Russian Encounter (1600–1945). Canadian Institute of Ukrainian Studies Press, Edmonton
Karatnycky A (2024) Battleground Ukraine: From Independence to the War with Russia. Yale University Press, New Haven
Kerikmäe T, Chochia A, Atallah M (2016) The Baltic States in the European Union. Oxford Research Encyclopedia of Politics. Oxford University Press. https://doi.org/10.1093/acrefore/9780190228637.001.0001/acrefore-9780190228637-e-186
Kerikmäe T, Joamets K (eds) (2017) The Law of the Baltic States. Springer, Cham
Kochenov D (2008) EU Enlargement and the Failure of Conditionality: Pre-Accession Conditionality in the Fields of Democracy and the Rule of Law. Kluwer Law International
Kochenov D, Janse R (2022) Admitting Ukraine to the EU: Article 49 TEU is the 'Special Procedure'. EU Law Live, 30 March 2022. Available at: https://ssrn.com/abstract=4083111 or https://doi.org/10.2139/ssrn.4083111 Accessed 5 February 2025
Kovziridze T et al. (2016) The EU-Ukraine Association Agreement: Trade and Economic Perspectives. European Foreign Affairs Review: 311–330
Krūma K, Statkus S (2019) The Constitution of Latvia – A Bridge Between Traditions and Modernity. In: Albi A, Bardutzky S (eds) National Constitutions in European and Global Governance: Democracy, Rights, the Rule of Law. TMC Asser Press, The Hague
Lannon E, Van Elsuwege G (2020) The EU-Ukraine Association Agreement and the Challenges of Implementation. In: Hillion C (ed) EU Enlargement: A Legal Approach. Hart Publishing
Lenaerts K, Gutiérrez-Fons JA (2010) The Constitutional Allocation of Powers and General Principles of EU Law. Common Market Law Review 47(6):1629–1669
Levits E (2000) Satversme un Eiropas Savienība [Constitution and the European Union]. Jurista Vārds, Nr. 23 (176)
Magen A (2007) Transformative Engagement Through Law: The Acquis Communautaire as an Instrument of EU External Influence. Journal of Common Market Studies 9(2):355–370
Mälksoo L (2016) Russian Approaches to International Law. Cambridge University Press, Cambridge
Mazur S (2024) On the Verge of the Next EU Enlargement. Accession Legal Framework: Conceptual Overview. Croatian Yearbook of European Law and Policy 20:105–126
Mehnert K (1981) Der Sowjetmensch [Soviet man]. Ullstein, Frankfurt
Merl S (2019) Entscheidungsprozesse in der Sowjetunion: Die Dominanz des Zentralkomitees der KPdSU [Decision-making processes in the Soviet Union: The dominance of the Central Committee of the CPSU]. In: Großbölting T (ed) Politisches Entscheiden im Kalten Krieg [Political decision-making in the Cold War]. Vandenhoeck & Ruprecht, Göttingen
Münkler H (2023) Welt in Aufruhr [World in turmoil]. Rowohlt, Berlin
Ohler C (2021) EUV Art. 49, para 23. In: Grabitz E, Hilf M, Nettesheim M (eds) Das Recht der Europäischen Union. Beck, Munich
Pech L, Scheppele K L (2017) Illiberalism Within: Rule of Law Backsliding in the EU. Cambridge Yearbook of European Legal Studies 19(1):3–47
Peters A (2011) Soft Law as a New Mode of Governance. In: Diedrichs U, Reiners W, Wessels W (eds) The Dynamics of Change in EU Governance. Edward Elgar Publishing

Pleines H (2014) Nach dem Ende der Sowjetunion. Sowjetunion II: 1953–1991 [After the end of the Soviet Union. Soviet Union II: 1953–1991], Informationen zur politischen Bildung. Bundeszentrale für politische Bildung (BPB)
Pleps J (2003) Kāds ir konstitucionālais pamats mūsu dalībai Eiropas Savienībā [What is the constitutional basis for our membership of the European Union?]. Jurista Vārds 23(281)
Pleps J (2024) Eiropas Savienības ietekme uz Latvijas tiesisko sistēmu [Impact of the European Union on the Latvian legal system]. Jurista Vārds 51/52 (1369/1370)
Rasnačs D (1995) Par korupcijas ierobežošanu [On curbing corruption]. Latvijas Vēstnesis. https://www.vestnesis.lv/ta/id/21352. Accessed 28 February 2025
Rometsch D, Wessels W (eds) (1996) The European Union and Member States: Towards Institutional Fusion? Manchester University Press, Manchester/New York
Schewe C (2013) Russia in the WTO: The Bear on a Leash? Russia in International Trade Disputes and the Added Value of a WTO Membership. Journal of World Trade 47:1171–1190
Schewe C, Aliyev A (2011) The Customs Union and the Common Economic Space of the Eurasian Economic Community: Eurasian Counterpart to the EU or Russian Domination? German Yearbook of International Law 54:565–608
Schewe C, Blome T (2021) The "Rule of Law Mechanism" and the Hungarian and Polish Resistance: European Law Against National Identity? Journal of the University of Latvia 14:49–67. https://doi.org/10.22364/jull.14.03
Schewe C, Buka A, Broks E (2024) Examining Ukraine's EU Candidate Status: (When) Does the Accession Process Turn from Political to Legal? Journal of the University of Latvia. Law 17:94–108. https://doi.org/10.22364/jull.17.06
Schimmelfennig F (2008) EU Political Accession Conditionality After the 2004 Enlargement: Consistency and Effectiveness. Journal of European Public Policy 15(6):918–937
Schlögel K (2017) Das sowjetische Jahrhundert [The Soviet century]. C.H. Beck, Munich
Snyder F (1993) The Effectiveness of European Community Law: Institutions, Processes, Tools and Techniques. The Modern Law Review 56(1):32
Terhechte J (2017) Art. 49 EUV. In: Pechstein M, Nowak C, Häde U (eds) Frankfurter Kommentar zu EUV, GRC und AEUV. Mohr Siebeck, Tübingen
Tridimas T (2006) The General Principles of EU Law. Oxford University Press
Tsygankov A (2015) Russia, Ukraine, and the Shift in Great Power Relations. International Affairs 72(4):971–985
Vachudova MA (2019) Corruption and Compliance in the EU's Post-Communist Members and Candidates. Journal of Common Market Studies 57(1):105–122
Van der Loo G, Van Elsuwege P, Petrov R (2014) The EU-Ukraine Association Agreement: Assessment of an innovative legal instrument. EUI Department of Law Research Paper 2014/09
Wagner M (2024) Affective polarization in Europe. European Political Science Review, 16(3):378–392

Edmunds Broks is an Assistant Professor and Dr.iur. at the Faculty of Law, University of Latvia.

Christoph Schewe is a Professor and Dr.iur. at the University of Applied Sciences Kiel-Altenholz/Reinfeld, Germany.

Arnis Buka is an Assistant Professor and Dr.iur. at the Faculty of Law, University of Latvia.

Lolita Buka is a Lecturer and Ph.D. at the Faculty of Law, University of Latvia.

Chapter 18
European Union and Core International Crimes (CIC): Support of Ukraine in the Fight Against Impunity

Vitalii Gutnyk

Contents

Abstract This chapter argues that while many international law actors neglect their obligations to combat impunity and maintain international law and order, the European Union is a driving force in the fight against impunity for core international crimes (CIC) committed on the territory of Ukraine; it supports both national investigations in the EU States Parties and international criminal justice. The European Union played an important role in Ukraine's ratification of the Rome Statute and supported the ICC in investigating international crimes committed in Ukraine after Russia's full-scale invasion of Ukraine. Domestic investigations of core international crimes allegedly committed in Ukraine have been launched in at least 14 EU Member States and Eurojust's coordination of national authorities allows for an effective fight against impunity. The raised issue is the fighting of impunity and future peace treaties with Russia and in any case the fight against impunity and justice should be served, and all those who committed international crimes to be held accountable.

V. Gutnyk (✉)
Faculty of Law, Vilnius University, Vilnius, Lithuania
e-mail: vitalii.gutnyk@lnu.edu.ua

Ivan Franko National University of Lviv, Lviv, Ukraine

I. Isokaitė-Valužė and H. Šinkūnas (eds.), *The European Union 2004-2024*,
https://doi.org/10.1007/978-94-6265-718-2_18

Keywords Fight against impunity · International crime · International Criminal Court · International law · EU law · Ukraine

18.1 Introduction

Russia committed blatant aggression, violating all principles of international law on which the international legal order is built as a result of the direct armed invasion of Ukraine in 2022. Unlike in 2014, when Russia's armed aggression began with the occupation of Crimea and continued in certain areas of the Donetsk and Luhansk regions, on 24 February 2022 the aggressor openly showed its face, forcing the inhabitants of Ukraine to wake up to the sounds of sirens and explosions.

Millions of Ukrainians were forced to leave their homes fearing for their lives. Many of them became witnesses or victims of core international crimes (CIC) committed during the armed aggression of the Russian Federation in Ukraine. Most Ukrainians found refuge in the EU Member States.[1]

It is worth agreeing with I. Isokaitė-Valužė's and G. Grigaitė-Daugirdė's opinion that Russia is clearly violating its obligations on a huge scale, including jus cogens norms, as it "distorts and abuses international law and acts against the rule of law".[2] Russia's armed aggression against Ukraine is a challenge both for Ukraine and for the entire civilized world because the aggression was committed not by just any state, but by a permanent member of the UN Security Council that possesses nuclear weapons. Will the international community be able to restore law and order and hold Russia and those responsible for international crimes accountable? It is obvious that if international law is not restored and the perpetrators are not punished, armed aggression against Ukraine could become a turning point in modern history, becoming a "permission" for other states to commit similar actions. Justice cannot wait, any expectations give rise to thoughts of impunity for the commission of CIC, which in turn provokes new crimes with new victims.

Russia's direct invasion of Ukraine in 2022 forced the European Union and its member states to rethink their role in countering CIC committed on the territory of third states and to take additional steps in implementing the idea of the fight against impunity of those who brazenly violate the international legal order. Obviously, human dignity, freedom, democracy, the rule of law, respect for human rights and other European values are worthless when CIC are committed.

The purpose of this study is to analyse the European Union's support in the fight against impunity for CIC committed during the Russian Federation's war against Ukraine. The main tasks of this research: to consider the role of the European Union as a driving force in the fight against impunity for CIC committed on the territory

[1] See Estimated number of refugees from Ukraine recorded in Europe and Asia since February 2022 as of July 2024, by selected country. https://www.statista.com/statistics/1312584/ukrainian-refugees-by-country/. Accessed 30 January 2025.

[2] Isokaitė-Valužė and Grigaitė-Daugirdė 2024, p. 41.

of third states; to analyse the problems of cooperation between the International Criminal Court and Ukraine, as well as the support from the European Union to the fight against impunity within the framework of international criminal justice; to identify the features of cooperation between states within the framework of the Eurojust regarding CIC; to characterize the problems of the universal jurisdiction of EU Member States regarding CIC committed in Ukraine.

The historical and legal method are applied to analyse the genesis of cooperation between Ukraine and the International Criminal Court. The comparative method is needed to contrast EU support in the fight against impunity within the framework of international criminal justice and national legal orders. Treaty interpretation methods are used to establish the content of treaty norms, in particular, the Rome Statute of the ICC.

18.2 The European Union as a Locomotive of the Fight Against Impunity for CIC

The armed conflict in Ukraine and the CIC that accompany it certainly force the EU to deepen cooperation in combating impunity. The European Union and its Member States exemplify best practices in the fight against impunity, aligning fully with its fundamental values. After all, how can we guarantee human dignity, freedom, democracy, and human rights if CIC are committed and the perpetrators go unpunished? Thus, ensuring such values requires the fight against impunity.

The fight against impunity for CIC is also linked to the principle of international law regarding respect for human rights, which includes *jus cogens* norms and obligations *erga omnes*.[3] This also implies an international legal obligation to combat the most heinous human rights violations—the commission of CIC.[4] Therefore, all states must, to maintain international law and order, take all possible measures to combat impunity.[5]

Undoubtedly, the United Nations, and especially its Security Council, should play the main role in the prevention of armed conflicts (and, as a result, committed CIC). However, concerning the aggressor—the Russian Federation, which is not only a permanent member of the UN Security Council but also possesses nuclear weapons, the UN toolkit proved to be completely ineffective.

However, if CIC are not combated, their consequences become felt in third countries as well. War crimes can be linked to arms trafficking or human trafficking (or even human organs) illegal trafficking of cultural property (as happened, for example, during the war in Iraq, at the initiative of various criminal groups, or in Syria).[6]

---

[3] Parker 1989, p. 414; Simonen 1999, p. 199.

[4] Sarkin 2012, p. 553.

[5] Yeneabat 2020, p. 44.

[6] Caianiello 2022, p. 221.

CIC can have consequences in the form of a refugee crisis, as a result of which hundreds of thousands, sometimes over a million people, seek refuge in the territory of other states, especially the EU.[7]

Therefore, within the EU, there is coordination of investigations and prosecutions of CIC between national authorities. At the centre of such coordination is Eurojust.[8]

In addition to combating CIC within the framework of national legal orders, the EU comprehensively supports international criminal justice. In particular, all EU Member States are States Parties to the Rome Statute of the ICC. In the EU, support for strengthening cooperation between EU Member States to prevent and combat CIC is coordinated through Eurojust and the European Network for the investigation and prosecution of genocide, crimes against humanity and war crimes.[9]

The financial support of the ICC by the EU member states throughout history has been the largest, and there is even talk of the ICC's financial dependence on the EU.[10] In addition to contributions to the regular budget, additional funding is provided by the EU. In 2024 for the Office of the Prosecutor Trust Fund on Advanced Technology and Specialized Capacity total contributions amounted to €7.2 million by the European Union.[11] The EU also financially supports separate ICC investigations. A few months after the start of the Russian Federation's direct armed invasion of Ukraine, funds were allocated to support the investigation of the International Criminal Court.[12]

In line with its obligations to the ICC, the EU should encourage States Parties to pay contributions to the ICC budget, as well as facilitate the accession to or ratification of the Rome Statute by third states and make efforts to develop training and assistance for judges, prosecutors, officials and lawyers in ICC-related work.[13]

An important step by the EU in the fight against impunity for CIC committed on the territory of third countries was the establishment of the Kosovo Specialist Chambers and Specialist Prosecutor's Office, which were created by the International Agreement between the Republic of Kosovo and the European Union of 23 April 2014 and an Amendment to the Constitution of the Republic of Kosovo: "Article

---

[7] *Ibid.*, p. 222.

[8] See Core international crimes. https://www.eurojust.europa.eu/crime-types-and-cases/crime-types/core-international-crimes. Accessed 2 February 2025.

[9] See Day of International Criminal Justice: Statement by the High Representative on behalf of the European Union. https://www.consilium.europa.eu/en/press/press-releases/2023/07/16/day-of-international-criminal-justice-statement-by-the-high-representative-on-behalf-of-the-european-union. Accessed 2 February 2025.

[10] Wiebelhaus-Brahm and Ainley 2023, p. 32.

[11] See International Criminal Court 2024, para 273.

[12] See Russian war crimes in Ukraine: EU supports the International Criminal Court investigation with €7.25 million. https://ec.europa.eu/commission/presscorner/detail/el/ip_22_3543. Accessed 2 February 2025.

[13] See Article 4 and Article 6 of the Agreement between the International Criminal Court and the European Union on cooperation and assistance (2006). Document 22006A0428(01). URL: http://data.europa.eu/eli/agree_internation/2006/313/oj. Accessed 2 February 2025; Article 3 of the Council Decision 2011/168/CFSP of 21 March 2011 on the International Criminal Court and repealing Common Position 2003/444/CFSP, 21 March 2011. Document 32011D0168. http://data.europa.eu/eli/dec/2011/168/oj. Accessed 2 February 2025.

162: The Specialist Chambers and the Specialist Prosecutor's Office", of 3 August 2015. Their work is actively supported by the EU, which covers the costs.[14] The setting up of the mentioned bodies became a great support for establishing justice and fighting against impunity for CIC, which were committed in Kosovo between 1 January 1998 and 31 December 2000.[15]

Why does the EU so strongly support the fight against CIC within the framework of international/hybrid criminal courts? Such significant attention is related with the fact that in the mentioned judicial institutions any person can be brought to criminal responsibility, despite possible immunities according to the norms of international or domestic law. Undoubtedly, immunities and official positions become an obstacle to responsibility within national legal systems. International criminal courts embody the collective interest of the international community in effectively ending impunity for *hostis humani generis.*[16]

However, regardless of whether the fight against impunity for CIC is taking place within the framework of the international or domestic legal order, a very important question arises: how to prevent the "heroization" of persons who have committed CIC, as well as the repetition of such crimes? After all, even the conviction of individuals for committing CIC by international criminal courts does not mean that they cease to be "heroes" for the population of their state. For example, after the conviction by the International Tribunal for the former Yugoslavia, there was no reassessment of the terrible consequences of CIC by those states and leaders who ordered the crimes to be committed, but on the contrary, in some cases, new "heroes" emerged. Those persons who were vindicated by the ICTY, and who, during investigations and prosecution declared their guilt for committing a crime, became "enemies" of their state.[17] Instead, some of those convicted by the ICTY for genocide, war crimes, or crimes against humanity have returned to their countries after serving their sentences and continue to be at the centre of political life in the Western Balkans; they either lead or are active members of influential veteran organizations close to the government.[18] Obviously, we need to think about this now, otherwise bringing them to justice will not prevent similar crimes in the future, but on the contrary, will cause vengeful sentiments among such "heroes" and their environment, and in the future will become the basis for committing similar crimes. It seems that the international community and especially the EU, as the locomotive in the fight against impunity for CIC, should put these issues on the agenda today.

---

[14] Cataleta 2022, p. 7.

[15] Mucaj 2021, p. 389.

[16] Shany 2010, p. 331.

[17] Strupinskienė 2023.

[18] *Ibid.*

18.3 Cooperation Between the International Criminal Court and Ukraine: The EU Support in the Fight Against Impunity

18.3.1 Ratification of the Rome Statute by Ukraine: A 26-Year Journey

On 1 January 2025, Ukraine became the 125th State Party to the ICC and the 20th state in the Eastern European region.[19] For Ukraine, this was a historic moment, which Ukraine has been moving toward for 26 long years. This time was a period of uncertainty, primarily due to political reasons and a lack of understanding of the benefits of joining the ICC.

Cooperation with the European Union played an important role in Ukraine's ratification of the Rome Statute. In particular, Ukraine had direct obligations to ratify the Rome Statute under Article 8 of the Association Agreement with the EU.[20] All EU Member States are parties to the Rome Statute of the ICC,[21] and the European Union has supported the ICC since 2000 through direct funding of outreach activities and projects aimed at the ratification of the Rome Statute.[22]

Ukraine actively participated in the drafting of the text of the Rome Statute. During the Diplomatic Conference of 15 June–17 July 1998, in Rome, the Ukrainian delegation submitted several proposals for improving provisions of the Draft Statute, in particular: (1) the use of nuclear weapons should become an *ipso facto* war crime;[23] (2) the specifics of sentencing in the event of multiple crimes;[24] (3) the procedure for electing judges must be based on the principle of equal representation of each geographical group of the ICC's States Parties.[25]

After the final text of the Statute was agreed upon, 120 states (including Ukraine) voted to adopt the Rome Statute on 17 July 1998. Ukraine signed the ICC Statute on 20 January 2000.[26]

However, after Ukraine signed it, the Rome Statute was not ratified due to the adoption of the Opinion of the Constitutional Court of Ukraine dated 11 July 2001,

---

[19] See ICC welcomes Ukraine as a new State Party, 2 January 2025. https://www.icc-cpi.int/news/icc-welcomes-ukraine-new-state-party. Accessed 2 February 2025.

[20] Association Agreement 2014.

[21] See The States Parties to the Rome Statute (2025) https://asp.icc-cpi.int/states-parties. Accessed 2 February 2025.

[22] See Day of International Criminal Justice: Statement by the High Representative on behalf of the European Union. https://www.consilium.europa.eu/en/press/press-releases/2024/07/16/day-of-international-criminal-justice-statement-by-the-high-representative-on-behalf-of-the-european-union. Accessed 2 February 2025.

[23] Ukraine: proposal regarding article 5, 1998, §1.

[24] Ukraine: proposal regarding article 77, as reproduced in document 1998.

[25] Ukraine: proposed amendment to article 37, para 7, 1998.

[26] Gutnyk 2015, p. 141.

which emphasized that "the possibility of such an addition to the judicial system of Ukraine is not provided for by Chapter VIII "Justice" of the Constitution of Ukraine".

On 2 June 2016, 15 years after the Constitutional Court of Ukraine adopted the Opinion, the Verkhovna Rada of Ukraine adopted amendments to the Constitution of Ukraine "regarding justice." The occupation of the Autonomous Republic of Crimea and the acceptance of the ICC's *ad hoc* jurisdiction preceded this.

Under the amendments, Article 124 of the Constitution of Ukraine was reworded, in particular, Article 124 (6) provides that Ukraine "may accept the jurisdiction of the International Criminal Court under the conditions specified in the Rome Statute of the International Criminal Court". By para 1 of the Transitional Provisions of the Amendments to the Constitution, the provisions of Article 124 (6) shall enter into force three years from the day following the date of publication of this Law, i.e. they entered into force on 30 June 2019.

Therefore, in its current wording, Article 124 of the Constitution provided an opportunity to ratify the Rome Statute and join the functioning of the ICC. Thus, Article 124 of the Constitution of Ukraine in its current wording has provided Ukraine with the opportunity to ratify the Rome Statute of the ICC and be involved in the full functioning of the ICC. As for other international criminal tribunals, the establishment of which Ukraine may be involved, there are no direct constitutional obstacles in this regard.

However, 5 years passed from the moment the amendments to the Constitution came into force until the ratification of the Rome Statute by Ukraine. First of all, such a delay in ratification was due to the fears of parliamentarians that Ukrainian political leaders or military personnel could be held criminally liable in the ICC. As S. Masol points out, such fears arose as a result of active campaigns of distortion and disinformation.[27]

On 21 August 2024, the Parliament of Ukraine adopted the Law of Ukraine "On Ratification of the Rome Statute of the International Criminal Court and Amendments Thereto". The ratification law entered into force for Ukraine on 1 January 2025.

In addition to the Rome Statute, amendments to Article 8 (war crimes), as well as amendments to the crime of aggression were ratified.[28]

Ukraine, upon ratification, made a declaration regarding war crimes by Article 124 of the Rome Statute, stating that "for seven years period after the entry into force of the Rome Statute for Ukraine, it will not recognize the jurisdiction of the ICC over the war crimes when the crime is alleged to have been committed by Ukrainian nationals".[29] Apparently, such a declaration was related to the parliamentarians' fears that the ICC would be able to hold Ukrainian military personnel accountable, rather than Russian ones. This argument has been heard in political discourse over the past 10 years as a justification for refusing to ratify the Rome Statute.

In the Rome Statute, Article 124 is quite special. As emphasized in international legal doctrine, the original purpose of this article was twofold: first, it contributed to

[27] Masol 2022, p. 174.

[28] *Ibid.*

[29] *Ibid.*

reaching a compromise on the text of Article 8 at the Rome Conference, and second, it sought to persuade hesitant States to sign the Statute by granting them a grace period to amend their national laws, military guidelines and procedures to conform to the Statute.[30] As the Diplomatic Conference in Rome drew to a close, France presented an informal proposal that the Court would not be able to exercise jurisdiction unless a State Party to the Statute had provided for such jurisdiction by general declaration or special consent. Since France had a large number of troops involved in peacekeeping missions in Africa, the country wanted to observe how the Court dealt with war crimes for some time before submitting itself to its jurisdiction.[31]

Ukraine became the third state to apply the temporary provision of Article 124 of the Rome Statute. The experience of France and Colombia was used.[32] On 13 August 2008, France withdrew its declaration regarding Article 124, and Colombia's seven-year period of limited jurisdiction expired on 31 October 2009.[33] Therefore, today Ukraine remains the only state that applies Article 124 and does not accept the jurisdiction of the ICC over war crimes when the crime was allegedly committed by its citizens.

Although Article 124 allows States Parties to waive the ICC's jurisdiction over war crimes for seven years, nationals of countries that have waived may still be prosecuted for genocide or crimes against humanity under the ICC Statute.[34]

18.3.2 Acceptance of the Jurisdiction of the ICC According to Article 12 (3) of the Rome Statute of the ICC by Ukraine

As a result of the Revolution of Dignity in 2013, the occupation of the Autonomous Republic of Crimea, and the beginning of armed conflict in the Donetsk and Luhansk regions in 2014, there was a need to involve international criminal justice to hold accountable those who committed CIC. The only possibility of involving the ICC was to accept its ad hoc jurisdiction under Article 12(3) of the Rome Statute. After all, even if Ukraine ratified the Rome Statute in 2014, this would not allow the ICC's temporal jurisdiction to be extended to crimes committed before ratification, but only to crimes that are to be committed after the ratification. The concept of *ad hoc* jurisdiction is associated with the principle of combating impunity and is an additional opportunity to bring to responsibility for CIC through the ICC.[35]

---

[30] Nemane and Gunjal 2015, p. 952.

[31] Scheers 2010, p. 304; Tabak 2009, p. 1086.

[32] France Declarations to the Rome Statute of the International Criminal Court 2000; Colombia Declarations to the Rome Statute of the International Criminal Court 2002.

[33] Tabak 2009, p. 1070.

[34] *Ibid.*, p. 1070; Nemane and Gunjal 2015.

[35] Tiribelli 2008, p. 16.

Ukraine has twice used the opportunity to exercise jurisdiction under Article 12(3) of the Statute. The first time Ukraine accepted jurisdiction was in February–April 2014 in respect of CIC committed during the peaceful protests in Ukraine from 21 November 2013 to 22 February 2014, and the second time—regarding CIC committed in Ukraine since 20 February 2014. Following Ukraine's acceptance of ad hoc jurisdiction, the ICC Prosecutor initiated a preliminary examination of both referred situations to determine whether they met the criteria for initiating an investigation. On 11 December 2020, the Prosecutor announced the completion of the preliminary examination on the situation in Ukraine.[36] However, before the start of the Russian Federation's direct armed invasion of Ukraine, these proceedings at the ICC had not yet progressed to the next stage.

18.3.3 ICC Investigation of International Crimes Following the Full-Scale Invasion of the Russian Federation in 2022 and the EU Support in the Fight Against Impunity

After the Russian Federation's armed invasion of Ukraine in February 2022, the question arose of intensifying cooperation with the ICC regarding investigation and prosecution for committed CIC. Since Ukraine was not a State Party to the Rome Statute, to expedite the decision to open an investigation, during March-April 2022, the "Situation in Ukraine" (CIC committed in Ukraine) was referred to the ICC by 43 States Parties.[37]

Why was the referral of the "Situation in Ukraine" by the States Parties important? The fact is that if ICC proceedings are initiated by a State under Article 12(3) of the Rome Statute, the ICC Prosecutor needs to obtain authorization for an investigation from the ICC Pre-Trial Chamber, so this takes significantly longer than in the case of a referral of the "situation" by a State Party to the Rome Statute or the UN Security Council.

---

[36] See Statement of the Prosecutor, Fatou Bensouda, on the conclusion of the preliminary examination in the situation in Ukraine, 11 December 2020. https://www.icc-cpi.int/news/statement-prosecutor-fatou-bensouda-conclusion-preliminary-examination-situation-ukraine. Accessed 2 February 2025.

[37] See Referral submitted by the Republic of Lithuania (2022) https://www.icc-cpi.int/sites/default/files/2022-04/1041.pdf; Referral letter submitted in coordination with 38 States Parties (2022) https://www.icc-cpi.int/sites/default/files/2022-04/Article-14-letter.pdf; Referral submitted by the Republic of North Macedonia (2022) https://www.icc-cpi.int/sites/default/files/2022-04/State-Party-Referral-North-Macedonia.pdf; Referral submitted by Japan (2022) https://www.icc-cpi.int/sites/default/files/2022-04/JAPAN_referral.pdf; Referral submitted by Montenegro (2022) https://www.icc-cpi.int/sites/default/files/2022-04/20220321164751497-ukraine-referral-montenegro.pdf; Referral submitted by Chile (2022) https://www.icc-cpi.int/sites/default/files/2022-04/20220401-Chile-Letter-to-OTP.PDF. Accessed 2 February 2025.

Therefore, the referral of the situation by the States Party, which included 31 EU Member States, enabled the ICC Prosecutor to decide to open an investigation on 2 March 2022.[38] As underlined C. Tarfusser and G. Chiarini, in the sum of referrals, the ICC Prosecutor opened the investigation of this situation without a separate preliminary examination. Instead, the Prosecutor decided to work within an already existent preliminary examination that started from both Declarations submitted by the Ukrainian Government in 2014 and 2015.[39]

A significant event in the context of the fight against CIC committed during the Russian armed aggression in Ukraine was the issuance of arrest warrants for suspects in war crimes and crimes against humanity. This step in the investigation stage is very important, because, both for the victims and for society as a whole, it is initially especially important to hear the names of those suspected of committing an international crime. Arrest warrants issued by the ICC oblige at least all States Parties to the Rome Statute to detain a suspect and extradite them to the ICC.[40]

Returning to the armed aggression of the Russian Federation in Ukraine, as of 1 February 2025, six arrest warrants have been issued. On 17 March 2023, Pre-Trial Chamber II issued arrest warrants for V. Putin and M. Lvova-Belova, who are suspected of committing war crimes in the form of illegal deportation of the population (children) and their illegal transfer from the occupied territories of Ukraine to the Russian Federation.[41] On 5 March 2024, arrest warrants were issued for two senior Russian military officers, S. Kobylash and V. Sokolov, who are suspected of committing war crimes and crimes against humanity for missile strikes on Ukrainian electrical infrastructure.[42] On 24 June 2024, Pre-Trial Chamber II of the ICC issued warrants of arrest for S. Shoigu and V. Gerasimov, in the context of war crimes and crimes against humanity (for missile strikes on Ukrainian electric infrastructure).[43]

However, the question may arise: why did the ICC issue arrest warrants for these crimes? After all, in the context of the Russian-Ukrainian war, these are not the most serious crimes. The answer is probably that these crimes are quite obvious and did not require obtaining a significant amount of evidence and conducting lengthy

---

[38] See Statement of ICC Prosecutor, Karim A.A. Khan QC, on the Situation in Ukraine: Receipt of Referrals from 39 States Parties and the Opening of an Investigation (2022) https://www.icc-cpi.int/news/statement-icc-prosecutor-karim-aa-khan-qc-situation-ukraine-receipt-referrals-39-states.

[39] Tarfusser and Chiarini 2023, p. 179.

[40] Zenginkuzucu 2021, p. 7.

[41] See Situation in Ukraine: ICC judges issue arrest warrants against Vladimir Vladimirovich Putin and Maria Alekseyevna Lvova-Belova (2023) https://www.icc-cpi.int/news/situation-ukraine-icc-judges-issue-arrest-warrants-against-vladimir-vladimirovich-putin-and. Accessed 2 February 2025.

[42] See Situation in Ukraine: ICC judges issue arrest warrants against Sergei Ivanovich Kobylash and Viktor Nikolayevich Sokolov. https://www.icc-cpi.int/news/situation-ukraine-icc-judges-issue-arrest-warrants-against-sergei-ivanovich-kobylash-and. Accessed 2 February 2025.

[43] See Situation in Ukraine: ICC judges issue arrest warrants against Sergei Kuzhugetovich Shoigu and Valery Vasilyevich Gerasimov (2024) https://www.icc-cpi.int/news/situation-ukraine-icc-judges-issue-arrest-warrants-against-sergei-kuzhugetovich-shoigu-and. Accessed 2 February 2025.

verification; the suspected Russian citizens publicly announced that they had these made decisions or given orders.

Despite the positive trends related to the issuance of arrest warrants, there is already a negative experience of the ICC's cooperation with the Government of Mongolia regarding the execution of arrest warrants within the framework of the "Situation in Ukraine" investigation. Thus, the suspect V. Putin visited Mongolia (State Party to the ICC) on 3 September 2024. As a reason for not complying with its obligations to cooperate, the Mongolian government emphasized that "Mongolia "recognize[d] that, under customary international law, President Putin, as a sitting head of state of a third country, is entitled and shall enjoy immunity ratione personae and ratione materiae", and that it 'ha[d] not identified any rule in customary international law that excludes or renders the immunity of heads of state inapplicable when their arrest is sought by an international criminal court". Mongolia continued by asserting that "[t]he person specified in the request enjoys immunity and privileges according to the existing international customary norms and legal principles" and that "proceeding with the request would result in breach of Mongolia's pre-existing legal obligations".[44] On such an argument, Pre-Trial Chamber II, "recalled its classified response to the submissions of another State Party issued in the context of a prior consultation process under article 97 of the Statute and notified to all States Parties, including Mongolia, whereby it found that "personal immunity of officials, including Heads of third States, is not opposable in proceedings before the Court, nor a waiver of immunity is required under article 98 of the Statute".[45] In sum, Pre-Trial Chamber II found, that "Mongolia failed to comply with its international obligations under the Statute by not executing the Court's request for the arrest and surrender of Mr Putin while he was on Mongolian territory; referred the matter of Mongolia's non-compliance with the request for arrest and surrender of Mr Putin to the Assembly of States Parties through the President of the Court in accordance with regulation 109(4) of the Regulations".[46]

The EU also regretted that Mongolia did not comply with "its obligations under the Statute to execute the arrest warrant" and underlined that "the EU supports the investigations by the Prosecutor of the ICC in Ukraine and calls for full cooperation by all State Parties".[47]

[44] See Situation in Ukraine. ICC-01/22-90. Finding under article 87(7) of the Rome Statute on the non-compliance by Mongolia with the request by the Court to cooperate in the arrest and surrender of Vladimir Vladimirovich Putin and referral to the Assembly of States Parties, 24 October 2024, Para 6. https://www.icc-cpi.int/sites/default/files/CourtRecords/0902ebd1809d1971.pdf. Accessed 2 February 2025.

[45] *Ibid.*, para 6.

[46] *Ibid.*, p.17.

[47] See European External Action Service 2024.

18.4 Cooperation Between States Within the Framework of Eurojust Regarding CIC Committed in Ukraine

Eurojust was established in 2002 "to improve judicial cooperation between the Member States further, in particular in combating forms of serious crime".[48] Today, the legal framework for the functioning of Eurojust is provided for by the Regulation (EU) 2018/1727 of the European Parliament and of the Council of 14 November 2018 on the European Union Agency for Criminal Justice Cooperation (Eurojust), which Eurojust defined as "as a Union body with legal personality, to stimulate and to improve coordination and cooperation between competent judicial authorities of the Member States, particularly in relation to serious organised crime".[49] Eurojust also coordinates the work of national authorities (both the EU Member States and third countries) in the investigation and prosecution of transnational crimes).[50]

Eurojust was established to ensure the EU's objective of a high level of security for its citizens within an area of freedom, security and justice. This is achieved by preventing and combating crime, and this should be done through closer cooperation between the police and the judiciary.[51]

Based on the above, Eurojust has become the central unit for the cooperation between states regarding CIC committed in Ukraine. It coordinates national investigations and evidence gathering and organizes meetings with all countries conducting investigations.[52]

According to Eurojust, more than 20 countries, including 14 EU Member States, have launched national investigations into CIC allegedly committed in Ukraine, either on the basis of nationality, passive legal personality or universal jurisdiction.[53] In such a situation, Eurojust's coordination of national authorities allows for a more effective fight against impunity for CIC committed.

Eurojust's work in the context of CIC committed in Ukraine focuses on the following areas: (1) the Joint Investigation Team (JIT); (2) the Core International Crimes Evidence Database (CICED); (3) the International Centre for the Prosecution of the Crime of Aggression against Ukraine (ICPA); (4) the EU Network for investigation and prosecution of genocide, crimes against humanity, and war crimes (the Genocide Network); (5) the EU Freeze and Seize Task Force.[54]

---

[48] See Council decision of 28 February 2002 setting up Eurojust with a view to reinforcing the fight against serious crime. Document 32002D0187.

[49] *Ibid.*

[50] See European Union Agency for Criminal Justice Cooperation: Who we are. https://www.eurojust.europa.eu/about-us/who-we-are. Accessed 2 February 2025.

[51] Souminen 2008, p. 220.

[52] See Eurojust Consolidated Annual Activity Report 2023, 26 June 2024. p. 16. https://www.drugsandalcohol.ie/41421/2/eurojust-consolidated-annual-activity-report-2023.pdf. Accessed 2 February 2025.

[53] *Ibid.*, p. 15.

[54] See Eurojust and the war in Ukraine. https://www.eurojust.europa.eu/eurojust-and-the-war-in-ukraine. Accessed 2 February 2025.

The JIT was established in March 2022. Ukraine, Lithuania, Poland, Estonia, Latvia, Slovakia and Romania are states members of the JIT.[55] The Office of the Prosecutor (OTP) of the ICC[56] and the Europol[57] joined the JIT as separate participants. The JIT aims to facilitate investigations and prosecutions in the relevant states, as well as those that may be referred to the ICC.[58] This is the first time the OTP participating in a JIT investigated alleged CIC, which opens a significant opportunity for the implementation of the proactive complementarity policy of the ICC.[59]

Undoubtedly, to prove committed CIC, a reliable evidence base is required, that is collected by various states. That is why in 2023 Eurojust established the CICED with the aim "to preserve, store and analyse evidence of CIC".[60] In addition to the evidence itself, the CICED will also contain a register with information about who provided the evidence, as well as the type of crime to which it relates.[61] The CICED's special role is in the safe storage of evidence, which is difficult to achieve in Ukraine today.[62]

Given the issues of the crime of aggression, in particular the lack of *ratione materiae* jurisdiction of the ICC over Russian aggression, the ICPA was established in 2023 as a unique judicial hub of Eurojust to support national investigations into the crime of aggression of the Russian Federation in Ukraine. The ICPA's work is aimed at preparing for and facilitating future prosecutions of the crime of aggression, regardless of the jurisdiction in which they will be brought.[63] Such work on collecting evidence of the crime of aggression is needed today, in the early stages of the commission of this crime, as is the search for a common strategy for the investigation and criminal prosecution of the crime of aggression.[64] Although the work of the ICPA does not involve a political debate on the establishment of the Special Criminal Tribunal for the Crime of Aggression of the Russian Federation against

---

[55] See Joint investigation team into alleged crimes committed in Ukraine. https://www.eurojust.europa.eu/joint-investigation-team-alleged-crimes-committed-ukraine. Accessed 2 February 2025.

[56] See Statement by ICC Prosecutor, Karim A.A. Khan QC: Office of the Prosecutor joins national authorities in Joint Investigation Team on international crimes committed in Ukraine. https://www.icc-cpi.int/news/statement-icc-prosecutor-karim-aa-khan-qc-office-prosecutor-joins-national-authorities-joint. Accessed 2 February 2025.

[57] See Europol participates in joint investigation team into alleged core international crimes in Ukraine. https://www.europol.europa.eu/media-press/newsroom/news/europol-participates-in-joint-investigation-team-alleged-core-international-crimes-in-ukraine. Accessed 2 February 2025.

[58] See Joint investigation team into alleged crimes committed in Ukraine. https://www.eurojust.europa.eu/joint-investigation-team-alleged-crimes-committed-ukraine. Accessed 2 February 2025.

[59] Yudan and Suhong 2023, p. 112.

[60] See Core International Crimes Evidence Database (CICED) https://www.eurojust.europa.eu/publication/core-international-crimes-evidence-database-ciced. Accessed 2 February 2025.

[61] *Ibid.*

[62] Hill 2024, p. 248.

[63] See International Centre for the Prosecution of the Crime of Aggression against Ukraine. https://www.eurojust.europa.eu/international-centre-for-the-prosecution-of-the-crime-of-aggression-against-ukraine. Accessed 2 February 2025.

[64] Aksamitowska 2024, p. 390.

Ukraine, it is clear that this body will support the Tribunal, especially in the context of collecting and safeguarding evidence.[65]

The Genocide Network was established in 2002. Its goal is to foster collaboration between practitioners, as well as with non-governmental organizations and international bodies, to serve as a central hub for sharing information and knowledge on combating CIC.[66]

Since March 2022, Eurojust has also been participating in the EU Freeze and Seize Task Force, established by the European Commission to ensure the effective implementation of EU sanctions against Russian and Belarusian oligarchs. Eurojust identifies links between persons and companies subject to sanctions and collects information necessary for asset confiscation.[67]

Hence, Eurojust has an important place in the fight against impunity for CIC committed in Ukraine. It is the central hub that coordinates the efforts of national authorities to investigate and prosecute CIC committed during the Russian war against Ukraine. However, the EU should already today provide stronger support for the establishment of a Special Tribunal for the crime of aggression or consider other mechanisms to combat this crime. The crime of aggression is a "mother" crime for other CIC. Without prosecuting the crime of aggression, it is impossible to avoid other armed conflicts and new CIC.

18.5 Universal Jurisdiction of EU Member States and CIC Committed in Ukraine

As a general rule, states that have a connection with a suspected person or CIC must prosecute or extradite such persons to another state that wishes to do so, in other words, the principle of *"aut dedere, aut judicare"* applies.[68]

Under ordinary circumstances, a state does not have the right to extend its criminal jurisdiction to crimes committed on the territory of other states, or if the suspects or victims are not its citizens. The application of the principle of universal jurisdiction is based on the fact that some crimes (war crimes, crimes against humanity, genocide) are so core that they become a matter of concern to the international community.

---

[65] Šniutytė-Daugėlienė 2024.

[66] See Genocide Network. https://www.eurojust.europa.eu/judicial-cooperation/practitioner-networks/genocide-network; Supporting judicial authorities in the fight against core international crimes factsheet. https://www.eurojust.europa.eu/publication/supporting-judicial-authorities-fight-against-core-international-crimes-factsheet. Accessed 2 February 2025.

[67] See EU Freeze and Seize Task Force. https://www.eurojust.europa.eu/eu-freeze-and-seize-task-force. Accessed 2 February 2025.

[68] Such obligations arise from Article 1, Article 6, Article 7 of the Convention on the Prevention and Punishment of the Crime of Genocide (1948), Article 49 of the First Geneva Convention (1949), Article 50 of the Second Geneva Convention (1949), Article 129 of the Third Geneva Convention (1949), Article 146 of the Fourth Geneva Convention (1949).

Therefore, to avoid impunity the principle of universal jurisdiction is provided[69]; international law provides all states with the ability to exercise extraterritorial jurisdiction and prosecute persons suspected of crimes committed on the territory of third states[70] without reference to the place of commission, the nationality of the suspect or victim, or any other connection between the crime and the state conducting the criminal proceedings.[71] The basis of universal jurisdiction is the principle that such crimes harm the international order as a whole.

Before the full-scale invasion by the Russian Federation in 2022, criminal proceedings under universal jurisdiction were being conducted in several states, but after 2022 their number increased significantly and is expected to increase given the persistence of the failed conflict.[72] Interestingly, armed aggression has led to a rethinking of the range of crimes subject to universal jurisdiction in the EU member states. For example, the crime of aggression, which traditionally was not a crime subject to universal jurisdiction,[73] today is subject to this jurisdiction at least in four of the EU State Members (Estonia, Latvia, Lithuania, Poland).[74] At least 23 of EU Member States exercise universal jurisdiction over genocide, crimes against humanity and war crimes.[75]

However, the question arises: do EU Member States have the right or obligation to apply the principle of universal jurisdiction to CIC committed in Ukraine?

Universal jurisdiction for CIC is linked to existing norms of international law *jus cogens* and obligations *erga omnes*.[76] Therefore, every state is obliged to fight against impunity for CIC committed on the territory of a third state, using the principle of universal jurisdiction.[77] To effectively use universal jurisdiction, such a state must have sufficient evidence about the commission of CIC on the territory of a third state.

The principle of universal jurisdiction is sometimes criticized. Thus, G. Fletcher notes that the first court to hear the case has the de facto authority to decide the fate of the accused, and the whole world will have to rely on their (possibly) unjust verdict.[78] One can agree with this opinion only on the condition that a state that applies the principle of universal jurisdiction has poor standards of fair trial, and investigation and prosecution are used for political motives. In EU Member States, which have the highest standards of fair trial, such a situation is improbable.

---

[69] Bassiouni 2001, p. 82; Advisory Service on IHL of the ICRC 2021.

[70] International Commission of Jurists 2015, p. 76.

[71] Cryer et al. 2010, pp. 50–51.

[72] See Eurojust: At a Glance: Universal Jurisdiction in EU Member States. https://www.eurojust.europa.eu/sites/default/files/assets/at-a-glance-universal-jurisdiction-in-eu-member-states.pdf. Accessed 2 February 2025.

[73] Cryer et al. 2010, p. 51.

[74] See Eurojust: At a Glance: Universal Jurisdiction in EU Member States. https://www.eurojust.europa.eu/sites/default/files/assets/at-a-glance-universal-jurisdiction-in-eu-member-states.pdf. Accessed 2 February 2025.

[75] *Ibid.*

[76] Chopra 1999, pp. 4-5.

[77] *Ibid.*

[78] Fletcher 2003, p. 584.

Another question that arises regarding universal jurisdiction is: how effective can it be compared to territorial jurisdiction in the context of CIC committed in Ukraine? It is obvious that universal jurisdiction is an additional tool in the fight against impunity and cannot be as effective as domestic territorial jurisdiction.[79] However, on the other hand, given the specifics of the crimes committed and the inability of Ukraine to bring to justice the persons who committed such crimes, primarily due to their hiding in the Russian Federation, the application of universal jurisdiction by EU member states may become a means of collecting evidence and a prerequisite for closer cooperation between states in the fight against impunity.

One of the most difficult problems is covering the universal jurisdiction of EU Member States to crimes committed by the highest officials of the Russian Federation who enjoy immunity from prosecution.

Following the arrest of former Chilean President Augusto Pinochet by British authorities in October 1998, the principle of universal jurisdiction became a subject of debate. Before this case, this basis of jurisdiction had not been applied often, although it has long been recognized.[80] After the Pinochet case, the principle of universal jurisdiction began to be applied in practice, but the practice of states was quite different. As for state officials of third states, some states preferred the principle of immunity of such persons, while others proceeded from the need to apply the principle of fighting against impunity regardless of any immunities.

One of the turning points in the conceptualization of the principle of universal jurisdiction over state officials was the case concerning the Arrest Warrant of 11 April 2000 (Democratic Republic of the Congo v. Belgium) of the International Court of Justice (ICJ). The ICJ in the Judgment emphasized that "the issue and circulation of the arrest warrant of 11 April 2000 by the Belgian authorities failed to respect the immunity of the incumbent Minister for Foreign Affairs of the Congo and, more particularly, infringed the immunity from criminal jurisdiction and the inviolability then enjoyed by Mr. Yerodia under international law".[81] The ICJ has recognized the priority of the immunity of state officials from foreign criminal jurisdiction over the application of the principle of universal jurisdiction over CIC.

It appears that the mentioned Judgement of the ICJ was erroneous. In essence, the ICJ recognized the primacy of immunity of the highest state officials over the most significant human rights violations (in this case, crimes against humanity and war crimes). With this approach, it seems that from the position of the ICJ, international law has returned to the times when the anthropocentric vision of international law was almost absent and only the state and its political interests determined the essence of international law.

In the last decade, there has been a positive trend in the covering of criminal jurisdiction to CIC committed by state officials of third states, which is related to the work of the UN International Law Commission (ILC), which in 2007 decided to include the topic "Immunity of State officials from foreign criminal jurisdiction"

[79] Hall 2008, p. 401.

[80] Orentlicher 2008, p. 127.

[81] International Court of Justice 2002, para 75.

in its work program. The ILC has completed in first reading the draft Articles on the immunity of state officials from foreign criminal jurisdiction; work on this topic is in progress.[82] According to Article 7 of the Draft, in the event of such persons committing the crime of genocide, crimes against humanity, war crimes, crime of apartheid, torture or enforced disappearance, immunity *ratione materiae* does not apply.[83] Hence, any state will be able to investigate and prosecute for the commission of one of these crimes.[84]

However, the question arises, what is the use of such a draft now? Perhaps, among other things, it should become an impetus for discussing the existence of customary norms of international law regarding the non-application of immunities in the case of the commission of CIC. In the context of the armed invasion by the Russian Federation, such a Draft of the ILC may become an additional argument for the legitimacy of the investigation and prosecution within the framework of the domestic legal systems of the EU Member States of state officials of the Russian Federation for CIC.

18.6 Conclusions

The EU is a driving force in the fight against impunity for CIC. It supports both national investigations and international criminal justice. No other integration entity has such a deep understanding of the need to combat impunity for CIC committed in third countries.

The EU supports the ICC in investigating CIC committed in Ukraine after Russia's full-scale invasion of Ukraine: 31 EU Member States referred the "Situation in Ukraine" to the ICC; the financial support provided to the ICC in its investigation is quite significant; EU Member States and the OTP of the ICC are participants in the JIT of Eurojust.

Cooperation with the EU played an important role in Ukraine's ratification of the Rome Statute. In particular, Ukraine had direct obligations to ratify the Rome Statute under Article 8 of the Association Agreement with the EU. Ukraine, upon ratification, made a declaration regarding war crimes by Article 124 of the Rome Statute, stating that "for a seven-year period after the entry into force of the Rome Statute for Ukraine, it will not recognize the jurisdiction of the ICC over war crimes when the crime is alleged to have been committed by Ukrainian nationals." Apparently, such a declaration was related to the parliamentarians' fears that the ICC would be able to hold Ukrainian military personnel accountable, rather than Russian ones. This argument has been heard in political discourse over the past 10 years as a justification

[82] See Immunity of State officials from foreign criminal jurisdiction: Analytical Guide to the Work of the International Law Commission. https://legal.un.org/ilc/guide/4_2.shtml. Accessed 2 February 2025.

[83] International Law Commission 2022.

[84] *Ibid.*

for refusing to ratify the Rome Statute. Today Ukraine remains the only state that applies Article 124 and does not accept the jurisdiction of the ICC over war crimes when the crime was allegedly committed by its citizens.

Domestic investigations of CIC allegedly committed in Ukraine have been launched in 14 EU Member States. Eurojust's coordination of national authorities allows for a more effective fight against impunity for these CIC.

Today, the EU probably needs to provide stronger support for the establishment of a Special Tribunal for the crime of aggression, which is the "mother" crime of other CIC, or to think about other mechanisms to combat this crime. Without prosecuting the crime of aggression, it is impossible to avoid other armed conflicts and new CIC. It seems that after having the experience of establishing the Kosovo Specialist Chambers and terrible armed aggression in a state neighbouring the EU, the establishment of such a Tribunal based on the Agreement between the EU and Ukraine would be a crucial step in the fight against impunity for the crime of aggression. This would be one more confirmation of the EU's leadership in the fight against impunity for CIC.

Another very comprehensive issue that needs to be addressed is fighting impunity and future peace treaties with Russia. Already today, some EU Member States, which are also ICC States Parties, in particular Hungary and Slovakia, are declaring their readiness to accept the suspect V. Putin on their territory for peace negotiations and to guarantee his safety and non-extradition to the ICC. Are EU sanctions being considered for such states? And what will the EU do with all investigations after peace is concluded? Fight against impunity and justice should be served and all those who committed CIC should be held accountable.

References

Aksamitowska K (2024) International Centre for the Prosecution of Russia's Crime of Aggression against Ukraine and the Role of New Technologies and Justice Hubs in the Fight against Impunity. Polish Yearbook of International Law 43:381–392. https://doi.org/10.24425/pyil.2024.152309

Bassiouni MC (2001) Universal jurisdiction for international crimes: historical perspectives and contemporary practice. Virginia Journal of International Law 42. 81–161

Caianiello M (2022) The Role of the EU in the Investigation of Serious International Crimes Committed in Ukraine. Towards a New Model of Cooperation? European Journal of Crime, Criminal Law and Criminal Justice 30(3–4):219–237. https://doi.org/10.1163/15718174-30030002

Cataleta M (2022) The Kosovo Specialist Chambers, an international tribunal inside the national judicial system. Journal of International Criminal Law 3(1):1–9. https://doi.org/10.22034/jicl.2022.144695

Chopra J (1999) Establishing universal jurisdiction. Brown Journal of World Affairs 6(1):4–5

Cryer R, Friman H, Robinson D, Wilmshurst E (2010) An Introduction to International Criminal Law and Procedure, 2nd edn. Cambridge University Press. https://doi.org/10.1017/CBO9780511760808

Fletcher G (2003) Against universal jurisdiction. Journal of International Criminal Justice 1(3):580–584

Gutnyk V (2015) International Criminal Court: prospects for criminal prosecution of the international crimes committed in Ukraine in 2013–2015. Revista Moldovenească de Drept Internațional și Relații Internaționale 3 (37):139–148

Hall K (2008) Universal Jurisdiction: It's Back. American Society of International Law Proceedings 102:397–404

Hill S (2024) International efforts to collect evidence related to Russia's aggression against Ukraine. Saint Louis University Law Journal 68(2):243–256

International Commission of Jurists (2015) International Law and the Fight Against Impunity - A Practitioners Guide. https://www.icj.org/wp-content/uploads/2015/12/Universal-Fight-against-impunity-PG-no7-comp-Publications-Practitioners-guide-series-2015-ENG.pdf. Accessed 31 January 2025

Isokaitė-Valužė I, Grigaitė-Daugirdė G (2024) Invocation of International (Treaty) Law Principles Against an Aggressor State: Suspension, Restriction of Membership Rights, Expulsion? Kyiv-Mohyla Law and Politics Journal 10:19–50. https://doi.org/10.18523/kmlpj320035.2024-10.19-50

Masol S (2022) Ukraine and the International Criminal Court: Between *Realpolitik* and Post-truth Politics. Journal of International Criminal Justice 20(1):167–190. https://doi.org/10.1093/jicj/mqac012

Mucaj A (2021) The Kosovo Specialist Chambers and Specialist Prosecutor's Office paradox. International Criminal Law Review 21(2):367–390

Nemane V V, Gunjal I D (2015) Article 124 of the Rome Statute of the International Criminal Court: 'transitional provision' or 'the right to (convenient) opt-out'. International Criminal Law Review 15(5): 949–969. https://doi.org/10.1163/15718123-01505004

Orentlicher D F (2008) Universal Jurisdiction: A Pragmatic Strategy In Pursuit Of A Moralist's Vision. In: Sadat L, Scharf MP (eds) The Theory and Practice of International Criminal Law. Brill Nijhoff, Leiden, The Netherlands. https://doi.org/10.1163/ej.9789004166318.i-448.17

Parker K (1989) Jus cogens: compelling the law of human rights. Hastings International and Comparative Law Review 12(2):411–464

Sarkin J (2012) Why the prohibition of enforced disappearance has attained jus cogens status in international law. Nordic Journal of International Law 81(4):537–584

Scheers I (2010) From Rome to Kampala: an analysis of article 124 of the Statute of the International Criminal Court. International Criminal Law Review 10(3):301–324. https://doi.org/10.1163/157181210X507840

Shany Y (2010) In defence of functional interpretation of article 12(3) of the Rome Statute. Journal of International Criminal Justice 8(2): 329–344

Simonen K (1999) Internal Conflicts and Protection of Fundamental Human Rights as an Obligation Erga Omnes. Finnish Yearbook of International Law 10:191–208

Šniutytė-Daugėlienė M (2024) Future collaboration and cooperation of the International Centre for the Prosecution of the Crime of Aggression against Ukraine (ICPA) with the Special Tribunal. Seminar on the Special Tribunal for the Crime of Aggression against Ukraine – What role for regional organisations such as the Council of Europe? 10 April 2024. https://rm.coe.int/eurojust-intervention-on-icpa-cahdi-seminar-2783-5752-3465-v-1/1680af5e70. Accessed 31 January 2025

Souminen A (2008) The past, present and the future of Eurojust. Maastricht Journal of European and Comparative Law 15(2):217–234. https://doi.org/10.1177/1023263X0801500204

Strupinskienė L (2023) Life After Conviction at the International Criminal Tribunal for the former Yugoslavia: Mapping the Empirical Reality. Journal of International Criminal Justice 21(1):113–135. https://doi.org/10.1093/jicj/mqad010

Tabak S (2009) Article 124, war crimes, and the development of the Rome Statute. Georgetown Journal of International Law 40(3): 1069–1100

Tarfusser C J, Chiarini G (2023) Without specific declaration of jurisdiction and ratification: Procedural weaknesses of the International Criminal Court's investigation into the Russo-Ukrainian war. Texas Tech Law Review 56(1):171–184

Tiribelli C (2008) The Exercise of Jurisdiction of the International Criminal Court: A Legal and Political Compromise which Renders its Effective Functions a rather Complicated Matter. Sri Lanka Journal of International Law 20(1):1–24. https://jil.law.cmb.ac.lk/past-issues/volume-20-issue-1/

Wiebelhaus-Brahm E, Ainley K (2023) The evolution of funding for the International Criminal Court: Budgets, donors and gender justice. Journal of Human Rights. 22(1):31–46. https://doi.org/10.1080/14754835.2022.2156276

Yeneabat D (2020) Fighting against Impunity in Ethiopia: An Emphasis on Crime against Humanity. Beijing Law Review, 11: 43–63. https://doi.org/10.4236/blr.2020.111004

Yudan T, Suhong Y (2023) The Joint Investigation Team in Ukraine: An Opportunity for the International Criminal Court? Chinese Journal of International Law 22(1):103–119. https://doi.org/10.1093/chinesejil/jmad005

Zenginkuzucu D M (2021) Enforcement of the Cooperation Obligation with the ICC for the Accountability under International Criminal Law. Journal of International Criminal Law 2(1):1–17. https://doi.org/10.22034/jicl.2021.128764

International Legal Documents, Practice of International Courts and Other Sources

Advisory Service on IHL of the ICRC (2021) Universal Jurisdiction over War Crimes – Factsheet. https://www.icrc.org/en/document/universal-jurisdiction-over-war-crimes-factsheet. Accessed 31 January 2025

Agreement between the International Criminal Court and the European Union on cooperation and assistance (2006). Document 22006A0428(01). http://data.europa.eu/eli/agree_internation/2006/313/oj. Accessed 31 January 2025

Amendment of the Constitution of the Republic of Kosovo (2015) Article 162: The Specialist Chambers and the Specialist Prosecutor's Office. www.scp-ks.org/sites/default/files/public/amendment_of_the_constitution_-no_24.pdf. Accessed 31 January 2025

Association Agreement (2014) between the European Union and its Member States, of the one part, and Ukraine, of the other part. Document 22014A0529(01)

Colombia Declarations to the Rome Statute of the International Criminal Court (2002). https://treaties.un.org/pages/ViewDetails.aspx?src=TREATY&mtdsg_no=XVIII-10&chapter=18&clang=_en. Accessed 31 January 2025

Constitution of Ukraine (1996). https://zakon.rada.gov.ua/laws/show/254%D0%BA/96-%D0%B2%D1%80#Text. Accessed 31 January 2025

Council of the European Union (2011). Decision 2011/168/CFSP of 21 March 2011 on the International Criminal Court and repealing Common Position 2003/444/CFSP, 21 March 2011. Document 32011D0168. http://data.europa.eu/eli/dec/2011/168/oj. Accessed 31 January 2025

European External Action Service (2024) Mongolia: Statement by the Spokesperson on the visit of the Russian President. https://www.eeas.europa.eu/eeas/mongolia-statement-spokesperson-visit-russian-president_en. Accessed 31 January 2025

France Declarations to the Rome Statute of the International Criminal Court (2000). https://treaties.un.org/pages/ViewDetails.aspx?src=TREATY&mtdsg_no=XVIII-10&chapter=18&clang=_en. Accessed 31 January 2025

International Court of Justice (2002) Case concerning the Arrest Warrant of 11 April 2000 (Democratic Republic of the Congo v. Belgium), Judgment. https://www.icj-cij.org/sites/default/files/case-related/121/121-20020214-JUD-01-00-EN.pdf. Accessed 31 January 2025

International Criminal Court (2014) The First Declaration lodged by the Government of Ukraine accepted ICC jurisdiction with respect to alleged crimes committed on Ukrainian territory from 21 November 2013 to 22 February 2014. https://www.icc-cpi.int/sites/default/files/itemsDocuments/997/declarationRecognitionJuristiction09-04-2014.pdf. Accessed 31 January 2025

International Criminal Court (2015) The Second Declaration extended this time period on an open-ended basis to encompass ongoing alleged crimes committed throughout the territory of Ukraine from 20 February 2014 onwards. https://www.icc-cpi.int/sites/default/files/iccdocs/other/Ukraine_Art_12-3_declaration_08092015.pdf. Accessed 31 January 2025
International Criminal Court (2022). https://www.icc-cpi.int/sites/default/files/2022-04/20220401-Chile-Letter-to-OTP.PDF. Accessed 31 January 2025
International Criminal Court (2024) Report of the Committee on Budget and Finance on the work of its forty-fifth session (ICC-ASP/23/25), https://asp.icc-cpi.int/sites/default/files/asp_docs/ICC-ASP-23-25-ENG.pdf. Accessed 31 January 2025
International Law Commission (2022) Immunity of State officials from foreign criminal jurisdiction: Texts and titles of the draft articles adopted by the Drafting Committee on first reading. UN Doc: A/CN.4/L.969. URL: https://daccess-ods.un.org/access.nsf/Get?Open&DS=A/CN.4/L.969&Lang=E. Accessed 31 January 2025
Opinion of the Constitutional Court of Ukraine (2001) In the case on the constitutional submission of the President of Ukraine on the provision of an opinion on the compliance of the Constitution of Ukraine with the Rome Statute of the International Criminal Court (Rome Statute case), July 11, 2001. Case N 1-35/2001 N 3-в/2001. https://zakon.rada.gov.ua/laws/show/v003v710-01#Text. Accessed 31 January 2025
Regulation (EU) 2018/1727 of the European Parliament and of the Council (2018). Document 32018R1727. Current consolidated version: 31/10/2023
Resolution of the Verkhovna Rada of Ukraine (2014) Statement of the Verkhovna Rada of Ukraine to the International Criminal Court on the recognition by Ukraine of the jurisdiction of the International Criminal Court over the commission of crimes against humanity by senior state officials, which led to particularly grave consequences and mass murder of Ukrainian citizens during peaceful protests in the period from November 21, 2013 to February 22, 2014. https://zakon.rada.gov.ua/laws/show/790-18#Text. Accessed 31 January 2025
Resolution of the Verkhovna Rada of Ukraine (2015) On the Statement of the Verkhovna Rada of Ukraine "On the recognition by Ukraine of the jurisdiction of the International Criminal Court over the commission of crimes against humanity and war crimes by senior officials of the Russian Federation and leaders of the terrorist organizations "DPR" and "LPR", which led to particularly grave consequences and mass murder of Ukrainian citizens", February 4, 2015. https://zakon.rada.gov.ua/laws/show/145-19#Text. Accessed 31 January 2025
Ukraine: proposal regarding article 5 (1998). UN Doc. A/CONF.183/C.1/L33.
Ukraine: proposal regarding article 77 (1998). UN Doc. A/CONF.183/C.1/WGP/L.6.
Ukraine: proposed amendment to article 37, paragraph 7 (1998). UN Doc. A/CONF.183/C.l/L31/Rev.l/Add.l

Vitalii Gutnyk is a dr. and professor of international law at the Ivan Franko National University of Lviv and the Law Faculty of Vilnius University.

Chapter 19
European Union Law in the Case-Law of the Lithuanian Constitutional Court: Still an Open Question?

Egidijus Kūris

Contents

Abstract The chapter deals with the constitutional aspects of Lithuania's accession to the European Union, including the referendum on the accession, held in 2003, and the constitutional amendments aimed at enabling the accession. It is demonstrated that the Constitutional Court had a significant role to play in the process, both before and after the accession. A special emphasis is put on the EU law-friendly interpretation in the Constitutional Court's case-law of the relationship between the EU law and Lithuanian law, and the rule of collision as formulated by the Constitutional Court in 2006. This rule consolidates the Constitution's supremacy vis-à-vis EU law, but at the same time postulates the primacy of application of EU law vis-à-vis all other domestic legal acts. It is shown that the Court itself departed from this rule in 2017, and then reverted to it in 2020.

Keywords Constitution of the Republic of Lithuania · Constitutional amendments · Constitutional Court of the Republic of Lithuania · Court of Justice of the European Union · European Union law · EU law-friendly interpretation · Lithuania's accession to the European Union · Referendum · Rule of collision

---

E. Kūris (✉)
Faculty of Law, Vilnius University, Vilnius, Lithuania
e-mail: egidijus.kuris@tf.vu.lt

I. Isokaitė-Valužė and H. Šinkūnas (eds.), *The European Union 2004-2024*,
https://doi.org/10.1007/978-94-6265-718-2_19

19.1 Introduction

When Lithuania was marking the tenth anniversary of her membership in the European Union (hereinafter also 'EU', 'Union'), the trajectory taken during these ten years was assessed overall positively, even if it was acknowledged that in certain fields the breakthrough did not happen or was lower than expected.[1] The second decade added to this generally positive assessment,[2] even in the face of various structural inadequacies that the EU suffers from. It is not surprising that official sources portray Lithuania's EU membership as undoubtedly a success story, with a high dose of apologetics and little (if any) criticism.[3] Indeed, it would be difficult to argue otherwise, because many of Lithuania's obvious achievements in the last two decades are related to her EU membership. Public support for EU membership has slightly decreased in the last years, but remains high.[4]

The positive assessment of Lithuania's EU membership relates more to the better standard of living, economic growth and enhanced national security, and seems to be less associated with the common legal space of the EU. But being a common legal space does not mean that all domestic law of EU Member States is subordinated to EU law, in particular owing to the declared recognition of their constitutional identity.[5] The EU project does not envisage complete unification of its Member States' law, therefore the relationship between the latter and EU law will always not be devoid of tensions. In interpreting this relationship, national constitutional (and equivalent) courts overall aim at ensuring harmony between domestic law and EU law (which does not exclude the possibility of abusing this notion.[6] This can be said, although perhaps with less certainty, about the Court of Justice of the European Union (hereinafter also 'CJEU'). But there is no wand which would guarantee that the coveted harmony is achieved.

The phrase 'an open question?' in the title of this chapter may look provocative, at least for some, because so much has been done to 'close' it. To wit, the 2004 Constitutional Act "On Membership of the Republic of Lithuania in the European Union" (hereinafter also 'the Constitutional Act' or 'the Act') was meant to dot all the i's and cross all the t's, by establishing the EU law's being a constituent part of Lithuania's legal system and, in the case of collision, its 'supremacy' over Lithuania's legal acts. On the surface, this looks like total subordination. Not really, for the final arbiter on what the Constitution (a constituent part of which the Act is[7]) says is

---

[1] Maniokas 2015; Švedas 2014.

[2] Vitkus 2024.

[3] Permanent Representation of the Republic of Lithuania to the European Union 2024; State Data Agency 2024.

[4] Fitzgerald 2023.

[5] Maes 2024.

[6] Scholtes 2023.

[7] Lithuania's Constitution is a composite codified document, which consists of five separate Acts. Apart of the Act called the Constitution, adopted in the 1992 referendum (sometimes called 'the main body of the Constitution'), it includes, as the Constitution's constituent part, four other Acts.

the Constitutional Court, whose interpretation of EU law's supremacy clause is, as we shall see, not so straightforward. The phrase 'an open question?' therefore not only looks provocative—it indeed is. And this is just one aspect of contradictions in Lithuania's path to the EU, which was not consistent from the perspective of its own law. In view of Lithuania's achievements related to her EU membership, this may sound like a heresy. But it is not and I turn to demonstrating that.

19.2 Amendments to Articles 47, 119 and 125 of the Constitution

The timeline of Lithuania's joining the EU is well known. In August 1991, less than a week after the collapse of the putsch in Moscow which eventually led to the collapse of the USSR, the European Community (hereinafter 'EC') recognised Lithuania's independence. In the course of the dialogue between Lithuania and the EC, Lithuania committed to adopt *acquis communautaire*. In July 1994, the Free Trade Agreement was signed between the EU and Lithuania, and in December they started negotiations on the Association Agreement, which was signed on 6 December 1995. Two days later, Lithuania submitted a formal request for admission. In 1999, she was invited to the membership negotiations, which were completed in 2002. The Accession Treaty was signed with Lithuania and the other nine new Member States in April 2003. In May, the referendum was held, in which more than 90% of those participating voted in favour of the accession. The Treaty was ratified by the Seimas (parliament) in September 2003. On 1 May 2004 Lithuania acceded to the EU, and in August of that year the Constitution was supplemented by the Constitutional Act "On Membership of the Republic of Lithuania in the European Union", which constitutionalised Lithuania's EU membership. In addition, other constitutional amendments were made to enable the very accession to the EU, and one (as it appeared much later, ill-fated) was made after it to enable Lithuania's membership in the Economic and Monetary Union of the EU. Further, I deal with these amendments, albeit not in strict chronological order. I begin with the amendments to Articles 47, 119 and 125 of the Constitution.

Two of them, adopted prior to the 1992 referendum, were indicated in the initial wording of Article 150 of the Constitution: the Constitutional Law "On the State of Lithuania" of 11 February 1991, and the Constitutional Act "On the Non-Alignment of the Republic of Lithuania to Post-Soviet Eastern Unions" of 8 June 1992. In 2004, Article 150 was supplemented by two other entries: the Law "On the Procedure for the Entry into Force of the Constitution of the Republic of Lithuania" of 25 October 1992, and the Constitutional Act "On Membership of the Republic of Lithuania in the European Union" of 13 July 2004. It is noteworthy that the first of these new entries, although adopted together with the 'main body of the Constitution', initially was not considered to be the Constitution's constituent part, but the Constitutional Court interpreted that it was its constituent part, irrespective of whether it was mentioned in Article 150 or not. Constitutional Court, Case 1/02, Ruling, 29 October 2003.

Article 47 was amended twice. It, in its initial wording, prohibited the acquisition of land to foreign nationals. In 1996, the conditions for foreign nationals to acquire and own non-agricultural land in Lithuania were mollified, which was one of the conditions for the signing of the Association Agreement. The 2003 amendment lifted the restrictions to EU nationals for acquiring land, internal waters and forests, but a 'constitutional law'[8] had to determine the conditions for the acquisition. As agreed with the European Commission, a seven-year transitional period was established for the full enjoyment of the right of acquisition, and consolidated in the respective 'constitutional law'. The transitional period had to end in 2011, but the Government negotiated its extension for three more years. Still, having obtained the Commission's agreement, the Seimas forgot to inscribe the extension into the 'constitutional law'. This meant that the extension did not take place under Lithuanian law. Only after many to-and-fros an amendment to the 'constitutional law' was adopted in November 2011. The extended period had to end on 1 May 2014. As that date approached, 300,000 signatures of citizens were collected to initiate the referendum on the restoration of the initial wording of Article 47, but it, held in June 2004, failed because of the low turnout.[9] In this context the Constitutional Court adopted a ruling,[10] in which it began formulating the doctrine of limitations on the amendments to the Constitution. That case was related to the central bank (see below) and not related to this particular referendum (which was at that time in its early stage of signature collection), but a message was sent that constitutional amendments which destroyed 'the harmony of constitutional regulation as integrity' were not permitted under the Constitution. Said doctrine was later further developed and expanded, initially in the case already related to the failed referendum but decided after it,[11] and then in 2000.[12] One line of development was that constitutional amendments are not permitted, if they run contrary to Lithuania's commitments stemming from its EU membership (of course, until she remains an EU Member State).

Coming back to the amendments to Article 47 of the Constitution, there was a certain paradox stemming from their sequence and wording. The 1996 amendment explicitly consolidated Lithuania's geopolitical orientation to the EU by stipulating that 'foreign subjects' entitled to acquire agricultural land in Lithuania had to meet the 'criteria of European and transatlantic [i.e. NATO] integration', as defined in a 'constitutional law'. The 2002 amendment was worded so that the mentioning of Lithuania's European integration was omitted. Hence the paradox: the amendment which did not enable Lithuania's EU membership, mentioned it as an aspiration (albeit in other words), whereas the later one which enabled it by removing one of

[8] The name 'constitutional laws' is misleading and indeed unfortunate. They do not have the force of the Constitution and are not part of it. But their legal force is higher than that of ordinary laws, and their adoption and amendment is subject to a more complicated procedure (Para 3, Article 69 of the Constitution).

[9] Kūris 2022, pp. 439–441.

[10] Constitutional Court, Case 22/2013, Ruling, 24 January 2014.

[11] Constitutional Court, Case 16/2014-29/2014, Ruling, 11 July 2014.

[12] Constitutional Court, Case 5/219, Ruling, 30 July 2020. Kūris 2023, pp. 123–126.

the major obstacles on this path was silent on this matter. The topic of EU membership reappeared in the Constitution only with the coming into force of the 2004 Constitutional Act.

Another constitutional amendment which was needed for Lithuania's acceding to the EU was related to municipal elections. Initially, the right (both active and passive) to take part in municipal elections was reserved only for Lithuanian citizens. In 2002, Article 119 was amended so that now it permitted participation of foreign nationals in municipal elections.[13] Today[14] it would be difficult to explain why this right was extended not only to the nationals of the EU Member States but also to those of other foreign states, including those clearly unfriendly to Lithuania and the EU. A few months later, in December 2002, the Constitutional Court disqualified the 'constitutional law' which postponed the coming into force of that amendment for a later date, so it could not be applied to the municipal elections which took place in December 2002,[15] which, when the Court delivered its ruling, were already a *fait accompli*. The Court based its finding on the consideration that, under the Constitution, the 'constitutional law', being of lower force than the amendment itself, could not limit the operation of the latter. This finding produced an oxymoron 'unconstitutional constitutional law'. In hindsight, the 2002 amendment to Article 119 should be held as having entered into force in July 2022, but that *ex post* rationalisation could have no effect on the 2002 municipal elections, in which foreign nationals did not take part under the *a posteriori* disqualified 'constitutional law'.

The most controversial was the amendment to Article 125, and this controversy showed up many years after the amendment was adopted. It was adopted in 2006, when Lithuania had already been in the EU for two years. Para 2 of Article 125, in its original (1992) wording, established the exclusive right of the Bank of Lithuania, i.e. the central bank, to issue currency, which from 1993 was litas. Lithuania aspired to introduce the euro, for which this provision was an obstacle, therefore it had to be abandoned. In 2006, it was abolished (simply deleted). In parallel, in order to ensure the independence of the central bank and the status of the Chairperson of its Board (in particular in order to secure his or her position against arbitrary dismissal from office by the political branches of state power), Para 3 of Article 125 was supplemented by the provision that the "legal status of the Chairperson of the Board of the Bank of Lithuania, as well as the grounds for his release from duties, shall be established by law". As it soon appeared, the expectation that the euro would be introduced in 2007, were overly optimistic, but the amendment was there and could wait for better times. In the end, the euro was introduced in 2015.[16] It seems

[13] This was not the only amendment of Article 119, but others were unrelated to the EU. Namely, this Article was amended in 1996 (effective in 1997)—it extended the term of municipal councils from two to three years. The 2002 amendment extended it to four years. In 2022, Article 119 (and some others) were amended to introduce direct elections of mayors of municipalities.

[14] In particular, in the face of the ongoing Russian war against Ukraine and subversive activities in many countries, including the EU Member States.

[15] Constitutional Court, Case 49/2000, Ruling, 24 December 2002.

[16] A provocative question, though never seriously raised, would be: on what formal constitutional basis litas continued to be issued by the Bank of Lithuania in 2007–2015.

that the amendment to Article 125 would have not given rise to any controversy, had there not been another amendment proposed in 2013. The latter was completely unrelated to the central bank,[17] still, it was controversial both on its merits and (even more) from the standpoint of the procedure of its adoption, because its final version was submitted not by 1/4 of Seimas Members or 300,000 citizens, but by a Seimas committee. The procedure of the proposed new amendment followed that of the 2006 amendment. Few could have predicted that those who proposed the new amendment would take such a defensive stance and would attempt to justify their motion on the basis of a dubious precedent from 2006. But they did much more than that. The Seimas *in corpore* applied to the Constitutional Court with the request to examine the constitutionality of the 2006 amendment on the central bank. Without exaggeration, this was the instrumentalisation of the Court. What was at risk was the introduction of the euro, scheduled for 1 January 2015. As it was perceived then, if the Court found the 2006 amendment unconstitutional, the central bank's exclusive power to issue currency would be restored, and a repeated amendment would have to undergo a full procedure which, at best, would last close to a year. Also, the repeated amendment would have become a card in various *quid pro quo*.[18] It was obvious that the Seimas, which challenged the 2006 amendment, expected that the Constitutional Court would not dare to disqualify it. But it did dare.[19] It found the amendment unconstitutional on account of the deficiency of the procedure of its adoption. Thus, in addition to the oxymoron 'unconstitutional constitutional law', Lithuania obtained an 'unconstitutional constitutional amendment'. True, while unconstitutional constitutional amendments are not unknown in some countries as, *inter alia*, a tool against populist and abusive constitution-making,[20] the very idea

[17] It was related to the execution of the judgment of the European Court of Human Rights in *Paksas v. Lithuania* (no. 39432/04, Judgment, 6 January 2011), which required that the prohibition to stand in parliamentary elections for the person, who has been removed from office or whose parliamentary mandate has been revoked in impeachment proceedings, is made not termless. The relevant constitutional amendment was passed only in 2022.

[18] The procedural issue in question was raised in public discourse in October 2013 (a confession: for the first time, by the author of this chapter). The debate exploded. The proposed new amendment was brought to a halt. On 7 November 2013, the Seimas adopted the resolution, requesting that the Constitutional Court examines the constitutionality of the 2006 amendment. Had the Court not prioritised this case and examined it without special celerity, it would have been decided in late spring or summer of 2014, at the earliest. Only then the motion to amend Article 125 could have been submitted to the parliament. On constitutional amendments, the Seimas must vote twice, with an interval of no less than three months (and a qualified majority is needed during each vote). Thus, the first vote could take place in summer, the second in October or even November 2014. At best, the amendment would have entered into force one month later, that is to say, in December 2014. If the *quid pro quo* were not reached, the amendment was not adopted, the new motion on the same matter might be submitted no earlier that after one year. The English and Portuguese call these *quid pro quo* deals, respectively, *horse trading* and *comércio de cavalos*; Italians and Estonians, respectively, *mercato delle vacche* and *lehmakauplemine*; and Lithuanians call them *pokiliminiai susitarimai* or *pokiliminiai sandoriai*—under-carpet dealings.

[19] Constitutional Court, Case 22/2013, Ruling, 24 January 2014.

[20] Barak 2011; Dixon and Landau 2015; Roznai 2017; Albert 2018; Roznai and Hostovsky Brandes 2019.

of their possibility still roils the minds of those who consider that, as a matter of principle, no court should invalidate what has been consolidated by the parliament as a constitutional provision.

Be that as it may, the predictions, that the introduction of the euro might be thwarted by the finding of the unconstitutionality of the 2006 amendment, did not materialise. The Constitutional Court, in a real *tour de force*, did not restore the validity of the earlier Para 2 of Article 125 of the Constitution, which was abolished in 2006. In its interpretation, Lithuania being the EU Member State, has undertaken commitments related to its membership in the Economic and Monetary Union of the EU and the abandonment of the national currency, once the conditions for the introduction of the euro were fulfilled (which in 2014 was a confirmed fact). This, in and of itself, did not allow for the restoration of that previous provision. Paradoxically enough, the current wording of Article 125 is published in all official sources (including the register of legal acts, but also on the Constitutional Court's internet page) with a peculiar note after the text of two of its paragraphs[21] which states that the law amending Article 125, "in view of the procedure of its adoption, is in conflict with Para 1 of Article 147 of the Constitution of the Republic of Lithuania".[22] Paragraph 1 of Article 125, wherein it is established that "[i]n the Republic of Lithuania, the Bank of Lithuania shall be the central bank, which belongs to the State of Lithuania by right of ownership", has been left intact. The note leaves an uninformed readership guessing as to what is the force of the second[23] paragraph, which establishes that "[t]he procedure for the organisation and activities of the Bank of Lithuania, its powers, and the legal status of the Chairperson of the Board of the Bank of Lithuania, as well as the grounds for his release from duties, shall be established by law". Very few would turn for clarity to the Court's ruling, where it is explained that the content of the formally disqualified provisions of that Paragraph stem from the Constitution, in particular from the Constitutional Act.

19.3 The 2003 Referendum and Beyond

Now, back to 2003. The Accession Treaty was signed in April, the accession was scheduled for 1 May 2004, but there remained one constitutional question, a fundamental one: did the forthcoming membership mean that Lithuania sacrificing its sovereignty? The opponents of membership were pointing to numerous constitutional provisions, which, in their interpretation, prohibited Lithuania from giving

---

[21] Instead of the previous three, the second of them, which consolidated the Bank of Lithuania's exclusive right to issue currency, being abolished.

[22] The note goes on by adding (in square brackets, whose function is somewhat confusing) that, "[i]n accordance with the ruling of the Constitutional Court of 24 January 2014, from the day of the official publication of this ruling, Paragraph 2 of Article 125 of the Constitution may not be applied. This does not mean that Article 125 of the Constitution comes into force in the wording effective before the entry into force of the Law Amending Article 125 of the Constitution".

[23] Formerly the third.

away even part of its sovereignty to any international union, EU or other (see below). To overcome such arguments, which, it must be underlined, were based on direct citations from the Constitution, a clear expression of the will of the people was needed, which could be convincing only if obtained by a referendum. For the authorities (which were pro-EU), the anticipated difficulty was not the exact percentage of votes cast for membership, as it was predicted that it would be high, but the turnout of the electorate. Had the latter not reached 50%, this would have made the referendum legally ineffective, notwithstanding the percentage of votes cast for the accession; if it was only slightly higher than the threshold, even the formally positive outcome could amount to a public relations disaster, especially if the majority of 'yes' votes was not overwhelming. The authorities therefore gave it their all to attract as many voters as they could. In the end, the referendum was a success: the turnout was 63%, out of which almost 90% voted 'yes'.[24] Is all well that ends well? It depends.

When the opponents of the membership (clearly less numerous today than in 2003–2004, but even then they were in the minority) question the 2003 referendum, they usually mockingly bring up the action of a retail chain, when a buyer, having shown to the cashier the sticker which certified that he or she voted in the referendum, could buy washing powder, a chocolate bar, a can of lemonade or a bottle of beer for a symbolic Lithuanian cent. Unsavoury as it might look, this was a private initiative. Other critics pointed to the national TV broadcaster's prime time edition on the eve of the referendum, where high-ranking politicians (such as the Speaker of the Parliament, ministers and so on) urged the voters not only to show up tomorrow but to vote 'yes'—in defiance of the statute which prohibited any last-day agitation. But it is seldom remembered in the public discourse what was done by the Seimas in terms of statutory amendments, aimed at attracting more voters to the ballot-boxes at whatever cost. Some of these amendments later became the object of constitutional review—and did not pass the test.

More specifically, one amendment aimed at a greater attraction of voters belonging to ethnic minorities. In several constituencies, where Russian or Polish minorities constituted a sizeable portion of the population (10% and more), voters belonging to these minorities could, if they wished, receive ballots not in Lithuanian, which was the state language, but in their native languages. The Seimas thus connived at the fact that, thirteen years after the restoration of independence, some Russian- and Polish-speaking citizens looked for such privileges, and indulged those who considered it to be normal that they were not able (even if in fact they were) or did not want to answer 'yes' or 'no' to the question of state importance. What is more, the parliament even did not attempt to conceal that this statutory amendment was related to the particular referendum on Lithuania's accession to the EU, for the ballots in other languages were foreseen only for referenda on Lithuania's membership in international organisations, as if the usage of plural form of the latter word made any sense. In 2006, this amendment was struck down by the Constitutional Court as unconstitutional,[25] but then Lithuania's EU membership was already a new reality.

[24] Over 91 per cent of the valid ballots.

[25] Constitutional Court, Case 25/03, Ruling, 10 May 2006.

The Court found it important to provide its ruling with the proviso that its finding did not, in and of itself, constitute a basis for challenging the results of the 2003 referendum or its legal outcomes.

Another statutory amendment pertained to the referendum's duration: it allowed to conduct the referendum not on one day. This new provision was made use of, and the referendum was held on two consecutive days, 10 and 11 May (unlike any other before it). With time, the Seimas's appetite grew. In 2018 it passed another statutory amendment, which allowed for conducting a referendum not on two consecutive days but on two days with an interval of two weeks. Again, this amendment was tailored to the particular referendum, in this case the forthcoming referendum on the introduction of multiple citizenship, which was scheduled for 2019. Multiple citizenship is allowed by the Constitution only in exceptional instances,[26] but public opinion has become generally in favour of easing this restriction or even lifting it altogether. However, this can be done only by a referendum and not by a vote in the parliament. Moreover, it is required that the majority of all eligible voters vote in favour of the proposal, which makes the success of such referenda very hard to achieve. The two-week interval was adjusted for the 2019 presidential elections: if the President was not elected in the first round, a second round was to be held after two weeks (which indeed was the case). This amendment was recognised as unconstitutional by the Constitutional Court, along with the respective provision of the Seimas resolution by which the referendum on multiple citizenship was announced.[27] Accordingly, the referendum had to be held on one day, which coincided with the first round of presidential elections. It failed, though not necessarily owing only to the striking down of the two-week interval. The Court's ruling covers a variety of subjects and is very comprehensive. At the same time it raises some questions, which can be answered only if the Court's arguments are read in their entirety. Although some fragments of the ruling may be read as suggesting that a referendum held on two (or more) consecutive days would not be blameworthy in and of itself, it transpires that, to hold such an 'extended' referendum is not allowed under the Constitution, irrespective of what the subject matter of the referendum may be and what extraordinary circumstances may have arisen in the state. In this context, the 2019 ruling has a serious gap, which is very much relevant to the long-forgotten 2003 referendum. Namely, it contains no proviso which would be similar to the one explicitly provided for in the 2006 ruling in the ballot language case. The Court mentioned that all but one of the referenda were held on a single day, that 'one' being the referendum on Lithuania's EU membership, which was held on two days. This would allow the EU-sceptic camp (small as it is now) to criticise that referendum as being held in violation of the Constitution (even if in 2003 there was no official constitutional doctrine which would prohibit a two-day referendum). But it is too late to brandish fists after the fight, therefore such criticism would bring about nothing in law or practice, especially in view of the fact that the Constitutional Court, on numerous occasions, has consolidated Lithuania's EU membership as

---

[26] As interpreted by the Constitutional Court in its ruling of 13 November 2006 (Case 45/03-36/04) and several subsequent rulings and decisions.

[27] Constitutional Court, Case 18/2018, Ruling, 15 February 2019.

consolidated in the Constitution. Also, such criticism might be rejected on the basis of the explicit mention of the 2003 referendum (both days) in the Constitutional Act, which is the Constitution's constituent part. Nevertheless, it is startling that the results of the one and only two-day referendum which presumably was held in disregard of a constitutional prohibition (if it was applicable since the day of the Constitution's coming into force in 1992) were themselves elevated to the level of the Constitution. For this reason, too, a proviso with a reference to the 2003 referendum would not have been redundant. Why did the Court choose to omit it (or not consider it), would be a question to which no answer has been provided.

19.4 The 2004 Constitutional Act, the Constitution for Europe, and the Lisbon Treaty

The 2003 referendum paved the way both for the ratification of the Accession Treaty and the adoption of the Constitutional Act, to which I now turn. In most states which aspired for EU membership in 2003–2004, heated discussions took place as to whether membership did not amount to the giving away of the states' sovereignty.[28] In this regard, Lithuania was no exception. The opponents of membership understood sovereignty as the state's unrestricted power to make decisions on all matters of policy, both domestic and foreign. They relied on Articles 1–4 of the Constitution, wherein sovereignty and independence were mentioned in categorical terms; on Article 7, which enshrined the supremacy of the Constitution; and on Article 14, which enshrined the Lithuanian language as the state language. The proponents of membership underlined not only its advantages, but also the fact that, owing to international law and states' interdependence, sovereignty did not mean (and never meant) absolute absence of constraints on state decision-making. But even among the supporters of membership there were many who were of an opinion that, in order to be on the safe side and not to compromise the very idea of EU membership, an explicit basis for it had to be provided in the Constitution. Thus, it was agreed that an intervention in the Constitution's text was necessary. The mandate for such intervention was given by the 2003 referendum. As to what precisely had to be changed in the Constitution, various proposals were voiced. One was to amend Chapter I of the Constitution. Its Articles could be amended only by a referendum, but the risk of its failure was high (it would have been a second referendum on a similar matter in less than two years, so a low turnout could be expected) and this idea was abandoned. Some were proposing the addition to the Constitution of a separate Chapter on the EU, but—where? The main body of the Constitution consists of the Preamble, fourteen Chapters and the non-numbered section entitled 'Final Provisions', the last numbered Chapter XIV (before the 'Final Provisions') being 'The Alteration of the Constitution'. Thus, the new Chapter could be included only before Chapter XIV. Even if this addition seemed like something which could be

[28] Albi 2005.

done by the Seimas, the question remained whether it would not call for re-numbering of subsequent chapters, including Chapter XIV. And here was the rub, the provisions of Chapter XIV (like those of Chapter I) could be altered only by a referendum. Hardly very many voters would have understood the sense of a referendum on such a technical issue, and this after the people had already expressed their will regarding EU membership. Thus, the idea of a separate Chapter was also a non-starter. Finally, it was agreed by all parties on the political spectrum (except diehard opponents) that the Constitution was to be supplemented by a separate Constitutional Act, which would not only rely on the will of the people expressed in the 2003 referendum and consolidate the basic tenets of Lithuania's EU membership, but also underline, in some form, the conviction that the membership was compatible with national sovereignty, whatever meaning the word 'sovereignty' entailed. That Constitutional Act had to become a constituent part of the Constitution, like the two other acts already mentioned in Article 150 of the Constitution (which it in the end became).

Said is easier than done. It was easier to reach an agreement than to implement it. The first vote on the Constitutional Act (and its inscription in Article 150) took place on 30 March. However, the Constitution requires a second vote on its amendment, which has to be held not earlier than after three months. Lithuania became a EU Member State on 1 May 2004, on which day the procedure of the adoption of the Constitutional Act was completed. The delay was related, at least by some, to the so called 'Paksasgate',[29] i.e. the impeachment of the President of the Republic, which plagued Lithuania for several months (the President was removed from office on 6 April). But this explanation, even if not completely baseless, is not an excuse. Be that as it may, the second vote on the Constitutional Act took place only on 13 July, and the Act came into force on 14 August 2004. Being late is being late. For more than three months Lithuania was in the EU without a constitutional basis, having, so to say, smuggled herself into the Union. Any rationalisation that, for becoming an EU Member State, no constitutional amendment was needed, would not hold water, because why in the end was that amendment adopted? Of course, the EU could not care less about this purely domestic legal problem. Still, one could wonder how, during that three-and-a-half-month period, a case on the constitutionality of an EU legal act or a domestic act based on EU law would have fared in the Constitutional Court or an administrative court.[30] This, however, would be futile guesswork, for no such hypothetical cases were initiated. Anyway, as of 14 August 2004 Lithuania was an EU Member State not only under the Accession Treaty, but also under her own Constitution. The Constitutional Act was meant to complete and crown the series of constitutional amendments aimed at permitting Lithuania's membership in the EU. As it turned out, it did not permit the membership—it *ex post facto* legalised it and approved of it as a new reality.

---

[29] I have borrowed the term from Taube 2008.

[30] The Constitutional Court examines compliance with the Constitution of legal acts, adopted by the Seimas, the President of the Republic, and the Government (and it has self-assumed the right to examine the constitutionality of acts adopted in referenda, but no such case was ever brought before it). Administrative courts examine the constitutionality of all other legal acts, including the acts of ministers, municipality legislation, etc.

In the preamble of the Constitutional Act, it is underlined that the Seimas, by 'adopt[ing] and proclaim[ing]' the Act, executes the will of the citizens, as expressed in the 2003 referendum. Also, the Seimas has expressed its conviction that the EU respects human rights and fundamental freedoms and that Lithuania's membership will contribute to their more efficient securing; that the EU "respects the national identity and constitutional traditions of its Member States"; and that it seeks to ensure Lithuania's fully fledged participation in the European integration, her security and the welfare of its citizens. More specifically, it is consolidated that: Lithuania as a EU Member State "shall share with or confer on the European Union the competences of its state institutions in the areas provided for in the founding Treaties of the European Union and to the extent it would, together with the other Member States of the European Union, jointly meet its membership commitments in those areas, as well as enjoy membership rights" (Article 1); "[t]he norms of European Union law shall be a constituent part of the legal system of the Republic of Lithuania"; "[w]here it concerns the founding Treaties of the European Union, the norms of European Union law shall be applied directly, while in the event of the collision of legal norms, they shall have supremacy over the laws and other legal acts of the Republic of Lithuania" (Article 2); "[t]he Government shall inform the Seimas about the proposals to adopt the acts of European Union law"; "[a]s regards the proposals to adopt the acts of European Union law regulating the areas that, under the Constitution of the Republic of Lithuania, are related to the competences of the Seimas, the Government shall consult the Seimas"; "[t]he Seimas may recommend to the Government a position of the Republic of Lithuania in respect of these proposals. The Seimas Committee on European Affairs and the Seimas Committee on Foreign Affairs may, according to the procedure established by the Statute of the Seimas, submit to the Government the opinion of the Seimas concerning the proposals to adopt the acts of European Union law"; "[t]he Government shall assess the recommendations or opinions submitted by the Seimas or its Committees and shall inform the Seimas about their execution following the procedure established by legal acts" (Article 3); "[t]he Government shall consider the proposals to adopt the acts of European Union law following the procedure established by legal acts"; "[a]s regards these proposals, the Government may adopt decisions or resolutions for the adoption of which the provisions of Article 95 of the Constitution are not applicable" (Article 4).

While the Seimas was too slow in adopting the Act, and later erred in amending Article 125 of the Constitution, it championed among all EU Member States with regard to the Treaty Establishing a Constitution for Europe (hereinafter—'Constitution for Europe'), signed on 29 October 2004 and sealed on 8 November 2004. Outrunning all other parliaments (or electorates, where the Constitution for Europe was subject to ratification by popular vote), the Seimas ratified it on 11 November 2004, with most of its members not even having read it. This extraordinary speediness was related to the purely domestic political conjuncture. 11 November was the last day of work of the parliament elected in 2000; on 15 November the newly elected parliament was scheduled to convene, with all the following consequences, including trade-offs concerning the re-distribution of influence, bearing on the formation of the new parliamentary majority and the new Government, the approval of the

Government's program etc. There was a risk that the ratification of the Constitution for Europe might become a card in these trade-offs. Few Seimas members doubted its ratification in other EU Member States, and perhaps ever fewer looked into its substance. Although some praised the Seimas for this celerity,[31] an unpleasant aftertaste remained. But the ratification was fallacious also from a formal legal point. Under the Constitution, laws must be promulgated, that is to say, officially published in their entirety and an international treaty, ratified by a law, becomes its part and acquires the force of the law. On 25 November 2004 the law by which the Constitution for Europe was ratified was published in the official gazette. Still, here it occupied only two and a half lines, which said that the Treaty Establishing a Constitution for Europe was ratified. The law was not accompanied by the text of the Constitution for Europe itself; this text was published in the EU's *Official Journal* only on 16 December 2004. However, its translation into Lithuanian was so hastily performed[32] that a review was needed, which took two years. The corrected translation was published on 2 November 2006, when the Constitution for Europe was already history, having been killed by the voters in France and The Netherlands.[33] Still, the Lithuanian law by which the Constitution for Europe was ratified was never annulled and is marked in the official register as being 'in force'.

The Seimas fared better with the Lisbon Treaty. It was signed on 12 December 2007 and sealed on 18 December 2007. The Seimas ratified it on 8 May 2008.[34] The text of the Lisbon Treaty, too, did not accompany the publication, in the official gazette, of the law by which it was ratified. However, now this non-publication in a domestic source was permitted under the amended Law on International Treaties (Article 16, amendment of 2005). The Seimas refused to consider the petition requesting to apply to the Constitutional Court for the examination of whether the Lisbon Treaty and its ratification not by a referendum was in conformity with the Constitution. Had such application been lodged, one could predict that the Court's response would have been that the Constitution was not departed from. Still, that case would have been useful for the clarification of the meaning of the constitutional provision that "[o]nly laws that are published shall be valid" (Para 2, Article 7), whose meaning might have changed with Lithuania's membership in the EU, as it is inconceivable from the practical point of view that all EU legal acts must be dubbed in Lithuanian sources.

---

[31] E.g., the doyen of the diplomatic corps (the Apostolic nuncio) in his speech before the newly elected parliament on 15 November 2004.

[32] To give a funny, but at the same time sad, example, in the Lithuanian translation, there was a mention of the date of '31 September 2007'. Article 38 of the Protocol on the Treaty and the Act of Accession of the Czech Republic, the Republic of Estonia, the Republic of Cyprus, the Republic of Latvia, the Republic of Lithuania, the Republic of Hungary, the Republic of Malta, the Republic of Poland, the Republic of Slovenia and the Slovak Republic. *OJ, C 130*, 16 December 2004.

[33] In referenda held, respectively, on 29 May 2005 and on 2 June 2005. The Constitution for Europe was rejected by 54% of French voters and 64% of Dutch voters.

[34] In this case, the champion was Hungary, whose Parliament ratified the Lisbon Treaty on 17 December 2007, that is to say, even before it was sealed.

Coming back to the 2004 Constitutional Act, it created, even if *ex post facto*, the legal basis for Lithuania's EU membership.[35] It also established the rules of adoption, by the Seimas and the Government, of decisions pertaining to Lithuania's position concerning the proposals to adopt EU acts. But regarding the latter, the text of certain provisions of the Act is unclear, at least to a certain extent.

According to the first provision of Article 4, the Government shall consider the proposals to adopt EU acts "following the procedure established by legal acts". This says virtually nothing, for in Lithuanian law-making tradition it is self-evident that any act of the Government may be adopted only according to a legally established procedure. But what exactly should be that procedure regarding the proposals to adopt EU legal acts? The second provision of the same Article attempts to clarify this matter, yet it does not succeed. It is stipulated that the Government "may adopt decisions or resolutions for the adoption of which the provisions of Article 95 of the Constitution are not applicable". In this regard, Article 95 establishes in this regard that: the Government "shall decide the affairs of state governance at its sittings[36] by adopting resolutions by a majority vote of all the members of the Government" (Para 1); the "resolutions <…> shall be signed by the Prime Minister and the Minister of the respective area" (Para 2). It is not clear which, if not all, of these provisions are not applicable to the decisions and resolutions regarding the proposals to adopt EU acts. In 2018, the Constitutional Court, found one of the provisions of the Law on the Government to be in conflict with para 1 of Article 95 of the Constitution on account that it did not require these decisions and resolutions to be adopted by a majority vote of all the members of the Government.[37] The Court examined this matter *ex propriu moto*, as the case under its examination concerned the legality of the dismissal, by a Government resolution, of the Director of the State Food and Veterinary Service, which had nothing to do with EU law. As to the other requirements of Article 95, the Court was lenient: it interpreted that the decisions and resolutions in question might be adopted not in the Government's sittings, but in "other organizational forms of the Government's activity", such as Government's conferences, and that they not necessarily had to be signed by both the Prime Minister and the Minister of the respective area. The Court did not specify who was vested with the power to sign these acts, leaving this matter to the appreciation of the law-makers. As to the possibility to use "other organizational forms of the Government's activity", the Court found no fault in that the 'form' envisaged in the Law on the Government was Government's conferences, usually held before the formal sittings and amounting to prologues to them; this allows the Government to be speedy and formal in adopting the decisions on the matters on its agenda, because they had been already discussed at the conferences and respective decisions had been approbated in principle.

There is a tricky point though, a linguistic one. The word used in Article 95 of the Constitution for marking the acts of the Government by which the "affairs of state

[35] In assessments the idea that this was done *ex post facto* is often omitted. See, e.g., Jarukaitis 2024, p. 41.

[36] I.e. meetings (*posėdžiai*), but 'sittings' is used in the Constitution's official translation.

[37] Constitutional Court, Case 5/2017, Ruling, 2 March 2018.

governance" are decided, is *nutarimas*. It is (and always was) translated into English as 'resolution'.[38] With the advent of the Constitutional Act, two more terms were introduced for marking the Government's decisions on the proposals to adopt EU acts: *sprendimas* and *rezoliucija*. The first one of them is (and always was) translated as 'decision', the second—which must not come as a surprise even to those having no command of the Lithuanian language—as 'resolution". Such translations appear also on the Court's internet page, which leaves the non-Lithuanian readership guessing as to the difference between 'resolutions' mentioned in Article 95 of the main body of the Constitution and 'resolutions' mentioned in Article 4 of the Constitutional Act. The Constitutional Court could clarify this, but the official translation of its 2 March 2018 ruling has not been provided: what we get on the Court's internet page is the note that "[i]nformation is being prepared".

More importantly, the Constitutional Act needed to be interpreted also from the standpoint of the relationship between the EU law and Lithuanian law. As mentioned, according to Article 2 of the Act, "[t]he norms of European Union law shall be a constituent part of the legal system of the Republic of Lithuania", and "[w]here it concerns the founding Treaties of the European Union, the norms of European Union law shall be applied directly, while in the event of the collision of legal norms, they shall have supremacy over the laws and other legal acts of the Republic of Lithuania". It is not unlikely that some of the drafters of this provision might have been so Eurocentric that they envisaged full subordination of Lithuania's law, not even excluding the Constitution, to EU law. At the same time, the pressure not to abandon the supremacy of the Constitution was too strong to be dropped off the scales. This explains references, in the preamble of the Act, to the EU Member States' national identity and constitutional traditions. In 2006, the Constitutional Court provided an interpretation of the provisions of Article 2 of the Act.[39] It interpreted them in a broader constitutional context. Its starting position was that the Accession Treaty was an international treaty. Under the Constitution, '[i]nternational treaties ratified by the Seimas of the Republic of Lithuania shall be a constituent part of the legal system of the Republic of Lithuania' (Para 3, Article 138), and "[i]n implementing its foreign policy, the Republic of Lithuania shall follow the universally recognised principles and norms of international law, shall seek to ensure national security and independence, the welfare of the citizens and their basic rights and freedoms, and shall contribute to the creation of the international order based on law and justice" (Para 1, Article 135). In addition, Lithuania's adherence to universally recognised principles of international law was declared in the Act "On the Restoration of the Independent State of Lithuania" on 11 March 1990. In the words of the Constitutional Court, "the observance of international obligations undertaken on its own free will, respect to the universally recognised principles of international law (as well as the

---

[38] The same goes for the resolutions of the Seimas, which are sub-statutory acts.

[39] Constitutional Court, Case 17/02-24/02-06/03-22/04, Ruling 14 March 2006. It is in this ruling that the Court first stated that, by the Constitutional Act, Lithuania's membership in the EU was 'constitutionally confirmed', which was one balanced way of stating that it was legitimised *ex post facto*. Prepositions matter. In Lithuanian, there is a difference between *patvirtinta*, the word used in the ruling, and *įtvirtinta*, which would be better suited for marking an *a priori* permission.

principle *pacta sunt servanda)* are a legal tradition and a constitutional principle of the restored independent State of Lithuania". Although international treaties are ratified by law (i.e. statute) and have the force of law (i.e. statute),[40] this does not mean that "Lithuania may disregard its international treaties, if a different legal regulation is established in its laws or constitutional laws than that established by international treaties". Consequently, "in cases when national legal acts (*inter alia,* laws or constitutional laws) establish a legal regulation which competes with that established in an international treaty, then the international treaty should be applied". The same goes for the EU law: in its regard, the Constitution "establishes *expressis verbis* the collision rule, which consolidates the priority of application of European Union legal acts in the cases where the provisions of the European Union arising out of the founding Treaties of the European Union compete with the legal regulation established in Lithuanian national legal acts (regardless of what their legal force is), save the Constitution itself".

Thus, the Constitutional Court avoids a head-on with EU law on the issue of which of the two systems (which co-exist but also can compete) is supreme in its legal force. For the purposes of application of EU law, it has made their formal confrontation irrelevant. It coined the algorithm of the primacy of application of EU law. EU law, being of extra-national origin, is still part of Lithuania's law ("constituent part of the legal system of the Republic of Lithuania"), but, like international treaties, it is not part of its national law, which only the legal acts adopted by Lithuanian institutions (or voters) are. The Constitution is not able to endow any legal instrument a higher legal force than that of its own: it only has enabled EU law to be part of Lithuania's legal system and has established that it must be applied, whatever the legal force of the competing norms, if the presumption holds that the respective EU regulation stems from the EU's founding Treaties. The issue of supremacy of either Lithuanian or EU law may arise only when EU law collides with the Constitution—then the Constitution prevails. In the collision rule cited above, the words 'save the Constitution itself' are central and crucial: without them, this rule would not be what it is, and the supremacy of the Constitution would be an empty quiver of air.

At the same time, efforts are put to interpret domestic law, including the Constitution, so that collisions are prevented. The Constitutional Court professes the EU law-friendly approach. If, however, this method does not work, the only way to achieve harmony between EU law and the Constitution is a constitutional amendment. This is nothing new. Germany changed its *Grundgesetz* in order to comply with the EU law provisions that allow women's military service. Poland changed its Constitution in order to able to comply with her obligations related to the European Arrest Warrant. France had drafted amendments to her Constitution in anticipation of the coming into force of the ill-fated Constitution for Europe, but the killing of it by its own electorate (and that of The Netherlands) made them unnecessary.

[40] Constitutional Court, Case 22/94, Conclusion, 24 January 1995; Constitutional Court, Case 8/95, Ruling, 17 October 1995; Constitutional Court, Decision, 25 April 2002; Constitutional Court, Decision, 7 April 2004.

19.5 New Adventures of the Rule of Collision

The rule of collision, coined in 2006, was repeated in the Constitutional Court's follow-up ruling of the same year,[41] and then in 2007 in the decision of 8 May 2007, adopted in the case on the constitutionality of one of the provisions of the Law on Electricity, by which the Constitutional Court applied for a preliminary ruling from the Court of Justice of the European Union regarding the provisions of one of the directives of the European Parliament and of the Council.[42] In its judgment,[43] the CJEU ruled that, *inter alia*, the provisions in question had to be interpreted as leaving a broad discretion to the national legislator. With that in mind, the Constitutional Court found no violation of the challenged statutory provision.[44] But the CJEU distorted the Constitutional Court's case-law by incorrectly citing the rule of collision: it deliberately cut off the last four words 'save the Constitution itself'; as it appears, the provisions of the directive in question would have been interpreted in the same way also without this ungainly shenanigan. It is understandable that the CJEU guards the serenity of EU law, but the jealousy with which it is guarded calls for being tempered. It is only a rhetorical question whether the CJEU would have dared to cut off the crucial fragment of a constitutional rule, had it been applied by, say, *Bundesverfassungsgericht* or *Conseil constitutionnelle* (in whose interpretation the Treaty of Lisbon could be ratified only after the French Constitution was respectively amended). So much to the respect to the Member States' national identity and constitutional traditions on behalf of the CJEU, or at least on behalf of that particular five-judge composition.

Be that as it may, it has become commonplace for the Constitutional Court to rely both on the provisions of the EU primary and even secondary law and on the case-law of the CJEU. At times, in order to obtain additional arguments for its reasoning, it even slows down the examination of a case before it, if it is known that the CJEU is about to deliver a judgment in a case where the issue under examination is the same as in the case before the Constitutional Court. For instance, it waited until Lithuania lost its case to the European Commission regarding right-hand-vehicles,[45] and then delivered the judgment finding that the Lithuanian domestic regulation was unconstitutional.[46] Even more symptomatic was the Court's ruling on the reunification of same-sex families,[47] wherein arguments are drawn from the CJEU judgment

---

[41] Constitutional Court, Case 30/03, Ruling, 21 December 2006.

[42] Constitutional Court, Case 47/04, Decision, 8 May 2007.

[43] CJEU, Case C-239/07, *Julius Sabatauskas and Others*, Judgment, 9 October 2008, ECLI:EU:C:2008:551.

[44] Constitutional Court, Case 47/04, Ruling, 4 December 2008.

[45] CJEU, Case C-61/12 *European Commission v. Republic of Lithuania*, Judgment, 20 March 2014, ECLI:EU:C:2014:172.

[46] Constitutional Court, Case 18/2012, Ruling, 6 February 2015.

[47] Constitutional Court, Case 16/2016, Ruling, 11 January 2019.

of 5 June 2018.[48] But such jurisprudential transplants do not mean that the EU law replaces national constitutional law; the case-law of the CJEU is the source of its development, among others. The Constitutional Court has stated, not once, that it is a source of interpretation of Lithuania's law, which notion covers also constitutional law—the case-law of the CJEU is not the source of constitutional law *per se*, but the source of its interpretation.[49]

If one would want to crystallise a trend in the above-described developments pertaining to the constitutional aspects of Lithuania's EU membership, it may be described in the following way. There were not so few constitutional boulders on Lithuania's path to the EU, both before she became its Member State and after that. They had to be removed. Some of them were removed by the Seimas by means of constitutional amendments, but at times, when removing one boulder, the parliament rolled in another one, even if inadvertently, which then had to be removed by the Constitutional Court (as when the Seimas manipulated the conditions for the 2003 referendum or was late to adopt the 2004 Constitutional Act).

However, when removing the boulders, the Constitutional Court brought in one itself. In 2017 it applied for the preliminary ruling from the CJEU regarding the provisions of one of the regulations of the European Parliament and of the Council in the case in which a piece of domestic legislation pertaining to the trade in milk was challenged.[50] In the Court's own words, "European Union law is a source of the interpretation of law of the Republic of Lithuania, *inter alia*, the Constitution in the areas where, under Article 1 of the Constitutional Act <…>, the Republic of Lithuania shares with or confer[s] on the European Union the competences of its state institutions". Then the Court added: "As the areas of agriculture and internal market fall under shared competence between the European Union and the Member States, there are no grounds for interpreting the provisions of the Constitution linked to these areas, *inter alia*, Article 46 thereof, in a different manner than the specified areas are regulated by European Union law". The new formula left virtually nothing of the supremacy of the Constitution even vis-à-vis EU regulation. In the decision, there is no mention of the rule of collision. No difference is drawn between *actes clairs* and *actes eclairés*. On top of that, no difference is drawn between the primary law of the EU (the founding Treaties) and its secondary law—directives and regulations, which are subject to frequent changes, which, in their turn, depend on various conjunctures, and whose conformity with the primary law of the EU cannot be *a priori* and unconditionally presumed. This new doctrine, if doctrine it was,[51] was

[48] CJEU, Case C-673/16 *Relu Adrian Coman and Others v. Inspectoratul General pentru Imigrări, Ministerul Afacerilor Interne*, 5 June 2018, ECLI:EU:C:2018:385.

[49] This thesis was first formulated with regard to the case-law of the European Court of Human Rights, but then extended to the case-law of the CJEU (which then was still called Court of Justice of the European Communities). Constitutional Court, Case 12/99-27/99-29/99-1/2000-2/2000, Ruling, 8 May 2000; Constitutional Court, Case 30/03, Ruling, 21 December 2006.

[50] Constitutional Court, Case 11/2016, Decision, 20 December 2017.

[51] One commentator, a former Constitutional Court and CJEU judge, commented that "[s]uch an approach <…> more than clearly demonstrate[d] its jurisprudential orientation" (Jarašiūnas 2024, p. 707). Another former Constitutional Court judge was, mildly put, less enthusiastic. She noted that,

repeated in the Court's final ruling in the same case, adopted, upon reception of the CJEU's preliminary ruling.[52] On closer inspection, one would hardly find anything in the constitutional dispute before the Court which would have justified this 'doctrinal development'.

But 'it ain't over 'til it's over'.[53] In a decision adopted only two months later,[54] the Court reverted to the rule of collision, undeservedly forgotten in the trade in milk case. The impression is that, in its case-law, two doctrines strangely cohabit: one asserts the supremacy of the Constitution and the rule of collision, and the other ignores or even denies it by endowing any piece of secondary EU legislation the status of the obligatory source of interpretation of the Constitution. Not only politics, but also hasty and superficial constitutional construction makes strange bedfellows.

19.6 Conclusion

Now I must correct myself. The provocative words 'an open question?' in the title of this chapter were inscribed in 2003, when I agreed to give a presentation at a conference, on the basis of which this chapter is written. Then the above-mentioned strange cohabitation was here-and-now. But today it looks more like an isolated aberration of the past, or is slowly becoming one. The reason for such assessment is the new ruling of the Constitutional Court,[55] where the rule of collision is referred to as the Court's long-standing position. On the other hand, the doctrinal anomaly of the trade in milk case has not been cited in any of the subsequent acts of the Constitutional Court. Even so, its explicit correction would do no harm (especially because it does not look like it would require great effort to accommodate it with the rule of collision by providing an explanation).

If the return to the rule of collision marks the Constitutional Court's return to constitutionalist approach, then the question of EU law's treatment in the Lithuanian Constitutional Court's case-law may not be said to be 'open' any longer. Constitutionalists would welcome that.

Nevertheless, as the two cohabiting formulas have not been accommodated yet in any of the Court's acts, some confusion remains. Therefore, the provocative words

---

the new formula notwithstanding, "the constitutional doctrine [on the supremacy of the Constitution over the EU law] remains relevant", as it was "developed for many years" (Birmontienė 2024, p. 702). There was also a more critical assessment by the same author, who reproached the Constitutional Court for providing no adequate reasoning of the change of the long-standing doctrine (Birmontienė 2020, pp. 88–90, 98–99). See also: Kūris 2024, pp. 12–13.

[52] Constitutional Court, Case 11/2016, Ruling, 6 February 2020. See also: Constitutional Court, Case 16/2016, Ruling, 11 January 2019; Constitutional Court, Case 10-A/2022, Ruling, 7 June 2023.

[53] Lenny Kravitz, It Ain't Over 'Til It's Over. From: *Mama Said*, Virgin, 1991.

[54] Constitutional Court, Decision no. KT70-A-S65/2020, 8 April 2020.

[55] Constitutional Court, Decision no. KT9-S9/2024, 24 January 2024.

have been retained in the title of this chapter—with the addition of the word 'still' before them. Time will tell.

References

Books and Articles

Albert R (2018) Constitutional Amendment and Dismemberment. The Yale Journal of International Law 43:1–84
Albi A (2005) EU Enlargement and the Constitutions of Central and Eastern Europe. Cambridge University Press, Cambridge
Barak A (2011) Unconstitutional Constitutional Amendments. Israel Law Review 44:321–341
Birmontienė T (2020) Konstitucinė teisė ir Europos Sąjungos teisė: Kas diktuoja teisės sistemų sąveikos ribas? [Constitutional Law and European Union Law: Who Dictates the Boundaries of Interaction between the Legal Systems?] In: Žilinskas J et al. (eds) XXI amžiaus iššūkiai tarptautinei teisei: Liber amicorum Sauliui Katuokai [Challenges of the 21st Century to International Law: Liber Amicorum Saulius Katuoka]. Constitutional Court of the Republic of Lithuania, Vilnius, pp 73–99
Birmontienė T (2024) Traditions of Lithuanian Constitution al Law. In: Jočienė D et al. (eds) Thirty Years of Constitutional Justice: Tempore et Loco. Constitutional Court of the Republic of Lithuania, Vilnius, pp 693–703
Dixon R, Landau D (2015) Transnational Constitutionalism and a Limited Doctrine of Unconstitutional Constitutional Amendment. International Journal of Constitutional Law 13:606–638
Jarašiūnas E (2024) Is the Concept of Constitutional Identity an Obstacle to Cooperation between the Constitutional Court and the Court of Justice of the European Union? In: Jočienė D et al. (eds) Thirty Years of Constitutional Justice: Tempore et Loco. Constitutional Court of the Republic of Lithuania, Vilnius, pp 704–70
Jarukaitis I (2024) Dvidešimt Lietuvos Respublikos metų Europos Sąjungos teisinėje erdvėje: Integracija teisės pagrindu veikia [Twenty years of the Republic of Lithuania in the legal space of the European Union: a law-based integration works]. In: Vitkus G (ed) Lietuvos narystės Europos Sąjungoje dvidešimtmetis: Pokyčiai ir perspektyvos [Twenty Years of Lithuania's EU Membership: Changes and Perspectives]. Vilniaus universiteto leidykla, Vilnius, pp. 35–47
Kūris E (2022) Lithuania. In: Griller S et al. (eds) National Constitutions and EU Integration. Hart, Oxford/London/New York/New Delhi/Sydney, pp 427–457
Kūris E (2023) Doctrinal Experimenting with the Constitution in Lithuania: On the Structure of the Constitution, the Non-Amendability of Constitutional Provisions, and the Legal Force of 'Pre-Constitutional' Acts. Review of Central and East European Law 48:65–133
Kūris E (2024) Brussels in Strasbourg: Theoretical Reflections on the Impact of the European Union Law on the Case-Law of the European Court of Human Rights. Teisė 131:8–22
Maes C (2024) The Notion of Constitutional Identity and Its Role in European Integration. Brussels: European Parliament. https://www.europarl.europa.eu/RegData/etudes/STUD/2024/760344/IPOL_STU(2024)760344_EN.pdf. Accessed 30 March 2025
Maniokas K (comp.) (2015) Pirmasis Lietuvos dešimtmetis Europos Sąjungoje: Transformacija ar imitacija [The First Decade of Lithuania's Membership in the European Union: Transformation or Imitation]. Vilniaus universiteto leidykla, Vilnius
Roznai Y (2017) Unconstitutional Constitutional Amendments: The Limits of Amendment Powers. Oxford University Press, Oxford
Roznai Y, Hostovsky Brandes T (2019) Democratic Erosion, Populist Constitutionalism and the Unconstitutional Constitutional Amendment Doctrine, at https://ssrn.com/abstract=3394412

Scholtes J (2023) The Abuse of Constitutional Identity in the European Union. Oxford University Press, Oxford
Švedas G (ed) (2014) Lithuanian Legal System under the Influence of European Union Law. Faculty of Law, Vilnius University, Vilnius
Taube C (2008) Liability of Heads of State: 'Paksasgate'. In: Frändberg Å et al. (eds) Festskrift till Anders Fogelklou [Festschrift for Anders Fogelklou]. Iustus Förlag, Uppsala, pp 275–285
Vitkus G (ed) (2024) Lietuvos narystės Europos Sąjungoje dvidešimtmetis: Pokyčiai ir perspektyvos [Twenty Years of Lithuania's EU Membership: Changes and Perspectives]. Vilniaus universiteto leidykla, Vilnius

Other Documents

Lithuania's Constitution and Legislation

Constitution of the Republic of Lithuania (with amendments), at https://lrkt.lt/en/about-the-court/legal-information/the-constitution/192. Accessed 30 March 2025
Law on International Treaties of the Republic of Lithuania (Lietuvos Respublikos tarptautinių sutarčių įstatymas). *TAR*, no. 0991010ISTAIII-1248 (in Lithuanian; *TAR* stands for the national register of legal acts)

Constitutional Court Case-Law

Constitutional Court, Case 22/94, Conclusion, 24 January 1995. https://lrkt.lt/en/court-acts/search/170/ta990/content. Accessed 30 March 2025
Constitutional Court, Case 8/95, Ruling, 17 October 1995. https://lrkt.lt/en/court-acts/search/170/ta983/content. Accessed 30 March 2025
Constitutional Court, Case 12/99-27/99-29/99-1/2000-2/2000, Ruling, 8 May 2000. https://lrkt.lt/en/court-acts/search/170/ta1160/content. Accessed 30 March 2025
Constitutional Court, Decision, 25 April 2002. https://lrkt.lt/en/court-acts/search/170/ta1202/content
Constitutional Court, Case 49/2000, Ruling, 24 December 2002. https://lrkt.lt/en/court-acts/search/170/ta1214/content. Accessed 30 March 2025
Constitutional Court, Case 1/02, Ruling, 29 October 2003. https://lrkt.lt/en/court-acts/search/170/ta1346/content. Accessed 30 March 2025
Constitutional Court decision of 7 April 2004. https://lrkt.lt/en/court-acts/search/170/ta1265/content
Constitutional Court, Case 25/03, Ruling, 10 May 2006. https://lrkt.lt/en/court-acts/search/170/ta1346/content. Accessed 30 March 2025
Constitutional Court, Case 17/02-24/02-06/03-22/04, Ruling, 14 March 2006. https://lrkt.lt/en/court-acts/search/170/ta1331/content. Accessed 30 March 2025
Constitutional Court, Case 45/03-36/04, Ruling, 13 November 2006. https://lrkt.lt/en/court-acts/search/170/ta1331/content. Accessed 30 March 2025
Constitutional Court, Case 30/03, Ruling, 21 December 2006. https://lrkt.lt/en/court-acts/search/170/ta1325/content. Accessed 30 March 2025
Constitutional Court, Case 47/04, Decision, 8 May 2007. https://lrkt.lt/en/court-acts/search/170/ta1400/content. Accessed 30 March 2025
Constitutional Court, Case 47/04, Ruling, 4 December 2008. https://lrkt.lt/en/court-acts/search/170/ta1425/content. Accessed 30 March 2025

Constitutional Court, Case 22/2013, Ruling, 24 January 2014. https://lrkt.lt/en/court-acts/search/170/ta850/content. Accessed 30 March 2025
Constitutional Court, Case 16/2014-29/2014, Ruling of 11 July 2014. https://lrkt.lt/en/court-acts/search/170/ta859/content. Accessed 30 March 2025
Constitutional Court, Case 18/2012, Ruling, 6 February 2015. https://lrkt.lt/en/court-acts/search/170/ta869/content. Accessed 30 March 2025
Constitutional Court, Case 11/2016, Decision, 20 December 2017. https://lrkt.lt/en/court-acts/search/170/ta1843/content. Accessed 30 March 2025
Constitutional Court, Case 5/2017, Ruling, 2 March 2018. *TAR*, no. 2018-03510 (in Lithuanian)
Constitutional Court, Case 16/2016, Ruling, 11 January 2019. https://lrkt.lt/en/court-acts/search/170/ta1915/content. Accessed 30 March 2025
Constitutional Court, Case 18/2018, Ruling, 15 February 2019. https://lrkt.lt/en/court-acts/search/170/ta1922/content. Accessed 30 March 2025
Constitutional Court, Case 11/2016, Ruling, 6 February 2020. *TAR*, no. 2020-14609 (in Lithuanian)
Constitutional Court, Decision no. KT70-A-S65/2020, 8 April 2020. https://lrkt.lt/lt/teismo-aktai/paieska/135/ta2117/content (in Lithuanian). Accessed 30 March 2025
Constitutional Court, Case 5/2019, Ruling, 30 July 2020. https://lrkt.lt/en/court-acts/search/170/ta2220/content. Accessed 30 March 2025
Constitutional Court, Case 10-A/2022, Ruling, 7 June 2023. *TAR*, no. 2023-11301. Accessed 30 March 2025 (in Lithuanian)
Constitutional Court Decision no. KT9-S9/2024, 24 January 2024. https://lrkt.lt/lt/teismo-aktai/paieska/135/ta2954/content (in Lithuanian). Accessed 30 March 2025

EU Legal Acts

Treaty Establishing the Constitution for Europe. *OJ, C 130*, 16 December 2004 (not entered into force)

Case-Law of the Court of Justice of the European Union

Case C-239/07, *Julius Sabatauskas and Others*, Judgment, 9 October 2008, ECLI:EU:C:2008:551
Case C-61/12 *European Commission v. Republic of Lithuania*, Judgment, 20 March 2014, ECLI:EU:C:2014:172
Case C-673/16 *Relu Adrian Coman and Others v. Inspectoratul General pentru Imigrări, Ministerul Afacerilor Interne*, 5 June 2018, ECLI:EU:C:2018:385

Case-Law of the European Court of Human Rights

Paksas v. Lithuania, no. 39432/04, Judgment, 6 January 2011

Other Sources

Fitzgerald R (2023) Clear support for EU membership for most European countries but emotional attachment to the nation state endures, at https://encompass-europe.com/comment/clear-support-for-eu-membership-for-most-european-countries-but-emotional-attachment-to-the-nation-state-endures. Accessed 30 March 2025
Kravitz L (1991) It Ain't Over 'Til It's Over. From: Mama Said, Virgin

Permanent Representation of the Republic of Lithuania to the European Union (Lietuvos nuolatinė atstovybė ES) 2024. Film: The Return that Changed Us [Sugrįžimas, kuris mus pakeitė]. https://www.youtube.com/watch?v=GdeT22g2iDo&ab_channel=Lietuvosnuolatin%C4%97atstovyb%C4%97ES. Accessed 30 March 2025

State Data Agency (Valstybės duomenų agentūra) 2024. 20 metų narystės: Sėkmės skaičiai. [20 Years of Membership: Figures of Success]. https://osp.stat.gov.lt/20-metu-narystes-es-sekmes-skaiciai. Accessed 30 March 2025

Egidijus Kūris is a Prof. Dr. (HP), a professor at the Law Faculty of Vilnius University, a former Justice (1999–2008) and President (2002–2008) of the Constitutional Court of the Republic of Lithuania and a former Judge at the European Court of Human Rights (2013-2024).

Chapter 20
Legal Mechanism of European Values Implementation as a Key Requirement on the Way to Ukraine's Accession to the European Union

Mykhailo Mykiyevych and Volodymyr Motyl

Contents

Abstract This chapter analyses the core values of the European Union (EU) as a key precondition for EU membership and the legal mechanism of their implementation in the legal order of Ukraine. The authors analyse the content of the written and unwritten criteria for EU membership and compare them with the core values enshrined in Article 2 of the TEU: human dignity, freedom, democracy, equality, the rule of law and respect for human rights, in particular those of persons belonging to minorities. The authors also examine the normative content of the duty to respect and

M. Mykiyevych (✉)
Faculty of Law, Vilnius University, Vilnius, Lithuania
e-mail: mykhailo.mykievych@lnu.edu.ua

M. Mykiyevych · V. Motyl
Faculty of International Relations, Ivan Franko National University of Lviv, Lviv, Ukraine
e-mail: volodymyr.motyl@lnu.edu.ua

I. Isokaitė-Valužė and H. Šinkūnas (eds.), *The European Union 2004-2024*,
https://doi.org/10.1007/978-94-6265-718-2_20

promote values. The accession procedure and its impact on the implementation of values by the candidate country, as well as the significance of other EU instruments designed to prepare for accession and their impact on the implementation of values by the candidate country are also examined (Association and Stabilisation Agreements, IPA III, Twinning, TAIEX, TASCO, SIGMA). The final section analyses the main reforms carried out by Ukraine to implement EU values, in particular in the field of media, the fight against corruption and protection of national minorities. Restrictions on constitutional rights and freedoms in connection with the introduction of martial law are examined for compliance with Ukraine's international legal obligations. The authors investigate the state of implementation of EU values in the constitutions of Ukraine and in the judicial practice of Ukrainian courts. Recommendations are also formulated to improve the implementation of EU values in the legal system of Ukraine.

Keywords EU values · EU law · EU membership criteria · EU membership procedure · EU accession support instruments · EU accession negotiations

20.1 Introduction

The European Union today is not only an economic and political Union, but above all a Union of values. Adherence to values is not only a requirement for EU member states, but respect for and promotion of EU values is a key requirement for countries wishing to join the EU. The core values reflect the written and unwritten criteria for EU membership and are closely interrelated. In addition, the EU contains a wide range of instruments to prepare candidate countries for EU membership, from Association Agreements to various programmes aimed at ensuring that candidate countries and third countries adhere to EU values. The EU also contains a number of mechanisms to ensure compliance with EU values for EU member states, including a special procedure for violations of the values.

Ukraine, which became a candidate for EU membership on 22 June 2022 and officially launched accession negotiations on 25 June 2024, faces a significant challenge in securing values. This task is complicated by the challenges of a war for survival caused by aggression from the Russian Federation, as well as by restrictions in legislation due to martial law. The authors analyse the key challenges and progress of Ukraine in implementing EU values in the legal order of Ukraine.

20.2 "Respect and Promotion of Values" as a Prerequisite for EU Membership

Adherence to and respect for the EU values enshrined in Article 2 of the TEU is not only an obligation of the states that are members of the European Union, but is also a requirement for countries that want to become EU members.

Thus, Article 49 of the TEU provides that "any European State which respects the values referred to in Article 2 and is committed to promoting them may apply to become a member of the Union". The need to respect the values enshrined in Article 2 has been repeatedly emphasised by the Court of Justice of the European Union.[1] In addition, the Court has repeatedly emphasised that compliance with the values enshrined in Article 2 TEU is a condition for the enjoyment of all rights arising from the application of the Treaties by the Member State concerned. Consistency with these principles cannot be limited to the obligation of a candidate country to comply with them in order to join the EU and which can be neglected after accession.[2]

It is quite clear from a systematic interpretation that this refers to the values of respect for human dignity, freedom, democracy, equality, the rule of law and respect for human rights, in particular those of persons belonging to minorities. However, it is necessary to clarify what exactly is required of such states and what actions are included in the concepts of "respect for values" and "promotion of values". Let us also analyse in more detail the place of the requirement of "respect for and promotion of values" in the system of criteria for EU membership.

20.2.1 What Does "European State" Mean?

In addition to respect for values, Article 49 itself mentions two other criteria for EU membership candidates. First, the application can only be submitted by a state. This means that membership is not possible for international organisations or other subjects of international law. It is quite clear that such states must be internationally recognised, and in no case can such pseudo-states as Transnistria, Ossetia or Abkhazia, which were the result of the Russian Federation's military aggression against neighbouring states, claim this status. Nor can, for example, the state of Sylvania or "Sealand", which was established in 1967 on the Fort Rose naval platform off the coast of the United Kingdom, make a claim, as it has not been recognised by any state.

---

[1] CJEU (2021a) Judgment of the Court (Grand Chamber), Repubblika v Il-Prim Ministru, C-896/19, ECLI:EU:C:2021:311, para 63. CJEU (2021b) Asociaţia 'Forumul Judecătorilor din România' and Others v Inspecţia Judiciară and Others, C-83/19, C-127/19, C-195/19, para 162.

[2] CJEU (2022), Judgment of the Court, Hungary and Republic of Poland v European Parliament and Council of the European Union, Case C-156/21, ECLI:EU:C:2022:97, para 126.

As for the requirement of Europeanness, this criterion should not be understood in a purely geographical sense,[3] but also in a political and cultural sense, as the historical and cultural aspect[4] and the spiritual aspect[5] are important. In this regard, countries that are not geographically part of Europe are definitely not eligible to apply. On the other hand, the possibility of membership is theoretically possible for states that straddle the border between Europe and Asia, such as Georgia or Armenia.[6] The question of whether a country that is close to Europe in social and economic terms, but geographically outside of it, such as Israel, can apply for membership is rather ambiguous.[7] It seems that historical, cultural and spiritual affinity is more important than socio-economic proximity. This is what German scholars emphasise: "Europe is not just a geographical concept, not just a political and economic community and a common market... Europe is above all a community of spirit, history and values of the Christian West".[8] Some authors associate Europeanness with the Acquis: "Europe cannot be defined according to strict geographical boundaries [...] with the help of the seas, mountains, rivers and lakes. It can be defined from the inside, with the great movements that continue to cross, and that run since a very long time: political, economic, intellectual, scientific, artistic, religious and spiritual movements".[9] In our opinion, this approach interprets the Acquis too broadly. From our perspective, Europeanness is manifested primarily in respect for the values enshrined in Article 2 of the TEU.

20.2.2 Respecting and Promoting Values: Active and Passive Aspects

As for the terms respecting and promoting EU values, they do not clearly define what measures or actions are expected of states wishing to become EU members, but based on a literal interpretation, it is clear that they are expected to behave proactively. This can be confirmed by a historical interpretation and comparison of the Amsterdam and Lisbon Treaties. While Article 49 of the TEU, or Article O in the old Amsterdam version, contained only the term "respect", the Lisbon Treaty also included the term "promote or disseminate", so it is clear that passive behaviour is not enough and that action is required to implement the values.

Czech scholars believe that the requirement to respect EU values enshrined in Article 49 includes the so-called "passive and active aspects". In their opinion, the passive or static aspect includes, for example, constitutionally enshrined protection

[3] European Union 1993; European Council 1998; European Commission 1989, 1998.

[4] Cremer 2002, p. 321.

[5] Pechstein 2012, p. 313.

[6] Tomášek and Šmejkal 2024, p. 1510.

[7] Oppermann 1999, pp. 800–801.

[8] Blumenwitz et al. 2005, p. 6.

[9] Cagiano de Azevedo et al. 2013, pp. 189–195.

of fundamental rights and accession to the ECHR, while the active or dynamic aspect includes an independent judiciary and functional mechanisms for the protection of fundamental rights.[10]

On the other hand, the term "respect" for values can be interpreted as certain measures in the domestic legal order, while the promotion of protection can be understood as certain actions of the state in the international arena, in particular within international organisations, international judicial bodies, or in bilateral relations between states, aimed at protecting and ensuring the values enshrined in Article 2 of the TEU.

Respect for values is not only a criterion for starting negotiations, but also for submitting an application. That is, it is not enough to assure that the state will respect human dignity, the rule of law, democracy and human rights at some point in the future, but rather that such respect must be ensured at the application stage.[11]

Prior to the entry into force of the Amsterdam Treaty, there were requirements for the political system of candidate countries as unwritten accession requirements. For example, as early as 1978, the European Council in its statement on democracy stressed that "democracy and respect for human rights are essential elements of EU membership".[12]

20.3 Criteria for EU Membership

In preparation for the accession of the Eastern and Central European states to the EU, these requirements were specified and approved in the decisions of the European Council in 1993 in Copenhagen, and thus became known as the Copenhagen criteria. Paragraph 7 of the European Council's Concluding Observations stated that membership requires the following from a candidate country:

- Stability of the institutions guaranteeing democracy, the rule of law, human rights and respect for and protection of national minorities (political criterion),[13]
- the existence of a functioning market economy, as well as the ability to cope with competitive pressures and internal market forces of the Union (economic criterion),
- ability to assume the obligations of membership, including compliance with the objectives of political, economic and monetary union (legal criterion),
- The ability of the Union to accept new members while maintaining the momentum of European integration.[14]

---

[10] Tomášek and Šmejkal 2024, p. 1510.

[11] Pechstein 2012, p. 310.

[12] European Council 1978.

[13] European Council 1998.

[14] European Council 1993.

Paragraph III A of the Conclusions of the European Council in Madrid on 15-16 December 1995 referred to the need to "create the conditions for the gradual, harmonious integration of the candidate countries, in particular by developing market economies, adjusting their administrative structures and creating a stable economic and monetary environment".[15]

In December 2006, the European Council also noted that an "enlargement strategy based on consolidation, conditionality and communication, combined with the EU's capacity to integrate new members, forms the basis for a renewed consensus on enlargement".[16]

In the case of the Western Balkan countries, additional membership conditions were laid out in the so-called Stabilisation and Association Process, which mainly concern regional cooperation and good neighbourly relations.[17]

The above-mentioned criteria are in fact always mentioned by the European Commission and are used as a basis for assessing the compliance of candidate countries with the EU accession criteria.

20.3.1 Unwritten Criteria for EU Membership

Some scholars write about the so-called unwritten criteria for membership - the economic constitution and implementation of the Aquis of the European Union. On the other hand, these requirements can hardly be called unwritten, since para 1.25 of the Conclusions of the European Council in Madrid on 15-16 December 1995 pointed to the need to comply with the Aquis Communautaire, which includes the common policies of the European Union. A special emphasis on the implementation of the Acquis by the candidate countries was placed in the Commission's Agenda 2000 report.[18] These criteria are closely related to the political and legal criterion and the economic criterion.

An economic constitution refers primarily to an economic order based on the principles of a market economy and free competition. This requirement was imposed on candidates for membership even before the Maastricht Treaty,[19] and the European Council in Copenhagen in 1993 pointed out the need to modernise the economies of the candidate countries from Central and Eastern Europe, which had weakened after 40 years of planned economies, to ensure their rapid transition to market economies.[20] It is currently included in Article 120(2) TFEU: "The Member States and the Union shall act in accordance with the principle of an open market economy with free

[15] European Council 1995.

[16] The Council of the European Union 2006.

[17] Mokra 2020, p. 38.

[18] European Council 2000.

[19] Pechstein 2012, p. 311.

[20] European Council 1993.

competition, favouring an efficient allocation of resources, and in compliance with the principles set out in Article 119".

Article 119(1) TFEU also mentions the principles of an open market economy and free competition: "For the purposes set out in Article 3 of the Treaty on European Union, the activities of the Member States and the Union shall include, as provided in the Treaties, the adoption of an economic policy which is based on the close coordination of Member States' economic policies, on the internal market and on the definition of common objectives, and conducted in accordance with the principle of an open market economy with free competition". Thus, these requirements were transformed from unwritten criteria for membership into a treaty obligation of the Member States. It should be noted, however, that the existence of a market economy is not a prerequisite for the start of negotiations, unlike respect for the values enshrined in Article 2 of the TEU, which must be ensured before negotiations can begin.

Another unwritten criterion is the implementation of Aquis. It should be noted at the outset that the term "acquis" of the European Union and *acquis communautaire* need to be distinguished terminologically. Prior to the entry into force of the Maastricht Treaty, there was only an "acquis communautaire". In the Commission's opinion of 19 January 1972 on the accession of Denmark, Ireland, Norway,[21] the United Kingdom and Northern Ireland to the European Communities, the Aquis Communautaire was broadly described as follows: "whereas in joining the Communities the applicant states accept without reserve the treaties and their political objectives, all decisions taken since their entry into force, and the action that has been agreed in respect of the development and reinforcement of the Communities".[22] When Greece joined the EU, this term was somewhat specified in detail: "It is an essential feature of the legal system set up by the treaties establishing the Communities that certain of their provisions and certain acts of the Community institutions are directly applicable, that Community law takes precedence over any national provisions conflicting with it, and that procedures exist for ensuring the uniform interpretation of this law; and whereas accession to the communities entails recognition of the binding force of these rules, observance of which is indispensable to guarantee the effectiveness and unity of community law".[23]

The Accession Acts stipulate, inter alia, that the new member states will recognise and abide by the principled positions, statements, and opinions of the EU bodies not only within the framework of the former Community law, but also the Common Foreign and Security Policy, as well as the former third pillar of EU law. Thus, the candidate countries undertake to implement not only the Aquis Communautaire, but also the Aquis of the entire European Union including the Schengen Aquis, as well

[21] At that time, Norway's application was "frozen", as Norway's membership was not supported in a referendum on 26 September 1972, when 53.5% of the population voted against the country's accession to the EU. Later, a similar referendum was held in 1994, with 52.2% of the population voting against. One of the reasons was the fishing quotas that Norway would have to adhere to after joining the EU.

[22] European Communities 1972, p. 2.

[23] European Commission 1979, p. 3. European Communities 1972, p. 2.

as international EU treaties into their domestic legal order.[24] The Aquis criterion is divided into 35 chapters that reflect the EU's legal heritage. Particularly important in the context of EU values are Chapter 10, Chapter 24 and Chapter 25, which reflect the values of democracy and the rule of law.

Of course, even if a particular state meets the criteria, there is no obligation to automatically accept it into the EU. In addition, the EU institutions and member states involved in the accession process have a fairly wide margin for subjective assessment of whether a particular state meets the EU membership criteria.

On the other hand, even if some countries do not yet fully meet the criteria for membership, the EU can be "patient". An example of this is the accession process of Romania and Bulgaria. It was agreed that the verification mechanism for these countries would be applied even after their accession.[25]

20.3.2 Correlation of Values and Membership Criteria

It is worth comparing the criteria for membership with the text of Article 2(1) of the TEU, which enshrines the values of the EU: "The Union is founded on the values of respect for human dignity, freedom, democracy, equality, the rule of law and respect for human rights, including the rights of persons belonging to minorities".

As we can see, the political criterion practically duplicates the provisions of Part 1, Article 2, mentioning democracy, the rule of law, respect for human rights and protection of national minority rights. There is no mention of freedom, equality and human dignity, which in principle can be included in respect for human rights. Thus, a close relationship between Article 2, Article 49 of the TEU and the Copenhagen criteria can be traced, although given the abstract and political nature of the Copenhagen criteria, it is difficult to speak of their identity.

Thus, as we can see, a certain level of respect for and protection of EU values must be ensured at the stage of application to the EU. At the same time, at the application stage, it is clear that the level of protection of EU values may not yet reach the level required of countries that are already EU members in accordance with Article 2 of the TEU. Therefore, a certain institutional stability is expected at the beginning of the negotiations, and in the course of pre-accession preparations, negotiations, and immediately after accession, candidate states improve the situation with the promotion and protection of EU values by interacting with EU institutions and member states, as well as receiving guidance and recommendations from them.[26] Let us take a closer look at how the accession process works and how it affects the safeguarding of values.

---

[24] Pechstein 2012, p. 311.

[25] Euractiv 2007.

[26] Seidl 2017, p. 90.

20.4 EU Accession Process and Securing Values

As we know, once the application is accepted, the EU accession procedure begins. Let us take a closer look at it from the point of view of the requirements for compliance with and protection of EU values.

The procedure for accession is not clearly defined and Article 49 covers only certain elements, while others have already been developed in the practice of states. The accession procedure consists of 2 stages: the application procedure and the negotiation procedure.

The first stage consists of the following steps:

1. Submission of an application for accession by a candidate country to the Council;
2. Communications from the European Parliament and national parliaments of EU member states;
3. The Commission prepares an opinion on the application based on a detailed analysis of the economic situation and legal system of the candidate country, as well as the level of implementation of the Acquis;[27] the Commission gives a positive opinion only if the political criterion is sufficiently met;[28]
4. The Council adopting a unanimous decision to launch negotiations.[29]

In case of a positive decision to initiate negotiations, the accession procedure is initiated:

1. Development by the Commission and approval by the candidate country of a framework for negotiations, including the guiding principles and principles of negotiations, the subject matter of negotiations, and the procedure;
2. Accession negotiations are held in the framework of ministerial conferences chaired by the President of the Council and attended by members of the Commission;
3. Completion of negotiations;
4. The Commission's opinion on accession;
5. Consent of the European Parliament by majority vote;
6. Unanimous decision of the Council;
7. Ratification by the candidate country;
8. Ratification by member states.

According to the Council's decision on the procedure for accession negotiations of 8–9 June 1970, the Council has a key role in the accession process and its conduct, the Committee of Permanent Representatives is responsible for preparing the negotiations, and the Commission may submit proposals on all matters relating to accession, and on behalf of the Council, the Commission may work out proposals together with

---

[27] In this process, the Commission uses a questionnaire. If the applicant country does not fully meet the criteria in a particular area, the Commission formulates recommendations on certain measures or reforms that need to be implemented to move forward.

[28] European Commission 2022a.

[29] *Ibid.*

the candidate country to solve specific problems arising in the accession process.[30] It should be noted that under the new methodology, no chapter of negotiations will be closed until the benchmarks for the rule of law chapters (23—judiciary and fundamental rights and 24—justice, freedom and security) are met.[31] This confirms that adherence to the values, and in particular the rule of law, is key to EU accession.

The key to completing the accession process is the Council's decision, the accession treaty, and ratification by all EU Member States. The accession documents themselves do not provide a unified framework for verification of compliance with EU values and political and legal criteria, but in Commission opinions, progress reports and other documents are generally grouped into 2 blocks: (1) democracy and rule of law; (2) human rights and protection of national minorities.[32]

In the Commission's report on Ukraine, which complemented the Commission's Communication on EU Enlargement Policy 2023, cluster 1 places the rule of law in the same group as human rights and democracy and public administration reform.[33]

The Commission's Enlargement Strategies do not follow this grouping. Whereas the European Commission's opinion on Greece's 1979 accession application gave priority to democracy and human rights, the 2011 Enlargement Strategy placed the main emphasis on the rule of law, and the Commission's Communication on EU Enlargement 2020 placed the rule of law, functioning democratic institutions and public administration at the forefront.[34]

20.5 Other Tools for Preparing Candidates for Admission

An important tool for preparing candidate countries for EU accession at the stage before accession negotiations are opened is the Association and Stabilisation Agreements concluded by the European Union on the basis of Article 217 TFEU.[35] They serve as the legal basis for preparing the country for accession. To monitor compliance with the objectives set out in such agreements, bilateral ministerial-level Association or Stabilisation Councils are established, consisting of representatives of the country and the EU, which meet at regular intervals or as needed. Since enlargement in 2004, such agreements have paid particular attention to the accession criteria to ensure that they are sustainably met. Action Plans are developed and regularly monitored to achieve the objectives of the agreements. The success of the objectives is ensured by a system of incentives and sanctions, which includes primarily the SAA, as well as the accession process itself.

---

[30] The Council of the European Union 1970.

[31] European Commission 2022a.

[32] Seidl 2017, p. 89.

[33] European Commission 2023b.

[34] European Commission 2020.

[35] Former Article 315. The agreements concluded with the countries of Central and Eastern Europe were called European agreements.

Such agreements contain the so-called "conditionality clauses" or "evolutionary clauses",[36] which make the validity of the provisions of the Association Agreements or the effect of certain components (e.g. trade preferences) dependent on compliance with the EU values enshrined in them. The EU-Ukraine Association Agreement contains such provisions in Article 478 in conjunction with Article 2. Thus, in case of violation of the values enshrined in Article 2, the suspension of any rights or obligations under the provisions of this Agreement, including those specified in Title IV ("Trade and Trade-related Matters") of this Agreement, may be applied.[37] In such cases, the rule of holding bilateral consultations within three months, as provided for in Article 478(3), does not even apply.

It should be noted that the European Association Agreements concluded with Central and Eastern European states were not as strict in terms of adherence to values. For example, the European Association Agreement between the European Communities, the Member States and Poland mentions values only in the preamble. It mentions "the common values shared by the contracting parties" and "the transition to a new political and economic order based on the rule of law and human rights, including the legal and economic framework for a market economy, a multiparty system with free and democratic elections".[38] Article 2 of this document also mentions "Poland's integration into the Community of Democratic States" and values in the Association and PCA agreements. No provisions on conditionality, similar to those contained in Article 478 of the EU-Ukraine Association Agreement, are contained in this Agreement or in the European Association Agreements. This indicates that the European Union is now more demanding of third countries and candidate countries' compliance with the EU's core values than it was before.

In this regard, the Commission's 2014 Communication on Enlargement Strategy is particularly noteworthy, which, in the context of the rule of law, stated that countries wishing to join the EU must have established and maintained the proper functioning of the institutions necessary to ensure the rule of law, and in the process of accession they must demonstrate a practical ability to implement the values on which the EU is built.[39]

In addition to the provisions of the Association and Stabilisation Agreements, the EU has other instruments to ensure EU values with countries wishing to join the EU. Thus, back in 2007, IPA I (Instrument for Pre-Accession Assistance) came into force, which was replaced by IPA II in 2013, and IPA III was approved in 2021 for the period up to 2027. This instrument for pre-accession assistance to candidate countries aims to support candidate countries in carrying out legal, institutional, economic and social reforms, aligning them with EU values and implementing norms, standards and policies. It is also an important financial instrument of the so-called positive conditionality with a budget of almost €15 billion.[40]

---

[36] Petrov 2018, p. 60.

[37] Ugoda 2014.

[38] European Union 1993.

[39] European Commission 2014.

[40] European Commission 2023d.

Also, even before the accession process begins, citizens of the candidate countries have access to various EU programmes and projects, civil society initiatives, academic mobility programmes such as Erasmus or Erasmus Mundus, can travel without visas and enjoy other benefits of free trade.

An important tool is Twinning, which is an institution-building and new form of direct technical cooperation between the authorities of EU member states and beneficiary countries, or a kind of inter-institutional partnership. Twinning aims to help beneficiary countries improve and strengthen the institutional and regulatory capacities of public authorities, their structure, human resources, and management capacity, which should facilitate the implementation of EU legislation (*acquis communautaire*). This tool includes various trainings, study tours and mentoring, and is based on the principles of learning from best practices and learning by doing.[41]

An important tool is also TAIEX (Technical Assistance and Information Exchange instrument of the European Commission) to support authorities in the approximation, application and enforcement of EU law and to learn about best practices through workshops, expert visits and study tours.[42]

The TASCO (Technical Assistance for Civil Society Organisations) programme provides technical support to civil society organisations and includes them in the EU's annual monitoring.

The EU also has a joint initiative with the OSCE to strengthen the capacity of government institutions, SIGMA (Support for Improvement in Governance and Management). The programme has been running since 1992 and assists in the preparation and implementation of reforms, budgeting, preparation of strategies, action plans and prioritisation.[43]

The above-mentioned programmes are more focused on incentives. At the same time, the EU also has a sanction mechanism for countries wishing to become EU members. First of all, this concerns the provisions on suspension of Association or Stabilisation Agreements, which, although they have become quite common, are rarely used in practice, as in 2006 in relation to Serbia. Then, on 3 May 2006, the EU suspended negotiations with Serbia-Montenegro over the refusal to arrest Ratko Mladic, who was suspected of genocide and war crimes, including the massacre of about 8000 Muslims in Srebrenica in 2005 and the siege of Sarajevo.[44]

Once the accession negotiations are launched, a positive and negative conditionality mechanism is also applied, depending on the fulfilment of the criteria and monitoring results of the EU Commission. In addition to the sanctions already mentioned above, the suspension of accession negotiations in general (disequilibrium clause) or the suspension of negotiations on certain sections of the Aquis, which constitute the so-called negative conditionality, may be applied.

Another tool was used in the accession negotiations with Romania and Bulgaria. In this case, Article 39 of the Accession Protocol provided for the possibility of

[41] European Commission 2024b.

[42] European Commission 2024a.

[43] Sigma 2024.

[44] Al Jazeera 2006.

postponing accession for a year if there were serious concerns that the candidate country would not be able to fulfil the obligations arising from membership.

As practice has shown, values and their adherence have become a key criterion for rapprochement with the EU for countries that aspire to join the EU, and EU instruments and programmes to ensure adherence to values have become a key to transforming the political, legal and economic systems of candidate countries, especially those that were influenced by totalitarian systems.

20.6 Implementation of EU Values by Ukraine on Its Way to the EU

20.6.1 EU Values and Constitution of Ukraine

Although the development and reception of European values on the territory of Ukraine has a thousand-year history and in our opinion began with the founding of Greek cities-polis in the Northern Black Sea region of Ukraine, let us consider in more detail their implementation at the present stage, in particular at the level of the main law—the Constitution of Ukraine.

Commitment to EU values is confirmed by the 1996 Constitution of Ukraine. Article 1 of the Constitution of Ukraine proclaims that Ukraine is a sovereign and independent, democratic, social, rule of law state. In accordance with Article 3 a person, his/her life and health, honour and dignity, inviolability and security are recognized in Ukraine as the highest social value; human rights and freedoms and their guarantees determine the essence and orientation of the activity of the State. The State is answerable to the individual for its activity. To affirm and ensure human rights and freedoms is the main duty of the State. According to Part 1 and Part 2 of Article 28, "no one may be subjected to torture, cruel, inhuman or degrading treatment, treatment or punishment. Also, Chapter II of the Constitution of Ukraine (Articles 21–69) contains a detailed catalogue of human rights, which reflects the provisions of the Universal Declaration of Human Rights and, to a large extent, the Charter of Fundamental Rights of the EU. Thus, the Constitution of Ukraine reflects the basic values on which the European Union is based—democracy, the rule of law, human dignity and respect for human rights. Although freedom and equality are also mentioned in Chapter II of the Constitution of Ukraine, it seems appropriate, given their fundamental nature for the EU, to move them to the General Principles, i.e. Chapter I of the Constitution of Ukraine.

Of course, filling these provisions of the Constitution with a content that will correspond to the understanding of these values in the EU will depend on the law-making, legal interpretation and application of the law, and in particular on the Constitutional Court of Ukraine, which can interpret the constitution in accordance with Ukrainian legislation. As part of further preparations for membership, Ukraine, in our opinion, should supplement the Constitution with provisions that would determine the place of EU law and EU values in the legal order of Ukraine, since currently the Constitution of Ukraine contains only Article 9, which enshrines the primacy of international treaties in case of conflict with the provisions of Ukrainian law, but, in our opinion, is not sufficient for the "introduction" of EU law and basic values as its core into the legal system of Ukraine. Such a "European clause" could provide that Ukraine participates in the European Union, which is based on fundamental values and undertakes to promote the implementation of these values in the legal system of Ukraine by giving primacy to the EU law and providing for the possibility of transferring certain sovereign powers to the EU with the consent of the constitutional majority of the Verkhovna Rada of Ukraine.

The Constitution of Ukraine not only contains provisions that reproduce the values of the EU, but also consolidates the foreign policy course towards membership in the EU and NATO. Thus, the Preamble states: "confirming the European identity of the Ukrainian people and the irreversibility of Ukraine's European and Euro-Atlantic course". Paragraph 5 of Article 85 of the Constitution of Ukraine, which regulates the powers of the Verkhovna Rada of Ukraine, refers to "the implementation of the strategic course of the state for Ukraine's full membership in the European Union". Article 116 of the Constitution of Ukraine states that the Cabinet of Ministers of Ukraine "ensures the implementation of the strategic course of the state for Ukraine's full membership in the European Union". Article 102 of the Constitution of Ukraine outlines the powers of the President to guarantee this process: "The President of Ukraine is the guarantor of the implementation of the strategic course of the state for the acquisition of full membership of Ukraine in the European Union."

Ukraine's path to the EU began even before the approval of the Constitution of Ukraine with the signing of the Partnership and Cooperation between Ukraine and the EU in 1994 Agreement which replaced the Trade and Cooperation Agreement of 1989 between the European Community and the former Soviet Union. Ukraine's strategic foreign policy goal is to become a full-fledged member of the EU. Although the Partnership and Cooperation Agreement between Ukraine and the EU of 1994 did not mention Ukraine's future membership in the EU, the preamble indicated commitment to the core values of the EU:

"CONVINCED of the paramount importance of the rule of law[45] and respect for human rights, particularly those of minorities, the establishment of a multiparty system with free and democratic elections and economic liberalization aimed at setting up a market economy";[46] Article 1 mentioned among the objectives of the partnership "[t]o support Ukrainian efforts to consolidate its democracy" and to the basic principles of partnership Article 2 took "[r]espect for the democratic principles and human rights as defined in particular in the Helsinki Final Act and the Charter

[45] Ugoda 2004.

[46] It should be noted that "rule of law" (верховенство права) in the official translation was "primacy of legislative acts" (верховенство закону). This small difference was in our opinion a consequence of the post-Soviet "disease" of the legal system, since in the Soviet Union, to which Ukraine was forcibly annexed for 70 years, the concept of the primacy of legislative acts, not the rule of law, dominated. At the same time, this concept was purely declarative in nature, since the Soviet Union was a totalitarian state, and none of the elements of the rule of law were ensured in practice.

of Paris for a New Europe…" are the basis of domestic and foreign policy. This provision was confirmed in the second section of this chapter where values were recognized as "an essential element of partnership "which underpin the internal and external policies of the Parties and constitute Agreement".[47] Thus, it emphasized 3 main principles—the rule of law, respect for human rights and a key component of democracy—free and democratic elections.[48]

The Association Agreement between Ukraine and the EU placed even greater emphasis on values. On the one hand, the common values on which the European Union is built, namely democracy, respect for human rights and fundamental freedoms and the rule of law, are included in the Preamble among the key elements of the Agreement. The Preamble of the Agreement also mentions the common values on which relations between Ukraine and the EU are based: "...democracy, the rule of law, respect for human rights and fundamental freedoms...". Article 1 mentions value-based convergence among the goals, and Article 7 mentions gradual rapprochement between the Parties based on common values.[49]

Based on the provisions of Article 49 of the TEU and the requirements of its own Constitution, Ukraine submitted its application for accession to the EU on 28 February 2022. On 7 March 2022, the Council of the EU requested the European Commission to provide an opinion on this application. On 17 June 2022, the European Commission approved the opinion with an assessment.[50] The Commission assessed Ukraine's application for membership as to whether it meets the membership criteria set by the European Council and also evaluated Ukraine's progress in fulfilling its obligations under the Association Agreement. The introduction to the Opinion states: "The aspiration to belong to the European Union has been an important priority for Ukraine, its governments and citizens for many years. It has been the main motive for democratic change over the past decade and the driver of a number of key reforms based on European values." In the final part of the Commission's Opinion, it was noted that "Ukraine is a European state that has reaffirmed its commitment to the values on which the European Union is based". It was stated that "Ukraine has demonstrated the resilience of its institutions, which guarantee democracy, the rule of law, human rights and respect for and protection of minorities". In view of this, the Commission recommended that Ukraine be granted candidate status, and subsequently, on 22 June 2022, Ukraine was granted candidate status by the European Council.[51]

It should be noted that the European Commission's recommendation to grant Ukraine the prospect of becoming an EU member was not unconditional and included 7 steps-recommendations that had to be implemented by the end of 2022 to start accession negotiations. The European Commission's report of 1 February 2023 on Ukraine's application for EU membership noted that Ukraine had fully implemented

[47] Ugoda 2004.

[48] *Ibid.*

[49] *Ibid.*

[50] European Commission 2022c.

[51] European Commission 2022b.

the European Commission's recommendations on judicial reform and media legislation. The latest report of the European Commission showed Ukraine's further progress in creating an effective legal mechanism for the implementation of European values. In particular, it was determined that Ukraine has fully implemented the recommendations on the reform of the Constitutional Court, as well as on anti-money laundering legislation and law enforcement reform. In addition, significant progress has been made in fulfilling the remaining requirements. Thus, Ukraine has clearly demonstrated its desire and determination to live up to European values and standards and to implement them in its national legal order. This was confirmed by the European Council's decision to start negotiations on Ukraine's accession to the EU, the approval of the negotiation framework in March 2024, and the official start of negotiations on Ukraine's accession to the EU on 25 June 2024.

The Commission's recommendations were essentially to implement the Aquis Communautaire and EU values in Ukraine's legal system. That is why, despite the Russian Federation's aggressive war against Ukraine, Ukraine has launched large-scale legislative reforms, in particular in the areas of the rule of law, freedom of speech, democracy, and protection of national minorities. The Commission has repeatedly noted progress, including progress in implementing recommendations on media and judicial reform,[52] anti-money laundering and other areas,[53] but there are still a number of challenges.

In addition to the Constitution, the Association Agreement containing basic EU values as essential elements is a key tool for the implementation of the EU's core values in the legal system of Ukraine. As an international treaty, it has primacy in relation to national legislation, and also provides for the promotion of the basic values of the EU. (i) The Supreme Court of Ukraine in its decision of 17.07.2018 in case No. 910/14972/17 (the case on the claim of Zentiva) applied the priority of Article 198 of the Association Agreement in comparison with the national legislation of Ukraine; (ii) The Supreme Court as part of the panel of judges of the Economic Court of Cassation in its decision of 04.07.2019 in case No. 910/4947/18 (Kanzhut case) came to the legal position that Article 198 of the Association Agreement can be applied as a norm of direct action, since it establishes new standards for the protection of intellectual property rights. In other words, these two decisions put a bold end to the scientific discussions on the impossibility of applying the norms of the Association Agreement as norms of direct application without a special law.

Let us look at some of the reforms adopted to implement EU values and law in Ukraine's legal system.

---

[52] European Commission 2023c.

[53] European Commission 2023a.

20.6.2 Media Reform

On 31 March 2023, the Law of Ukraine "On Media"[54] came into force. It was developed in response to the recommendations of the European Commission and was among its main requirements. It was prepared with the involvement of a wide range of the public and experts, and its main goal was, on the one hand, to implement the European Union Directive on Audiovisual Media Services 2010/13/EU[55] as amended by EU Directive 2018/1808 of 14 November 2018,[56] and, on the other hand, to codify disparate legal acts and regulations in the media sector by unifying and eliminating contradictions. This legal act amended and supplemented dozens of laws and launched a thorough reform in the media sector.

The main provisions and innovations of the law include the following:

- Prohibition of censorship and consolidation of freedom of media activity on the principles of freedom of expression, freedom of dissemination, exchange and receipt of information, freedom of activity of media entities, including free determination of the content of media information, as well as prohibition of restrictions in this area;
- It regulates areas that were previously unregulated or only partially regulated, such as online media, audiovisual services on demand and shared access platforms;
- It introduces procedures and instruments to ensure financial transparency of media entities, as well as transparency of ownership structure, through the publication of relevant reports and data on the ownership structure and ultimate beneficiaries. The law also contains provisions to ensure competition. Thus, no individual or legal entity or group of individuals may control more than 35% of the national, regional or territorial audiovisual media market;
- Regulates in detail the status of the national regulator—the National Council of Ukraine on Television and Radio Broadcasting—and provides the regulator with broad opportunities to restrict access to channels and services of Russian Federation providers, as well as the content of linear channels on video sharing platforms;
- EU media access to the Ukrainian market is liberalised: reception or retransmission of radio channels, TV channels, programme catalogues originating from EU member states, as well as other radio channels, TV channels, programme catalogues whose content meets the requirements of the European Convention on Transfrontier Television, is not restricted;
- Defines the procedure for licensing and registration of media entities and prescribes the procedure for registration of foreign linear media; at the same time, according to Article 66, linear media originating from EU member states do not require such registration for distribution in Ukraine by audiovisual service providers;

[54] Zakon 2023a.

[55] EU 2010.

[56] EU 2018.

- Defines the minimum share of European product on national television at 50%, and the share of the state language on national television at 90%;
- It more clearly defines the procedure for the responsibility of various media actors and defines different categories of violations. It also provides for measures to be taken in case of violations by Ukrainian and foreign media in accordance with the 1998 European Convention on Transfrontier Television;
- Enshrines the specifics of legal regulation in the context of armed aggression.

Thus, the law creates a legal framework for ensuring media freedom, prohibiting censorship and guaranteeing transparency and predictability of their activities. The law simplifies the access of EU media to the Ukrainian media market, which gives grounds to expect an increase in the presence of EU media products and EU media market participants in Ukraine. The law paves the way for the use of international mechanisms for holding media market participants accountable, in particular those provided for by the 1998 European Convention on Transfrontier Television. The law also strengthens the position of the Ukrainian language in the media space and restricts access to the media of the Russian Federation, which will help reduce the amount of disinformation and fake news spread by the aggressor country in the media space of Ukraine.

20.6.3 Reform of Legislation on National Minorities

On 1 July 2023, the Law of Ukraine "On National Minorities (Communities) of Ukraine" of 13 December 2022[57] came into force, which was supplemented by the Law amending this Law of 21 September 2023 (entered into force on 8 November 2023).[58] The Law is based on the Council of Europe's 1995 Framework Convention for the Protection of National Minorities and the 1992 European Charter for Regional or Minority Languages.

The law prohibits direct and indirect discrimination against persons belonging to national minorities and guarantees a number of rights, including the right to: (1) self-identification; (2) freedom of public association and peaceful assembly; (3) freedom of expression of views and beliefs, opinion, speech, conscience and religion; (4) participation in political, economic and social life; (5) use of the language of a national minority (community); (6) education, including in the languages of national minorities (communities); (7) preservation of the cultural identity of a national minority (community).

The law provides for the free provision of textbooks (including electronic ones) to students of complete general secondary education belonging to national minorities (communities), as well as state assistance in training and advanced training of

---

[57] Zakon 2023b.

[58] Zakon 2023c.

pedagogical and scientific-pedagogical staff in the languages of national minorities (communities).

It should be noted that the law provides additional rights and guarantees for languages that are official languages of the European Union, languages of national minorities (communities) to which the provisions of the European Charter for Regional or Minority Languages apply. Thus, the law provides for the use of national minority languages for this category of public events, in the media, and in publishing. In settlements traditionally inhabited by persons belonging to national minorities (communities), or where such persons constitute a significant part of the population, it is allowed to use inscriptions of official names in the language of national minorities on the signs of local self-government bodies, communal enterprises, announcements, signs, pointers, signs, messages, inscriptions and other publicly posted textual, visual and audio information, as well as during election campaigning. The condition is that such information is duplicated in the state language. It should be noted that these additional rights under the law do not apply to the official language of the aggressor state, i.e. the Russian Federation.

For the first time, this law establishes at the legislative level the powers of a central executive body—the State Service for Ethnic Policy and Freedom of Conscience (SESS)—to implement state policy in the field of protection of the rights and freedoms of persons belonging to national minorities or communities. At the regional level, on the initiative of national minority organisations, it is envisaged to establish centres of national minorities. The task of such centres should be to provide institutional and technical conditions for meeting the cultural needs of national minorities.

On the basis of this law, subordinate legal acts are being developed to implement its provisions, including the methodology for the use of languages of national minorities (communities) in settlements and the Concept of the state programme "Unity in Diversity" until 2032.

The adoption of this law was the result of a recommendation from the European Commission and the implementation of international legal acts. The law will help to ensure the exercise of the rights of persons belonging to national minorities. The rights to use and develop national minority languages are particularly extensive for languages that are official languages of the European Union, as well as for languages of national minorities (communities) to which the provisions of the European Charter for Regional or Minority Languages apply.

20.6.4 Reforming Anti-money Laundering Legislation

On 17 October 2023, important amendments to the Law of Ukraine "On Prevention and Counteraction to Legalisation (Laundering) of the Proceeds of Crime, Terrorist Financing and Financing of the Proliferation of Weapons of Mass Destruction"[59]

[59] Zakon 2023d.

on Politically Exposed Persons (hereinafter referred to as the Law on Politically Exposed Persons).[60] The adoption of this law was an important precondition for receiving international financial assistance. The Law establishes the obligation of primary financial monitoring entities to apply a risk-based approach when servicing clients who are politically exposed persons, members of their families, or persons related to politically exposed persons in order to establish a reasonable level of risk to business relations (conducting a financial transaction without establishing business relations), and to prevent unreasonable refusal to conduct financial transactions and/or establish (continue) business relations. This obligation remains in place even after the PEP ceases to perform significant public functions, but may be cancelled if more than twelve months have passed and the financial transactions conducted by the PEP during this time were low risk.

In case of violation or improper application of the risk-based approach to politically exposed persons, the subjects of primary financial monitoring will be liable for a fine of up to EUR 3,302,071.97.[61]

The implementation of this law will have a positive impact on the fight against corruption and money laundering, especially at the level of politically exposed persons, and will facilitate the receipt of international financial assistance from the European Union and the IMF.

20.6.5 Legality of Human Rights Restrictions as a Result of Martial Law

In the context of the ongoing armed aggression of the Russian Federation against Ukraine, which is accompanied by a commission of war crimes and crimes against humanity, the most questionable issue is whether the restrictions imposed by Ukraine on fundamental rights and freedoms are in line with Ukraine's international obligations and its accession to the EU.

On 24 February 2022, Presidential Decree No. 64 "On the Introduction of Martial Law" was adopted, which was approved by Law No. 2102-IX of 24.02.2022. This act provides a list of articles of the Constitution that may temporarily restrict the constitutional rights and freedoms of a person and citizen for the period of martial law. In fact, it provides that for the period of martial law, the constitutional rights and freedoms of a person and a citizen provided for in Articles 30–34, 38, 39, 41–44, 53 of the Constitution of Ukraine may be restricted. Article 64 of the Constitution of Ukraine provides certain restrictions on rights and freedoms, with an indication of the duration of these restrictions, may be imposed in martial law or a state of

[60] Zakon 2023e.

[61] According to Ukrainian Law fine in the amount of 100,000 non-taxable minimum incomes of citizens. The non-taxable minimum incomes of citizens as of 2025 is UAH 1514, i.e. the fine may amount to UAH 151,400,000, or at the exchange rate of the National Bank of Ukraine as of 6.04.2025 (45.85 UAH / 1 EUR, bank.gov.ua) EUR 3,302,071.97.

emergency. It is worth noting that derogation from obligations does not necessarily mean an admission that the state will not be able to guarantee the rights enshrined in the Convention. In practice, when declaring a derogation, a contracting state usually indicates that the measures it takes "may" involve a derogation from its obligations under the Convention.

Article 24 of the Law of Ukraine on martial law stipulates that Ukraine, in accordance with the International Covenant on Civil and Political Rights, in the event of martial law, shall immediately notify the States Parties to the Covenant through the UN Secretary-General of the restrictions on human and civil rights and freedoms that constitute a derogation from its obligations under the International Covenant, the extent of such derogations and the reasons for such a decision. It is worth noting that such special legislation was adopted in Ukraine in connection with the full-scale war of the Russian Federation against Ukraine.

With regard to the applicability of the state's international human rights obligations in the context of war and the temporary occupation of part of the territory, it should be noted that Article 4 of the International Covenant on Civil and Political Rights and Article 15 of the Convention for the Protection of Human Rights and Fundamental Freedoms provide for derogation from obligations in times of emergency, war or other public danger.

As for the possibility of holding elections during the war, according to Article 19 of the Law of Ukraine on the Legal Regime of Martial Law, it is prohibited to hold elections of the President of Ukraine, as well as elections to the Verkhovna Rada of Ukraine, the Verkhovna Rada of the Autonomous Republic of Crimea and local self-government bodies. Thus, if we do not take into account the issues of security for voters, the possibility of ensuring participation or the expediency of holding elections, their holding is possible from a legal point of view only after the end of the legal regime of martial law or after amendments to the Law of Ukraine on the Legal Regime of Martial Law.

Consequently, the introduction of martial law in Ukraine has led to a temporary restriction of certain constitutional rights and freedoms which constitutes a temporary derogation from its international obligations under Article 4 of the International Covenant on Civil and Political Rights and Article 15 of the Convention for the Protection of Human Rights and Fundamental Freedoms. Russian aggression and occupation of parts of Ukraine has led to massive gross violations of EU values. The continuation of Russian aggression poses a huge threat to EU values not only in Ukraine but also in EU member states.

20.6.6 European Values and Judicial Practice in Ukraine

First of all, the practice of courts of general jurisdiction and the Constitutional Court should be singled out. As for the courts of general jurisprudence, it should be recognized that there has been a significant shift in the implementation of fundamental rights and freedoms as exercised by judges due to the widespread application of the practice of the European Court of Human Rights and references to its decisions. The first court of general jurisdiction of Ukraine, which for the first time applied the provisions of the European Convention on Human Rights and the decisions of the European Court of Human Rights, was the Mykolaiv Regional Court of Appeal, which, during the consideration of an appeal against the decision of the Pervomaisky District Court on 6 May 2000, referred to Article 10 of the ECHR and the decision of the ECtHR Lingers v. Austria.[62]

Today, courts of general jurisdiction regularly refer to the provisions of the ECHR and the practice of the ECtHR not only to strengthen the argumentation of court decisions, but as a guide to what principles, values, and approaches should be laid as the basis for resolving a particular case. References to the case-law of the Court of Justice of the EU have become a kind of rule of good manners, and decisions containing them are considered more reasonable.

There is a number of cases in which the Ukrainian courts refer to the practice of European Court of Human Rights. First of all, it concerns the value of respect for human rights. And this fact confirms that through judicial proceedings and with its help, European values are being implemented in Ukraine.[63] Although the judgments of the Court of Justice of the EU, as well as the decisions of the European Court of Human Rights, are not sources of Ukrainian law.

It should be noted that not only the ECHR and the practice of the ECtHR are actively applied by the courts of Ukraine, but there are also numerous cases of reference to the practice of the Court of Justice of the EU, as well as to the Association Agreement.[64] As for the Constitutional Court of Ukraine, in its decisions it often refers to the decisions of the Constitutional Courts of the EU member states.[65]

[62] Repetskyy and Motyl 2005.

[63] Supreme Court of Ukraine 2024.

[64] Thus, the Kyiv District Administrative Court in its Decision No. 2/416 of 2008 referred to the decision of the Court of Justice in the case of Van Duyn v the Home Office. This in particular concerned the justification of the right of people with disabilities to social benefits from the state by the principles of legal certainty and legitimate expectations. The country's courts began to actively apply certain provisions of the Association Agreement as norms of direct action. The first case in which the norm of the Association Agreement was directly applied and in which the supreme legal force of the Association Agreement over national law was confirmed is the case of Zentiva. The Supreme Court in the case of Zentiva confirmed the supreme legal force of Article 198 of the Association Agreement in comparison with the provisions of national legislation. Ukraine (Supreme Court of Ukraine 2018), and later in the case No. 910/4947/18 of July 4, 2019, Article 198 was recognized as a norm of direct action, since it establishes new standards in the field of human rights protection (7.1.5) (Komarova 2025).

[65] Thus, in its Decision No. 6-p(II)/2021 of September 16, 2021, the Constitutional Court of Ukraine, when interpreting human dignity, referred to the relevant case-law of the European Court of Human Rights (judgment in the case of Kafkaris v. Cyprus of February 12, 2008, Tyrer v. the United Kingdom of April 25, 1978), in the practice of the Court of Justice of the European Union (C-337/98 Kingdom of the Netherlands v European Parliament and Council of the European Union of October 9, 2001), as well as a number of decisions of the Federal Constitutional Court of Germany, the Constitutional Tribunal of the Republic of Poland, the constitutional courts of the Republic of Lithuania, Romania and Hungary (para 2.2) (Constitutional Court of Ukraine 2021). Similarly, in Decision No. 3-p(II)/2023 of March 22, 2023, the Constitutional Court of Ukraine in para 2.4

Of course, this trend contributes to a deeper approximation of EU law and a unified interpretation of both EU law and the core values of the EU in particular. At the same time, although in general, it is allowed to apply the decisions of international courts when interpreting the norms of international treaties,[66] it was necessary to legislate at the level of law the decisions of the Court of Justice of the European Union and provide for the need to apply them in the interpretation of both Ukrainian and EU law, which is negotiable for Ukraine, in particular the Association Agreement with the EU, and the EU's core values, as its essential elements. A certain example can be para 1 of Article 17 of the Law of Ukraine on the Execution of Judgments and Application of the Practice of the European Court of Human Rights of 2006, which provides that Ukrainian Courts shall apply the practice of the European Court of Human Rights as a source of Ukrainian law in the consideration of the case.[67]

20.7 Conclusions

Thus, adherence to the EU's core values is a key precondition for EU accession. The obligation to uphold the values includes both a passive component and an active component related to the dissemination of values. Values and their protection are a key prerequisite for EU membership, and the content of the core values reflects both the basic criteria for EU membership and the requirement of European identity. The EU accession procedure requires the candidate country to implement EU values at various stages. In addition, the EU has a wide range of pre-accession support programmes to help candidate countries implement its values. Ukraine is moving decisively towards EU membership, implementing reforms aimed at implementing the EU's core values. At the same time, the country faces the challenge of reconciling this process with restrictions on constitutional rights due to the introduction of martial law, as well as violations of human rights and freedoms as a result of Russian aggression. The authors argue that such restrictions are consistent with Ukraine's international legal obligations to protect human rights. At the same time, the authors point out the need for further steps to form a mechanism for the implementation of EU values in the legal system of Ukraine. Such steps should, in particular, provide for implementation at the level of constitutional law by making some additions to the Constitution of

---

refers to Article 26 of the Charter of Fundamental Rights of the EU, as well as in para 4 to the decisions of the Constitutional Court of Portugal and the Federal Constitutional Court of Germany (Constitutional Court of Ukraine 2023).

[66] Thus, the Resolution of the Plenum of the High Specialized Court of Ukraine for Civil and Criminal Cases No. 13 of December 19, 2014: "On the Application of International Treaties of Ukraine by the Courts in the Administration of Justice" provided that "in case of difficulties with the application of international treaties of Ukraine, the courts in the administration of justice may use acts and decisions of international organizations, specialized bodies that have the authority to interpret the relevant international treaties or settlement of disputes on interpretation" (para 11) (Higher Specialized Court of Ukraine 2014).

[67] Zakon 2006.

Ukraine, as well as at the level of interpretation of the Constitution of Ukraine by the Constitutional Court of Ukraine, as well as at the level of application of law by courts of general jurisdiction.

References

Blumenwitz D, Gornig G H, Murswiek D (eds) (2005) Die Europäische Union als Wertegemeinschaft. Staats- und völkerrechtliche Abhandlungen der Studiengruppe für Politik und Völkerrecht (SVA) [The European Union as a community of values. Treatises on Constitutional and International Law of the Study Group for Politics and International Law (SVA)], vol. 22. Duncker und Humblot, Berlin

Cagiano de Azevedo R, Paparusso A, Vaccaro M (2013) Sovereignty and acquis communautaire: the new borders of the European Union. L'Europe en Formation 2(368):189–195. https://www.cairn.info/revue-l-europe-en-formation-2013-2-page-189.htm. Accessed 2 February 2025

Cremer H-J (2002) Art 49 (ex-Art.O). In: Caliess C, Ruffert M (eds) Kommentar des Vertrags über die Europäische Union und des Vertrags zur Gründung der Europäischen Gemeinschaft: EUV/EGV [Commentary on the Treaty on European Union and the Treaty establishing the European Community: TEU/TEC], 2nd edn. Luchterhand, Neuwied

Komarova T (2025) Rol' ukrayinskoyi sudovoyi vlady u procesi yevrointegratsiyi [The role of the Ukrainian judiciary in the process of European integration]. Supreme Observer, https://so.supreme.court.gov.ua/news/286/rol-ukrainskoi-(5.03.2025). Accessed 18 February 2025

Mokra L (2020) European Values as a Pre-Condition of Membership and their subsequent implementation. In: Čepo D (ed) European Values and the Challenges of EU Membership Croatia in Comparative Perspective. Centar za demokraciju I pravo Miko Tripalo, pp 35–60. https://tripalo.hr/wp-content/uploads/2020/10/European-Values-and-the-Challenges-of-EU-Membership-1-70.pdf. Accessed 19 February 2025

Oppermann T (1999) Europarecht: ein Studienbuch, 2nd edn. Beck, Munich

Pechstein (2012) Art. 49. In: Streinz R (ed) EUV/AEUV, 2nd edn. Verlag C.H. Beck, Munich

Petrov R (2018) EU Common Values in the EU-Ukraine Association Agreement: Anchor to Democracy? Baltic Journal of European Studies, Tallinn University of Technology 8(1)(24): 49–62

Repetskyy V, Motyl V (2005) Misce Konventsiyi pro zakhyst prav lyudyny ta osnovnykh svobod 1950 roku v pravoviy systemi Nimechchyny ya Ukrayiny Місце Конвенції про захист прав людин та основних свобод 1950року: Видавничий центр ім. І.Франка, Львів [The place of the Convention for the Protection of Human Rights and Fundamental Freedoms of 1950 in the legal system of Germany and Ukraine]. Publishing Center I. Franko, Lviv

Seidl J (2017) Beitrittsverfahren und Sanktionen als Sicherungsmechanismen für die Werte der Europäischen Union [Accession procedures and sanctions as safeguards for the values of the European Union]. PhD diss., University of Erfurt, Erfurt

Tomášek M, Šmejkal V (2024) Commentary on the Treaty on the Functioning of the EU, the Treaty on the EU and the EU Charter of Fundamental Rights [Commentary on the Treaty on the Functioning of the EU, the Treaty on the EU and the EU Charter of Fundamental Rights]. Wolters Kluwer ČR, Prague

CJEU Cases

CJEU (2021a) Judgment of the Court (Grand Chamber), Repubblika v Il-Prim Ministru, C-896/19, ECLI:EU:C:2021:311
CJEU (2021b) Judgment of the Court (Grand Chamber). Asociaţia 'Forumul Judecătorilor din România' and Others v Inspecţia Judiciară and Others. C-83/19, C-127/19, C-195/19, C-291/19, C-355/19 and C-397/19, ECLI:EU:C:2021:393
CJEU (2022) Judgment of the Court, Hungary and Republic of Poland v. European Parliament and Council of the European Union, Case C-156/21, ECLI:EU:C:2022:97

Cases of National Courts

Constitutional Court of Ukraine (2021) Decision No. 6-p(II)/2021 of September 16, 2021. https://zakon.rada.gov.ua/laws/show/v006p710-21#Text. Accessed 30 January 2025
Constitutional Court of Ukraine (2023) Decision No. 3-p(II)/2023 of March 22, 2023. https://zakon.rada.gov.ua/laws/show/v003p710-23#Text. Accessed 30 January 2025
Higher Specialized Court of Ukraine (2014) The Resolution of the Plenum of the High Specialized Court of Ukraine for Civil and Criminal Cases No. 13 of December 19, 2014: "On the Application of International Treaties of Ukraine by the Courts in the Administration of Justice". https://zakon.rada.gov.ua/laws/show/v0013740-14#Text. Accessed 15 February 2025
Supreme Court of Ukraine (2018) Supreme Court as a panel of judges of the Economic Court of Cassation in its Resolution on case No. 910/14972/17 of July 17, 2018 (the case Zentiva). http://iplex.com.ua/doc.php?regnum=75399206&red=100003444e13a9790034069f276c4b12b96dc5&d=5. Accessed 24 February 2025
Supreme Court of Ukraine (2021) Resolution of the Supreme Court of Ukraine as of 20 May 2021 in case No. 908/1550/19 [Resolution of the Supreme Court of Ukraine as of May 20, 2021 in case No. 908/1550/19]. https://reyestr.court.gov.ua/Review/97242697?fbclid=IwAR1qk5Xnodjp7Uu0Qv2bxb7wR0DVP_aFRvi6SyQbpB9B4YUd812wW0QZgfA. Accessed 26 February 2025
Supreme Court of Ukraine (2024) Comprehensive consideration of European integration legal aspects meets the tasks of implementing Ukraine's European integration policy – Chairman of the Administrative Court of the Supreme Court https://supreme.court.gov.ua/supreme/pres-centr/news/1631007/. Accessed 26 February 2025

EU Treaties, Legal Acts and Documents

EU Directive (2010) 2010/13/EU of the European Parliament and of the Council of 10 March 2010 on the coordination of certain provisions laid down by law, regulation or administrative action in Member States concerning the provision of audiovisual media services (Audiovisual Media Services Directive). https://eur-lex.europa.eu/eli/dir/2010/13/oj. Accessed 2 February 2025
EU Directive (2018) 2018/1808 of the European Parliament and of the Council of 14 November 2018 amending Directive 2010/13/EU on the coordination of certain provisions laid down by law, regulation or administrative action in Member States concerning the provision of audiovisual media services (Audiovisual Media Services Directive) in view of changing market realities. http://data.europa.eu/eli/dir/2018/1808/oj. Accessed 4 February 2025
European Commission (1979) Stellungnahme der Kommission vom 23. Mai 1979 zu dem Antrag der Republik Griechenland auf Beitritt zu den Europäischen Gemeinschaften. Amtsblatt Der

Europäischen Gemeinschaften [Commission Opinion of 23 May 1979 on the application for accession to the European Communities by the Hellenic Republic. Official Journal of the European Communities] Jahrgang Nr. L 291. 19.11.1979. 3. Available at https://eur-lex.europa.eu/legal-content/EN/TXT/PDF/?uri=CELEX:11979H/AVI/COM. Accessed 11 February 2025

European Commission (1989) SEC(89) 2290 final, Commission opinion on Turkey‘s request for accession to the Community. SEC (89) 2290 final/2, 20 December 1989

European Commission (1998) Legal questions of enlargement, Briefing No 23. CO; https://www.europarl.europa.eu/enlargement/briefings/pdf/23a1_en.pdf

European Commission (2014) Communication from the Commission to the European Parliament, the Council, the European Economic and Social Committee and the Committee of the Regions Enlargement Strategy and Main Challenges 2014-15, COM/2014/0700 final. https://eur-lex.europa.eu/legal-content/EN/TXT/?uri=CELEX%3A52014DC0700&qid=1726246271968. Accessed 9 February 2025

European Commission (2020) Commission staff working document Bosnia and Herzegovina 2020 COM (2020) 660 final, p.4. https://eur-lex.europa.eu/legal-content/EN/TXT/PDF/?uri=CELEX:52020SC0350. Accessed 9 February 2025

European Commission (2022a) From EU Membership application to Accession Negotiations: Frequently asked questions (DG NEAR). https://neighbourhood-enlargement.ec.europa.eu/system/files/2022-06/FAQ%20accession%20negotiations.pdf. Accessed 8 February 2025

European Commission (2022b) European Council 23-24 June 2022 presidency conclusion. Knowledge for Policy. https://knowledge4policy.ec.europa.eu/publication/european-council-meeting-23-24-june-2022-conclusions_en. Accessed 8 February 2025

European Commission (2022c) Commission Opinion on Ukraine’s application for membership of the European Union: COM(2022) 407 final. http://aei.pitt.edu/4475/1/4475.pdf. Accessed 8 February 2025

European Commission (2023a) Analytical Report following the Communication from the Commission to the European Parliament, the European Council and the Council Commission Opinion on Ukraine’s application for membership of the European Union, Brussels, 1.2.2023. http://surl.li/gsbcs. Accessed 7 February 2025

European Commission (2023b) Communication on EU Enlargement Policy, 690 final Brussels. https://neighbourhood-enlargement.ec.europa.eu/2023-communication-eu-enlargement-policy_en. Accessed 7 February 2025

European Commission (2023c) Commission staff working document Ukraine 2023 Report Accompanying the document Communication from the Commission to the European Parliament, the Council, the European Economic and Social Committee and the Committee of the Regions 2023 Communication on EU Enlargement policy, SWD(2023) 699 final

European Communities (1972) Dokumente betreffend den Beitritt des Königreichs Dänemark, Irlands, des Königreichs Norwegen und des Vereinigten Königreichs Großbritannien und Nordirland zu den Europäischen Gemeinschaften. Amtsblatt Der Europäischen Gemeinschaften [Documents relating to the accession of the Kingdom of Denmark, Ireland, the Kingdom of Norway and the United Kingdom of Great Britain and Northern Ireland to the European Communities. Official journal of the European Communities]. 15. Jg, Nr. L 73, 27.03.1972. 3. https://eur-lex.europa.eu/legal-content/EN/TXT/HTML/?uri=CELEX:11972B/AVI/COM. Accessed 25 February 2025

European Council (1978) Erklärung des Europäischen Rates zur Demokratie, Kopenhagen, 8. April, Bull-EG 3/1978, 6.09.2012, https://www.consilium.europa.eu/меді/48467/kopenhagen_april_1978__de_.pdf. Accessed 15 February 2025

European Council (1993) Conclusions of the Presidency - Copenhagen, 21-22 June 1993, SN 180/1/93 REV 1. https://www.europarl.europa.eu/enlargement/ec/cop_en.htm. Accessed 14 February 2025

European Council (1995) Madrid European Council, 15-16 December 1995 https://www.europarl.europa.eu/summits/mad1_en.htm

European Council (1998) Luxembourg European Council 12-13 December 1997 presidency conclusion
European Council (2000) Presidency report to the European Council on enlargement of the Union and Agenda 2000. https://www.europarl.europa.eu/summits/mad1_en.htm. Accessed 12 February 2025
European Parliament (2003) Presidency report to the European Council
European Parliament (2008) Briefing No 23 Legal issues of enlargement, 19 May 2008 Resolution, Part III (undated) https://www.europarl.europa.eu/enlargement/briefings/23a2_en.htm#B14. Accessed 11 February 2025
European Union (1993) Europe Agreement establishing an association between the European Communities and their Member States, of the one part, and the Republic of Poland, of the other part, Publications office of the European Union, Official Journal of the European Communities, No L 348/2, 31 December 1993. https://op.europa.eu/en/publication-detail/-/publication/83db0eca-ebb4-4409-825b-28cc8d7febc9/language-en. Accessed 15 February 2025
The Council of the European Union (1970) Beschluß des Rats betreffend das Verfahren der Beitrittsverhandlungen (8. und 9. Juni 1970) [Council Decision on the procedure for accession negotiations (8 and 9 June 1970)]. https://www.cvce.eu/content/publication/2005/7/8/95fb31bc-b3d2-47d5-8dab-66b2714e01cb/publishable_de.pdf. Accessed 25 February 2025
The Council of the European Union (2006) Presidency Conclusions - Brussels, 14/15 December 2006, 16879/06 https://www.consilium.europa.eu/ueDocs/cms_Data/docs/pressData/en/ec/92202.pdf. Accessed 24 February 2025
Ugoda (2004) Ugoda pro partnerstvo i spivrobitnyctvo mizh Ukrayinoyu u Evropeyskymy Spivtovarystvamy ta yikh derzhavamy chlenamy [Partnership and Cooperation Agreement between the European Communities and their Member States, and Ukraine] https://zakon.rada.gov.ua/laws/show/998_012#Text. Accessed 25 February 2025
Ugoda (2014) Ugoda pro Asociaciyu mizh Ukrayinoyu, z odniyeyeyu storony, ta Evropeiskym Soyuzom, Evropeyskym spivtovarystvom z atomnoyoy energiyi I yikhnimymi derzhavamy chlenamy, z inshoyoy storony vid 2014 [Association Agreement between Ukraine, on the one part, and the European Union, the European Atomic Energy Community and their Member States, on the other part, of 2014]. https://zakon.rada.gov.ua/laws/show/984_011#Text. Accessed 25 February 2025

National Laws

Zakon (2006) Law of Ukraine On the Execution of Judgments and Application of the Practice of the European Court of Human Rights of February 23, 2006
Zakon (2020) Law of Ukraine On Prevention and Counteraction to Legalisation (Laundering) of Proceeds from Crime, Financing of Terrorism and Financing of Proliferation of Weapons of Mass Destruction. https://zakon.rada.gov.ua/laws/show/361-20. Accessed 2 March 2025
Zakon (2023a) Zakon Ukrayiny Pro Media. https://zakon.rada.gov.ua/rada/show/2849-IX.zakon.rada.gov.ua/rada/show/2849-IX. Accessed 1 March 2025
Zakon (2023b) Law of Ukraine On National Minorities (Communities) of Ukraine https://zakon.rada.gov.ua/laws/show/2827-20#Text. Accessed 1 March 2025
Zakon (2023c) Law of Ukraine On Amendments to the Law of Ukraine "On National Minorities (Communities of Ukraine)" on the implementation of rights and freedoms of national minorities [Law of Ukraine On Amendments to the Law of Ukraine "On National Minorities (Communities) of Ukraine" Regarding Certain Issues of Exercising the Rights and Freedoms of Persons Belonging to National Minorities (Communities) of Ukraine]. https://zakon.rada.gov.ua/laws/show/3389-20#Text. Accessed 2 March 2025

Zakon (2023d) Law of Ukraine On the Protection and Enforcement of Legalisation (Protection) of Individuals with a Loan Loss, Financial Institutions and Financial Institutions for the Protection of the Property of a Client

Zakon (2023e) Law of Ukraine On amendments to the Law of Ukraine On the registration and enforcement of legalisation (detection) of individuals. Oderzhanyh zlochynnym shlyakhom, finansuvannym teroryzmu ta finansuvannym rozpovsyudzhennym zboyi masovoho znyshchennya shchodo politically znachushchykh osib [Law of Ukraine On Amendments to the Law of Ukraine "On Prevention and Counteraction to Legalisation (Laundering) of Proceeds from Crime, Financing of Terrorism and Financing of Proliferation of Weapons of Mass Destruction" Regarding Politically Exposed Persons]. https://zakon.rada.gov.ua/laws/show/3419-20#Text. Accessed 2 March 2025

Websites and Other Sources

Al Jazeera (2006) EU suspends Serbia talks. Al Jazeera News. https://www.aljazeera.com/news/2006/5/3/eu-suspends-serbia-talks. 25 January 2025

Euractiv (2007) 2007 accession for Bulgaria and Romania - with probation. Euractiv News. https://www.euractiv.com/section/enlargement/news/2007-accession-for-bulgaria-and-romania-with-probation/. Accessed 5 February 2025

European Commission (2023d) Instrument for Pre-accession Assistance (IPA) III - Performance. https://commission.europa.eu/strategy-and-policy/eu-budget/performance-and-reporting/programme-performance-statements/instrument-pre-accession-assistance-ipa-iii-performance_en. Accessed 7 February 2025

European Commission (2024a) TAIEX. https://neighbourhood-enlargement.ec.europa.eu/funding-and-technical-assistance/taiex_en. Accessed 5 February 2025

European Commission (2024b) Twinning. https://neighbourhood-enlargement.ec.europa.eu/funding-and-technical-assistance/twinning_en. Accessed 6 February 2025

Sigma (2024) SIGMA at a glance. https://www.sigmaweb.org/about/. Accessed 8 February 2025

Mykhailo Mykiyevych is a Doctor of law, a Professor, the Head of the Department of European Law of the Faculty of International Relations of Ivan Franko National University of Lviv and a professor at the Law Faculty of Vilnius University.

Volodymyr Motyl is a post-doc researcher, and an Associate Professor in the Department of European Law of the Faculty of International Relations of Ivan Franko National University of Lviv.

Chapter 21
Ukraine's Accession to the European Union: Legislative Dimension

Volodymyr Venher

Contents

Abstract The ongoing war has profoundly challenged the ability of law to regulate social and political life effectively. In this context, the Verkhovna Rada of Ukraine's legislative role is central to preserving the systemic coherence of the national legal order. The Ukrainian Constitution provides for the introduction of martial law, a special legal regime enabling the use of exceptional legal and administrative instruments. While these mechanisms expand the discretionary powers of public authorities to respond swiftly to wartime exigencies, they must also safeguard fundamental human rights. This chapter examines the Verkhovna Rada's legislative activity under martial law, focusing on how it upholds the core elements of the rule of law, such as legality, legal certainty, non-discrimination, the prohibition of abuse of power, and access to justice. The chapter presents a case-based analysis of specific sectors where wartime legislative interventions reveal tensions between emergency governance and constitutional guarantees. The chapter argues that when adopting new laws or amending existing ones, Parliament must carefully balance the imperatives of national security, the military's operational needs, and the individual's fundamental rights. From the perspective of EU accession, this requires prioritizing high-quality, predictable legislative regulation at the statutory level and institutionalizing safeguards that enable judicial protection of rights during martial law. Thus, the study underscores the importance of aligning wartime lawmaking with European standards of constitutionalism and the rule of law.

V. Venher (✉)
Faculty of Law, National University "Kyiv-Mohyla Academy", Kyiv, Ukraine
e-mail: venhervm@ukma.edu.ua

I. Isokaitė-Valužė and H. Šinkūnas (eds.), *The European Union 2004-2024*,
https://doi.org/10.1007/978-94-6265-718-2_21

Keywords EU accession · Parliament · Legislative discretion · System of legislation · Rule of law · Legality · Legal certainty · Access to justice

21.1 Introduction

Ukraine's prospective accession to the European Union (EU) signifies a multifaceted transformation, encompassing not only a geopolitical and economic reorientation but also a substantial constitutional and legislative metamorphosis. As a candidate country, Ukraine must align its legal and institutional frameworks with the *acquis communautaire*—the body of EU law—thereby undertaking one of the most extensive legal harmonization processes in its modern history. This transformation is not merely technical in nature; rather, it reflects deeper constitutional choices about the nature of sovereignty, the rule of law, and the relationship between domestic and supranational norms.

At the core of this process is the legislative dimension, encompassing both the adaptation of Ukraine's national legal order and the restructuring of its parliamentary and regulatory practices. The experience of previous waves of EU enlargement demonstrates that the national legal system must possess a sufficiently high level of capacity to implement the necessary legislative changes.[1] The Verkhovna Rada of Ukraine (Parliament), as the primary legislative authority, plays a pivotal role in this process. It is obligated to adopt and revise a multitude of laws across various sectors, encompassing environmental policy and competition law.[2] The challenge is further compounded by the ongoing war, which complicates institutional functioning and necessitates urgent yet systematic legal reform.

Furthermore, the process of legislative convergence between Ukraine and the EU will be constrained by the national constitutional framework of a post-Soviet state, excluding the mechanisms of relevant or devolved legislative practices and constitutional court activism that are present in some EU member states.[3] Achieving this objective demands a substantial degree of legal precision and political consensus, thereby averting inconsistencies and constitutional tensions. The overarching requirement is adherence to European values—namely, democracy, human rights, and the rule of law—as defined in Article 2 of the Treaty on European Union (TEU).[4] Consequently, Ukraine's legislative agenda functions as both a reflection of its constitutional identity and a conduit to its European future. For Ukraine, the entrenchment of these principles is not only a matter of aligning with EU standards but also a precondition for progressing along the path of accession. The rule of law functions as a foundational benchmark in the EU's enlargement policy, serving both

[1] Nicolaides 2012, p. 44.

[2] Emerson 2018.

[3] Sadurski 2012, p. 116.

[4] European Union (2016) Consolidated version of the Treaty on European Union. Official Journal of the European Union, C 202, 7 June, pp. 13–46.

as a normative compass and as a structural framework guiding legal reform and institutional integrity.

The principle of legality, which demands that all state action be grounded in law, that laws be accessible and foreseeable, and that legal certainty be preserved, is central to the rule of law.[5] In the context of Ukraine's accession, legality assumes particular salience given the country's historical struggles with legal pluralism and formal Soviet-style formal positivism.[6] The reinforcement of legality is contingent upon the adherence of legislative and executive actions to the constitutional mandates, their susceptibility to judicial review, and their implementation through transparent and accountable procedures. These elements are critical in building public trust, attracting foreign investment, and ensuring judicial independence—all of which are key indicators in the European Commission's annual enlargement reports.[7]

Furthermore, the EU's conditionality framework prioritizes the implementation of sustained and credible reforms in the domain of the rule of law. This encompasses the establishment of an effective system of public administration, the decentralization of power, and the empowerment of local self-government. Moreover, the establishment of effective anti-corruption institutions and the eradication of excessive political influence within the justice system are imperative. The Venice Commission and other Council of Europe institutions have repeatedly underscored the imperative for rule of law reforms to be substantive in nature, as opposed to a mere adherence to formalistic procedures. This emphasis signifies a cultural shift towards a paradigm of legality, as opposed to the mere engineering of institutions.[8] For Ukraine, the implementation of the rule of law is not merely a prerequisite for accession; it is also a strategy to enhance its democratic legitimacy and constitutional resilience, particularly in the context of the ongoing pressures of war and reconstruction.

The principles of legality and legal certainty are foundational elements of constitutional governance and require not only judicial oversight but also active, substantive engagement by the legislature. In accordance with Article 75 of the Constitution of Ukraine, the Verkhovna Rada is defined as the sole legislative authority in the state, bearing full responsibility for ensuring the coherence, stability, and legality of the national legal order.[9] This institutional role becomes particularly critical under

[5] European Commission for Democracy through Law (Venice Commission) (2011) Report on the Rule of Law. CDL-AD(2011)003rev. Council of Europe, Strasbourg, p. 10.

[6] Holovaty et al. 2021, p. 11.

[7] See, e.g. European Commission (2023) Ukraine 2023 Report. Brussels: European Commission, p. 6. https://enlargement.ec.europa.eu/ukraine-report-2023_en. Accessed 22 November 2024.

[8] See, e.g. European Commission for Democracy through Law (Venice Commission) (2020) Ukraine – Urgent Opinion on the Reform of the Constitutional Court, CDL-AD(2020)039-e. Council of Europe, Strasbourg. Adopted 11 December 2020. https://www.venice.coe.int/webforms/documents/?pdf=CDL-AD(2020)039-e. Accessed 22 November 2024; Parliamentary Assembly of the Council of Europe (PACE) (2017) Resolution 2145 (2017): The Functioning of Democratic Institutions in Ukraine, 25 January. https://pace.coe.int/en/files/23452/html. Accessed 22 November 2024.

[9] Verkhovna Rada of Ukraine (1996) Constitution of Ukraine, adopted 28 June 1996, as amended. https://zakon.rada.gov.ua/laws/show/254к/96-вр#Text. Accessed 22 November 2024.

conditions of martial law, where legal frameworks must be adapted to extraordinary circumstances without undermining constitutional values.

Despite the operational challenges posed by the full-scale Russian invasion, the Verkhovna Rada has continued to perform its law-making function, enacting emergency laws and amending existing statutes to ensure continuity of governance and protection of fundamental rights. In the wartime context, the Ukrainian Parliament has assumed a pivotal role in maintaining the integrity of the constitutional system through a series of legislative initiatives addressing decentralisation and judicial independence. In light of these considerations, the following analysis will be presented: a concise examination of the principles that govern the Ukrainian parliament's operations in the context of war and the relevant activities in these abovementioned areas.

21.2 Parliament in Wartime

Of fundamental importance during wartime is the preservation of the constitutional model governing the functioning of the legislature. The Constitution of Ukraine explicitly stipulates that the Verkhovna Rada shall not cease its operations during martial law. On the contrary, it is constitutionally mandated to remain in continuous session. Article 92 of the Constitution of Ukraine, which enumerates matters subject exclusively to regulation by law, provides no exceptions for states of emergency or martial law.[10] This constitutional design underscores the imperative role of the legislature in maintaining democratic oversight and legal certainty during crises.

Comparative experience during the COVID-19 pandemic illustrates that even under conditions of extraordinary disruption, the majority of national parliaments continued to function, albeit with procedural adjustments or limitations. Most legislatures opted for hybrid or remote sessions, preserving their law-making and oversight functions. Notably, only the parliaments of Cyprus and the Czech Republic temporarily suspended their activities, delegating certain powers to the executive.[11] This international precedent reinforces the constitutional position that emergency governance must not erode legislative authority but should instead ensure its adaptability and continuity.

Under conditions of martial law, the Constitution of Ukraine does not provide any mechanisms for the delegation of legislative authority by the Verkhovna Rada to other state actors. This contrasts with the constitutional frameworks of several European states (Belgium, Denmark), which, in exceptional circumstances, allow for the temporary transfer or expansion of executive legislative functions under strict legal

[10] *Ibid.*, Article 92.

[11] European Commission for Democracy through Law (Venice Commission) (2020) Interim Report on the Measures Taken in the EU Member States as a Result of the COVID-19 Crisis and Their Impact on Democracy, the Rule of Law and Fundamental Rights. CDL-AD(2020)018-e, adopted at the 124th Plenary Session (8–9 October 2020). Council of Europe, Strasbourg, pp. 64–65. https://www.venice.coe.int/webforms/documents/?pdf=CDL-AD(2020)018-e. Accessed 20 December 2022.

safeguards and time limitations.[12] Moreover, Ukrainian constitutional law does not foresee any expedited or emergency legislative procedure distinct from the ordinary process outlined in the Rules of Procedure of the Verkhovna Rada.[13] Consequently, the regular functioning of the legislature during wartime must be maintained, and its law-making activity must be responsive both to the exigencies of the armed conflict and the broader horizon of post-war recovery and reconstruction.

Notwithstanding the ongoing armed conflict, the Verkhovna Rada of Ukraine has continued to operate in full compliance with the constitutional framework, holding plenary sessions in person and maintaining its legislative function as the sole law-making body of the state. The continuation of in-person parliamentary procedures under martial law highlights the fortitude of Ukraine's institutional framework and exemplifies a constitutional dedication to democratic continuity, even during periods of crisis. The legislative process during this period has been marked by a remarkable degree of political consensus, with the majority of adopted laws receiving support from various political party factions, including members of the opposition.[14] This consensus-driven approach has contributed to political stability and facilitated rapid institutional responses to wartime exigencies without undermining the legitimacy of the legislative process. Notwithstanding the implementation of certain procedural simplifications intended to expedite the adoption of legislation in emergency contexts, the Verkhovna Rada persists in observing the fundamental stages of the legislative process, thereby preserving the formal integrity of parliamentary lawmaking.[15] However, due to ongoing hostilities and the imperative of protecting national security, the transparency and openness of parliamentary proceedings, particularly with respect to public access to deliberations and documentation, have been significantly curtailed even in 2023–2024, a few years under the pressure of extraordinary conditions.[16]

The Verkhovna Rada of Ukraine, in enacting new laws or amending existing ones, bears a heightened responsibility to ensure that urgent legislative responses are both proportional and coherent within the broader legal system. At the onset of a full-scale invasion, this encompasses not only the immediate response to regulatory requirements but also the anticipation of long-term legal ramifications of emergency legislation. In undertaking this action, the legislature is obligated to adhere to international legal standards and best practices. Notwithstanding the ongoing operation of the Verkhovna Rada under martial law, a number of wartime legislative practices

---

[12] See, e.g. Diaz Crego and Kotanidis 2020; European Commission for Democracy through Law (Venice Commission) (2020) Report – Respect for Democracy, Human Rights and the Rule of Law during States of Emergency: Reflections. CDL-AD(2020)014-e. Council of Europe, Strasbourg. https://www.venice.coe.int/webforms/documents/default.aspx?pdffile=CDL-AD(2020)014-e. Accessed 20 November 2024.

[13] For example, the Basic Law of the Federal Republic of Germany (Article 115d) provides for a special procedure for simultaneous adoption of a bill by the Bundestag and the Bundesrat at the request of the Government. See Jakab 2006.

[14] Venher et al. 2023, p. 63.

[15] *Ibid.*, pp. 6–8.

[16] Venher et al. 2024, pp. 6–9.

have emerged that give rise to concerns regarding their compatibility with Ukraine's constitutional framework and established democratic standards. It is noteworthy that there has been a discernible trend towards the de facto delegation of legislative powers to executive and other state authorities, despite the absence of constitutional grounds for such transfers. Moreover, wartime legislation has frequently entailed the narrowing of the scope of existing laws, the transfer of the powers of local self-government bodies to military administrations, and the introduction of special procedures for the dismissal of certain public officials. Furthermore, the limitation of parliamentary oversight powers in specific domains, rationalized on the basis of national security concerns, accentuates the constitutional discord between emergency governance and the tenets of legality, separation of powers, and democratic accountability.

In the course of this examination of the legislative endeavours of the Verkhovna Rada of Ukraine, it is essential to underscore a notable element that appears to be incompatible with the principle of legality. This involves the Parliament's practice of de facto evasion of legislative responsibility, either through the avoidance of regulation in specific domains or, more pertinently, through the explicit delegation of norm-making authority to subordinate authorities, thereby contravening constitutional stipulations concerning legislative exclusivity.

A substantive understanding of the principle of legality, as a fundamental component of the rule of law, requires recognition of its multiple dimensions. Central to this principle, however, remains the acknowledgment of the hierarchical supremacy of statute law within the national legal system.[17] This doctrinal position reinforces both formal and substantive aspects of legality. Formal legality emphasizes the necessity for public authorities to act solely on the basis of, within the limits of, and in the manner prescribed by law. As a rule, normative acts of executive authorities—specifically, those issued by the President of Ukraine and the Cabinet of Ministers—do not acquire elevated legal status or enhanced normative force merely by virtue of the extraordinary circumstances of war. These acts remain subordinated within the established hierarchy of normative legal acts, in which statutory law retains primacy and exclusive competence over matters enumerated in Article 92 of the Constitution of Ukraine.

Despite the constitutional principle of legislative exclusivity, the Verkhovna Rada of Ukraine has increasingly relied on the practice of legislative abstention, whereby it intentionally refrains from regulating specific matters by law, instead delegating norm-setting authority to subordinate legal acts. Notably, several wartime laws have expressly authorised the Cabinet of Ministers of Ukraine to determine exemptions for the movement of certain goods across the customs border; to establish rules for the lease of state and communal property that diverge from the provisions set out in the Law of Ukraine On the Lease of State and Communal Property; and to define

[17] European Commission for Democracy through Law (Venice Commission) (2011) Report on the Rule of Law. CDL-AD(2011)003rev. Adopted at the 86th Plenary Session (Venice, 25–26 March 2011). Council of Europe, Strasbourg. https://www.venice.coe.int/webforms/documents/default.aspx?pdffile=CDL-AD(2011)003rev-e. Accessed 20 November 2022.

the peculiarities of public procurement procedures applicable to entities covered by the Law of Ukraine On Public Procurement.[18] In these and similar cases, Parliament justifies such exceptions based on the extraordinary circumstances brought about by wartime conditions.

However, even during periods of martial law, the importance of legality is further accentuated. In such conditions, sub-legislative norm-makers may not only be tempted to regulate critical societal relations through executive or administrative acts. Still, they may also be compelled by the exigencies of wartime governance. Despite this practical pressure, the Ukrainian constitutional system does not allow to transfer legislative powers to other bodies, even under exceptional circumstances. Hence, the Ukrainian model maintains a strict interpretation of legislative exclusivity and legality, rooted in Article 6 and Article 92 of the Constitution of Ukraine, which enshrine the division of powers and the exclusive competence of parliament in adopting laws. In light of these considerations, the present study will also examine the impact of legislative activity on the organization of the separation of powers between state bodies and local self-government, as well as the principles of the functioning of justice.

21.3 Functioning of Public Authorities and Decentralisation

Legal certainty, as a fundamental element of the rule of law, is traditionally regarded in academic discourse as a standard for the quality of both legislation and its application. It encompasses such key characteristics as clarity, precision, intelligibility, and predictability of legal norms, along with the principle of non-retroactivity.[19] In the context of a legal system operating under the extraordinary conditions of martial law, these components assume renewed importance. The requirement of predictability is particularly vulnerable in wartime, when rapid, ad hoc legislative interventions may destabilise the coherence and foreseeability of the legal order. Nonetheless, legislative predictability must remain a guiding principle, even if it requires reinterpretation in light of security imperatives and emergency governance.

This discussion underscores a frequently disregarded facet of legal certainty from a constitutional law perspective: the necessity for a stable and coherent institutional framework within the public administration system. A critical component of Ukraine's EU accession is establishing a legislative framework that ensures the continued functionality of central and local government bodies under martial law. This framework must delineate these bodies' mutual interactions, competencies, and oversight mechanisms, ensuring their operational effectiveness.[20] This is imperative for safeguarding the constitutional model of public administration and upholding

[18] Venher et al. 2023, p. 42.

[19] Craig 1997, p. 467.

[20] See, e.g. European Commission (2023) Ukraine 2023 Report. Brussels: European Commission, p. 6. https://enlargement.ec.europa.eu/ukraine-report-2023_en. Accessed 22 November 2024.

the rule of law in its substantive sense, even under emergencies. Consequently, legal certainty evolves from a mere technical or procedural standard to a critical safeguard for democratic resilience.

In accordance with international standards governing the administration of territories during armed conflict, the establishment and functioning of special military administrations is a common legal mechanism. Ukraine's legal system reflects this normative approach. The Law of Ukraine "On the Legal Regime of Martial Law" provides that, alongside the existing organs of state power and local self-government, military administrations and military command authorities are vested with public authority during martial law.[21] Together, these actors form a complex institutional architecture, whose core functions include not only ensuring national security and resisting armed aggression but also imposing restrictions on constitutional rights and freedoms in a manner that is proportionate to the scale and nature of the threats faced.[22]

From a constitutional law perspective, the Ukrainian Parliament holds a pivotal role in shaping and maintaining a balanced regulatory framework for the operation of public authorities under martial law. This includes enacting laws that not only define the powers and responsibilities of military administrations but also ensure their coordination with elected governmental bodies in line with the principles of separation of powers, subsidiarity, and legal certainty.[23] In doing so, Parliament must secure both the effectiveness of emergency governance and the constitutional safeguards necessary to preserve democratic order during and after the conflict.

The effective functioning of public authorities during martial law must be both balanced and systematized in order to maintain constitutional legitimacy and administrative coherence. In this context, the legal regulation of military administrations and their interaction with state authorities and local self-government bodies becomes particularly significant. The Ukrainian experience demonstrates a complex and evolving model of institutional relations, particularly in the wake of Russia's full-scale invasion in February 2022.

Pursuant to the Law of Ukraine "On the Legal Regime of Martial Law," military administrations were introduced into the public authority system as temporary institutions endowed with a broad mandate to ensure public order, national security,

---

[21] Verkhovna Rada of Ukraine (2015) Law of Ukraine "On the Legal Regime of Martial Law", No. 389-VIII of 12 May 2015, as amended. https://zakon.rada.gov.ua/laws/show/389-19#Text. Accessed 22 November 2024.

[22] European Commission for Democracy through Law (Venice Commission), 2020. Respect for Democracy, Human Rights and the Rule of Law during States of Emergency. CDL-PI(2020)003rev. Council of Europe, Strasbourg, para 40. https://www.venice.coe.int/webforms/documents/?pdf=CDL-PI(2020)003rev-e. Accessed 22 November 2024.

[23] See, e.g. Constitution of Ukraine articles 6 and 19; see European Commission for Democracy through Law (Venice Commission), 2011. Report on the Rule of Law. CDL-AD(2011)003rev. Council of Europe, Strasbourg, pp. 6–7.

and the coordination of emergency responses.[24] On 24 February 2022, the President of Ukraine issued a Decree on the Establishment of Military Administrations, which created regional, district, and the Kyiv City military administrations, effectively replacing the existing local state administrations.[25] However, at that time, the law did not provide an unambiguous framework for the interaction between newly created military administrations and the elected local councils, particularly at the regional and district levels.

This legal gap resulted in potential ambiguities in statutory interpretation. Specifically, the provisions of Articles 4 and 15 of the Law of Ukraine "On the Legal Regime of Martial Law" could be construed in two different ways: either that the powers of elected local councils were fully terminated and thus not subject to reinstatement after the cessation of martial law, or that their functions were merely suspended, subject to resumption upon restoration of peacetime governance. Under the former interpretation, it would follow that extraordinary elections would be required to reconstitute local councils post-conflict, raising significant questions about democratic continuity and legal certainty.

To eliminate such ambiguities and prevent constitutional uncertainty regarding the status and authority of regional and district councils, legislative amendments were adopted in May 2022. These amendments modified the Law of Ukraine "On the Legal Regime of Martial Law," the Law "On Local Self-Government in Ukraine", and related statutes.[26] The revised provisions established a clear mechanism for the suspension (rather than termination) of local self-government powers in territories where military administrations are established. Additionally, they introduced a complex procedure for the formal transfer of competencies from local councils to military administrations, contingent upon a resolution by the Verkhovna Rada of Ukraine based on a submission from the President.[27]

This legal evolution underscores the importance of clarity, predictability, and proportionality in the regulation of exceptional governance mechanisms. It also reflects an attempt to maintain fidelity to the principles of the rule of law, democratic governance, and the separation of powers during times of extraordinary crisis.

Another crucial aspect of Ukraine's wartime governance concerns the limited establishment of military administrations at the level of settlements.[28] Although

---

[24] Verkhovna Rada of Ukraine (2015) Law of Ukraine "On the Legal Regime of Martial Law", No. 389-VIII of 12 May 2015, as amended. https://zakon.rada.gov.ua/laws/show/389-19#Text. Accessed 22 November 2024.

[25] President of Ukraine (2022) Decree No. 72/2022 on the Establishment of Military Administrations, 24 February.

[26] Verkhovna Rada of Ukraine (2022) Law of Ukraine No. 2259-IX on Amendments to Certain Laws of Ukraine Regarding the Functioning of Local Self-Government and Military Administrations under Martial Law, 12 May. https://zakon.rada.gov.ua/laws/show/2259-20#n19. Accessed 22 November 2024.

[27] *Ibid.*, Article 2(3).

[28] According to the Law of Ukraine On the Legal Regime of Martial Law, military administrations are to be formed at the level of individual settlements (*naselenyi punkt*), rather than at the level of territorial communities (*hromadas*). This distinction, while formally coherent within the statute,

hundreds of localities have been officially classified as active combat zones or temporarily occupied territories, military administrations have only been established in several dozen.[29] This selective approach reflects a deliberate state policy aimed at preserving democratic governance structures—even under the constraints of martial law—by prioritizing the continuity of elected local self-government over appointed military authority.

The relevant decisions adopted by the Verkhovna Rada in this regard should be viewed as reactive and pragmatic, aligning with a broader state policy that favours elected local councils over military administrations wherever possible. Without delving into a detailed assessment of the normative advantages or disadvantages of such an approach, it is important to emphasize the need for stable, clear, and predictable legal regulation in this sphere. The long-term configuration of local public governance structures is critical to democratic consolidation, and unpredictability in legal norms can significantly undermine the ability of public authorities to effectively safeguard human rights and fundamental freedoms at the local level.

Moreover, preventing the abuse of power and limiting administrative discretion is a particularly challenging task during wartime, especially when the authority and influence of military command structures are exceptionally high. While military necessity may justify temporary extraordinary measures, excessive centralization of power in military hands poses risks to democratic governance and civilian oversight. International standards on peacebuilding and post-conflict reconstruction consistently emphasize the need to avoid the overconcentration of power in military institutions,[30] recognizing that military actors, by their nature, are more directly aligned with wartime exigencies. In the context of European integration, it is crucial to preserve legislative mechanisms that ensure adherence to these fundamental principles. In Ukraine's case, this balance remains a key constitutional and policy challenge as the country navigates the complexities of wartime governance and democratic resilience. For military administrations operating in areas not directly affected by active combat, it is critically important to ensure mechanisms of active public oversight, adherence to the principles of openness and transparency, and the establishment of reasonable limitations aligned with national security concerns. These challenges must be addressed directly by the legislature, as any evasion of legislative regulation or transfer of normative powers to subordinate bodies risks undermining the requirements of the rule of law and may lead to violations of European democratic standards.

---

creates practical and legal complications in light of Ukraine's recent administrative-territorial reform of 2020, which consolidated local governance structures and significantly expanded the jurisdiction of local self-government bodies to cover multiple settlements within unified territorial communities.

[29] Ministry for Communities and Territories Development of Ukraine (2025) Order No. 376 of 28 February 2025 on Approval of the List of Territories in which Military Operations are (were) Conducted or Temporarily Occupied by the Russian Federation. https://zakon.rada.gov.ua/laws/show/z0380-25#Text. Accessed 15 May 2025.

[30] Hasebe 2012, p. 469.

21.4 Functioning of the Judiciary

The legislative regulation of access to justice during armed conflict presents a particularly complex constitutional challenge. Ensuring the continued and effective functioning of the judiciary under the extraordinary conditions of war is a task that implicates the foundational principles of the rule of law and democratic governance. Notably, the Constitution of Ukraine does not provide for any explicit derogations or exceptional procedures relating to the operation of the judiciary under martial law.[31] Rather, it presumes the continuity of judicial authority as part of the broader framework of constitutional order.

This position is reinforced in the legislative domain. Article 122(2) of the Law of Ukraine "On the Legal Regime of Martial Law" expressly stipulates that "the powers of courts, bodies and institutions of the justice system provided for by the Constitution of Ukraine may not be restricted under martial law".[32] This provision affirms the constitutional imperative that judicial institutions retain their full authority even during times of national emergency, reflecting Ukraine's formal commitment to the principle of separation of powers and judicial independence.

The significance of judicial independence in this context cannot be overstated. As constitutional scholar Mykola Koziubra has observed, judicial independence constitutes "a cornerstone laid into the very foundation of any democratic and lawful state".[33] Both institutional and functional guarantees of this principle—including the independence of judges, the irremovability of their office, and the integrity of judicial procedures—must therefore be preserved without erosion due to the exigencies of wartime governance.

While the broader issue of judicial functioning under martial law warrants separate and detailed examination, it is important to highlight the legislative dimension of this issue and the related constitutional guarantees of the right to a fair trial. Article 55 of the Constitution of Ukraine guarantees the right of every individual to protect their rights and freedoms through a court of law, and Article 6 of the European Convention on Human Rights, to which Ukraine is a party, affirms the right to a fair and public hearing by an independent and impartial tribunal.[34] Even during a state of war, access to justice and the effective operation of the judicial system must be maintained as a core element of constitutional democracy.

According to Article 92(1)(14) of the Constitution of Ukraine, the judicial system, the administration of justice, and the status of judges must be defined exclusively

---

[31] Verkhovna Rada of Ukraine (1996) Constitution of Ukraine, adopted 28 June 1996, as amended. https://zakon.rada.gov.ua/laws/show/254к/96-вр#Text. Accessed 22 November 2024.

[32] Verkhovna Rada of Ukraine (2015) Law of Ukraine "On the Legal Regime of Martial Law", No. 389-VIII of 12 May 2015, as amended. https://zakon.rada.gov.ua/laws/show/389-19#Text. Accessed 22 November 2024, Article 122(2).

[33] Koziubra 2007, pp. 3–9.

[34] Council of Europe (1950) Convention for the Protection of Human Rights and Fundamental Freedoms, Rome, 4 November 1950, Article 6; Verkhovna Rada of Ukraine (1996) Constitution of Ukraine, adopted 28 June 1996, as amended, Article 55.

by laws of Ukraine.[35] This constitutional requirement admits no exceptions, even in conditions of martial law. Despite this, the experience of judicial functioning under the full-scale Russian invasion revealed significant regulatory gaps, particularly in terms of emergency procedures and continuity of justice in occupied or combat-affected territories. With the imposition of martial law on 24 February 2022, it became immediately apparent that no comprehensive legislative framework was in place to guide the actions of judges or court personnel in situations of active hostilities, occupation, or other threats to the regular operation of courts.

In the absence of detailed statutory guidance, temporary measures were introduced by the Chief Justice of the Supreme Court and through resolutions of the Council of Judges of Ukraine.[36] These interventions served as emergency stopgaps to address procedural uncertainty. However, it is important to emphasise that neither the Constitution nor the legislation on the judiciary confers independent regulatory authority on these actors. The measures adopted were of a largely recommendatory nature and were issued in exceptional circumstances. In principle, such matters should have been regulated promptly and comprehensively by Parliament, in accordance with the constitutional requirement that questions concerning the judiciary be addressed through legislation.[37]

In response to the most urgent gaps, the Verkhovna Rada later amended the Law of Ukraine "On the Judiciary and the Status of Judges". Notably, new provisions empowered the Chief Justice of the Supreme Court to reassign territorial jurisdiction of cases when objective wartime conditions prevent a court from administering justice, provided that the High Council of Justice is unable to render a timely decision. This legislative innovation, codified in Article 147(7), partially addressed the operational challenges associated with territorial jurisdiction under martial law. Nevertheless, many procedural and institutional aspects of judicial work in wartime remain unresolved.[38]

The need for legislative regulation of various procedural matters—such as the secure conduct of hearings, remote participation in proceedings, and access to legal aid—remains acute. For example, as early as 2014, following the onset of the Russian military aggression and the launch of the Anti-Terrorist Operation (ATO), Parliament

---

[35] Verkhovna Rada of Ukraine (1996) Constitution of Ukraine, adopted 28 June 1996, as amended. https://zakon.rada.gov.ua/laws/show/254к/96-вр#Text. Accessed 22 November 2024.

[36] See, e.g. Recommendations to first-instance and appellate courts in the event of the capture of a settlement and/or court building, or the immediate threat thereof: Directive of the Chief Justice of the Supreme Court of 13 March 2022 No. 6/0/9-22, https://oda.court.gov.ua/userfiles/media/new_folder_for_uploads/dsa/rozp_6_VC_13_03_22.pdf. Accessed 24 November 2024; Decision of the Council of Judges of Ukraine of 24 February 2022 No. 9, http://rsu.gov.ua/uploads/news/risenna-rsu-no9-vid-240222-2de02988e4.pdf. Accessed 24 November 2024; Decision of the Council of Judges of Ukraine of 14 March 2022 No. 10, http://rsu.gov.ua/ua/documents?id=130&page=4&per-page=8. Accessed 24 November 2024.

[37] European Commission for Democracy through Law (Venice Commission) (2011) Report on the Rule of Law, CDL-AD(2011)003rev. Council of Europe, Strasbourg, pp. 16–18.

[38] Smokovych 2022, p. 28.

adopted a special law governing judicial proceedings in conflict-affected territories.[39] While still in force, this law has not been updated since 2017 and no longer fully reflects the contemporary realities of large-scale war. Moreover, its application in practice has been inconsistent and has revealed substantial organisational challenges, some of which have been addressed in the case law of the European Court of Human Rights.[40]

Although interim arrangements have ensured basic adherence to the principle of legality, the prolonged absence of comprehensive legislation poses significant risks to the right to a fair trial and to the constitutional doctrine of separation of powers. Continued reliance on non-legislative instruments to govern the judiciary during wartime could undermine judicial independence and create legal uncertainty about the validity of judicial decisions. In the context of Ukraine's accession to the European Union, the Verkhovna Rada has a constitutional obligation to uphold the integrity and institutional resilience of the judiciary through consistent and systematic legislative engagement in accordance with European rule of law standards.

In addition to the institutional dimension of judicial functioning, it is also important to consider an example of legislative regulation within a specific functional domain. The field of criminal justice is a particularly illustrative case because it demonstrates the need to balance high-quality legislation with the need for a rapid response to wartime challenges. At the same time, it underscores the importance of ensuring strict compliance with international human rights standards. This area clearly shows that effective, constitutionally grounded lawmaking is essential to maintaining the rule of law and aligning national practice with the legal framework required for Ukraine's integration into the European Union.

The constitutional principle of equality of all participants in judicial proceedings before the law and the court, as enshrined in Article 129(2)(1) of the Constitution of Ukraine, demands particularly rigorous protection in times of national emergency. This principle is foundational to the concept of adversarial criminal proceedings and is operationalised through various guarantees in the Criminal Procedure Code of Ukraine (hereinafter CPC). Notably, during the pre-trial investigation phase, the CPC ensures that potential infringements upon individual rights, particularly those of the suspect, are counterbalanced by judicial oversight of the actions of prosecutors and investigators. The institution of the investigating judge serves as a critical safeguard against the accusatorial bias of pre-trial proceedings by restraining the dominance of the prosecution.

However, Article 615 of the CPC introduces a special regime for criminal proceedings under martial law. Between March and July 2022, this chapter underwent several

[39] Verkhovna Rada of Ukraine (2014) Law of Ukraine No. 1632-VII "On the Administration of Justice and Criminal Proceedings in Connection with the Anti-Terrorist Operation". Adopted 12 August 2014. https://zakon.rada.gov.ua/laws/show/1632-18#Text. Accessed 22 November 2024.

[40] See, e.g. European Court of Human Rights (2021) Kurochenko and Zolotukhin v. Ukraine (Applications Nos. 20936/16 and 53257/16), Judgment of 11 February 2021; European Court of Human Rights (2021) Grankov v. Ukraine (Application No. 16800/16), Judgment of 11 February 2021.

substantive revisions.[41] Particularly controversial were the amendments of 14 April 2022, which permitted detention without a court order for up to 216 hours during martial law,[42] and which temporarily transferred several core functions of the investigating judge to the head of the respective prosecutorial authority in cases where judicial oversight was deemed objectively impossible.[43] These changes significantly disrupted the procedural balance between the prosecution and the defence, privileging the accusatory function at the expense of constitutional guarantees.

While some degree of procedural flexibility may be justified under martial law, the amendments were neither territorially limited nor temporally constrained. Moreover, they applied broadly across a wide array of criminal offences, many of which bore no clear nexus to conditions of active hostilities. This blanket approach had the effect of undermining the constitutional guarantee of judicial equality and the right to a fair trial, as recognised in Article 6 of the European Convention on Human Rights.[44] The legislative framework failed to establish meaningful procedural safeguards or proportional limitations, thereby increasing the risk of abuse and arbitrary detention.

Following domestic and international criticism, Parliament revised Article 615 in July 2022 to reintroduce a degree of judicial oversight and procedural safeguards.[45] However, concerns regarding proportionality remain, particularly with regard to temporal duration, geographic applicability, and the scope of crimes covered by the derogation. In wartime, changes to procedural legislation must be approached with caution because they can substantially affect judicial control over executive action,

[41] See, e.g. On Amendments to the Criminal Procedure Code of Ukraine and the Law of Ukraine "On Pre-Trial Detention" Regarding Additional Regulation of Law Enforcement Activities Under Martial Law: Law of Ukraine of 3 March 2022 No. 2111-IX, https://zakon.rada.gov.ua/laws/show/2111-20#n7. Accessed 12 November 2024; On Amendments to the Criminal Procedure Code of Ukraine and the Law of Ukraine "On Electronic Communications" Aimed at Increasing the Effectiveness of Immediate Pre-Trial Investigation and Countering Cyberattacks: Law of Ukraine of 15 March 2022 No. 2137-IX, https://zakon.rada.gov.ua/laws/show/2137-20#n78. Accessed 12 November 2024; On Amendments to the Criminal Procedure Code of Ukraine to Improve the Procedure for Conducting Criminal Proceedings Under Martial Law: Law of Ukraine of 14 April 2022 No. 2201-IX, https://zakon.rada.gov.ua/laws/show/2201-20#n45. Accessed 12 November 2024; On Amendments to the Criminal Procedure Code of Ukraine to Improve Certain Provisions of Pre-Trial Investigation Under Martial Law: Law of Ukraine of 27 July 2022 No. 2462-IX, https://zakon.rada.gov.ua/laws/show/2462-20#n61. Accessed 12 November 2024.

[42] Part 3 of Article 29 of the Constitution of Ukraine establishes the relevant 72-hour time limit. However, the provisions of Article 64 of the Constitution allow for the restriction of the rights guaranteed by this article under conditions of martial law.

[43] Verkhovna Rada of Ukraine (2022) Law of Ukraine on Amendments to the Criminal Procedure Code of Ukraine to Improve the Procedure for Conducting Criminal Proceedings Under Martial Law, No. 2201-IX of 14 April 2022, https://zakon.rada.gov.ua/laws/show/2201-20#n45. Accessed 22 November 2024.

[44] Council of Europe (1950) Convention for the Protection of Human Rights and Fundamental Freedoms, as amended by Protocols Nos. 11 and 14. Rome, 4 November 1950. https://www.echr.coe.int/documents/convention_eng.pdf. Accessed: 22 November 2024.

[45] Verkhovna Rada of Ukraine (2022) Law of Ukraine on Amendments to the Criminal Procedure Code of Ukraine to Improve Certain Provisions of Pre-Trial Investigation Under Martial Law, No. 2462-IX of 27 July 2022, https://zakon.rada.gov.ua/laws/show/2462-20#n61. Accessed 22 November 2024.

particularly that of pre-trial investigative authorities. These changes can violate not only the right to a fair trial, but also the broader requirements of the rule of law.

This example illustrates the reactive and sometimes emotionally charged nature of parliamentary responses to war, as well as the legislature's capacity to revise and recalibrate its regulatory approaches. Importantly, the shift in legislative position reflects the influence of advocacy by civil society and the expert community, in part. While not perfect, this case represents an attempt to balance the imperative to uphold the rule of law, particularly by implementing international human rights standards, with the exceptional demands of wartime governance. The latter often necessitate extraordinary and unconventional solutions by their nature, which poses a direct challenge to the consistency and restraint typically expected in legislative practice—especially within the context of Ukraine's aspirations for European integration.

21.5 Wartime Challenges

The Ukrainian legal system has long faced systemic challenges in protecting human rights, a fact that must be acknowledged and addressed within the framework of its European integration. According to official statistics from the European Court of Human Rights (ECtHR), Ukraine consistently ranked among the leading respondent states in terms of applications lodged, even prior to the full-scale Russian invasion.[46] This trend must be considered in legislative reforms and restructuring across all sectors of national law. There is an urgent need to ensure compliance with Article 6 of the European Convention on Human Rights, which guarantees the right to a fair trial. A significant proportion of ECtHR judgments against Ukraine concern violations of the right to a fair trial, the excessive length of judicial proceedings, and the absence of effective remedies.[47] These patterns underscore the necessity of aligning national legal standards with ECtHR jurisprudence as a precondition for accession to the European Union and highlight persistent structural deficiencies.

Ukraine's legal system faces unprecedented challenges in wartime that test the resilience of its constitutional framework and commitment to European legal standards. The imposition of martial law has temporarily suspended or modified several constitutional guarantees under Article 64 of the Ukrainian Constitution. Although practices such as military officers inspecting civilians' mobile phones at checkpoints are intended to safeguard national security, they raise serious concerns about privacy rights in the absence of statutory safeguards. Similarly, restrictions, including curfews and mandatory compliance with air raid alerts, are often imposed by military administrations and affect fundamental freedoms, such as the right to free movement (Article

[46] European Court of Human Rights. Statistical Reports. Council of Europe, Strasbourg. https://www.echr.coe.int/statistical-reports. Accessed 22 November 2024.

[47] European Court of Human Rights (2022) Violations by Article and by State 1959–2021. Council of Europe, Strasbourg, https://www.echr.coe.int/Documents/Stats_violation_1959_2021_ENG.pdf. Accessed 22 November 2024.

33 of the Constitution of Ukraine) and personal liberty (Article 29 of the Constitution of Ukraine). However, enforcement often lacks procedural clarity. The war has also complicated civil documentation and access to identity restoration services despite digital innovations, such as the Diia platform. Emergency legislation allowing extended working hours and limitations on evacuation, especially in critical sectors, has reshaped labour rights and raised constitutional questions about the right to life and family protection. Business owners in combat-affected regions face legal uncertainty regarding tax compliance, and housing destruction and the registration of births or deaths are difficult to process due to institutional disruptions. The most pressing concern is property requisition by military authorities without prior judicial oversight, which risks violating Article 41 of the Constitution. These developments underscore the urgent need for a wartime legal regime that safeguards constitutional rights while meeting national defence imperatives, particularly in light of Ukraine's aspirations for European Union membership.

With respect to the normative regulation of exceptional legal regimes, constitutional frameworks in the majority of European states are generally characterised by a degree of brevity and restraint. Although the procedures for declaring and terminating martial law are typically embedded within national constitutions, the more detailed normative and institutional regulation of how martial law is implemented and managed remains largely unresolved at the constitutional level. This legal gap is commonly addressed through ordinary legislation, to which constitutions often delegate the responsibility for specifying the modalities and effects of such exceptional measures. These measures can seriously harm human rights and the functioning of democratic institutions.[48] Such an approach reflects a broader pattern in comparative constitutional design, whereby constitutions define only the formal parameters of emergency powers, while leaving substantive shift between legislative and executive authorities.[49] While this division may enhance legal flexibility, it also raises significant questions regarding the adequacy of legal safeguards, the scope of delegated powers, and the potential for executive overreach under emergency conditions.[50]

The scope and legitimacy of restrictions on human rights under exceptional (special) legislation during a state of martial law remain highly contested and unresolved issues. In particular, the boundaries of permissible limitations raise complex constitutional questions that encompass substantive, institutional, and temporal dimensions. From the substantive perspective, Article 64 of the Constitution of Ukraine establishes the legal basis for determining the permissible scope of restrictions on human rights during martial law. Ukrainian legal scholarship has long engaged with the normative complexities, benefits, and limitations associated with

[48] European Commission for Democracy through Law (Venice Commission) (2020) Report – Respect for Democracy, Human Rights and the Rule of Law during States of Emergency: Reflections. CDL-AD(2020)014-e. Council of Europe, Strasbourg. Taken note of on 19 June 2020 by written procedure replacing the 123rd Plenary Session. https://www.venice.coe.int/webforms/documents/?pdf=CDL-AD(2020)014-e. Accessed 22 November 2024.

[49] Kettemann and Lachmayer 2022, p. 19.

[50] *Ibid.*, pp. 22–23.

applying this constitutional provision. Without delving into a detailed doctrinal analysis of specific rights, two overarching considerations merit attention.

First, para 2 of Article 64 authorises the imposition of additional, time-bound restrictions on certain rights and freedoms during a state of emergency.[51] These are conceived as supplementary limitations beyond those ordinarily permitted in peacetime. Accordingly, the "ordinary" scope of restriction applicable to a given right remains subject to legislative discretion, including under martial law conditions. For instance, Article 45(2) of the Constitution delegates to the legislature the authority to define the conditions under which labour rights may be exercised. Amendments to such peacetime laws continue to fall within the purview of the Verkhovna Rada and may occur independently of the special legal regime enacted under martial law.

Second, even concerning rights that are explicitly non-derogable under Article 64(2), those that cannot be restricted even during martial law, the legislature retains regulatory discretion concerning their scope and implementation in non-emergency settings. A clear example is the right to a fair trial guaranteed under Article 55 of the Constitution. Although formally inviolable during a state of war, the practical realisation of this right depends on structural and procedural factors such as judicial independence, court organisation, and access to remedies. Modifications to any of these parameters, judicial status, procedural rules, or institutional design, may, in practice, restrict the exercise of this right, even absent explicit reference to martial law considerations.

This approach reflects what V. Feldman has described as the theory of constitutional dualism, wherein two parallel regulatory frameworks operate concurrently: one tailored to ordinary conditions, and another to extraordinary emergencies.[52] Thus, when enacting legislation, the Ukrainian parliament must consider not only the restrictive provisions of Article 64(2) regarding emergency-specific legislation, but also the broader normative framework governing rights under peacetime conditions. Any adjustment to seemingly routine procedures or entitlements during martial law may lead to misapplication of legal norms and, ultimately, to a significant violation of the constitutional limits set out in Article 64.

The institutional dimension of human rights limitations during martial law constitutes a critical determinant of their practical enforcement. In particular, the absence of appropriate administrative and governance mechanisms—such as the failure to confer authority on a relevant public body or the non-establishment of a specialised institution—may result in certain rights becoming effectively unenforceable or, worse, entirely illusory. For instance, the constitutional guarantee under Article 56 of the Constitution of Ukraine, which prohibits the restriction of the right to compensation for material and moral damages caused by unlawful acts or omissions of public authorities, is rendered substantively meaningless in the absence of a legally defined mechanism for its implementation.

---

[51] Verkhovna Rada of Ukraine (1996) Constitution of Ukraine, adopted 28 June 1996, as amended. https://zakon.rada.gov.ua/laws/show/254к/96-вр#Text. Accessed 22 November 2024.

[52] Feldman 2005.

In this regard, the effective functioning of the public administration system under wartime conditions is essential to preserving both the reality of human rights protection and the overall integrity of the legal order.[53] During armed conflict, the operational priorities of public authorities necessarily shift toward the logistical and strategic needs of the armed forces and the humanitarian needs of the civilian population. This reorientation may entail institutional restructuring, including modifications to the organisation of executive bodies and the temporary limitation of local self-government. However, any such changes must be grounded in constitutional principles and be governed by legislation enacted by the Verkhovna Rada of Ukraine. The legitimacy of emergency governance structures thus depends not only on their responsiveness to the exigencies of war, but also on their adherence to the foundational norms of constitutionalism and the rule of law.

The temporal dimension of permissible restrictions on human rights under martial law represents one of the most complex aspects of constitutional regulation during states of emergency. This component requires a continuous and dynamic assessment of both the level of threat to national security and the appropriate scope of limitation for each specific right. According to Article 64 of the Constitution of Ukraine, any exceptional restriction on human rights and freedoms must be implemented with a clearly defined duration of applicability. However, neither the constitutional text nor the implementing legislation establishes precise timeframes, stages, or criteria for the initiation, continuation, or termination of such limitations.

The lack of a clear normative framework defining the temporal limits of emergency restrictions has sparked considerable debate within Ukrainian constitutional scholarship. Scholars emphasize the importance of distinguishing between short-term emergency measures, which are justified by immediate threats during active hostilities, and longer-term restrictions that may erode constitutional rights and violate the principle of proportionality if left unchecked. This issue is particularly pressing in the context of Ukraine's ongoing, geographically varied military conflict following Russia's full-scale invasion in February 2022. Under these conditions, the scope and duration of limitations on rights must regularly be reassessed and adjusted according to the evolving security situation in different regions.

Certain extraordinary measures, such as curfews, restrictions on assembly, and limitations on freedom of movement, were introduced in the early stages of the conflict and were initially justified by urgent security needs. These measures continue to play a role in safeguarding public order. However, as military and humanitarian conditions evolve, some of these restrictions may no longer be warranted or may require adjustment. According to the constitutional principle of proportionality, public authorities must periodically assess the necessity, scope, and territorial application of such measures. Furthermore, discretionary power exercised to impose or extend restrictions must adhere to the principles of legal certainty and democratic

[53] European Commission for Democracy through Law (Venice Commission) (2020) Report – Respect for Democracy, Human Rights and the Rule of Law during States of Emergency: Reflections. CDL-AD(2020)014-e. Council of Europe, Strasbourg. https://www.venice.coe.int/webforms/documents/?pdf=CDL-AD(2020)014-e. Accessed 22 November 2024.

oversight to prevent emergency practices from becoming entrenched beyond what the Constitution permits.

The Ukrainian legal system faces the crucial challenge of balancing national security needs with the constitutional obligation to protect individual rights. Developing a more detailed legal framework to define the temporal scope of rights restrictions under martial law would enhance legal clarity and reinforce the legitimacy and resilience of constitutional governance during periods of crisis. In line with constitutional principles governing public authority, the permissible scope of human rights restrictions under martial law must be recalibrated and clearly articulated in legislation. This underscores the critical role of legal certainty and the rule of law in emergency governance. The effectiveness and legitimacy of any restrictions—whether substantive, institutional, procedural, or temporal—depend directly on the quality and coherence of their legislative regulation.

In this context, the Verkhovna Rada of Ukraine, as the national legislature, plays a central constitutional role in establishing the fundamental parameters for the state's operation under martial law and in providing a responsive legal framework that can address wartime challenges and societal needs. Legislative adaptability and parliamentary oversight are essential to preserving democratic accountability during states of emergency. Due to the fluidity of the wartime environment and the varying impact of hostilities on different regions, the legislature must have the necessary tools to swiftly respond to new threats while adhering to constitutional principles.

In light of Ukraine's EU accession objectives, it is crucial to prioritize key areas of parliamentary activity that reinforce the systemic integrity of national legislation during wartime. This includes periodically reviewing emergency measures to ensure they are proportional, developing targeted legal protections for vulnerable populations in accordance with EU fundamental rights standards, and institutionalizing transparent procedures for introducing, overseeing, and repealing rights restrictions. Aligning these processes with EU rule-of-law benchmarks, such as legal certainty, accountability, and proportionality, strengthens Ukraine's constitutional democracy and is essential for meeting the legal and institutional criteria of EU membership. Without a coherent legislative framework grounded in the constitution that reflects these standards, the risk of arbitrary or disproportionate restrictions on fundamental rights increases. This undermines both domestic legitimacy and prospects for European integration.

21.6 Conclusions

Ukraine's Constitution and existing legislative framework provide a solid foundation for the state's European integration, even under the current exceptional circumstances of martial law. The key constitutional principles—such as the rule of law, the separation of powers, and the recognition of international treaties as part of the national legal order—align with the core values of the European Union, as enshrined in Article

2 of the Treaty on European Union. This compatibility offers a constitutional basis for systematic convergence with the *acquis communautaire*.

A critical component of this process is the consistent implementation of international human rights standards and the functional requirements of the rule of law. These elements should serve not only as objectives of legal harmonisation but also as constraints on excessive parliamentary discretion in law-making. In particular, ensuring legal certainty, proportionality, and the predictability of legislative acts must become structural safeguards against arbitrary legislative intervention in sensitive areas such as judicial independence, media regulation, and anti-corruption policy.

The further development of the legal system must be grounded in the principles of the rule of law, judicial independence, access to justice, and institutional resilience. Among the most pressing aims is the strengthening of the institutional independence of the judiciary, particularly with respect to shielding the courts from undue political influence. This includes addressing long-standing systemic challenges such as the persistence of post-Soviet judicial culture and decision-making patterns that undermine public trust in judicial impartiality.

In line with EU legislative practice, the admission process should involve the reallocation of regulatory competence from the level of primary legislation (acts of Parliament) to the domain of secondary legislation (regulations issued by executive or independent bodies), with strong and efficient safeguards. The constitutional supremacy and priority of parliamentary legislation (statutory laws) should be preserved. This evolution would allow for more flexible, technical, and EU-compliant rule-making, while preserving the core democratic oversight functions of the legislature.

Moreover, greater emphasis must be placed on strengthening constitutional review of legislative acts related to European integration. This includes equipping the Constitutional Court of Ukraine with the tools and independence required to evaluate laws for their conformity with both the national Constitution and binding European standards. At the same time, parliamentary oversight over public administration must be further institutionalised and clearly regulated, in order to ensure democratic accountability in the implementation of EU-aligned reforms. This is especially important in areas requiring coordination between national and supranational institutions, such as environmental regulation, data protection, and public procurement.

References

Craig P (1997) Formal and Substantive Conceptions of the Rule of Law: An Analytical Framework. Public Law

Diaz Crego M, Kotanidis S (2020) States of emergency in response to the coronavirus crisis: Normative response and parliamentary oversight in EU Member States during the first wave of the pandemic. European Parliamentary Research Service, Brussels. https://www.europarl.europa.eu/RegData/etudes/STUD/2020/659385/EPRS_STU(202)659385_EN.pdf. Accessed 20 November 2024

Emerson M (2018) Western European Economic Area: Convergence, divergence and implications for the EU and Ukraine. CEPS Policy Insight No. 2018/05. Centre for European Policy Studies, Brussels. https://cdn.ceps.eu/wp-content/uploads/2018/02/PI2018_05_ME_WEEA.pdf. Accessed: 22 November 2024

European Commission for Democracy through Law (Venice Commission) (2011) Report on the Rule of Law. CDL-AD(2011)003rev. Adopted at the 86th Plenary Session (Venice, 25–26 March 2011). Council of Europe, Strasbourg. https://www.venice.coe.int/webforms/documents/default.aspx?pdffile=CDL-AD(2011)003rev-e. Accessed 20 November 2022

European Commission for Democracy through Law (Venice Commission) (2020) Interim Report on the Measures Taken in the EU Member States as a Result of the COVID-19 Crisis and Their Impact on Democracy, the Rule of Law and Fundamental Rights. CDL-AD(2020)018-e. Council of Europe, Strasbourg. https://www.venice.coe.int/webforms/documents/default.aspx?pdffile=CDL-AD(2020)018-e. Accessed 22 November 2024

Feldman W (2005) Theories of emergency powers: A comparative analysis of American martial law and the French state of siege. Cornell International Law Journal 38(3):1041–1072. http://scholarship.law.cornell.edu/cilj/vol38/iss3/17. Accessed 18 November 2024

Hasebe Y (2012) War Powers. In: Rosenfeld M, Sajó A (eds) The Oxford Handbook of Comparative Constitutional Law. Oxford Academic, 21 November 2012, https://doi.org/10.1093/oxfordhb/9780199578610.013.0024. Accessed 23 November 2024

Holovaty S, Koziubra M, Matvieieva Y, Tseliev O, Venher V, Zaiets A, Zvieriev I (2021) Rule of Law Checklist at National Level: Case of Ukraine. In: Koziubra M (ed) Council of Europe and Centre for Research on the Rule of Law and its Implementation in Ukraine. National University of "Kyiv-Mohyla Academy", Kyiv

Jakab A (2006) German Constitutional Law and Doctrine on State of Emergency – Paradigms and Dilemmas of a Traditional (Continental) Discourse. German Law Journal 7(5):453–477. https://doi.org/10.1017/S207183220000479X

Kettemann M C, Lachmayer K (eds) (2022) Pandemocracy in Europe: Power, Parliaments, and People in Times of COVID-19. Hart Publishing, Oxford

Koziubra M I (2007) Pryntsypy verkhovenstva prava i pravovoi derzhavy: yednist osnovnykh vymoh [The principles of the rule of law and the rechtsstaat: the sameness of the fundamental requirements]. Naukovi zapysky NaUKMA. Yurydychni nauky 64:3–9

Nicolaides P (2012) Preparing for Accession to the European Union: How to Establish Capacity for Effective and Credible Application of EU Rules. In: Cremona M (ed) The Enlargement of the European Union (Oxford, 2003; online edn., Oxford Academic, 22 March 2012), https://doi.org/10.1093/acprof:oso/9780199260942.003.0003. Accessed 22 November 2024

Sadurski W (2012) Return of the Solange Ghost: the Supremacy of EU Law and the Democracy Paradox, Constitutionalism and the Enlargement of Europe (Oxford, 2012; online edn. Oxford Academic, 20 September 2012), https://doi.org/10.1093/acprof:oso/9780199696789.003.0004. Accessed 22 November 2024

Smokovych M I (2022) Dystantsiina forma pravosuddia yak harantiia bezpeky suddiv pid chas voiennoho stanu [Remote form of justice as a guarantee of judges' safety during martial law]. 3 Pravo Ukrainy 26–38

Venher V, Bondar M, Doroshenko B, Kyrychenko Y, Ivasyk S (2023) The Verkhovna Rada under War Conditions: Functioning of the Parliament during Martial Law. Internews Ukraine, Kyiv. https://internews.ua/storage/app/media/rang/VRU-under-war-conditions-ENG.pdf. Accessed 22 November 2024

Venher V, Doroshenko B, Bondar M, Ivasyk S, Kulakov A, Ihnatenko D, Ishchenko D (2024) Parliament in Wartime: How the Verkhovna Rada Functions during the Full-Scale War. Internews Ukraine, Kyiv. https://internews.ua/storage/app/media/rang/2024/3/parliamentinwartime/EN_Parliament_under_war_conditions_Ukraine.pdf. Accessed 22 November 2024

Volodymyr Venher is a dr., the Dean of the Faculty of Law of the National University of "Kyiv-Mohyla Academy", and an Associate Professor in the Department of Jurisprudence and Public Law.

MIX
Papier aus verantwortungsvollen Quellen
Paper from responsible sources
FSC® C105338

If you have any concerns about our products,
you can contact us on
ProductSafety@springernature.com

In case Publisher is established outside the EU,
the EU authorized representative is:
Springer Nature Customer Service Center GmbH
Europaplatz 3, 69115 Heidelberg, Germany

Printed by Libri Plureos GmbH
in Hamburg, Germany